CAD *for* Fashion Design *and* Merchandising

fb

CAD *for* Fashion Design and Merchandising

Stacy Stewart Smith

Fashion Institute of Technology, New York

Fairchild Books, Inc.
New York

Fairchild Books

An imprint of Bloomsbury Publishing Inc

175 Fifth Avenue　　　　　　　　　50 Bedford Square
New York　　　　　　　　　　　　　London
NY 10010　　　　　　　　　　　　　WC1B 3DP
USA　　　　　　　　　　　　　　　　UK

www.fairchildbooks.com

Library of Congress Cataloging-in-Publication Data
A catalog record for this book is available from the Library of Congress.
LOC number in process.

ISBN: 978-1-60901-063-8

Typeset by Mary Neal Meador and Carly Grafstein
Cover Design by Carly Grafstein
Cover Art: Stacy Stewart Smith
Photography by Stephen Sullivan and Stacy Stewart Smith
Printed in the United States by Thomson-Shore, Inc. Dexter, Michigan

To Mom, from your youngest son

Contents

Extended Contents

Preface

A Fashion Story

Seventy-five dollars and two gigantic suitcases filled with my fashion life were the sum of my worldly possessions. As I struggled through the doors of New York City's Port Authority bus station, I thought about what I had done. In the previous month, I had given notice to my employer, sold or given away most of my personal belongings, and left my friends and family behind to attend the Fashion Institute of Technology (FIT). Because of my talent and skills, a week later, I landed a part-time job in the garment center as an assistant designer, sketching freehand and making first patterns after school. In three months, I was working full time as a fashion designer. The year was 1987, and most computers in the garment center were used for business administration and accounting purposes.

A Return to College

I went on to enjoy a career for many years as a head fashion designer generating major trends in various markets and revenues that provided jobs and helped the economy. Somewhere in the midst of my career things changed, and I realized that I needed training. Before I returned to college, I studied desktop publishing for graphics, fashion, and textiles on the Macintosh platform at a computer center. I learned to use software programs such as Illustrator®, Photoshop®, and others. My career was drastically changed by this experience.

Figure P.1 © Gavin Hellier/Alamy.

A Fashion Educator Learns

Thanks to my computer skills, I was hired as a fashion design instructor at the Wood Tobé-Coburn School (a Bradford college). I was promoted to Professor of Fashion Design and continued to teach many dedicated and talented students. During this period, I also returned to college full-time to study fine arts. The load between full-time work and heavy semester course schedules was grueling, but I persevered and graduated at the top of my class with a BFA from the School of Visual Arts of New York (SVA). Ironically, I was also hired to teach courses in the Fashion Design Art department at FIT.

When I am asked what I am most proud of, I reply, "my students." Those who were dedicated always made the grade. Today, in the global apparel and accessories markets, just "making the grade" is not enough. You must possess computer graphics presentation skills.

Why *This* Textbook?

In the global apparel business, manufacturers need fashion personnel with professional computer skills. Just read the want ads; technical and creative designers who can develop their designs digitally are in demand. However, professional fashion computing is highly specialized, so it has to be taught. You can either learn it on the job or from someone in an academic setting. Often, because of these factors, appropriate training is out of reach.

Most fashion educators who teach technology courses will agree that there is a lack of textbooks written upon the subject of digital fashion design and illustration. Many of the books on the market magnify one program or another. Most of the graphics-centered software-based books available are too complicated and do not fit the needs of aspiring fashion students.

CAD for Fashion Design and Merchandising was written for the fashion design and merchandising student and is an effective learning aid for higher education and independent study. This book proposes an uncomplicated method for you to begin learning digital presentation skills at various stages of your academic journey. *Here's the good news!* Whether or not you draw well freehand, you can benefit from the tutorials and DVD extras.

The focus of *CAD for Fashion Design and Merchandising* is to teach you combined use of Illustrator® and Photoshop® for fashion careers. The book features men's wear and women's wear fashion design art and merchandising tutorials for creative and technical fashion design presentations.

The tutorials in this book offer techniques yielding dramatic effects through photographic and prerendered images available for use right from the two enclosed DVDs. You can use them with the tutorials, or use your own sketches and photos to challenge your skills, mastery, and technical acumen. Either way, you will develop your own digital fashion presentation style by applying the principles suggested through each tutorial. Furthermore, you will learn which applications, tools, filters, panels, etc., are appropriate to use for the best results.

Numbered Step-by-Step Tutorials

The tutorials in this book are designed so that you can follow them in easy steps right at your terminal. The figure numbers in the written steps correspond to adjacent screen grabs and photographs of the stages. You can choose where you want to start, stop, and return to a tutorial.

DVD Tutorials and Extras

The two accompanying DVDs contain the files needed to follow the textbook tutorials, along with additional tutorials, stock photos, clip art, and more. These files are arranged by chapter and labeled corresponding to the tutorial titles and numbers.

Terminology, Features, and Benefits

CAD for Fashion Design and Merchandising is a great resource for aspiring or professional fashion designers who do not possess strong drawing skills. Feel free to use the DVD templates along with your own creativity to develop an entire collection of apparel on the figure or digital flats. Fashion merchandisers will also enjoy the same ease of creating comprehensive presentation visuals. You will increase your knowledge and skills through consistent study, practice and application.

Both fashion and computing have their own languages. In this book fashion technology terms are highlighted in bold or italic typeface. Many definitions appear right in the manuscript, but space will not allow for every new term or catchphrase. For this reason, the book also contains a glossary, and it contains the terms most relevant to your academic success. Consult it if you read something that you do not understand. You can test your knowledge, and then consult the glossary to compare your accuracy.

Mac and PC

CAD For Fashion Design and Merchandising contains cross-platform instruction. Each tutorial also includes keyboard shortcut and menu sequences for Macintosh and PC users of Illustrator® and Photoshop®.

Adobe Software Compatibility

Anyone using Illustrator® and/or Photoshop®, no matter what the version, will be able to learn from *CAD for Fashion Design and Merchandising*. Please note, however, that this textbook was written using CS5® and CS5.5®, so the screenshots will not reveal the dark, customizable user interface of CS6. To view the CS6 interface, see the movie CS6_Adjust_User_Interface_Color.mov on ① Ch02. There are also notes and tips for using version CS6 throughout the text.

The full Adobe® upgrades appear about once every twelve to fourteen months, and recently the CS5.5 mid-cycle upgrade made a notable stir. Predictably, the current upgrade pattern will change again, and users will continue to ask the question of "Do I really need to upgrade?"

The fundamental needs of fashion computing are generic to all Adobe® versions. The publisher and I support the upgrades and decisions by Adobe® Systems, Inc. but prefer multi-version compatibility for academic instruction. Simlarly, the global apparel industry,currently uses different versions.

Compatibility with CS4 and Lower Versions

Users of Adobe® CS4 and lower versions can easily use the DVD tutorial files. However, you should note that when the Acrobat® pdf files are opened in lower versions of Illustrator®, the layers might become flattened. You may also need to cut and paste parts into new layers. For example, a tutorial may require that the parts of a croquis or apparel flat be placed on different layers. Before opening the DVD files, you should first carefully read through all the steps. Then, select, cut, and paste the parts into identical layers as shown in the text. The same issue may also occur in Photoshop®, and in some cases, cutting and pasting the parts may not be possible. However, the illustrated steps in this textbook are customizable and will prove to be an easy-to-follow companion. Additionally, in almost every tutorial within this textbook you will be able to use your own drawings, either hand rendered or digital, instead of the DVD files.

Compatibility with CS6 and Higher Versions

As for Adobe® CS6 and future upgrades of the Adobe® software bundle, users can easily adapt the tutorials. The relevant CS6 innovations have been included in this textbook and/ or featured in movies on the accompanying DVDs.

Illustrator® CS6 Upgrade Features

For fashion users, the most innovative and useful change in Illustrator® CS6 is the ability to seamlessly define pattern repeats with the new *Pattern Editor*. (See CS6_Pattern_Editor. m4v on ① Ch03) While this single upgrade feature is desirable, do not get too comfortable because it is likely that it will be improved in future upgrades. Moreover, since lower versions are still in wide use, learning the manual methods for digital patterns are essential.

Illustrator® *Live Trace* was revamped. It is now referred to as Image Trace, and there are some access modifications. (See CS6_Image_Trace.m4v on ① Ch06\Tutorial 6.1.) The ability to add gradient strokes is also another fine addition. (See CS6_Gradient_Stroke_ Panel_Options.m4v on ① Ch04\Tutorial 4.1.) Organizational features, such as the ability to change the title of a layer by highlighting and retyping, are also good to learn for saving time.

Photoshop® CS6 Upgrade Features

In Photoshop® CS6 the ability to create vector dashed line strokes that simulate machine stitches makes the raster program independent from Illustrator®. This was the missing link. Users can now draw flats totally in Photoshop.® (See ② Ch 12\DVD Extras\DVD Extra 12.2 CS6_Vector_Smart_Dashed_Lines.m4v.) There are many other interesting Photoshop® CS6 upgrade features, but they are not essential for fashion professionals.

Avoid "Skimming Through"

Many creative people like to skim through books. However, learning to operate computers and use digital graphics software for fashion design and merchandising requires the disciplines of focus and devotion. The tutorials in this book are multifaceted; you will learn many things about Illustrator® and Photoshop® in each tutorial. It is important that you complete all the steps in each tutorial. Some of the tutorials focus on men's wear and others feature women's apparel, but each is vital to your total development.

Manipulate, Do, and Then Undo

Another good suggestion that will help you to learn the programs is to open select DVD files and study their parts. Using the tools in Illustrator® and Photoshop®, pull apart the contents on each layer. Explore the files by manipulating them with the tools, panel features, filters, etc. Deliberately set out to change the look of the finished plates and make them your own. In time, you will become more comfortable with the programs and begin making your own electronic drawings. Once you have finished working on a file, you can press *Cmd+Z / Ctrl+Z* to remove or retrace your steps, save the file, or simply close it unsaved. Figure P.2 shows a MacBook Pro® laptop keyboard, revealing the command keys located on both sides of the spacebar. Pressing the Command keys (Mac) and Control keys (PC) are vital to completing the tutorials. You will learn more about these later.

Figure P.2 Mac Book Pro®. © Tim Graham/Alamy.

Figure P.3 Chuck Close in his studio.
© Gordon M. Grant/Alamy.

Figure P.4 Paintings by Gerhard Richter.
© Sandy Young/Alamy.

The Author's Fashion Design/Art Philosophy

Even though digital art, particularly fashion illustration, is used primarily for communication and not for art's sake, important parallels can be drawn from certain principles exampled in the fine arts. This book is based on those governing photorealism, which got its start in the United States during the 1960s. A few proponents of photorealism in painting include, but are not limited to, Chuck Close and Gerhard Richter (Figures P.3 and P.4). Creating **photorealism** through the means of painting is extremely difficult, requiring natural talent and years of practice to perfect. Few people actually master freehand photorealism through painting and drawing, but thanks to computer graphics software and photography, now almost anyone can create convincing and professional digital 3-D photorealistic fashion illustrations. The artistic possibilities are nearly unlimited, particularly since this book will instruct you how to use fashion photography, freehand rendering, and digital design processes.

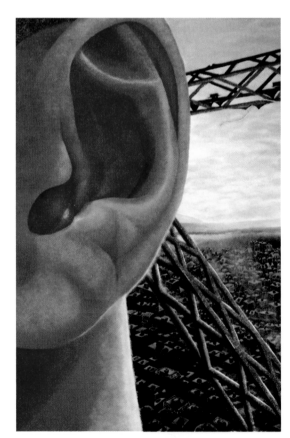

Abstractrealism and Virtual Digital Realism

As a digital purist, I am convinced that the goal of digital fashion illustration is to be as distanced from hand rendering as possible. My views have developed out of years of practice as a fine art painter with my own individual style that I call **abstractrealism** (Figure P.5). In this, portions of both realism (figurative) and abstract fine arts painting techniques are combined and placed in to environments with one or two-point perspective. Elements of motion and some spiritual and/or surreal contents are also a part of the composition.

Figure P.5 *Temptation,* oil on canvas by Stacy Stewart Smith.

As a result my digital fashion design art pedagogy falls into either one of two categories. The first begins with the real, and later adds the ideal. It is a procedure that I call **virtual digital realism**. Photography plays a major role in this technique. Fashion models, interiors, landscapes, and textile scans are digitized, then further appended to make them look three-dimensional. There are examples of virtual digital realism in films like *The Animatrix* (2003, Warner Bros.), directed by the Wachowski brothers (Figures P.6 and P.7), *Confessions of a Shopaholic* (2009, Touchstone Pictures), directed by J. P. Hogan, and James Cameron's epic motion picture *Avatar* (2009, Fox release).

Often, when virtual digital realism is used to create digital fashion illustration from photos, it gives the original human subjects a doll-like appearance. This is actually an advantage for digital fashion illustration. There are software programs which can help you to create these types of 3-D photo illusions; however, some are too reliant upon fixed photo character images. As these types of programs improve, they will gain greater use and possibly find their place in the garment industry. However, the best way to create virtual digital realism is to begin with an image-editing raster-based software program and add object-oriented vector software features.

Realistic Idealism and Fashion Abstractrealism

The focus of *CAD for Fashion Design and Merchandising* is **realistic idealism** (Figure P.8). This illustration technique begins with digitized freehand renderings and/or figurative photo

Figure P.6 Still from the Animatrix.
© David Crausby/Alamy.

Figure P.7 Still from the Animatrix.
© David Crausby/Alamy.

Figure P.8 Illustration by Stacy Stewart Smith.

LE CHAT JEANS GO PLACES

Figure P.9 Illustration by Stacy Stewart Smith.

resources. These are used to create idealized illustrations by using a vector graphics software program. Further applications of realist 3-D techniques are achieved by rasterizing these images, and then adding photographic collage, filters, and digital painting. In this book, the procedure of creating realistic idealism will be referred to as **"Digital Duo."** When these images are juxtaposed in total environments—for fashion illustration and presentation—they become **fashion abstractrealism** (Figure P.9).

The "Digital Duo" Modeling Agency Folder

Digitally enhanced photos of fashion models are located in a folder entitled *Digital Duo Modeling Agency* located on ①. The folder showcases three models whose avatar names are Ana (Figure P.10), Jade (Figure P.11), and Carl (Figure P.12), as well as anatomical shots to help you to render hands, feet, and more. Each model

Figure P.10 Ana

Figure P.11 Jade

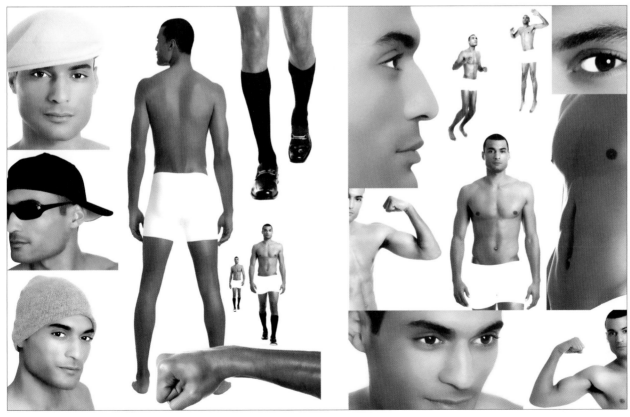

Figure P.12 Carl

has been selected to generate a variety of types. The photography has been retouched and altered to help you use the pictures with the software programs meeting standard fashion illustration proportions.

The Avatar Modeling Agency Folder

Although fashion illustration in editorials and advertisements has been missing in action since the early 1990s, digital fashion figures (fashion avatars), due to their flexible nature, are poised to take a premier position in fashion. Unlike their freehand counterparts, digital croquis can be used and manipulated repeatedly. With the added realism from photography, fashion avatars can even become top models. A few top models from the *Avatar Modeling Agency folder* on ② appear in a beach scene that is actually a Chapter 9 tutorial where you can make use of the avatar models to design a swimwear collection (Figure P.13). You will also learn to create your own "Digital Duo" fashion croquis figures.

"Digital Duo" Technical Design

Figurative fashion illustration is only a portion of what you will learn in this book. Every technique is also applied to the principles of technical design through 3-D conceptual flats/ floats and technical production flats for tech-packs. Traditional and innovative tutorials will teach you how to be prepared for a place in the global apparel industry.

Figure P.13 Illustration by Stacy Stewart Smith.

Chapter Preview

Chapter 1 will acquaint you with cross-platform desktop publishing for fashion techies. You will discover the parts of the computer. In addition, you will learn about the differences between Macs and PCs, keyboard etiquette, keyboard shortcuts, disk space, and resolution. This chapter prepares you for working with the Adobe programs.

Chapter 2 introduces you to basic vector software attributes through learning the tools, workspaces, panels, and features of Illustrator®. You will learn how to use the program and discover the basic interfaces, including the Menu Bar, Application Bar, and Control Panel options. Several practice exercises will teach you the art of creating Bézier Curves (curved line segments). The chapter culminates in a foundation tutorial that will teach you how to use the basic functions of Illustrator® and layer compositing.

Chapter 3 picks up the vector instruction pace and provides you with an increased command of Illustrator® through multifaceted tutorials. The use of appropriate measuring tools is stressed, and you will focus on the Character panel and type as a means to define textile pattern repeats. You will also get your chance to render apparel on the figure as a means to develop your eye for proportion. Clipping paths and digital spatial arrangement are stressed.

Chapter 4 makes great use of wedding attire as a means to teach vector creation of various textiles through panel features, such as velvet, lace, metals, novelties, and satin. You will also learn to create darts, tucks, creases, buttonholes, stitches, and more. The fashion figure is used and hands are featured in tutorials that will teach you how to design gemstones and add "bling" to a ring. You will use the new CS5 Perspective Grid Tool to create a garment in one-point perspective. The tutorials magnify both men's wear and women's wear garment details and categories.

Chapter 5 is all about the Photoshop® software interface. You will learn all about the tools, panels and features of the program. Layer compositing, Layer Styles, and file formats are stressed. The chapter contains one customer profile tutorial that will help you to gain control of what you have learned in the chapter. Some aspects of Photoshop® that teach scanning and the new Content Aware feature are introduced through DVD tutorials.

Chapter 6 proposes the Live Trace attributes of Illustrator® for your personal drawings and fashion photography. The tutorials in this chapter teach you how to avoid the digital floating figure and methods for developing digital contrapposto. You will develop critical thinking skills concerning placing, scaling, and dressing figures in reference to perspective. Textile scanning is introduced as a pattern repeat. You will be introduced to exporting files from Illustrator® to Photoshop® and develop storyboard compositions with multiple figures in two-point perspective. Digital intarsia sweater design and screen printing is demonstrated.

Chapter 7 introduces Photoshop® painting capabilities for fashion design and merchandising presentations, including digital mood boards, color boards, and conceptual flats. In a special tutorial, you will be guided through techniques that will enable you to use your own designs on figures or photographs and stage an actual interactive digital runway fashion show. In this chapter you will also learn to create, save, and reload Alpha Channel masks.

Chapter 8 is all about digital pattern repeats using Illustrator® and Photoshop®. You will learn how to create and define horizontal repeats, vertical repeats, and those that are comprised of both. In addition, you will be introduced to the Illustrator® Pattern Libraries and how to manage the Swatches panel. The Illustrator® Mesh Tool is introduced to help define abstract repeats that simulate tie-dye patterns. Moreover, you will learn how to use multiple Photoshop® filters to simulate couture quality textiles, create moiré effects, and more.

Chapter 9 is the digital color chapter, where you will learn about color modes, mixing gradients, and the color interfaces of both Illustrator® and Photoshop®. Included in this chapter is information on the new Kuler panel and a strong focus on creating color wheels. You will learn about color schemes, harmonies, and complements. The chapter includes a detailed explanation and application of the differences between CMYK and RGB. You will use the Photoshop® Lighting Effects filter to illuminate a club art gallery.

Chapter 10 will benefit anyone who needs to work with digital photography for fashion. You will learn color correction and repair torn photos. You will also learn how to use Photoshop® to restore and colorize black-and-white vintage photos. The HDR Toning filter demonstrates how to make the subjects in photos look years younger. The Photoshop® Spot Healing Tool and Clone Stamp Tool are featured.

Chapter 11 totally focuses on how to create digital male and female croquis in frontal and three-quarter views by using photos and Illustrator® tools, panel features, and filters. You will learn to simulate muscle tone and add realism to the upper body. The Illustrator® Skintones Library is used throughout the chapter to create a variety of ethnic fashion avatar types.

Chapter 12 makes use of the layer compatibility of both Illustrator® and Photoshop®. Croquis figures and apparel files are exported from one program to another and 3-D effects are created. A particular highlight of this chapter is a lesson in Vector Smart graphics, which enable you to update a portion of a file in Illustrator® while you work on the entire plate in Photoshop®. "Digital Duo" enhancements are stressed through Photoshop® tools and filters.

Chapter 13 introduces vector and raster graphics face and hair techniques for male and female croquis similar to those in Chapters 11 and 12. The chapter proposes a variety of methods to achieve dynamic results including the Illustrator® Hair Symbols, scans of hand-painted hairstyles, photography, and tool attributes in both programs. You will learn to create ethnic features for a variety of fashion avatars using "Digital Duo" techniques.

Chapter 14 focuses on technical design and digital flats. You will learn to maintain constant proportions in Illustrator® to create a variety of front and back views of technical production flats for men's wear and women's wear. Interactive files containing movable figure parts and fashion figure proportion scales enable you to morph apparel design parts from templates created with the Illustrator® Pen Tool and/or geometric shapes. Lessons in the book and folders on ② enable you to see the construction of a variety of flats and completed tech-packs.

Chapter 15 culminates the book with lessons that will help you to create a variety of color conceptual design flats for designer apparel. You will learn "Digital Duo" techniques to simulate fur, sequins, suede, leather, knits, marabou feathers, beading, lace, and other fine fabrics, treatments, and trims for men's wear and women's wear design portfolio presentations. The Appendix explains how to convert your files to create multiple-page slide show files.

Note from the Author

Although a concerted amount of time and energy were sacrificed to accurately prepare this publication and to make it as complete as possible, the information printed in it is "as is." Neither warranty nor fitness is implied concerning the information stated in this book. The author nor the publisher shall forever have neither liability nor responsibility to any person, group, or entity with respect to potential loss or damages that may arise from the use of the information in or emanating from this publication, nor the use of the programs, nor any stated, nor implied use of related and/or associated information, groups, individuals, entities, and affiliates.

Trademarks

The author and the publisher have made every effort to ensure that each and every trademark was capitalized and duly marked, and that all known procedures concerning trademarks were in compliance. The use of trademarks does not give credence to the information stated concerning it. The use of any trademark or registered term in this book does not imply validity or any presumed level of quality.

CAD for Fashion Design and Merchandising is an independent publication and has not been authorized, sponsored, or otherwise approved by Apple® in the United States and/or other countries.

CAD for Fashion Design and Merchandising is an independent publication and has not been authorized, sponsored, or otherwise approved by Microsoft® Corporation in the U.S. and/or other countries. Windows® is a registered trademark of Microsoft Corporation in the United States and other countries. The Windows® operating system is the property of Microsoft® Corporation.

Illustrator® and Photoshop® of the Creative Suite® are trademarks of Adobe® Systems incorporated in the United States and/or other countries. The use or mention of Illustrator®, Photoshop®, and all other Adobe products in this publication are not an endorsement by Adobe® Systems Incorporated.

Digital Design Duo

The coined phrase "Digital Duo" in this textbook will refer to the process of using object-oriented, vector-based digital art combined with image-editing raster-based digital art to create fashion illustrations and presentations. It is not a means on the part of the author and/or the publisher of *CAD for Fashion Design and Merchandising* to rename any specific software program(s) but simply a reference to the dual usage of the digital art forms for the purpose of instruction.

Kudos

I would like to thank my mother, who is my best friend and the source of my inspiration. To Don Canali, I extend my gratitude for my initial computer graphics instruction. Kudos to the fine art instructors at the School of Visual Arts of New York (SVA) and most especially Betty Tompkins, Paul Fortunato, and Peter Hristoff, who each lavished their expertise on me and helped to polish my artistic talent. I cannot forget my SVA art history professor, Ann Sargent Wooster, whose father, Harold Wooster, made a tremendous contribution to all of our lives by funding the research that helped to develop the personal computer and the Internet. Rev. Dr. Richard F. Christie, Sr., president of the Manhattan Bible Institute of New York, assisted me in ways too numerous to count. Thank you, Susan Cohan, for giving me my first opportunity to teach. Still more effusive thanks to the wonderful people I have met at the Fashion Institute of Technology. Olga Konzias, Jaclyn Bergeron, and the staff at Fairchild Books deserve applause for their tireless efforts and support, which helped me to become a published author. I would also like to acknowledge Liz Van Doren, whose editorial critique inspired me to reorganize this book and make it a more meaningful resource. Thanks to each model who wore my designs on runways during the early years, including Eloise, Gloria, Jackie, and others who helped me understand fashion anatomy. To all of my reviewers, colleagues, collectors, relatives, close friends, and others who have supported me in innumerable ways—thank you. I am grateful for the copyediting and administrative work that Diane Lane Root has contributed to this project; I cannot imagine having achieved the completion of the first draft without her expertise and friendship. Last, but certainly not least, to each student I have taught and to each one I shall teach after the publication of this book, thank you for taking with you a little part of me, to every desk wherever you go and to places where I could not go. Remember that "change" is the right fashion attitude to adopt.

Cross-Platform Desktop Publishing

1

Objectives

Currently, there are two types of computer platforms, Mac and PC. Macintosh computers run on the Mac OS (Mac Operating System) and PCs run on the Windows operating system. One of these is loaded on the central processing unit (CPU) of your computer. Each platform has its benefits, but the major advantage of both is the ability to create and print right from your desk—a process known as desktop publishing.

The goal of Chapter 1 is to acquaint you with the basics of both Mac and PC desktop publishing for fashion and graphics. You will be introduced to:

◉ The hardware, system software, and benefits of Mac and PC computers

◉ Basic Mac and PC keyboarding and mouse-clicking sequences

◉ Information highlighting current ports, drives, and peripherals

◉ Universal and system shortcuts for Mac and PC

◉ Screen resolution and disk space

◉ File formats

Fashion Techie Essentials

In order to work through the tutorials in this textbook you will need some essential hardware, software, and supplies. If you do not own a computer already, that will probably be your first purchase (Figure 1.1). Here are a few types of products to consider.

Mac Studio Hardware Requirements

Before 2005, Apple computers operated on processors known as **PowerPC**, but today they have **Intel**-based processors. *CAD for Fashion Design and Merchandising* requires that you use an Intel-based **Mac**. By the time you read this book, there will be new products and upgrades available, so the recommendations will be kept to the basics. If you are a first-time buyer, you should purchase a laptop, although there are a few promising all-in-one desktop models. Do your research on the products first and ask questions. Plenty of information is available online, but always speak to dealers and look at actual products before you make purchase decisions. Ask about discounts, especially for students. Visit the official Adobe website to discover the current hardware specifications necessary to run Illustrator® and Photoshop® on the Macintosh platform.

Mac System Software

The system software directs the basic functions of a computer. Each platform has its own system software, and Macintosh computers run on **Mac OS**. The current version, as of this publication, is **Mac OS X**. The company also gives names to its software versions. A recent upgrade is called **Mac OS X Mountain Lion** for Intel-based Macs.

Note: *If your Mac is not new, current upgrades of Adobe software will necessitate an upgrade of Mac OS to Lion or later versions. Visit the official Apple website for more information.*

Internal Parts of the Mac

The unique quality that distinguishes Macintosh computers, in addition to having been the leader in the concept of style, is their all-inclusiveness. Unlike PCs, which are usually customized, most Macintosh computers are built with set features and benefits. To some users, these restrictions are burdensome, but to others, they make using the Macintosh platform effortless. Apple customizes some of their products when they are purchased through their official website. The latest version of the system software offers some of the best user-friendly interfaces available.

Figure 1.1 When new products are launched, Macintosh users often stand in line at local Apple Stores, like this man who just left the Apple Store in London with a new iPhone. © Frantzesco Kangaris/Alamy.

Central Processing Unit or CPU

The **central processing unit** of a Mac is the portion of the computer referred to as the CPU. Its primary purpose is to tell the computer how to function by means of a program.

Hard Disk Drive

The computer's **hard disk drive** (Macs and PCs), or *hard drive*, is quite literally a disk inside your computer that has the capacity to store information. It is the computer's memory. Figuratively speaking, the combination of the CPU and the hard drive is the computer's brain. Disk space will be discussed later in this introductory chapter.

Ports

Ports are connectors that allow you to interface with the Internet, peripherals, wireless networks, and more, including **universal serial bus (USB)**, **Ethernet**, and **video graphics array (VGA)** ports.

Drives

In order to power feature devices built within the computer, the manufacturers have installed drives to run them. The DVD-ROM and the CD-ROM each provide useful functions and creature comforts such as playing movies, music, and more.

External Parts of the Mac

Most recently, the visual divide between Mac and PC has become less obvious. The sleek techno design and other benefits are available on both types of computers. Figure 1.2 shows some of the basic external parts of the MacBook Pro and the iMac.

Mac Clicking Sequence

Apple manufactures all types of **mouses** (plural for a computer mouse) with single and double-sided clickers in wireless and USB corded versions. Whichever mouse you choose (Mac or PC), try to remember the **clicking sequence**:

- Click once to select something.
- Double-click to open a file or to load an application.
- Click and drag to select multiple items, then open or move them.
- Right-click to access system and applications options menus.

The Mac Desktop

Before you can begin mastering the graphics software that will be used in the tutorials, familiarize yourself with the Macintosh desktop (Figure 1.3). The computer desktop is what you see on your monitor. Mac OS X features various background displays and screen savers. You can read through your manual to discover all the details of how to change things around. We will just familiarize you with the basics. The Mac desktop area is where you work. It's just like your physical desk.

The Menu Bar: At the top of the screen there is the **Menu Bar**. Use it to access the items that you see on the display with your mouse or trackpad and corresponding **cursor** (also known as the pointer). There are various items on the Menu Bar. When you click and hold them with your mouse, you will discover **pull-down menus** for each. This is only for the Mac OS X desktop menu. Each software application has its own Menu Bar items, so when you are using, for example, Illustrator® or another program, they will change. To return to the Mac OS system interface, click again on the desktop.

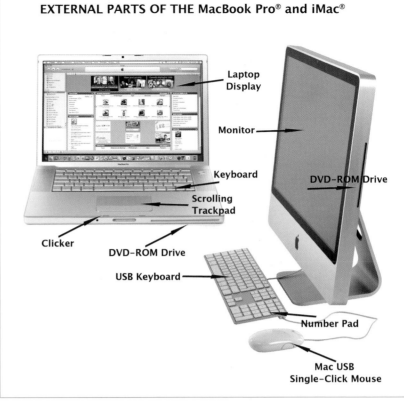

EXTERNAL PARTS OF THE MacBook Pro® and iMac®

Figure 1.2 © vario images GmbH & Co.KG/Alamy (left) and © Finnbarr Webster/Alamy (right).

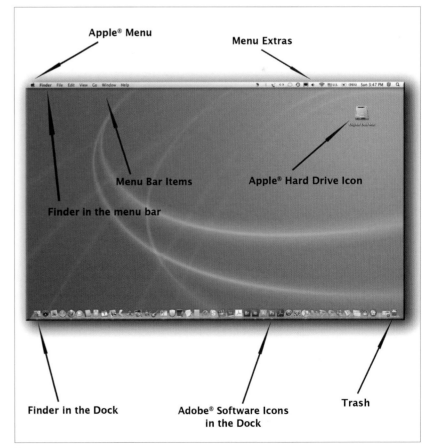

Figure 1.3

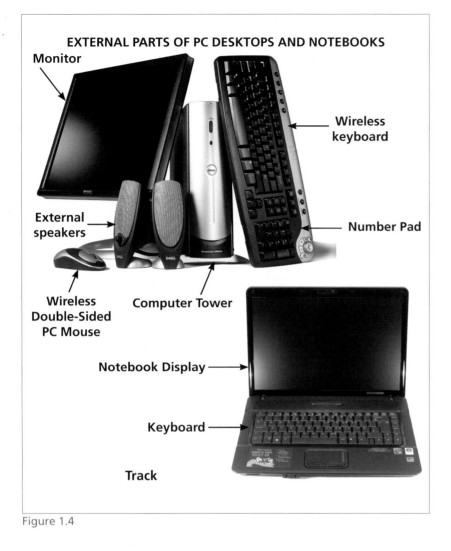

EXTERNAL PARTS OF PC DESKTOPS AND NOTEBOOKS

Monitor

Wireless keyboard

External speakers

Number Pad

Wireless Double-Sided PC Mouse

Computer Tower

Notebook Display

Keyboard

Track

Figure 1.4

Apple Menu and Finder: At the far left of the Menu Bar is an Apple icon referred to as the **Apple menu**. When you press and hold the **Apple icon**, an important menu will appear that allows you to scroll and perform basic functions such as accessing your **system preferences**, manually restarting or shutting down your computer, and more. There is also a **Finder** in the Menu Bar that when pressed reveals a menu where you might alter your Finder preferences, empty the trash, and perform other manual functions.

Widgets and Menu Bar Icons: On the right side of the Menu Bar are menu extras. These icons are divided between **widgets** (small application programs) and other application programs that provide auxiliary services such as a **wireless router**, **bluetooth** functions, and antivirus protection software (if installed). The appearance of these icons is customizable depending on how you set your system preferences. Usually, the system software will automatically install Menu Bar widgets and icons that allow you to access internal devices such as display settings, volume, date, and time.

Mac Dock: The Mac desktop currently features a **Dock** area, which has positioning and magnification features. You can place it on the bottom or sides of your screen. Your Apple menu can be set to magnify icons so that when you scroll over them with your cursor, they increase and decrease in scale. The Dock also provides easy access to the **Finder icon**, where you can view the menu contents of your hard drive/computer. On the right side of the Dock is the **Trash icon**, where you may drag and drop items to be deleted.

Hard Drive Icon: The only item that comes installed on the desktop is your Apple hard drive icon. When you double-click on it, the contents of your Mac are revealed in a window similar to that of the Finder.

PC Required Hardware

In order to operate Illustrator® and Photoshop®, you need a PowerPC running on the Windows operating system. Visit the official Adobe website for the latest system requirements and information.

PC Customization

The greatest advantage of PC computers is the fact that they can be customized to the preferences and lifestyles of the consumer. Another benefit is the ease of use with other interfaces that cater to the PC platform. Cross-platform users are surprised to discover the extra benefits and ease of downloads and Internet experiences for the Windows operating system versus those available for Mac users.

Basics: Parts of the PC, Ports, and Drives

Because various companies make PCs with different branding, they come in an endless variety of styles. It is impossible to predict what type of internal devices each company will feature as part of a particular customization. It is also difficult to predict where each company will place external features, such as ports and drives. The latest PC models have taken on the all-inclusive form of various products offered by Apple, including touch screen interfaces.

External Parts of the PC

Figure 1.4 shows some of the basic external parts of PC desktop and notebook models.

PC System Software

The system software that runs a PC is manufactured by Microsoft and is known universally as the Windows operating system. The recent version is the **Windows 7 operating system**, but older versions are still in use. The character of the Windows operating system differs from Mac OS in how you interface with the computer. Each additional software program, such as Illustrator® and Photoshop®, installed on a PC will have navigating differences from their Macintosh versions. They will also possess enough similarities to keep the programs familiar for both PC and Mac lovers.

PC Clicking Sequence

PCs usually come with a mouse that has a double-sided clicking function. The left side of the mouse performs functions similar to the Mac mouse. Use it to select, drag, and modify items and/or objects via pop-out menus.

PC Desktop

Gradually, over the years, both Apple and PC manufacturers have managed to develop some similar desktop interfaces. Because the Windows operating system runs PCs, they will all have similarities, but some features may not be available with certain types of hardware. PCs usually feature a dock at the bottom of the monitor that contains various icons allowing users instant access to applications with a click of the mouse. On the right side of the dock are widgets, and on the left side is the **Windows Start icon**. Use it to access all the contents and functions of your PC. The Windows operating system also installs certain icons on the desktop, including a **Recycle Bin** used for deleting files, and those allowing access to various application programs (Figure 1.5).

Note: Because PCs are in common universal use, we will detail visual information only as necessary in the tutorials.

Tutorial Software Requirements

In order to complete the tutorials in this book, you need to have Illustrator® and Photoshop® (Mac or Windows) installed on your computer. We will be using Adobe **CS5** in the tutorials, but most of the lessons may also be completed in other **CS** versions. However, in order to make the best use of the tutorial files on the DVDs, Adobe CS5 and higher versions are recommended.

Note: The release of **CS6** has introduced some great new features that will eventually revolutionize the way Illustrator® and Photoshop® are used in the global fashion industry. The essential differences between earlier versions will be noted throughout the chapters. You will be prompted to locate essential detailed instruction on the DVDs.

Software Bundles

The **Adobe Creative Suite** is the current "A" series of Adobe products encompassing a collection of bundled software packages for graphic design, web design, and video editing. The term **software bundle** refers to prepackaging of several different software programs for one price, usually installed together. The company offering a bundle saves money and markets the software at a promotional price. At the time of this writing, the current version is Adobe CS5 with a transition to CS6. The features of each version vary, and some users may not seek to upgrade each time Adobe makes changes. Each level of the Adobe Creative Suite is still in current use by consumers; however, higher versions are somewhat incompatible with lower versions.

Figure 1.5 This photo of a PC desktop is typical of the Windows 7 operating system and contains a dock, desktop icons, widgets, and the Windows logo.

Adobe Creative Suite

Although you only need Illustrator® and Photoshop® to complete the tutorials, you may want to go ahead and invest in the bundle in order to acquire the other relevant software. Besides, even with an educational discount, the cost is inexpensive compared to purchasing each of the programs separately. Shown in Figure 1.6 are the various software programs that are bundled in the Adobe Creative Suite.

Adobe Acrobat Professional® (Pro): Adobe Acrobat Pro® is used to view, create, manage, and edit Adobe's **Portable Document Format (PDF)** files that maintain the integrity of your work in a universal self-extracting format when shared.

Adobe Bridge®: Adobe Bridge® is a software program used to view and link files in the Adobe Creative Suite in an interface similar to a browser.

Adobe InDesign®: This program is used for creating multiple-page layouts where you can import vector graphics and photos, etc., combined with text formatting to facilitate desktop publishing of books, pamphlets, etc.

Adobe Illustrator®: Illustrator® is the most popular object-oriented, vector-based digital software used for drawing.

Adobe Photoshop®: Photoshop® is the most popular image-editing, raster-based digital software used for photo manipulation, retouching, drawing, and applying 3-D features.

Adobe Reader®: Adobe Reader® is a free, downloadable software program, created by Adobe Systems Incorporated, that enables you to open, view, and print PDF files, even without Adobe Acrobat Professional® installed on your computer.

Optional Supplies

You may choose to acquire or use the following optional supplies. In some cases these items are stan-dard equipment; however, they are not actually essential to the textbook tutorials. With each upgrade of the programs and the system software, the following information is subject to change.

Peripherals

Peripherals are input and output devices. Currently, most peripherals attach to computers via a universal serial bus (USB) port (Figure 1.7). Some peripherals, such as monitors and keyboards, are absolutely necessary. Others, such as digital projectors, external speakers, and web cams, are nonessential to digital design.

Input Devices

Input devices (keyboard, mouse, digital camera or scanner, etc.) import information into the computer.

Flatbed Scanners: A **flatbed scanner** is a tabletop electronic device used for digitizing documents and flat objects (Figure 1.8). You may need a fairly large flatbed model for digitizing your freehand illustrations, magazine tear sheets, vintage photos, trims, notions, and textile swatches. The settings on most scanners allow you to input the images at variable **spi**, or samples per inch. Many people confuse the resolution of scanners with the resolution of printers, which is **dpi**, or dots per inch. When we use the term **ppi**, or pixels per inch, which refers to monitors, even more confusion is added.

Contrary to popular belief, scanners are complicated devices; it would not hurt to ask questions before you make the decision to purchase one. Today, most scanner manufacturers refer to resolution as dpi. The higher the scanned resolution, the better the image will print; however, this also increases the size of the file. You should scan your images at a minimum of 300 dpi in order to generate digitized images that will be vivid and effective for various uses. The resolution of a file can always be reduced.

Graphics Tablets: Some fashion techies prefer the use of **graphics tablets** because they mimic the freeform flow of hand rendering (Figure 1.9).

Figure 1.6 A zoomed-in view of the Dock on a MacBook Pro reveals magnified icons from the Adobe Creative Suite CS5 including, from left to right: Adobe Acrobat Professional®, Adobe Bridge®, Adobe InDesign®, Illustrator®, Photoshop®, and Adobe Reader.

The Wacom® brand of tablets has become the must-have among fashion techies; their tablets come in a variety of sizes and models. Newer PC and Mac computers allow you to draw with the tip of your finger.

Note: Touch apps such as Photoshop® Touch and Adobe Collage are currently available for Android touch devices and may soon be available for iPads. Currently these apps augment full versions of Illustrator® and Photoshop® installed on laptop and desktop computers.

Digital Camera: Everyone uses digital cameras to capture images for inspiration in a format that is ready for immediate transfer to a computer. Even cell phones have them. You never know when you'll need an image to add to something that you are working on. A 10-megapixels or higher digital camera will take acceptable pictures.

Output Devices

Output devices (printers, monitors, digital projectors, etc.) are those that bring information out of a computer.

Printers: Although you probably could use a printer, it is not necessary for completing the tutorials in this book. To generate quality enlargements and storyboard prints, take your high-resolution files to any output image center. Owning a printer and purchasing paper and replacement ink cartridges can be more burdensome and expensive than simply having someone print for you. If you decide to purchase a printer, purchase an inkjet model. Epson has efficient, quality products that are advanced in technology, and the company stands behind their products. Some of their printers are capable of producing museum-quality prints (with appropriate media) in wide formats. Visit their website for more detailed information and product descriptions.

Saving, Storing, and Transferring Your Work

Because you will likely need to transfer your files from one computer to another, storage devices will come in handy. There are many ways to store data, and one may be to save your work right onto a campus network drive. Often this can be unreliable, and files do disappear. Therefore, before we discuss storage devices, a little information on file formats is apropos.

Popular File Formats

Throughout this book, you will be told to **save** your work, but you need to know which file formats to use. The **file format** is the character of the file and determines how it will communicate with applica-

Figure 1.7 A universal serial bus (USB) port. © Editorial Image, LLC/Alamy.

Figure 1.8 A flatbed scanner. © Niels Poulsen/Alamy.

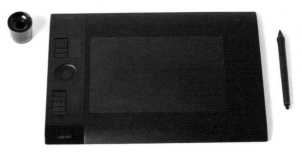

Figure 1.9 Graphics tablet. © Greg Gard/Alamy.

tions and system software. Each file format has its own extension beginning with a period or dot right after the file name. Both Illustrator® and Photoshop® have their own specific file formats:

- Illustrator®: .ai (for example, digital_duo_tutorial.ai)
- Photoshop®: .psd (for example, digital_duo_tutorial.psd)

These default file formats are first in the list of those offered in the **Save As** dialog box pull-down menus that you see when saving or updating a file. The default file formats allow you to continue to edit your work and will retain the file's layers. The trade-off for this convenience is an increased file size. You will learn more about layers later, but for now—unless otherwise instructed—in the tutorials, always save your work in the default file formats. It is also a good practice to save your files in the default formats first, and then save copies in additional file formats if needed. Each *Save As* dialog box in the Adobe programs has a *Copy* option. By choosing this option, you will always have at least one file that you can edit. This is especially true of Photoshop® files because other file formats can flatten (compress) your work. The following are a few file formats that you will find useful with this book.

Adobe PDF

The Illustrator® Portable Document Format is a transfer application that allows you to share your work and retain its integrity. This includes an ability to write the layers, so that when a file is opened in Illustrator® on another computer, it can be restored to its original state. The receiving computer must have the same version of Illustrator® or higher installed; otherwise, the file will appear flattened and lose some of its features. Save your work in this format when you need to send it by e-mail or to communicate with another platform or application. This format is readable on all computers with the free Adobe Reader®. Many of the enclosed DVD files have been saved in the PDF format, so that you can open them right in the programs.

Illustrator EPS

The **Encapsulated Post Script** format maintains high resolution and is the choice for printing high-quality images, especially for large production runs.

Photoshop PDF

This is the Photoshop® file format for a Portable Document Format file.

Photoshop JPEG

The **Joint Photographic Experts Group** extension will dramatically reduce your file size, but you will also lose your layers in the compression. The quality of the image will not be significantly reduced as long as it was high-resolution to begin with. Many of the enclosed DVD files have been saved in the JPEG format, so that you can open them right in the programs.

Photoshop EPS

This is the Photoshop® file format for an Encapsulated Post Script format.

Storage Devices

File saving is likely something that you are already familiar with, but periodically you will be reminded in the book to save and back up your work. If you are taking a course, ask your instructor for file requirements for submission of projects. Naturally, you will need something to store your files on as a backup to your computer. Here are some popular methods of storing your files.

Note: *Technology is changing, so some of the following devices are subject to extinction. The increasingly popular cloud technology allows you to save your work without a device via an app that will store it on a remote server. Other features include the ability to receive tech support and upgrades via a web browser.*

Portable External Hard Drives

Portable external hard drives are great for people who are working on public or communal computers (Figure 1.10). You can carry them with you if you need to store large files that cannot be contained on other storage devices. If you do not have ample disk space available on your home computer, purchase a desk model external hard disk drive.

USB Flash Drive

USB flash drives are a common method of storing digital information (Figure 1.11). They fit directly into the USB ports of your computers and are generally reliable as long as they are kept dry. Occasionally, they have a limited storage capacity and can become corrupt. They are also prone to hosting computer viruses.

Compact Discs

CD-ROMs (CD-R) and **DVD-ROMs (DVD-R)** are still the most reliable storage devices. **CD-RW** discs are rewritable. Just remember that nothing is forever, so back up your important files in a few places.

Adapters

In order to transfer data in and out of your computer, you will need the right adapters. Some computer manufacturers provide **adapters**, but others do not. Notebooks and laptops come with a power adapter cord to keep them charged. If you want to connect your unit to a projector or a flat-screen HDTV display, you may need a **video graphics array (VGA)** adapter (Figure 1.12). You will need an adapter that has a **digital visual interface (DVI)** connection on one side and a VGA connection on the opposite.

Table 1.1	How Disk Space Is Measured	
Unit	*Symbol*	*Value*
byte	B	unit
kilobyte	KB or Kbyte	1,000 bytes
megabyte	MB or Mbyte	1,000 kilobytes
gigabyte	GB or Gbyte	1,000 megabytes
terabyte	Tb or TB	1,000 gigabytes

Figure 1.10 Portable hard drive. © Metta foto/Alamy.

Figure 1.11 USB flash drive. © PaulPaladin/Alamy.

Figure 1.12 Video graphics array (VGA) adapter.
© Stockimages/Alamy.

Disk Space

Before you can begin the tutorials, you need to know that **disk space** is measured in **bytes**, **kilobytes**, **megabytes**, **gigabytes**, and **terabytes** (Table 1.1). The tutorial files on the enclosed DVDs have been saved as Adobe Portable Document Format (.pdf) files. The files were created at high resolution but were later reduced to save space. You can open the files in either Illustrator® or Photoshop® and update them to the version of the Adobe Creative Suite that is on your computer. The files were created in CS5, so if you open them in lower versions, the layers will be merged. The layers will be fine if you are opening the files with higher versions of Illustrator® and Photoshop®. You will learn more about this as you use the book.

After you locate a file on the DVDs, you will need to save it to a disk, and that is where disk space becomes an issue. Some disk space is used when you save a file to your computer, CD-R, portable hard drive, or flash drive. As you work with the file, you will also add to its size because each filter, stroke, fill, gradient, etc. from Illustrator® and Photoshop® increases it.

Naturally, the aim of all fashion presentation is the look, so a decent understanding of disk space is essential to creating proper files. Every disk has a size capacity. Newer computers can come with hard drives with hundreds of gigabytes of space. You should purchase a computer that has at least a 300 to 500 GB hard drive. Just so that you get an understanding, your portable hard drive might have as much as 400 GB of space. A CD-R can typically contain 700 GB of data, and a flash drive has about 20 GB of space.

Random Access Memory

Your system software and other applications will take up plenty of space. What is left over after your computer loads the system software and other

Figure 1.13 Image appears bitmapped when scanned at 20 dpi.

Figure 1.14 Same image appears sharper when scanned at 300 dpi.

applications is known as **random access memory (RAM)**. A graphics software program can use approximately 2 GB of disk space. The tunes that you download to your music player take up about 4 MB, and a full-color digital fashion illustration/presentation created at 300 dpi could take up as much as 30 MB. Depending on other factors, it can even be as much as several gigabytes.

Resolution

Understanding disk space and resolution are directly related. **Resolution** has to do with the visual quality of files for scanners and printers. The higher the resolution, the more space you will use. Fashion presentations, by their very nature, require high-resolution files, especially those that are to be printed. It is important for you to input files at high resolution so that your output print or display image will be of good quality. It is not possible to improve an image by increasing the resolution. For example, if you scan an image or import it from a digital camera at 20 dpi, the image will looked **bitmapped** (Figure 1.13). However, if you scan the same image at 300 dpi, you will get a clearer picture (Figure 1.14). Even if you reduce a "high-res" file through compression, the quality will still show through.

Keyboard Macros

One goal of this textbook is to encourage you to use the **shortcut commands**. In each tutorial you will notice that the shortcut/hotkey sequences are arranged in *italicized, blue text*. You can use **macros** to perform computing tasks by pressing **code keys** on your keyboard instead of using your mouse. You may have noticed that the **shortcuts** or **hotkeys** listed after the titles of operations in your hierarchical pull-down and **scroll menus**. They

are usually located directly to the right of the title. The purpose of learning the shortcut coding is to assist you with maintaining your creative focus and accuracy. This will enable you to keep your eyes on your work. Using the shortcuts will not necessarily increase speed except in routine or repetitious operations, and digital rendering is still a manual task like freehand drawing.

Mac Modifier Keys and Keyboarding

On the Mac the **Command keys** (⌘) are the main **modifier keys** used to facilitate multikey macros. The Command keys are located on each side of your spacebar. Proper keyboarding calls for you to depress them with your thumbs and reach for the other keys with your fingers to complete your command sequences. Use the left thumb for the left Command key and the right thumb for the right Command key. Do not cross your hand over the keyboard to reach the commands on the other side. This is definitely a sign of insufficient training. The Mac **Option**, **Control**, and **Shift** keys are also modifier keys. You can use them in a sequence with other keys to change their function. Some operations have single key shortcuts; particularly notable are those within the software programs that allow you to move around the toolboxes.

PC Modifier Keys and Keyboarding

In PC circles, similar rules apply to macros but the term hotkey is popular for modifier keys. On a PC the **Control key** replaces the Command key and the **Alt key** replaces the Option key. Similar keyboarding should be exercised by using the thumbs to depress modifier keys appropriately on each side of the keyboard. However, it is acceptable to use the pinky fingers to access the keys at the far left and right when performing a shortcut sequence. On all full keyboards, use the number pad at the right to enter mathematical information with your right hand instead of the numbers at the top. Avoid crossing over the keyboard to reach for keys when possible.

The Code Connectors

Because this textbook is being written for both Mac and PC platforms, there is the possibility of confusing the written code sequences. To keep things clear, the code language has been unified through the use of plus and "greater than" symbols, and instructions will be given using the formal titles of the keys themselves. Table 1.2 includes relevant keyboard modifier keys for both the Mac and Windows operating systems.

The plus (+) character will be used between Mac and PC keyboard shortcut sequences to let you know when to press a series of keys. Do not press the + key. Press those keys that it divides. For example: Press *Cmd+S / Ctrl+S* to save a file.

For Mac and PC menu sequences, the titles will be divided by the "greater than" (>) symbol. Do not press the > key. For example: Go to *Menu Bar > Edit > Define Pattern, and then press OK.*

Table 1.2   Relevant Keyboard Modifier Keys

Apple Mac OS X		Windows Operating System
⌘ (Command key)	=	B
⌥ (Option key)	=	(Alt key)
⇧ (Shift key)	=	(Shift key)
Fn (Function key)		(F1, F2, F3 etc.)

Chapter 1 Summary

There are endless varieties of options for desktop publishing on each computer platform and for various software applications. This book has been written to prepare you for creating fashion presentations using both Mac OS X and Windows operating systems. The shortcut or hotkey sequences will be listed for each platform in the tutorials; however, it is recommended that you commit to memory those manual functions that you perform repeatedly. With each software upgrade you should anticipate some changes in the sequences.

Personal computers and desktop publishing are now a way of life. In order to stay ahead of the competition, you will need to be committed to staying abreast of the latest technology. It is unnecessary to purchase each new gadget that appears on the market, but you should stay informed, especially concerning cloud technology, the introduction of new apps, and software upgrades. Your ability to speak intelligently about digital fashion presentation, technology innovation, and their end use through desktop publishing for the apparel industry will take you far up the ladder of success.

Chapter 1 Self-Assessment

1. Can I name the system software that runs a PC?
2. Can I name the current system software for Apple computers?
3. In computing, do I know what is meant by the term customization?
4. Can I name the basic parts of the Mac desktop?
5. Do I know how the central processing unit is different from the hard disk drive?
6. Do I know which port(s) on a computer allow access to peripherals?
7. Can I name the external parts of Mac and PC computers?
8. Do I know how the Finder is different from the Start icon?
9. If I wanted to e-mail someone a file, but I was not certain if the recipient would be able to open it, do I know what type of file format to use?
10. Do I know how disk space is measured?
11. Do I know what the acronym RAM stands for?
12. Can I locate and properly use the Command key on Macintosh computers? Am I familiar with and do I practice proper keyboarding?
13. Do I know which modifier key on the PC keyboard is equal to the Command key?
14. Do I know how many megabytes are in 1 gigabyte?
15. Am I familiar with the latest features of the system software that I'm using?

Basic Vector Design Skills with Illustrator®

2

Objectives

Chapter 2 introduces you to object-oriented vector graphics for both the Macintosh and PC platforms. The basic rendering features of Illustrator® will be explored through an overview of the Illustrator® desktop interface and software features. The information in this chapter and practice exercises will help you to become familiar with the program's tools and panels, and assist you in learning to draw electronically. This chapter is just the foundation; you will become familiar with each important aspect of the program as you advance in the tutorials to come. The Chapter 2 objectives include:

- ◉ Understanding vector software attributes

- ◉ Setting up and saving Artboards

- ◉ Arranging and saving Workspaces

- ◉ Exploring and organizing the basic Illustrator® panels and docks

- ◉ Utilizing tools in the Tools panel

- ◉ Operating the functions of the Stroke panel

- ◉ Discovering the Illustrator® Menu Bar, Application Bar, and Control Panel

- ◉ Learning various ways to navigate the Illustrator® window

- ◉ Using the Fill and Stroke buttons in the Tools panel

- ◉ Mixing spot colors and saving swatches

- ◉ Coordinating Layer Compositing to organize your work

Figure 2.1
Upper portion of the PC Illustrator® Tools panel.

Figure 2.2
Fill and Stroke buttons on the Illustrator® Tools panel.

Working with Illustrator®

Developed by Adobe Systems Incorporated, Illustrator® is the foremost vector software program. **Vectors** are parameters that mark a position in digital space. In Illustrator® they are called anchor points. **Vector software** is object-oriented, so shapes are used in combinations to create composite images. This is also referred to as **vector art** or **vector animation**.

There are many ways to use Illustrator®: You can operate it manually through the Menu Bar with a mouse, stylus, or touch-sensitive technology, or via keyboard shortcut combinations. Illustrator® offers a multiplicity of digital capabilities that you can access by clicking icons that activate program functions. Most of these icons correspond to the basic principles of graphic design, but fine arts capabilities are slowly being integrated with each product update. In addition to the many ways to access the program, there are also several ways to accomplish some of the same tasks. The lessons in the book will not cover every method—just those that are appropriate for what is essential. Active experimentation with the program and communication with the Adobe online community, your instructor, and/or your personal network of techie friends and associates will provide the rest.

Loading and Artboards

When Illustrator® is loaded, you will see the program's interface and window, but a new document must be set up in order to begin using the program. Pressing *Cmd+N / Ctrl+N* will reveal a **New Document Profile** dialog box. Dialog boxes are prompts on the screen containing fields that require the user to enter information before a computer program carries out a command. In this chapter you will simply use the default settings and press the OK button. However, in the tutorials to come, each new document will require its own settings. If the Illustrator® logo and opening menu appears before the window opens, simply press the link/button that allows you to create a new document. Create a letter-size document, and a white window will appear with a tab. In this window is a rectangular shape outlined in black known as the **Artboard** or printable area. It can be customized to sizes up to 227 × 227 inches.

Illustrator® Tools Panel

When the program is loaded, you should find that the **Tools panel** appears on the left side of the program's window. This is the default position, but it can be anchored to the right with the other panels, or you can float it anywhere else on the screen. If the Tools panel is not visible, go to *Menu Bar > Window > Tools* to show it.

Note: *In Illustrator® CS6, the interface, by default, will be dark gray. The CS6 user interface color can be customized via the Preferences. See CS6_Adjust_ User_Interface_Color.mov on ① Ch 02.*

The Illustrator® Tools panel is the most important panel of the program. You cannot maneuver without it. The Tools panel is divided into six parts, including a column of tools. You will learn to use the Tools panel effectively as you complete the tutorials; however, it will be to your advantage to take time out to experiment with each tool. Box 2.1 on page 15 shows the Illustrator® CS5 tool names and keyboard shortcuts for Macintosh computers. The red characters next to each tool correspond to the names and shortcuts listed in the gray shaded area of the figure. These are the same for Mac and PC. By pressing these codes on the keyboard, you can switch from one tool to another. Some tools do not have a keyboard shortcut, while others within a suite of tools share one. Place your cursor over the Tools panel to view a display of the names and the keyboard shortcuts for each tool.

Note: *Information concerning new relevant CS6 tools will be discussed in the tutorials or via DVD extras where prompted.*

Moving and Converting the Tools Panel

At the top of the Tools panel is a bar (Figure 2.1). To move the panel around your window, click on the double set of broken lines right beneath it and drag the panel to another position. The same action works with other panels as well. Inside this dark gray bar is a twin arrow icon that you can click to convert the Tools panel from a single column to a double column formation of the tools. The bar also contains a small "o" (Mac) or "x" (PC). Click on these to close the Tools panel. To show it again, go to *Menu Bar > Window > Tools*.

Tools Panel Attributes

Figure 2.2 shows the area beneath the tools, which contains the **Fill button** on the left and the **Stroke button** on the right. You will use them to alter the appearance of selected objects. The default attributes of the Fill and Stroke are a Fill of white and a Stroke of black. In this state, the Fill is always in the front overlapping the Stroke button. The double-sided arrow that you see allows you to swap the contents of the Fill and Stroke. The icon in the lower left corner restores the default attributes. If you would like to change the **Fill** of a selected object, select it first, and then click on the Fill box in the Tools panel before making changes by selecting colors, gradients, or patterns. Remember, the Fill box must be selected, and in the front position. To adjust the **Stroke**, follow the same instructions, but make sure the Stroke is selected and in the front position within the Tools panel.

Box 2.1: Tool Names and Keyboard Shortcuts

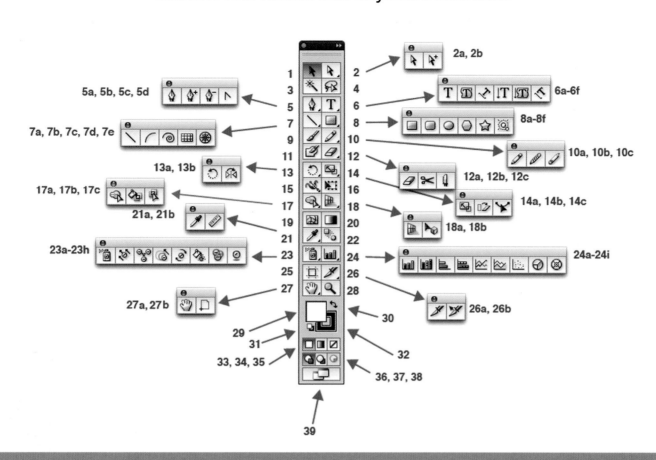

1. Selection Tool (V)	8c. Ellipse Tool (L)	18a. Perspective Grid Tool (Shift+P)	24h. Pie Graph Tool
2a. Direct Selection Tool (A)	8d. Polygon Tool		24i. Radar Graph Tool
2b. Group Selection Tool	8e. Star Tool	18b. Perspective Selection Tool (Shift+V)	25. Artboard Tool (Shift+O)
3. Magic Wand Tool (Y)	8f. Flare Tool		26a. Slice Tool (Shift+K)
4. Lasso Tool (Q)	9. Paintbrush Tool (B)	19. Mesh Tool (M)	26b. Slice Select Tool
5a. Pen Tool (P)	10a. Pencil Tool (N)	20. Gradient Tool (G)	27a. Hand Tool (H)
5b. Add Anchor Point Tool (+)	10b. Smooth Tool	21a. Eyedropper Tool (I)	27b. Print Tiling Tool
5c. Delete Anchor Point Tool (-)	10c. Path Eraser Tool	21b. Measure Tool	28. Zoom Tool (Z)
	11. Blob Brush Tool (Shift+B)	22. Blend Tool (W)	29. Fill (X); click to activate
5d. Convert Anchor Point Tool (Shift+C)	12a. Eraser Tool (Shift+E)	23a. Symbol Sprayer Tool (Shift+S)	30. Swap Fill and Stroke (Shift+X)
6a. Type Tool (T)	12b. Scissors Tool (C)	23b. Symbol Shifter Tool	31. Default Fill and Stroke (D)
6b. Area Type Tool	12c. Knife Tool	23c. Symbol Scruncher Tool	
6c. Type on a Path Tool	13a. Rotate Tool (R)	23d. Symbol Sizer Tool	32. Stroke (X); click to activate
6d. Vertical Type Tool	13b. Reflect Tool (O)	23e. Symbol Spinner Tool	
6e. Vertical Area Type Tool	14a. Scale Tool (S)	23f. Symbol Stainer Tool	33. Color (<)
6f. Vertical Type on a Path Tool	14b. Shear Tool	23g. Symbol Screener Tool	34. Gradient (>)
	14c. Reshape Tool	23h. Symbol Styler Tool	35. None (/)
7a. Line Segment Tool (\)	15. Width Tool (Shift+W)	24a. Column Graph Tool (J)	36. Draw Normal (Shift+D to switch modes)
7b. Arc Tool	16. Free Transform Tool (E)	24b. Stacked Column Graph Tool	37. Draw Behind (Shift+D to switch modes)
7c. Spiral Tool	17a. Shape Builder Tool (Shift+M)		
7d. Rectangular Grid Tool	17b. Live Paint Bucket (K)	24c. Bar Graph Tool	38. Draw Inside (Shift+D to switch modes)
7e. Polar Grid Tool	17c. Live Paint Selection Tool (Shift+L)	24d. Stacked Bar Graph Tool	
8a. Rectangle Tool (M)		24e. Line Graph Tool	39. Change Screen Mode (F)
8b. Rounded Rectangle Tool		24f. Area Graph Tool	
		24g. Scatter Graph Tool	

Figure 2.3
Fill and Stroke options on the Illustrator® Tools panel.

Figure 2.4
Drawing Modes on the Illustrator® Tools panel.

Figure 2.5
Screen Mode icon on the Illustrator® Tools panel.

Figure 2.3 reveals Fill and Stroke options, such as access to the **Color panel**, the **Gradient panel**, and a **None icon** button. Click on the None icon button when you do not want a Fill and/or Stroke on a selected object. **Figure 2.4** contains the Tools panel's **drawing modes**, which are (from left to right) the default **Draw Normal** mode, a **Draw Behind** mode (draw behind a shape), and a **Draw Inside** mode (draw inside a shape). At the bottom is a screen mode icon (**Figure 2.5**). Change the **screen mode** to suit your viewing preferences by clicking on this icon and scrolling to either of three settings: **Normal Screen Mode**, **Full Screen Mode with Menu Bar**, or **Full Screen Mode**. To return to the default Normal Screen Mode, press the Escape button on the keyboard.

Tool Tear-Off Menus

Those tool icons with small black dots/arrows/triangles in their lower right corners have **tear-off menus** revealing hidden tools. You can show hidden tool suites by clicking and holding the current tool. (**Box 2.1** exhibits all of the Tool panel's tear-off menus.) You can also scroll to the bar at the right side; when it is highlighted, click and pull the menu onto your page. The tear-off menus will help you to access specific tools quickly by placing them near your work area. Click and hold the **title bar** to move them around the page.

Watch the **QuickTime** movie AI_Tools_Panel.mov located on ① Ch02. The short film demonstrates how to access and manipulate the Tools panel. You will need a current version of the **QuickTime player** installed on your computer. Free downloads for Mac and PC are available from the Apple website.

Illustrator® Preferences

Illustrator® contains a comprehensive panel of **Preferences** (preferred operating options). With them you can adjust the general functions of the software program to fit your particular needs for any project. Find the **Preferences Menu** at *Menu Bar > Illustrator > Preferences (Mac)*, or *Menu Bar > Edit > Preferences (PC)*. In Illustrator®, a **Preferences button** is located in the Control Panel for easy access when you are in Full Screen Mode with Menu Bar. Selecting this button causes a Preferences dialog box to appear. Scroll the menu to make adjustments; press OK to keep the changes, or Cancel to exit the menu (Figure 2.6).

The Preferences menus adjust a variety of functions, but the areas you will need later include **General**, **Units**, **Guides & Grid**, and **Smart Guides**. While the default settings are fine for most of your basic functions, we will return to the Preferences menus throughout the tutorials to enable specific aspects of the program.

The Illustrator® Window, Desktop, and Help

Most colleges have both PC and Mac labs, so it is useful for you to become acquainted with each version of Illustrator®. The same is true of many apparel and accessory manufacturers. You will need to be able to work on whichever platform is available to remain competitive in the job market. As mentioned in Chapter 1, each program that you load on your computer has a different desktop interface. The Mac and PC versions of Illustrator® are equally comprehensive. Although the program functions are identical in both versions, they do appear slightly dissimilar, and a few things are located in different places. On Macs, the Menu Bar is separate, the Application Bar is in the middle, and the Control Panel, by default, is right under it. The Illustrator® PC version has the Menu Bar and Application Bar together at the top, and the Control Panel is under it. **Figure 2.7** reveals the basic parts of an Illustrator® desktop for Mac. **Figure 2.8** reveals the basic parts of an Illustrator® desktop for PC. Study the desktop elements identified by the arrows. Use the glossary to define the terms. The rest will be provided in the practice exercises and tutorials.

Most of the Illustrator® window functions for Mac and PC are the same. You can scroll the pages up and down, or right and left. The icons to close or collapse a window on the Mac are in the upper left corner of the window title bar (red to close, yellow to collapse, and green to fit the window to the screen). In the PC version, these options are on the opposite side of the window and have self-explanatory icons for the same functions.

Illustrator® Window Options

At one point, you will need to open more than one window. When you do, you will notice that Illustrator® docks them together with tabs in what they refer to as an **Application Frame**. To arrange the windows, go to *Menu Bar > Window > Float in Window* or *Float All in Windows*. You can restore the windows to the consolidated docked position, too.

Preferences

General ▼

Keyboard Increment: 0.0139 in

Constrain Angle: 0 °

Corner Radius: 0.17 in

OK
Cancel
Previous
Next

☐ Disable Auto Add/Delete ☑ Double Click To Isolate
☐ Use Precise Cursors ☐ Use Japanese Crop Marks
☑ Show Tool Tips ☑ Transform Pattern Tiles
☑ Anti-aliased Artwork ☐ Scale Strokes & Effects
☐ Select Same Tint % ☐ Use Preview Bounds
☑ Append [Converted] Upon Opening Legacy Files

Reset All Warning Dialogs

Figure 2.6 Illustrator® Preferences menu.

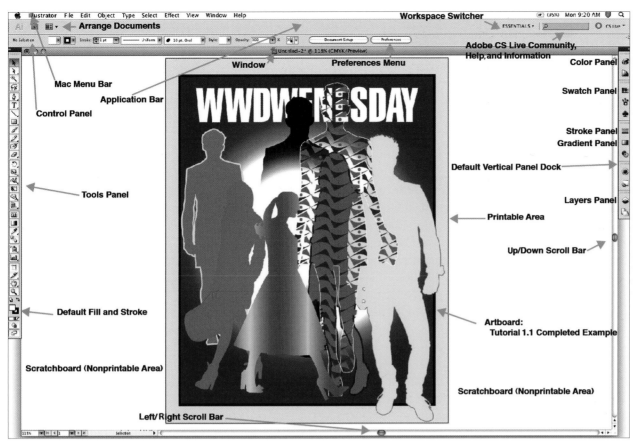

Figure 2.7 Basic parts of the Illustrator® CS5 desktop for Mac.

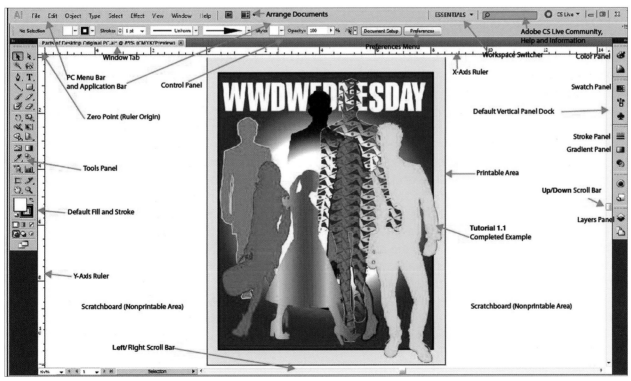

Figure 2.8 Basic parts of the Illustrator® CS5 desktop for PC.

Arrange Documents

Use the **Arrange Documents menu** for various viewing options. You can select any window simply by clicking on its tab. Windows can be rearranged by clicking and dragging them by these tabs. To float a window, click and drag the tab out of the docked group. To close a window, click "x" in the tab, or press *Cmd+W / Ctrl+W*.

The Application Bar

The CS5 **Application Bar** houses those functions that assist the user and augment the program, including the Illustrator® logo, a button that will take you to Adobe Bridge® (a program used to access and organize files), the Arrange Documents menu icon, and the Workspace Switcher. In addition, there is a search field that will take you to Adobe Community Help. The application's menu is located in the Application Bar (Figures 2.7 and 2.8).

Illustrator® Workspaces

A **Workspace** is simply your preferred working desktop. Illustrator® allows you to work with preset or saved Workspaces. We will set up and save various Workspaces throughout the tutorials to make learning and applications easier.

The Illustrator® **Workspace Switcher** is located in the Application Bar. Familiarize yourself with the various preset Workspaces by **tipping** (clicking on an arrow to access a hidden menu) the **arrow pointer**. The menu offers a series of grouped panels and docks them, by default, on the right of the window. Once you select and save your preferred Workspace, you will not have to set it up each time you open the program (Figures 2.7 and 2.8).

Saving Workspaces: The preset Essentials Workspace and the Painting Workspace will be close to what we need for our exercises and tutorials; however, you may choose to make changes. To remove panels from the dock located on the right side of your window, click on the tab of the panel you want to remove. Drag it onto the Artboard and close the panel. To reunite the panel with the dock, click and drag it near the dock until it becomes translucent; you will see a blue line. This is an indication that the program is **meshing** with the dock and the area is called a **Drop Zone**. To extend a panel, click the arrows on its top bar. Panels can be arranged in almost limitless combinations to facilitate the most useful Workspace for your particular task. Take some time to experiment with them. Also consult the Help menu.

If you want to save the adjusted Workspace, click on the Workspace Switcher, and then scroll to Save Workspace. When the Save Workspace dialog box appears, give the new Workspace an appropriate name in the highlighted field. You may also delete Workspaces here in the Manage Workspace section. When you choose this option, a dialog box will appear. Select any Workspace that you have saved and click the *Delete Workspace* icon at the bottom.

The Control Panel

The **Control Panel** is a hub for other panel/tool functions, and provides quick access to them. In Illustrator®, the Control Panel can be docked at the top or the bottom of your Workspace by clicking and holding the hidden menu icon on the right side and scrolling to the option. You can also float the Control Panel by pulling it from its tab at the right onto the page. To replace it, just drag it back beneath the Menu Bar until you see the Drop Zone.

The Control Panel can be customized to suit your working requirements; however, some of the Illustrator® panel attributes appear in it by default. One of these is the **Document Setup button**, which allows you to return to the document setup and make changes to the page attributes. You can also access or change the Fill, Stroke, brushes, styles, or Opacity, and select similar objects with a click of your mouse and by scrolling to the various options. The hidden menu can also be used to select functions of the program that you would like to reveal in the Control Panel by checking the appropriate boxes. For example: If the Align box is checked, each time that you select two or more objects, the **Align panel** options will appear in the Control Panel. If you do not want certain panel options to show in the Control Panel, simply uncheck them in the hidden menu (Figures 2.7 and 2.8).

Note: *When nothing else is selected, you can also access the Preferences menu via a button in the Control Panel.*

Illustrator® Panels

Panels contain associated functions allowing you to create effects through a single interface. Illustrator® features easy-to-use panels that relate to the principles of graphic design, technical sciences, fine arts, and more. There are essential panels that you will use constantly and others that you will use only for special projects. Key features of many of the panels include a row of icon buttons at the bottom, which allow you to add and delete, among other features. In addition, each panel that we shall use in this book has a hidden menu at the right side where you can access additional panel options. You will learn to use the panels and functions that will best service you as a fashion student and professional.

Managing Panels

No matter what size Artboard you work on, you will often need screen space, because panels can block your actual working area. However, in Illustrator®, panels can be moved, hidden, docked, collapsed, and stacked. One option is for you to keep your panels on an area referred to as the **Scratchboard** (the nonprintable area outside of your Artboard).

Showing and Hiding Panels: Panels may be shown opened, as icons, with names in groups, and/or stacked in **vertical docks**. Some panels toggle visibility via keyboard shortcuts (usually **function keys**). By default, panels will be shown in the preset Workspaces in various ways. They will generally be stacked as open or icon docks pinned to the right of the Workspace. This stack of panels is referred to as a default vertical dock.

To show panels as icons with names, place your cursor on the side of the panel until you see a double-sided arrow. Pull the panel open to a desirable width. The panel's name will show. You can show the panels that you will need; you can also completely hide, or close them. To close a panel, click the small button on the left of its title bar (Mac) or click the "x" in the title bar at the right (PC). If you have closed all your panels and wish to create a new vertical dock, drag the panel(s) to the right edge of your Workspace until you see a Drop Zone. Toggle the visibility of your panels, including the Tools panel, by pressing *Tab*.

Docking Panels: By default, the panels are docked in groups horizontally. For example, when you show the Layers panel, it will be docked with the **Artboard panel**. You can remove panels from these groupings by clicking and dragging their tabs. Move an entire panel by clicking and dragging the title bar at the top. Panels can be docked vertically or horizontally. To do this, drag a panel or docked group of panels below or at the side of another until it turns translucent and you see a blue line. Figure 2.9 shows a grouping of panels that appear with the **Transform panel**.

Collapsing and Resizing Panels: The panels can also be collapsed into icons only by clicking on the twin arrow icon in their title bars. To collapse an open panel, click on the title bar. Panels may be resized by moving your cursor to the edges and pulling the double-sided arrow that appears.

Basic Color Panels: There are several ways to choose, mix, and apply color to your work in Illustrator®. Since you will be applying color to either Strokes or Fills, the easiest way to do this is to click once on the Stroke or Fill icon in the Tools panel. When you do, a simple Color panel will appear (for more on color, see Chapter 9).

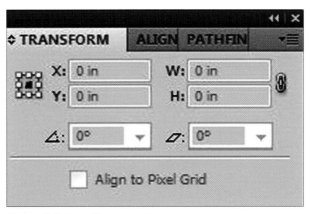

Figure 2.9 Transform panel.

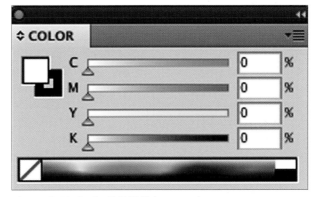

Figure 2.10 Basic CMYK Color panel.

Color Panel Details: You can use the Color panel to mix **spot colors**. The term is borrowed from its original use in printing when inks are used for a single run. In the case of computers it refers to hues mixed by the user for a single use. The two uses become similar under the umbrella of desktop publishing. Spot colors can be mixed for whichever color mode you are working in by moving the sliders or typing in percentages. Figure 2.10 shows the **Basic CMYK Color panel's** set of four sliders. Each slider adjusts one of the colors (cyan, magenta, yellow, and black). To mix a new spot color, move the sliders and the results will appear in the preview Fill or Stroke of the panel. When you are satisfied with a color that you have mixed, click and drag the swatch into the **Swatches panel** and give it an appropriate name by double-clicking on the swatch and typing the name into the Swatch Name field of the Swatch Options dialog box. When you save your work, that color will always appear in the Swatches panel each time you open the file. For now, you will only use the Basic CMYK Swatches panel, which is shown in Figure 2.11. In Chapter 9 you will learn more about digital color.

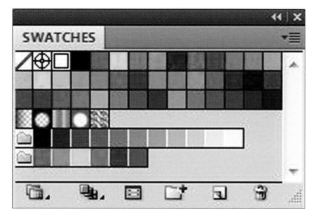

Figure 2.11 Basic CMYK Swatches panel.

Swatches Panel Details: The Basic CMYK Swatches panel (for four-color printing processes on paper) or the **Basic RGB Swatches panel** (for three-color printing processes using light) usually appears in the vertical panel dock depending on the color mode you selected when you opened the New Document Profile dialog box. You can also locate the Swatches panel by going to *Menu Bar > Window > Swatch Libraries > Default Swatches.* The panel consists of primary, secondary, and intermediate colors along with select neutrals, grays, brights, gradients, fades, and default patterns. At the bottom of the panel are buttons offering access to the Swatches panel attributes. From left to right these include:

- **Swatch Libraries** menu: Allows quick access to other default swatches.

- **Show Swatch Kinds** button: Allows you to show only color or gradients, etc.

- **Menu Swatch Options** button: Alters the properties of a selected swatch.

- **New Color Group:** Creates a folder where swatches can be organized.

- **New Color:** Creates a new spot color swatch that can be mixed.

- **Delete Swatch:** Permanently removes it from the Swatches panel.

By clicking and holding the hidden menu icon on the right side of the panel in the title bar, you can access additional Swatches panel attributes and features.

Navigator Panel: The **Navigator panel** (Figure 2.12) allows you to easily move about the page. The main feature of this panel is its **Proxy Preview Area** (red box) that mirrors the larger page view. You can move this red box to change your view to a specific area of the page. When you place your cursor inside the Proxy Preview Area, the cursor's icon will turn into a grabber icon that looks like the **Hand Tool (H).** Use it to move the page view within the Proxy Preview Area. The actual Hand Tool (H) located in the Tools

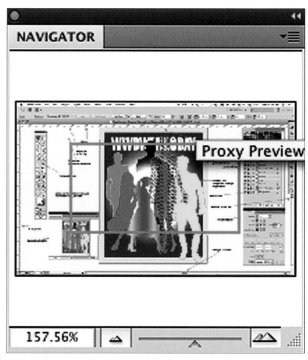

Figure 2.12 Navigator panel.

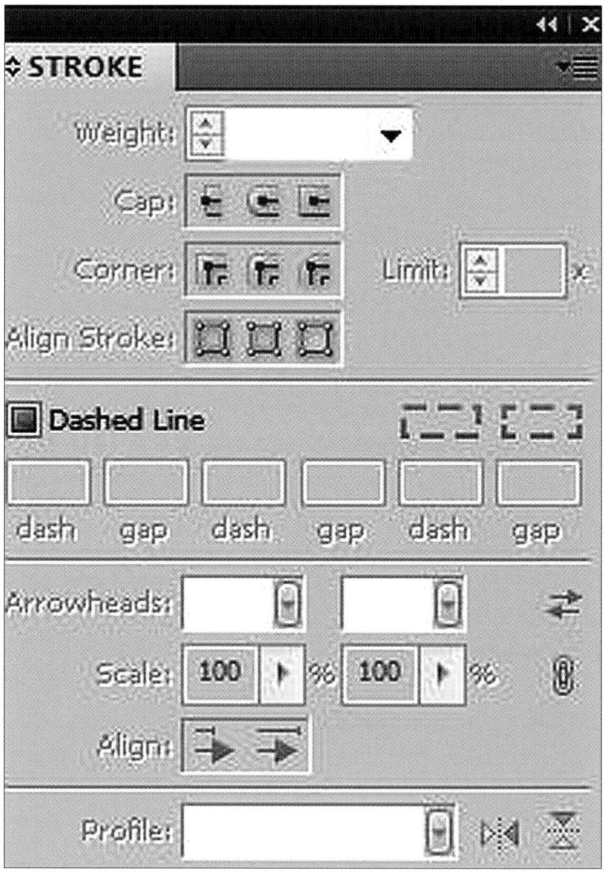

Figure 2.13 Stroke panel.

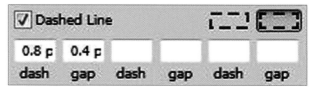

Figure 2.14 The Aligns Dashes to Corners and Path Ends icon is selected.

panel allows you to grab the Artboard and move the page within the window. At the bottom of the Navigator panel, from left to right, are a percentage scale, a **zoom-out** icon, a **Zoom Slider**, and a **zoom-in** icon. Each of these also corresponds to both the Proxy Preview Area and the window view of your page.

Stroke Panel: The **Stroke panel** (Figure 2.13) allows you to create solid or dashed outlines of various widths. A feature of Illustrator® CS5 and CS6 gives you the ability to narrow or widen a color line segment at specific areas via the **Width Tool** (Shift+W), which will be examined later.

The Stroke panel is divided into four sections. The top section allows you to adjust the basic attributes of a stroke or a line. The **Stroke Weight** is the thickness of the line. The **Stroke Cap** and **Stroke Corner** are features that alter the look of a line with one or more corners. The **Stroke Limit** adjusts the sharpness of the corners. **Align Stroke** gives you an option to position the Stroke relative to the path of a shape, either inside, outside, or centered on a line segment. These basic features are useful when you are creating apparel details for production technical flats.

The **Stroke Dashed Line**, when checked, allows you to customize the look of your dashes by entering numeric information into the dash and gap areas. For example, a dash of .04 pt and a gap of .04 pt with a Weight of 0.25 pt. could resemble sewing-machine stitches—give or take a point. The exact amount is up to you. Figure 2.14 shows the **Aligns Dashes to Corners and Path Ends** icon in the Stroke panel's Dashed Line section highlighted on the right.

Stroke Weight, for our purposes, should be measured in points instead of the default inches. To change the Stroke Weight to points or other options, go to *Menu Bar > Preferences > Units*, or *Menu Bar > Edit > Preferences > Units*.

Create and adjust instant arrowheads on the ends of paths by choosing options from the **Stroke Arrowheads** menu. The **Stroke Profile** enables you to transform the look of your lines to various preset widths similar to what you can do with the CS5 and CS6 Width Tool (Shift+W). One fashion illustration benefit here is the ability to simulate embroidered or trim edges such as passementerie.

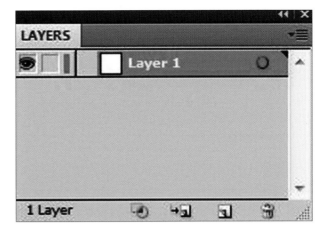

Figure 2.15 **Layers panel.**

Layers Panel

The Layers panel keeps the various parts of your digital renderings separate and allows you to work effectively without other objects, on the same layer, being in the way. To open the Layers panel, go to *Menu Bar > Window > Layers.* Figure 2.15 exhibits the Layers panel, as it appears when a new document is opened in Illustrator®. The Layers panel has icons on the left that look like eyes, which enable you to see what is on that particular layer. If you **toggle off** one of the eye icons with your cursor, whatever is on that layer will not be visible on the Artboard. To the right of the visibility icon for each layer is a **lock icon**. If it is not showing, click into the blank square area, and it will appear. This icon will **toggle on** and toggle off your ability to access that layer. When a selected layer is locked, a small pencil icon with a strikethrough will show if you attempt to apply anything to the Artboard. To make changes on the selected layer, simply toggle off the lock icon.

Layer Compositing: The use of different layers in the digital creative process is called layer compositing. It is a professional technique that will help you to work effectively on a single object at a time within a file containing many objects. Additionally, layer compositing is a great way for teams of people to work on the same project at various times, because it makes it easier to begin where someone left off in the production process. This saves time that would be wasted on moving parts out of the way, and reorganizing. You

TIP: **Adjusting Stroke Attributes**

A line segment must be selected, and the Stroke box must be in the front position before you can adjust the Stroke attributes. The Stroke Weight, Stroke Dashed Line, and other attributes should be adjusted for each project to maximize the overall presentation. This is important when rendering technical production flats, which often require more than one Stroke Weight. More will be discussed in Chapter 14.

will learn to use layer compositing in the tutorials of this book, because this feature was built into the program to assist you. It will also make the tutorial steps easier to follow. Naturally, each person will develop preferred work disciplines; computer operational protocols even extend to groups.

Merging and Flattening Layers: Layers can be exported from Illustrator® to other Adobe software programs. You can also merge certain layers and even flatten them all into one. These options are available in the hidden menu at the right side of the panel or by selecting all of the layers (hold the Shift key) and then pressing *Cmd+E / Ctrl+E*. When you do this, all the layers will be condensed into one layer. Each function has its specific advantages. Illustrator® was designed with these capabilities to assist printing production, color separation, and the ability to work on a clean visual surface when tackling complicated and lengthy rendering projects. Figure 2.16 exhibits the Layers panel.

Sublayers: If you click on the white pointer of a layer, you will see its sublayers. These usually contain the separate parts of the objects on that particular layer. Although you could add items to sublayers below a layer, it is not recommended that you do so in the tutorials to come. Because the sublayers are hidden, it becomes difficult to manage them when you are learning. Create a **new layer** instead by clicking the **New Layer icon** at the bottom of the panel.

Identifying Layers: You can name each layer by double-clicking on the layer itself. Identify the layer with an appropriate name when the **Layer Options** dialog box appears. In CS6, highlight the default title and then rename it. Click and hold the hidden menu for more Layer Options.

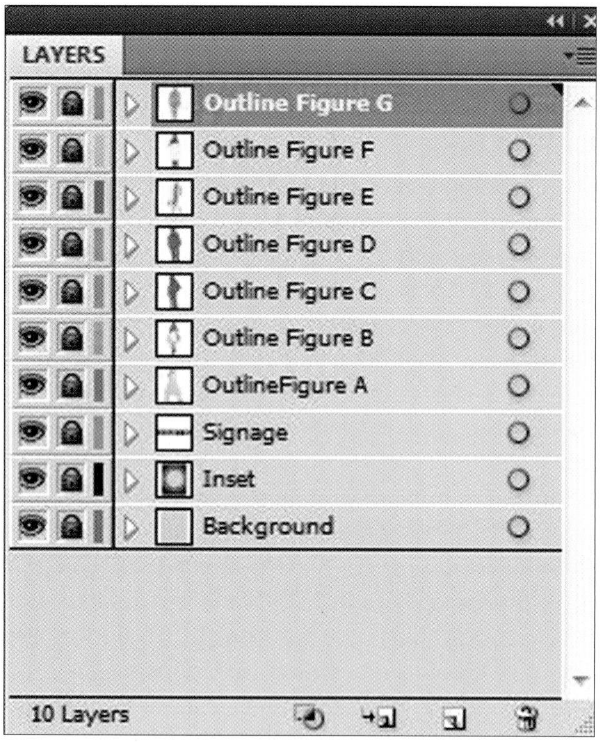

Figure 2.16 Layers panel with compositing.

Highlight Color: You can also identify your layers with a highlight color. Even if the object has no color Fill or Stroke, the highlight color will show on your screen, although it does not print. The hidden Layer Options menu and the Layers Options dialog box are shown in Figures 2.17 and 2.18, respectively.

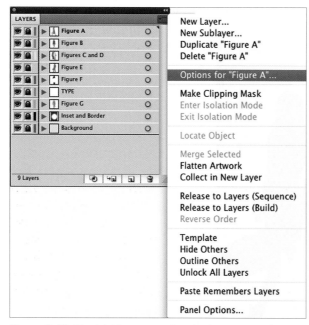

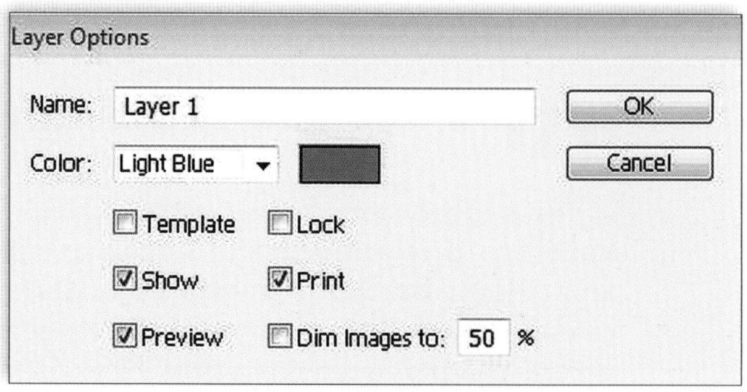

Figure 2.17 The hidden menu for the Layers panel allows users to select options for a selected layer.

Figure 2.18 Layer Options dialog box.

There are various layer features in the dialog box, which you can check on or off for a particular layer. For now, you only need to check the **Show**, **Print**, and **Preview boxes**. Their titles describe their functions in reference to the layer contents. Checking these settings will allow whatever you create on a particular layer to function properly on the screen and/or if you want to print the completed project. In addition, there is a small circular icon on each layer on the right that allows you to target and move an object on each layer. When you click on it, the objects on that layer will be selected, and the highlight color will appear in a small square to the right.

Basic Rendering Skills with Illustrator®

Now that you have been introduced to Illustrator® and learned some of the essentials of how to interface with the program through its tools, panels, docks, preferences, etc., let us move on to learning how to draw electronically. In this section, you will focus upon building skill and dexterity using the program to render with the mouse, a trackpad, or a stylus tablet. You will be introduced to the following:

- Drawing with the Pen Tool (P) and the Pen Tool Suite of tools

- Practicing the functions of the Selection Tool (V)

- Manipulating paths and anchors with the Direct Selection Tool (A)

- Completing a Curved Scale Exercise

- Creating shapes with marquee formations

- Creating Bézier Curves

- Completing four Bézier Curves practice exercises

- Developing comfort and speed when drawing electronically

By learning to render digitally with the Illustrator® **Pen Tool (P)** through the creation of straight paths and **Bézier Curves** (referred to as curved line segments), you will build confidence. To help you garner skills, three textbook exercises and four practice exercises have been prepared for study and application. One of the practice exercises is printed in the book and the others are located on ①. These textbook exercises and practices, along with your course curriculum, will enhance your digital rendering skills and command of Illustrator®.

Digital Software:
The New Tool of Fashion Illustration and Technical Design

Because you are embarking on or continuing a career in fashion, you will need to be able to draw electronically (also referred to as **digital drawing**). There is no way of getting around this. Today, fashion illustration consists of apparel on the figure and **digital flats** (also **conceptual flats**). Then there is the **production technical flat**, which is used to facilitate **tech-packs**. Recent upgrades to Illustrator® have fused it with certain qualities of Photoshop®, and this has resulted in digitally engineered combinations of vector and raster fashion illustration/animation. In this book, the fashion presentation features of Illustrator® are being presented separately from Photoshop®, at least for now, but later we will combine the techniques of the tools, panels, features, and filters of both programs.

Illustrator® has an edge on global apparel manufacturing, since most of the basic digital communication of apparel production (now termed **technical design**) is facilitated through vector art and raster art that mimics it. The practice is pervasive, and as time passes, computer illustration and technical design will completely dominate the fashion industry. However, digital fashion art will never replace hand-rendered illustration completely.

The chief goal of Chapter 2 is to introduce you to **electronic drawing**. The fundamentals include creating curved paths and straight paths (open or closed) to be filled and/or stroked. Through applying the principles outlined in this chapter, you will be able to use the Illustrator® Pen Tool (P) to complete basic types of digital drawing by tracing photo imagery. You will also be introduced to shape tools to expand your digital rendering capacity.

Do not become intimidated by the program. With all its seeming complexity, Illustrator® actually has just a handful of features essential to fashion presentation. The rest of its functions represent many creative options that you will explore as you advance in skill. However, it is of the utmost importance that you work on the practice exercises in this chapter until you are comfortable with electronic drawing.

Vector Software and Line Segments

Illustrator® uses vectors: digital coordinates that represent parameters (the confined extent and form of a line between fixed points). The purpose for this in electronic drawing is to create paths (**line segments**). Line segments are drawn between parameters (**anchor points**) and may be either curved or straight. A line segment can be visible or invisible. Curved line segments are professionally termed Bézier Curves after a French engineer, *Pierre Bézier*, made them popular in the 1960s when he designed automobiles for Renault.

In vector-based software programs like Illustrator®, Bézier Curves are used to create smooth,

Exercise 1: Bézier Curve Scale

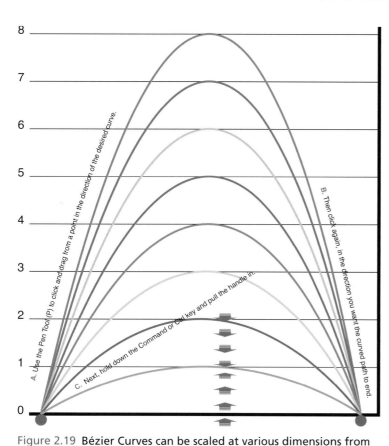

Figure 2.19 Bézier Curves can be scaled at various dimensions from the same parameters.

Load Illustrator® and press *Cmd+O / Ctrl+O*. In the Open dialog box, locate the file Exercise_1.pdf on ① Ch02. Save the file to your computer. Work from the copy, and return to this exercise anytime. When you have opened this file in Illustrator®, locate the Layers panel by going to *Menu Bar > Window > Layer* or finding it in the vertical panel dock. With the panel showing, click on the lock icons to unlock the layers labeled 2 through 9. Leave the other layers locked. Select the various curved line segments on the *Bézier Curve Scale* chart with the Direct Selection Tool (A), and then move the handles that appear. Zoom out to select the end points of the handles. You may also scroll upward to locate them. Use the handles to move the various colored lines to different levels. This will help you understand the function of manipulating curved line segments, which can be scaled from the same anchor point positions. It will also better prepare you for the practice exercises. See also Bezier_Curve.mov on ① Ch02.

rounded, or curved line segments that can be scaled without limitation and combined with straight paths to create endless varieties of geometric and organic forms. When a line segment is clicked with the **Direct Selection Tool (A)**, a handle appears. This looks like a line with a small square at the end. You can reshape any line segment by moving its **handle**. Simply click on the line segment, then hold and drag the handle in any direction to make adjustments. Figure 2.19 in Exercise 1 demonstrates how Bézier Curves can be scaled at various dimensions from the same parameters. The anchor points and line segments are visible for each level shown.

TIP: Viewing Tool Tips and Smart Guides

You can view tool rendering tips and position indicators by toggling on your Smart Guides. Press *Cmd+U / Ctrl+U*, and each time you touch an anchor or a path, you will see a small notice. To toggle off the Smart Guides, use the same shortcut sequence.

Creating Paths in Illustrator® with the Pen Tool (P)

A simple method of creating paths in Illustrator® involves the use of its Pen Tool (P). Figure 2.20 identifies indicators, which appear to the right of the Pen Tool (P) icons; their functions are below. Take a moment to study these **tool tips**; you will see them again soon. Recognizing the tool tips will help you master the Pen Tool (P) and other tools that will be used in the tutorials.

Straight Path Clicking Sequence

To become familiar with the Pen Tool (P), open a new letter-size document in Illustrator® by pressing *Cmd+N / Ctrl+N*. Press OK when the dialog box appears. Select the Pen Tool (P) from the Tools panel, using the default Stroke of black at 1 pt (point) and work with a Fill of None. Click once with the Pen Tool (P), then click again in another place on your Artboard to create a line segment. Box 2.2 demonstrates the three essential steps for how to create a straight path. See Figure 2.21 and follow the steps listed in Exercise 2 to learn how to create line segments.

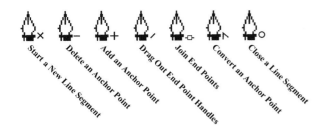

Start a New Line Segment   Delete an Anchor Point   Add an Anchor Point   Drag Out End Point Handles   Join End Points   Convert an Anchor Point   Close a Line Segment

Figure 2.20 Functions of the Pen Tool (P) indicators.

TIP: Toggling Tools

If you select the Direct Selection Tool (A), and then select the Pen Tool (P), you will be able to alter anchor points and line segments without switching tools. Just press the modifiers *Cmd* or *Ctrl* and hold them to make adjustments.

Box 2.2: How to Create a Straight Line Segment with the Pen Tool (P) in Illustrator®

1. Fill — Stroke

2. Starting Anchor Point

3. Destination Anchor Point

Step 1:

Use a Fill of None and a Stroke of Black from the Illustrator® Tools panel.

Step 2:

Select the Pen Tool (P) from the Tool panel, then click from your starting point to create a new path with an anchor point.

Step 3:

Click again toward your destination point to create the line segment.

Closing Paths

The main characteristic of vector art is a flat and car-toon-like appearance of filled and/or stroked shapes that makes it suitable for certain presentations, but not all. This look is great for technical flats, which are used by contractors in conjunction with garment specifications to help create patterns and samples. You must learn to render combinations of curved and straight line segments. The paths can be con-nected by anchor points to make closed shapes that will create the parts of digital flats and croquis fig-ures such as arms, sleeves, legs, or pants.

Closed paths are **shapes**. When these shapes are filled and/or stroked with color, patterns, gradi-ents, etc., they assist in the creation of vector art. Some of the tutorials in this book require shapes (closed paths) without broken line segments. When using the Pen Tool (P), you will notice a small circle on the side of the icon that appears when you have correctly closed your line segments.

Performing a Marquee and Creating Shapes

Illustrator® boasts a few tools that create ready-made basic geometric shapes, such as the **Rectangle Tool**

(M), **Rounded Rectangle Tool**, **Ellipse Tool (L)**, **Polygon Tool**, and **Star Tool**. They are located in the Tools panel with a hidden tear-off menu (Box 2.1 on page 15). You can use these tools when you need quick but accurate closed paths that you can modify as to Fill, Stroke, and scale.

To use these tools, you will need to perform what is known as a **marquee formation**. The term comes from the same name given to the illumi-nated rectangular marquee usually seen in front of a theater. The correct way to **perform a marquee** is to select a tool, then click and drag, from an upper left to a lower right destination. Technically, you are creating an invisible rectangular area that will be the base for the size and position of your geometric objects. You can also perform a mar-quee and select several objects with the **Selection Tool (V)** or Direct Selection Tool (A), or increase the view of a particular area with your Zoom Tool (Z). Figure 2.22 displays Illustrator® shapes created by performing a marquee with shape tools, with default Fill and Strokes from the CMYK Swatches panel. Practice performing marquees by complet-ing Exercise 3.

Exercise 2: Correct Line Segments

Creating proper Bézier Curves is tricky and takes a little practice. This figure illustrates the steps for creating them. To help you memorize the steps for creating Bézier Curves, locate Exercise_2.pdf on ① Ch02. Save the file to your computer or another storage device. You can also print the file and keep it as a handout for practice. Observe the steps of the Exercise_2.pdf file, then open a letter-size document in Illustrator®. Repeat the following instructions until you have mastered Bézier Curves.

1. Use a Fill of None and a Stroke of black (or any other color) from the Illustrator® Tools panel.

2. Select the Pen Tool (P) from the Tools panel, then click and drag from your starting point to create a new curved line segment with an anchor point.

3. Click again toward your destination point to create the curved line segment.

4. Hold the *Cmd key* or *Ctrl key* to toggle the Pen Tool (P), turning its icon and function temporarily into a Selection Tool (V) or a Direct Selection Tool (A). This depends upon which tool you select before you select the Pen Tool (P).

   Note: *When you release the Cmd key or Ctrl key, the Pen Tool (P) will reappear.*

5. Keep your finger on the key and use the Selection Tool (V) or Direct Selection Tool (A) to move the handle. Adjust your curved line segment. Depending on your settings, a **Bounding Box** (a visual rectilinear nonprintable parameter of a selection) will appear around your curved path. Use the Bounding Box to resize the shape, or press *Cmd+H / Ctrl+H* to hide it. Repeat the process as many times as needed.

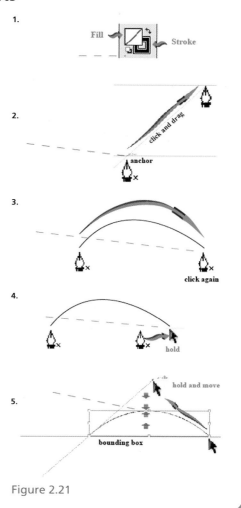

Figure 2.21

Exercise 3: Marquee Shapes

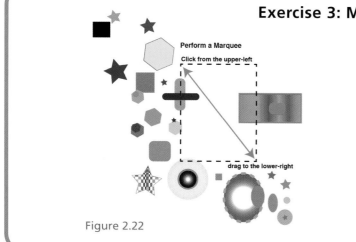

Figure 2.22

Load Illustrator® and open the file Exercise_3.pdf located on ① Ch02. It will look similar to Figure 2.22. When you have the file opened in Illustrator®, unlock Layer 1, then select the objects with the Selection Tool (V). You can resize the shapes with highlighted Bounding Boxes. As a quick exercise, duplicate the shapes that have been created using the shape tools. Fill your shapes with various Fills and Strokes from the CMYK Swatches panel or explore and use the **Swatch Libraries** menu by clicking the icon located at the lower left corner of the Swatches panel.

TIP: Adjusting Stroke Width

Use the Width Tool (Shift+W) along with the preset Stroke panel Profile options to change the width of the strokes you apply to various shapes. To use the Width Tool (Shift+W), simply click on a stroke and move the mouse to adjust the width of a portion of that segment. You can repeat the procedure and make adjustments with the same tool.

If you are new to Illustrator®, you will benefit from plenty of practice. Before you attempt to digitally render croquis and digital flats in Illustrator®, you may need to repeat the four practice exercises in Tutorial 2.1 a few times. These practice exercises ask you to trace over the profile images of three models and a necklace with the Pen Tool (P) and the Pencil Tool (N). You will also learn how to exclude the contents of negative space and create severe Bézier Curves by tracing near-perfect circular shapes. These practices will strengthen your ability to create Bézier Curves and straight line segments, manipulate paths, and create perfectly closed shapes. The exercises present simple tasks that will form a solid foundation for your work in subsequent chapters where you will consistently use the Pen Tool (P), the Pencil Tool (N), the Selection Tool (V), and the Direct Selection Tool (A). You will also make great use of these tools with the others in the **Pen Tool Suite**:

- Use the **Pen Tool (P)** to create straight and curved line segments.
- Use the **Add Anchor Point Tool (+)** to create more definition by clicking to add anchors to an existing path.
- Use the **Delete Anchor Point Tool (-)** to remove anchors on an existing path.
- Use the **Convert Anchor Point Tool (Shift+C)** to change a straight angle into a curve and vice versa.

Because these tools and their functions are vitally important to your success, they will be stressed throughout the book. Once you feel that you have mastered the function of these tools, you should advance to rendering more sophisticated practice exercises on your own, such as scanning and tracing your own drawings or magazine photos. Each practice exercise in Tutorial 2.1 opens with its own set of instructions, and the instructions for Practice 1 (Ana) appear below.

Watch the movie Bezier_Curves_With_Ana.mov located on ① Ch02\Tutorial 2.1. This movie actually shows the completion of Practice 1 (Ana), but you can also use it as a reference for Practice Exercises 2 through 4.

1. Load Illustrator®. Press *Cmd+O / Ctrl+O* to open the file Practice_1.pdf located on ① Ch02\Tutorial 2.1. Save a copy of the file in the .ai format on your computer. Work from the copy. This file features a profile view of the model Ana (Figure 2.23). Open the Layers panel; study the file. Drag the *Completed Demo* layer to the Trash icon in the Layers panel.

Figure 2.23

2. Lock the other layers and create a new layer above them with the Create New Layer icon (next to the Trash icon in the Layers panel). Double-click on the new layer. When the Layer Options dialog box appears, label it *Practice_1* or appropriately for whichever practice you are completing.

3. Choose a Stroke of yellow from your default Illustrator® Basic CMYK Swatches panel, along with a Fill of None.

4. Select the Pen Tool (P) as demonstrated in Bezier_Curves_With_Ana.mov and trace around the model's profile.

5. Try switching to the Pencil Tool (N), especially to outline the model's chignon, but be sure to connect with the anchors. The outline must be unbroken, but if a break is discovered, select both ends with the Direct Selection Tool (V), then press *Cmd+J / Ctrl+J* to join the two line segments.

6. Once you have completed the shape, you will see a small circle tool tip on the side of the Pen Tool (P). This indicates that you have successfully rendered an unbroken digital silhouette of the model's profile.

7. Swap the Fill and Stroke with the double-sided arrow icon in the Tools panel to view the shape.

8. Save your work.

Continue to practice Bézier Curves by completing Practice_2.pdf, Practice_3.pdf, and Practice_4.pdf, which are located on ① Ch02\Tutorial 2.1. Once you have mastered these exercises, scan and trace other images until you are comfortable creating straight and curved line segments with the Pen Tool (P), Pen Tool Suite of tools, and both the Selection Tool (V) and the Direct Selection Tool (A).

TIP: **Adding Anchors**

Use the Add Anchor Point Tool (+) to add an anchor to a line segment if you need one, and the Delete Anchor Point Tool (-) to remove unwanted anchors. You can manipulate the paths or the anchors with the Direct Selection Tool (V). To move the entire completed shape, use the Selection Tool (A). If you find a pointed angle or straight path that you want to make curved, select an adjacent anchor point with the Convert Anchor Point Tool (Shift+C), then pull out and twist.

Chapter 2 Summary

Chapter 2 presented a basic overview of the Illustrator® software attributes. You learned to create a new document with a specified Artboard, and then to arrange and save Workspaces. You discovered the Illustrator® Menu Bar, Application Bar, and Control Panel and were introduced to the tools, panels, and docks. In your studies and the exercises, you interacted with the Illustrator® Fill and Stroke boxes in the Tools panel. You learned the functions of the Stroke panel sections, which should help you create shape details and dashed lines. Further exploration of the tools and panels revealed various ways to navigate around the Illustrator® window and mix spot colors and showed you how to save color swatches.

Layer compositing was stressed to teach you how to organize your work. Then you learned to draw with the Pen Tool (P) and the Pen Tool Suite of tools. You also used these tools in conjunction with the functions of the Selection Tool (V) and the Direct Selection Tool (A) to help manipulate paths and anchors. In addition, you were introduced to the art of performing a marquee with tools to create shapes, make selections, and zoom in on areas.

Chapter 2 taught you how to draw electronically and prepare you for the tutorials in later chapters. A major task was presented with several textbook and DVD practice exercises designed to teach you how to create, manipulate, and master Bézier Curves by tracing images.

Chapter 2 Self-Assessment

What should you know before proceeding to Chapter 3? Ask yourself the following questions, and if you can answer them with ease, then you are ready to go to the next chapter. If not, read Chapter 2 again, and repeat the textbook and DVD practice exercises.

1. Do I possess a moderate to strong ability to render digitally with the Pen Tool (P) through the creation of straight paths and Bézier Curves (referred to as curved line segments)?

2. Can I draw a straight path in Illustrator®?

3. Can I use the Pen Tool Suite effectively, including the Pen Tool (P), Add Anchor Point Tool (+), Delete Anchor Point Tool (-), and Convert Anchor Point Tool (Shift+C)?

4. Can I render the basic outline of any shape using the tools and features of Illustrator®?

5. Do I create proper shapes and close them?

6. Do the shapes I render consist of unbroken line segments?

7. Do I know how to create basic shapes with the various Illustrator® shape tools by performing a marquee?

8. Do I know most of the tool names and can I recognize their icons?

9. Do I know how to use the Workspace Switcher to set my preferred desktop?

10. Do I know how to make effective use of the Layers panel and all of the organizational attributes of layer compositing?

11. Am I able to access the Illustrator® Preferences menu, and do I know how to use it to adjust my Stroke Weight units?

12. Can I create a spot color in the Color panel and save it into the Swatches panel?

Digital Fashion Illustration Foundation with Illustrator®

3

Objectives

Chapter 3 reinforces the features of Illustrator® through three tutorials that will unfold more tools, panels, and functions of the program. The goal is to help you to further develop your command of the Illustrator® interface, and to improve your digital illustration capabilities through numbered step-by-step instructions. By completing the tutorials in this chapter, you will accomplish the following objectives:

◎ Increased command of Illustrator® tools, panels, and features

◎ Understand proper file setup including placing and embedding

◎ Reinforce rendering of straight paths and curved line segments

◎ Learn appropriate digital measuring tools, including rulers, guides, grids, and the Zero Point

◎ Support concepts of typography through the use of the Character panel

◎ Sample the use of gradients, patterns, and fades

◎ Create all-inclusive digital page layouts with compelling backgrounds and develop a sense of spatial arrangement of figures

◎ Comprehend the working parts of repeat patterns

◎ Render apparel and accessory items on the figure

◎ Make clipping masks and compound paths

This tutorial introduces you to additional attributes of Illustrator® with an emphasis on using the Pen Tool Suite. You will use these tools to create fashion figure silhouettes for a colorful digital presentation. By completing each of the steps, you will learn the foundation for rendering digital fashion croquis, using front pages from the fashion news periodical *Women's Wear Daily* (*WWD*).

This respected source of fashion reporting worldwide celebrated 100 years of publication in 2010. The June 21, 2012, cover of the online version of *Women's Wear Daily* (WWD.com) features current trends and fashion news affecting all facets of fashion (Figure 3.1). A copy of the June 1910 *Women's Wear Daily* newspaper is a testament to the fact that the news periodical has changed over the decades (Figure 3.2).

It is recommended that you complete the exercises in Chapter 2 and Tutorial 2.1 before beginning this tutorial. Use the files provided on ① Ch03\Tutorial 3.1.

Step 1: Import the Completed Example

Insert ① into your computer. Load Illustrator® and press *Cmd+O / Ctrl+O* to open the file entitled Tutorial_3.1_Example.pdf, which is in the Ch03\Tutorial 3.1 folder. An Open dialog box will appear. Select the file from the menu and click Open. *The file was saved in a portable document format (.pdf), but it will open as an Illustrator® file with compositing of nine locked layers.* If you do not see the Layers panel, go to *Menu Bar > Windows > Layers* to show it, or press *F7* (PC). On certain Mac keyboards, especially the MacBook Pro, hold the **fn** key (short for Mac function) and then select the F7 key. You may need to activate your function keys in the **Keyboard & Mouse Preferences** menu. Save the file to your computer.

Note: *If you are working on a classroom computer, save the file on the desktop and then save a copy to your external drive. Work from the copy on the computer's desktop to maximize the computer's speed and prevent system crashes.*

Step 2: Familiarize Yourself with the Completed Example

This completed example has been provided to assist you in learning Illustrator®. As you advance in the tutorials, increase your knowledge, and garner new skills, you will not need completed example files.

Figure 3.1 Screenshot of WWD.com, June 2012.

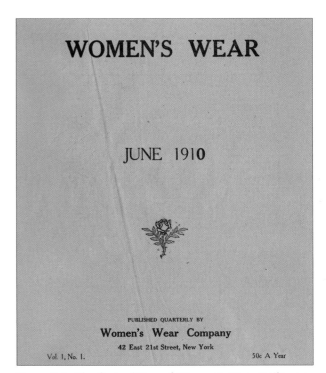

Figure 3.2 The first edition of *Women's Wear Daily* was published in 1910. Courtesy of WWD.

Study the file and show the Layers panel. Toggle on and toggle off the visibility icons. Each figure has been rendered on a layer; unlock them at random. Use the Selection Tool (V) to move the silhouetted figures around the page. Then press *Cmd+Z / Ctrl+Z* and **Undo** your moves to revert the file to its original condition (Figure 3.3).

Step 3: Convert the Tutorial Files

Also on ① Ch03\Tutorial 3.1 are six Adobe Acrobat (.pdf) files labeled A.pdf, B.pdf, C_and_D.pdf, E.pdf, F.pdf, and G.pdf. Double-click on these files to open them. You will see *WWD* covers with silhouetted closed line segments stroked in color around photographs of fashion models. These outlined shapes were rendered with the Pen Tool (P) in Illustrator®. The Adobe.pdf file allows you to view but not alter the page.

Step 4: Test the Fill and Stroke

Once you have the files open in Illustrator®, they will be docked into a single window. Click the Illustrator® Arrange Documents button located in the Applications Bar (Mac) or Menu Bar (PC), and choose *6-Up*. Select each file and perform a **Fit-in-Window** by pressing *Cmd+0 / Ctrl+0* (Figure 3.4).

Show the Layers panel. Each file contains two layers, except for C_and_D.pdf, which contains three. The bottom layer is the *WWD* cover photo file. On the layers above it are the outlined silhouettes (strokes) of the models. Unlock these layers individually and select each of them. Press *Cmd+A / Ctrl+A* to Select All.

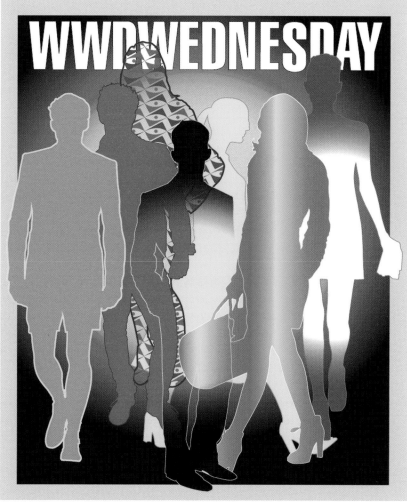

Figure 3.3 Completed example of Tutorial 3.1.

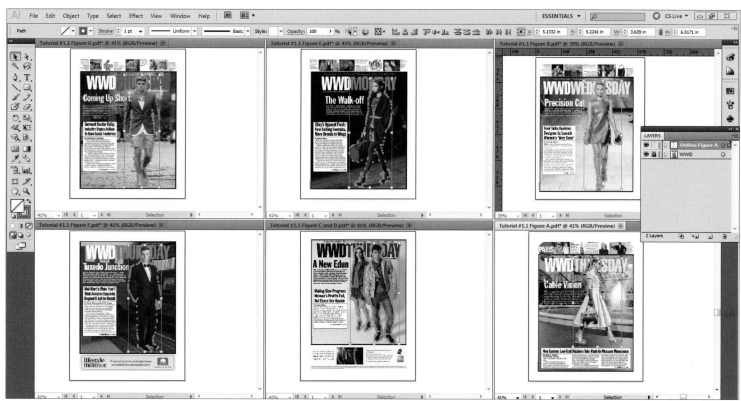

Figure 3.4 Each individual file shown here is on a layer with the outlines highlighted as selections.

Bounding Boxes

Depending on your settings, a highlighted rectilinear Bounding Box may appear around the figures when you select them. Bounding boxes represent the parameters of vector objects. Use them to manually **scale** (alter the size and dimensions) of objects by adjusting the sides with the Selection Tool (V) (Figure 3.4).

> **TIP: Scale Proportions**
>
> **When scaling, always hold the Shift key to constrain the proportions; otherwise, the image will be distorted.**

Rotating Objects with Bounding Boxes You can rotate any vector object with its Bounding Box by bringing your cursor toward the corners. When you see the cursor icon convert to a double-sided curved arrow, click and rotate the Bounding Box in the desired radial direction.

Hiding Bounding Boxes The Bounding Box feature in Illustrator® is useful; however, it can also obscure the rendering process. Toggle it off, if necessary, by pressing *Shift+Cmd+B / Shift+Ctrl+B*. You can also go to *Menu Bar > View > Hide (or Show) Bounding Box*.

Clearing Negative Spaces

Some of the figures contain outlines of the negative spaces between hair, arms, legs, etc. This was explained in *Tutorial 2.1 Practice 2* and is reinforced here. To exclude the negative space when you fill the outlines, show the **Pathfinder panel** by going to *Menu Bar > Window > Pathfinder*. You can also memorize the Pathfinder panel's keyboard shortcut, which is *Shift+Cmd+F9 / Shift+Ctrl+F9*. With all the shapes selected on a layer, click the **Exclude** button. The negative space will now be cleared. Do this for each file. The green arrow in Figure 3.5 points to the Pathfinder panel's Exclude option.

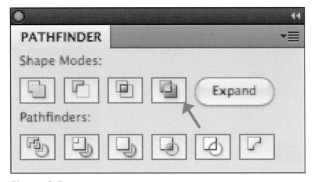

Figure 3.5

Creating New Fills and Strokes

Click on the Fill box in the Tools panel to bring it forward; then select each figure's outlined Stroke separately. Now select a Fill color, pattern, or gradient from the Basic CMYK Swatches panel. Do the same for the Stroke. You can also use the Stroke panel to create a dashed line and other attributes as described in this chapter. Figure 3.6 shows each file with a different fill.

> **TIP: Show Swatches Panel**
>
> **If your Swatches panel shows without any color swatches, add them by clicking the Swatch Library Menu button at the lower left corner of the panel. When the menu appears, scroll to the Default Swatch Library, then to Basic CMYK Swatches. To permanently add the swatches to your file, select them and use the option in the hidden menu on the upper right side.**

Step 5: Create Your Own Women's Wear Daily Front Page

To create your own *WWD* mock front page, begin with a new file. Load Illustrator® and create a new page by pressing *Cmd+N / Ctrl+N*. A New Document dialog box appears. This dialog box has a few fields that require information. Place your cursor into the field labeled Name and type *wwd_cover*.

New Document Profile for Tutorial 3.1

In the pull-down menu adjacent to the New Document Profile field, choose **Custom**. We will work on one Artboard. The *document size* will be *Letter*; the *Units* should be in *inches*. Highlight the icon showing the figure in **Portrait Orientation**. Do not change the Bleed information; it should be zero on all sides. We will discuss Bleeds later on pages 42-43.

Below this section is another one labeled *Advanced*. Tip the arrow pointer at the left. Your **Color Mode** should be CMYK. The **Raster Effects** should be set on High (300 ppi, which stands for *300 pixels per inch*). Use the Default preview mode. Now click OK at the upper right of the dialog box. A New Document Profile is shown in Figure 3.7.

Step 6: Create a New Artboard and Workspace

A new Artboard will appear in your window Workspace. Whatever panels you have used previously will show and the vertical panel dock will be as you left it the last time you used the program; however, for this exercise the Essentials Workspace is ideal. You will need to have your Tools panel, Layers panel, Navigator panel, Align panel, Swatches panel, Gradient panel, Color panel, Transform panel, and Pathfinder panel showing in the vertical panel dock or floating on the Workspace. Some of these are already located in the default vertical dock of the Essentials Workspace. Go to *Menu Bar > Window* to locate the rest, then go to *Menu Bar > Windows Workspace > Save Workspace* to label the new Workspace *wwd_tutorial_one*. Figure 3.8 shows this window and Workspace.

Step 7: Save Your Work

Now save your work by pressing *Shift+Cmd+S / Shift+Ctrl+S* or go to *Menu Bar > File > Save As*. Follow your normal saving procedures for Mac or PC. Remember the three important things to do when saving files for the DVD exercises and tutorials:

1. Save your file in a specific location. Create a new folder on your computer and name it so that you can remember the contents. Do this by selecting the Folder button in the Save dialog box.

2. Give your file an appropriate title. Use the tutorial numbers and your initials. Many techies use all lowercase letters and underscores to separate words. If you are taking a course, follow the instructor's directions for saving files, but always use your name or initials in the title.

3. Choose a proper file format. In this case, it will be Illustrator® (.ai) Mac or (.AI) PC. Other popular Illustrator® file formats include Illustrator® EPS (.eps) and Adobe PDF (.pdf). Each file format has an extension that will follow the title of your file preceded by a period. For example, a file for Mary Ann Doe might appear as: Tutorial_3.1_mad.ai.

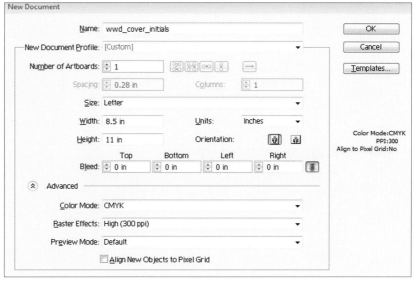

Figure 3.6

Figure 3.7

Figure 3.8

TIP: Saving and Backing Up

Work smart! Always periodically save your files somewhere on your computer, and then back up your work on an external storage device between the steps of the tutorials. Failure to follow this advice could result in the complete loss of a file.

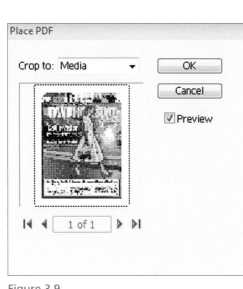

Figure 3.9

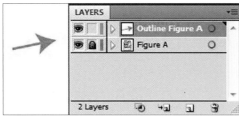

Figure 3.11

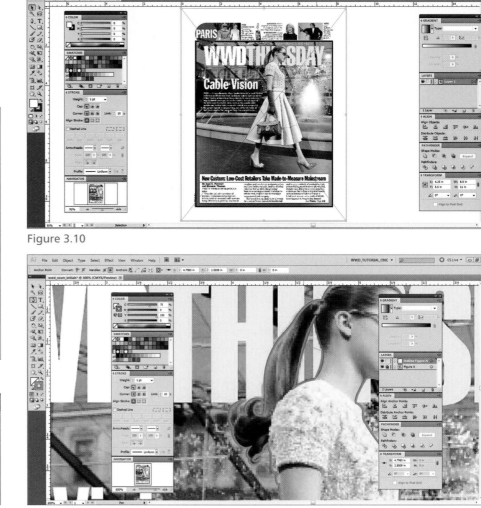

Figure 3.10

Figure 3.12

Step 8: Place Your *Women's Wear Daily* File

Place your *WWD* cover file into your document by going to *Menu Bar > File > Place*. When the Place dialog box appears, locate any of the ① Tutorial 3.1 files. There are six files in alphabetical order. A good way to start would be with A.pdf. Select this file, and import it into your Illustrator® file by clicking the Place button at the lower right of the dialog box. A Place PDF dialog box appears. Select *Crop to Media* from the pull-down menu (Figure 3.9).

How to Embed a Placed File

When the file appears on your Artboard, it will have a highlighted cross formation. The *WWD* photo file should align itself with the letter-size Artboard you set up, but you may reposition or scale it if needed. While it is still selected, accept the placed file by clicking the **Embed** button located in the Control Panel. Files that are placed into others need to be embedded, so that they will become a part of the new document. Again, if you do not click the Embed button, you may need to link the photo to your file

each time you open it. Figure 3.10 exhibits the placed file before it has been embedded.

Show your Layers panel by pressing *F7* on your keyboard, selecting it from the vertical panel dock, or going to *Menu Bar > Window > Layers*. This *WWD* photo file will be placed on *Layer 1*. Double-click this layer and rename it as *Figure A*. Lock the layer as indicated by the arrow in Figure 3.11.

Step 9: Render Your Silhouetted Figure(s)

At the bottom of the Layers panel next to the Delete Layer icon is a New Layer icon. Click on it to create *Layer 2*. It will be positioned above the *Figure A* layer. Now, name *Layer 2* to correspond with the one below it as *Outline Figure A*.

Choose a Fill of None and a Stroke of any color to create your outline. Use your Pen Tool (P) to trace the same outline appearing around the figure, then click away on the desktop, and trace the negative spaces separately. You can also use the Pencil Tool (N). Figure 3.12 shows the area of the negative space at the back of the neck on Figure A; the green outline is near completion.

Step 10: Repeat and Reposition the Layers

Repeat Step Seven, Step Eight, and Step Nine for each of the five remaining figure files on ① Ch03\ Tutorial 3.1. Place them all in the same file, and create one new layer at a time above each of the *WWD* cover photos. Save and back up your work.

Note: Figures C and D only require one combined new layer. The photo files will obscure the layers beneath them, so lock and toggle off their visibility icons in order to see your outlines. Figure 3.13 shows the completed layer compositing of all 13 layers with the visibility of the WWD *covers toggled off.*

Step 11: Fill and Arrange Your Figures

Select the outlines that you rendered on each layer and fill each with a different color, gradient, or pattern from the Basic CMYK Swatches panel. Change the Stroke color to make interesting contrasts with the Fill contents of each silhouette. In addition, try increasing the *Weight* in the Stroke panel or using dashed lines. Use the Selection Tool (V) to arrange your figures on the page. There is no particular standard, but you should keep the silhouettes inside the Artboard.

The Reflect Tool

Use the **Reflect Tool (O)** to change the direction of one or more of the figures. Select the figure you wish to change, then double-click on the Reflect Tool (O). When the *Reflect Options* dialog box appears, choose *Vertical* and enter *90°*. This action will flip your figure. Figure 3.14 shows the figure outlines filled and arranged with one selected, and then reflected vertically 90°.

Render Signage

Prior to its latest redesign, *Women's Wear Daily* featured the day of the week as part of its masthead. We will incorporate this design into our lesson. Usually this **signage** (in visual graphics, "signage" is text used to communicate to a target audience) is combined in a page layout with the figurative fashion photography. The typography for the days of the week differentiate the periodical's daily features and have no set attributes, but they often consist of bold white and/or colored letters. Toggle on the visibility of any of the *WWD* covers in your file that are on layers labeled *Figure A, Figure B*, etc. Choose a weekday shown on any of the covers and create a new layer above it. Label this layer *Signage*. Again, toggle off the visibility of any layers that might obscure your view. Lock all the other layers.

Step 12: Set Up Typography

Typography is the term used to denote the art of creating and setting type. For the purposes of this step, we will focus on the **baseline** and **cap height** of the type. The baseline is where the type rests; cap height designates the vertical length of capital letters. To help you understand this portion of Tutorial 3.1, a file entitled WWD_WEDNESDAY.pdf containing completed signage is available on ① Ch03\Tutorial 3.1. Study the file before you begin rendering the signage.

Zero Point (Ruler Origin)

Show the rulers by pressing *Cmd+R / Ctrl+R* or go to *Menu Bar > View > Rulers*. In the upper left corner, where the **x-axis** (horizontal ruler) and the **y-axis** (vertical ruler) join, there is a small white square space called the **Zero Point**, also referred to as the **Ruler Origin**. Just as in algebra where there is a zero between negative and positive integers, the same concept exists here. To help clarify the length and width of the letters of the signage, move the Zero Point by clicking the small white square between the rulers, then dragging and placing it at the upper left

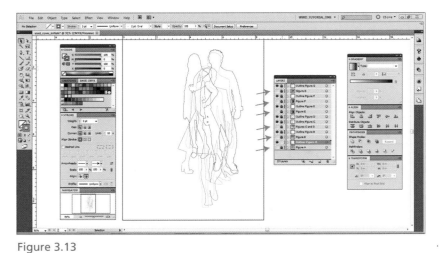

Figure 3.13

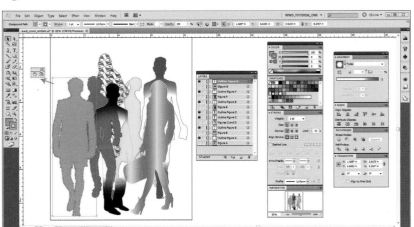

Figure 3.14

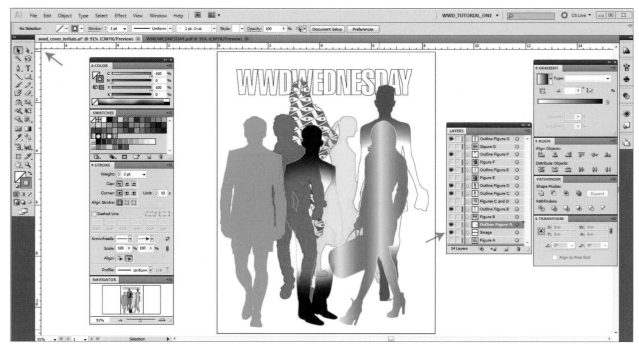

Figure 3.15 The green arrows point to the Zero Point (ruler origin).

corner of the first character. When you do this, the 0 in the horizontal ruler and the vertical ruler will join at that position. You can use this technique to maintain uniform height and width of the letters as you create them. Just move the Zero Point to the top left of each character as you create its outline. Later we will use the Zero Point to help you position the figures. In Figure 3.15, the Zero Point area between the rulers is identified at the upper left, a new layer labeled *Signage* was created, and the sample signage from the DVD is displayed as a part of the page layout.

Guides & Grid

The horizontal and vertical lines of basic **Guides** are used to assist alignment. You can click and pull horizontal Guides from the horizontal ruler and vertical Guides from the vertical ruler. Use the Guides to help you define straight planes for rendering and locating the apex of curved line segments. You can alter Guides via the Preferences Menu by going to *Menu Bar > Illustrator > Preferences > Guides & Grid* or *Menu Bar > Edit > Preferences > Guides & Grid*. When the dialog box appears, select a color from the pull-down menu in the Guides section. (You may also show Guides as dots or lines.) To adjust the functional attributes of Guides, go to *Menu Bar > View > Guides*. Then choose to Hide Guides, Lock Guides, Clear Guides, etc. When these features are activated, a check mark appears next to their menu titles. Each attribute has a command as well as a particular shortcut that you should commit to memory. You can toggle the Guides by pressing *Cmd+; (semicolon) / Ctrl+; (semicolon)*.

The Basic Grid

Straight paths like those needed to create typography may also be assisted through the use of the **Grid**. The Grid consists of repetitious perpendicular lines that can be used to calculate visual space. You can toggle the Grid by pressing *Cmd+' (apostrophe) / Ctrl+' (apostrophe)*. To customize the Grid, go to *Menu Bar > Illustrator > Preferences > Guides & Grid* or *Menu Bar > Edit > Preferences > Guides & Grid*. (You may show the Grid as dots or lines.) An essential feature of the Grid is the option to show it in front or in back of objects. Uncheck the **Grids in Back** box if you prefer them in front of the signage. You may find the basic Grid limiting, because it may not align perfectly with your signage. In that case, reposition it or use the **Rectangular Grid Tool**.

Rectangular Grid Tool

This tool allows you to customize a small Grid over a specific area, which can also be filled or stroked. It is located in the Tools panel in position 7d within the tear-off menu of the **Line Segment Tool (\\)** and has no keyboard shortcut. To use this option, first select the Rectangular Grid Tool from the Tools panel and perform a marquee over your signage. Double-click on the tool to reveal the *Rectangular Grid Tool Options* dialog box. This allows you to change the default cell dimensions, the number of horizontal and vertical dividers, as well as the fill, frame, and skew features.

While your Rectangular Grid is still selected, stroke it with any color at a .25 pt weight. Lock the selection by pressing *Cmd+2 / Ctrl+2* or go to *Menu Bar > Object > Lock > Selection*.

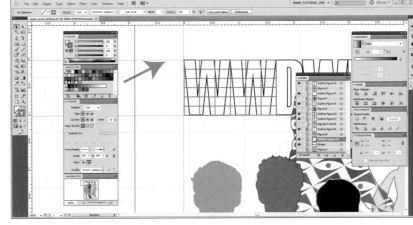

Figure 3.16 The green arrow points to the upper left corner of the grid where the Zero Point has been moved.

Figure 3.17 Align panel

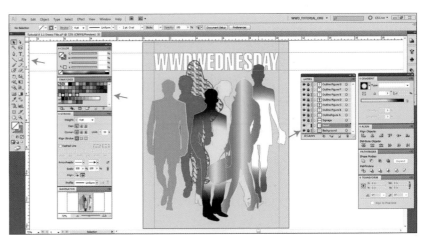

Figure 3.18 The green arrow on the right points to the Background layer.

Step 13: Render Your Signage

Using what you have learned about straight and curved line segments, render your signage on the layer you have created. Trace the outline of the headline that you chose for your project. The Pen Tool (P) should suffice for this job. Carefully outline each character separately, using the Guides to establish a baseline, cap height, and the straight planes of the letters. To maintain control, lock each of them on the layer as you render them by selecting the letter, then pressing *Cmd+2 / Ctrl+2*. A model's head may hide some of the letters in the original image. This presents a great opportunity to solve a problem. Try to render the hidden portion of the letters using the Illustrator® features that you have learned, but be creative.

Aligning the Signage

Adjusting space between letters or characters is called **kerning**. The headline letters in the tutorial files are close to each other, but are a signature of the *WWD* iconic branding, so kerning, in this case, would be inappropriate. However, some adjustments may be essential to improving the aesthetics of the set type.

The Align panel is used to organize the position of objects in relationship to one another. Use the actual cover images as a guide for placement, then distribute your letters evenly on a line with the Align panel. To show the Align panel, go to *Menu Bar > Window > Align* or press *Shift+F7*. To straighten the letters, arrange them in the correct order with the Selection Tool (V), then select them all and click the **Vertical Align Bottom** icon in the Align panel. The letters will automatically move into place. The Align panel shown in **Figure 3.17** is also used for creating regimented patterns like stripes and plaids, and for the alignment/distribution of buttons on garments.

Step 14: Apply Finishing Touches

Create a Background layer (**Figure 3.18**, Layers panel) with the Rectangle Tool (M) the size of your Artboard. You can do this by simply performing a mar-

quee and adjusting the Bounding Box to fit. Fill it with a solid color and a Stroke of None. This layer must be below all the others or you will obscure everything.

Drag the original *WWD* figure layers (sample completed demos) to the Trash icon at the bottom of the Layers panel. You can make changes to the arrangement or aesthetics of your layout, and can change the relative size of your outlined figures by using the **Scale Tool (S)**. Select a figure, then double-click on the Scale Tool (S). When the Scale dialog box appears, reduce or increase the scale *Uniform* by percentage. If you want to scale the pattern within a selection, just uncheck *Objects*. This will allow you to scale only the pattern by percentage, and prevent you from scaling the shape.

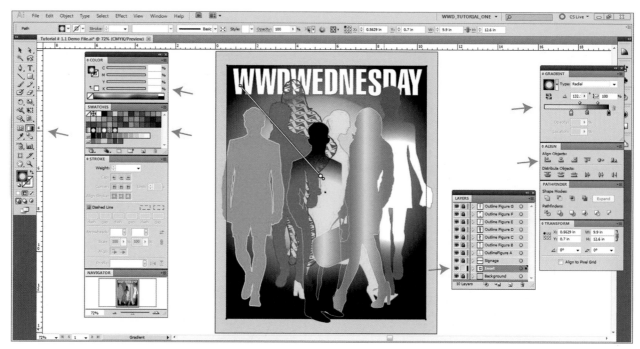

Figure 3.19 The green arrows point to all the tools and panels that have been used.

You can also use the **Rotate Tool (R)** to turn selected figures or objects on an angle. If you double-click on this tool, check *Patterns* only; then you can rotate them by degrees.

Step 15: Create an Inset

1. Select the background rectangle you made and press *Cmd+C / Ctrl+C*. Then create a new layer right above the background and name it *Inset*.

2. Paste the copy into this layer by pressing *Cmd+V / Ctrl+V*.

3. Fill the pasted rectangular shape with a color or a gradient from the CMYK Swatches panel, as shown in the completed example.

4. With the pasted inset selected, click the Scale Tool (S) in your Tools panel.

5. Double-click on the Scale Tool (S) and enter 90% into the field to reduce the rectangular object evenly.

6. Select both the Background and the Inset. Go back to the Align panel. First click **Horizontal Align Center** and then the **Vertical Align Center** to make the shapes equidistant.

7. Use the Selection Tool (V) to select, and then tweak the placement of the shapes by nudging them with the arrow keys.

Step 16: Work with Gradients and Fades

The default options of the **gradients** (blends of two or more colors) and **fades** (blends of transparency and one or more colors) in the Basic CMYK Swatches panel are limited. But you can change the colors of any gradient or fade by adding or replacing spot colors on the Gradient panel.

1. Click anywhere on the **CMYK Spectrum bar** at the bottom of the Swatches panel, then adjust the sliders until you have the color you want.

2. Drag and drop this Fill color onto the **Gradient Bar** in the Gradient panel.

3. Move the sliders around in the Gradient panel to adjust the distribution of the blends.

4. Create a **Radial gradient** or a **Linear gradient**. You can also drag colors from the Swatches panel. When you have the gradient color mix that you want, select either Radial or Linear in the *Type* pull-down menu.

5. Drag the Fill box containing the gradient and drop it into the Swatches panel.

6. Double-click on the new gradient or fade swatch in the Swatches panel and give it an appropriate name.

7. Next, select the inset and then the new gradient swatch that you have already created. With the inset selected, use the **Gradient Tool (G)** in the Tools panel to adjust the gradient's position and distribution of color by striking across it. You can move the sliders that appear to further tweak your gradient. Figure 3.19 shows a finished example of an adjusted gradient in an inset.

TIP: Gradient Libraries

Explore the Illustrator® Gradient Libraries by going to *Menu Bar > Window > Swatch Libraries > Gradients.*

Box 3.1

In the Transform panel select the upper left corner Reference Point selector. Next, select the Outline Figure(s) and enter the following corresponding coordinates in the Transform panel x and y fields, then press Enter. Illustrator® will move the objects to the exact positions based on the upper left corner of their Bounding Boxes.

(Outline Figure A)	x = 3.6"	y = 2.9"
(Outline Figure B)	x = 7.165"	y = 1.7053"
(Outline Figure C)	x = 2.9"	y = 1.4"
(Outline Figure D)	x = 2.0"	y = 2.5"
(Outline Figure E)	x = 4.8632"	y = 2.7834"
(Outline Figure F)	x = 3.5762"	y = 3.4904"
(Outline Figure G)	x = 0.3"	y = 2.7993"
Signage	x = 0.862"	y = 0.8527" (aligned and grouped)

Step 17: Use the Transform Panel

The Transform panel is used to designate positions on the Artboard and Workspace in reference to the Zero Point, the x-axis, and the y-axis. Use it to set up the dimensions of selected objects based on a **Reference Point** of the Bounding Box that contains them. In Illustrator®, every Bounding Box has nine reference points corresponding to the Transform panel Reference Point (a selector icon in the upper left of the panel), no matter what their shape. These are top left corner, top center, top right corner, midleft, center, midright, bottom left corner, lower center, and lower right corner. When you select one of these positions in the panel, you are telling Illustrator® that you want to arrange the selected objects in relation to that exact position. In this tutorial, we will use the Transform panel to position objects on the page. Follow these steps:

1. Select the Transform panel from your default vertical panel dock or show it by going to *Menu Bar > Window > Transform*. In the upper left of the Transform panel is a Reference Point selector. It consists of nine boxes. Each box represents an area of the object's Bounding Box.

2. Select the upper left corner reference point. Next, click and drag the Zero Point and place it at the upper left corner of your Artboard to set the page as the placement area. Then select a figure (but keep the other layers locked), and type the coordinating "x" and "y" positions (see Box 3.1) into the appropriate fields of the Transform panel. The program will move the object based on the upper left corner of the Bounding Box to the positions indicated by the measurements on both the x-axis and the y-axis.

Figure 3.20

3. Press Enter to reposition the figures on the page. Repeat this procedure until you have repositioned each figure. In Figure 3.20, Outline Figure G is juxtaposed with the others by the designer entering "x" and "y" coordinates in the Transform panel.

4. Perform a Fit-in-Window by pressing *Cmd+0 / Ctrl+0*, to view and inspect your completed work on the Artboard in relation to the window size. Adjust the figures manually with the Selection Tool (V) if you prefer coordinates other than those from Box 3.1.

5. **Flatten** or **Merge** your layers if needed. Simply go to the hidden menu at the side of the Layers panel and scroll to Flatten Artwork. If you want to unify certain layers, they must be selected first before merging (*Cmd+E / Ctrl+E*).

TIP: **Transform Panel Options**

You can also use the Transform panel to specify the width, height, and rotation of selected objects.

Could you imagine being limited to purchasing just three pairs of leather shoes per year? That is exactly what happened in the U.S. when consumer goods, including nylon stockings, were rationed to support war production. Figure 3.21 shows the cover of the October 1941 issue of *Vogue* magazine featuring autumn shoes and nylons illustrated by Carl Erickson. Certainly, consumers who read this issue never saw the World War II rations mandate coming.

Today, consumers are still obsessed with signature accessories, especially designer brands. Logo-clad accessories have helped to create a fashion frenzy to the extent that even their knock-offs are in demand. Nearly all fashion shoes and accessories purchased in the U.S. are imported, making careers in accessory design and merchandising attractive. Accessory production, like apparel, is also communicated through digital means.

In order to provide practice and to help you develop your digital rendering skills for foot and leg poses, enhance your ability to work with type, and sharpen both your critical thinking and artistic acumen, in this tutorial, you will design a line of shoes and hosiery inspired by your name and/or initials. Tutorial 3.2 builds upon the fundamentals of Tutorial 3.1 and will provide instruction for the following:

- Document bleeds to assist printing storyboards
- Use of typography as a creative catalyst
- Digital accessory design and merchandising
- Digital rendering of male and female fashion leg poses via tracing of fashion photography
- Translucency via the Transparency panel
- Digital simulation of shading through tools and filter combinations
- How to create pattern repeats made from type
- How to use the Illustrator® Type on a Path Tool
- The Color Guide panel, the Color Picker, and the Color Libraries
- Graphic Styles panel techniques
- Combined use of the Symbols Sprayer Tool (Shift+S) and the Symbols Libraries

To help you complete this tutorial, files have been provided on ① Ch03\Tutorial 3.2. You'll also be instructed to use additional figurative photo files from the ① Digital Duo Modeling Agency.

Note: *This tutorial will use photography. Because figurative photography tends to look wider than the needs of fashion illustration, these photos have been elongated. As we advance in the tutorials, further distortion will be your choice.*

Step 1: Create a New Document and Workspace

Load Illustrator® and create a new file by pressing *Cmd+N / Ctrl+N*. When the New Document dialog box appears, enter the information that you see in Figure 3.22, then click OK.

Bleeds

Bleeds appear in this tutorial as a red rectangle around your printable area. Bleeds indicate to a printer that the image is to be printed borderless (printed to the edge of the page). In this case, we

Figure 3.21 **The October 1941 issue of** *Vogue.*

Figure 3.22

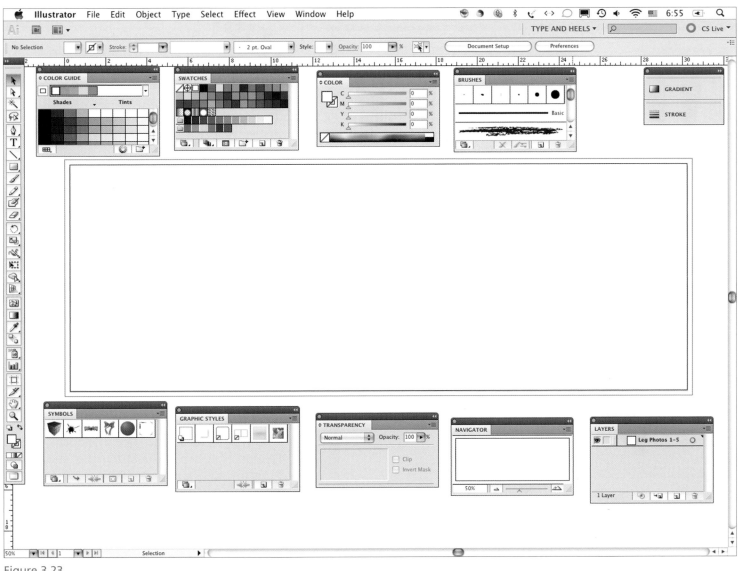

Figure 3.23

want a clean look with equilateral bleeds of 0.25 inches on all sides. This will leave a margin for error in printing, scoring, mounting, etc.

1. Show the Layers panel, Navigator panel, Color panel, Swatches panel, Color Guide panel, Brushes panel, Transparency panel, Graphic Styles panel, Gradient panel, Stroke panel, and Symbols panel.

2. Go to the *Application Bar > Workspace Switcher > Save Workspace.*

3. When the Save Workspace dialog box appears, type the title of this tutorial, *TYPE AND HEELS*, into the *Name* field and click OK.

The window and Artboard will look something like Figure 3.23, depending upon your arrangement of the panels. Remember to save and back up your work.

Step 2: Place, Arrange, and Align the Leg Photos

Place photos from ① Digital Duo Modeling Agency into the file:

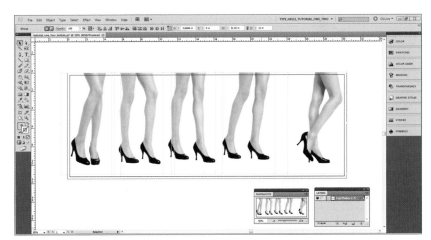

Figure 3.24

- For women's footwear and hosiery presentations, use any three files from the folder Anatomical Poses\Female\Leg and Shoe Poses (**Figure 3.24**).

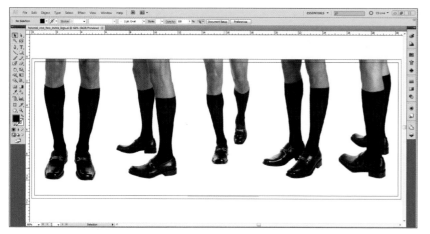

Figure 3.25

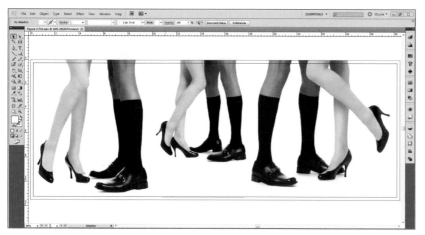

Figure 3.26

- For men's footwear and hosiery presentations, use any five files from the folder Anatomical Poses\Male\Leg and Shoe Poses (**Figure 3.25**).

- For footwear and hosiery presentations featuring men and women, use any four files from the folder Anatomical Poses\Couples Leg and Shoe Poses (**Figure 3.26**).

To set up your photos similar to those shown in Figures 3.24–26, double-click on the default layer in the Layers panel, and rename it *Leg Photos 1–5.* Select and Embed each photo, then arrange them across the width of the page (**Figure 3.24**). The white background of each photo should not cover other leg images, and the images must not extend outside the Artboard. However, at the top of the Artboard the images will extend to the bleed. When you have made your arrangement, follow these steps:

1. Press *Cmd+R / Ctrl+R* to show your Rulers.

2. Pull the Zero Point from the Ruler Origin and place it at the upper left corner of the bleed rectangle.

3. Go to *Menu Bar > Window > Transform* to show the Transform panel. Select the upper left corner button in the Reference Point selector.

4. Press *Cmd+A / Ctrl+A* to Select All.

5. Show the Align panel by going to *Menu Bar > Window > Align*, then click Vertical Align Top. This will align the photos at the top.

6. Type 0 in the *y* field of the Transform panel options, then press the Enter key to position the selected photos at the top of the bleed.

Step 3: Create Outlines of the Legs and Shoes

1. Lock the layer labeled *Leg Photos 1–5,* then use the Create New Layer icon at the bottom of the panel to add a new layer. Label this layer *Legs A.*

2. Beginning on the left side of the Artboard, use the Pen Tool (P) with a Stroke of any color and a Fill of None to trace the outline of the legs in the photos. Try and render the legs as if they were in stockings.

TIP: **Bleeding Color**

The bleed in the tutorial example is red, but you can change the color in the Guides & Grid section of the Illustrator® Preferences menu. The bleed will not show unless you toggle it on with the Guides by pressing *Cmd+; (semicolon) / Ctrl+; (semicolon).*

TIP: **Photo Options**

Certain nuances of the curves in the photographs will give your renderings an enhanced presence, and others may be unattractive. If needed, use the photo images of barefoot poses located on ① Digital Duo Modeling Agency\Anatomical Poses. They will help you with rendering the stocking feet. It is not necessary to render each toe. You will trace the shoes later.

3. Turn on your Smart Guides. Toggle them by pressing *Cmd+U / Ctrl+U.*

4. Increase the view by performing a marquee with the Zoom Tool (Z) or press *Cmd++ (plus) / Ctrl++ (plus).* The actual key would be the equal symbol (=), but the plus symbol (+) is commonly used to describe this particular shortcut. In addition, the page view can be repositioned manually with the Navigator panel's Proxy Preview Area.

5. Beginning with the first pair of legs on the left, render the outline of the rear or right leg, first (whichever is applicable to the pose) in a Stroke of red (or any color) with a Fill of None. Observe the other leg photos to imagine the parts that you cannot see. Begin by selecting the Direct Selection Tool (A), then the Pen Tool (P) to enable you to toggle the two tools. Trace the top portion at the bleed, click on one side of the leg, and hold the Shift key to create a straight line segment, then click again, on the other side. The Smart Guides will help you to see the path. If necessary, temporarily hide the Bounding Box by pressing *Shift+Ctrl+B.* Continue your rendering in controlled Bézier Curves until you have created a closed shape; then select it, and lock the selection by pressing *Cmd+2 / Ctrl+2.*

6. Render the outline of the front or forward leg, but use a Stroke of green with a Fill of None.

7. Repeat these actions for each pair of legs on separate layers labeled *Legs B, Legs C, Legs D,* and *Legs E.* Remember that it is important that each leg is rendered as a separate shape.

8. Save and back up your work periodically.

Figure 3.27 shows the look of the Artboard and layer compositing of Step Three after the renderings are completed. The Stroke of each leg shape has been toggled to the Fill. The file Step_Three_Example_Women.pdf has been provided on ① Ch03\ Tutorial 3.2 so you can examine this completed step. Open the file in Illustrator®, unlock the layers, then press *Option+Cmd+2 / Alt+Ctrl+2* to unlock the shapes on the layers. Figure 3.28 is an example using a male model's photo.

Step 4: Switch the Legs

You may have discovered that you are able to exchange some of the legs with others from another set.

1. Pair up some of the green legs with copies of the red legs. Select, copy, and paste the desired legs. Change the Fill colors on the copies, so that you can easily identify your changes. Figure 3.29 shows how various changes to leg pairs can affect the mood of a pose.

2. Make alterations to the shapes with the tools in the Pen Tool Suite if needed and use the Direct Selection Tool (A) to move anchor points and paths by clicking and dragging.

3. Scale certain leg shapes by constraining the proportions of the Bounding Box (hold the Shift key). Make realistic changes to the legs; do not alter the foot positions. Again, align the legs at the top of the bleed. Save and back up your work.

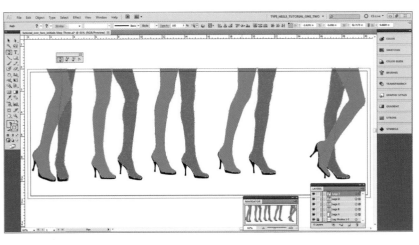

Figure 3.27

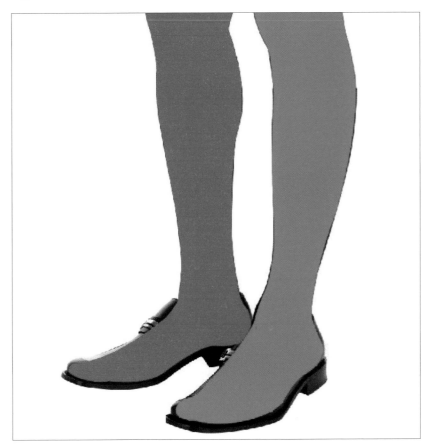

Figure 3.28

Figure 3.29

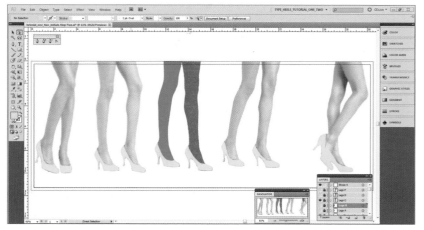

Figure 3.30

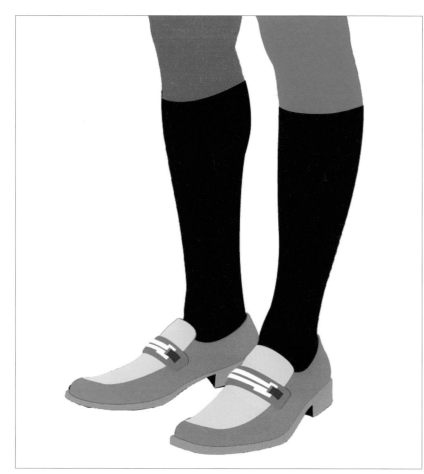

Figure 3.31

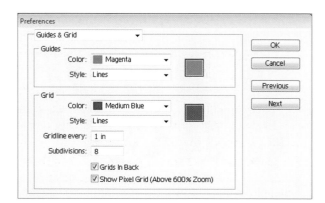

Figure 3.32

Step 5: Render the Shoes

The female model is wearing black leather pumps with a slight platform. The photo image will create an edgy classic silhouette when digitally rendered. You will not be able to tell that they were platforms when you view them filled with a color.

Create a new layer above all the layers and carefully render the shoes in each photo with the Pen Tool (P). Choose a color that is easily seen on black. Use the same color for all the shoes. Once you have traced around their forms, select them and press Shift+X to Swap the Fill and Stroke in the Tools panel. Toggle off the visibility of the leg layers to view the shoes in relation to the photos. Keep them on one layer for now. We will copy and paste a few later on. Completed digital renderings of the shoes are shown in Figure 3.30. Figure 3.31 shows the development of men's shoes. The file Step_Five_Example_Men.pdf has been provided on ① Ch03\Tutorial 3.2 so you can examine this completed step.

Step 6: Create a Logo Pattern

Lock all the layers and create a new layer above them labeled *Logo Pattern*. The Artboard is filled with images, so the Scratchboard will become the canvas for creating a pattern from various fonts. Use the Guides and the Grid as a structure. Set your Grid Preferences by clicking the button in the Control Panel or by going to *Menu Bar > Illustrator > Guides & Grid* or *Menu Bar > Edit > Preferences > Guides & Grid*. Use the settings in Figure 3.32. Toggle on the Grid by pressing *Cmd+' (apostrophe) / Ctrl+' (apostrophe)*. Zoom in on an area of about 12 square inches with the Zoom Tool (Z). Pull Guides to accentuate the boundaries of this area.

Select the Type Tool (T) and click in the upper-left corner of the area on the Scratchboard that you marked with Guides. Go to *Menu Bar > Type > Font* and select an interesting typeface from 12 pt to 24 pt. You could use the Font pull-down menu in the Control Panel to do this as well. However, unless you are familiar with various fonts, their titles alone will not help you. Type your name, initials, or anything you want in various ways on one line, as close to the boundaries as possible until you cannot go farther than the right side of the space. You may leave spaces between letters, or the names may be flush against each other. Use bold, italic, or both. Be creative. After you retype the name or initials on this line a few times, it may cross the guideline or be just shy of it. Type the spelling of the name(s) or the initials as close to the boundaries as possible. Repeat the steps about eight times until you cannot fit any additional rows of type into the space.

The Character Panel and Tracking

Because Illustrator® is not a word-processing software program, most designers do not use it for page layouts. However, Illustrator® does have some comprehensive typography capabilities and features. The **Character panel** provides a few of these benefits. When you select the type or the Type Tool (T), the Character panel appears in the Control Panel. You can also go to *Menu Bar > Window > Type > Character* to float the panel.

Set Tracking: In Tutorial 3.1, we learned about the concept of kerning, which relates to the space between letters. Now the space between entire bodies of text, known as **tracking**, needs adjusting. You will need to adjust the tracking of each row until it is flush with the right boundary of your Guide or Grid space to prevent gaps in the pattern that will be defined. To do this, select each row individually and reduce or increase the amount of tracking in the Character panel in the lower right section. Notice that the icon that represents tracking is also highlighted. Use the double-sided arrows on the left side to track the highlighted text in individual increments. Figure 3.33 identifies the tracking section of the Character panel. The font Rosewood Std is highlighted and ready for tracking in Figure 3.34.

Set Leading: Above the gauge that allows you to set the tracking for selected text is area that adjusts the spaces between lines of text. **Leading** is the amount of blank space between lines of text. You may need to adjust the leading in your entire body of text; however, some spaces between lines may need to be adjusted more than others. To adjust one line but not all, select the line and then use the double-sided arrows of the leading gauge in the Character panel to move the line up or down. Exercise restraint. Be careful not to cause the baselines and the cap heights to converge. Figure 3.35 shows the combination of tight leading and tracking suitable for a defined pattern repeat.

Step 7: Outline the Type

Now that you have set the type, select it with the Selection Tool (V) and go to *Menu Bar > Type > Create Outlines* or press *Shift+Cmd+0 / Shift+Ctrl+0*. Each character will be transformed from type to vector shapes.

Step 8: Color and Flip Type

1. Ungroup the type while it is selected by pressing *Shift+Cmd+G / Shift+Ctrl+G*.

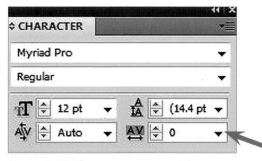

Figure 3.33 **The green arrow points to tracking.**

Figure 3.34

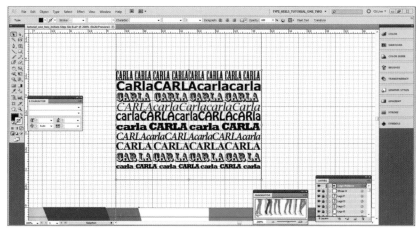

Figure 3.35

2. Repeat this until each character can be selected. Use the Selection Tool (V) to select words or entire rows with a marquee.

3. Use the Reflect Tool (O) to flip the selections horizontally (Figure 3.36).

4. Now, flip the selections vertically. This will give your pattern a two-way effect, which is important to textile design because it allows the pattern pieces to be cut in opposite directions. In the case of this exercise, the two-way design will accommodate reading the pattern from various directions in the hosiery.

Figure 3.36

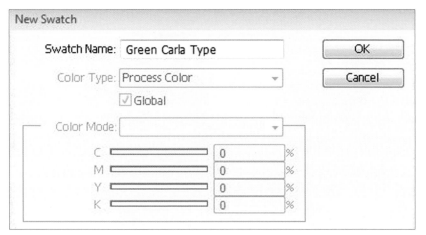

Figure 3.37

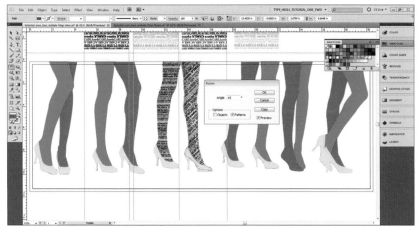

Figure 3.38

5. Afterward, select the rows, words, or letters, and fill and/or stroke them with any fashion color combinations.

6. Next, select, copy, and paste the type, then try different color combinations by changing the Fill and Stroke as shown in Figure 3.36.

Step 9: Define and Fill

Select each group of outlined type and go to *Menu Bar > Edit > Define Pattern* or use the CS6 Pattern Editor. A New Swatch dialog box appears. In the Swatch Name field, type in an appropriate title for your pattern and press OK (**Figure 3.37**). The swatch will appear in the Swatches panel. Repeat the steps and create several different patterns in various fashion color combinations. Save your work to retain the new swatch each time you open the file.

Fill the Shapes

Select any of the leg shapes that you rendered from the *A–F* Layers, then select the Fill box in the Tools panel, and choose one of the new pattern swatches that you defined from the Swatches panel. Your pattern will appear placed in the shape as if it were hosiery. This is great, but there are many more options; we will cover some of them in this tutorial. Save and back up your file.

Step 10: Scale the Pattern

Select any of the leg shapes that you rendered, then select the Fill box in the Tools panel. Afterward, select any new pattern that you have defined. The shape will be filled with your pattern, but the scale of the pattern may need adjusting.

Note: *Gradients may be used to fill Strokes in Illustrator® CS6. If you are operating lower versions of Illustrator®, do not fill your Stroke with a pattern or gradient. This may prevent printing or cause your computer to crash.*

To scale the pattern:

1. Select the leg(s) that you filled with the new pattern swatch you defined, then double-click on the Scale Tool (S) in the Tools panel.

2. When the Scale dialog box appears, choose the *Uniform* button, but uncheck *Shape* at the bottom in the *Scale Options* section. **Figure 3.38** shows the leg shapes filled with defined patterns. The left leg shape has been scaled to 60% of its original size.

Step 11: Color Guide Panel

The **Color Guide panel** will help you to manage fashion color schemes, harmonies, and stories. It provides suggestions for these from your selected object's Fill and Stroke colors and patterns in the Tools panel. Illustrator® calculates color changes based on your artwork. This allows you to mix and preview various color combinations before you actually accept them and without having to redefine a pattern swatch.

You can limit the scope of your color scheme by selecting the button at the lower left corner of the Color Guide panel. It limits your colors to those within predetermined Color Libraries. Just scroll to one of the Color Libraries and these colors will appear in the **Color Guide Harmony Rules** selector at the top of the panel. Use the Color Libraries to select color schemes based on fine art, nature, etc. Once you choose a color story, click the **Save Color Group to Swatch panel** button located at the bottom right of the Color Guide panel. A copy of the row of colors shown in the Color Guide Harmony Rules selector window will now be available in your Swatches panel. To affect the colorways in the defined type pattern:

1. Select one of the legs that have been filled with a pattern.

2. Show the Color Guide panel by going to *Menu Bar > Window > Color Guide*, or press Shift+F3.

3. Zoom in on the legs so that you will be able to view color combinations.

4. The Harmony Rules selector window at the top of the Color Guide panel has a hidden pull-down menu that reveals various color schemes. Click on any combination you like (Figure 3.39).

5. Click the **Edit or Apply Colors button** (color wheel icon) at the bottom of the panel.

6. Click OK to accept the new color scheme when the **Recolor Artwork** dialog box appears (Figure 3.40).

7. Other options include clicking the **Randomly change color order button** to allow the panel to alter the colorway or the **Randomly change saturation and brightness button** to alter the actual colors. Both are located at the bottom right of the **Current Colors Field** within the Recolor Artwork dialog box shown in Figure 3.40.

About the Recolor Artwork Options

At the top center of the Recolor Artwork dialog box is a **Get colors from selected art button**. When selected, the colors will show in the Current Colors field below it. The *Color Groups* area on the right side contains those that you have saved to your Swatches panel. Below this to the left is a color scale based on the color mode you are currently using. In this case, it is CMYK. To change the colors in your artwork/pattern:

1. Select the current color.

2. Click on the smaller color box to the right of the longer one.

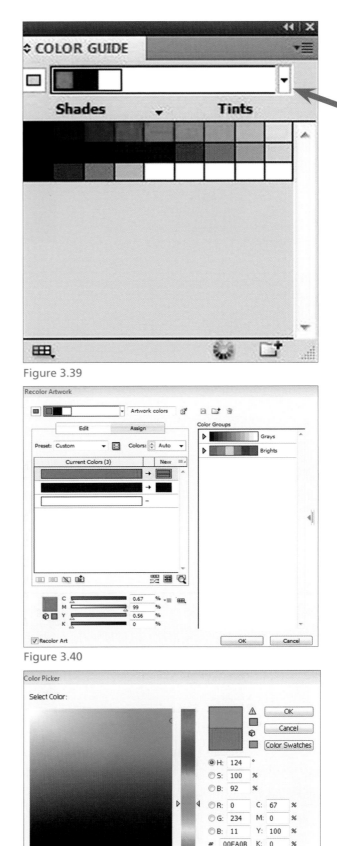

Figure 3.39

Figure 3.40

Figure 3.41

3. Select from the Color Swatches or click on the Color Models button to show the Color Picker (Figure 3.41). Slide the spectrum selector to the desired color, then click into the field to select a new color, and click OK.

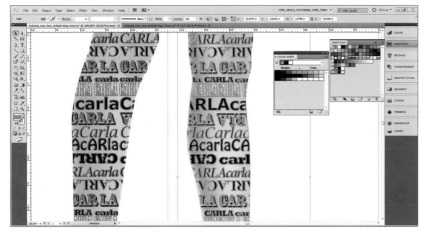

Figure 3.42

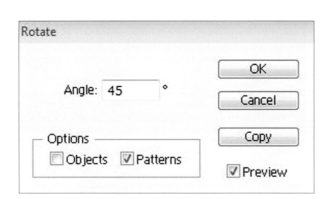

Figure 3.43

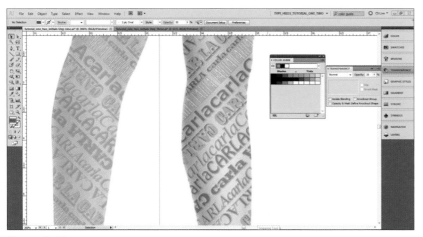

Figure 3.44

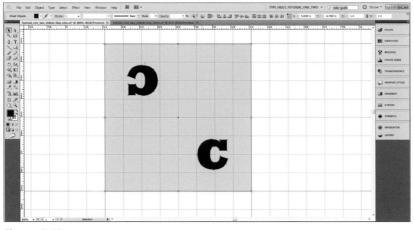

Figure 3.45

4. In the Recolor Artwork dialog box, accept the new color, or to continue making changes, repeat the procedure for the same or another color in the Current Color field. To add the color group changes to your swatches within the dialog box, select the icon that looks like a folder with a plus symbol to its right.

5. To accept the overall changes, click OK at the bottom of the Recolor Artwork dialog box.

6. If you forgot to add the color group within the Recolor Artwork dialog box, click the icon at the bottom right of the panel or scroll to the option in the hidden menu of Color Guide panel. Repeat this process to create many different color harmonies. Figure 3.42 shows the effects of the changes to the actual pattern on the right leg. Both the Color Guide panel and the Swatch panel contain the new colorway.

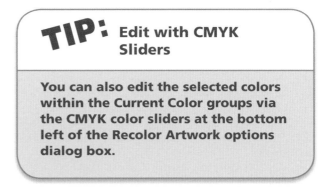

TIP: Edit with CMYK Sliders

You can also edit the selected colors within the Current Color groups via the CMYK color sliders at the bottom left of the Recolor Artwork options dialog box.

Step 12: Rotate the Pattern

Depending on the type of pattern that you create, you may want to rotate it within the shape. To do this, select the object and then double-click on the Rotate Tool (R). When the Rotate dialog box appears, select patterns and uncheck *Objects*, as shown in Figure 3.43. If you want your pattern to flow diagonally in reverse, enter a minus sign in front of the degree that you entered in the *Angle* section field. Spend some time figuring out which angles work best for your presentations.

Step 13: Use the Transparency Panel

The **Transparency panel** has more complicated features than we need for this tutorial, but its primary function is to make selected objects translucent. In fact, we could use the *Opacity* feature in the Layers panel, but doing so would affect the entire layer instead of a single object. To affect your pattern, select the shape where you have it filled and show the Transparency panel. You can also press *Shift+Cmd+F10 / Shift+Ctrl+F10*. Figure 3.44 reveals the beauty of the basic Transparency panel function: the left leg has been reduced to 20% and the right leg to 40%.

Create a Transparency Pattern

Follow the steps you used to create the type pattern but this time use only one to three initials. Then do the following:

1. Select the Illustrator® Rectangle Tool (M) from the Tools panel, and hold the Shift key while performing a marquee to create a shape that is 1 inch on all sides. It should have a Fill of any color and a Stroke of None.

2. Use the Transform fields in the Control Panel to make further adjustments. Enter 1 inch for the width and 1 inch for the height, then press Enter.

3. With the square selected, show the Transparency panel and reduce it to about 15%.

4. Using the same color Fill, select the Type Tool (T), and create the initials or a single character in any font from 24 to 36 pt.

5. Go to *Menu Bar > Type > Create Outlines*. Figure 3.45 shows the letters and square transparent space selected and ready to be defined.

6. Copy and paste the character(s). Rotate the character(s) 180°, then toggle the Grid, and position them (Figure 3.46). Leave some space at the sides so that the repeat will not look crowded.

7. Select the square and the outline, then define the pattern.

8. Fill a leg shape, and make adjustments as necessary. The defined transparency pattern is shown on the right in Figure 3.46.

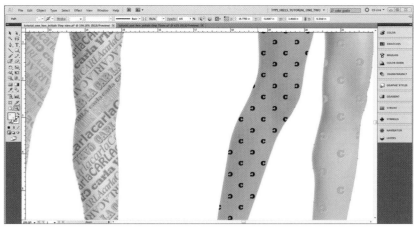
Figure 3.46

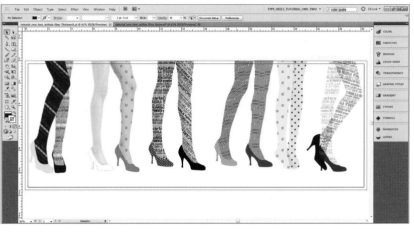
Figure 3.47

Step 14: Fill All the Legs with Patterns

It is time to fill in each of the legs that you rendered with a text pattern. Use all of the options explained in this tutorial and develop your color forecast and design concept. If you prefer, a Stroke of color can be added to the shapes in a *Weight* of 0.15 pt or less. Figure 3.47 shows all the legs and shoes filled with a color and/or a pattern. Some objects filled with patterns have been placed on top of the same shape in a solid color. The left leg and foot in Figure 3.48 shows the development of a men's wear presentation.

Step 15: Finish the Shoes

The patterned hosiery accessorizes the shoes in this presentation. Fill the shoes with a single color or present various styles and colors. Try the tools and features that you have already learned and be creative. Add bows or other shapes but keep the presentation marketable. Some shoes and legs will need to be placed on a different layer to create the proper illusion.

Figure 3.48

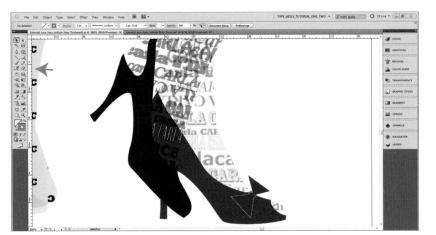

Figure 3.49

Figure 3.50

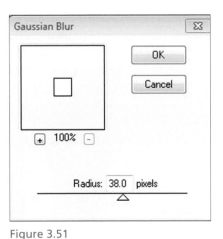

Figure 3.51

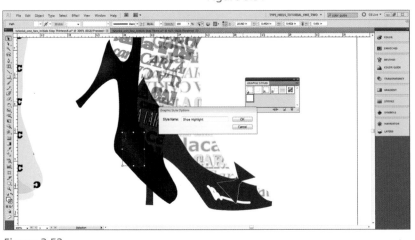

Figure 3.52

The Eraser Tool

Use the **Eraser Tool** (Shift+E) to remove parts of the shoes, such as the toe to create peep-toed styles (Figure 3.49). You could erase the back of the shoe to make sling-backs or mules. The Eraser Tool (Shift+E) is easy to use: just zoom in on the area and click and drag to erase. If the diameter of the brush size needs adjusting, double-click on the icon in the Tools panel to find the *Eraser Tool Options*.

The Blob Brush Tool, Gaussian Blur, and Graphic Styles

The **Blob Brush Tool** (Shift+B) can help add highlights or create shadows on the shoes. It is different from the Brush Tool (B) because it creates a random shape that is a selection rather than a stroke. The effects you will generate may not be as great as what you will later achieve with the "Digital Duo" processes, but it is an effective vector solution. Follow these steps:

1. Select the Blob Brush Tool (Shift+B).

2. Select the Fill color that you want to use. You may need to adjust the brush size in the Control Panel, or by double-clicking on the brush's icon in the Tools panel.

3. Lock the objects on the layer by selecting them and pressing *Cmd+2 / Ctrl+2*.

4. Use the Blob Brush Tool (Shift+B) to create highlights or shadows (Figure 3.50).

5. Select the shapes that you painted with the Selection Tool (V) and go to *Menu Bar > Effects > Blur > Gaussian Blur*.

6. When the Gaussian Blur dialog box appears, move the Radius slider to a Radius of 38.0 px, or whatever works for your selection, then click OK (Figure 3.51). The effects will be similar to the blue shoe in Figure 3.48 or the black shoe in Figure 3.52.

The **Graphic Styles panel** is used to save combination effects like the one you just created with the Blob Tool (Shift+B) and the Gaussian Blur filter. With the object with the filter selected, show the Graphic Styles panel by going to *Menu Bar > Window > Graphic Styles* or click Shift+F5. Click the New Graphic Style icon located at the bottom of the panel next to the Trash icon. When the Graphic Style Options dialog box appears, enter an appropriate name. When you save your work, the new graphic style will be available for you to use again. To use the Graphic Style, select any object, and then select the Graphic Style swatch. Explore the other options on your own and consult the Adobe Help menu.

Step 16: Further Fashion Distortion

Because the vector processes can make your renderings from photos appear a bit heavy, you may want to elongate the legs. To do so, simply unlock all the layers and everything on them. Perform a marquee across the bottom of the legs including the shoes with the Selection Tool (V), then pull the legs down by the Bounding Box. Some of the pairs may need further distortion by pulling in the width. Do not overexaggerate the elongation of the legs.

Step 17: Finishing Touches

Illustrator® has many creative options. This tutorial would not be complete without showing you how to use the Brushes panel and the Symbols panel.

The Brushes Panel

You can access the **Brushes panel** by going to *Menu Bar > Window > Brushes* or by pressing *F5*. Here you will find libraries of preset brushes that you can use and access directly through the panel at the lower left. For this tutorial, we will only use the Brushes panel to create a line made from type. Proceed by doing the following:

1. Select any font and use the Type Tool (T) to enter any name or phrase using the keyboard. The fictitious designer name Carla Rossi fits well with the hosiery; it was selected, and then turned into outlines as described previously.

2. With the outlines selected, click the Create New Brush icon at the lower right of the panel. A New Brush dialog box appears (Figure 3.53). Select **Pattern Brush**, then click OK. A pattern brush will be one that repeats itself on a line.

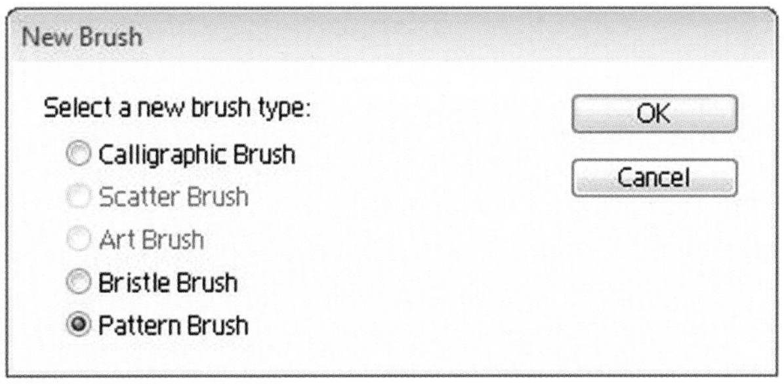

Figure 3.53

3. When the Pattern Brush Options dialog box appears, do not touch anything. Just click OK, and the new type brush will appear in the window options of the Brushes panel.

4. Create a line, beneath the shoes, from curved line segments as if the legs were walking on a line of type, as shown in Figure 3.54. Delete some of the photos to produce exciting effects. If parts of the photos that you retain show from beneath the edges of your work, select and diminish them with the Gaussian Blur filter. It creates an easy and attractive shadow.

5. Select the line and then the Stroke box in the Tools panel, or press the X key on the keyboard to automatically bring it to the front.

6. Next, select the new brush in the Brushes panel to become your line of type. If you need to make adjustments to the scale, just double-click on the brush in the panel window and make them in the Pattern Brush Options dialog box. You can also use this brush freehand with the Brush Tool (B) or the Pencil Tool (N).

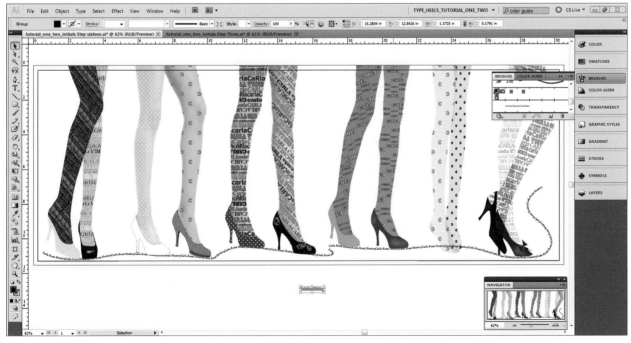

Figure 3.54

Symbols Panel

The **Symbols panel** works in conjunction with the **Symbol Sprayer Tool** (Shift+S). There are too many options to name here, so just spray a few symbols as final touches, like the flower on one shoe, a red bow on another shoe, and a butterfly to finish the type pattern brush. Try a few different symbols.

Show the Symbols panel by pressing *Shift+Cmd +F11 / Shift+Ctrl+F11*, or go to *Menu Bar > Window > Symbols*. You could create your own symbol from any drawing, and then select and save it with the New Symbol icon at the bottom of the panel. However, because the Illustrator® symbols libraries are extensive, it would be easy just to pick a few things.

At the lower left of the panel is a Symbols Libraries Menu button. Click it and scroll to open any of them that interest you. The default symbols, the Flowers symbols and the Nature symbols, were fine for the example, but you may want to choose others. Figure 3.55 shows the Symbols panel and a few libraries docked vertically. As the libraries appear, choose the symbols of interest to you, then use the Symbols Sprayer Tool (Shift+S) to place a symbol of your choosing somewhere on the page. If you press too hard or move your cursor, the sprayer will place more symbols than you want. Use the Navigator panel's Proxy Preview Area to zoom in and inspect your work. Do not forget to properly save and back up your file. Figure 3.56 shows the completed Tutorial 3.2 example with several symbols applied.

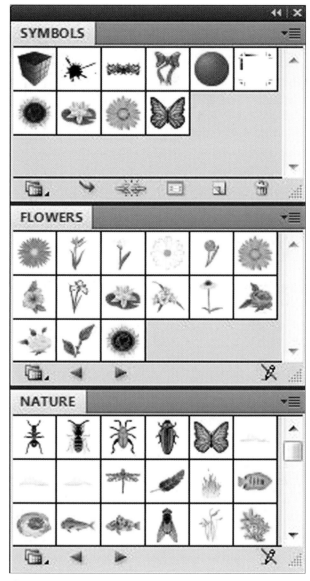

Figure 3.55

Figure 3.56 **Illustration by Stacy Stewart Smith.**

This tutorial was inspired by a Pablo Picasso oil painting on canvas entitled *Girl Before a Mirror*, 1932 (Figure 3.57). In the painting a blond girl gazes at her image, but in this tutorial, our fashionista gazes at either of her two possible dates, Brad 1 or Brad 2. One of them has entered her room by surprise. This project combines retouched and distorted fashion photography and vector graphics processes. The goal of this multipart exercise is to:

- Create clipping masks.

- Learn to prepare compound paths.

- Introduce the Photoshop® Effects Gallery within Illustrator®.

- Apply seamless pattern repeats.

- Define a tile repeat pattern.

- Further develop electronic drawing skills.

It is recommended that you complete all previous exercises and tutorials before beginning this tutorial. Use the files provided on ① Ch03\Tutorial 3.3.

Step 1: Create a New Document

Load Illustrator® and open a letter-size CMYK document without bleeds in portrait orientation. Name the file *date_with_brad*. Type your name or initials after this title. The New Document dialog box is shown in Figure 3.58.

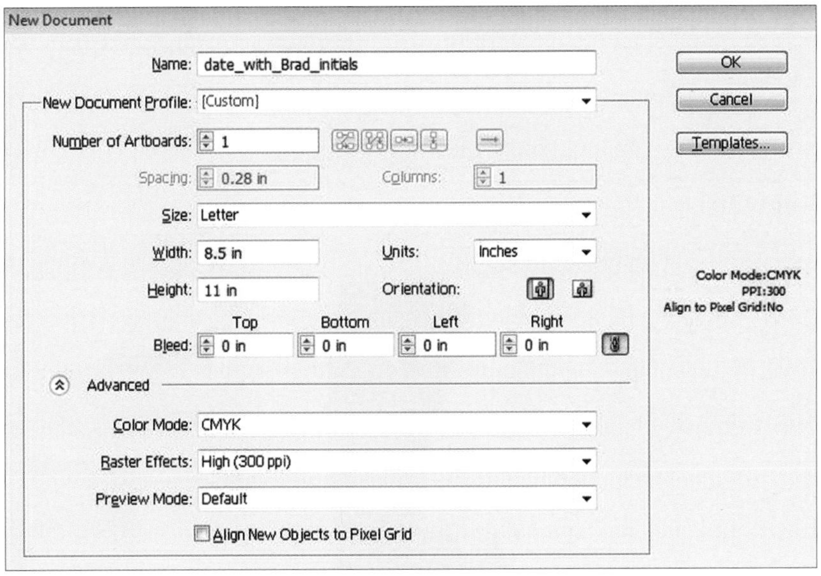

Step 2: Prepare Your Workspace

Prepare and save your Workspace as previously instructed. Show the panels you prefer or use the Essentials Workspace, which will suffice for this tutorial. Save the file to your desktop and back up the file on an external storage device. Do this throughout the tutorial.

Step 3: Exclude to Create a Clipping Mask

A **clipping mask** is a shape that can be used to block out areas of images. Follow these steps to create the first clipping mask in this tutorial:

1. Open the file Girl_Before_a_Mirror.pdf.

2. Rename the default *Layer 1* with the file's title *Girl Before a Mirror*. Select the image and lock it on the layer by pressing *Cmd+2 / Ctrl+2*.

3. Locate the file Outline_Girl.pdf in ① Ch03\Tutorial 3.3. Open the file in Illustrator®, then copy and paste it on the same layer.

Figure 3.57 *Girl before a Mirror*, Pablo Picasso, 1932. Museum of Modern Art. Digital Image © The Museum of Modern Art/Licensed by SCALA/ Art Resource, NY.

Figure 3.58

Figure 3.59

Figure 3.60

Figure 3.61

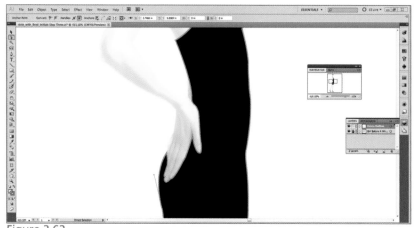

Figure 3.62

4. Perform a marquee to select both the outline and the negative arm space. Change the contents to a Fill and a Stroke of None, and then place the selection in alignment with the image of the girl.

5. Use the Navigator's Proxy Preview Area to inspect the alignment (Figure 3.59). The image and the outline are not exact matches. This is intentional. Make adjustments using the Direct Selection Tool (A) and others if needed (Figure 3.60).

6. To block out the white background of the figure, you must first select the grouped outline and the negative space shape.

7. Show the Pathfinder panel and click the *Exclude* button on the top row at the right. This will exclude the negative space.

8. With the outline and negative space shape still selected, press *Shift+Cmd+G / Shift+Ctrl+G* to ungroup the shapes.

9. Hold the Shift key and also select the figure file *Girl Before a Mirror*. The outlines must be on top of the image file.

10. With all three items selected, go to *Menu Bar > Object Clipping Mask > Make*.

11. Now the figure can be placed on any background. The negative space and the white background that came with the rasterized image will be masked.

12. Create a temporary background below the figure with the Rectangle Tool (M), and then select a temporary Fill color to reveal and inspect the mask (Figure 3.61).

13. Fill the background mask with white for now, and then select and group the objects. Lock the layer.

Step 4: Trace the Dress

Create a new layer and name it *Dress Outline*. Use the Pen Tool (P) to trace the outline of the dress on the fashion figure in a Stroke of color that you can easily see. Do not cover the figure's hand; trace around the shape of it instead. The Navigator panel will be helpful here (Figure 3.62).

Step 5: Create a Triple Flare Dance Skirt

The girl in this tutorial has a dance date. A great dance dress should consist of a simple element, plus a skirt that moves or swings with each step. We have the simple element in the haltered bodice, but something a little more dramatic is needed for the skirt. A sheer flare skirt in three tiers should do the trick.

Create a new layer and name it *Skirt,* then follow these steps:

1. Begin by creating a simple shape with the Pen Tool (P) upon which each flounce will hang, such as the one pictured with a Stroke of lime green in Figure 3.63.

2. Select, then lock this object on the layer by pressing *Cmd+2 / Ctrl+2*.

3. Continue using the Pen Tool (P) to create a flounce that descends to about half the length of the object that you just created.

4. Use the Pencil Tool (N) to create the scalloped hem the same as the bottom of the first shape. Attach the hem to the bottom of the first shape.

5. Lock the flounce on the layer by selecting it, then pressing *Cmd+2 / Ctrl+2*, but continue working on the *Skirt* layer to create two additional flounces. One will begin at about half the length of the first object and overlap the second.

6. Lock the flounce after you create it. Figure 3.64 displays the flounce in a Stroke of magenta.

> ## TIP: Hemline Variations
>
> **You can use your own imagination and try a different hemline instead of the one in the tutorial. Why not render your flounces with an asymmetrical back or a longer tulip, handkerchief, or tango hemline?**

The final two flounce shapes (Figure 3.65) require repeating this procedure, but they will follow the curved line at the top of the first object and overlap the last one you rendered. Lock the *Skirt* layer and save your work.

Step 6: Place the Date

Our girl has to choose between two possible dates, both named Brad (Figure 3.66). They appear to her in an oval full-length mirror. The two Brads were modeled from the same photo. To place the date, perform the following procedures:

1. Create a new layer above the rest entitled *Brad in Mirror*.

2. Locate the files Brad1.pdf and Brad2.pdf on ① Ch03\Tutorial 3.3.

3. Select and use the Scale Tool (S) to reduce the shape uniformly to 88% of its size.

4. Lock this layer (Figure 3.67).

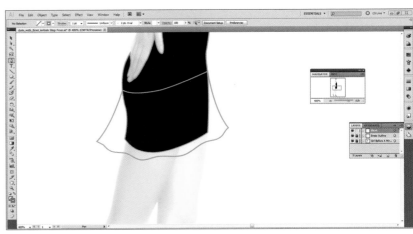

Figure 3.63

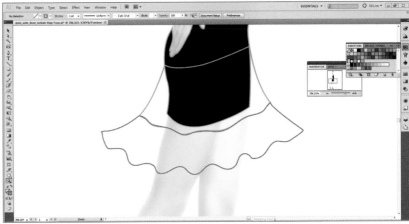

Figure 3.64

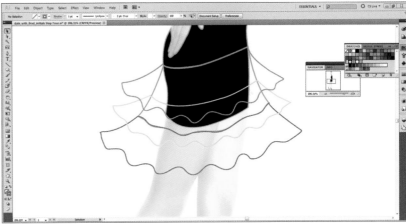

Figure 3.65

Figure 3.66

Figure 3.67

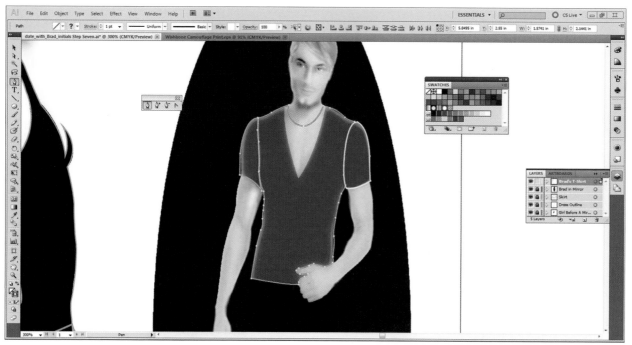

Figure 3.68

Step 7: Render Brad's T-Shirt

Create a new layer above *Brad in the Mirror*. Using the Pen Tool (P), Pencil Tool (N), or both, render Brad's T-shirt. The sleeve shapes should be separate from the T-shirt front. The neckline could be converted to a crew neck (Figure 3.68).

Step 8: Create Brad's New Camouflage-Print T-Shirt

Brad is wearing the right look, but a T-shirt made of a pattern might give it a boost on the dance floor. Camouflage prints have been popular since the 1980s. This one is a conversational print composed of wishbone-like shapes. Follow these steps to define the camouflage pattern repeat:

1. Load Illustrator® CS5, then open the file Wishbone_Camouflage_Repeat.pdf located on Ch03\Tutorial 3.3. The file contains a tile repeat pattern that must be defined. Notice that some parts of the pattern repeat protrude outside of the rectangle shape filled with color underneath. The rectangle shape is the **ground tile** of the pattern. Beneath this shape is another one with a Fill of None and a Stroke of None, referred to as a **Repeat Bounding Box**. This is not the same Bounding Box as was discussed earlier because it is being used for a different purpose and does not contain an object. This one tells Illustrator® CS5 (and earlier versions) how to repeat a pattern. If you pull Guides on all sides of the rectilinear ground tile, you would identify where one part of a pattern ends and continues on the opposite side (Figure 3.69).

2. Press *Cmd+A / Ctrl+A* to Select All. Create a new layer in the file: *date_with_brad*. Name this new layer *Wishbone Camouflage*. Copy and paste the repeat into this layer. Do not shift any of the elements or the repeat may develop highly visible fractures. Place it on the Scratchboard.

Avoiding Hairline Fractures

3. Before defining the print, take precautions to avoid creating **hairline fractures**. When creating the pattern repeat, the motif must be positioned within the ground tile properly. The Repeat Bounding Box must be below all the objects, and aligned with the

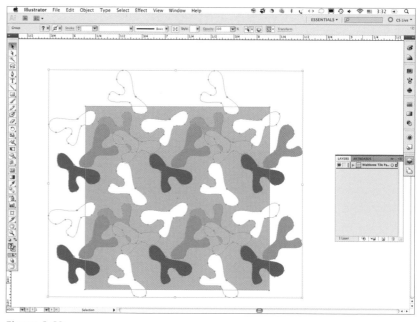

Figure 3.69

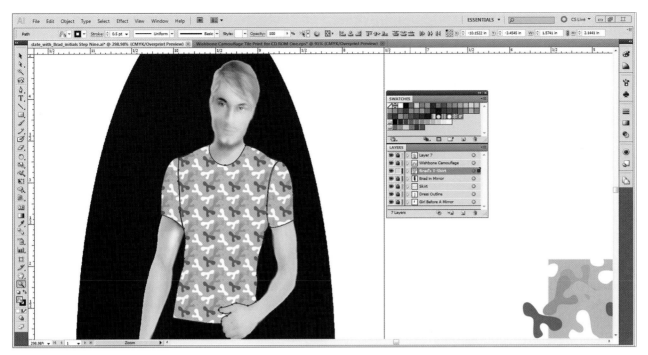

Figure 3.70

ground tile. Whatever parts of the motif protrude from the ground tile on one side must enter it on the opposite side. This technique requires practice. A hairline fracture in the defined pattern may result if any of the parts are not in proper alignment. Because this is not a book about textiles, we can accept some imperfection that is not too obvious. Often, what looks like a hairline fracture may just be a problem appearing only on the screen. To investigate if there is indeed a hairline fracture in the print, zoom in on the area, or better yet print a copy. In most cases, the repeat will be of a scale that it will not show when printed.

4. The Wishbone Camouflage tile repeat has been created, but you must still define it. **Defining a pattern** is a procedure in Illustrator® that allows you to create a continuous repeat that can be used to fill objects by selecting it in the Swatches panel.

Note: The following steps are suggested for defining patterns using CS5 and earlier versions, but you can use the same repeat parts in CS6 without the ground tile.

5. Lock all the other layers in the file *date_with_brad*. With the entire repeat selected, go to *Menu Bar > Edit > Define Pattern*. When the New Pattern dialog box appears, enter *Wishbone Camouflage*. A new swatch will appear in your Swatches panel.

Note: If you are using CS6, select the parts and then go to Menu Bar > Object > Pattern > Make. When the Pattern Editor appears, use the setting to redesign or recolor the repeat and make it seamless.

6. Select the T-shirt parts you created and the Fill in the Tools panel, then select the new Wishbone Camouflage swatch in the Swatches panel.

7. Stroke the T-Shirt parts with a *Weight* of .05 pt in any suitable color.

8. The pattern can be scaled to about 30% with the Scale Tool (S), or change the color via the Color Guide panel as discussed in Tutorial 3.2. In Figure 3.70, Brad 1 is clad in this new Wishbone Camouflage patterned T-shirt.

Note: If you fill an object with a pattern defined in CS6, the program will update the changes that you make with the Pattern Editor until you save it.

Merge Layers

9. Illustrator® allows you to merge two or more selected layers. Hold the Shift key, then select the *Wishbone Camouflage, Brad's T-Shirt*, and *Brad in the Mirror* layers.

10. Merge the three layers via the option in the Layer panel's hidden menu or press *Cmd+E / Ctrl+E*.

11. Rename the layer *Brad in Mirror*.

Step 9: Create a Vintage Printed Dress

Repeat the procedures of Step Eight, but use the file Arts_and_Crafts.pdf on ① Ch03\Tutorial 3.3 to define a tile pattern repeat. The motif will not protrude from the ground tile.

1. Create a new layer in the file *date_with_brad*, then name it.

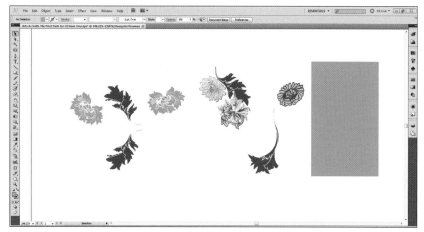

Figure 3.71

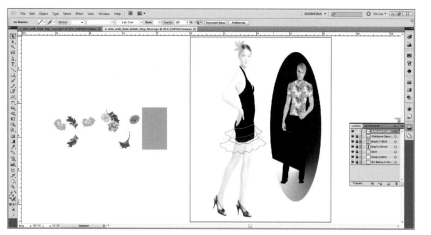

Figure 3.72

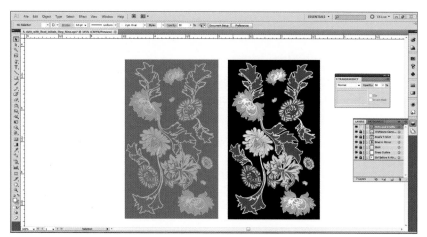

Figure 3.73

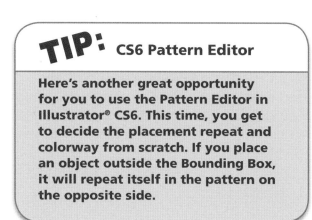

TIP: CS6 Pattern Editor

Here's another great opportunity for you to use the Pattern Editor in Illustrator® CS6. This time, you get to decide the placement repeat and colorway from scratch. If you place an object outside the Bounding Box, it will repeat itself in the pattern on the opposite side.

2. Open the file in Illustrator®, select the parts with the Selection Tool (V), then place them on a new layer with the same name (Figure 3.71). This print will be used for the dress.

3. Move the repeat to the Scratchboard as shown in Figure 3.72.

Step 10: Create Chiffon Fabric with the Transparency Panel

In Tutorial 3.2 we examined the attributes of creating sheer effects with the Transparency panel. Follow the steps below for CS5 and earlier. For CS6, use the transparency options available in the Pattern Editor.

1. Select the parts of the Arts and Crafts repeat, and arrange them onto the ground color rectangle. The Color Guide panel can be used to change the colors.

2. Select the Arts and Crafts repeat and open the Transparency Panel.

3. Reduce the *Opacity* to at least 50%. Figure 3.73 shows the parts of the Arts and Crafts repeat arranged onto the ground (left), and the results of the Transparency panel (right).

Figure 3.74

Step 11: Define, Fill, Stroke, and Scale

Define the pattern as previously instructed. Recolor the pattern of both the dress and Brad's T-shirt if desired. Select the dress shapes and fill them in with the pattern by selecting it in the Swatches panel. A complementary Stroke of color is also a nice finishing touch at 0.25 pt. Figure 3.74 shows the defined pattern in the dress.

Step 12: Create the Mirror

Now that everyone is dressed, it's time to add some finishing touches.

1. Toggle off the visibility of the *Arts and Crafts* layer and the *Wishbone Camouflage* layers.

2. Lock the layers and create a new one above the layer labeled *Brad in the Mirror*.

3. Give this new layer the title *Mirror, Mirror*.

4. Locate the file named Mirror_Mirror.pdf on ① Ch03\Tutorial 3.3 and open it in Illustrator®.

5. Unlock the layers, select the objects, then copy and paste them into your file on the *Mirror, Mirror* layer. In addition to the instructional letters, this file contains renderings of the following:

   A) The ornamental frame, which was created with the Ellipse Tool (L) and the *Decorative Border* brush from the Brushes panel.

   B) The illusion of glass that will cover Brad, which was created with the Ellipse Tool (L) and filled with a Linear gradient. White was added to the Fade to Black swatch located in the Default CMYK Swatches panel by dragging and dropping it on the bar of the Gradient panel. Pull off the Transparency slider to avoid a fade.

   C) A copy of the ellipse from "B" without a fill that will be used to create a Compound Path from part "D."

   D) A gradient-filled ellipse that will become a base for the frame.

   E) Stand parts for the mirror that have been grouped and filled with gradients.

   F) The ellipse filled with black, which will become a floor shadow.

Figure 3.75 shows the parts pasted into the *Mirror, Mirror* layer.

Step 13: Use the Gaussian Blur Filter

Brad 1 was created from a photo that was originally the image of Brad 2, but this is digital fashion illustration, not photography. Therefore, we shall use the Gaussian Blur filter to create a greater illusion of Brad. To do this, select the placed file of Brad and

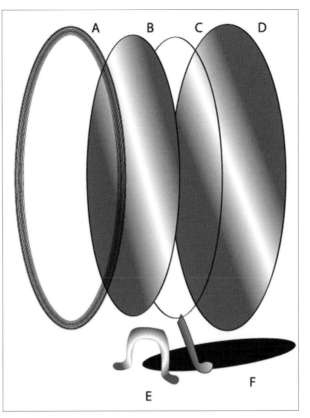

Figure 3.75

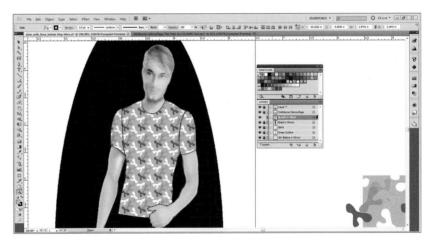

Figure 3.76

the parts of his T-shirt, which you rendered and filled with the pattern. Go to *Menu Bar > Effect > Blur > Gaussian Blur* and enter 3.0 or whatever effect you prefer. The effects of the Gaussian Blur filter at a Radius of 3.1 px are seen in Figure 3.76.

Step 14: Clipping Mask and Glass Transparency

Transparent backgrounds surrounding raster images can change to solid white rectilinear Bounding Boxes when they are imported to vector software. Later you will learn to solve this problem in different ways. A clipping mask can hide the white areas and re-create the silhouette of the images they contain. This

Figure 3.77

Figure 3.78

Figure 3.79

would not be an issue if we were creating an image with a white background, but we will eventually fill our background with a color or a print. To create a clipping mask, you need an outline of the vector shape that you wish to form. In this case, it is the simple elliptical shape of the mirror. This shape has been created for you, so follow these steps:

1. Select the *Mirror, Mirror* layer and *Brad in the Mirror* layer by holding the Shift key.

2. Merge the two layers by scrolling in the Layer panel's hidden menu to that option. The images will now all appear on the *Brad in the Mirror* layer.

3. To create the clipping mask, copy and paste the object labeled *C*. Arrange it over the image of Brad so that the image is inside the ellipse (**Figure 3.77**).

4. Complete this step by selecting both the image of Brad and the copy of object *C*. Do not select Brad's T-shirt.

5. Go to *Menu Bar > Object > Clipping Mask > Make*. You can also use the shortcut method by pressing *Cmd+7 / Ctrl+7*. The elliptical shape of the mirror will now be defined. You will need to send this object to the back in order to restore the printed T-Shirt shape by going to *Menu Bar > Object > Arrange > Send to Back*. The shortcut for this function is *Shift+Cmd+[(left bracket) / Shift+Ctrl+[(left bracket)*.

6. Afterward, reposition the T-shirt shape over Brad's image, select both objects and press *Cmd+G / Ctrl+G* to group them (**Figure 3.78**).

Mirror Glass

Create the illusion of glass by selecting the object labeled *B*. Place it in front of Brad's image as shown in **Figure 3.79**. The oval needs to be somewhat centered, but you can adjust the position as you progress. While the shape is selected, use the Transparency panel to reduce the *Opacity* to at least 30%. Adjust the sliders of the Gradient panel as shown in **Figure 3.80**. Use the Illustrator® Gradient Tool (G) to change the direction of the light by clicking and dragging near the selected object.

Step 15: Create the Frame as a Compound Path

A **Compound path** is the manual procedure that is also performed by the Exclude option of the Pathfinder. The frame consists of part *C* and part *D*. Select the two and center them using the Align panel options as shown in **Figure 3.81**. Our goal is to exclude the center. We could use that option in

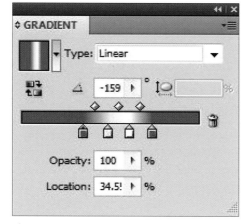
Figure 3.80

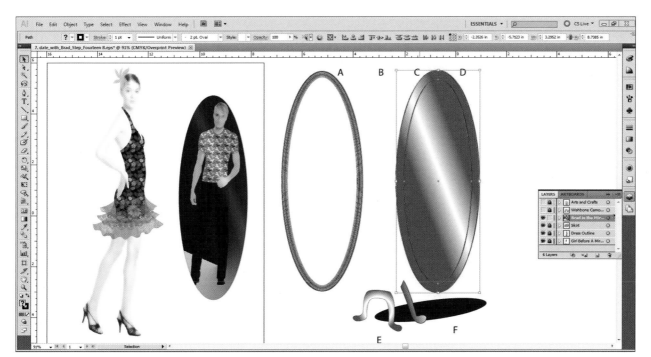

Figure 3.81

Figure 3.82

the Pathfinder panel, but there's another way to perform this task. With the two shapes selected, go to *Menu Bar > Object > Compound Path > Make.* The center ellipse will disappear, leaving an open area. Move the frame on top of the mirror (Figure 3.82).

Step 16: Use the Chrome Filter

Illustrator® is loaded with all sorts of cool **filters** that allow you to generate near-realistic effects on vector and raster images within the program. The **Chrome filter** transforms the look of flat vector graphics to that of 3-D metal in the **Photoshop® Effects Gallery**.

TIP: Right-Click

Certain options that are introduced throughout the book may also be accessed by right clicking with a double-headed mouse.

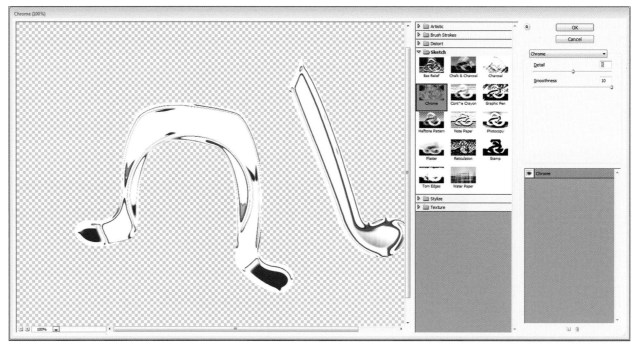

Figure 3.83

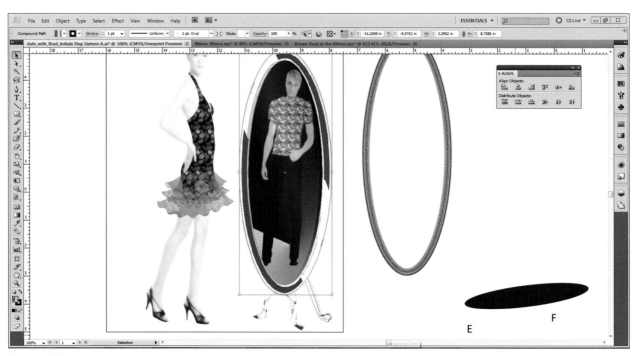

Figure 3.84

Move part *E* into position, then select it and the frame and go to *Menu Bar > Effect > Sketch > Chrome*. When the Chrome filter options window opens (Figure 3.83), adjust the *Detail* and the *Smoothness*, then click OK. Figure 3.84 shows the results of the Chrome filter upon the frame and stand.

TIP: Try Filters

You can try other filters instead of Chrome. There are plenty to choose from in the Photoshop® Effects Gallery. Just select the icons and be creative.

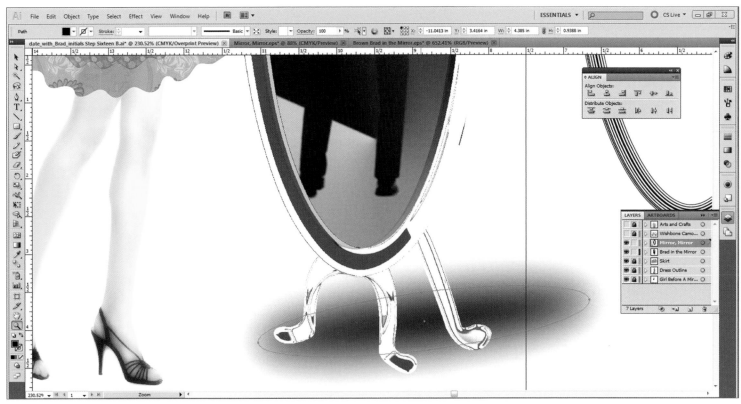

Figure 3.85

Step 17: Gaussian Blur Shadow

Select part *F* and place it beneath the mirror. Use the Gaussian Blur filter with a Radius of 70.0 px. It does not matter if it extends outside of the printable area Figure 3.85.

Step 18: Set the Detail Frame

Place part *A* on top of the frame as shown in Figure 3.86.

Step 19: Add Objects from the Symbols Libraries

"Brad! Hey, Brad! You forgot to bring your date some flowers!" You can add a few on the *Brad in the Mirror* layer with the Symbol Sprayer Tool (Shift+S) and the Symbols panel (Figure 3.87).

Step 20: Create a Simple Geometric Tile Pattern

In the background of the original painting *Girl Before Mirror*, Picasso painted a background likely inspired by the diamond-shaped patterned costumes of harlequins, which were also one of his favorite subjects. Follow these steps to create a similar pattern:

1. Create a 1-inch square with the Rectangle Tool (M) by holding the Shift key while performing a marquee. This will be called your ground tile. Use the Transform options in the Control Panel and the Grid to ensure accuracy.

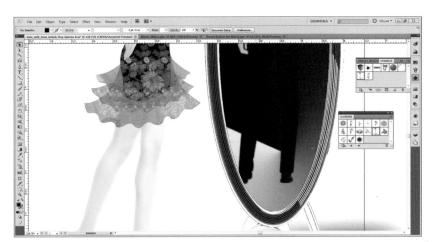

Figure 3.86

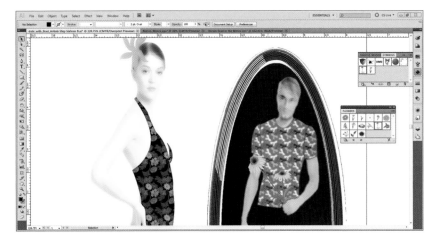

Figure 3.87

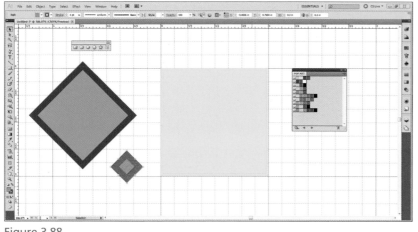

Figure 3.88

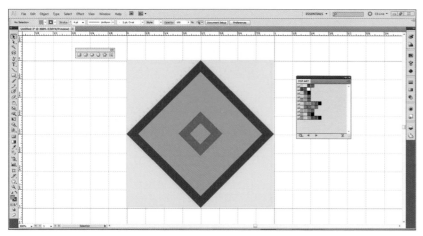

Figure 3.89

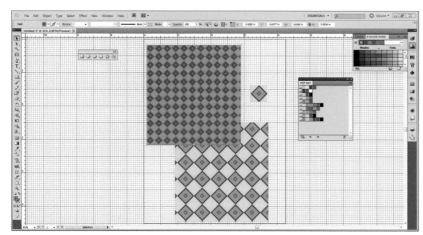

Figure 3.90

2. Choose your Fill color from the **Pop Art Color Library** by going to *Menu Bar > Window > Swatch Libraries > Art History > Pop Art*.

3. Select, copy, and paste the ground tile twice to create your **motif**.

4. Reduce the first copy to 70% and the second copy an additional 30%.

5. Select and rotate the copies 45° with the Rotate Tool (R) options.

6. Fill and stroke the copies with various **Pop Art colors**. Stroke them in contrasting or complementary colors using a 4 pt *Weight* on the larger copy and a 2 pt *Weight* on the smaller one.

TIP: **Align Strokes**

On the larger square, align with the options in the Stroke panel. This will keep the shape from protruding from the sides of your ground tile (Figure 3.88).

7. Select and center the copies by clicking the Horizontal Align Center icon, then Vertical Align Center icon in the Align panel to even the motif.

8. Group and place the motif on top of the ground tile, then select and center all the objects (Figure 3.89).

9. Define the pattern by selecting all the objects and going to *Menu Bar > Edit > Define Pattern*.

10. Name the pattern *Picasso Harlequin*.

11. Fill the background of your Artboard with the new patterned swatch.

12. Scale the pattern and/or recolor it with the Color Guide panel options for a modern art feeling (Figure 3.90). Take things further by selecting all or parts of your presentation and adding filter effects. Save and back up your work.

Figure 3.91 shows the completed file with a Harlequin pattern background.

Figure 3.91 Illustration by Stacy Stewart Smith.

Chapter 3 Summary

Now that you have had even greater exposure to the Illustrator® tools, panels, and features, you should be ready to go on to more advanced tutorials. In this chapter, you learned important Illustrator® fundamentals, such as proper file setup, placing and embedding objects, setting up document bleeds, and using proper file-saving techniques. Moreover, in the tutorials you actually rendered both straight paths and curved line segments, which is a big step to mastering electronic drawing. In addition, you learned to define, rotate, and scale patterns. You used the Color Guide panel to recolor patterns, and you made them translucent with the Transparency panel.

You also learned to make clipping masks and compound paths to assist you in creating all-inclusive digital page layouts with compelling environments. These procedures were proposed to help you develop a sense of digital spatial arrangement between figures and objects by exploring color gradients, fades, and Photoshop® Effects Gallery filters in Illustrator®. In addition, you examined concepts of typography through signage, and used the Character panel options. You learned to make use of digital measuring tools including the x-axis and y-axis (rulers), Transform panel, Align panel, Guides, Grids, the Rectangular Grid Tool, the Zero Point, and more.

The multidimensional lessons in this chapter have taught you foundation skills that later chapters will build upon. Later tutorials will teach you how to render croquis figures and apparel. You will make good use of what you learned about rendering footwear and hosiery in this chapter. This chapter should also have provided you with a basis for understanding leg and foot poses by tracing images from ① Digital Duo Modeling Agency. You learned from both the men's wear and women's wear aspects in these tutorials. This is a practice that you should continue as you advance in the chapters.

Chapter 3 Self-Assessment

If you have indeed followed the tutorials and learned from them, you are ready to meet the digital challenges of Chapter 4. However, before you proceed, ask yourself the following questions to determine if you are really ready. If the answers come easily, move on, but if not, repeat the Chapter 3 tutorials until you can answer them.

1. Do I know the shortcut sequences for the following:
   * Group
   * Ungroup
   * Toggle Rulers
   * New Document
   * Toggle Smart Guides
   * Selection Tool
   * Direct Selection Tool
   * Pen Tool
   * Add Anchor Point Tool
   * Delete Anchor Point Tool
   * Convert Anchor Point Tool
   * Undo
   * Hide/Show Bounding Box

2. Do I know the purpose of the None icon button in the Tools panel?

3. Do I understand how to create a Graphic Style and can I communicate its usefulness to my design process?

4. Can I list the procedures for defining a pattern repeat in Illustrator®?

5. Do I know the difference between a gradient and a fade in Illustrator®?

6. Can I explain in detail the location and function of the Illustrator® Zero Point?

7. Do I really know what a clipping mask is and how to make one?

8. Can I explain the procedures for recoloring selected objects with the Illustrator® Color Guide panel?

9. Can I briefly articulate the functions of leading, tracking, and kerning in relationship to signage?

10. Can I explain to someone how to flip a pattern in an opposite direction?

11. Do I know the meaning of the terms Merge and Flatten in reference to layer compositing?

12. Can I simulate true bias in a pattern repeat within a selected object? Do I know how to do this with the Rotate Options dialog box?

13. Can I explain the purpose of a dialog box?

14. Do I know how to scale a pattern within an object in Illustrator®?

15. Can I make good use of the Photoshop® Effects Gallery?

16. Do I understand the importance of the Shift key when scaling objects?

17. Do I know why it is important to click the Embed button after placing an object into Illustrator®?

18. Can I elaborate on why and how the Transform panel's Reference Point selector affects the Bounding Box of an object in reference to the panel options and both the x-axis and the y-axis?

Mastering Vector Tools for Apparel Design and Presentation

4

Objectives

In Chapters 2 and 3 the basics of working with Illustrator® were emphasized. In this chapter, fashion apparel and accessory tutorials are used to teach digital apparel design and presentation techniques using Illustrator®. The tutorials in this chapter will also prepare you for rendering technical flats, jewelry, and accessories. Specific focus is given to:

- ◎ Textile rendering: Velvet, lace, sheers, novelties, satin

- ◎ Apparel concepts: Dresses, skirts, pants, shirts, jackets

- ◎ Treatments: Flares, darts, tucks, creases, buttons, buttonholes, stitches, gathers, ruffles, appliqué, cascades, beading, pocket flaps, collars, cuffs

- ◎ The figure: Arms, hands, fingers

- ◎ Accessories: Precious metals, gemstones, gloves, stockings, socks, rings, tiaras, earrings, necklaces, veils, bow ties, cummerbunds, shoes

- ◎ The Symbol Tool Suite

- ◎ The Flare Tool, Magic Wand Tool, and Brushes panel

- ◎ The Illustrator® Pattern, Gradient, Brush, and Symbols Libraries

Using Wedding Attire as a Design Paradigm

Men's wear and women's wear make up a large portion of the entire apparel market, but women's wear is larger. Because this book cannot cover all of the apparel categories, it must focus on the types of apparel that are common to both sexes. A solution exists in wedding attire. The bride's attire is usually ultrafeminine and the groom's garments represent the finest examples of tailoring. The two looks are a quintessential standard of digital design and illustration, so they will be used to teach fundamental digital apparel illustration techniques.

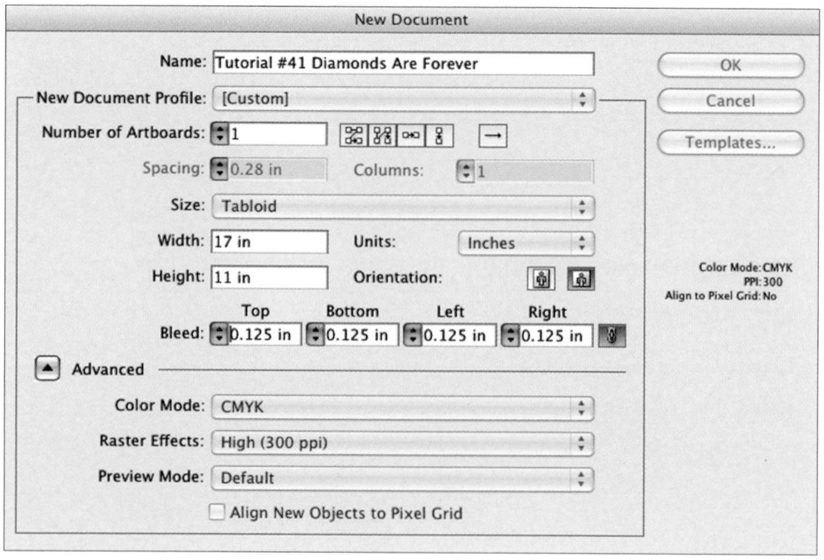

Figure 4.1

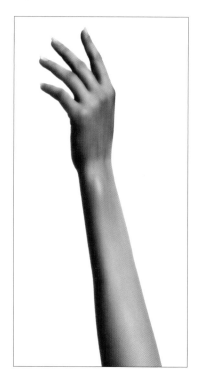

Figure 4.2

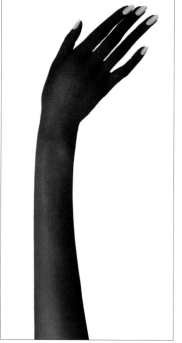

Figure 4.3

Before the wedding can take place, someone needs to propose, and provide an engagement ring. The first tutorial focuses upon hands, gloves, and the creation of a multifaceted gemstone set in a precious metal. You will learn to use Illustrator® gradients, tools, filters, Smart Guides, the Transform Tool, and the Flare Tool while strengthening your electronic drawing skills. Through the steps of this tutorial, you will create digital illusions and mathematical structures and render an engagement ring on a velvet-gloved hand as an editorial page layout for a fashion magazine, a storyboard, and an accessories presentation.

Use the files provided on ① Ch04\Tutorial 4.1 to complete this tutorial.

Step 1: Prepare a New Document and Workspace

Load Illustrator® and prepare a new document as shown in Figure 4.1. Name the file *Diamonds Are Forever*. Save and back up the file.

Step 2: Locate the Fashion Avatar Hand

Two files are available for this tutorial: Female_Avatar_Hand_1.pdf and Female_Avatar_Hand_2.pdf. Each file is located on ① Ch04\Tutorial 4.1. The files contain images of idealized female arms that were manipulated in Photoshop® (Figures 4.2 and 4.3). As intimated in the Preface, they are examples of virtual digital realism, which is a digital photo-retouching and painting technique. You will learn more about this later.

Place and Embed the file of your choice on *Layer 1*. Rename the layer *Avatar* or anything that reminds you of the image.

Step 3: Rotate the Image

Select the image and double-click on the Rotate Tool (R). A dialog box appears. Enter 90° and the image flips horizontally as shown in Figure 4.4. Click on the landscape orientation button, because the tutorial starts with the hand in a horizontal position to establish the perspective of your drawing.

Step 4: Create a Glove with the Pen Tool (P)

On a new layer entitled *Glove*, use any drawing tool to render the shape of the fashion avatar's arm as shown in Figure 4.5. When you have completed the shape, select and fill it with a dark hue, then lock the layer.

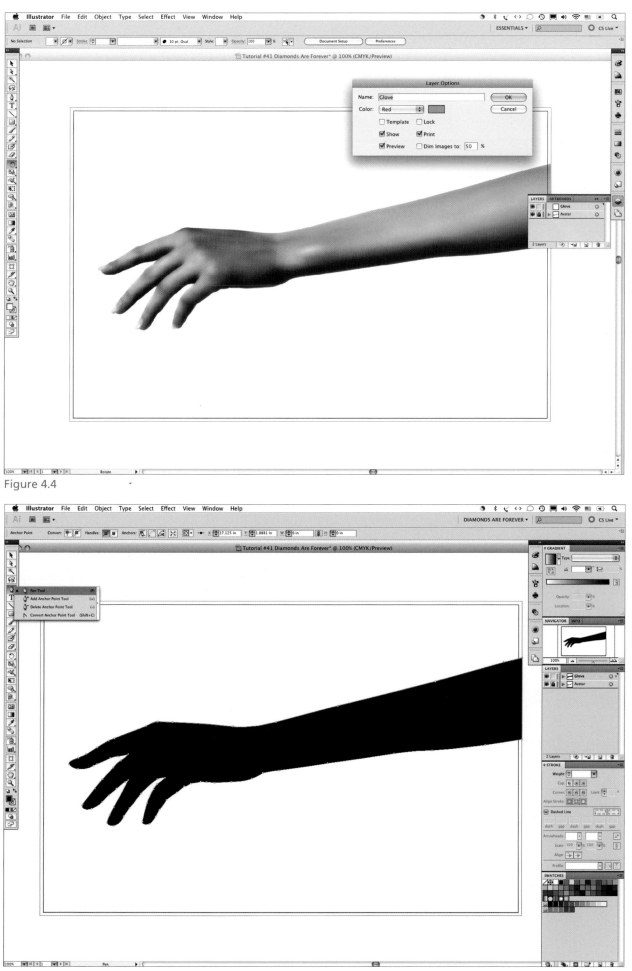

Figure 4.4

Figure 4.5

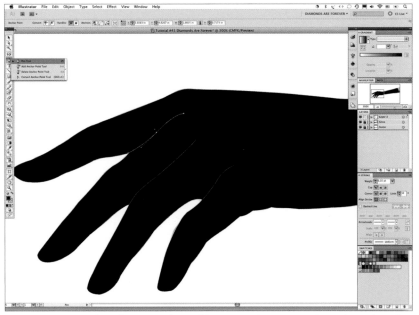

Figure 4.6 A Stroke of gray and no Fill was used to create the selected paths.

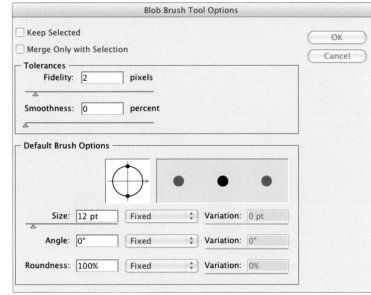

Figure 4.7

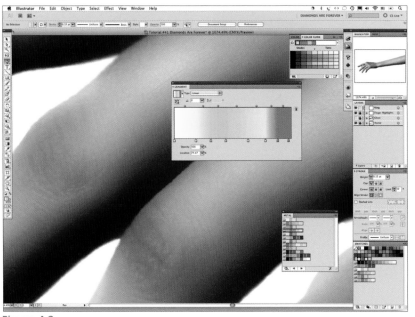

Figure 4.8

Step 5: Create Highlights with Various Tools and Filters

Toggle off the visibility of the *Glove* layer, and create a new layer entitled *Glove Highlights*. Render the outline of the knuckles and the curvature of the fingers with any drawing tool as shown in Figure 4.6. Select the highlights and go to *Menu Bar > Effects > Blur > Gaussian Blur*. When the dialog box appears, enter 4.0 to 6.0 px in the *Radius* scale. Some adjustments may be needed, but the result should yield a blurred line that will replicate the effects of light on velvet.

Step 6: Use the Blob Brush Tool Options

As an alternate, or in addition to the tools introduced previously, try the Blob Brush Tool (Shift+B) to create the highlights in Step Five. The default brush size will be too large for your needs, but you can adjust it to about 2 pt by double-clicking on the tool to obtain the Blob Brush Tool Options as shown in Figure 4.7.

Step 7: Create Metallic Illusions with Gradients

Illustrator® contains comprehensive Swatch Libraries organized into panels. One such library is called *Metal*. Go to *Menu Bar > Window > Swatch Libraries > Metal* to view it. In this library, you will find solid hues that you can use to create digital metallic illusions much like a fine artist would do with paint.

Illustrator® Swatch Library Folders

For this tutorial, you can create a gradient from various hues grouped in a folder in the Metal Library. The metallic illusion is greater as a gradient because it allows for a natural blending of various hues. To use the colors in the folder, simply drag the folder icon in the Metal Library to your Swatch panel. The folder appears beneath your default swatches with the associated hues as shown in Figure 4.8.

To use the colors as a gradient, double-click on the Gradient Tool (G), then drag the individual swatches to the bottom of the Gradient Bar. Discard the colors that you do not want by pulling them off the bar. Remember, you can save the gradient by pulling, dragging, and dropping the swatch that appears in the Gradient panel to your Swatches panel. Use the Color Guide panel to generate additional associated hues. Always label any swatch that you save to the Swatches panel with an appropriate name.

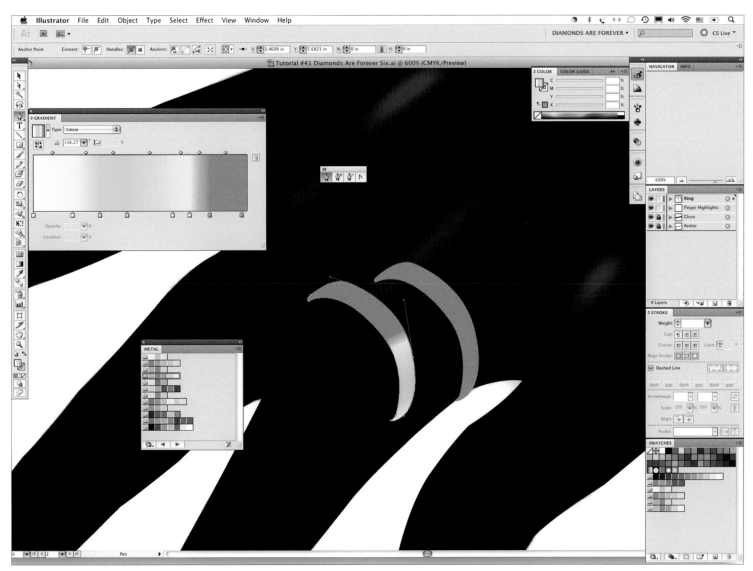

Figure 4.9

Step 8: Create the Ring

Render a simple shape around the ring finger with the Pen Tool (P). Fill the shape with a gradient and adjust the gradient sliders by selecting the Gradient Tool (G), then clicking and dragging on the page. Copy and paste the ring shape (Figure 4.9).

In Illustrator® CS6 you can create a gradient stroke. Watch the movie CS6_Gradient_Stroke_Panel_Options.m4v.

Step 9: Create a Simple 3-D Illusion

Place the copy of the ring shape on top of the other, but a bit offset, as shown in Figure 4.10. Select the shape on the top and adjust the gradient as instructed in Step Seven. The color blend should be slightly different from the shape on the bottom, so adjust the gradient accordingly. This creates a 3-D illusion.

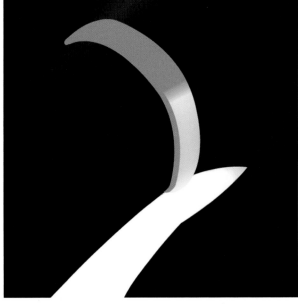

Figure 4.10

Step 10: Smart Guides Preferences for Angles

Although this tutorial deals with accessories, most fashion designers and merchandisers will find the need for the illustrated gem that you will learn to create. Essentially, you will form a radial structure (lines diverging from one central location point) in the shape of a 12-sided polygon. You will need to use the Smart Guide's **Construction Guides** option for this portion of the tutorial. Follow these steps to set the Smart Guides:

1. Adjust the Smart Guide Preferences on a Mac by going to *Menu Bar > Illustrator > Preferences > Smart Guides*. On a PC, go to *Menu Bar > Edit > Preferences > Smart Guides*.

2. When the Preferences dialog box appears, choose *30° Angles* in the *Display Options* pull-down menu.

3. Choose a highlight color.

4. You can also choose various tool tips. For this tutorial you only need to check *Anchor/Path Labels* (alerts identifying anchors or line segments) and *Construction Guides* (highlighted lines to help you draw perfect paths). You will use them to draw from one side of the radial structure through the center, to the opposite side. They will activate when you are creating paths on 30° angles, including 0° (completely horizontal), 30°, 60°, 90° (completely vertical and perpendicular to zero degrees), 120°, and 150° angles based on a central radius. When you have set your preferences as shown in **Figure 4.11**, click OK.

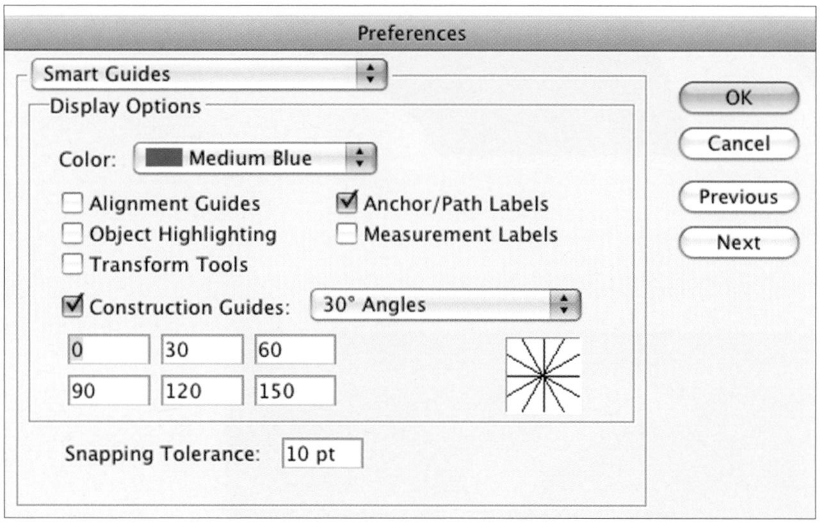

Step 11: Create a Perfect Circle and Center

1. Select the Ellipse Tool (L) and hold the Shift key to form a perfect circle by creating a marquee in a Stroke of black (0.5 pt *Weight*) with a Fill of None.

2. Use the Transform panel options to check the width and height of your shape's bounding box. The dimensions should be identical. Round off the measurements to 1-inch square by selecting the circle and then entering the information into the *Width* and *Height* fields.

3. Afterward, press Enter.

Smart Guide Center

1. Turn on the Smart Guides by pressing *Cmd+U / Ctrl+U*.

2. Test this by selecting the Pen Tool (P) and positioning it to touch the boundary (stroke) of the circle. If you see a **tool tip**, such as "path" or "anchor," next to the tool icon, it indicates that the Smart Guides are active. If you do not see the tip, repeat Step Ten.

3. Once you have your Smart Guides working, use them to find the center of the circle (**Figure 4.12**).

4. Scroll with your Pen Tool (P) until you see the word "center."

Step 12: Render 30° Angles

1. After you find the center, pull your cursor down vertically until you see a 90° tool tip and a Smart Guide, as shown in **Figure 4.13**.

2. Slowly move the cursor to the bottom of the circle until you see both the Guide and the word "anchor," then click on the circle.

3. Move the cursor through the center again, allowing the 90° Smart Guide to appear, and find the "anchor" point on the opposite side of the circle.

4. When the Smart Guide appears, click on the edge of the circle. You will have rendered a straight line at 90°.

5. Select the line and lock it by pressing *Cmd+2 / Ctrl+2*.

6. Repeat this procedure at 0°, as indicated by the perpendicular black path shown in **Figure 4.14**.

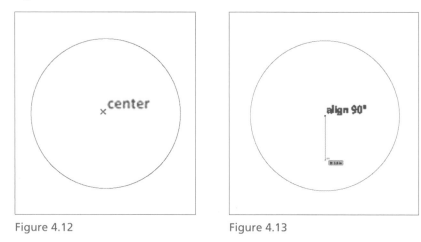

Figure 4.11

Figure 4.12

Figure 4.13

Step 13: Lock the Lines and Find the Angles

1. Locate each of the 30° angles and render straight angles that touch the edges of the circle with the aid of the Smart Guides.
2. Lock each line before rendering the next (Figure 4.15).

Step 14: Finish the Lines and Inspect

When you have rendered the six angled lines creating a radial structure, inspect them to be certain that each line is locked and touches the circle. The lines, like the circle, should have a Stroke of black (0.5 pt *Weight*) and a Fill of None.

Step 15: Create a Polygon

Use the Pen Tool (P) to create a polygon by clicking on the ends of each line as shown in Figure 4.16. The tool tips will indicate when you should click by displaying the word "anchor."

Step 16: Create the Second Polygon

1. Copy and paste the polygon.
2. Select the copy, then double-click on the Scale Tool (S).
3. Reduce the size uniformly by 50%.
4. Select both polygons and center them using the Align panel options.
5. Position them as shown in Figure 4.17.

Step 17: Create a Wedge Segment

In order to construct the lower facets of the diamond, we need to create 12 wedge shapes like the one in Figure 4.18. Use the Pen Tool (P) to create the shape from the angles of the structure. Again, click on the angles when the word "anchor" appears until the shape is closed.

Step 18: Copy, Paste, and Rotate the Wedges

After you render the first wedge shape, fill it with any color (Figure 4.19).

Step 19: Use the Guides for Placement

1. Copy and paste the wedge, and then double-click on the Rotate Tool (R).
2. Enter 30° into the *Angle* field.
3. Position the copy into the space adjacent to the original.
4. Use the lines you created with the Smart Guides to maintain accuracy.

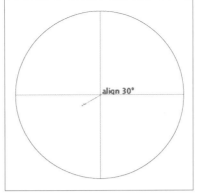
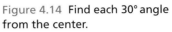
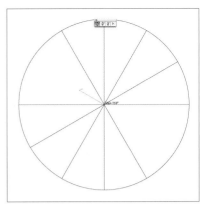

Figure 4.14 Find each 30° angle from the center.

Figure 4.15

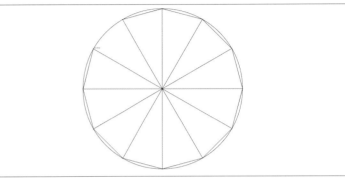

Figure 4.16

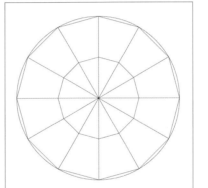
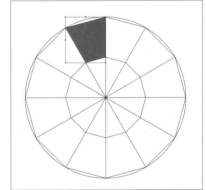

Figure 4.17

Figure 4.18

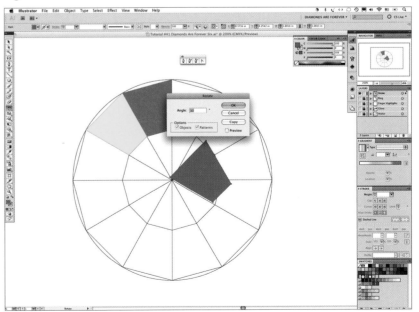

Figure 4.19

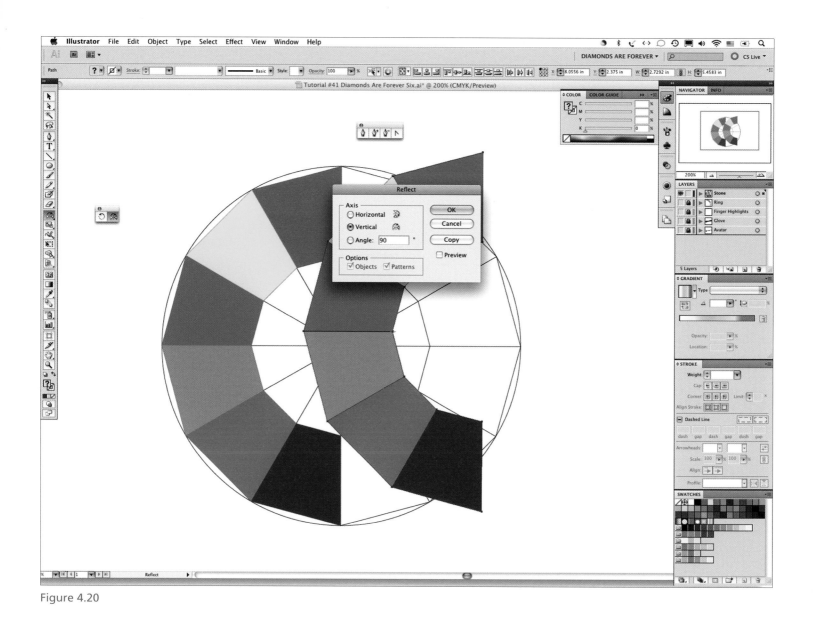

Figure 4.20

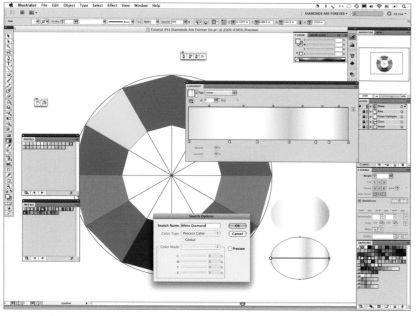

Figure 4.21

Step 20: Group, Copy, Paste, and Reflect

1. This procedure should be repeated six times.

2. Copy, paste, and then rotate the last copy created each time.

3. Inspect the wedges to be certain that they are precisely in place.

4. A good way to do this is to use various colors.

5. When all the shapes are in place, select them with the Selection Tool (V), and then group them by pressing *Cmd+G / Ctrl+G*.

6. Copy and paste the group as shown in Figure 4.20.

7. Reflect the copy and place it on the opposite side of the radial frame (Figure 4.21).

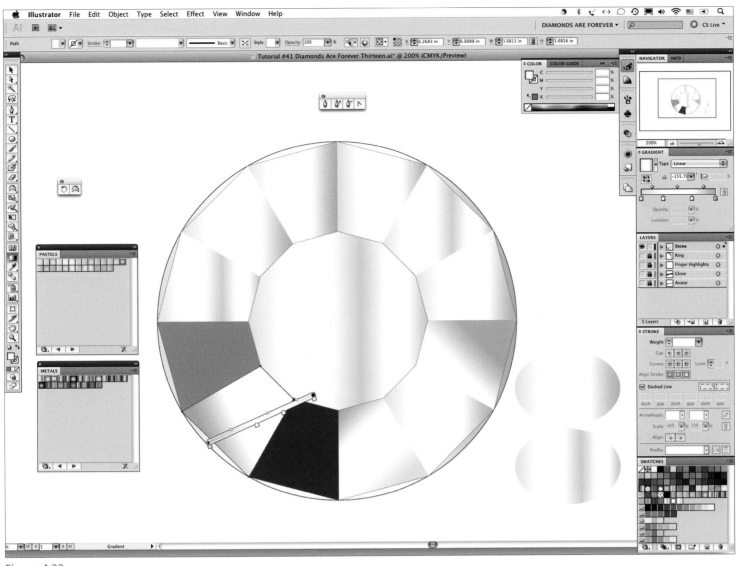

Figure 4.22

Step 21: Use the Gradient Color Libraries

1. Now that you have all the wedges and polygons in place, it is time to fill the shapes with gradients from the Gems and Jewels Gradients Library.

2. Go to *Menu Bar > Window > Swatch Libraries > Gradients > Gems and Jewels*.

3. Use any of the gradients to create the gem of your choice. To simulate a blue-white diamond, use the white gold gradient from the Metals Gradient Library and blue violet from the Pastel Gradient Library.

4. Add white to each, and then redistribute the sliders until you obtain convincing blends of the two separate gradients as shown in Figure 4.22.

5. Save each of these to the Swatch panel.

Step 22: Fill and Adjust the Segments

1. Fill the wedges and the smaller polygon with the gradients colors that you chose or mixed for the gemstone (Figure 4.23).

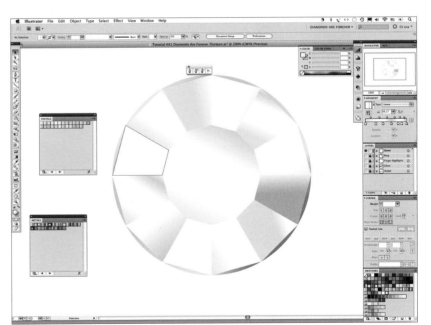

Figure 4.23

2. Adjust the direction of the gradient with the Gradient Tool (G) and the gradient sliders to simulate the reflection of light.

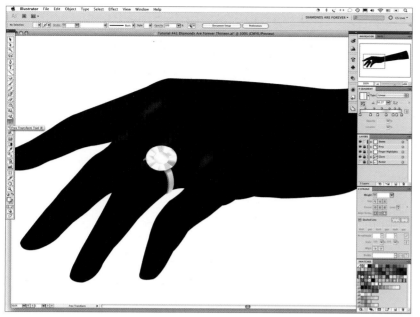

Figure 4.24

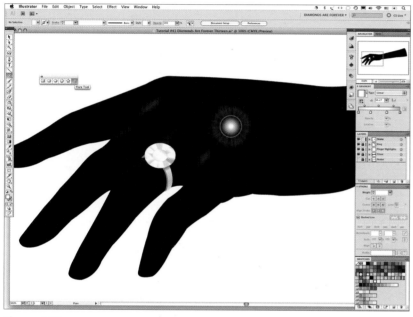

Figure 4.25

Figure 4.26

Step 23: Add Finishing Touches to a Diamond

1. To complete the illusion of the gem, leave one or several facets in solid white or a coordinating hue.

2. Fill the larger polygon with the same metallic color that you used for the ring in Step Eight.

3. Select and group all the parts.

4. Unlock and move the structure to your Scratch-board.

Step 24: Use the Free Transform Tool (E)

The illustrated stone is a digital 3-D illusion, but it was created in a frontal view. The gloved hand is posed at a slightly three-quarter angle. To skew the gem, use the **Free Transform Tool (E),** which helps to angle objects in perspective.

1. Select the grouped parts, then the Free Transform Tool (E).

2. Click and drag with the tool to turn the gem from the top as if you were tilting it.

3. You may need to try a few different angles before you obtain a believable position. Figure 4.24 depicts the result of the Free Transform Tool (E). The gem-stone has been positioned realistically on top of the ring. Press *Cmd+Z / Ctrl+Z* to undo moves if needed.

Step 25: Use the Flare Tool

The **Flare Tool** creates the illusion of light flashes. It is located in the Tools panel within the hidden menu of the shape tools. Select it, then marquee to create a brilliant flash of digital light (Figure 4.25).

Step 26: Add "Bling" to the Ring

Select the flare and place it on the ring to add "bling" as in Figure 4.26.

Step 27: Flare Tool Options

The Flare Tool Center, Halo, Rays, and Rings can be adjusted to increase or decrease its visual effect. Double-click on the tool to obtain the options dialog box shown in Figure 4.27.

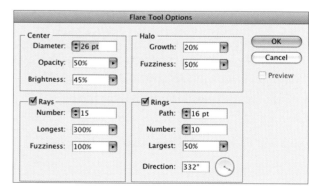

Figure 4.27

Figure 4.28 To complete the look of the page, create a striking colored background beneath the glove. Use the Rectangle Tool (M) and position the edges to your bleed.

The bridal industry is huge, representing millions of weddings globally each year. Designing gowns for the bride, bridesmaids, the mother of the bride, and flower girls can advance your fashion career. Whether you are targeting the bridal or evening wear markets or looking to open your own boutique, learning to show your design concepts digitally with Illustrator® will help you communicate with your clients effectively.

In this tutorial, you will use Illustrator® to render a wedding gown and accessories upon a croquis. You will learn to fill shapes with gradients that have the look of satin, define lace patterns, and simulate organdy. In addition, you will establish the proper proportion of a simple garment on the figure, create flare shapes in a skirt, and use brushes for trims. Follow the tutorial exactly or develop your own design concepts. Additional features of this tutorial include the formation of a simulated environment with an aisle and chandelier.

Use the file provided on ① Ch04\Tutorial 4.2 to complete this tutorial.

Step 1: Prepare a New Document and Workspace

1. Load Illustrator® and create a new document entitled *Wedding Gown*. The file should be 11×14 inches in portrait orientation with no bleeds. The Color Mode should be CMYK.

2. Place and Embed into this document the file Ines_Avatar.jpg from ① Ch04\Tutorial 4.2.

3. Arrange your preferred panels onto your window and save the workspace.

This file exhibits a female croquis figure created completely in Illustrator® from an idealized photograph of a real fashion model (**Figure 4.29**). The file shows the improved capabilities of Illustrator®, which can now create some simulated realism and 3-D effects. Study the figure closely. Each part was originally created as a shape on a separate layer. The file that you are using in this tutorial is a flattened image of the original. Use it for the tutorial as a practice exercise. Later, you will learn how to create your own croquis by using Illustrator®.

Step 2: Mask the Background

1. Follow the instructions from Tutorial 3.3 Step Three and create a clipping mask around the croquis, so that the white background of the rasterized image and the negative spaces of the bride's figure will not show.

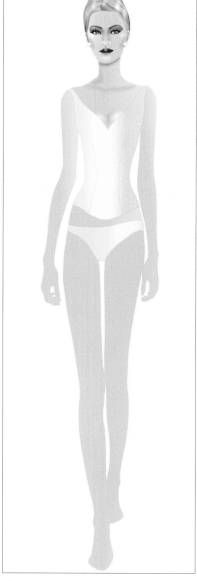
Figure 4.29

Figure 4.30

2. Change the title of *Layer 1* to *Bride Croquis*.

3. Lock the layer.

Step 3: Create Stockings

The bride is wearing a bodice and panties. Add sheer white stockings using the Pen Tool (P) and the Transparency panel options (**Figure 4.30**).

Step 4: Create Bridal Satin Pumps

You learned how to create shoes with the Pen Tool (P) in Chapter 2. Render bridal slippers as shown in **Figure 4.31**. The Fill used in the figure is the Opal gradient from the Gradients Swatch Library.

Step 5: The Skirt

Render a skirt shape with the Pen Tool (P) as shown in **Figure 4.32**.

Step 6: Create a Background

1. Create a *Background* layer beneath the *Bride Croquis* layer.

2. Use the Rectangle Tool (M) to create a shape that is the size of the page, and fill it with the Sky 9 gradient or any other.

3. Use the Gradient Tool (G) to adjust the gradient so it is lighter on the left of the page.

4. Pull a vertical Guide from the y-axis and place it on the right of the figure as shown.

5. Use the Guide as the temporary structure for simulating the apex of the red carpet on a **horizon line** (Figure 4.33).

6. The apex should begin at the bottom of the croquis's right leg. Use the Pen Tool (P) to create a red carpet starting from the edges of the page.

Step 7: Create a Lace Skirt

Illustrator® has Pattern Libraries that contain optical patterns without backgrounds. Some of these are suitable to use with motifs from the Symbols libraries. Follow these steps to choose a motif, **Flatten Transparency**, and define a lace repeat:

1. Locate a suitable pattern and symbols.

2. Pull a few swatches from these libraries onto your Artboard.

3. Flatten the swatches by selecting them and going to *Menu Bar > Object > Flatten Transparency*.

4. Check the boxes as shown in Figure 4.34 to make them editable as vector outlines. In this tutorial, the Knit pattern repeat was pulled from the Decorative Classic Pattern Library. A Fill of None and a Stroke of white were used for the lace. When such patterns are pulled onto the Artboard, you will notice when selected that they also contain a Bounding Box (Figure 4.35).

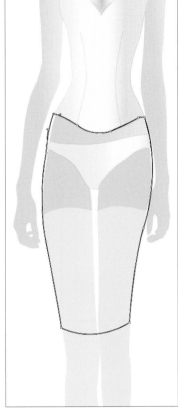

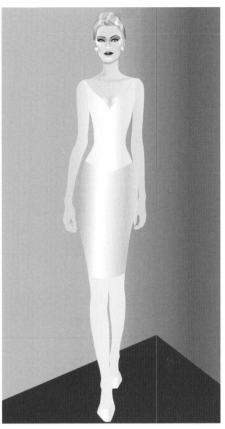

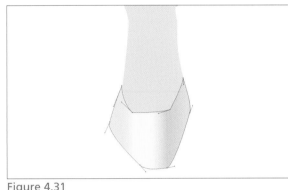

Figure 4.31

Figure 4.32

Figure 4.33 A cropped view of the entire page.

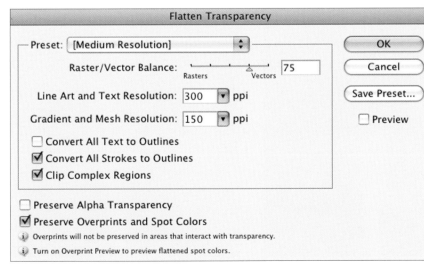

Figure 4.34

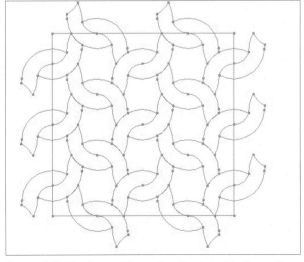

Figure 4.35 The Repeat Bounding Box is inside the pattern.

To create a floral motif, the Daisy symbol was pulled from the Flowers Symbols Library (Figure 4.36). After following the steps on the previous page, copy, scale, and arrange the daisies inside the Repeat Bounding Box. Select the repeat and define the pattern as outlined in Tutorial 3.2 Step Nine. To create a lace overlay for the skirt, copy, paste, and fill the shape with the newly defined Daisy Lace pattern.

Step 8: Use Ellipses to Demarcate the Sweep of a Skirt

As a guide for rendering the contour and sweep of a voluminous skirt, use the Ellipse Tool (L) to create oval shapes that will guide your digital drawings and serve as the shape of the hem. In Figure 4.37, three elliptical shapes were rendered to help guide the design of the lower skirt.

Figure 4.36

Step 9: Delete Half of the Ellipse

Once you decide how you want to shape the skirt, use one of the ellipses to make the hem. Delete the top of the ellipse as shown in Figure 4.38 by selecting it with the Direct Selection Tool (A) and pressing Delete.

Step 10: Create the Sides of the Skirt

Create the sides and top of the lower skirt. If needed, use the additional ellipses to help calculate the curves (Figure 4.39).

Step 11: Add Flares to the Hem

Use the Add Anchor Point Tool (+) to create curves along the hem by adding anchor points. Pull the curves into place with the Direct Selection Tool (A), shown in Figure 4.40.

Step 12: Create the Flare Shapes

Create cone shapes with the Pen Tool (P) to look like flowing flares, and then place them on top of the main shape of the skirt. The shapes do not need to be closed at the top, but should be curved at the bottom to serve as the shapes of the hem protruding from the main shape as shown in Figure 4.41.

Step 13: Fill and Gather

1. Select and fill the cone shapes with the gradient.
2. Adjust the gradients with the Gradient Tool (G) to appear as shadows in the folds and highlights on the flares.
3. Group the shapes and lock them on the layer.

Figure 4.37

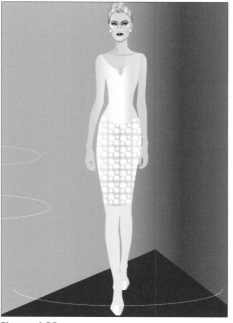

Figure 4.38

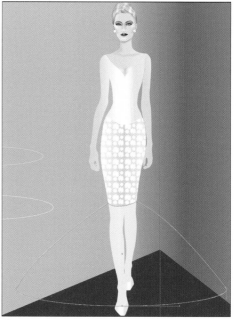

Figure 4.39

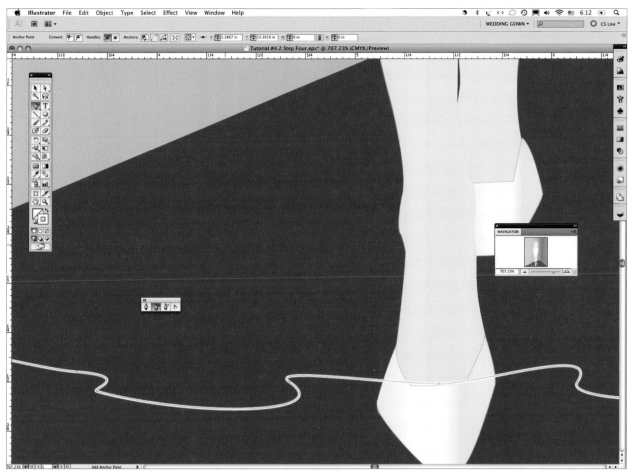

Figure 4.40 The Reshape Tool can also be used to create the effects in the hem.

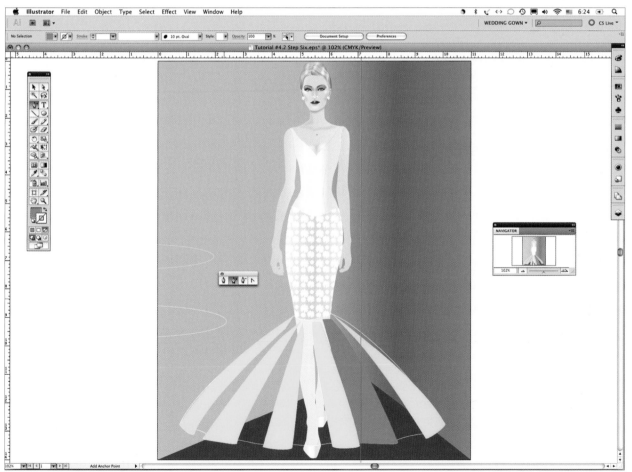

Figure 4.41 Place the cones in a natural arrangement as they represent flares of fabric.

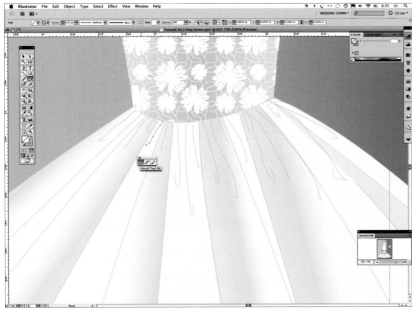

Figure 4.42

Figure 4.43

Figure 4.44

4. Afterward, use the Pencil Tool (N) to create gathers with a 0.5 pt Stroke of a coordinating color and a Fill of None (Figure 4.42).

5. Unlock the objects. Select the objects and the gather lines, then group them.

Step 14: Make a Sheer Underskirt

1. With the lower parts of the skirt selected, reduce the *Opacity* of the Transparency panel to 78%. Figure 4.43 displays the dramatic development of the wedding gown silhouette with the underskirt now appearing in opalescent organdy.

2. Copy and paste the skirt to create a second skirt; position it slightly above the original.

Step 15: Create a Layer of Lace

1. Paste another copy of the underskirt by pressing *Cmd+V / Ctrl+V* a second time.

2. Select the second copy and adjust the *Opacity* in the Transparency panel to 100%.

3. Fill the shape with the lace pattern.

4. Rotate the angle of the lace pattern (only) of the cone shapes to 45° by selecting them and double-clicking on the Rotate Tool (R).

5. Place the lace flounce slightly above the other two as shown in Figure 4.44.

Step 16: Enlarge the Artboard and Plan the Layout

1. Use the Artboard Tool (Shift+O) to increase the width of the Artboard on the right side to 17 inches. To accept the change, select any tool.

2. Unlock the *Background* layer and select the rectangular shape filled with the gradient. Drag the shape to fill the page. The gradient will readjust itself, but if you wish, readjust it with the Gradient Tool (G).

3. Lock this shape, and then select the aisle carpet triangular shape.

4. Add an anchor point at the top to create a trapezoid. The top and bottom of the trapezoid (carpet runner) will be parallel, but the sides will have varied angles to resemble a view in perspective as

Figure 4.45

shown in Figure 4.45. The apex of the trapezoid will be approximately 13 inches on the x-axis. The horizon line (top) will rest at about 10.75 inches. You can also use the CS5 Perspective Grid Tool (Shift+P) for this procedure as seen in Tutorial 4.4.

5. To make the carpeted aisle more convincing, add an arched door filled with white.

6. With the arch selected, go to *Menu Bar > Effects > Blur > Gaussian Blur*.

7. Set the Radius to 40 px, or whatever you prefer.

8. Create a ray of light beaming down the aisle with a 10 pt *Weight* Stroke of white, or whatever works.

9. Select the stroke and use the Gaussian Blur filter with a Radius of 42 px to complete the illusion (Figure 4.46).

10. Lock the *Background* layer.

Figure 4.46

Figure 4.47

Step 17: Make a Trim with the Brush Panel

Illustrator® also has **Brush Libraries**. You can use them with the **Brush Tool (B)** and the Stroke area of the Tools panel. The look of a re-embroidered Alençon lace is shown placed on the top and bottom of the bodice in Figures 4.47 and 4.48. It was created with the Scalloped Pattern in the Elegant Curl & Floral Brush Set Library.

Step 18: Add Digital Appliqué and Lace Galloons

As shown in Figure 4.49, a lace galloon appliqué can be created from the repeat of your lace. A galloon is a cut-out motif trim from the main yardage. Galloons are often used as badges, collars, or trims on lingerie and evening apparel. To enhance this type of digital appliqué, you could also use additional brush shapes and other techniques that you have already learned. In the tutorial example, the appliqué is being used as a type of decorative badge. The badge was copied, and the original was stroked in a shadow of a coordinating color. The copy was then set slightly offset on top to create the illusion of dimension and showcase the motif (Figure 4.50). Use your own creativity along with Illustrator® to design interesting galloons, appliqués, and embroideries using the

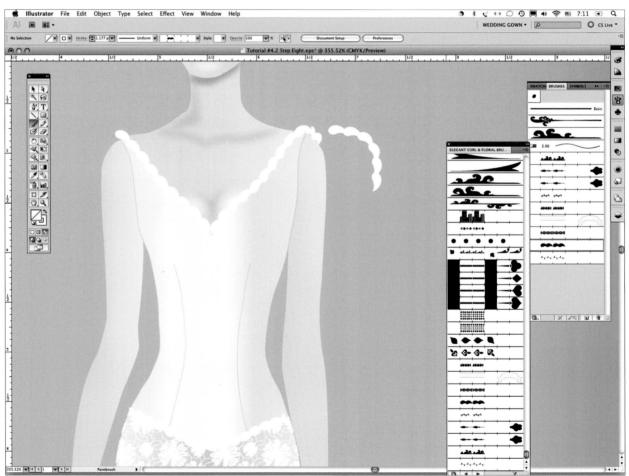

Figure 4.48

techniques learned in previous chapters as well as in this chapter.

Step 19: Create a Digital Bouquet

Add a bouquet of flowers with the Flowers Symbols Library and the Symbol Sprayer Tool (Shift+S). Use the Symbol **Scruncher Tool** to bring the symbols closer together (Figure 4.51). If you prefer, render your own special bouquet.

Step 20: Flares and Chandeliers

Figure 4.52 exhibits the completed example of Tutorial 4.2. Use a variety of tools, libraries, filters, and panels to create the chandelier.

Figure 4.49

Figure 4.50

Figure 4.51

Figure 4.52

What bride would be complete without someone to marry? The wedding industry includes men's apparel, especially the tuxedo, morning coat, and tailcoats. In this tutorial you will use the digital tools, panel options, and filters attributes of Illustrator® to design and render basic men's wear apparel and accessories on a male croquis, but the technique that you learn will also help you to create digital flats.

Use the file Brad_Avatar.pdf provided on ① Ch04\ Tutorial 4.3 to complete this tutorial. The file is a male croquis figure created in Illustrator® from an idealized photograph of a fashion model (Figure 4.53).

Step 1: Prepare a New Document and Workspace

1. Load Illustrator® and create a new document entitled *Meet the Groom* with your initials (Figure 4.54). The file should be 11×14 inches in portrait orientation with no bleeds. The Color Mode should be CMYK.

2. Place and Embed into this document the file Brad_Avatar.pdf.

Step 2: Mask the Background

Follow the instructions from Tutorial 3.3 Step Three and create a clipping mask around the croquis, so that the white background of the rasterized image and the negative spaces of the groom's figure will not show. Change the title of *Layer 1* to *Groom Croquis*. Lock the layer.

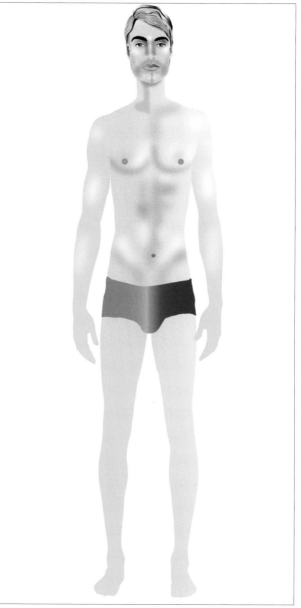

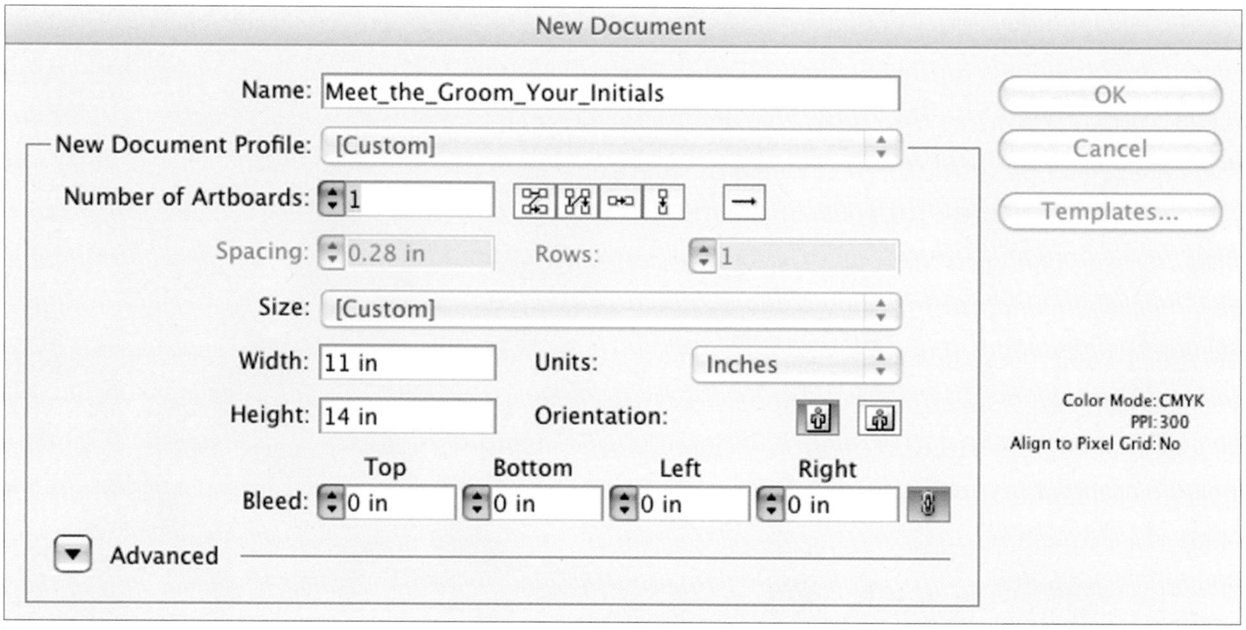

Figure 4.53

Figure 4.54

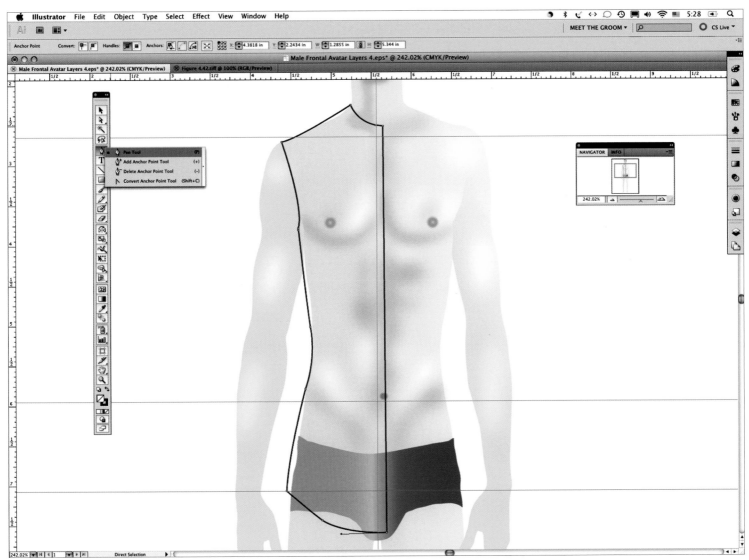

Figure 4.55

Step 3: Render a Tuxedo Shirt Left Front

Create a new layer entitled *Tux Shirt*. Use the Pen Tool (P) to render the shape consisting of straight and curved line segments as seen in Figure 4.55. Begin with a Stroke *Weight* in black of 0.5 points.

Step 4: Fill and Create a Bib

Fill the shape with white, and then render a bib shape similar to the one in Figure 4.56.

Step 5: Add Stripes to Simulate Tucks

1. Copy and paste the bib shape.

2. Keep the Stroke but fill the shape with a stripe from the Basic Graphics Lines Pattern Library or draw your own with the Pen Tool (P) while holding the Shift key to create paths from the top to the bottom of the bib accordingly.

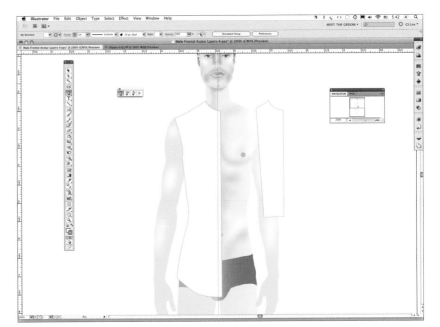

Figure 4.56

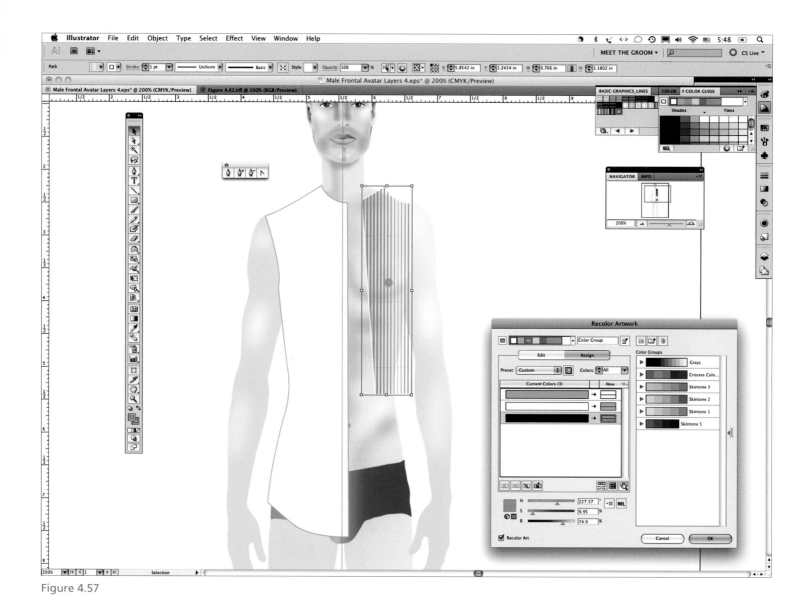

Figure 4.57

Figure 4.58

3. The pattern used in Figure 4.57 is the Undulating Fine Lines Pattern. Recolor the stripes using the Color Guide panel. Scale the pattern so that it fits in the shape.

4. Place the bib shape on top of the left shirt front.

5. Align and group the two shapes, then copy and paste them. Reflect the shapes to create the right side of the shirt shown in Figure 4.58.

Step 6: Create the Shirt Sleeve

1. Render the sleeve, and then make a copy (Figure 4.58).

2. Reflect the copy vertically with the Reflect Tool (O).

3. Because this pose is nearly symmetrical, you may only need to make slight alterations to the bottom position with the Direct Selection Tool (A).

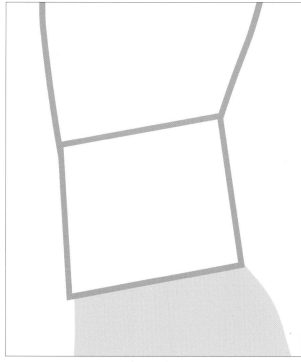

Figure 4.59 A simple cuff shape.

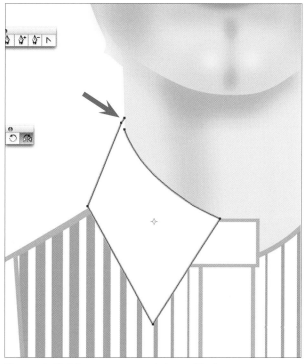

Figure 4.60 **The open curved shape illusion.**

4. Position all the objects, and then lock them on the layer.

5. Add cuff shapes using the Rectangle Tool (M) as shown in **Figure 4.59**.

Step 7: Create the Shirt
Collar Stand and Collar

1. Use the Rectangle Tool (M) to create a collar stand. Lock the shape.

2. Above the stand, use the Pen Tool (P) to create the collar.

3. Begin at the side of the neck. Click and drag, then click again toward the center front on top of the stand to create a Bézier Curve.

4. From there, click straight down onto the upper chest area to make the collar spread.

5. From the tip of the collar, click onto the shoulder, and click again toward the side of the neck but above your original starting point.

6. The collar bends around the neck, so create a small curve to suggest the fold as in **Figure 4.60**. Reduce the Stroke *Weight* on the collar shape to 0.25 pt.

7. To create the other side of the collar, copy, paste, and double-click the Reflect Tool. Click on the 90° vertical button in the Reflect dialog box.

Step 8: Draw a Simple Bow Tie

A simple bow tie can be rendered on a new layer by adding anchor points to the center top and bottom of a rectangle.

1. Use the Direct Selection Tool (A) to pull the points toward the shape's center.

2. Create a knot with the Ellipse Tool (L). Naturally, you could take this concept further on your own by rounding the edges and adding slight details, but filling the shapes with a gradient will do for now.

3. Copy the tie shape and fill it with the default 20% or 30% gray.

4. Add the Gaussian Blur filter with a Radius of 38 px to create a drop shadow as shown in **Figure 4.61**.

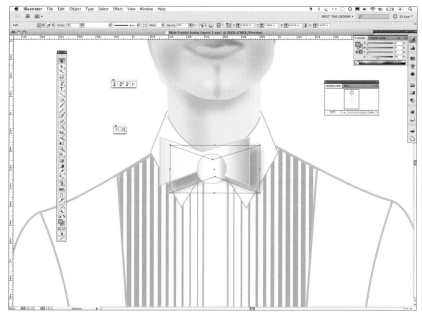

Figure 4.61

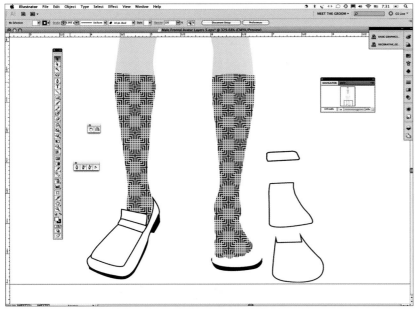

Figure 4.62

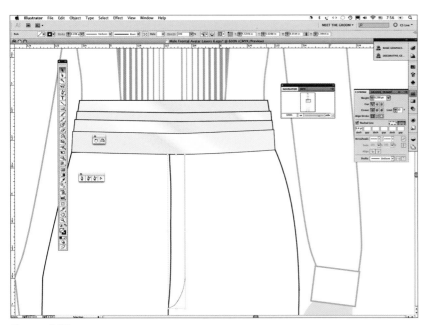

Figure 4.64

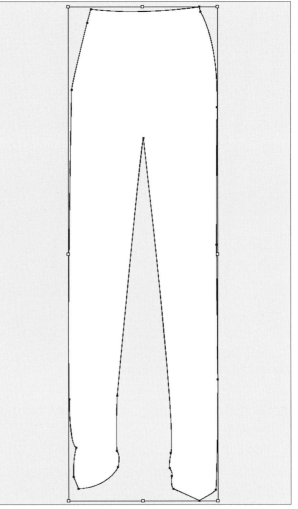

Figure 4.63 Pants on figures can have a hem break.

TIP: Shoe Styles

Shoe styles go out of fashion just like apparel. Digital illustration gives you an advantage because you can simply change the look of parts in your drawings.

Step 9: Render Men's Loafers

Creating shoes and socks for men will be easy if you completed Tutorial 3.2 and used the male model photos from ① Digital Duo Modeling Agency. The basic parts for creating men's loafers with a square toe from a frontal view are demonstrated in Figure 4.62. Create the parts with the Pen Tool (P), and then place each shape upon the other. Render shoes and socks on a separate layer. In the tutorial example, a pattern was chosen from one of the Illustrator® libraries. Try creating your own from what you have learned in previous tutorials.

Step 10: Create Pants Details

Use any of the Illustrator® drawing tools to create the pant silhouette on the croquis. In this tutorial, the shape can be in one piece, but later you will need to separate the pants legs (Figure 4.63). Four rectangular shapes were stacked to create the illusion of a cummerbund waistband (Figure 4.64). Each shape was filled with the same gradient, but the angles were adjusted separately with the Illustrator® Gradient Tool (G). The fly of the pants was generated with a 0.4 pt. *Dashed Line* in the Stroke panel.

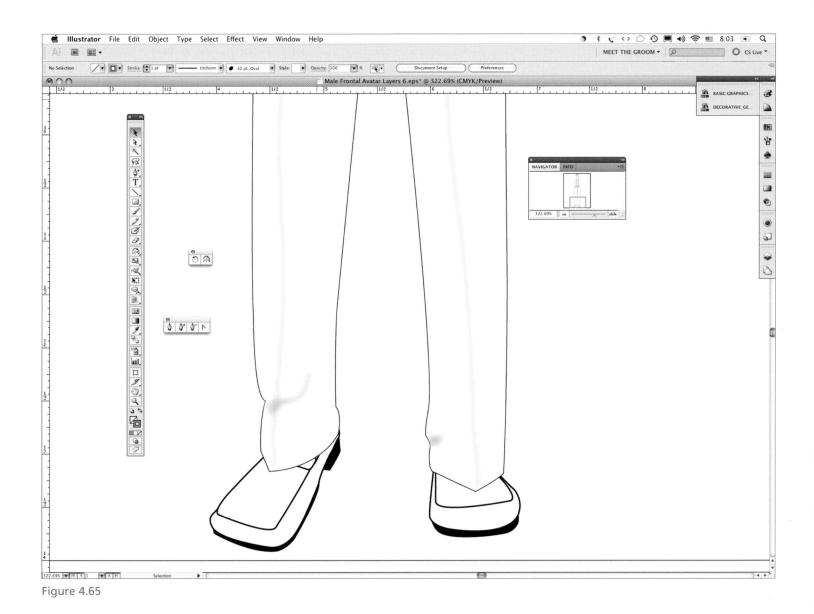

Figure 4.65

Step 11: Detail Folds and Creases with the Blob Brush Tool

Create pant creases and fold details with the Blob Brush Tool (Shift+B) and the Gaussian Blur filter. The default 20% gray was used in the example of the break in Figure 4.65.

Step 12: Make Studs from Symbols

Use the Symbols Library to create studs for the tuxedo shirt, or design your own. Those shown in Figure 4.66 are in the Heirloom Symbols Library.

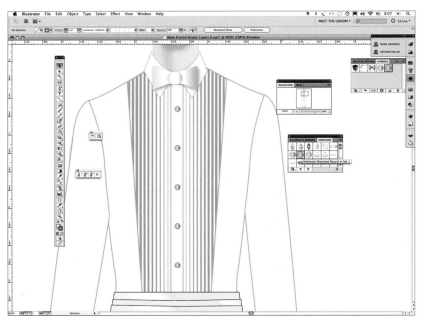

Figure 4.66

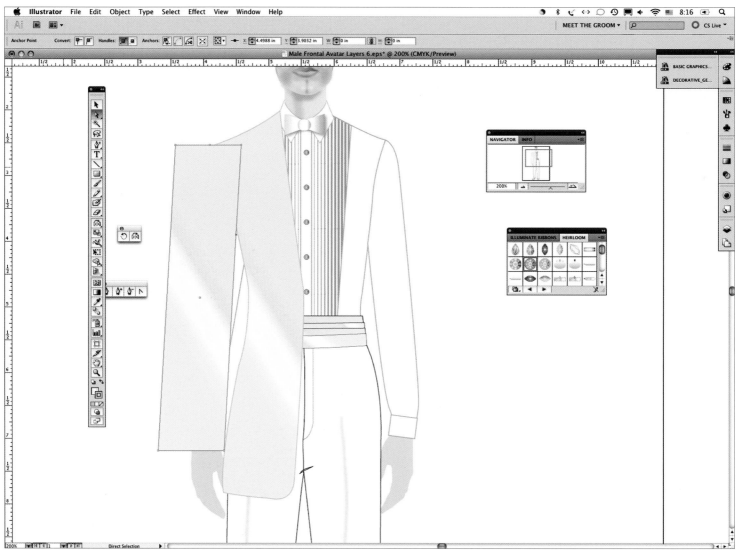

Figure 4.67

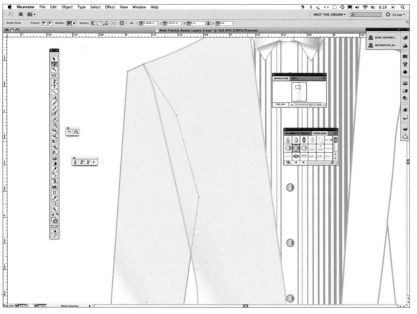

Figure 4.68

Step 13: Design a Tailored Jacket

Create a new layer entitled *Tuxedo Jacket*. Render the jacket and sleeve shapes as shown in Figure 4.67. The sleeve can be morphed from a rectangle. Add anchor points to the shoulder, the underarm, and the cap. Place the sleeve shape behind the jacket shape by selecting it and then pressing *Shift+Cmd+[(left bracket) / Shift+Ctrl+[(left bracket)* (Figure 4.68).

Step 14: Convert the Sleeve Cap

Use the Convert Anchor Point Tool (Shift+C) to round off the point on the sleeve cap as pictured in Figure 4.69.

Step 15: Create a Shawl Collar

Use the Pen Tool (P) to create a shawl collar. You used this technique demonstrated in Step Seven to simulate the roll of the collar at the side of the neck. Create a copy of the shape and use the Gaussian Blur filter to render a shadow beneath the shape (Figure 4.70). If you used a gradient to fill the jacket, adjust the angle with the Gradient Tool (G) and sliders.

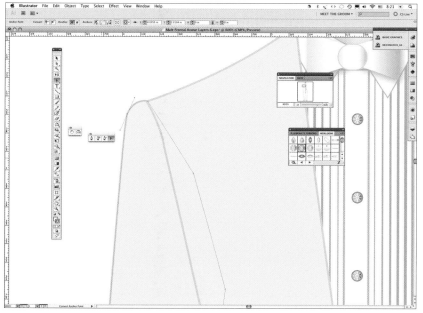

Figure 4.69

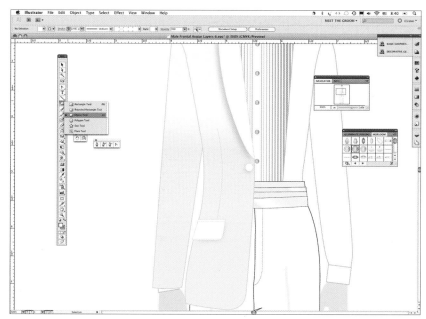

Figure 4.71

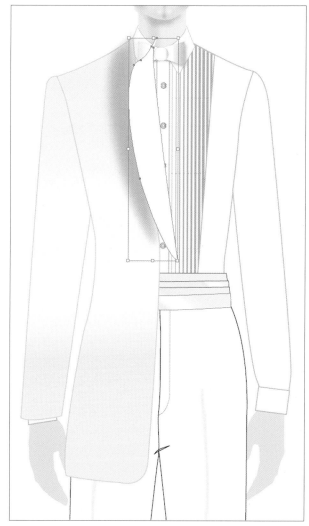

Figure 4.70

Step 16: Pockets and Buttons

Shape Tools will generate great results for creating pockets and buttons as shown in Figure 4.71. A full view of the developing look is shown in Figure 4.72.

Step 17: Create Button Accents and Buttonholes

1. A drop shadow beneath the button is a nice accent and is easily achieved with a copy, a Fill of 20% gray, and the Gaussian Blur filter (Figure 4.73).

2. To create a keyhole buttonhole, combine a small elliptical shape with a triangle by using the Combine option of the Pathfinder panel.

Figure 4.72

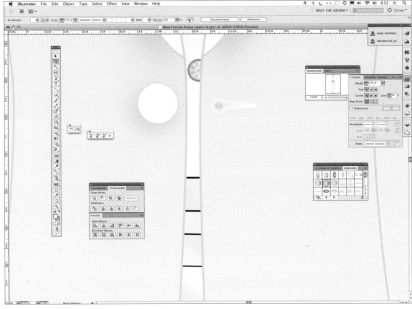

Figure 4.73

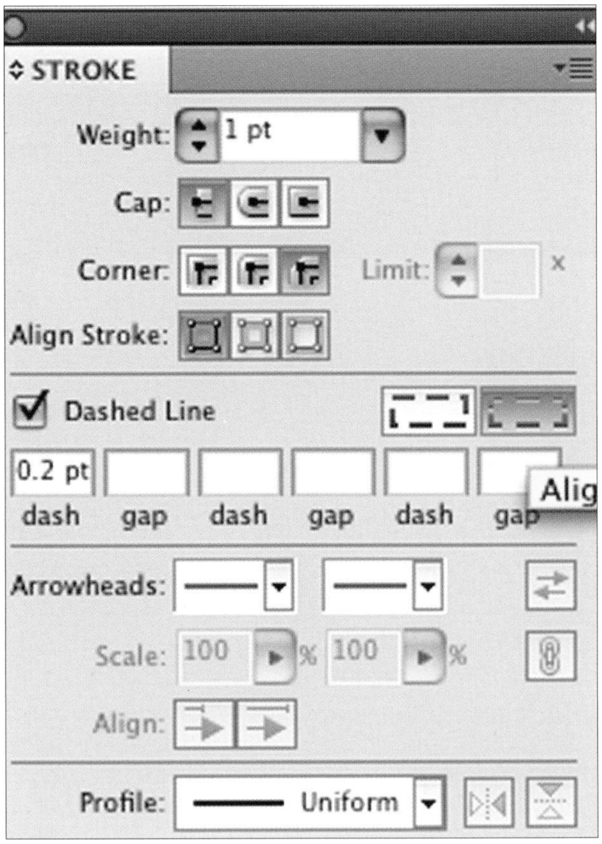

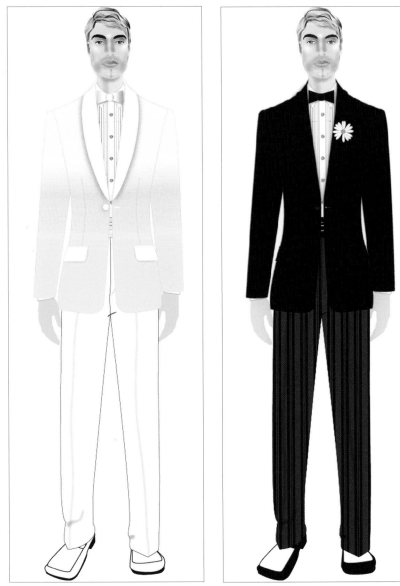

Figure 4.75

Figure 4.76

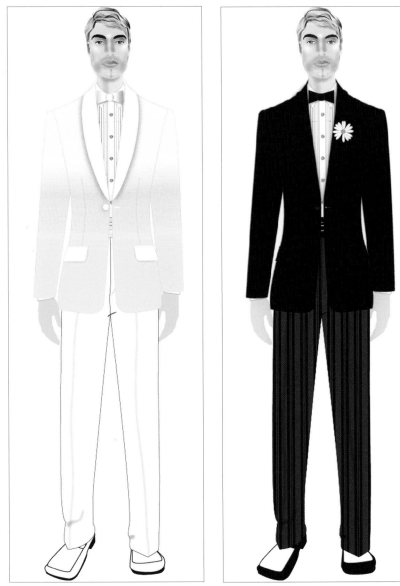

Figure 4.74

3. The Pathfinder panel's *Combine* option will merge the two selected shapes. It is located on the top left of the panel.

4. Fill the shape with a gray color.

5. Use a Stroke with a *Weight* of 1 pt and a Dashed Line of 0.2 pt. Check the Aligns Dashes to Corners, Bevel Join Corner, and other features in the Stroke panel (Figure 4.74). These are small details, but they make an impressive digital presentation.

Step 18: The Complete Groom

The completely dressed groom croquis is shown in Figure 4.75.

Step 19: Black Tie Option

If a black tie look is what you desire, try using a thin soft gray for the Stroke and a Fill of black. Using the Gaussian Blur filter will help if you want to soften the lines. A striped pant is not a bad idea either (Figure 4.76).

Some apparel and accessory items trail the figure in the distance. The Illustrator® **Perspective Grid Tool (Shift+P)** will help you learn to digitally render a wedding veil in the proper perspective.

Step 1: Prepare a New Document and Workspace

Load Illustrator® and open the file that you completed in Tutorial 4.2. The example file is pictured in Figure 4.77.

Step 2, Part A: Use the Perspective Grid Tool

The Illustrator® (CS5 and CS6) Perspective Grid Tool (Shift+P) was originally designed to help illustrators create simulated landscape and architectural perspective. You can use it in fashion illustration to help create the proper perspective of figures in environments or in relation to other figures, such as placing figures on a runway. In this tutorial, you will use the Perspective Grid Tool (Shift+P) to render the drapery of a simple veil in 1-point perspective. The Perspective Grid Tool (Shift+P) can also be used for 2-point and 3-point perspectives. We will not be using all of the functions of the Perspective Grid Tool (Shift+P) in this tutorial. When you click on the Perspective Grid Tool (Shift+P), it appears on your Artboard in 2-point perspective. Go to *Menu Bar > View > Perspective Grid > One Point Perspective > [1P-Normal View]*, and the grid will change as shown in Figure 4.78. You can also use *Cmd+Shift+I / Ctrl+Shift+I* to hide this tool in your window.

The grid will appear with a **Plane Switching Widget** in the upper left corner of your Artboard. Depending on the perspective that you use, select a side as an active **grid plane**. Draw objects on the active plane to represent them from a viewer's perspective on that particular plane.

The white dot that you see in the middle is resting on the **horizon line**. This dot represents your **vanishing point**. It can only be moved along the horizon line to the left or the right. To move the entire grid, select the white diamond shapes at the lower sides. To adjust the green **Horizontal Grid**, select and pull the dotted circle button at the lower center of the grid. You can adjust the Left Grid with a similar icon beneath it. Pull the Horizontal Grid to the front of the red carpet at the edge of the page (Figure 4.79).

Figure 4.77

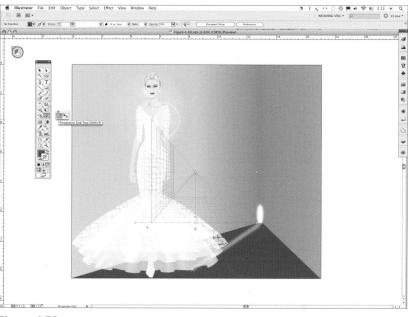

Figure 4.78

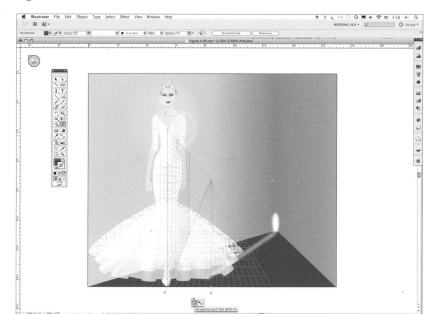

Figure 4.79

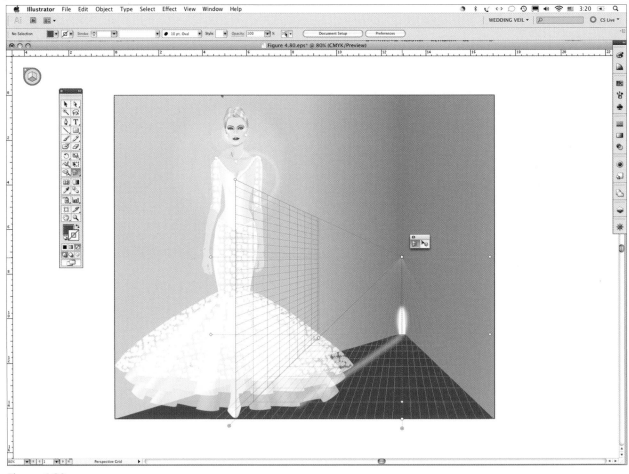

Figure 4.80

Step 2, Part B: Adjust the Horizon Line

Move the vanishing point to the right and above the glowing arch as shown in Figure 4.80. The horizon line must be moved toward the top of the trapezoid or somewhere in the lower portion of the arch. You will need to make this decision. Figure 4.81 shows the vanishing point in the middle of the arch as if it were outside the building, which might be accurate. However, the goal is to locate the perspective of the drapery in alignment with the perspective of the aisle. To accomplish this, pull the top horizon line down until the diamond shapes of the Horizontal and Left Grids align with the vanishing point. Position the **Left Grid** in the center of the croquis and pull the diamond shape to the top of the head (Figure 4.82).

Step 3: Render the Veil in Parts

Design a veil for the bride in three parts, using the Left Grid in reference to the vanishing point and the croquis. Use various colors to help you maintain the concept of dimension. The back of the veil is yellow and was placed on a layer below the figure, but the sides in this example are on a layer above the figure shown in blue and green (Figure 4.83).

Step 4: Adjust the Veil

Adjust the veil so that the effect of virtual gravity and the illusion of perspective enhance the presentation as shown in Figure 4.84. Remember, in 1-point perspective, objects appear smaller in the distance.

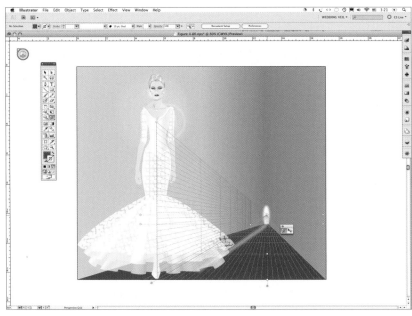

Figure 4.81

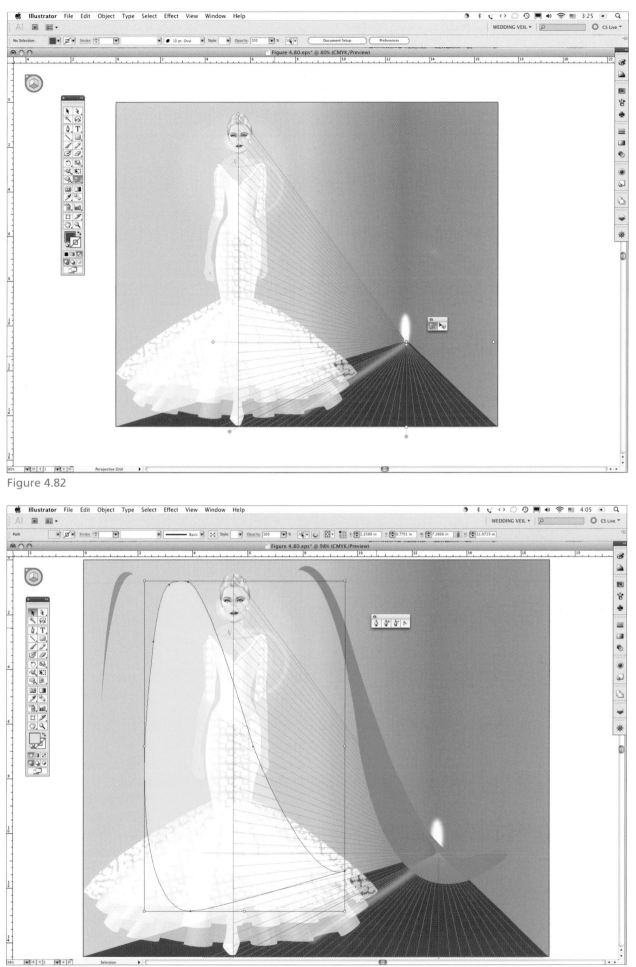

Figure 4.82

Figure 4.83

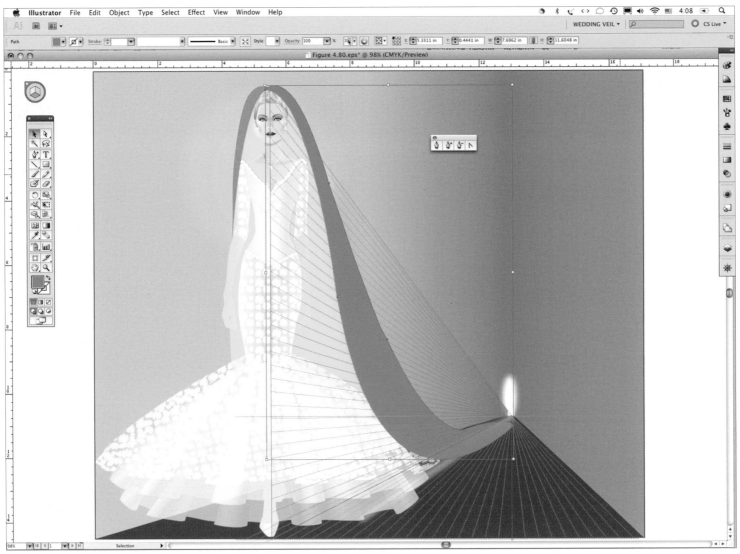

Figure 4.84

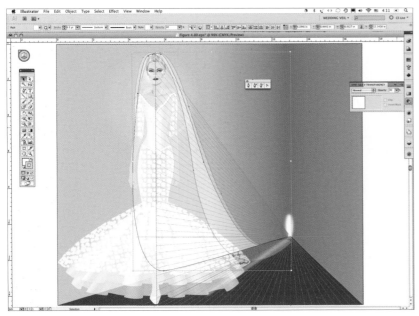

Figure 4.85

Step 5: Use Transparency

Select the parts of the veil and fill them with white or whatever color you prefer. Use the Transparency panel to reduce the *Opacity* of the objects as shown in Figure 4.85.

Step 6: Add Details

Add details to the veil. Use the Symbols Libraries or Illustrator® Brushes, or alternatively, make your own symbols or brushes. If you prefer, create another veil shape that covers the bride's face. Figure 4.86 shows the bride wearing a tiara constructed from the same digital diamond from Tutorial 4.1.

Step 7: Reposition Parts

Use the Direct Selection Tool (A) to reposition any parts. The completed bride is shown in Figure 4.87, but where is the groom? All the apparel and accessory items have been digitally designed and the couple is fully dressed for their special day in Figure 4.88.

Figure 4.86

Figure 4.87

Figure 4.88 Illustration by Stacy Stewart Smith.

As a means to make a connection between the human touch of traditional fashion illustration and the digital techniques of Illustrator®, this tutorial combines digital processes and digitized freehand line drawings. The skills taught here are the foundation for digital fashion design and essential to styling fancy details for women's and children's wear apparel. The tutorial includes the following:

- An introduction to the Symbol Tool Suite to make new Symbols from freehand artwork. You will learn how to add dashes of color to freehand drawings with the Symbol Stainer Tool. You will bunch together objects with the Symbol Scruncher Tool, and then resize or twirl them with the Symbol Sizer Tool or the Symbol Spinner Tool, respectively.

- The creation of lace repeat patterns and how to use such patterns in conjunction with freehand art to create unique presentations.

- An explanation of the capabilities of the Brushes panel through the creation of lace trims and treatments, such as flared ruffed edges and scalloped lace trims.

This tutorial should be followed as written, using the files provided on ① Ch04\Tutorial 4.5. This way, you will get the most out of the lesson without having to do a lot of preparation. However, you're encouraged to scan and enhance your own similar black ink, watercolor, or marker fashion sketches. The designs need to have fancy details like those illustrated in the tutorial example. After your freehand sketches are scanned, they will need to be placed in Illustrator®, embedded, digitized in the Color 6 or the Color 16 feature of Live Trace CS5 or Image Trace CS6, then Expanded in order to make full use of the tutorial features. For more information on the features of Live Trace, see Chapter 6, which focuses on the subject.

Step 1: Prepare a New Document and Workspace

1. To follow the tutorial example, load Illustrator® and create a new file using the information from the New Document dialog box shown in Figure 4.89. Then, open the file Catch_the_Bouquet.pdf on ① Ch04\Tutorial 4.5.

2. Once the file has been imported, save it, then set up and save a Workspace as *Catch the Bouquet*. The file will open in a window and look similar to Figure 4.90.

3. Show the Layers panel, and then unlock the objects on the layer by pressing *Cmd+2 / Ctrl+2*. The figures have been placed on one layer with the illustrated apparel, but each figure is a separate selection.

Step 2: Use the Magic Wand Tool (Y) to Select Color

Illustrator® has a **Magic Wand Tool (Y)**. Like its Photoshop® counterpart, this tool selects objects by color. It is useful when you need to select colors from complicated patterns in order to quickly recolor them.

1. Select, copy, and then paste each figure into a separate layer (Figure 4.91).

2. Name the layers according to the color of each bridesmaid, for example, *Blue Bridesmaid, Green Bridesmaid,* etc. The color-coding in this tutorial will make it easy for you to navigate through the steps.

3. Place each figure in alignment with the apparel and lock the layers.

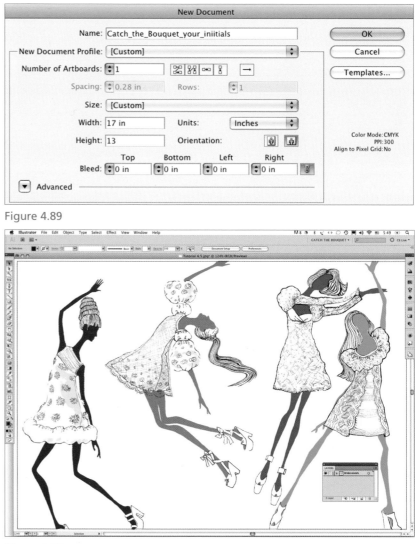

Figure 4.89

Figure 4.90

Figure 4.91 The parts in this example can be selected by color because it was Live Traced (Image Traced in CS6).

Step 3: Create a New Symbol from the Artwork

Many users love the ease of computer graphics programs but wish to retain the freehand look of their drawings. The example file is a digitized freehand drawing that has been Live Traced with Color 16. Now that the line work has been converted into vector outlines, you can use segments of the illustrations to make Symbols or brushes in Illustrator®.

1. Select a motif as shown in Figure 4.92, then show the Symbols panel.

2. Use the hidden menu and scroll to New Symbol or click on the New Symbol icon at the bottom of the panel. The icon for your Symbol will immediately appear in the Symbols panel.

3. Double-click on it to give it a title.

4. Once you save your file, the new Symbol will appear with your file each time that you open it.

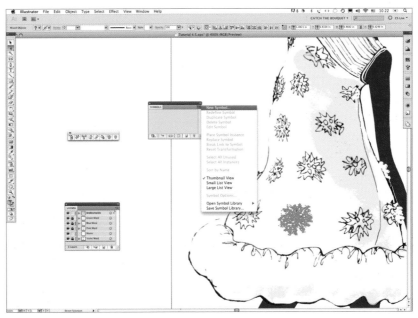

Figure 4.92 Use the Direct Selection Tool (A) to select a motif.

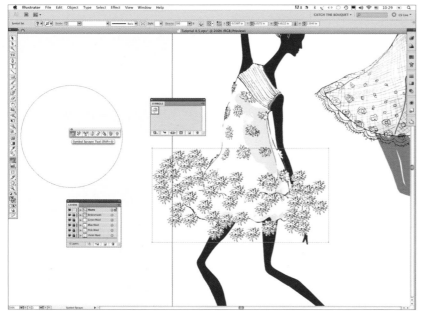

Figure 4.93

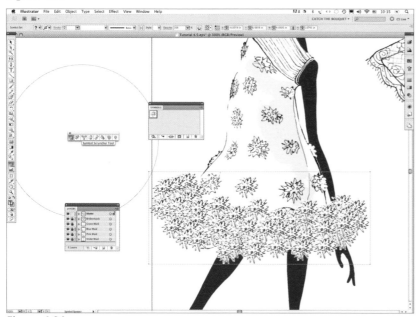

Figure 4.94

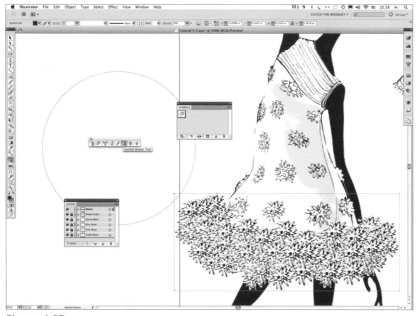

Figure 4.95

The Symbols Tool Suite

1. Select the Symbol that you just made, then use the Symbol Sprayer Tool (Shift+S) to apply the motif to the area at the hem as pictured in Figure 4.93. The tool will continue to place additional symbols as long as you hold the clicker. This tool spreads the symbols out, so it must be used in conjunction with other tools in the suite to control the placement and to personalize the presentation of the objects.

2. To move the Symbols closer together, select the **Symbol Scruncher Tool** or select the Bounding Box to resize the objects and pull them closer.

3. If you prefer to randomly rearrange the Symbols, use the **Symbols Shifter Tool**.

4. Click with your mouse to push the motifs together until you obtain a desired shape. Alternate the use of tools as needed.

5. If you would like to rotate some of the Symbols, use the **Symbol Spinner Tool**. To achieve maximum results, you will need to move around the "mass of Symbols" and push inward. Figure 4.94 shows the combined benefits of these tools.

It seems like a lot of work, but the benefits are tremendous when you are trying to create collections that have exact details that must be replicated. In a way, the process supersedes freehand rendering and saves time. A design team using this approach will be able to generate a large body of work and maintain the aesthetics and hand of a single artist. This technique is especially important for those working with licensors.

Step 4: Stain the Symbols

Just when you thought that the Symbols could offer no more, the **Symbols Stainer Tool** actually tints the color of a selected Symbol. It will not work on solid black, but it works perfectly on line drawings that have been scanned in color when a Fill color has been selected.

1. Select the Fill Box in the Tools panel and then sample the color of the Bridesmaid croquis with the Eyedropper Tool (I).

2. Select the Symbol motifs at the bottom of the dress with the Selection Tool (V).

3. Use the Symbols Stainer Tool to apply the Fill color by clicking over the bottom of the dress (Figure 4.95).

Step 5: Use the Symbol Sizer Tool

1. Create a new Symbol from the motifs in the Pink Bridesmaid's dress.

2. Use the Symbol Sizer Tool to vary the scale of the objects, then sample the color of the figure with the Eyedropper Tool (I) and use the Fill color with the Symbol Stainer Tool (Figure 4.96).

Figure 4.96

Step 6: Create Lace Trim Brushes

Instead of having to repeatedly draw lace or other fine ornamentals like schiffli embroidery or passementerie trims, you can render them once, then define a brush. You will be able to use the brush to place the trim on any drawing that is digitized. You can either freehand the trims, digitize them, or use a combination of both techniques. Once you make your repeat in Illustrator®, you will be able to use the digital trim with the freedom and organic curves of a brushstroke.

Creating a Pattern Brush with Digital Tools and Hand-Rendered Drawings

A pattern brush functions with the Paintbrush Tool (B). Follow these steps to create a lace trim brush:

1. Toggle on the Grid, and then use any drawing tool to create a repeat pattern within the framework of a rectilinear space. The brush will not have breaks if the top of it is defined as the longest point of the repeat. Illustrator® will match whatever is on one side with the opposite side. Because brushes are generally used as trim and these are relatively small, you may notice slight imperfections. This can work to your advantage, however, because imperfections are often the hallmark of a designer's signature.

2. Use the Pencil Tool (N) and others to create a scalloped Chantilly lace galloon repeat (Figure 4.97).

3. Group, copy, and paste the repeat, and then stroke it with a gray color. The copy should remain white. Do this in order to create a slight 3-D illusion.

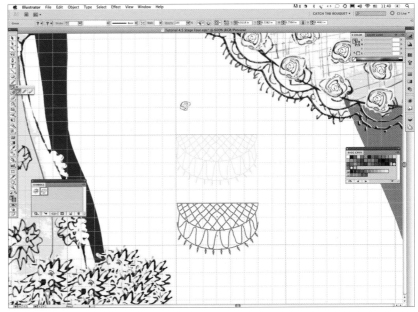

Figure 4.97

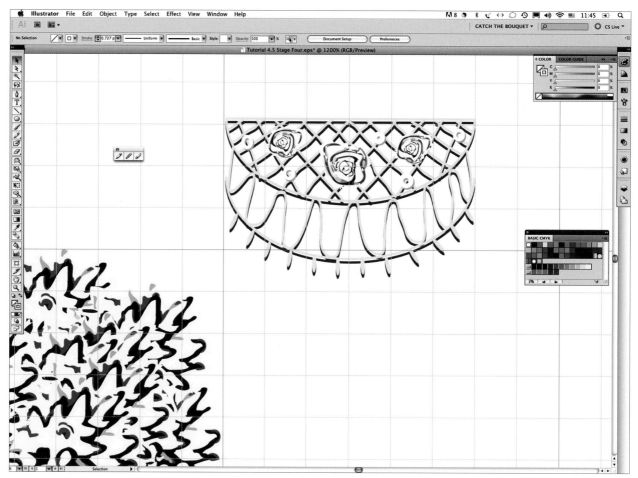

Figure 4.98

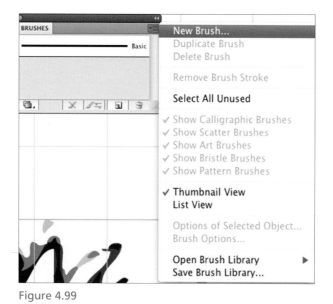

Figure 4.99

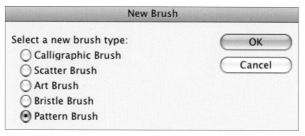

Figure 4.100

4. On top of this, place floral Symbols (originally freehand drawings) in varied sizes or use those in the Symbol Tool Suite (**Figure 4.98**).

5. Select all the objects in the repeat, then scroll to the New Brush option in the hidden menu of the Brushes panel as shown in **Figure 4.99**.

Step 7: Work with Brush Options

1. When the New Brush dialog box appears, select the button next to *Pattern Brush* as in **Figure 4.100**.

2. Afterward, a Pattern Brush Options dialog box appears (**Figure 4.101**). The default settings are fine for this simple type of brush. Just make sure that the word "original" is selected in the lower left field. This word identifies the selected object.

Step 8: Add Brush Flexibility

1. You can also define the repeat as a pattern, and then use it as a coordinating brush.

2. Choose from any of the patterns that appear in the field from which to create New Brushes.

3. The icon of the brush will appear in place of the strikethrough (**Figure 4.102**).

4. Give the brush an appropriate name and click OK.

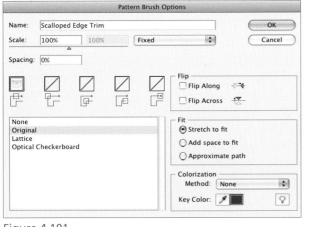

Figure 4.101

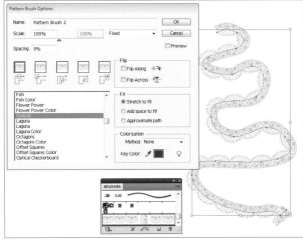

Figure 4.102

Step 9: Test and Resize Brushes

1. Select your New Brush in the Brushes panel and use the Brush Tool (B) to test it with a swirling Stroke across the Artboard.

2. If the brush is not a good fit for your needs, double-click on its icon in the Brushes panel.

3. When the Pattern Brush Options dialog box appears as shown in Figure 4.103, simply push the Scale slider to make an adjustment and click OK. A smaller dialog box labeled **Brush Change Alert** then appears.

4. Select *Apply to Strokes* to affect the brush marks already on your Artboard.

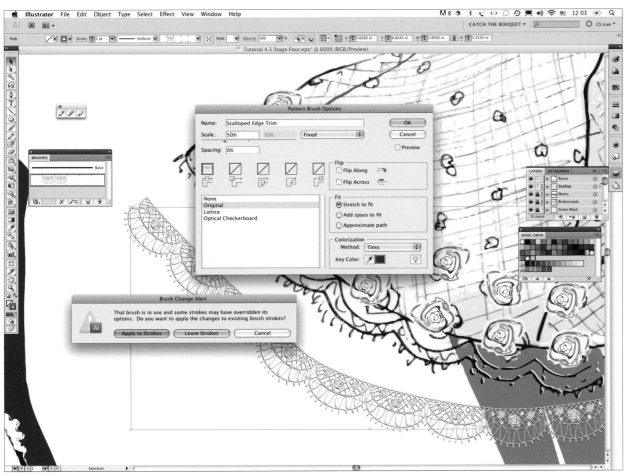

Figure 4.103

Step 10: Add Color to Brushes

1. Select the Stroke box in the Tools panel and change the color.

2. Select a *Method* from the pull-down menu in the colorization section of the Pattern Brush Options dialog box and click OK. Two rows of the brush trim worked beautifully in Figure 4.104.

Note: *A sample of the lace brush is available in the file Scalloped_Lace_Trim.pdf on* ① *Chapter04\Tutorial 4.5. To use the brush with the Brush Tool (B) or another drawing tool, locate it in the Brushes panel.*

Step 11: Create Lace Patterns

The most beautiful lace patterns stem out of personal ideas. The important thing to remember is that lace can be both organic and geometric. The background for lace is usually some kind of lattice pattern. To create a lace all over pattern for the Blue Bridesmaid's dress, begin with a small square shape with a Fill of None and a Stroke of white. Copy and paste the square, then make a copy. Shadow the original by changing the color of the copy and increasing its stroke *Weight* (Figure 4.105).

Step 12: Simulate Weight in the Lace

To create lace that does not have that flat look associated with vector graphics, use the Stroke panel options to change the alignment of the line and to produce a 3-D look. The stroke on the shadow square should be outside the line and the white square's stroke should be inside. Select each square separately, then use the appropriate Align Stroke option in the panel. Afterward, use the Align panel to center the objects as shown in Figure 4.106.

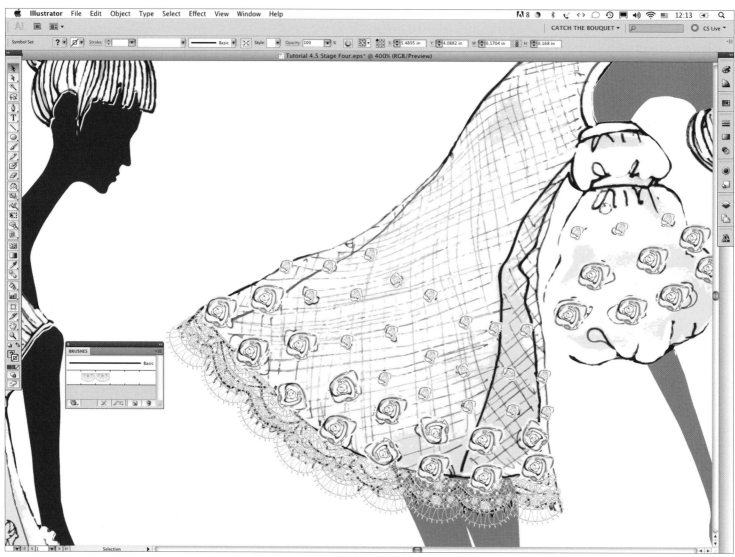

Figure 4.104

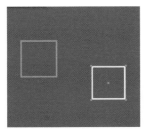
Figure 4.105

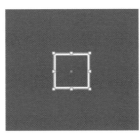
Figure 4.106

Figure 4.107

Figure 4.108

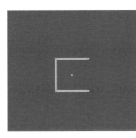
Figure 4.109

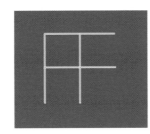
Figure 4.110

Step 13: Remove Bulk

To remove the bulk that will accumulate when the sides double up on the repeat, eliminate them. Simply use the Direct Selection Tool (A), marquee over them, and then press Delete (Figure 4.107). Do the same for the bottom portion.

Step 14: Stack the Repeat

Group the objects, then copy and paste them (Figure 4.108). Stack them and use the Align panel to ensure even placement. You should have an "F" formation as shown in Figure 4.109.

Step 15: Align

Group, copy, and paste the "F" formation, then use the Align panel to position the objects. Zoom in to ensure that there are no gaps (Figure 4.110).

Step 16: Organic Motifs on Geometric Forms

Use a combination of tools including the Spiral Tool, which creates swirls reminiscent of the Art Nouveau era. The Arch Tool may also add beauty to your lace. Use these and/or other designs, including your own motifs from the Symbols panel. Figures 4.111 and 4.112 show the development and placement of the

Figure 4.111

Figure 4.112

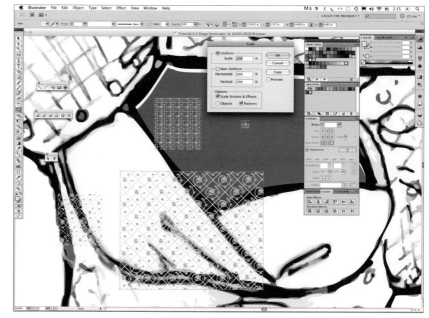

Figure 4.113

Figure 4.114

floral motif and spiral structure that is placed on the geometric formations. If you are using version CS5 or lower, be certain that no parts of the motif protrude outside the Bounding Box that appears when everything is selected.

Note: The Illustrator® CS6 Pattern Editor allows you to create repeats that extend the lines of the motif and Bounding Box. Select them and go to Menu Bar > Object > Pattern > Make and then use the Pattern Editor to make changes.

Step 17: Define the Lace Pattern

Select everything, then go to *Menu Bar > Edit > Define Pattern*. Give the pattern a name that

you will recognize later. You can also create a brush from any pattern that you define. Check the pattern and try scaling it. Lace patterns always look great rotated on a 45° angle. This keeps them from looking like plaids and checks. Figure 4.113 shows a defined lace pattern that has been scaled.

Step 18: Fill with the New Lace Pattern

To improve the design of the dress on the Blue Bridesmaid, the Pencil Tool (N) was used to trace near the lines of the original lines. The sweep was increased and then the shapes were filled with the lace pattern, which was then scaled to 300% (Figure 4.114).

Step 19: Create a Ruffled Edge

A simple as it may seem, even the best illustrators have difficulty drawing ruffles. Fortunately, they are not as difficult to manage digitally as they are by hand. The Green Bridesmaid's ruffled neckline could use some help. To create the ruffle as a brush, begin with a rectilinear shape. Use the Grid if needed. To simulate the flares, render several different cone shapes with rounded bottoms a bit shy in height of the rectangle, as practiced in Tutorial 4.2. Leave the tops open as shown in Figure 4.115.

Step 20: Positioning the Flares

Place the cone shapes randomly on the rectangle. They should not protrude outside of the top but should flow naturally from the bottom as shown in Figure 4.116. Use the Direct Selection Tool (A) to reshape some of them and use the Reflect Tool (O) Options to flip a few horizontally.

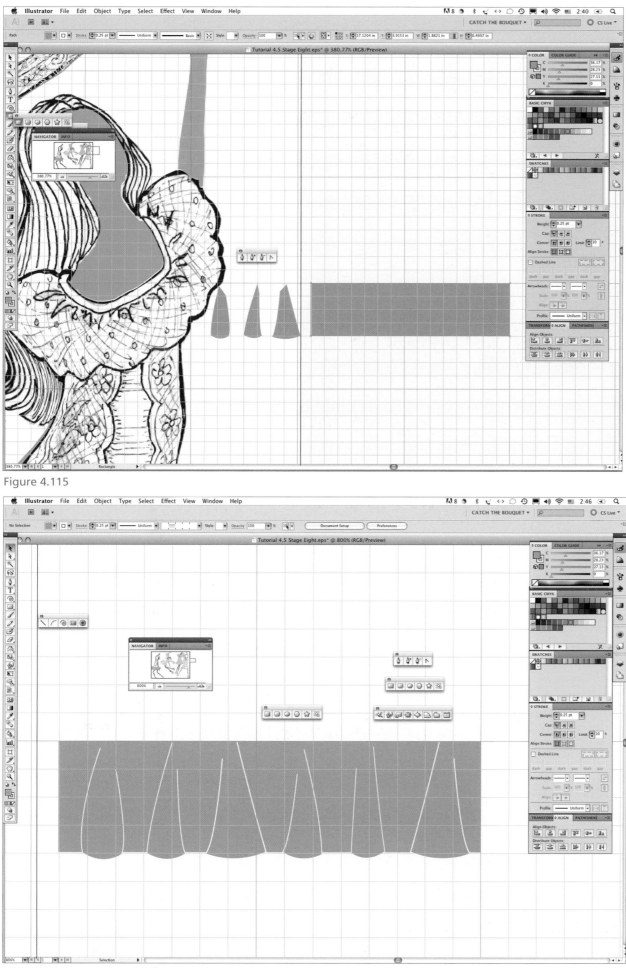

Figure 4.115

Figure 4.116 The random placement of the cone shapes helps to create the illusion of actual flares.

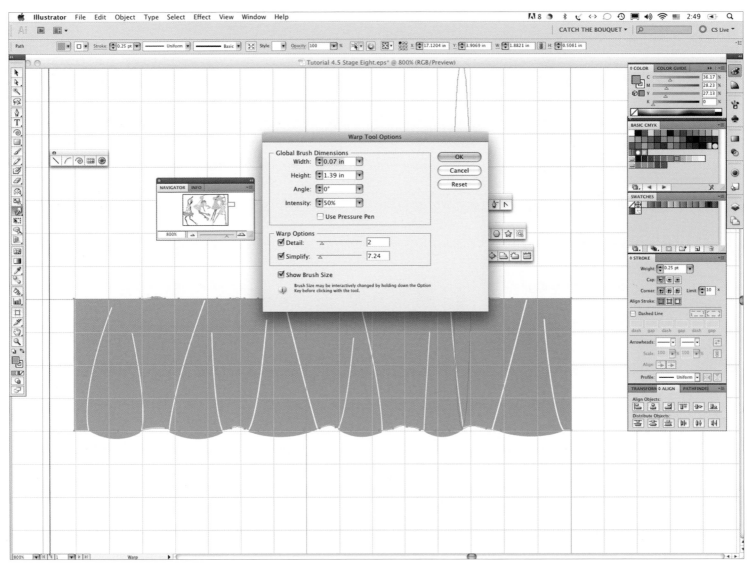

Figure 4.117 Warping the bottom of the rectangular shape will give it a concave look in relationship to the cone shapes.

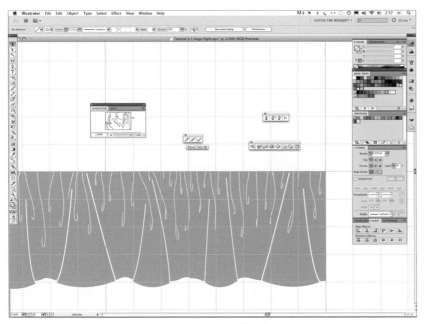

Figure 4.118 Vary the length and spacing of gathers.

Step 21: Use the Warp Tool

Select and lock the cones *Cmd+Z / Ctrl+Z*. Use the **Warp Tool (Shift+R)** to shape the areas of the rectangle that are between the cones. Double-click on the tool to access its options, specifically to adjust the width, because the default brush size is quite wide. Figure 4.117 shows both the Warp Tool Options dialog box and the effect it had on creating the curved lines at the bottom of the rectangle in the example.

Step 22: Adding Gathers or Shirring Effects

To render the look of gathers or shirring, use the freehand look generated by the Pencil Tool (N) as pictured in Figure 4.118. Notice that the Stroke *Weight* has been reduced and that the lengths and curvature vary. These lines should be created without a fill. Keep them aligned with the top edge.

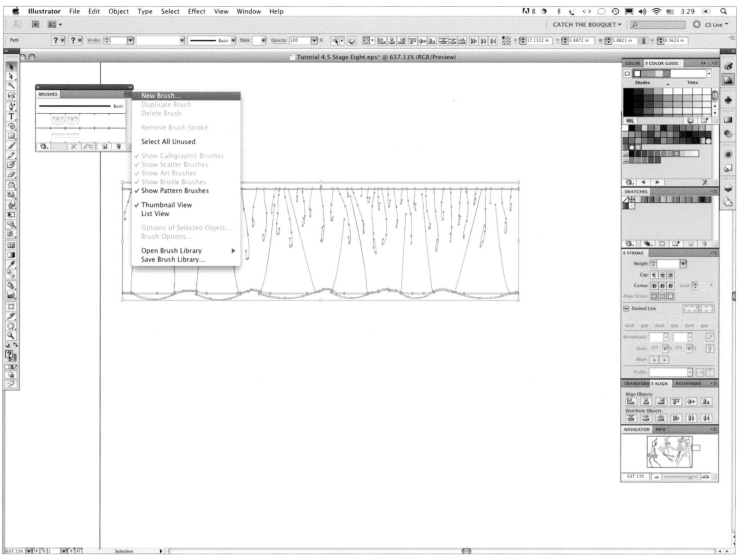

Figure 4.119 Unlock the cones before proceeding to define the brush pattern. Maximize the versatility of the brush by filling it with white. You can make these changes by double-clicking on its icon in the Brushes panel.

Step 23: Create a New Brush

This technique for creating ruffles and flares can be used as is, but you can create a brush as well. Add details to the hem such as stitches with the *Dashed Line* in the Stroke panel and a trim at the top. Select everything and proceed to define a pattern. You can create a new brush from the pattern as previously instructed (Figure 4.119). Define all the angles as discussed in Step Eight. Figure 4.120 illustrates the new ruffled collar, and the completed example is shown in Figure 4.121.

Note: *A sample of the ruffle edge brush is available in the file* Ruffled_Edge.pdf *on ① Ch04\Tutorial 4.5. To use it, simply open the file in Illustrator® and select it in the Brushes panel. Learn how to create cascades by watching the demonstation of* Cascade_Demo_1. m4v.

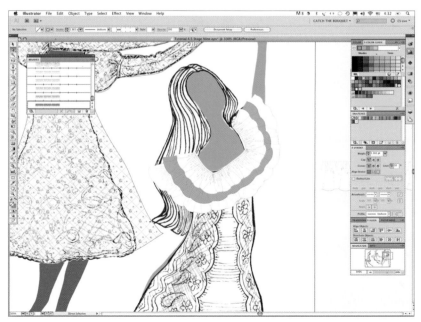

Figure 4.120

Chapter 4 Summary

Chapter 4 was filled with tutorials that aim to strengthen your Illustrator® rendering skills and teach you to apply the benefits of the Photoshop® Effects Gallery. Ask yourself the following questions to determine if you should proceed to Chapter 5.

Chapter 4 Self-Assessment

1. Am I able to digitally simulate a precious gem by using the tools and gradients in Illustrator®? Do I know how to adjust the Flare Tool?

2. Can I define a simulated translucency for sheer textiles?

3. Do I know how to render buttons and button-holes, and align dashes to corners and path ends in Illustrator®?

4. Can I create a simple environment or backdrop for my fashion designs/presentations in Illustrator®?

5. Can I use the features of Symbols Tool Suite in Illustrator® to enhance my apparel designs? Can I define an all-over lace pattern from a rendered motif, and create a ruffle brush?

6. Do I know how to make effective use of the Illustrator® Smart Guides to create geometric shapes and perfect 30° angles?

7. Can I use the Illustrator® Pen Tool (P) to render simple apparel and accessory items on a figure?

8. Can I create a simple lace pattern from a default pattern in Illustrator®? Do I know how to flatten the transparency of an object, so that I can use it as part of a motif, and then define it as a pattern?

9. Flares in a skirt can be simulated by rendering what shapes on top?

10. What part of a shirt is generally rendered under the collar at the front of the neck where the button is placed? Do I understand how to simulate the neck curvature of a collar on a figure?

11. The Illustrator® Perspective Grid Tool (Shift+P) can be used to render what types of apparel on the figure?

12. Can I create a new Symbol from my own art-work?

13. Do I know how to make a lace-patterned brush?

14. Can I use the Warp Tool to reshape selected cones?

Figure 4.121 **Illustration by Stacy Stewart Smith.**

Basic Raster Skills with Photoshop®

Objectives

In this chapter, you will be exposed to the latest version of the number one image-editing software program: Photoshop®. Although it may appear intimidating to the beginner, many of its capabilities are similar to those offered in Illustrator®. Both programs possess tools, panels, filters, and menu options. A goal of this chapter is to acquaint you with these common benefits, including the Photoshop® Pen Tool (P) and the Photoshop® Direct Selection Tool (A). Chiefly, the fundamentals of the program will be introduced. This chapter also includes a tutorial that will teach you how to prepare a digital customer profile storyboard. Because our scope is specialized, we will not attempt to unveil all the functions of Photoshop®; rather, the fundamentals of the program will be introduced, including:

- ❂ The Photoshop® Tools panel

- ❂ Photoshop® Layer Compositing

- ❂ The use of Photoshop® Layer Styles

- ❂ Photoshop® file-saving formats

- ❂ Scanning and manipulating freehand drawings

- ❂ File exporting and "Digital Duo" techniques

Image-Editing Raster-Based Digital Art

Image editing is the process of altering images. The foundation of image-editing software is rooted in the convergence of fine art movements and the infancy of printing technology that began with the appearance of Neo-Impressionism in 1886. Pointillism, invented by the French painter Georges Seurat (the founder of Neo-Impressionism), may have been a chief catalyst of digital image editing. Seurat painted dots of pure color to create compositions that "blend" in the eye when seen at distances. The technique is made apparent by his masterpiece *Bathers at Asnières (Une Baignade, Asnières)*, oil on canvas, 1884 (Figure 5.1). The tenets of Pointillism and other Neo-Impressionist techniques, such as painting daubs, advanced published photography through printmaking techniques, and color prints helped to generate an overwhelming public allegiance to periodicals, especially magazines. In the aftermath (by the middle of the 20th century), the advent of television and network broadcasting packaged these concepts for the digital age and the Internet.

Figure 5.1 *Bathers at Asnières (Une Baignade Asnières)*, oil on canvas, 1884, by Georges Seurat. The Art Archive/Hermitage Museum Saint Petersburg.

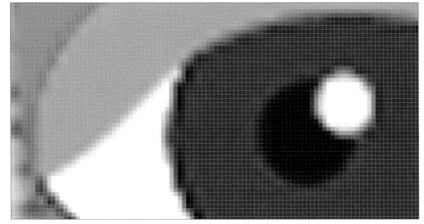

Figure 5.2 A zoomed view in Photoshop® reveals a grid and pixels.

Raster Art, Pixels, and Bitmaps

In Photoshop®, images are digitized by pixels (tiny squares of color placed by the program onto a numbered grid). This grid is a bitmap of a monitor (Figure 5.2). Digital art composed of pixels is known as *raster art*.

The fashion industry uses Photoshop® primarily to edit photos, but the program offers much more, including, but not limited to, digital design, animation, and **digital painting**. Photoshop® possesses similar interface capabilities as Illustrator®, but the purpose for using them is quite dissimilar. It is possible to use raster-based software independent of vector software; however, in the author's opinion, the best presentations derive from combinations of both. These "Digital Duo" techniques will be explored in this and later chapters.

Photoshop® File Formats

Save your work by pressing *Shift+Cmd+S / Shift+Ctrl+S* or go to *Menu Bar > File > Save As*. Follow your normal saving procedures for Mac or PC. You learned the three important things to do when saving files for the book and DVD exercises and tutorials in Tutorial 3.1. They are:

1. Save your file in a specific location.
2. Give your file an appropriate title.
3. Choose a proper file format.

Each file format has an extension that will follow the title of your file, preceded by a period. The important Photoshop® file formats that you will use in this book are:

- **Photoshop® (.psd)** Saving your files in the default Photoshop® format allows you to retain your layer compositing as long as you do not flatten them.

- **JPEG (.jpg)** Used for files with reduced resolution (72 to 150 dpi) to send images via e-mail or for posting purposes on the Internet. Once the resolution of an image has been set, the JPEG format maintains the lowest file size that can still generate a quality print. This file format will flatten your layers, so always retain a copy of the original .psd file before saving the .jpg format.

- **Photoshop PDF (.pdf)** This file format allows you to share files without communication problems. It also allows you to maintain the integrity of your files when imported. You can save your layer compositing and view the contents in Adobe Acrobat Pro® or open and edit the files in Photoshop®. Through Acrobat Pro®, PDF files can be assembled into multiple-page slide shows (see appendix).

The Photoshop® Tools Panel

Photoshop® has a Tools panel containing 60 to 65 different tools, depending upon which version you are running. Not all of the tools are immediately visible (Figure 5.3). The panel does not have floating tear-off features like Illustrator®. Hidden tools are accessible by clicking and holding the default tools that have a black lower right corner. Most of the tools within the same suite have identical shortcuts.

Note: To access the next tool in the suite, you simply hold the Shift key and continue to press the code until you reach your desired tool.

The Photoshop® Tools panel can generally be separated into eight categories: drawing, painting, selection, navigation, formatting, image editing, typography, and administration.

Moving and Converting the Tools Panel

The Photoshop® Tools panel can be converted from a single column to a double column of tools just like the one in Illustrator® (Figure 5.4). These basic functions were discussed in Chapter 2. By now, you should have no problem experimenting with the panel, so press *Cmd+N / Ctrl+N* to open a new letter-size document and get started.

Tools Panel Attributes

The Photoshop® Tools panel does not have a Fill or a Stroke box like Illustrator®. Instead it contains a **Set Foreground Color** box and a **Set Background Color** box (Figure 5.5). These boxes provide quick color, pattern, or gradient Fills and Strokes of selected areas and shapes. The Set Foreground Color box is the automatic fill used for indicating visual objects. The Set Background Color box offers an immediate alternative fill option. The contents of the two boxes can be swapped using the double-sided arrow icon above them on the right. In addition, a default Foreground and Background Color icon is located above the boxes on the left. Click it to return to black and white.

In image-editing software each pixel is actually an individual container for color. **Pixels** are like the tiny components of an image. Because pixels form images, they can be altered in many ways. They can even be masked. Unlike vector art where an entire shape becomes a selection, a segment of pixels within an area can be manipulated, while those masked areas within the same region are not affected by any changes that you make. The Photoshop® Tools panel has an **Edit in Quick Mask Mode (Q)** icon at the bottom of the tools panel that provides immediate access to this option by converting painted areas to quick selections (Tutorial 7.2 on page 211).

Photoshop® Tools Panel and Related Panel Review

Because the Photoshop® tools cannot be detached from the panel column like the Illustrator® Tools panel, they must be introduced individually. The following is a review of the tools and related panels from CS5. Photoshop® CS6 does not contain significantly different tools from CS5; however, some upgraded features will be mentioned as necessary. Keep in mind that each tool also has options that you can adjust in the Options Bar.

Note: To avoid confusion, software titles are written before the tools or panel names that are shared by both programs, for example, the Photoshop® Zoom Tool (Z) and the Illustrator® Zoom Tool (Z).

Rendering Tools

Use the following tools and panels in Photoshop® to render or assist in rendering:

The Pen Tool Suite: Because we have already journeyed into mastering the Pen Tool (P) and Bézier Curves in earlier chapters using Illustrator®, an extensive discussion concerning the creation of Bézier Curves would be redundant. The five tools in the Photoshop® Pen Tool Suite (Figure 5.6) function similarly to those with the same names in Illustrator® except the paths they make, when filled, are separate from the shaped objects that they can produce.

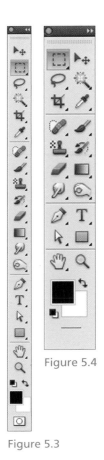

Figure 5.4

Figure 5.3

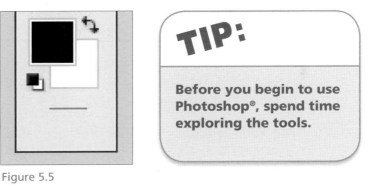

Figure 5.5

TIP:

Before you begin to use Photoshop®, spend time exploring the tools.

Figure 5.6 Photoshop® Pen Tool Suite.

Pen Tool   P
Freeform Pen Tool   P
Add Anchor Point Tool
Delete Anchor Point Tool
Convert Point Tool

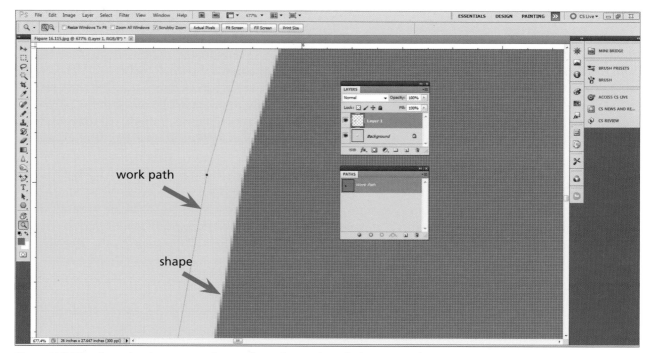

Figure 5.7 The shape has been moved away from the work path that created it.

Think of a path created with the Photoshop® Pen Tool (P) as a cookie cutter. You can use the path repeatedly to produce the same shape with different fills and strokes in the same document, even on the same layer. The editing tools can affect the shapes because they are composed of pixels and will appear on layers. The work paths are merely containers for rendering in a manner similar to vector art and appear only on the levels of the Paths panel.

The Photoshop® Freeform Pen Tool (P) performs like the Illustrator® Pencil Tool (N). It creates anchors and paths. In Figure 5.7, a work path has been moved to the left of a shape that was created from its parameters. The shape takes on the raster bitmap as indicated by its pixel edges.

The Path Selection Tool: The Photoshop® **Path Selection Tool (A)** functions like the Illustrator® Selection Tool (V). It allows you to select and move paths, but not the filled shapes they create (Figure 5.8).

The Direct Selection Tool: The Photoshop® Direct Selection Tool (A) manipulates paths only. It will not affect the shapes they create. It modifies paths just like the Illustrator® Direct Selection Tool (A) (Figure 5.9).

Using the Paths Panel: The Photoshop® **Paths panel** works in conjunction with any shape that is created with the Photoshop® Pen Tool (P) or the **Free-form Pen Tool (P)** (Figure 5.10). When a shape is rendered, a work path appears. Use the Paths panel when working with shapes (*work paths*) created on the same layer that you want to keep separate. The panel can affect each path created as to its fill or its stroke, or you can load them as selections (*rasterize them*), etc. Use the buttons at the bottom of the panel to access these features, which include the following (from left to right): Fill path with the foreground color, Stroke path with brush, Load path as selection, Make work path from selection, Create new path, and Delete current path.

Note: In CS6 there are options that allow you to add a layer mask, as well as add dashed lines to selected strokes.

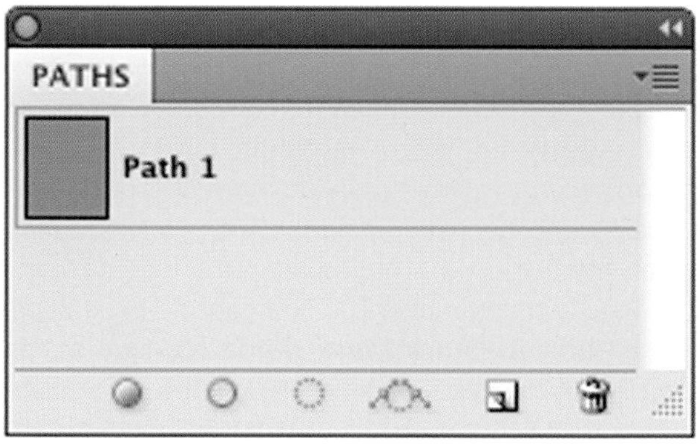

Figure 5.8

Figure 5.9

Figure 5.10 Photoshop® Paths panel.

Eraser Tool Suite: Photoshop® has a family of eraser tools. They offer various cleanup options (Figure 5.11). The **Photoshop® Eraser Tool (E)** is your main eraser option. It provides direct freeform contact with objects and expunges any area that it touches based on the diameter of a brush.

The **Background Eraser Tool (E)** deletes pixels of any object below the one on which you are working. The **Magic Eraser Tool (E)** erases pixels of the same color. Use it to erase a particular colored area within a pattern or photo.

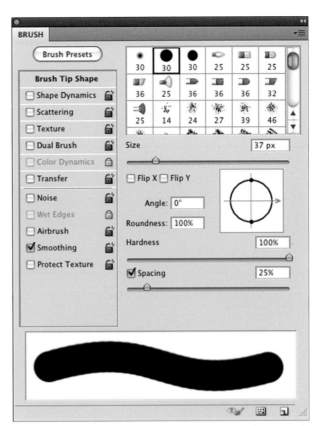

Figure 5.12 Photoshop® Brush panel.

Figure 5.11

TIP: Erase Reduced Opacity

Through the settings available in the Options Bar, you can also erase using a reduced *Opacity* mode that allows you to create sheer effects within solid objects. This is a terrific way of simulating burnout, sheer elements of a garment, and flocked textile patterns.

Painting Tools

The following tools and panels will assist the digital painting process:

Brush Panel: Use the options in the **Photoshop® Brush panel** to adjust the attributes of each brush preset. Figure 5.12 shows the Brush panel including a menu of brush types and a slider that allows you to change the size. Right-click your mouse to access this portion as a mini menu when you are using a tool like the Photoshop® Eraser (E) to make adjustments. On a trackpad, hold two fingers and press the clicker.

Brush Tool: The **Photoshop® Brush Tool (B)** shown in Figure 5.13 is used for digital painting and may be adjusted as to type, size, and function through the Options Bar and the Brush Presets panel.

Pencil Tool: The **Photoshop® Pencil Tool (B)**, unlike the Illustrator® Pencil Tool (N), acts like a brush and does not leave a trail of anchor points. Use it to render fine to thick lines.

Color Replacement Tool: This tool allows you to replace the color of an object with applied Strokes of a new color from the Set Foreground Color box. The **Color Replacement Tool (B)** does not work when the color is black or white. An attempt to replace a specific hue with these color absences will result in varied grays (Figure 5.13).

Mixer Brush Tool: The **Mixer Brush Tool (B)** blends two or more colors, gradients, and/or patterns (Figure 5.13).

Figure 5.13

Brush Presets Panel: The Photoshop® **Brush Presets panel** (available in CS5 and CS6) offers preset options for each individual brush. It is pictured in Figure 5.79 on page 145.

Gradient Tool: The **Photoshop® Gradient Tool (G)** provides blends of two or more color fills (Figure 5.14).

Paint Bucket Tool: The **Paint Bucket Tool (G)** in conjunction with the Set Foreground box is used for the random fills of objects and/or color areas. This tool is located in a hidden suite with the Photoshop® Gradient Tool (G) (Figure 5.14).

Figure 5.14

Eyedropper Tool: The **Photoshop® Eyedropper Tool (I)** samples a color with a click and places it in the Set Foreground box (Figure 5.15).

Color Sampler Tool: The **Color Sampler Tool (I)** allows you to place up to four temporary color samples in a file for referencing via the Info panel (Figure 5.15).

Figure 5.15

History Brush Tool: This tool works as a brush to return areas gradually to their original state when you opened the file. The **History Brush Tool (Y)** is a great asset to have when retouching photos, especially when you like the changes that you have made to an image in some areas, but do not care for what happened in others. Click on the areas that you want to restore (Figure 5.16).

Art History Brush Tool: The **Art History Brush Tool (Y)** allows for the use of fine art painting techniques from images through various adjustment options available in the Brush panel (Figure 5.16).

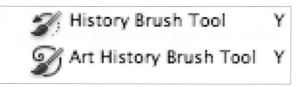

Figure 5.16

Selection Tools

These tools generate selected or shaped areas:

The Marquee Tool Suite: This suite of tools creates shaped selected areas with the **Rectangular Marquee Tool (M)**, the **Elliptical Marquee Tool (M)**, the **Single Row Marquee Tool**, and the **Single Column Marquee Tool**. The presence of "marching ants" always indicates selected areas (Figure 5.17).

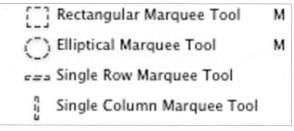

Figure 5.17

The Lasso Tool Suite: These tools create freeform selected areas with the **Lasso Tool (L)**. The **Polygonal Lasso Tool (L)** creates freeform angular selections from point to point. The **Magnetic Lasso Tool (L)** adheres digital pins to the outer parameter of objects, and then creates a selection when the shape is closed (Figure 5.18).

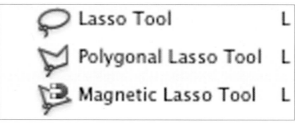

Figure 5.18

Shape Tools: The shape tools generate the forms associated with their titles, which are filled with the contents of the Set Foreground box (Figure 5.19). The **Custom Shape Tool (U)** makes flat symbols from preset vector mask logos and clip art libraries located in the **Photoshop® Options Bar**. You can also create and save your own shapes. The tools in this suite create vector masks on the Paths panel. Paths can be manipulated by their anchors with selection tools just as you learned to do in Illustrator®.

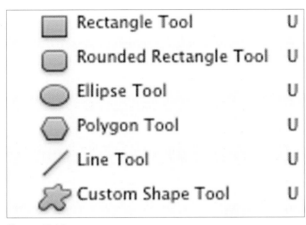

Figure 5.19

Quick Selection Tool: The Photoshop® **Quick Selection Tool (W)** allows you to make freeform selections in brushlike strokes. It also has settings in the Options Bar that allow you to alter its tolerance, brush size, and selection type, and to adjust the selection edge. We will not use all the features of this tool (Figure 5.20).

Photoshop® Magic Wand Tool: The **Photoshop® Magic Wand Tool (W)** selects pixels by color and has settings in the Options Bar that adjust sensitivity (tolerance) and other behavioral capabilities that we will not need to cover in this book. It is one of the most useful tools in the program; you will rely upon it frequently. Certain functions such as adding or subtracting from selected areas may be easier to access with the keyboard shortcuts; however, this is a matter of personal preference. You will need to experiment with the tool and develop your own technique (Figure 5.20).

Figure 5.20

Navigational Tools

These tools will help you to move objects and/or assist with page navigation:

Move Tool: The Move Tool is the first tool in the panel (Figure 5.21). Use it to reposition objects, selections, etc.

Figure 5.21

Hand Tool: Use the **Photoshop® Hand Tool (H)** to move around the page. Press the space bar to toggle this capability (Figure 5.22). This tool also works in conjunction with the Proxy Preview Area of the **Photoshop® Navigator panel**.

Rotate View Tool: The **Rotate View Tool (R)** randomly changes the page orientation based on a radius (Figure 5.22).

Figure 5.22

Zoom Tool: The **Photoshop® Zoom Tool (Z)** is the last tool in the panel and allows the user to view the document at various distances (Figure 5.23). The zoom features of the program can also be activated with *Cmd++ (plus) / Ctrl++ (plus)* to zoom in. To zoom out, press *Cmd+(minus) / Ctrl+(minus)*. The zoom features also work with the slider options in the Navigator panel.

Figure 5.23

Formatting Tools

The tools in this section will help you alter the format of your page:

Crop Tool: The **Crop Tool (C)** can be used to reduce the size of the canvas or change its orientation by performing a marquee, then clicking inside the highlighted area (except the center) to accept the changes (Figure 5.24).

Slice Tool: The **Slice Tool (C)** is used to isolate areas of a file or photo in order to save and place them on Web pages (Figure 5.24).

Slice Select Tool: The **Slice Select Tool (C)** is used to select and reposition slices. To save a specific slice of a photo or file, go to *Menu Bar > File > Save for Web & Devices....* In the dialog box, you have the option of saving all the slices or just the one that you have selected (Figure 5.24).

Ruler Tool: The **Ruler Tool (I)** measures distances with a click and drag. The recorded information as to position, width, and height will appear in the Options Bar (Figure 5.15 on p.120).

Figure 5.24

Image-Editing Tools
The image-editing tools enable you to alter pixels:

Spot Healing Brush Tool: Use the **Spot Healing Brush Tool (J)** to eradicate blemishes, spots, and marks that are surrounded by acceptable areas. This tool is one of several used for photo retouching (Figure 5.25).

Healing Brush Tool: With this tool you can sample desirable pixels near a problem area by clicking and holding down with the Option key (Mac) or the Alt key (PC). Use the **Healing Brush Tool (J)** to reposition desirable pixels, color, patterns, etc. Options Bar options offer a variety of means to personalize this for each user (Figure 5.25).

Patch Tool: The **Patch Tool (J)** is best used to sample selected problem areas such as tears or damaged areas of photos. When the selection is moved to a desirable area, the Patch Tool replaces the selection with the image of the second position. This tool is useful for retouching, to create instant pattern fills, or to reposition pattern repeats within a rendering. One of its greatest benefits is the removal of tattoos (Figure 5.25).

Red Eye Tool: The name says it all. With a click, the tool covers red eye. However, on small files sizes with images of subjects who have ruddy or brown skintones, the **Red Eye Tool (J)** can produce a black eye. The tool can be adjusted in the Options Bar, and is accessible with a panel of Photoshop® retouching favorites (Figure 5.25).

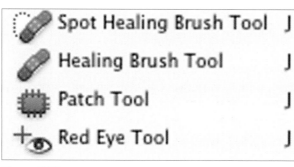

Figure 5.25

Clone Stamp Tool: With the **Clone Stamp Tool (S)** you can sample an area of pixels by clicking and holding down the Option key (Mac) or the Alt key (PC) and place them with a click in another area (Figure 5.26).

Pattern Stamp Tool: The **Pattern Stamp Tool (S)** can sample an area of patterned pixels; click and hold down the Option key (Mac) or the Alt key (PC) and place them with a click or a swipe in another area to continue a repeat (Figure 5.26).

Figure 5.26

Blur Tool: Use the Blur Tool to defocus pixels (Figure 5.27).

Sharpen Tool: Use the **Sharpen Tool** to focus pixels (Figure 5.27).

Smudge Tool: The Smudge Tool smears pixels (Figure 5.27).

Dodge Tool: The **Dodge Tool (O)** brightens pixels with a brushstroke (Figure 5.28).

Note: *The term* dodge *is taken from the photography darkroom technique that avoids or decreases the exposure of select areas in a photograph.*

Figure 5.27

Burn Tool: The **Burn Tool (O)** darkens pixels with a brushstroke (Figure 5.28). Obviously, the Burn Tool (O) takes its name from actual burn tools used by photographers in darkrooms to overexpose areas in photos.

Sponge Tool: Use the **Sponge Tool (O)** to saturate or desaturate (make grayscale) pixels with a brush (Figure 5.28).

Figure 5.28

Typography Tools

The typographic capabilities of Photoshop® are offered through the following tools that can be adjusted through the **Photoshop® Character panel**, the Paragraph panel, the Options Bar, and other features of the program:

Horizontal Type Tool: Use the **Horizontal Type Tool (T)** to type across the file using a variety of fonts in various sizes. In Photoshop®, type can be treated as an object that can take on most of the features and the various effects the program offers.

Note: Each section of type will appear on a separate layer.

Vertical Type Tool: You can type from top to bottom with the **Vertical Type Tool (T)** (Figure 5.29).

Horizontal Type Mask Tool: The **Horizontal Type Mask Tool (T)** allows you to create horizontal type as selections that can be filled or stroked. You can type horizontally and mask out areas, leaving just the shape of the characters with whatever is beneath them showing through the characters (Figure 5.29).

Vertical Type Mask Tool: The **Vertical Type Mask Tool (T)** allows you to create vertical type as selections that can be filled or stroked. You can type vertically and mask out areas, leaving just the characters with whatever is beneath them showing through the characters (Figure 5.29).

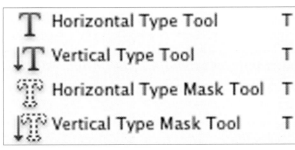

Figure 5.29

An Administrative Tool

Photoshop® has one administrative tool:

Note Tool: The **Note Tool (I)** allows users of a file to leave notes that can be posted as reminders or to give instructions (Figure 5.15 on p.120).

Tool Presets Panel: To discover which tools possess preset functions, select them and show the **Tool Presets panel** (Figure 5.30). If a preset is available, try it out. You can also use the panel to set new presets for tools. Simply select a tool, set particular options, such as mode, opacity, etc., then click the Create New Tool Preset icon at the bottom of the panel. A Preset dialog box appears allowing you to give your preset a title. To use the preset when you open Photoshop®, select it from the panel.

Note: The preset will also retain color information.

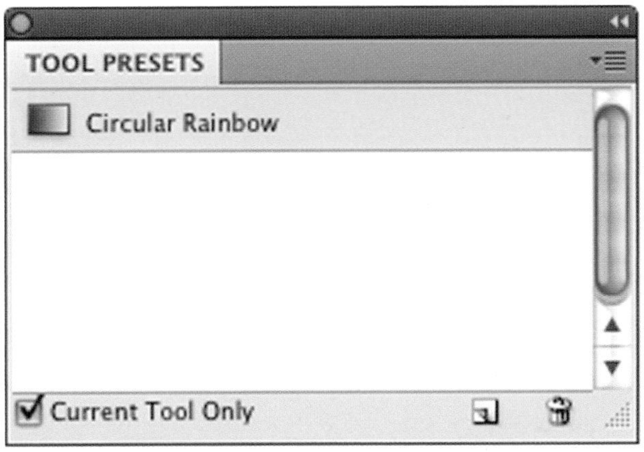

Figure 5.30 Photoshop® CS5 Tool Presets panel.

Photoshop® Preferences

To access the **Photoshop® Preferences** menus, go to *Menu Bar > Photoshop > Preferences > General (Mac)* or *Menu Bar > Edit > Preferences > General (PC)*. In CS5 and CS6, the Preferences menus are similar and offer identical choices in both Mactinosh and Windows operating systems. On the left side is a column of categories including *General, Interface, File Handling, Performance, Cursors, Transparency & Gamut, Units & Rulers, Guides, Grid & Slices, Plugins,* and *Type*. Select a category to view adjustment menu options. Generally, you will not need to change the settings; however, there are a few issues that will arise as we proceed to the tutorials.

History and Cache, History Panel, and History States

The **Preferences dialog box** category has an area on the right labeled *History & Cache*. It works with

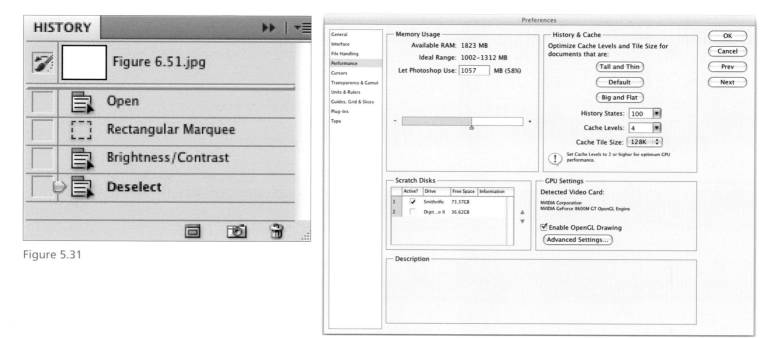

Figure 5.31

Figure 5.32

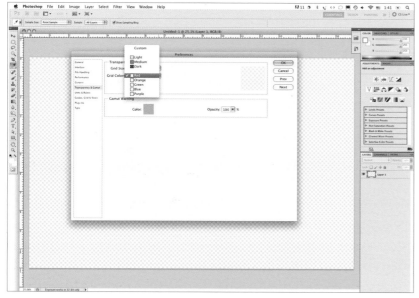

Figure 5.33 Photoshop® CS5 Custom Preferences.

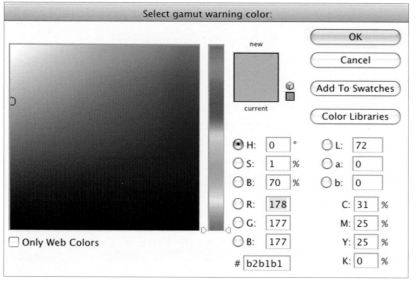

Figure 5.34

the **History panel**, which by default allows you to undo up to 20 steps (Figure 5.31). Adjust the settings in the *History States* to give you the ability to undo more actions. In Figure 5.32, the *History States* have been set to 100. Keep in mind that retaining more steps in a file will use up more RAM.

Transparency & Gamut

When you open a new document in Photoshop®, you will see a checkered background. This represents **digital transparency** (colorless pixels). In the Preferences menu's *Transparency & Gamut* category, you can select specific colors for the checkered background from the color samples. Click on them and use the Color Picker to specify your choice(s). There are also a few preset color combinations. In Figure 5.33, the setting was changed to red and white.

The **gamut** is the capacity of your computer to interpret colors. When a particular color or range of colors in your working file falls out of the color RGB color mode gamut, a warning signal appears in the Color Picker and in the Color panel.

Note: *The default color mode for Photoshop® is RGB, but when we refer to proofing colors for output, CMYK is the primary option for the tutorials in this book. If you need to know exactly which colors might be a problem for your output device, go to Menu Bar > Proof Setup > Working CMYK. Afterward, go to Menu Bar > View > Gamut Warning. You can also press Shift+Cmd+Y / Shift+Ctrl+Y. The areas will show in the default gamut color (gray) shown in the Preferences menu. To change the color, click on the sampler in the gamut options section*

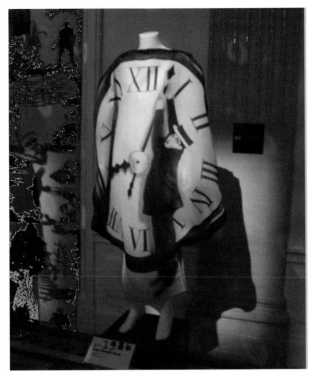

Figure 5.35 Photograph by Stacy Stewart Smith.

(Figure 5.34) and use the Color Picker. In Figure 5.35, the gamut color was changed to Day-Glo green, so that issues in the photo could be identified easily.

Note: If large areas fall into the gamut, select and convert them or otherwise convert the entire file to the RGB color mode by going to Menu Bar > Image > Mode > RGB Color.

The Photoshop® Window, Desktop, and Help

Navigating your way around the Photoshop® window will be much easier now that you have completed the Illustrator® exercises in previous chapters. The Mac version in Figure 5.36 and the PC version (Figure 5.37) are nearly the same. A few features are located in different places. Take a moment to open the program and study the window, desktop, and features.

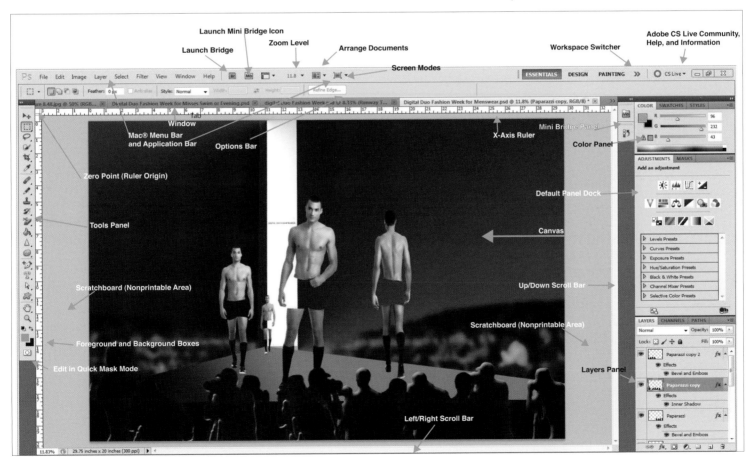

Figure 5.36 Photoshop® CS5 Mac desktop interface.

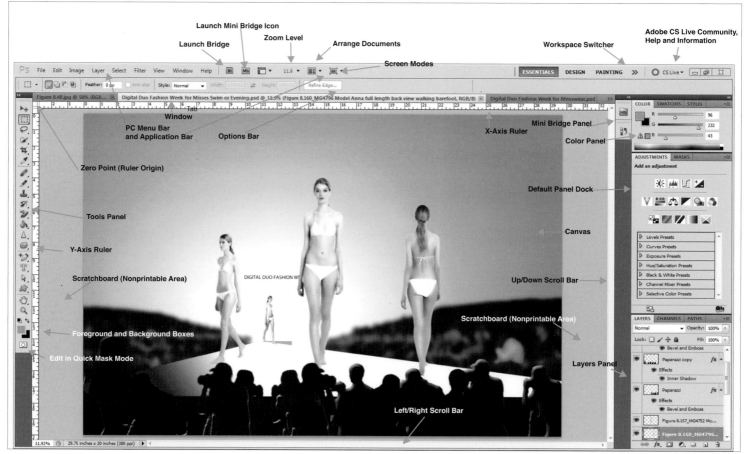

Figure 5.37 Photoshop® CS5 PC desktop interface.

Note: *The Photoshop® CS6 window interface color theme is, by default, dark gray, but it can be changed back to the classic platinum look of CS5 and lower versions via the Preferences menu.*

Photoshop® Window Options

Just as in Illustrator®, you can open more than one window at a time in Photoshop®. The program will dock the windows, but it will leave identifying tabs for you to manage the view.

Arrange Documents

Click the **Photoshop® Arrange Documents button** located in the Application Bar to uncover various viewing options (Figures 5.36 and Figure 5.37).

The Application Bar and Mini Bridge

Because users of image-editing software programs work with photos and other images, Adobe has positioned **Launch Bridge** and **Launch Mini Bridge buttons** in the **Photoshop® CS5 Application Bar**. These will come in handy, especially as you begin to work with many different files. Use the Launch Mini Bridge option to access an organized view via a panel within the program. When you click the icon in the Application Bar, the Mini Bridge panel opens. The Launch Bridge icon will actually open the program.

Note: *In CS6, Mini Bridge appears at the lower left corner of the Application frame of the Essentials Workspace and is slightly more comprehensive than in the earlier version. In addition, the horizontal arrangement leaves more room for viewing your work.*

Photoshop® Workspaces

The Workspace options are located on the right side of the Application Bar. The default settings are actually fine for most projects. However, you can save your own new arrangements of panels by clicking and holding the double arrows of the **Photoshop® Workspace Switcher**. Scroll to the option of choice to activate additional features.

Saving Workspaces

In Photoshop®, you can save a Workspace by creating one via the Workspace Switcher in the Options Bar.

The Options Bar

The Photoshop® Options Bar hosts additional tool options.

Photoshop® Support Center

The Photoshop® Support Center offers answers to questions with the click of the Help button located in the Application Bar (PC) and in the Menu Bar (Mac).

Managing Photoshop® Panels

Showing and Hiding Panels

Like Illustrator®, panels are the main method to access program features in Photoshop®. Many of the panel functions can be figured out easily. The tutorials will explain the panels as they are needed.

Layers Panel

The **Photoshop® Layers panel** is one of the most essential. The panel provides organization and an ability to apply filters to certain objects but not others.

When you open a file/image in Photoshop®, the default layer is the *Background* layer. This layer is the raster environment for the file and cannot be altered as long as it is named *Background*. Double-click on a layer in order to rename it. You can also right-click to access menu options in order to make changes.

Creating Layers and More

Selected layers can be identified by a color highlight. Use the Create a New Layer icon at the bottom of the panel to build your layer compositing. Toggle on and off the visibility of any layer with the eye icon at the left. To title a layer, double-click on the name. This creates a highlight field where you can type. Layers can also be linked. Hold the Shift key to select two or more layers, and then click the **link icon** (chain) at the bottom left side of the panel.

Layer Groups

To help users organize various aspects of a singular project, Photoshop® has folders known as **Layer Groups**. They can house and hide many layers. You can create a Layer Group by clicking the folder icon at the bottom of the panel. Figure 5.38 identifies Layer Group 1, containing Layer 2, while Layer 1, which is outside the group, is positioned below it. To hide the layers in a group, click the pointer on the left.

Preparing for Digital Duo Fashion Week

Several times per year in different locations around the globe, fashion houses showcase their latest creations in highly publicized marketing venues during what is known as Fashion Week. At these events, fashion shows are staged and scheduled for an "A-list" crowd including store buyers, journalists, and celebrities (Figures 5.39 and 5.40). They receive formal invitations and take front-row seats close to the actual runway. The "fashion crowd" (general public or industry professionals without confirmed reservations) usually stands outside until the A-list crowd locates their seats. When all the seats are filled, occasionally a "standing only" overflow crowd is admitted. Fashion Week events are often sponsored by huge corporations. The paparazzi come for photo-ops of celebrities, models, and fashion designers.

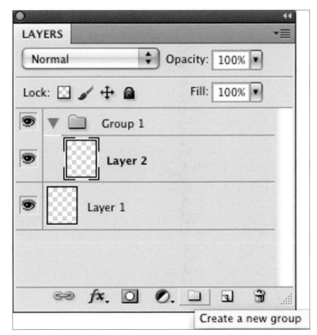

Figure 5.38 Photoshop® Layers Panel.

Figure 5.39 Designers show their latest lines to A-list celebrities and fashion industry elites during Fashion Week. © Frances Roberts/Alamy.

Figure 5.40 © Rudy K. Lawidjaja/Alamy.

Now you get your chance to be a part of the fashion in-crowd through a series of fashion design and merchandising tutorials that begin in this chapter. In Chapter 7 you will get the opportunity to prepare for the **Digital Duo Fashion Week**. The digital storyboards that you create using Photoshop® will consist of the following categories: a customer profile board, a mood board, a color forecast board, and design presentations. These represent the apparel design and fashion merchandising stages of product development. Then you will complete an additional digital storyboard representing the fashion marketing stage for a runway fashion show at Digital Duo Fashion Week. You can choose to follow the men's wear tutorials using the digital runway file shown in Figure 5.36, as well as the women's wear runway (Figure 5.37), or you can design your own digital environment.

The largest market segment for apparel is women's wear. Apparel for men and children are separate markets. Most retail buyers identify the needs of a consumer in a fragment market, and then market segments are further divided. They are usually specialized and are categorized by apparel type. For instance, to maintain focus, a major retailer may hire buyers who only purchase women's woven tops or bottoms, men's outerwear, etc.

Apparel product developers must have an understanding of the image and lifestyle of a consumer type. This is also known as designing for a *target market*.

The Task

In this tutorial, you will assemble a digital storyboard that identifies and promotes a typical consumer in a target market. A digital customer profile storyboard should consist of photographs of the ideal consumer type, as well as images reflecting the lifestyle choices most likely associated with such an individual, including but not limited to the following categories: housing, transportation, income level, professional status, accessories, grooming, hobbies, habits, nutrition, exercise, marital status, family life, entertainment, etc. To help you complete this tutorial, assorted images have been provided on ① Ch05\Tutorial 5.1. You'll also make use of the figurative photo files from the ① Digital Duo Modeling Agency.

Although the actual market segment includes couture, designer, bridge, juniors, young men's, etc., we will limit the tutorial specialization to designer or contemporary sportswear for women's wear and/or men's wear. This provides four possible fashion exercises on which to practice product development and marketing skills, and to build Photoshop® expertise. The information below details the tutorial target markets.

The Designer Sportswear Market

This market has no age restrictions. Consumers select a designer brand based on its aesthetics and attributes. Apparel for men or women is considered "designer" when it is made of better fabrics and possesses a signature look. A designer line may be known for its silhouette, color, embroidery, fabrications, or fit, or for any number of luxurious qualities. Individuals who purchase designer clothing consider fashion to be a means of self-expression.

Designer labels attract anyone who does not mind paying the high cost for exclusive attire. The price of designer sportswear may range from several hundred dollars to thousands of dollars. Designer clothing may contain some hand detailing, treatments, or notions that are difficult to produce. Most designer clothing is exhibited at runway fashion shows during a market week and made available to consumers via branded specialty boutiques and department stores.

The Contemporary Sportswear Market

This market targets an urban professional who is 25 to 50 years of age; it includes a strong advertising campaign, online shopping, exclusive sales offers, and promotional events. The contemporary customer is usually a working professional whose economics prohibit purchasing apparel that does not have an immediate purpose. They may also own some designer clothes that they wear on special occasions, but they prefer to limit their apparel purchases to items that they need to replace in their wardrobes.

Women's contemporary sportswear sold in department stores is marketed below bridge sportswear, but is often sold on the same floor as designer diffusion (secondary lines). For men, this category falls right beneath the designer men's wear market. Many contemporary brands also manufacture accessories and fragrances. Fashion companies producing apparel for a specific consumer will follow similar trend information and inspiration. The textiles and garment construction of contemporary sportswear is considered to be of moderate to better quality and is sold at prices ranging from $60 to $600 in freestanding boutiques, department stores, and increasingly online. Some renowned fashion designers also cater to the contemporary sportswear market. Kenneth Cole, A|X Armani Exchange (Figure 5.41), Banana Republic, AK Anne Klein, and Club Monaco are a

Figure 5.41 Fashion House Giorgio Armani uses the retail marketing concept of Armani Exchange to appeal to a wider contemporary market. © uk retail Alan King/Alamy.

![New document dialog box](Figure 5.42)

New

Name: customer_profile_initials

Preset: Custom

Size:

Width: 17   inches

Height: 11   inches

Resolution: 300   pixels/inch

Color Mode: RGB Color   8 bit

Background Contents: Transparent

▼ Advanced

OK
Cancel
Save Preset...
Delete Preset...
Device Central...

Image Size:
48.2M

Figure 5.42

Figure 5.43

Figure 5.44

few popular brands as of this writing. Recent retail marketing concepts for the contemporary market include specialty shops for both men and women at the same boutique.

Step 1: New Document and Workspace

Double-click on the Photoshop® application icon. When the program loads, press *Cmd+N / Ctrl+N*, and a New Document dialog box will appear (Figure 5.42). Enter an appropriate name that includes your initials and the information shown in the fields. Use a high resolution if you would later like to print the completed work.

Note: *In the tutorial exercises of this chapter, all the digital documents will be set at 17×11 inches; however, you may choose to use portrait orientation instead. At all times, feel free to interpret the tutorial instructions to fit your needs.*

Step 2: Place and Arrange the Photo Images

Select a number of relevant images from ① Ch05\ Tutorial 5.1, or use the images you have scanned that identify and promote your targeted customer/ market. For each image, go to *Menu Bar > File > Place* to add it to the tutorial file that you created in Step One. To accept the file and remove the X running through it, double-click on the image. Repeat this process until you have placed the images that you need to identify your customer. Images placed into the file in Figure 5.43 are on separate layers and illustrate examples of the contemporary sportswear market for women.

Moving and Transforming Pictures

Use the Move Tool (V) to reposition each of the photo images by selecting the layer they are on, and then selecting the tool. Click and drag the objects around the canvas. To resize the images, go to *Menu Bar > Edit > Free Transform* or press *Cmd+T / Ctrl+T*. Hold the Shift key to constrain the proportions of the images, resize the image using the Bounding Box, and then double-click inside it to accept the new size (Figure 5.44).

Reordering Layers

Photoshop® has a Layers panel, and each of the layers can be **reordered**. If a certain image needs to be placed below another, locate it, then select the layer and pull it to the new position above or below other layers. You will notice the results in your window immediately. Double-click on the titles of the layers and type in new titles so that you can remember what is on each one.

Arrange the pictures in a manner that is easy for others to see and understand. Layouts with images placed horizontally and vertically are called rectilinear. They are easy to read as digital compositions because they leave an impact while giving the eye a rest (Figure 5.44).

Step 3: Reshape Images

The files on ① Ch05\Tutorial 5.1 all contain rectilinear images. Zoom in closer by using the Navigator panel to inspect the shapes for problems such as unevenness, darkened or lightened edges, etc.

Rasterize Smart Objects

You may have placed some of your own images into the file, which include those that act more like vector objects. Called **Smart Objects**, they can be converted from raster to vector and back again within the file. Smart Objects would cause some problems in this tutorial because they cannot be edited by the Photoshop® tools and filters, but we will use them later. To ensure that things go smoothly and before you begin to make alterations, rasterize the layers by going to *Menu Bar > Layer > Rasterize > All Layers*.

Cropping Images on Layers

To crop an image on a layer without affecting the rest of the file, select it, then marquee inside the image with the Rectangular Marquee Tool (V). With the marching ants flashing, press *Shift+Cmd+I / Shift+Ctrl+I* to Inverse the selection as shown in Figure 5.45. It will now include the area around the image up to the original selection. Press Delete to accept the cropped shape. To deselect the image, press *Cmd+D / Ctrl+D*. Try the same steps using the Elliptical Marquee Tool on another image/layer (Figure 5.46).

Step 4: Delete Imperfections with the Spot Healing Brush Tool

Spots or debris may have come along with some of your images. You may have noticed a few on the image of the woman holding the handbag. To delete the flaws, use the Spot Healing Brush Tool (J). Adjust the brush size in the Options Bar to correspond to the size of the problem. Locate a spot and click on it. Photoshop® will calculate and copy the good pixels surrounding the problem area, then replace the debris/spot with them as if it were never there. Success depends largely on the combination of the brush size and the condition of the surrounding pixels. This technique is not always effective on the edges of images, nor does it perform well on the transition of shapes like the edge of clothing. Compare the two photos in Figure 5.47. The image on the right has been retouched with the Spot Healing Brush Tool (J). Check the other images for spots, and use the Spot Healing Brush Tool (J) to delete them.

Figure 5.45

Figure 5.46

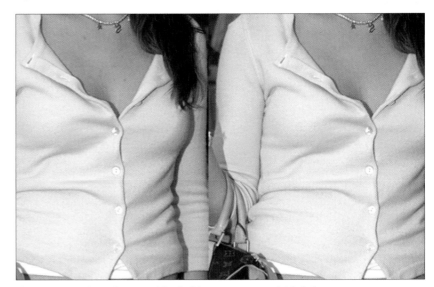

Figure 5.47 Blemishes on skin (left) were removed (right).

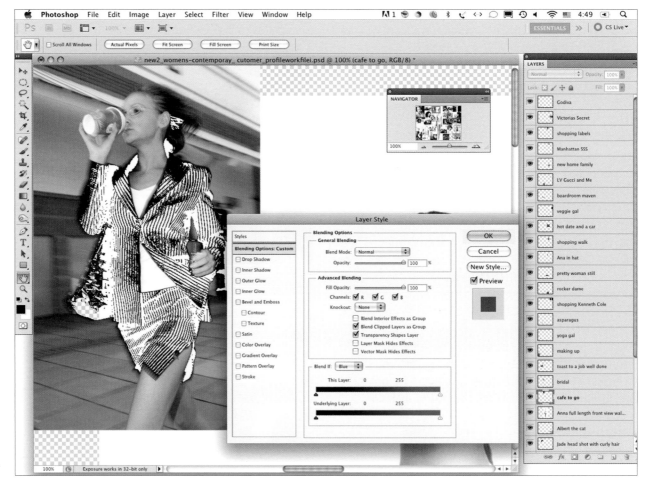

Figure 5.48 **Blending options can add an illustration effect to photography.**

Adding Layer Styles

Because each of the images is on a separate layer, effects and filters can be added to any of them, without affecting the others. **Layer Styles** contain various filter options that can add blending, shadows, glowing, beveling, embossing, color overlays, pattern overlays and more at the touch of the *fx* icon located at the bottom of the Layers panel. To access Layer Styles, double-click on the *fx* icon or on a layer but not on its title. Collectively, Layer Styles can improve the appearance of your work and add 3-D touches. The Layer Style dialog box (Figure 5.48) reveals the available Styles on the left. Selecting it and fine-tuning the settings can adjust each of these presets.

Multiple Layer Styles

You can add more than one Layer Style to an object by simply checking Styles on the left side of the dialog box, selecting the Layer Styles you desire, and adjusting the settings for each.

Readjusting Layer Styles

Layer Styles can be altered repeatedly. A layer containing an *fx* icon signals that Layer Styles are beneath it. Tip the pointer to select any of the Styles

appearing on separate sublayers. This will take you directly to the Layer Style dialog box where you can make alterations. You can also toggle off the visibility of a particular Layer Style and delete it if needed. The main reason to use Layer Styles in CS5 and earlier versions of Photoshop®, rather than creating permanent effects with the tools, filters, etc., is the flexibility it offers. Experiment with Photoshop® to discover what works best for you.

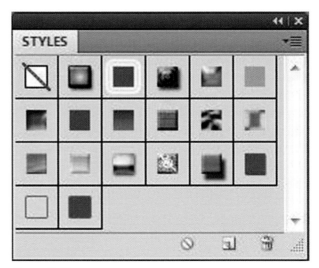

Figure 5.49

Figure 5.50 A coordinating orange hue was selected from another photo with a click of the Eyedropper Tool (I).

Styles Panel

You can also use the **Styles panel** to select a preset group of Layer Styles or to save your own (Figure 5.49). Going to *Menu Bar > Window > Styles* accesses the Styles panel. The default styles are shown when you open the Photoshop® Essentials Workspace, but more are available by clicking the hidden menu. To apply a Style preset, select the layer, then the Style. To remove a Style, select the Clear Style icon at the bottom of the panel. To add one or more styles that you have created, select the layer where the Layer Style appears, then click into an empty space on the Styles panel. Give the new preset an appropriate name and click OK.

Step 5: Use Blending Options

The **Blending Options** can be used to fade out the image on a layer as if it were disappearing. It has been used here to diminish the subject's apparel and hair (Figure 5.48). The transparent pixels—that are now showing through—will allow images added below them to be visible. The Elliptical Marquee Tool (M) was used to create and fill with color the oval that appears from behind the image of the woman with a cup of coffee in Figure 5.50. Follow these steps to fill a selection of Marching Ants with a color:

1. Go to *Menu Bar > Edit > Fill.*

2. Choose Color from the pull-down menu in the Fill dialog box. When the Color Picker appears, choose a color from the range in the Spectrum Bar on the left, and then click anywhere in the larger field to select an exact hue. You can also select a hue from something already in the file with the Eyedropper Tool (I) that automatically appears. Click OK once you have made your selection.

3. Click a color from the range in the Spectrum Bar on the left side of the Color Picker.

4. Click anywhere in the larger field to select an exact hue. You can also place another photo beneath it or fill the shape with a pattern.

Step 6: Create a Drop Shadow

To add another Layer Style to the same object on a layer, check the Style of choice. You can add an instant shadow to a shape with the **Drop Shadow** feature. Use the settings to adjust the attributes of the filter, including its color. To change it, click on the default black box on the right side of the blend mode. The Color Picker appears, allowing you to choose a different hue. Click OK when you are done to return to the Drop Shadow options. Experiment

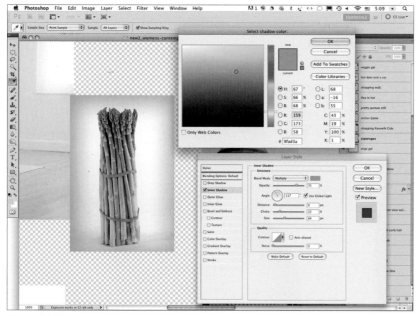

Figure 5.51

Figure 5.52

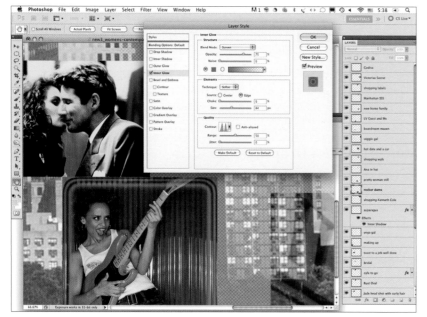

Figure 5.53

with the settings in order to become familiar with them. Use *Distance, Spread,* and *Size* to move, enlarge, and define the shape of the shadow. If you check the *Global Light* box, the styles will all take on similar light effects. To move the drop shadow manually, place the cursor over the image, then click and drag the shadow into place. In **Figure 5.50**, a blue drop shadow has been pulled to the lower right and adjusted to soften the edges. The presence of the drop shadow makes the shape of the picture appear to float above a surface.

Step 7: Create an Inner Shadow

The **Inner Shadow** Layer Style offers nearly everything that you can do with a drop shadow. In **Figure 5.51**, the automated Eyedropper Tool (I) was used to select the color of the asparagus via the Color Picker. The **Noise** scale added the graininess. To change the shape of the Inner Shadow, try different options in the **Contour** pull-down menu.

Step 8: Adjust the Opacity

To enhance your presentation, add a layer by clicking the new layer icon at the bottom of the Layers panel. Place an image that reveals an aspect of your customer profile, such as a cityscape or an interior, onto the new layer and rasterize it via the hidden menu option at the upper right of the panel. To scale the image so that it fills the entire background, press *Cmd+T / Ctrl+T* and pull in the corners while holding the Shift key. Reduce the *Opacity* of the photo in the Blending Options section of Layer Styles. Advanced blending can reduce the Opacity of certain colors and not others within the RGB color mode. For more options, try a different **Blend Mode**. In **Figure 5.52**, a photo of New York City was added to the tutorial example, and the Fill *Opacity* was reduced to 63%.

Step 9: Create Outer Glow and Inner Glow

To add a warm effect to your photos, use an Inner Glow or an **Outer Glow** as a type of vignette to frame the overall shape. In **Figure 5.53**, the Inner Glow Style dialog box option reveals adjustments to the *Color, Opacity, Contour,* and other settings that are reflected inside the photo at the bottom of the window. A basic example of an Outer Glow is shown at the top left.

Step 10: Use Bevel and Emboss

A very essential and widely used Layer Style, **Bevel and Emboss**, is used to create quick convex 3-D effects. Checking the Contour box below it will add softness to the curving transition. In the *Style* section, you can choose the type of bevel. The **Depth** setting adjusts how far the transition goes into the

Figure 5.54

image. Because Bevel and Emboss has both a **Highlight Mode** and a **Shadow Mode**, you can change the mode, color, and Opacity of each. Checking **Anti-aliased** will prevent the program from distorting any vector-based imagery that you imported. In Figure 5.54 the oval-shaped photo on the left has been enhanced by Bevel and Emboss. The Drop Shadow Layer Style can also be used by clicking on the style settings shown in the Layer Style dialog box on the right.

Step 11: Add Satin and Effects

The **Satin** Layer Style also adds a 3-D appearance to flat surfaces and makes them look as if they are softly contoured like the shiny textile weave of the same name. Settings allow you to adjust the color, Contour, and more (Figure 5.55).

Figure 5.55

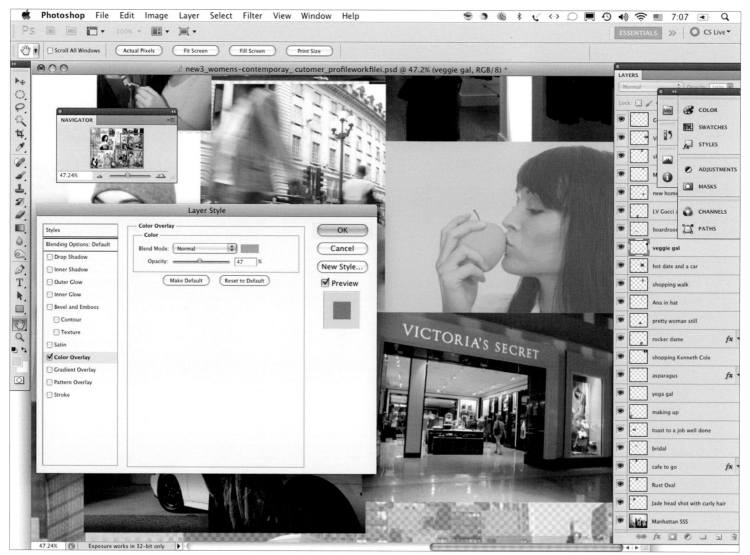

Figure 5.56 Clicking on the color sample allows you to change the Color Overlay via the Color Picker.

Figure 5.57

Step 12: Create a Color Overlay

Adding a **Color Overlay** Layer style is a quick and effective way to add a sophisticated touch and artistic contrast to a photo collage. The settings in the dialog box are few and self-explanatory. Just click on the color sample to change the hue with the Color Picker (Figure 5.56).

Step 13: Gradient Overlay and Stroke

A gradient can add a cool misty touch to a photo. The **Gradient Overlay** Layer Style filter combination allows you to overlay default gradients, and/or any gradients that you create and save, to the file. Reduce the Opacity accordingly to create the proper effect. The key is to treat each photo individually and to consider the entire composition. The white fade of Foreground to Transparent is an excellent choice for the photo on the left in Figure 5.57. It matches the car color and adds mood to the composition. Additional Layer Style options are also available, such as Stroke.

Figure 5.58 Photoshop® Pattern Overlay Layer Style.

Step 14: Apply a Pattern Overlay and Stroke

A **Pattern Overlay** is a great way to add texture to an image in Photoshop®. Patterns can communicate trend direction and transform awkward photocompositions. In Figure 5.58, a textile swatch was scanned and added via the pull-down menu of the Pattern option. The effect has taken the emphasis off the headless subject. You can also change the *Mode* as well as adjust the *Opacity* and the *Scale* of your chosen pattern. Patterns work well with strokes. To add the stroke, select the object and go to *Menu Bar > Edit > Stroke* for more options, such as width in pixels, color, etc. A drop shadow gives this image dominance in an area filled with visual information. To add color to the composition, a layer was added below the others and filled. The transparent areas above it filter the color, adding another great effect to various areas.

Step 15: View Your Work

To view your completed work in **Full Screen Mode**, go to *Menu Bar > View > Full Screen Mode*. An information dialog box concerning navigation appears. You can return to **Standard Screen Mode** by pressing *F* or *Esc*. The completed example tutorial is shown in Figure 5.59. A completed sample of a men's contemporary customer profile storyboard is shown in Figure 5.60.

TIP: Design Your Own

To practice making digital customer profile storyboards, create a trend from your imagination using your own photos. Skim through magazines, books, vintage photos, and Internet resources to find quality images that reflect both your creativity and a customer for the designer sportswear market. Scan the photos and assemble your page, using the format demonstrated previously.

Step 16: Saving Your Work in the Photoshop® Format

Save the customer profile storyboard file(s) that you created in the Photoshop® format if you want to retain your layer compositing.

Note: *Future tutorials will have you work with your storyboard files, so save them in a location that you'll have access to later.*

Figure 5.59 Illustration by Stacy Stewart Smith.

Figure 5.60 Illustration by Stacy Stewart Smith.

This tutorial teaches you how to digitize and enhance the overall look of your own freehand sketches. You will apply digital procedures to a scanned, multipart freehand illustration, then import and repair the files in Photoshop®. To help you complete this tutorial, a scanned freehand illustration has been provided on ① Ch05\Tutorial 5.2, or you can choose to use your own illustration on a white background.

The Photoshop® interface has several preset Workspaces: Essentials, Design, Painting, etc., but set up your own by showing the panels you will need, then save the Workspace by going to *Menu Bar > Window > Workspace > New Workspace*. When the *New Workspace* dialog box appears, name and save it. For this tutorial, you will only need the Layers panel, the Navigator panel, and the **History panel**, which allows you to go back a few steps for ease of reference.

Step 1: Import Freehand Drawings

Use Your Drawings

If you plan to use your own freehand sketches for this tutorial, you will need to import the image into Photoshop® with an input device. If you own a small flatbed scanner, you will need to scan larger images in separate pieces, then photo-retouch the breaks. If you do not own a scanner, or if you want to avoid the repair process, take a photo with a digital camera that has a resolution of 10 megapixels or higher.

Use the Provided DVD Sketch

If you prefer, follow the tutorial as exampled by locating the files Couture_Bride_A.pdf and Couture_Bride_B.pdf on ① Ch05\Tutorial 5.2. These files should be opened in Photoshop®. Figures 5.61 and 5.62 show the tutorial example images as they were in the preview window of a small-format scanner.

Step 2: Adjust the Canvas Size

In Photoshop®, the size of the work area may be too small for your various images. You will need to change the **Canvas Size** of the first image that you open into the program, and then place the others into the same file. The Canvas is a type of working space that defines the parameters of your page behind your images. It is literally your adjustable file dimensions.

To change the space to fit your multipart images, go to *Menu Bar > Image > Canvas Size*. In the dialog box, change the *Width* and *Height* to suit the size of your image. The image below this allows you to

Figure 5.61 Scanned half of a large illustration.

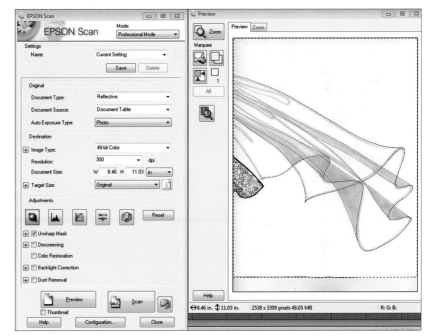

Figure 5.62 Keep the settings to scan multiple parts.

TIP: Taking Photographs

Lay your work flat on a surface, but avoid using a flash. Try lighting the area with regular incandescent lights or take the photos outside during the daytime.

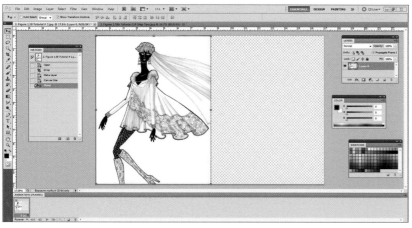

Figure 5.63

choose where you want to anchor the image in reference to the canvas. For now just leave it on the default center position. To complete the tutorial example, use the measurements in the Canvas Size dialog box shown in Figure 5.63. When you have completed this, click OK, and your file will look something like 5.64, revealing the gray-and-white checkered background that represents **transparent pixels**.

Step 3: Place Your Files in Photoshop®

Place your files one at a time into the canvas area by going to *Menu Bar > File > Place* as shown in Figure 5.65. You can accept the files in this program by clicking on the images that will appear with a cross formation.

Use the **Move Tool (V)** to position the files by clicking and dragging them. Each file appears on its own layer, bearing the names of the files that you have already placed. Check this by going to *Menu Bar > Window > Layers*, or simply show them by clicking on the layer icon if it appears in your vertical panel dock. The fashion illustrations should match almost seamlessly, as shown in Figure 5.66.

Step 4: Flatten Your Work

Before you begin to repair the rest of your digital illustration, you need to use the Flatten Artwork option of the Layers panel. Scroll to this option in the hidden menu at the right side of the layer. The flattened layer will be renamed Background.

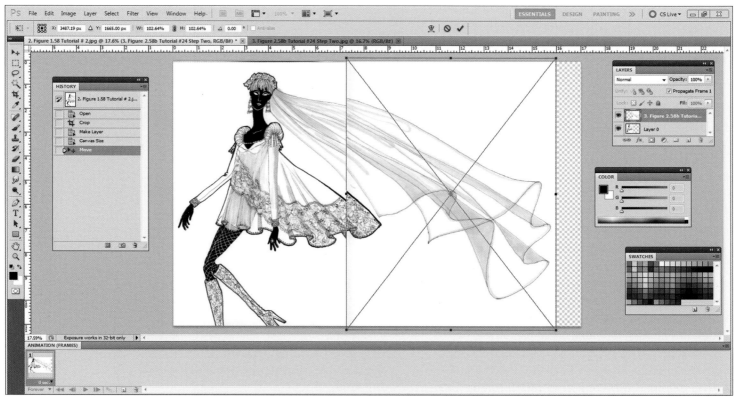

Figure 5.64

Figure 5.65

Figure 5.66

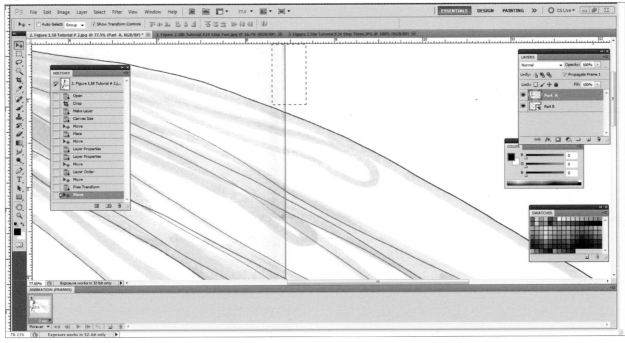

Figure 5.67

Step 5: Delete the Stains in Photoshop®

Use the Eyedropper Tool (I) to sample the exact color of the background with a click. The color will appear in the Tool panel's **Foreground Box** at the bottom of the panel. Afterward, select the **Rectangular Marquee Tool (M)** from the Tools panel. Use it to marquee around those areas of the background on the top layer where a shadow has stained the edges of the paper (Figure 5.66). Your selected area will be surrounded by the flashing "marching-ant" indicators (Figure 5.67). Press Delete and a Fill options dialog box appears (Figure 5.68). Fill the space with Foreground Color (or white if using the tutorial file) from the *Use* pull-down menu and click OK. The

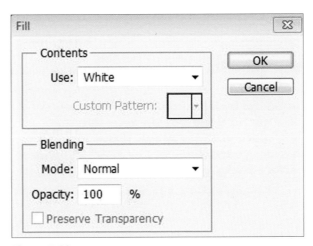

Figure 5.68

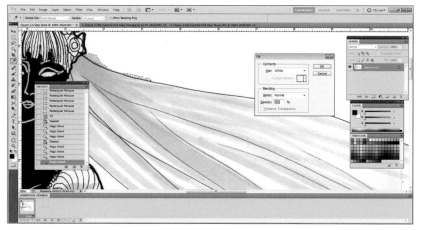

Figure 5.69

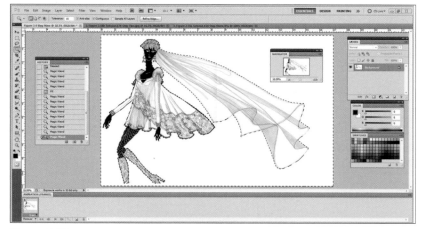

Figure 5.70

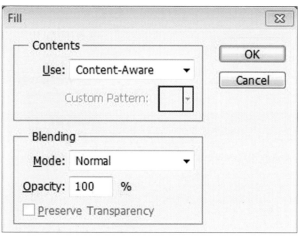

Figure 5.71

TIP: **Add and Subtract from Selections**

You can add to a selection by holding the Shift key when clicking on another area. Hold the *Option key / Alt key* while clicking on the space with the Magic Wand Tool (W) to subtract an area from your selection. **Figure 5.70** shows a selection of the entire background.

stain will be covered with the color that you sampled with the Eyedropper Tool (I). Repeat this action in various places to clean up the illustration.

TIP: **Changing the Background Layer**

Photoshop® will not allow you to delete the Background layer. To make any permanent changes to this layer, including repositioning it above other layers, you will need to rename the layer. Simply double-click on the layer, then click OK in the New Layer dialog box.

Step 6: Use the Photoshop® Magic Wand Tool to Select and Delete Areas

The Photoshop® **Magic Wand Tool (W)** selects pixels by color similarity. When you select the Magic Wand Tool (W), options appear in the Options Bar. The **Tolerance** option tells Photoshop® how much variation in a color you want to allow in your selection. A low-level Tolerance will select fewer ranges of a hue. In the example, the Tolerance has been reduced to 10. Click on areas with the Magic Wand (W) like those shown in **Figure 5.69**. Investigate the selection before you fill it, because some areas of the illustration may have been included. **Deselect** by pressing *Cmd+D / Ctrl+D*, then reduce the Tolerance of the Photoshop® Magic Wand Tool (W) before reselecting the background. Next, press Delete and fill the Contents with the appropriate color.

Repeat this step at random where needed around your artwork to slowly restore the correct color of your background. When you have removed most of the imperfections, slightly increase the Tolerance and use the Magic Wand (W) to select the entire background.

Step 7: Use the Photoshop® Content-Aware Feature to Restore Deleted Portions of the Image

Some areas of your illustration may have been selected and filled along with the background when you used the Magic Wand (W) tool. If you are using version CS5 and higher, the feature **Content-Aware** can approximate the old fill based on a selected adjacent area. To use this feature, select the affected area with any selection tool.

Note: *You must also select some of the surrounding area of the illustration and the background, too. Then press Delete.*

Scroll the *Contents Use* menu to *Content-Aware* (Figure 5.71). Photoshop® will do the rest. Figure 5.72 shows a deleted area that has been selected and is about to be filled using Content-Aware. The full restoration was completed in Figure 5.73. Content-Aware can also be used to restore the color of areas as in the example of Figure 5.74. The completed tutorial example is shown in Figure 5.75.

Note: *The effectiveness of the Photoshop® Content-Aware feature depends upon the surrounding imagery. Often, multiple smaller selections rather than larger ones generate better results.*

Figure 5.72 **Before Content-Aware**   Figure 5.73 **After Content-Aware**

Figure 5.74

Figure 5.75 Illustration by Stacy Stewart Smith.

Digital software can be used to create fashion presentations without any hand-rendered drawings. However, do not throw away your pencils and markers just yet; there will always be an interest in the human touch. Although fashion design sketches are usually composed of quick and stylized signature lines in pen on paper, most do bear the distinct signature of the designer. Many consider these sketches to be collector's items. As a result, apparel and accessory manufacturers and retailers periodically use fashion illustration to market products.

Fashion illustration in advertising took a hiatus after the 1990s when the supermodel era was in full force and photography became the standard. However, recently top fashion magazines, both printed and online, have shown a renewed interest. Even animation is enjoying a boom.

Most fashion colleges support digital correction as a part of their art and design curriculum. This will become even more important as designer sketches and fashion illustrations again take their rightful places in online advertising. With a global fashion market hungry for new ideas, now is a great time to show off both freehand and digital skill sets. Without a doubt, the combination packs a powerful punch and presents a fresh aesthetic when you are interviewing for potential employment or internship opportunities.

Fashion designers possessing strong drawing talent often do not give much attention to small details in their sketches. This is chiefly caused by the size of standard fashion figures; details are usually too small to see with the naked eye. For example, the freehand drawing of the croquis that was used in Tutorial 5.2 has a face that is approximately 1 inch square. From a distance, the lines that compose the image look fine, but under the scrutiny of digital image-editing software, when placed on a monitor, some undesirable imperfections and a few drawing problems are evident (Figure 5.76).

In this tutorial, Illustrator® and Photoshop® procedures will be applied to the same freehand illustration to improve its overall surface and beauty. This process will give your drawings a slightly 3-D look. In order to complete this tutorial, you need to begin with the same Photoshop® file that you completed in Tutorial 5.2. For your convenience, the file Completed_Couture_Bride.pdf is available on ① Ch05\ Tutorial 5.3. This high-fashion illustration from Tutorial 5.2 (or one similar) will enhance your learning capacity because it has been rendered in grayscale but scanned in color. It has many details. You will begin this tutorial by using Photoshop®, and then open your file in Illustrator®. Later, you will export the file back to Photoshop® to add filters and toning adjustments.

Figure 5.76

Step 1: Content-Fill in Photoshop®

In Tutorial 5.2, you learned how to select areas with the Photoshop® Magic Wand Tool (W) and how to fill these areas with color, or to use the Content-Aware function of Photoshop®. Continue this process to fill the body area of the scanned illustration with black.

Step 2: Use the Smudge Tool to Contour

The Photoshop® **Smudge Tool** (Figure 5.77) is located in position 13 of the Photoshop® Tools panel (Figure 5.78). It blends colors the way fine art painters might do by using their fingers. The tool's icon looks like a hand with the index finger extended as if smudging a surface. When you select this tool, the Options Bar offers you a selection of brushes from which to choose. Click on the pointer next to the brush icon, and a pop-out menu reveals a chart where you may choose a suitable brush. You may also show the **Brush Presets panel** by going to *Menu Bar > Window > Brush Presets* (Figure 5.79). The **Diameter and Hardness** of each brush can be adjusted within this panel. The first brush in the panel, called a *Soft Round,* is perfect for now.

Note: You can also access the Brush Presets panel by a holding the Command key (Mac) and clicking, or right-clicking (PC).

In the Photoshop® Options Bar, the Smudge Tool's *Mode* should be *Normal* and the *Strength* about 40%. Adjust the brush to an appropriate size. Use the Smudge Tool to blend any harsh lines or areas that appear unpainted. Figure 5.80 shows the results of using the Smudge Tool to resurface and contour shapes and lines in the face of the example.

Step 3: Use the Photoshop® Blur Tool

Many freehand drawings, particularly life drawings, are created with blurry effects made by smudging and toning. One digital solution in Photoshop® is the **Blur Tool** (Figure 5.81). Add a few soft highlights with the Photoshop® Brush Tool (B) by selecting a grayscale swatch color from the Swatches panel. Resurface the drawing in matching hues by alternating brushes and lowering *Opacity* and the *Flow* in the Options Bar. After this, use the Blur Tool to blend the tool effects and soften the lines (Figure 5.82). Work on the entire

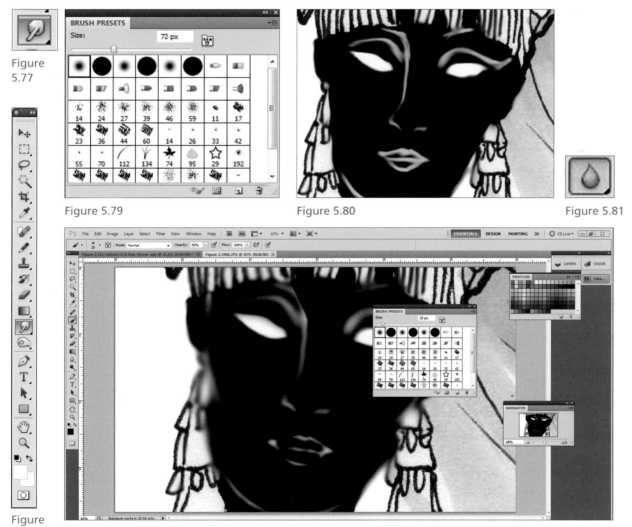

Figure 5.77

Figure 5.79

Figure 5.80

Figure 5.81

Figure 5.78

Figure 5.82

Figure 5.83

figure using various tools to create the realistic look of photography. If you have taken drawing classes, it will not be difficult for you to imagine where things should go. If not, use a photo reference from ① Digital Duo Modeling Agency. Figure 5.83 shows greater digital development and drawing correction.

Step 4: Use the Photoshop® Liquify Filter

Go to *Menu Bar > Filter > Liquify* or press *Shift+Cmd+X / Shift+Ctrl+X*. The image appears in a window like the one in Figure 5.84. The **Liquify filter** allows you to move selected portions of your image around as if they were being transformed by water, or in this case, by a breeze or wind. This is a great filter for transparencies or anything that needs careful warping, especially patterns and floating fabric. The Liquify filter also works wonders for flowing hair that is on a separate layer. The veil needs a little work because it looks too stiff, so give it some motion in the "digital water."

Figure 5.84 **Before Liquify filter.**

The Liquify filter options window is comprehensive and contains a Tools panel on the left and the Effects options on the right. All the functions are far too complex to explain at this level, so we will keep it simple. You can always experiment on your own. Select the **Forward Warp (W)** Tool.

Note: *The Liquify Tools panel keyboard shortcuts are applicable only while the window is open.*

Next, select a large brush, and use it in gradual steps to pull out portions of the flowing parts of the veil or whatever you are working on at this stage. When you are done, click OK. The completed Liquify filter effect on the veil is shown in Figure 5.85.

The History Panel

To compare the before-and-after results, show the **History panel** by going to *Menu Bar > Window > History*. The bottom step will be highlighted. Select the steps above this to temporarily go back in your digital development of the illustration up to the opening file view that you see at the top of the panel. When you're done, select the step at the bottom to return to your current stage.

The History panel, by default, has a cache of 20 steps. To change the amount for a particular project, you must change the preferences. To increase the amount of steps that you can Undo, go to *Menu Bar > Photoshop > Preferences > Performance > History & Cache (Mac)* or *Menu Bar > Edit > Preferences > Performance > History & Cache (PC)*. Look for the History States area, and then change the amount of steps by entering a number.

TIP: History Panel

If you are using a PC mouse, simply right-click on the History panel to access the Interface options. If you are using a trackpad, hold two fingers on the pad and click for the Interface Options.

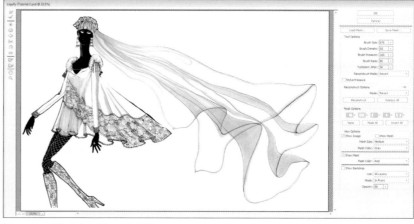

Figure 5.85 After Liquify filter.

Step 5: Save Your Work in Photoshop®

Save and back up your file on an external storage device. Save the file in the Photoshop® JPEG (.jpg) format. Give the file an appropriate name or keep it the same, but add your initials to the title.

Step 6: Open the File in Illustrator®

Load Illustrator® and open the file that you saved in Step Five. You will need to adjust the Artboard via the **Artboard Tool** (Shift+O). When you see the document size boundaries, pull them to crop the page (Figure 5.86).

Figure 5.86

Step 7: Create Layers

Label Layer 1 *Gothic Couture*, and then create another layer and label it *Detail Work*. Lock the *Gothic Couture* layer and select the *Detail Work* layer.

Step 8: Convert Symbols to Line Art in Illustrator®

The Illustrator® Symbols Libraries are filled with artwork that you can use without the Symbol Sprayer Tools (Shift+S). Take a moment to look through the various Symbols and choose one or more to add to your drawing. Because the tutorial example has a crown of roses, the Flowers Symbol Library is ideal.

Select one of the Symbols and drag it onto your Artboard. With it still selected go to *Menu Bar > Object > Flatten Transparency*. A dialog box with many options appears. The default settings are fine. Make sure you have checked both *Convert All Strokes to Outlines* and *Clip Complex Regions*. These settings ensure that the raster art you are converting to vector art maintains the shape pictured and that it will create editable paths. Figure 5.87 shows the Flatten Transparency dialog box with the appropriate settings for this tutorial along with scaled artwork pulled from the Flowers Symbol Library. To make the changes to the Transparency, click OK. You will then be able to select, fill, and stroke the drawing in Illustrator® (Figure 5.88).

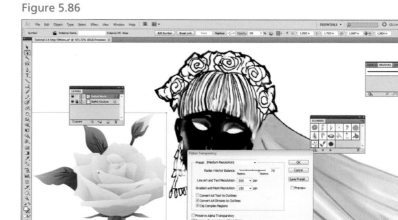

Figure 5.87

Figure 5.88

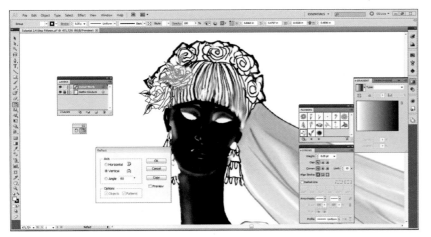
Figure 5.89

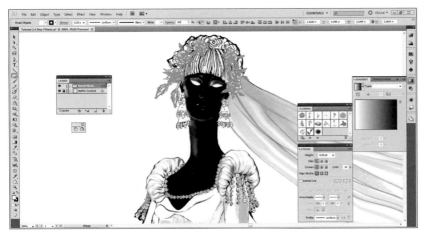
Figure 5.90

Figure 5.91   Figure 5.92

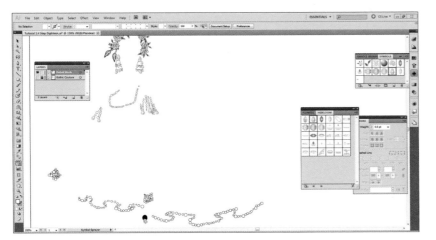
Figure 5.93

Step 9: Add More Symbols as Details

Continue to use other Symbols as instructed in Step Eight. Repetition is sometimes a good thing. Vary the scale, and reflect and rotate objects to keep them looking natural (Figure 5.89). Do not attempt to cover the entire drawing with Symbols; just add touches that will bring out the intended beauty of the work and allow much of the drawing to show through. Figure 5.90 shows the beginnings of "Digital Duo" development.

Step 10: Make Adjustments with the Pen Tool (P)

Some of the lines may be too soft. To rectify this, use the Illustrator® Pen Tool (P). Shown here are further adjustments to the mouth in Figure 5.91, and to the lashes in Figure 5.92.

Step 11: Add Details with the Illustrator® Shape Tools

The high-fashion Goth-inspired trapeze dress in this illustration has pearls, beads, jewels, and lace details. Some of the sketch quality should be retained, but other details, like the pearls, need enhancements. The Ellipse Tool (L) was used to create the finishing touches (Figure 5.91).

Step 12: Complete the Details

Use as many vector tools as you would like, but they should complement your drawing. Shown in Figure 5.93 are the completed vector additions on the *Detail Work* layer.

Step 13: Add Filter(s) to Complete Your Work

Depending on your illustration and end use, you may want to add a few additional filters from the Photoshop® Effects gallery to your work in Illustrator®. Go to *Menu Bar > Effect > Artistic > Paint Daubs*. In Figure 5.94, the **Paint Daubs** filter enhances the painterly details already on the illustration.

Note: The Photoshop® Effects Gallery bridges the gap between vector and raster digital art by providing filters that would typically apply only to raster interfaces. Many of the filters are available in both programs.

Step 14: Save Your Work in Illustrator®

Save and back up a copy of your Illustrator® file. Use the Illustrator® (.ai) format.

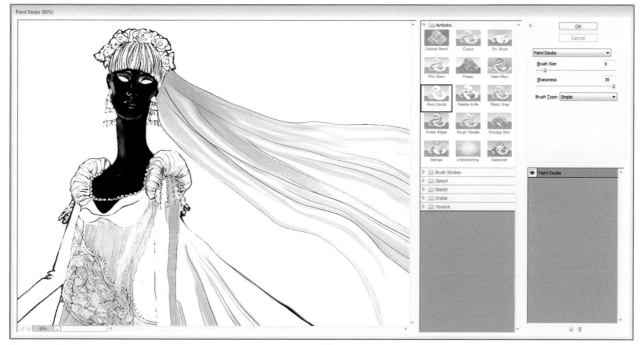

Figure 5.94

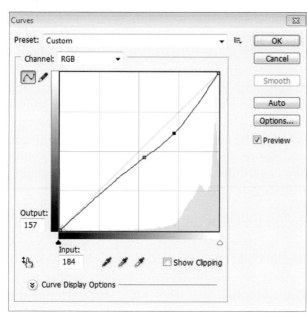

Figure 5.95

Step 15: Export Your File to Photoshop®

We are not yet finished using "Digital Duo" procedures. A simple way to retain your layer compositing without closing the program or saving it to another format like Acrobat Pro® is to export the file. In the Illustrator® window, go to *Menu Bar > File > Export*. When the *Export* dialog box appears, choose *Photoshop® (.psd)* in the Format menu, and then click Save. Save the new Photoshop® file—containing the layer compositing that you created in Illustrator®—in the same location of the copy you saved in Step Fourteen.

Step 16: Open and Inspect the Exported (.psd) File

Double-click on the exported Photoshop® file to open it. The objective of exporting the file and maintaining the layers is to keep the vector art drawings separate from the original drawing, so that you can create effects for each separately. By selecting the layer where the drawing is, you can add raster effects, but preserve the look of certain vector details.

Step 17: Restore Toning with Curves

If you lost a little contrast in tone on either layer, restore it with the **Curves** controls by going to *Menu Bar > Image > Adjustments > Curves*. They can also be shown by pressing *Cmd+M / Ctrl+M*. The Curves option enables you to make slight to dramatic adjustments of the overall luminosity and the tone of an image. It does this by moving the straight diagonal line in positions above and below its starting point. Through Curves, you can bring light or shadow into a specific area of your work instead of affecting the whole. Adjust the line only slightly, then glance at the preview. If it is not what you intended, click *Auto* to restore the default setting. Try again, and anchor the curve line in a few places, then push the adjustment line up or down carefully until you have what you want. If you like the changes, click OK to accept them (Figure 5.95).

Step 18: Add a Lens Flare

To add a very worldly and photographic effect to the animated look of your work, try a **Lens Flare** filter, which will also give the work greater warmth and

Figure 5.96

Figure 5.97

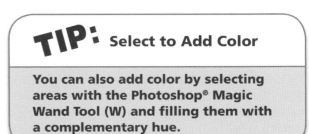

Figure 5.98

dimension. Go to *Menu Bar > Filter > Render > Lens Flare* and choose an option from the dialog box shown in Figure 5.96. The completed full view with the Lens Flare added is shown in Figure 5.97.

Step 19: Use the Hue/Saturation Control

If the result of the Lens Flare adds too much color to your work, you can diminish the saturation of specific colors with the **Hue/Saturation** control by going to *Menu Bar > Image > Adjustments > Hue/Saturation*. Choose the color that you want to adjust and move the sliders. In the case of the tutorial example, the Saturation level of the *reds* will be adjusted with the controls shown in Figure 5.98.

Step 20: Use the Photoshop® Levels Feature

The Lens Flare added good elements, but along with it came a dusty haze that took away some of the illustration's luster. The Photoshop® **Levels** feature can help to bring it back to life. Go to *Menu Bar > Image > Adjustments > Levels* or press *Cmd+L / Ctrl+L*. There is a **histogram** in the Levels option dialog box (Figure 5.99). It shows where your image is positioned related to highlights (shown in white). If all the dark spaces in the histogram are closer to one side as shown, it means that there may be too much light in the image. The histogram allows you to adjust the input levels of shadows by moving the black slider. You can also pull the gray slider, which represents the midtones, and the white slider (highlights) toward each other to make slight to dramatic changes to the distribution of light in your work. Figures 5.100 and 5.101 show examples of adjustments made by using Levels.

Step 21: Finish

Use the Navigator panel's Proxy Preview Area to examine your completed tutorial file for any imperfections and delete them with the available tools. The completed example shows dramatic changes and improvements made to a fashion illustration for haute couture. This is the result of using a combination of freehand fashion illustration, object-oriented digital software, and image-editing digital software (Figure 5.102).

TIP: Select to Add Color

You can also add color by selecting areas with the Photoshop® Magic Wand Tool (W) and filling them with a complementary hue.

Figure 5.99

Figure 5.100

Figure 5.101

Figure 5.102 Illustration by Stacy Stewart Smith.

Chapter 5 Summary

If you completed all the tutorials in this chapter and have studied the Photoshop® tools, panels, filters, layers, and functions, then you are ready to proceed to Chapter 6. Below are a few questions that you should ask yourself before moving on.

Chapter 5 Self-Assessment

1. Can I locate, identify, and explain the function of the tools in Photoshop® CS5 Tools panel?

2. Can I locate, identify, and explain the function of the Photoshop® CS5 panels, such as the Brush panel, Channels panel, Color panel, History panel, Transform panel, Paths panel, and Layers panel?

3. Do I understand the function of Layer Styles, and am I able to use them appropriately.

4. What are Blending Options? How can they be used to enhance my work on various layers?

5. Which Photoshop® tools are considered painting tools?

6. What are pixels, and how do they assist image-editing?

7. How can I increase the amount of Undo steps in Photoshop®?

8. Can I name the selection tools and describe their functions?

9. Do I know what the Free Transform shortcut sequence is?

10. How is complete transparency indicated visually in Photoshop®?

11. Do I know what I must do when opening a new document in Photoshop®, if I want to print it out at a high quality?

12. Can I describe the differences between the Photoshop® Pen Tool (P) and the one in Illustrator®?

13. Do I know what a work path is?

14. Which Photoshop® file format do I select if I want to send a picture via e-mail?

15. If I want to retain my layers, which file format should I select when saving my work?

16. Do I know how to scan and reposition large files by importing them into Photoshop®, and can I repair the file(s) seamlessly using Content-Aware, Blur Tool, and other features of the program?

17. Can I use the Photoshop® Magic Wand (W) to select areas by color?

18. Can I make effective use of the Photoshop® Liquify filter to improve my freehand drawings?

19. Can I make use of the Photoshop® Lens Flare filter?

20. Do I know how to adjust the histogram in the Levels settings?

Tracing Figurative Fashion Art and Photography

Objectives

Chapter 6 explores the attributes of Illustrator® Live Trace and the Live Paint Bucket Tool (K) through various multifaceted presentation exercises. To help you create compelling digital fashion art and merchandising resources, the tutorials are image-based and make use of fashion photography, freehand drawings, and/or computer-generated renderings. You will learn to use Live Trace with a combination of filters to mimic freehand drawing effects. You will also develop sensitivity to drawing male and female digital croquis within virtual environments. The tutorials are suitable for the functions of CS6 Image Trace.

This chapter is multifaceted, so you will use both Illustrator® and Photoshop® and learn to:

◉ Treat the figure as an object with weight and volume

◉ Develop an understanding of digital contrapposto

◉ Exercise critical thinking concerning figure proportion and perspective

◉ Use a textile scan to fill objects

◉ Analyze the composition of the digital fashion face and hair through color separation techniques via Illustrator® Live Trace

◉ Compose digital figurative compositions in two-point perspective

◉ Use the figure as a pictorial image on apparel intarsia sweater design and on screen prints

Tutorial 6.1 combines fashion design, fashion merchandising, photography, and fine art with the **Live Trace** attributes of Illustrator®. Live Trace allows you to convert rasterized images into vector selections.

Note: In CS6 Live Trace is called Image Trace.

In this exercise, you will:

- Make use of both Illustrator® and Photoshop®.
- Use Live Trace and Live Paint.
- Design your own denim sportswear items.
- Scan textiles to define them as patterns.
- Create a presentation for any apparel market.

Note: This is a "Digital Duo"-based tutorial, so the files will be exported from Illustrator® to Photoshop® for further enhancements.

Figure 6.1 *Grace*, 2008, oil on canvas by Stacy Stewart Smith.

To help you complete this tutorial, images have been provided on ① Ch06\Tutorial 6.1. Figure 6.1 exhibits an image of the oil painting *Grace*, 2008, by Stacy Stewart Smith, which is the primary file for this tutorial. The composition shows a skewed image of a man walking across a portion of the Eiffel Tower in his underclothes holding a balancing rod. The composition, proportion, and angle of the painting make it a great candidate for a fashion advertisement poster.

TIP: Make It Your Own

Once you have completed the tutorial using the provided files, you are encouraged to re-create the presentation using your own illustrations, photographs, and/or images from the ① Digital Duo Modeling Agency.

Step 1: Open a New Document in Photoshop®

Load Photoshop®, then open the file Grace.jpg on ① Ch06\Tutorial 6.1. Save and back up the file. At this point, you may choose keep the walking man as depicted in the original artwork or replace him with another figure. Steps Two through Six explain how to incorporate a new image into the artwork. If you decide to keep the walking man in place, skip to Step Seven.

Step 2: Use the Photoshop® Lasso Tool to Select the Figure

Note: The Photoshop® Content-Aware feature is required in order to replace the walking man with another figure in the original artwork. Users of CS4 and lower should use the alternate file Grace_Sans_Crosswalker.jpg if they wish to use their own figure in this tutorial.

1. To substitute the walking man image, select it with the Photoshop® Lasso Tool (L) shown in Figure 6.2. The Lasso Tool (L) makes freehand selections that will yield marching ants like those shown around the image of the walking man in Figure 6.3.

2. Click and hold your mouse until you have created a selection in one movement around the figure. If you find it too difficult to do this in one movement, select one area at a time.

Figure 6.2

3. To add to the selection, hold the Shift key and then select another adjacent area around the figure. Continue this procedure until you have selected the entire image.

4. Selected areas should be close to the figure, but not precisely at the edge. If you lose your selection, press *Cmd+Z / Ctrl+Z* to undo a move.

TIP: Photoshop® Undo

In Photoshop®, pressing Undo again will only toggle back to the former stage of production. If you need to undo more than one move in Photoshop®, press *Option+Cmd+Z / Alt+Ctrl+Z.*

Figure 6.3

Figure 6.4

Step 3: Use the Photoshop® Content-Aware Feature

Delete the selected area by going to *Menu Bar > Edit > Clear* or press Delete. Selected areas filled with the Photoshop® Content-Aware feature will replace the selection with a composite of what is outside it. With the marching ants flashing, follow these steps:

1. Go to *Menu Bar > Edit > Fill*.

2. In the Fill dialog box, choose Content-Aware and then click OK to allow Photoshop® to fill in the background.

3. Deselect by pressing *Cmd+D / Ctrl+D*.

4. Select the Photoshop® Zoom Tool (Z), marquee over an area where the selection was, and check the filled selection. If you are not satisfied with the results of Content-Aware, try reselecting the figure more precisely, especially around the foot areas.

5. A fracture could have occurred, creating a ghost silhouette. If so, one way to rectify the problem is to use the **Content-Aware Scale** to increase the size of the selection and cover the imperfection. To do this, simply follow these steps:

- Reselect your marching ants by using the Undo shortcut.

- While they are flashing, go to *Menu Bar > Edit > Content-Aware Scale*. A Bounding Box will appear around the selection.

- Hold the Shift key to constrain the proportions, then slightly increase the size of the shape. This will cover the fracture. The results of Content-Aware are shown in Figure 6.4. This image is now the background.

Step 4: Use the Photoshop® Magic Wand Tool to Select a Figure

Open any three-quarter walking photo from the ① Digital Duo Modeling Agency. Figure 6.5 is an ideal photo of Ana because although she appears to be walking, she's actually in a pose, which demonstrates perfect **contrapposto** (Italian for counterpose). The weight of her body in this standing pose is all on one leg, and the action of her shoulders and waist are at angles opposite to those of the hips and legs. This makes the composition more convincing and relaxed. Poses in contrapposto will prevent the development of a **digital floating figure**, which is a common mistake. Digital floating figures occur when freehand figurative drawings or photos are digitized and placed in front of a background photo, painting, illustration, etc. Because images scanned into computers are brought into a virtual environment—unlike flat paper—if the poses are not in contrapposto, they will appear as flat floating puppets. If you decide to use your own image(s), choose or create those that have similar composition. In addition, the steps will be easier to follow if the photo or illustration has a single color background.

In Tutorial 5.2 Step Six, you learned to select areas by color, using the Photoshop® Magic Wand Tool (W). Follow these steps in order to proceed with this tutorial:

1. Select the Photoshop® Magic Wand Tool (W) from the Tools panel.

2. Reduce the *Tolerance* in the Control Panel to 6.

3. Select the background of your image.

4. If the selection overruns into the figure as it does in Figure 6.6, select the Lasso Tool (L).

Figure 6.5

5. Use the Lasso Tool (L) to select the marching ants that have overrun into the figure's image by encapsulating them while holding the Shift key and clicking. Draw from the inside up to the edge to add the overrun marching ants to the selection. When you release the clicker, the selection should be clean to the figure's edge, but will include all of the background around the figure and any negative spaces (Figure 6.7).

6. To select the figure instead of the background, press *Shift+Cmd+I / Shift+Ctrl+I* to **Inverse** the selection. The inversed selection of Ana's walking pose is shown in Figure 6.8.

7. Leave the marching ants running; do not deselect.

Step 5: Use the Photoshop® Move Tool to Drag-and-Drop the Figure

The term **drag-and-drop** is used to describe the entire procedure of grabbing a selected image and moving it to another file. Now that you have successfully removed the figure from the original artwork and have prepared a new figure to replace it, drag-and-drop the selected image into the background file (without the walking man from Step Three), using these steps:

1. Place the file of your figure (with the marching ants flashing the selection) next to the file of the background. Both files should be side by side.

2. Select the Photoshop® Move Tool (V), shown in Figure 6.9. Use it to click on the selected figure.

3. Hold the clicker while dragging-and-dropping the figure into the background file.

Note: You may see a Paste Profile Mismatch dialog box (Figure 6.10), if the color profile of the file does not match the file in which you are placing it. This is a warning that tells you that Photoshop® will convert the profile to match the destination file.

The completed procedure should now reveal a copy of the figure without the outline placed in the background file (Figure 6.11).

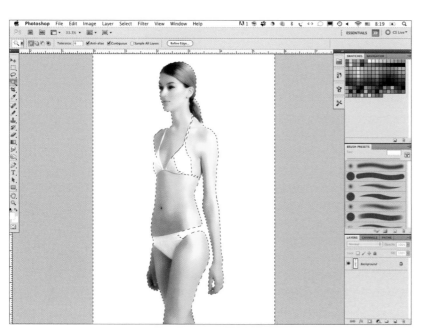

Figure 6.6

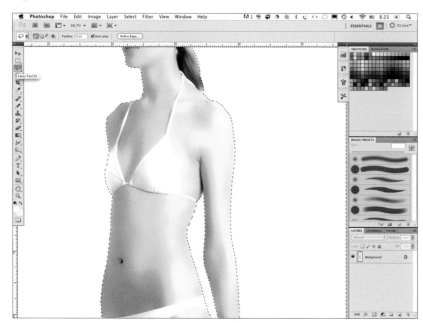

Figure 6.7

Figure 6.8

Step 6: Use the Photoshop® Free Transform Option to Scale the Figure

1. A layer for the figure was created when it was dragged-and-dropped into the background file.

2. Select this layer and press *Cmd+T / Ctrl+T* to scale the figure with the Photoshop® **Free Transform** option.

Figure 6.9

Figure 6.10

3. A Bounding Box appears around the figure. Pull in the Bounding Box while holding the Shift key to constrain the proportions (Figure 6.12).

4. Save your file(s) in the Photoshop® format. Also, save a copy in the .jpeg format, and back up your file(s).

Altering Images with Photoshop® Transform Options

More image-altering options are in the **Photoshop® Transform** menu. To explore the functions of **Perspective**, **Rotate**, **Transform**, **Flip**, **Distort**, **Skew**, and others, go to *Menu Bar > Edit > Transform*, and then scroll to the option(s). Each will yield a Bounding Box or grid that you can adjust to alter a selection or everything on a selected layer. Combined Transform options can help you to alter the pose of your figure and create more believable contrapposto.

Note: *This tutorial will continue in Illustrator®.*

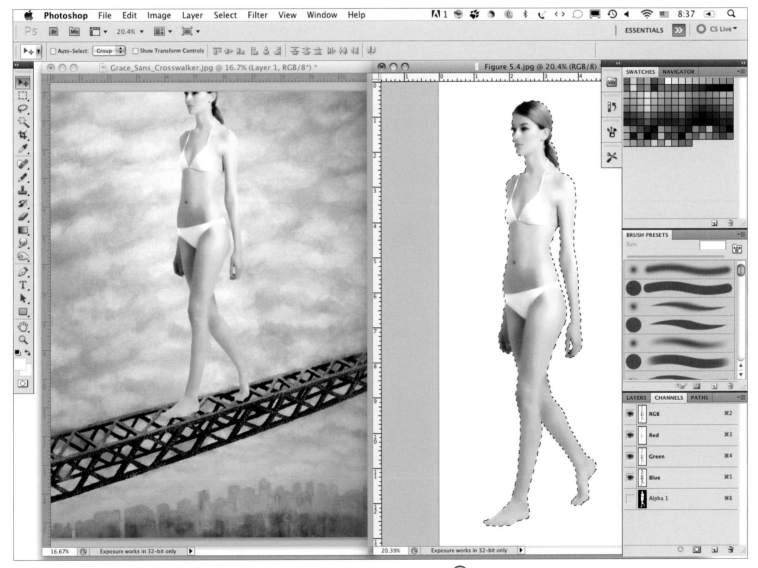

Figure 6.11 If you are using Illustrator®, only open the file Grace_with_Ana.jpg on ① instead of dragging and dropping the Photoshop® file as shown above.

Figure 6.12

Step 7: Create a New Document in Illustrator®

1. Whether you are using the original artwork or an alternate image, create a new document in Illustrator®.

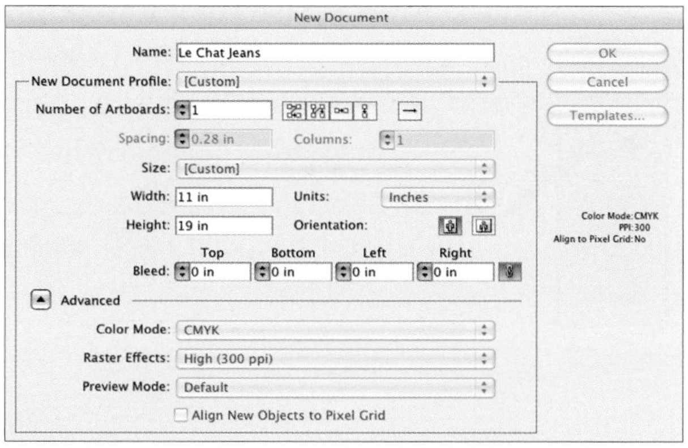

Figure 6.13

2. The Artboard size for this tutorial is 11×19 inches based on the files available on ①. These dimensions are ideal for a small poster. Figure 6.13 shows the Illustrator® New Document dialog box and all the required data.

3. When you have entered the information as shown, click OK, then save the file on your computer.

Step 8: Place the Required Files in Illustrator®

You will need at least two Photoshop® files to continue working on this tutorial in Illustrator®. These files are located on ① Ch06\Tutorial 6.1. The first file is the original image of the painting entitled Grace.jpg, with the man walking holding a balancing pole. You may also use the file with an alternate

Figure 6.14 Aerial view of the Seine from the Eiffel Tower. Photograph by Stacy Stewart Smith.

figure that you prepared with instructions from Steps Two through Step Six instead of this file. The second file, Rive_Gauche.jpg, is an aerial view from the Eiffel Tower showing the Seine River (Figure 6.14). Once you have placed the files of your choice on separate layers, Embed them. Figure 6.15 displays the layer compositing and the files before embedding.

Step 9: Position the Files in Illustrator®

Align the files as shown in Figure 6.16. Figure 6.17 shows the development of the tutorial with the image of Ana walking. Select the Rive_Gauche.jpg

photo and scale the Bounding Box to fit the space at the bottom of the Artboard beneath the background image. Pull the photo toward its center, then adjust the top and the bottom to fit the remaining space. This will give the landscape image more convincing visual perspective in comparison to the painted background, as exhibited in Figure 6.18.

Step 10: Select and Live Trace the Photo in Illustrator®

Live Tracing converts raster images to vector outlines, making them editable.

Figure 6.15

Figure 6.16

Figure 6.17

Figure 6.18

Figure 6.19

1. Select the Rive_Gauche.jpg photo and Live Trace it as Color 6 located in the center of the Control Panel.
2. Use the adjacent pull-down **Tracing and Presets menu** to locate the Color 6 option. It transforms your images into just six different colors (Figure 6.19). *Tracing Options* are also available in this menu. Use them to alter a preset or save specific settings.

Note: *Some images take longer than others to Live Trace. If you see a dialog box indicating that the tracing will proceed slowly, just click OK. Watch* CS6_ Image_Trace.m4v *on* ① Ch06\Tutorial 6.1.

Step 11: Change the Color Sections into Vector Outlines

Click the **Expand** button in the Control Panel to change the color sections into vector outlines in Illustrator®. This gives each outline more definition. The selected outlines are shown in Figure 6.20.

Step 12: Check the Individual Live Trace Expanded Selections

Go to the *Smart Guides Preferences* menu. In the Smart Guides dialog box, check all the *Display Options*. Then toggle on your Smart Guides to highlight all the individual selections created by Live Trace as Color 6.

Step 13: Use the Illustrator® Direct Selection Tool to Define Live Trace Groups

In order to use the Live Paint Bucket Tool (K), you first need to make outlines of the image **Live**. This will make them recognizable as areas that can be affected by the Live Paint Bucket Tool (K). The process is simple when the image contains fewer **Faces**. These are shapes created by intersecting outlines termed **Edges**. When a Live Trace image is Live, the Faces and Edges can be filled with color, gradients, and patterns.

The Rive_Gauche.jpg photo with Live Trace as Color 6 has many complex paths. If you attempt to make the entire photo Live, it might crash the program. To avoid this potential problem and proceed to define the Live areas, follow these steps:

1. Select the Fill box in the Tools panel, then select a color that you would like to add to the photo.
2. Select the Direct Selection Tool (A), then click on several Faces that were outlined by Expanding the Live Traced image.

3. While the Faces are selected, press the K key on your keyboard to toggle to the Live Paint Bucket Tool (K), then click into the selection until it is filled with the color in the Fill box. This will not only make all the selections the same color, but it will also make them individually Live. You will be able to fill each selected Face with the contents of the Live Paint Bucket Took (K).

4. The Live Paint Bucket Tool (K) fills selected areas with color, gradients, patterns, etc. Use it to fill some of the Faces and Edges created by Live Trace Color 6 with the colors of the Impressionism Color Library. You can also select colors from those in the painting with the Eyedropper Tool (I). Save these spot colors to the Swatches panel if you plan to use them again. Select the color you want in the Swatches panel; the two colors adjacent to it appear on both sides of the Live Paint Bucket Tool (K) icon. To swap colors, use the arrow keys, then click into a selected Live area to fill it.

5. If you receive the **Live Paint tip** as shown in Figure 6.21, it means that you have not actually made that area Live before you used the tool.

6. The results are revealed in new colors in the photo (Figure 6.21).

Step 14: Render Jeans, Scan Fabric, Define, and Fill

Place a cropped, rectilinear shape of a textile from a Photoshop® file. Once placed, select it and then define it by going to *Menu Bar > Edit > Define Pattern* as previously discussed (Figure 6.22). For your convenience, Denim_Swatch.jpg is available on ① Ch06\Tutorial 6.1. If you would like to scan your own fabric, use a swatch that is much larger than the area that you will fill. This will give you the ability to scale the pattern without the edges becoming a checked repeat. In addition, set your scan resolution to 300 dpi to ensure a quality image, but reduce the file size later (See Boxes 15.2 and 15.3 on pages 484 and 488).

Figure 6.20

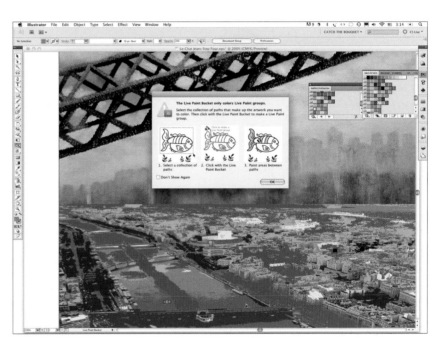

Figure 6.21

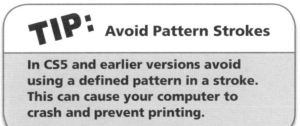

Figure 6.22

Figure 6.23

Use what you have learned in the previous tutorials to design denim sportswear for your featured model using the Illustrator® drawing tools. Render them on separate layers, and then fill them with the textile(s) that you have scanned and defined. In Figure 6.23, Ana is wearing a denim skirt and halter created with the Illustrator® Pen Tool (P), dashed lines of .04 at .5 pt *Weight*, and filled with the *Denim_ Swatch* pattern scaled to 50%. The button was created with the Ellipse Tool (L) and a gradient.

TIP: Tilde to Move Patterns

In Illustrator® you can redistribute defined patterns by selecting each shape and holding the Tilde key (above the Tab key) on your keyboard. Move the pattern with a click and drag. This allows you to reposition the defined pattern slightly within the shape and show a different section of the repeat. This will make your digital illustration less flat and mimic what happens when apparel items are constructed with patterned textiles.

Step 15: Freehand and Scan Option

You can also print your posed figure and use it as a template to hand-render **conceptual action flats** (see Tutorial 14.10 on page 451). Action flats (also floats) have gained popularity in specific markets, especially young men's, juniors, and children's wear. They are used for presentation storyboards, and they sometimes augment technical production flats in tech-packs. Color drawings on solid, light-colored paper will be sufficient. Scan the drawings, then Place them in Illustrator® as art (Figure 6.24).

Step 16: Use Photo High Fidelity to Remove White Space

When you scan an image, the file is rasterized. These images are sometimes surrounded by white space when placed into vector software, especially in earlier versions of Illustrator®. To remove the background, Live Trace the images with the **Photo High Fidelity** preset, so you do not lose the look and the details. Use the Direct Selection Tool (A) to select and delete the areas as shown in Figure 6.25. Some of the white fragments and stray paths of the original drawing may need to be selected individually and then deleted (Figure 6.26).

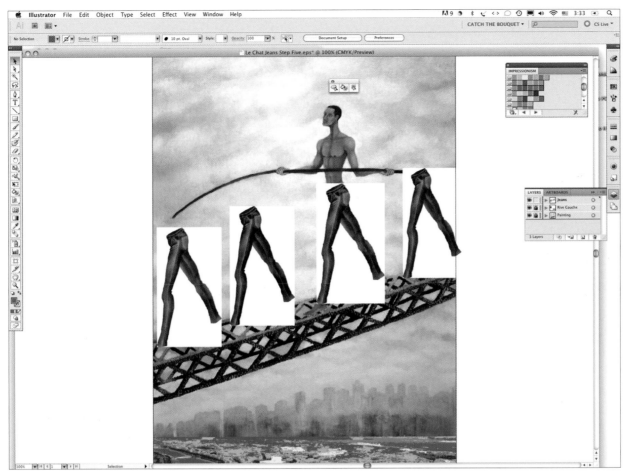

Figure 6.24

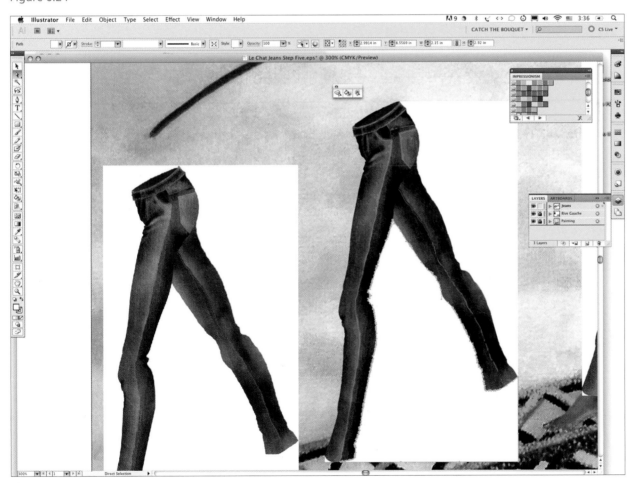

Figure 6.25

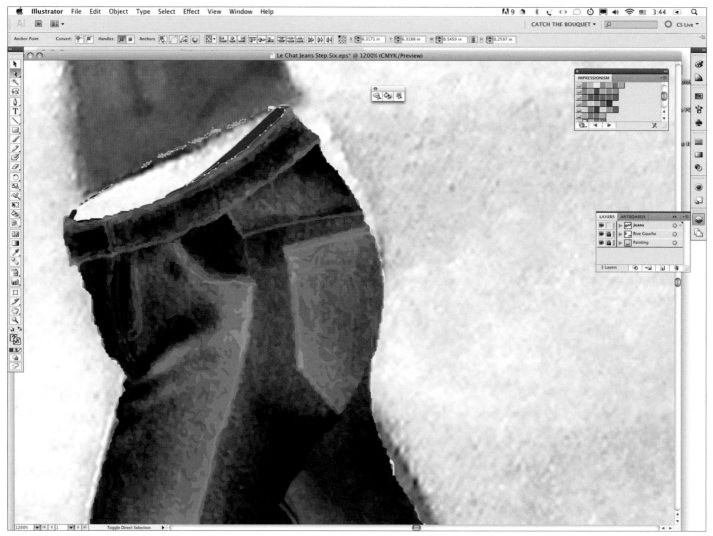

Figure 6.26

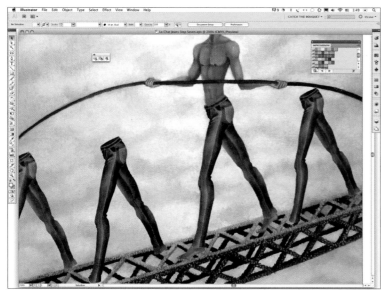

Figure 6.27

TIP: **File Size**

Reduce your file size to 150 dpi.

Note: *In Illustrator® CS6 you can place rasterized images without the white background (See Tutorial 12.2 on page 347).*

Step 17: Position Your Action Flats

Position the action flats as shown in Figure 6.27.

Step 18: Add Filters

To give the Rive_Gauche.jpg photo the look of a fine art painting, select it and then go to *Menu Bar > Effects > Artistic > Sponge.* Experiment with the settings once you see the window as shown in Figure 6.28. Use a small brush size until you get the look you desire. The finished look is shown in Figure 6.29.

Step 19: Add Whimsical Extras

A sure way to be remembered after an interview is to add whimsical additions to a few of your presentations. The combination of techniques and media used in this tutorial qualify it as fashion abstractrealism. The self-contained environment depicted tells a story and will sell your designs and add a special quality to your presentation. Use whimsical additions

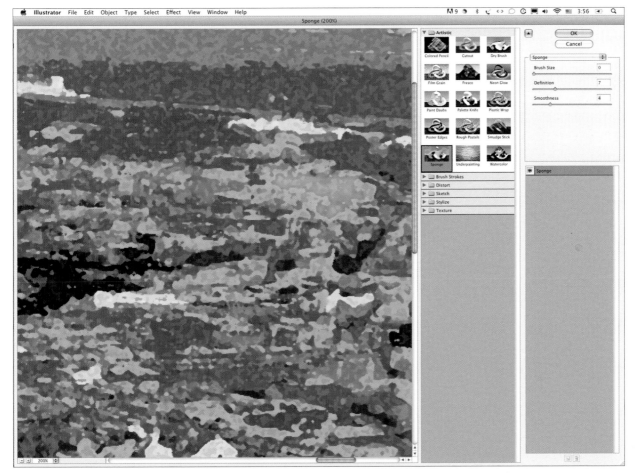

Figure 6.28 The Photoshop® Sponge filter gives images a painterly effect.

Figure 6.29

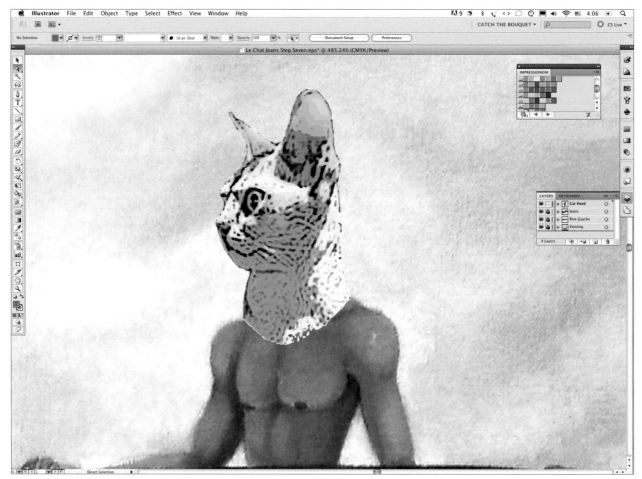

Figure 6.30

Figure 6.31

Figure 6.32

to personalize your presentation. In Figure 6.30, a cat's head was used as a mask.

The full impact of this small gesture is revealed in Figure 6.31. Naturally, everyone has different tastes. Try something out of your own imagination, but keep it lighthearted and pleasant.

Add Signage

Signage, as you have learned in earlier tutorials, is a great way to capture the attention of your viewer. It can also reveal your personality through design. The slogan *Le Chat Jeans Go Places* in Figure 6.32 complements the cat mask. In Figure 6.33, a scaled run-

Figure 6.33

Figure 6.34

way pose of Jade from the ① Digital Duo Modeling Agency was added as an element of surprise.

Fill Live Faces with Patterns

More drama is added by selecting the Denim swatch from the Swatches panel. Make the River Seine in the Rive_Gauche photo Live, then use the Live Paint Bucket Tool (K) to fll the Faces. In Figure 6.34 the denim-filled River Seine draws a parallel to denim washes as a marketing tool.

Step 20: Inspect and Save Your File

The completed posters are shown in Figure 6.35.

Figure 6.35 Illustration by Stacy Stewart Smith.

This tutorial combines the look of freehand illustration with the principles of fine art screen-printing. You will use Live Trace in various ways to design a poster invitation for a fashion show. The techniques used here are based on early poster art and make use of Illustrator®. The concept of employing multiple Artboards is also introduced.

To help you complete this tutorial, four files have been provided for you on Ch06\Tutorial 6.2. You may also choose to scan and use one or more of your own freehand fashion figures, as long as it was drawn on white paper. If you own a Wacom® tablet, you can replace the Paris_Signage.eps file with a different poster title written in your own handwriting.

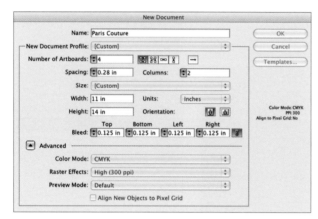

Figure 6.36

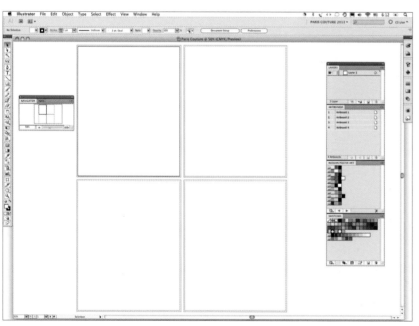

Figure 6.37

Step 1: Prepare a New Document with Four Artboards

Load Illustrator® and use the specifications of Figure 6.36 to open a document with four Artboards, as shown in Figure 6.37. Artboards are a good way to stay organized, and they work well in conjunction with layer compositing. The Artboard panel is located in the panel dock associated with the Layers panel (Figure 6.37). Like the other panels, it has a hidden menu whereby you can manage the stacking order, delete Artboards, organize them, etc. The Artboard feature works particularly well with the Live Trace features because of the need to separate colors within one layer. Using layers will keep you focused on the creative aspects of your work without having to reposition your view of the window or toggle off the visibility of layers to see other objects.

Set up your Workspace. The one in this tutorial makes use of the Navigator panel, the Swatch panel, the Layers panel, the Artboard panel, and the Russian Poster Art Color Library. The Workspace of the tutorial example has been named *Paris Couture 2013*. Save your file to your computer with a similar appropriate name.

Step 2: Place and Embed the Required Files

Having four Artboards on one layer makes it easy for you to locate, place, and Embed the four image files provided on Ch06\Tutorial 6.2 (Figure 6.38). If you are using more elements, you can place more than one object in an area. The Artboards are all on one layer; you can add more if you need them by using the hidden menu items located at the upper left side of the panel.

Note: *When you fit the image on your screen by pressing Cmd+0 / Ctrl+0, only the first Artboard will show. Zoom out to show all the Artboards in the window.*

Step 3: Live Trace the Moulin Rouge in 16 Colors

Begin with the photo entitled Moulin_Rouge.jpg. The photo has been altered to give the iconic red windmill atop of the famed Moulin Rouge an austere look. This cabaret is a major tourist attraction in Paris. Although the photo was taken during the day, we will turn it into a night scene. Select the photo, and Live Trace it with Color 16, located in the Control Panel presets menu (Figure 6.39).

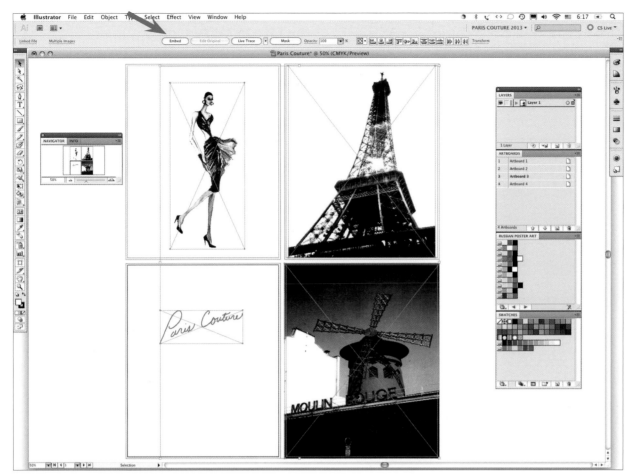

Figure 6.38 Always press the Embed button to secure selected placed images.

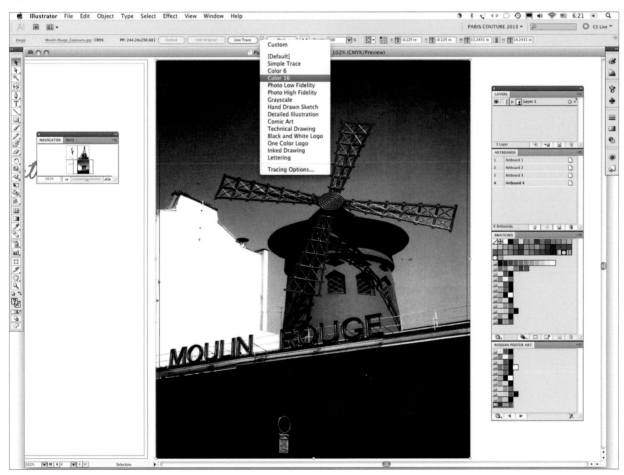

Figure 6.39 The Illustrator® CS5 and earlier Live Trace menus can be accessed from the Control Panel.

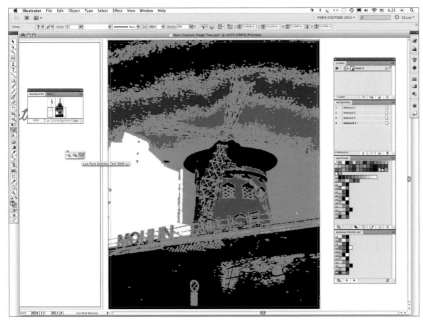

Figure 6.40

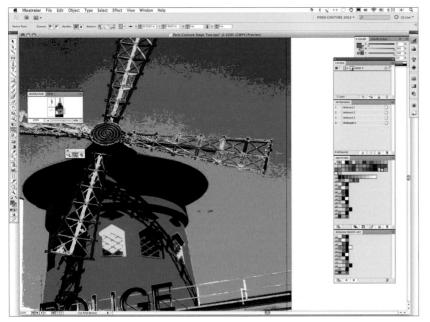

Figure 6.41

Step 4: Select to Inspect the Outline

Figure 6.40 reveals the outlines created by Live Trace Color 16 after it was Expanded. The limited color palette has eliminated many of the subtle hues associated with daytime. The sky is divided into fewer than 10 selectable areas and has a wonderful arrangement of cool blues in the example photo, but be creative and make it your own.

Step 5: Color the Image with the Live Paint Bucket

Russian Poster Art, which possessed a strong element of Socialist Realism, was popular from 1919 through the 1930s. The posters were composed of vivid primary and secondary colors and masterfully used black, red, and white along with elements of photomontage. A similar palette of colors is located in the Illustrator® Russian Poster Art Color Library. To create a sharp image, limit your color palette to six to ten colors from this library. Use the Live Paint Bucket Tool (K) to fill multiple selected areas.

Step 6: Add Photo-to-Illustration Accents

Use the Live Paint Bucket Tool (K) to recolor photos by selecting a few Live areas to repeat a color accent. Do not apply color to every element. Leave a few parts as they were traced. In other places, you may want the same color for two or more adjacent Faces. The yellow accents of Figure 6.41 are reminiscent of streetlight reflections. Save and back up your file.

Step 7: Use a Fade, Vignette, or Gradient

A **Vignette** is similar to a Fade, except it contains transparency and color in radial formation. Vignettes can be used to frame an area with soft color by creating a clearing that allows the white background of the Artboard to show. Make a Vignette with two colors as shown in Figure 6.42, and create the illusion of the moon or whatever comes to mind. Use the Gradient Tool (G) to resize and reposition the transparent space in the center.

Learn how to create gradient strokes as offsets in Illustrator® CS6 by watching the video CS6_Gradient_Stroke_Offset.m4v ① Ch06\Tutorial 6.2.

Step 8: Place a Warhol-Like Screen Print Offset

Since we are working with art posters, why not introduce a bit of screen-printing technique? Andy Warhol used mistakes to suggest movement and depth by offsetting the placement of certain screens in his art-making process. Figure 6.43 showcases the advantage of this practice.

1. Select all the other artwork on the Artboards, then press *Cmd+2 / Ctrl+2* to lock the selections on the layer.

2. Use the Illustrator® Magic Wand Tool (Y) to select all the Faces filled with a specific color. Do not choose areas with very large bold shapes because this technique works best with smaller elements.

3. Cut, paste, and group them. Reposition the selections slightly offset from their originally scored position.

Figure 6.42

Figure 6.43 Offset images create movement, as seen in the image above.

Figure 6.44

Figure 6.45

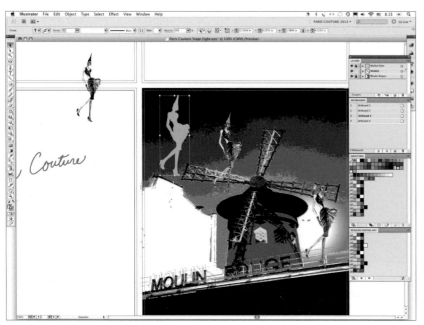

Figure 6.46

Step 9: Live Trace, Expand, and Isolate Your Figure(s)

1. Live Trace the figure Couture_Babe.jpg with Photo High Fidelity (Figure 6.44), then Expand the image. Do the same if you are using your own figure(s) instead.

2. Use the Direct Selection Tool (A) to isolate and delete the backgrounds, including the negative spaces, and then make them Live as instructed previously.

3. In this tutorial, some white areas, including stray points and fragments, will enhance the look. Follow these steps, but use a Live Trace method appropriate for your drawings. For instance, if your drawing has only one color, select another preset from the Live Trace menu in the Control Panel.

Step 10: Scale and Reduce the Eiffel Tower to a Chapeau

1. Scale the image Tour_Eiffel.jpg.

2. Use the Simple Trace option of Live Trace.

3. Place the Eiffel Tower on the croquis's head (Figure 6.45).

Note: Feel free to design your own hat and other accessories instead of using the provided file.

Step 11: Copy, Paste, and Recolor with the Live Paint Bucket Tool

1. Group the hat with the figure, then copy and paste the image a few times.

2. Use the Live Paint Bucket Tool (K) to recolor apparel and accessory elements of each figure and differentiate them from each other (Figure 6.45).

Step 12: Scale the Figures to Create the Illusion of Distance

1. Scale the figures to create the illusion of perspective.

2. Select one and double-click on the Scale Tool (S).

3. Select Uniform and Scale Strokes and Effects.

4. Reduce figure by 10% successively.

Note: You may need to make further adjustments by selecting the figures and holding the Shift key to constrain the proportions, then resizing the Bounding Box.

Step 13: Place the Figures

1. Create a new layer.

2. Copy and paste the figures into it.

3. Select and move them from their Artboard onto the area of the Moulin_Rouge.jpg image (Figure 6.46).

Figure 6.47

TIP: Variations

To make a more compelling presentation, replace some of the croquis with others wearing various designs from a signature collection. Try to place some walking in the opposite direction on a layer below the others.

Step 14: Place the Title and Add Finishing Touches

1. Create a new layer.
2. Copy and paste the title into it.
3. Select and move the title from its Artboard onto the area of the Moulin_Rouge.jpg image.

Be creative with your placement by adding additional colorful finishing touches as needed (Figure 6.47).

Step 15: Create Signage and Save

1. Select, cut, and paste the entire completed poster into a new layer, and delete the extra Artboards.
2. Add some interesting text to your presentation using a sans serif font, and save and back up your file. An example of the completed tutorial is pictured in Figure 6.48.

TIP: CS6 Image Trace

For more information on how you can use the CS6 Illustrator® instructions of this tutorial, watch the movie CS6_Image_Trace.m4v on ① Ch06\Tutorial 6.1.

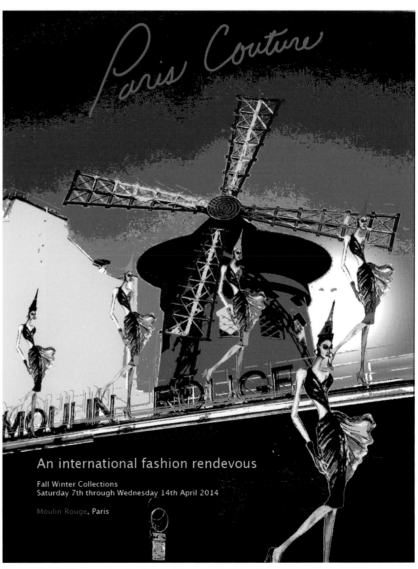

An international fashion rendevous

Fall Winter Collections
Saturday 7th through Wednesday 14th April 2014

Moulin Rouge, Paris

Figure 6.48 Illustration by Stacy Stewart Smith.

Figure 6.49a March 1928 issue of *Vogue.* © Condé Nast.

Figure 6.49b February 1928 issue of *Vogue.* © Condé Nast.

Figure 6.49c April 1933 issue of *Vogue.* © Condé Nast.

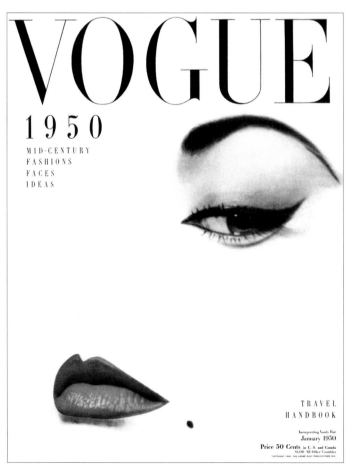

Figure 6.49d January 1950 issue of *Vogue.* © Condé Nast.

Vogue magazine has been the premier source for fashion and lifestyle information since the first issue was published in 1892. Long before photography became the primary means of representing style, fashion illustrators were hired to create covers and advertisement layouts for the pages of periodicals like *Vogue*. The January 1950 cover of *Vogue* is actually a photo by Erwin Blumfield of the legendary model Jean Patchette (Figure 6.49d). The cover shows only her beautifully shadowed and penciled eye, red lipstick on a pouty mouth, and her signature mole. The goal of this tutorial is to help strengthen your ability to use portions of photographs and other images to make strong statements. This assemblage technique is termed photomontage.

To help you complete this tutorial, the file Vogue_1950.jpg has been provided for you on ① Ch06\Tutorial 6.3. You can also use any of the images in the subfolder named Extra Vogue Covers.

Step 1: Open, Embed, and Live Trace a Modeling Agency File

Create a single 11×14 inch Artboard in CMYK without bleeds (Figure 6.50). Place and Embed Ana_frontalview_glam.jpg (Figure 6.51) from ① Digital Duo Modeling Agency\Ana\Glam Headshots. Select the image, use the Photo High Fidelity preset of Live Trace, then Expand the image.

Note: *The* ① *Digital Duo Modeling Agency offers a variety of headshots for you to choose from. Test your creativity by choosing an alternate image.*

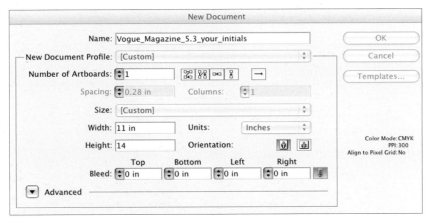

Figure 6.50

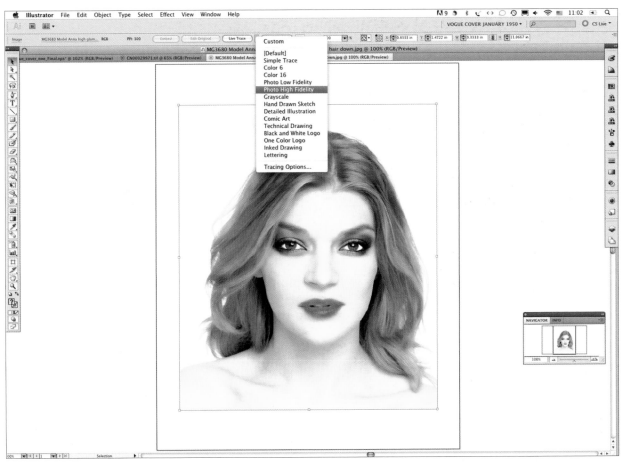

Figure 6.51 Live Trace the image in Photo High Fidelity.

Figure 6.53

Figure 6.52

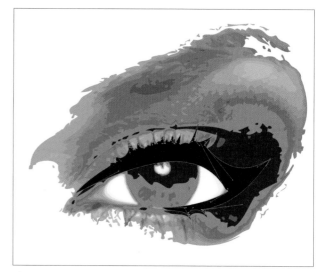

Figure 6.54

Step 2: Select and Delete Portions of the Face

Use the direct Selection Tool (A) to delete portions of the image (Figure 6.52).

Step 3: Select, Copy, Paste, and Alter Areas of Interest

1. Use the Illustrator® Direct Selection Tool (A) to marquee and select specific areas.

2. Copy and paste certain parts that you can reuse, such as an eye or eyebrow (Figure 6.53).

3. Recolor them to add greater contrast and create a striking look (Figure 6.54).

Step 4: Use the Blob Brush Tool and the Gaussian Blur Filter

The Illustrator® Middle Ages Color Library offers a palette suitable to the eye color and the model's makeup on the original cover of *Vogue*. Use the Blob Brush Tool (Shift+B) to create shadow areas, then select the object and add the Gaussian Blur filter to make them appear smoky and blended like real eye makeup (Figure 6.55).

Step 5: Draw the Haute Couture Brow

Paris designers send models down the haute couture runways with exaggerated lashes and brows reminiscent of 1950s Hollywood movie stars or drag superstars. The look features perfectly penciled brows. Sometimes they are drawn above the actual brow area. The Pencil Tool (N) was used in Figure 6.56 to create the shape; then the **Width Tool** (Shift+W) was used to add the contour. To replicate this effect, click with the Width Tool (Shift+W), and pull in the brow end to make the shape thinner on that side. On the brow front, pull out to increase the width and alter the shape (Figure 6.57).

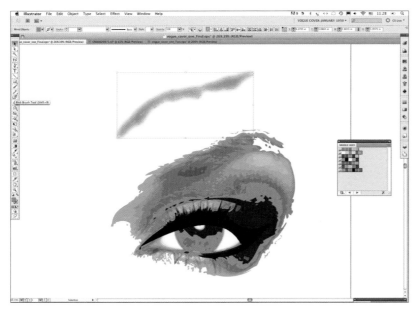

Figure 6.55

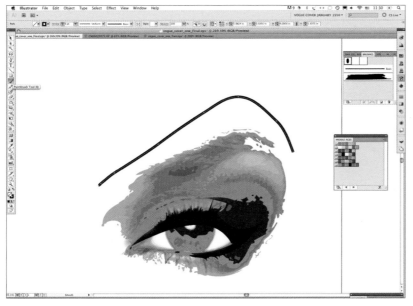

Figure 6.56

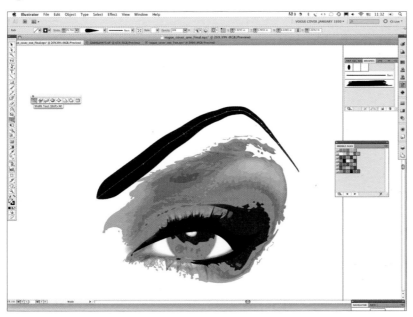

Figure 6.57

Note: *The Width Tool (Shift+W) is a feature of versions CS5 and CS6. If you are using version CS4 or lower, use the Pen Tool (P) to draw the haute couture brow.*

Step 6: Delete Stray Points

Go to *Menu Bar > Object > Path > Cleanup* and select the options you want to remove. Use **Cleanup** to rid the illustration of all unpainted paths and stray points, especially around the mouth, as seen in Figure 6.58. You can also select and delete the objects.

Step 7: Create Lip Accents and Exaggeration

The lip color is a bit drab for this presentation. Try filling the areas with brighter hues (Figure 6.59). Do not neglect to color the inside of the mouth. Afterward, use the Pen Tool (P) to develop a kissable pout.

Send the shape to the back by pressing *Shift+Cmd+[/ Shift+Ctrl+[*. After this, create a shadow below the lower lip with the Blob Tool (Shift+B) and then use the Gaussian Blur filter (Figure 6.60).

Step 8: Examine and Tweak

Zoom out to examine your work. Select the parts to scale or rotate them if needed. Figure 6.61 illustrates the dramatic completion of the art portion of this tutorial.

Step 9: Simple Trace the Vintage Vogue Cover File

Open the file Vogue_1950.jpg located on ① Ch06\ Tutorial 6.3 in Illustrator®. Select, then Simple Trace the file via the *Live Tracing Presets and Options* located in the Control Panel.

Figure 6.58

Figure 6.59

Figure 6.60

Figure 6.61

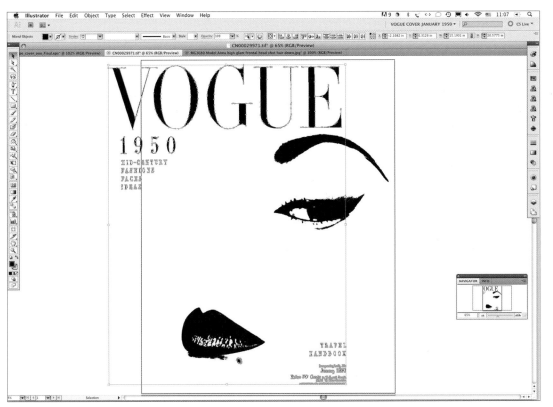

Figure 6.62

Figure 6.63

Figure 6.64

Step 10: Select and Copy the Typography

If you choose not to attempt to re-create the typography, just select, copy, and paste the type into your file (Figure 6.62).

Step 11: Use New Fonts and the Character Panel

To create a challenge for yourself, find suitable fonts to re-create the typography using the kerning, leading, and tracking attributes of the Illustrator® Character panel (Figure 6.63). You were introduced to these concepts in Tutorial 3.2.

Step 12: Finish the Cover

Inspect your work and save your file. A completed example that has a similar feeling to the original *Vogue* cover is shown in Figure 6.64.

Step 13: Try Various Backgrounds

You can also add new twists to your presentation to personalize it even further. In Figure 6.65, gradients from the Spectrum Gradient Library provide a contemporary aesthetic. Go to *Menu Bar > Window > Swatch Libraries > Gradients > Spectrums* to access the multicolored gradients.

VOGUE

2014

Digital Age
Fashions
Faces of the 50s
Ideas

TRAVEL
HANDBOOK

Incorporating Vanity Fair
January 2014
WWW.VOGUE.COM
COPYRIGHT 2013 THE CONDE NAST PUBLICATIONS INC.

Figure 6.65 Illustration by Stacy Stewart Smith.

Tutorial 6.4
SCREEN PRINTS AND INTARSIA
PATTERNS IN ILLUSTRATOR®

In this tutorial, you will learn how to use Illustrator® to create your own simple screen print designs for T-shirts and intarsia motifs for knitted apparel. An intarsia is a knitting technique used to create a placed design consisting of several colors. This tutorial uses two images: Ana_3Q_Pigtails.jpg from ① Digital Duo Modeling Agency\Ana\Headshots with Pigtails and Carl_3Q_baseball_cap.jpg from ① Digital Duo Modeling Agency\Carl\Headshots with Hats. Once you have completed the tutorial using the provided files, you are encouraged to re-create the presentations using your own photos or illustrations.

Step 1: Prepare a New Document with 12 Artboards

Load Illustrator® and create a new document with 12 Artboards on two rows using the specifications indicated in Figure 6.66.

Step 2: Place and Trace Headshot Photos

Place, Embed, then Live Trace Ana_3Q_Pigtails.jpg and Carl_3Q_baseball_cap.jpg using the Color 6 preset in the Illustrator® Control Panel. Expand the images and delete the backgrounds as shown in red on Figure 6.67.

Note: *The top row with the headshot of Ana will represent the steps for creating an intarsia motif, and the bottom row using Carl's image will represent screen-printing procedures.*

Step 3: Recolor the Outlines

To create fashion-worthy images, use the Color Guide panel to recolor your images as shown in Figure 6.68.

TIP: Color Standards Background

One of the colors in your design could just be representative of the ground or fabric color, such as white or black. This is a money-saving screen-printing technique. It would save you from needing to have an additional screen produced.

Figure 6.66

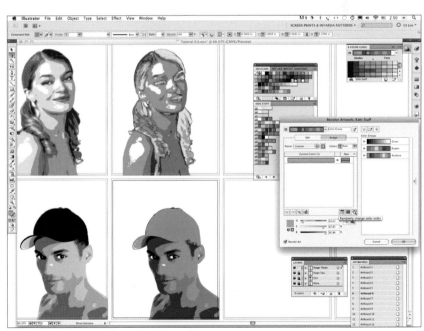

Figure 6.67

Figure 6.68

Step 4: Create a Screen Print

Fashion designers and merchandisers should know how the general screen-printing process operates. Naturally, computer software has made everything easier, but reaching production minimums needed to market your own ideas can be costly. The basic principle behind the screen-printing process is color separation. Each color requires a separate screen. Even the most complicated screen prints are only the sum of their parts. Thanks to Illustrator®, finding the colors is easier than ever. The Artboard in Figure 6.69 shows that there are eight colors in this developing screen print composition.

Step 5: Use the Illustrator® Magic Wand Tool to Separate Colors

Lock all the other objects on the Artboards and select each color separately. Select, copy, and paste them below on the Scratchboard, or scale them and place them in the Artboard on the lower right as shown in Figure 6.70.

Basic Screen-Printing Procedures

If you wanted to create an actual hand-pulled screen print of the image, you would need to prepare a silk screen for each color. Each color image(s) would be drawn onto a silk screen today, (not actually made of silk). The nonprintable areas would be blocked out with a solution. Once the screens had been properly prepared, each color would be applied to a surface one at a time. A score point(s) would mark the placement, so that the colors were applied accurately in registration. The paint would be placed into the screen print box and pushed through the unblocked design on the screen with the force of a squeegee. This entire process can be facilitated manually or automated with specialized machinery.

Naturally, there is a lot more involved in the production process if you are working to produce large lots of apparel. Again, knowledge of screen print design is a valuable asset to any fashion designer or merchandiser seeking employment. Adding a few concepts to your portfolio collections is a sure way to be remembered.

Step 6: Create a Multicolored Intarsia Motif with the Grid

To create an intarsia motif, begin by setting the *Preferences* for your *Guides & Grid* to 20 Subdivisions within each inch (Figure 6.71). This setting is the closest to graph paper for hand knitting with a medium-gauge yarn. Select certain areas in the outlines and fill them with the same colors in adjacent shapes to keep the image from becoming too abstract. Compare the image of Figure 6.72 with the one in Figure 6.68. Toggle on your Grid.

Figure 6.69

Figure 6.70

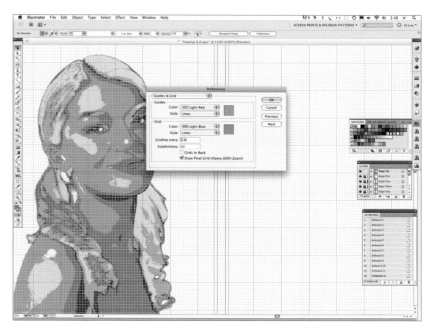

Figure 6.71

Step 7: Scale the Motif

An intarsia pattern can only be successful if the scale of the image allows you to see the design based on the yarn gauge. You will need to select a design that accommodates for the medium-to-large grid spaces generated with hand knitting and this tutorial. For a different project, you can adjust the grid to suit any gauge.

Intarsia patterns that have fine details may not be suitable for this particular grid. The tutorial Artboard is 8.5×11 inches, which is sufficient to fill the front of a fitted top. If you want to use artwork or photography that has some fine details, select it, and then scale it by double-clicking on the Scale Tool (S). In the Scale dialog box, enter 150% to 175% into the *Uniform* field and click OK. Figure 6.72 shows the scale increase of this more intricate design, which now covers a knitted area approximately 13×17 inches. A motif with less detail may not require such a vast increase in scale.

Figure 6.72

Step 8: Rasterize the Image with the Effects Menu

Years ago, designers had to draw these charts painstakingly by hand, but with Illustrator® now all you need to do is select the color separations and go to *Menu Bar > Effects > Rasterize*. In the dialog box (Figure 6.73), click the *Other* button and enter 20 ppi. Then check the **Transparent button**. This prevents the image from being surrounded by white boxes. You do not need to touch the other default settings.

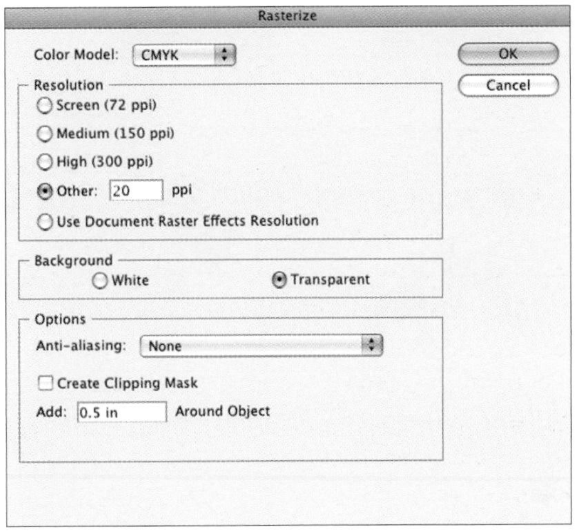

Figure 6.73

Step 9: Create a Perfect Intarsia Pattern

Figure 6.74 shows the successful creation of an intarsia motif. The sections match the grid space and the design would be easy to reproduce by hand using a medium-gauge yarn.

Step 10: Review and Application

Pictured in Figure 6.75 are all the steps for creating simple intarsia patterns and screen prints. You should have accomplished the following:

Intarsia Grid (top row)

- Stage One shows the original image/artwork.
- Stage Two shows the image/artwork after Live Trace Color 6.
- Stage Three shows the results of the Color Guide panel.
- Stage Four shows adjustments made by selecting and manipulating Faces and Edges with the Direct Selection Tool (A). Colors are also rearranged.
- Stage Five contains finalized artwork with color standards.
- Stage Six shows the completed intarsia motif scaled 175%.

Figure 6.74

Figure 6.75

Screen Print (bottom row)

- Stage One contains the original image/artwork.
- Stage Two shows the image after Live Trace Color 6.
- Stage Three shows the results the Color Guide panel.
- Stage Four a color was added.
- Stage Five another color was added.
- Stage Six eight color screens are placed on the bottom and lower right.

Step 11: Scale the Intarsia Design

Place a copy of your intarsia design into a new file where you plan to work on a digital sweater design. You will find that the scale is too large to fit the average design illustration on a figure or a flat. If you do scale it to fit, you risk losing the image. To prevent this, uncheck *Scale Strokes and Effects* in the *General* sec-

tion of the *Preferences* menu. Then select the intarsia design and scale the selection to fit the apparel illustration by pulling in the Bounding Box while you hold the Shift key to constrain the proportions.

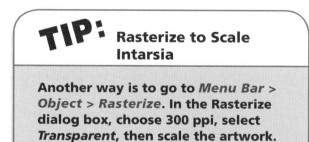

TIP: Rasterize to Scale Intarsia

Another way is to go to *Menu Bar > Object > Rasterize*. In the Rasterize dialog box, choose 300 ppi, select *Transparent*, then scale the artwork.

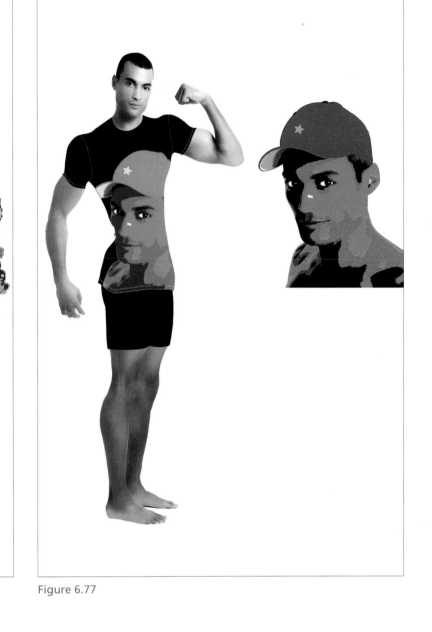

Figure 6.76

Figure 6.77

Step 12: Design an Intarsia Sweater

Use the tools, filters, and panels in Illustrator® to create a simple sweater design. Place a copy of the scaled intarsia design onto your sweater design. Select all the objects and use the Color Guide panel to recolor the design and intarsia motif to coordinate the color/shades. Figure 6.76 shows Ana wearing an intarsia design bearing her own image.

Step 13: Design a T-Shirt

Render a T-shirt or another apparel item for the screen print that you designed. If you would like to use the oversized crop method shown in Figure 6.77, follow the procedure of Step Eleven, scale up the screen print, then create a clipping mask (Tutorial 3.3) from the T-shirt front that you created. Use the Stroke panel *Dashed Lines* to create topstitching and use any other tools or features to enhance your presentation.

The High Jump Defense tutorial presents a number of digital challenges. At the forefront of these is the concept of creating believable **two-point perspective** in a digital layout. The Illustrator® Perspective Grid Tool (Shift+P) was introduced in Chapter 4 to demonstrate one-point perspective, but two-point perspective presents challenges that many fashion designer/illustrators avoid.

Fashion designers and fashion merchandisers can benefit from this tutorial because it combines design with marketing and presentation techniques. It will yield a large-format print for a storyboard that measures 30 x 30 inches when printed. The **resolution independent** quality of vector art will produce vivid prints. Later, the print can be adhered to foam core board, and fabric swatches, trims, and other elements could be added.

Step 1: Prepare a New Document for a Storyboard with a Bleed

Load Illustrator® and create a large storyboard format file as indicated by the specs shown in the Illustrator® New Document dialog box of **Figure 6.78**.

Step 2: Place and Embed a Headshot in Illustrator®

1. Open Daryl_MVP.jpg from Ch06\Tutorial 6.5 in Illustrator®.

2. Place the image into the file that you created in Step One, and position it near the lower left corner of the Artboard.

3. Scale the image if needed and rename *Layer 1* as *MVP*. The placement of the *MVP* headshot is shown in **Figure 6.79**.

Step 3: Use Live Trace Photo High Fidelity to Trace and Expand the Headshot

1. To eliminate the white background surrounding the image of the MVP, select it, then Live Trace it, using the Photo High Fidelity preset.

2. Expand the image, and delete the attached background.

3. Lock the layer.

Step 4: Place, Embed, Trace, and Expand Action Photos

1. Make use of each file in Digital Duo Modeling Agency\Carl\Basketball Action Shots.

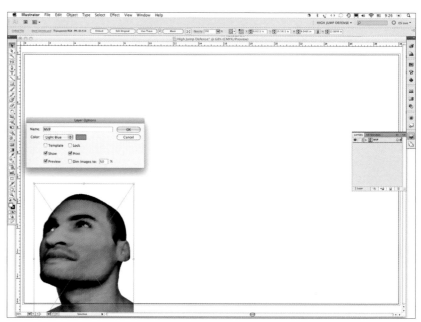

Figure 6.78

Figure 6.79

2. Place each figure on a separate layer and assign names to them that you can remember.

3. Embed, Live Trace Color 6, and Expand each file. **Figure 6.80** shows all the images on the Artboard.

Step 5: Use Two-Point Perspective

1. Select the Perspective Grid Tool (Shift+P).

2. Go to *Menu Bar > View > Perspective Grid > Two Point Perspective > [2P Perspective Normal View]*.

3. When the grid appears, you may opt to move the middle diamond shape, at the bottom, upward to decrease the amount of division lines.

4. Readjust the horizon line to about the 13-inch position on the y-axis.

5. Pull the visual plane to the bottom of the Artboard and the height to the top at 17 inches on the x-axis (**Figure 6.81**).

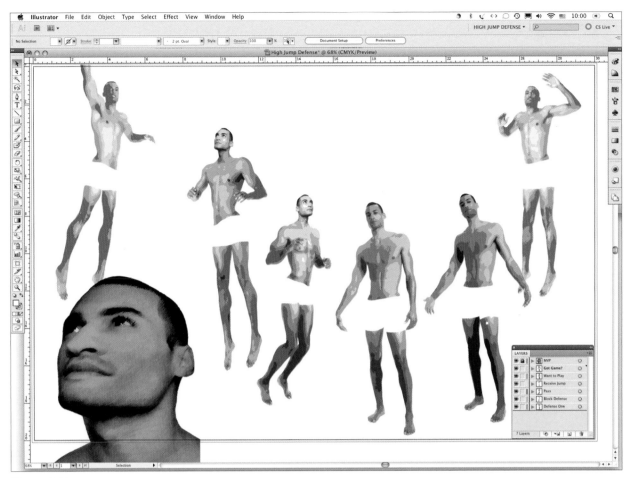

Figure 6.80

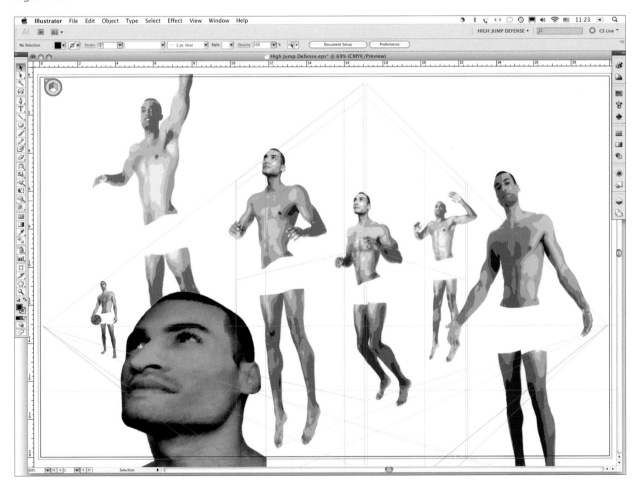

Figure 6.81

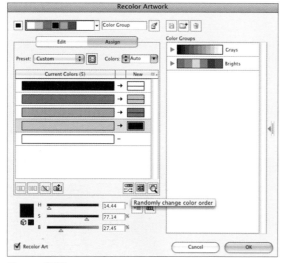
Figure 6.82

Step 6: Turn the Photographs into Digital Illustration

By now you have learned to experiment with different aspects of Illustrator® to produce various outcomes. Start this process by selecting the players and randomly changing the colorways with the Color Guide panel (Figure 6.82).

Step 7: Create a Background and Design Clothing

Gradually build the look of your presentation by adding a background layer below each player's layers that will fill the space between the foreground edge of the composition and the horizon line. Use the Rectangle Tool (R) to create two separate shapes touching the horizon line (Figure 6.83).

Step 8: Create an All-Inclusive Mood

Add more details and experiment further with the color, gradients, clothing, and composition. Also draw a basketball and floor markings with the Pen Tool (P) (Figure 6.84).

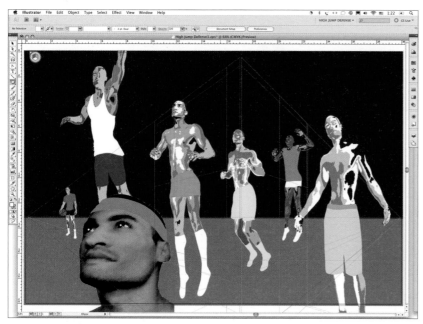
Figure 6.83

Step 9: Work with Patterns

Another element of digital design is the use of patterns and texture. The tutorial example features socks and underwear for men. The Illustrator® Pattern Libraries are extensive, but if you are already comfortable with defining pattern repeats, use your imagination and develop your own. Figure 6.85 shows the details of the various briefs and shorts with filled patterns.

Step 10: Add Shadows and Details

To take away that weightless appearance of the players, add a floor shadow with the Blob Brush Tool (Shift+B) and the Gaussian Blur filter (Figure 6.86). Place the shadows on a layer by themselves.

Note: *The tutorial continues in Photoshop®.*

Step 11: Export Your Illustrator® File to Photoshop®

To generate a few enhanced effects, you can export this file to Photoshop® (Figure 6.87). Go to *Menu Bar > File > Export*, and in the Export dialog box, choose the Photoshop® PSD format at the middle area. Click Save and the new Photoshop® file will be saved in the same location as the original Illustrator® file.

Step 12: Open and Crop the File in Photoshop®

Locate, open, and use the **Crop Tool (C)** to clean up the presentation. To use this tool, select it and marquee. You can adjust the Bounding Box to a precise area, then double-click anywhere except the center to accept the changes (Figure 6.88).

Figure 6.84

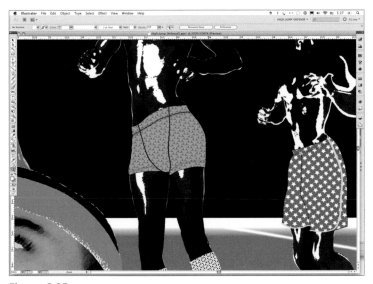

Figure 6.85

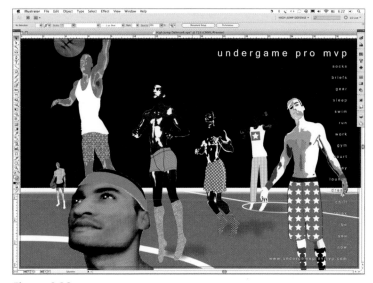

Figure 6.86

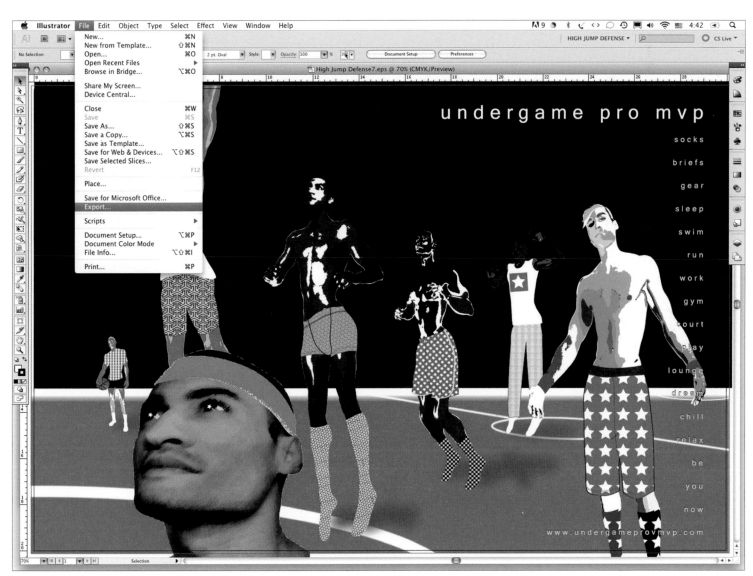

Figure 6.87 Illustrator® window shows the menu for exporting a file.

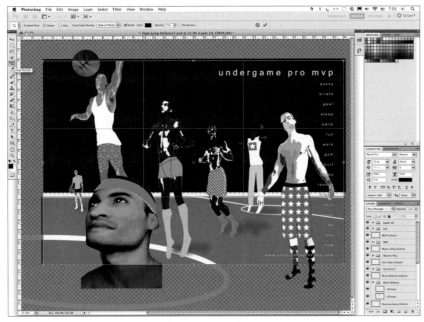

Figure 6.88 The same file has been opened in Photoshop®.

Step 13: Investigate the Layer Compositing

You may have noticed that the transfer of layer compositing also brought with it a few extra folders. In order to affect the parts, locate the sublayer that contains them. To do this, tip the pointer next to each folder, select the sublayers, then toggle off the **visibility icon** (eye). If an object disappears, that means it is located on the selected sublayer. The layer compositing is shown in **Figure 6.89**.

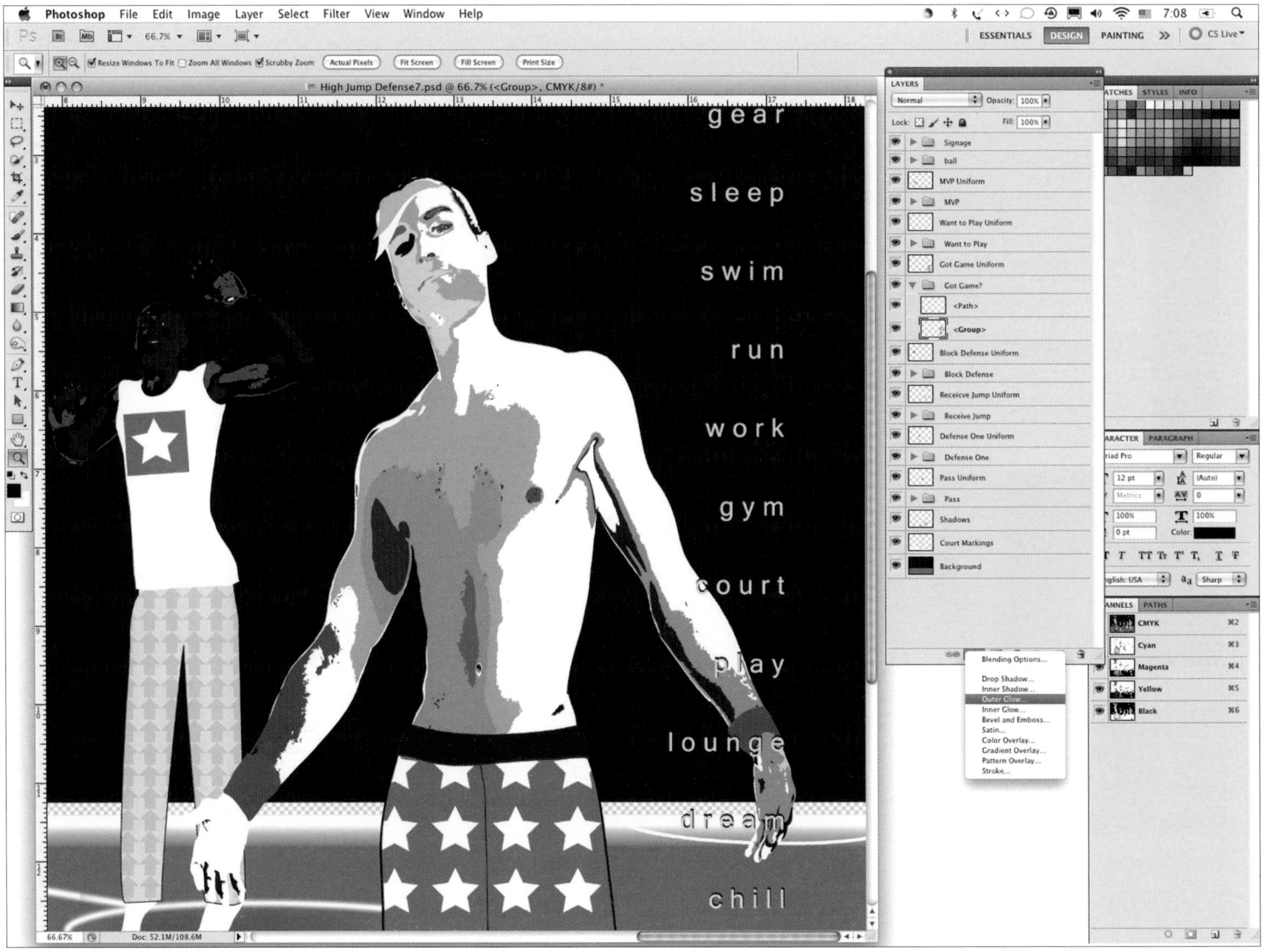

Figure 6.89

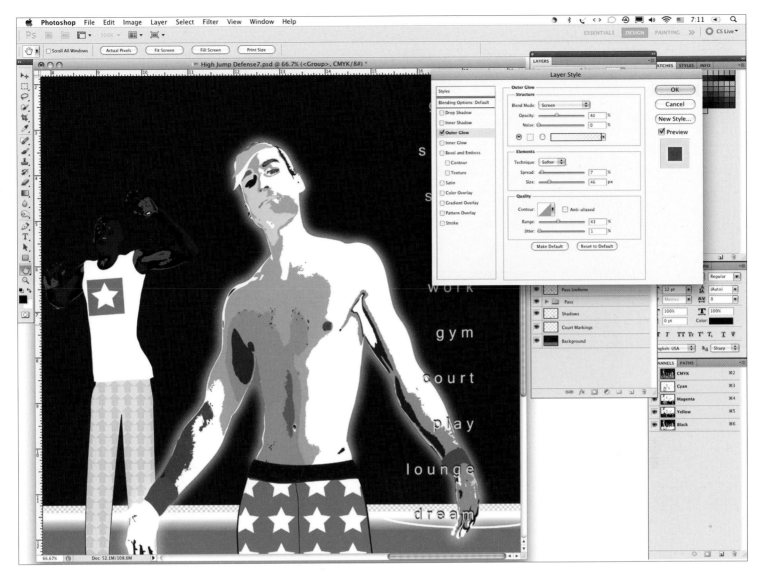

Figure 6.90

Step 14: Use Layer Styles to Enhance Your Work

Layer Styles are filters that help give dimension to your vector art on specific layers. If everything you created were on one layer, the Layer Styles would change the entire work. That would not be desirable. Select a layer that you would like to modify, then press the *fx icon* at the bottom of the Layers panel to activate the Layer Style options dialog box (Figure 6.90).

In the Layer Style options dialog box, you will notice a list of options on the left. You can add as many Layer Styles as you would like to a specific layer by selecting them and adjusting the settings separately. An **Outer Glow** adds a simulated aura around the objects on a selected layer. Experiment with the other options and settings.

Note: *When the Global Angle of a specific Layer Style is checked, it will automatically take on the light source of the other layers.*

To toggle off the visibility of a Layer Style, locate it in a sublayer and press the eye icon. You can also delete the Layer Style by dragging it to the Trash icon.

Figure 6.91

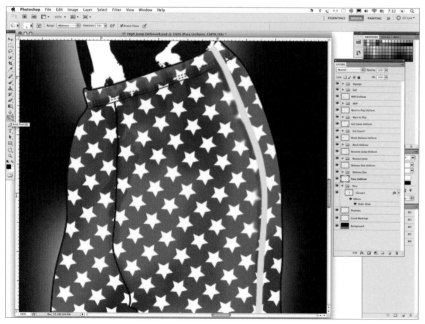

Figure 6.92

Step 15: Use the Burn Tool

The **Photoshop® Burn Tool (O)** shadows colors. Use it to create shaded areas in the clothing, especially wrinkled or shirred effects like in the shorts pictured in Figure 6.91.

Step 16: Use the Dodge Tool

The opposite of the Burn Tool (O) is the **Photoshop® Dodge Tool (O)**. They both share the same keyboard shortcut. Use the Dodge Tool (O) to highlight areas, particularly those that protrude, such as the convex portions of folds (Figure 6.92).

Note: *Both the Burn Tool and the Dodge Tool (O) have settings that can be adjusted in the Photoshop® Options Bar. It is a good practice to use lower settings and gradually build up the effects.*

Step 17: Make Inner Shadows and Gradient Overlays

Adding additional Layer Style features can create attractive results. An **Inner Shadow** will add toning to the object on a selected layer (Figure 6.93). **Gradient Overlays** can create illusions of contouring if the Opacity is lowered.

Step 18: Tint the Shadows

Inner Shadows and other elements of Layer Styles can be tinted. The one in Figure 6.94 has given a tanned glow to the form of the character.

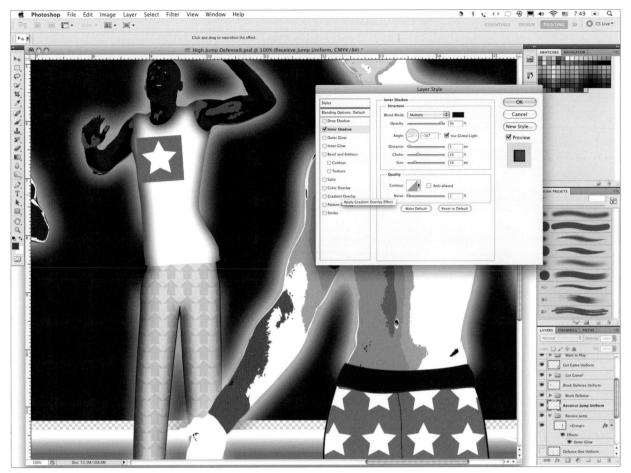

Figure 6.93

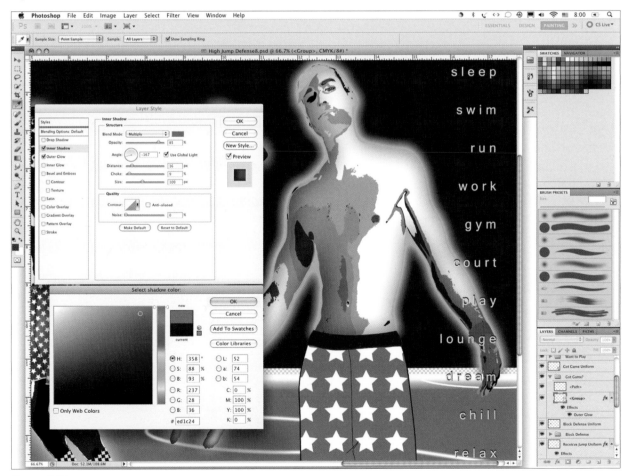

Figure 6.94

Figure 6.95 Illustration by Stacy Stewart Smith.

Step 19: Bevel and Emboss to Finish

The **Bevel and Emboss** Layer Style is commonly used to simulate 3-D realism. Try using it on some of the clothing elements. The size, spread, and Opacity of this Layer Style all play important roles in its successful application. In the finished story-board (Figure 6.95), Layer Styles and tool attributes were added to the clothing elements and also to some of the croquis. The perspective of the horizon line was slightly tilted, a drop shadow was added to the signage, and the small figure on the left was rescaled.

Exercise 6.1

Now that you have learned how to use the fundamentals of both Illustrator® and Photoshop®, rethink Tutorial 6.5 as a women's wear presentation. Use your own drawings or images of Ana and Jade from the Digital Duo Modeling Agency on ①. Try designing swimwear or loungewear. Use your imagination.

Chapter 6 Summary

Chapter 6 was a tour de force of tutorials designed to develop your Illustrator® skills, especially the use of the Live Trace features. Although the visuals suggest a fixed aesthetic for each tutorial, alternative presentations could be created. As an alternative exercise, challenge yourself to re-create your own versions of the tutorials. For example, take photos of your own illustrations, friends, family, or even classmates, and then position them in Tutorial 6.5: High Jump Defense. You will discover that each of the tutorials can be personalized; just add your own touch and use your imagination and creativity. Once you have practiced these tutorials, answer the questions in the Self-Assessment. If you can answer them with ease, proceed to Chapter 7. Review and/ or repeat the Chapter 6 tutorials if you sense difficulties.

Chapter 6 Self-Assessment

1. Do I understand how to add Layer Styles to particular layers in my Illustrator® files?

2. Have I tried all of the Illustrator® Live Trace preset options?

3. Do I know what the Expand button does when it appears during Live Trace?

4. Do I really know how to use the Illustrator® Paint Bucket Tool (K), the Illustrator® Magic Wand Tool (Y), and the Illustrator® Eyedropper Tool?

5. If someone asked me what the difference is between the Illustrator® Faces and Edges, could I give an explanation? Could I also tell someone the differences between Photo High Fidelity and Color 16 in Illustrator®?

6. Do I really understand the purpose for using multiple Artboards, and can I actually set up or add them to a file in Illustrator®?

7. Do I know which Illustrator® tool to select and use if I want to convert a simple line segment into a beautiful fashion eyebrow?

8. Can I make effective use of the Illustrator® tool to establish two-point perspective? Can I name this tool, set up a proper Artboard, add figures, and then scale them appropriately in my presentation(s)?

9. Can I use Illustrator® to create an intarsia sweater graph? Can I separate colors for screen-printing procedures?

10. I know I can open an Illustrator® file in Photoshop®, but can I effectively export the layers? In addition, can I name and describe the function for at least seven tools or features in Photoshop® that can be used to enhance exported images?

Chapter 6 DVD Extra

Develop your expertise with Illustrator® Live Trace by completing the following DVD Extra tutorial. This tutorial can be found on ① Ch6\ DVD Extra 6.1.

DVD Extra 6.1

This tutorial challenges you with the task of creating a digital illustration totally from fashion photography (Figure 6.96). You will use the Live Trace features of Illustrator® to separate the parts of a photo, as well as filters to add fine art and illustration characteristics to your project.

Figure 6.96

Fashion Design, Presentation, and Exhibition with Photoshop®

7

Objectives

Chapter 7 contains a series of fashion design and merchandising tutorials that demonstrate the painting benefits of Photoshop®. You will also have an opportunity to exercise your own freehand electronic drawing skill while you master the tools, panels, and filters of the program.

Because Photoshop® provides superior benefits to fashion illustration through a multiplicity of options, you must consider the types of brushes and the input devices to use for each project. By the very nature of our physical/mental attributes, each digital artist will need something different. However, a digital drawing tablet is suggested for use with some of the tutorials. In this chapter, you will:

◎ Examine and exercise Photoshop® digital painting capabilities that mimic those used by traditional fine art painters

◎ Draw freehand with digital brushes to develop fashion concepts and illustrations

◎ Obtain a fuller understanding of the Brush panel, and adjust the settings to create brushes that yield painterly, bristle strokes, and/or wet-looking edges associated with fine art washes, drips, or watercolor techniques

◎ Design mood, color, and inspiration digital storyboards using Photoshop®

◎ Create Alpha Channels to save selections

◎ Design a fashion show for Digital Duo Fashion Week using what you have learned and executed in the chapter tutorials

Tutorial 7.1
THE DIGITAL MOOD BOARD

A fashion mood board sets the tone of a burgeoning trend in a target market. Use the customer profile storyboard that you created in Tutorial 5.1 to help you design a digital mood board and identify a trend for a target market. There are many ways to create mood boards, but they all require research and assembly. Digital mood boards can be put together within minutes if you have your images already scanned. The only difficult part is staying focused and making a strong statement with images, textile swatches, trims, and some market inspiration.

Using Apparel Images for Inspiration

There are two basic ways to develop the digital fashion mood board. The first method involves actual fashion trends. In the apparel industry, professionals make educated predictions by either subscribing to trend-forecasting publishers or shopping the global market for ideas. They carefully select images and sample swatches for their intrinsic characteristics. They then assemble the mood boards. The objective is to convey strong visual fashion messages without using images of the current apparel trends. Nearly a year or more in advance of a market, the product development team will present anywhere from five to twenty mood boards at a meeting.

Note: Some companies prefer to show their color inspiration separately from mood boards. Often the two are inseparable because color may be the trend.

Using Nonapparel Images to Inspire

Although it is sometimes practiced in apparel product development, images of current fashions should not be used on mood boards as inspiration for the clothing itself, particularly in markets like designer and bridge sportswear. For you this is extremely important because the last thing you want is for viewers to love the ideas of the designer's clothing/trends more than they do your illustrations/designs. Another method of creating fashion mood boards is to use images that allude to ideas, rather than actual fashion photos. Couture and designer markets should set trends rather than follow them, so fine art, vegetation, animals, minerals, and almost anything can become a source of inspiration to convey their artistic direction.

Fashion Trend Theory

Fashion trend theory is not an exact science. It is anyone's guess when a particular one will be in demand, but savvy fashion professionals make solid predictions based on the sales climate, and then test new merchandise. For example, it usually takes at least a year for trends that were shown in the couture or designer markets to slowly appear in mass (popular priced) sportswear markets. Thanks to the Internet, global fashion market weeks and comprehensive information can be shared almost instantaneously.

Trends fade quickly, so in order not to date the visuals, this tutorial is not being based on actual trends. Instead, the DVD images for the Chapter 7 Tutorials were selected based on a single idea for three different mock trends that will work for either men's wear or women's wear presentations. They include:

- **Metal Minimalism:** Contemporary and retro images with a futuristic appeal such as metals, textiles, trims, architecture, artifacts, raw materials, and landscapes in tones of metallic silver, soft grays, and neutrals.

- **Nouveau Passage:** Inspired by the Art Nouveau international design style and Paris culture, images include fine art painting, sculpture, landmarks, textiles, vintage interiors, antique furniture, birds, and jewelry in tints, tones, and shades of teal green, amber, beige, hunter, and gold.

- **Refuge Revisited:** Imagine an urban professional living in a country environment. The images magnify nature, especially autumn trees, dried plants, bark, fine art installations, lace, quilts, fruit, and ribbons in gold, burgundy, natural, taupe, and navy.

The aim is to demonstrate the procedures for creating fashion mood boards using Photoshop®. You will also be introduced to additional Photoshop® tools, panels, and filters.

The Mood Board Task

Use one of three sets of images from ① Ch07\ Tutorial 7.1 or digitize the following types of images for each trend that you identify, then create your fashion mood board by following the tutorial steps Here is the formula for a mood board image:

- Interior views of a room
- Exterior, architecture, or landscape images
- Fine art, but not fashion-related
- Four to six photos of fabric swatches
- One to three trims and/or notions
- One historical, ethnic, or technology image
- One home furnishings element
- One "life" image (anything relevant to the mood that is alive). For example: a plant, an elephant, a school of fish, a butterfly, etc.
- A word or simplified phrase that personifies the trend in an appropriate font

Note: *If you decide to use your own photos, remember that all of the images for one trend must contain a unified marketing concept and aesthetic. The files must also be scanned at the same resolution (suggested: 150 to 300 dpi).*

Step 1: Set Up Your New Document in Photoshop®

Load Photoshop®. Press *Cmd+N / Ctrl+N* to create a new document. In the New dialog box, enter the information shown in Figure 7.1 into the fields and click OK.

Step 2: Place Your Chosen Theme Files

Go to *Menu Bar > File > Place* and locate each of the files that you will use for this mood board (Figure 7.2). We will be using images from ① Ch07\ Tutorial 7.1\Refuge Revisited for the example. You may choose the photos shown here or pick images from the other two available themes (*Metal Minimalism* or *Nouveau Passage*). Scanning your own images is ideal, so try to use a combination of your own photos along with those available on the DVD.

Figure 7.1

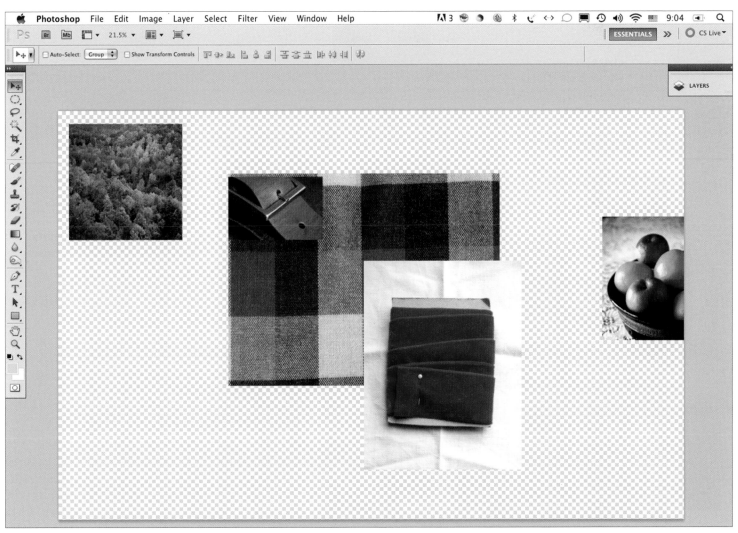

Figure 7.2 Place and position relevant images on your canvas. They will appear on separate layers with the titles you give them.

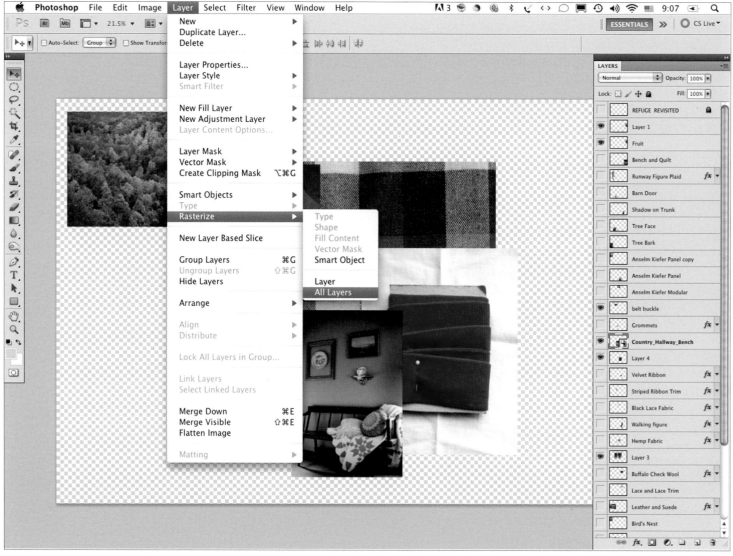

Figure 7.3 Rasterize all the layers.

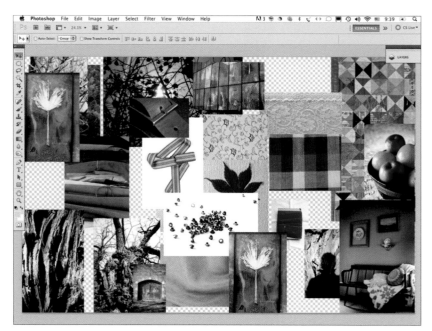

Figure 7.4

Step 3: Rasterize All Layers

Make certain that all your layers are rasterized. Go to *Menu Bar > Layer > Rasterize > All Layers* as illustrated by Figure 7.3.

Step 4: Resize and Reposition the Images

Select each layer and press *Cmd+T / Ctrl+T* to Free Transform the images. Hold the Shift key and constrain the proportions while you resize the Bounding Box. Double-click inside the box to accept the changes (Figure 7.4).

Step 5: Set Up and Save a Workspace

The Photoshop® default Essentials Workspace settings are fine for this tutorial, but they do contain some panels that will not be used, and those panels should be hidden. To do this, close the Adjustments, Masks, Styles, and Mini Bridge panels.

Figure 7.5

New Workspace

Name: Refuge Revisited Mood Board

Capture
Panel locations will be saved in this workspace.
Keyboard Shortcuts and Menus are optional.
☐ Keyboard Shortcuts
☐ Menus

Save
Cancel

Figure 7.6

The Photoshop® Workspace switcher is located in the Application Bar. If you are using a PC, the Application Bar is in the same location as the Menu Bar. On a Mac the Application Bar rests below the Menu Bar. Look on the right side (Figure 7.5), and then press the double arrows to locate the hidden menu. Scroll to New Workspace and its dialog box appears. Enter an appropriate title and click Save (Figure 7.6).

Step 6: Identify and Rename the Layers

As you Place the images into the file, double-click on each new layer and rename it so you can recognize where each is located (Figure 7.7).

Step 7: Use the Magic Wand to Select and Delete Pixels

Some pictures may contain solid backgrounds that can be deleted. Choose the Photoshop® Magic Wand

LAYERS

Normal   Opacity: 100%

Lock: ☐ ✐ ✤ 🔒   Fill: 100%

Fall Trees

Fruit

Belt Buckle

Grommets

Velvet Ribbon

Striped Ribbon Trim

Black Lace Fabric

Hemp Fabric

Lace and Lace Trim

Antique Quilt

Jacquard Herringbone

Leather and Suede

Buffalo Check Wool

Anselm Kiefer Panel

Tree Face

Old Barn

Anselm Kiefer Modular

Natural Lace Flowers Sky

Bird's Nest

Tree Bark

Barn Door

Shadow on Trunk

Bench and Quilt

Figure 7.7

Figure 7.8

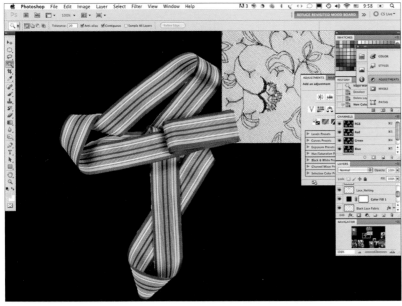

Figure 7.9

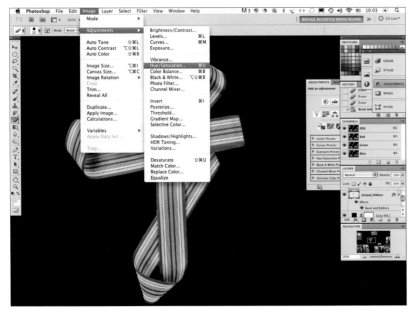

Figure 7.10

Tool (W), select the area, and press Delete. You may need to adjust the *Tolerance* in the Options Bar. To select multiple areas, hold the Shift key. The white background was removed from the striped ribbon trim in Figure 7.8.

Step 8: Use Adjustment Layers to Clean Up Images

1. Deselect by pressing *Cmd+D / Ctrl+D.* Select the layer below the one you are working on.

2. Click the Create New Fill or **Adjustment Layer** icon at the bottom of the Layers panel. It looks like a black-and-white ellipse.

3. A menu appears. Choose *Solid Color* and a new layer will be added below the one you are working on. Use the Color Picker to select a contrasting background color to help you see the areas that need cleaning up.

4. Zoom in closer; use the Photoshop® Eraser Tool (E), as well as others, to clean the selection (Figure 7.9).

5. The Blur Tool rids the edges of any unsightly white areas by blending them into transparent pixels. Use a small brush and try not to move into the interior of the image.

6. The Layer Style Bevel and Emboss may help the image retain its 3-D look.

7. When you are done, drag the *Adjustment* layer to the Trash icon at the bottom of the panel.

8. Save and back up your work.

Step 9: Change Color

You may find that the color of certain images is confining. To adjust or change the color of an image in order to create a more harmonious mood board, select a layer and go to *Menu Bar > Image > Adjustment > Hue/Saturation* (Figure 7.10).

1. The Hue/Saturation dialog box appears. Because you have not created any presets, use the Default. In the section below this, you can either choose to adjust the entire image from the *Master* or click the icons to reveal exact hues to adjust.

2. Because the ribbon in the tutorial example is monochromatic, only reds will be adjusted. To change the color, push the *Hue* slider (Figure 7.11).

3. To intensify the color or to make it more grayscale, use the *Saturation* slider.

4. The *Lightness* slider will brighten or darken the image.

5. To change a specific color, use the automatic Eyedropper to select the hue from the image, then adjust the sliders accordingly (Figure 7.12).

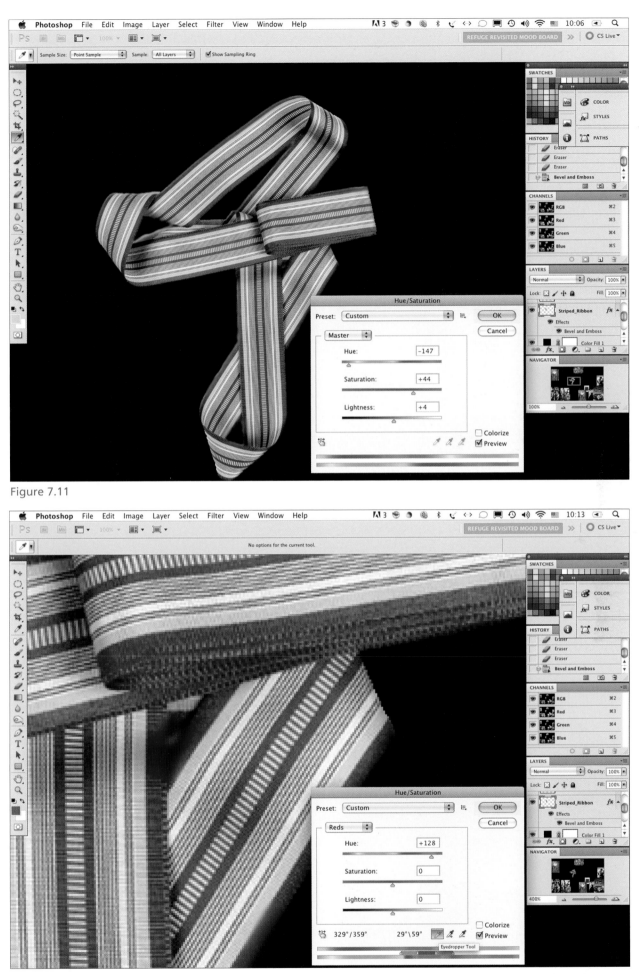

Figure 7.11

Figure 7.12

Figure 7.13

Figure 7.14

Step 10: Arrange the Fabric and Trims

Because the mood board is the personification of a fashion trend, textiles and trims are the primary means to convey the apparel message. Use the Move Tool (V) to arrange these images in one area. If necessary, reorder the layers so that the textile and trims layers are adjacent to each other. Consider the arrangement, size, colors, etc. Lock and/or toggle off the visibility of the other layers. Make changes by using what you have already learned in this and in previous chapters (Figure 7.13).

Step 11: Rotate the Images

To rotate an object that is on a layer, press *Cmd+T / Ctrl+T* to Free Transform. When you see the Bounding Box, bring your cursor to the corner and a double-sided arrow will appear. Rotate the object (Figure 7.14), and then double-click inside the box, except for the center, to accept the new position.

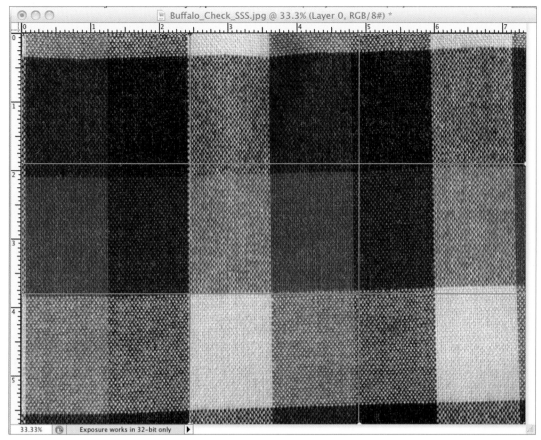

Figure 7.15

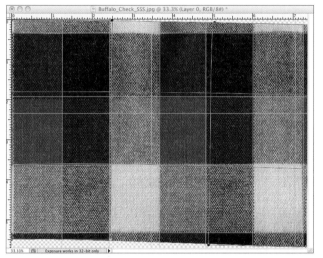

Figure 7.16

Figure 7.17

Step 12: Warp Scanned Textile Images

Scanned textile patterns, especially stripes, checks, and plaids, often appear slightly skewed. To correct this, use the Photoshop® **Warp** filter.

1. Select the layer and go to *Menu Bar > Edit > Transform > Warp*. A gridded Bounding Box will appear around your image (Figure 7.15).

2. If you cannot see the Warp grid well, pull Guides from the rulers to help gauge the perpendicular planes. If the Guides do not show, toggle them on by pressing *Cmd+;(semicolon) / Ctrl+; (semicolon)*, then adjust the simulated warp and weft of the digital pattern image with the Warp's grid divisions. The changes will not make the repeat perfect, but you will be able to refine the appearance (Figure 7.16).

3. Select the Check (Commit transform) icon in the Options Bar on the right to accept the changes.

Note: *If you are having difficulty with the alignment, try rescanning the fabric.*

4. Use the Crop Tool (C) to fit the check pattern into a rectangle. The pattern repeat should begin on the top and left sides, then repeat on the bottom and right (Figure 7.17).

Figure 7.18

Figure 7.19

5. Lock the other layers, but link the fabric and trim layers by selecting them while holding the Shift key, and then clicking the chain icon at the bottom of the panel. **Figure 7.18** shows the completed arrangement of fabric swatches and trims.

Step 13: Locate and Resize a Background Image

Select one of your images to serve as a background. Resize it using the instructions in Step Four and pull the layer to the bottom (Figure 7.19).

Step 14: Unlock and Reposition the Additional Images (Figure 7.20)

Step 15: Use the Colored Pencil Filter

Select one of your layers with an organic image and use the **Colored Pencil filter**. Go to *Menu Bar > Filter > Artistic > Colored Pencil*. Use the settings in Figure 7.21 or make further adjustments by pushing the sliders.

Figure 7.20

Figure 7.21 Colored Pencil filter.

Step 16: Use the Paint Daubs Filter

The **Paint Daubs filter** will take the edge off some of your more cluttered images. Go to *Menu Bar > Filter > Artistic > Paint Daubs*. Depending on the image, you may not need to make any changes to the default settings (Figure 7.22).

Figure 7.22 **Paint Daubs filter.**

Step 17: Use the Rough Pastels Filter

The **Rough Pastels filter** will instantly give any photo the appearance of a work of digital fine art (Figure 7.23).

Step 18: Use the Cutout Filter

Some images have too much information. The Cutout filter will eliminate some of the superfluous information (Figure 7.24).

Step 19: Use the Spatter Filter

Because we are heading in the direction of illustration, why not try the **Spatter filter**? The settings allow you to generate a painterly look from an otherwise ordinary photo source (Figure 7.25).

Step 20: Add Silhouetted Figures

If you completed Tutorial 3.1, then you probably have saved some figure silhouettes. Open the Illustrator® file for that assignment and copy, then paste a few figures into the Photoshop® file. A small Paste dialog box will appear. Check the *Paste as Pixels* option and click OK (Figure 7.26). The figures will appear on separate layers. Rename and reposition the layers.

Step 21: Define a Pattern from a Swatch

Select a patterned swatch like the buffalo check supplied with the *Refuge Revisited* images. Use the Rectangular Marquee Tool (M) to create a selection around an identifiable repeat. Try to be as precise as possible. Copy and paste the selection. Photoshop® will create a new layer for the swatch that you pasted. Below that new layer, temporarily create an Adjustment layer filled with a solid color so

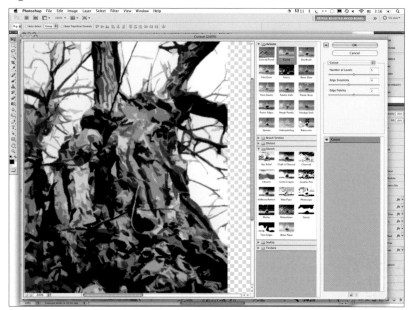

Figure 7.23 **Rough Pastels filter.**

Figure 7.24 **Cutout filter.**

Figure 7.25   **Spatter filter.**

Figure 7.26

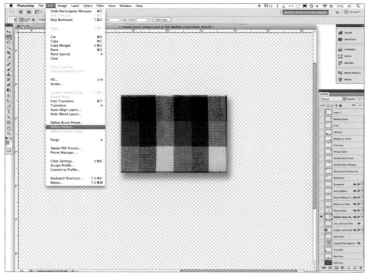

Figure 7.27

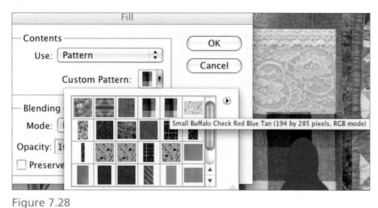

Figure 7.28

that you can see it easily. Scale the pattern to a size that would comfortably fit into a rendered garment on the page by pressing *Cmd+T / Ctrl+T*. Reselect the repeat with the Rectangular Marquee Tool (M), and then go to *Menu Bar > Edit > Define Pattern* (Figure 7.27). In the dialog box, give the pattern an appropriate name and click OK.

Step 22: Fill and Be Creative

To use the pattern that you have defined, select an object, then go to *Menu Bar > Edit > Fill*. In the Fill dialog box, scroll to the pattern in the *Use* area as shown in Figure 7.28. The pattern will fill the selected area of the figure. The Bevel and Emboss effect and the Stroke Layer Styles will enhance the look.

Be creative with the settings, using everything that you have learned to make this mood board your own. Add or delete images, and try filters, Layer Styles, as well as the tools and panel features to enhance your presentation. The blending options available in the Layer Style menu were used to further enhance the completed tutorial example in Figure 7.29.

Note: *Do not forget to add signage; it makes a nice final touch.*

Figure 7.29 Illustration by Stacy Stewart Smith.

Communicating Style through Color Trends

Photoshop® has great capacity for mixing colors because of the nature of pixels. New improvements to the program, particularly those associated with digital painting, take it to an even higher level. This tutorial is a short, but vitally important, exercise aimed at teaching you how to construct digital fashion-color forecasting information. You should note that this is different from the science of color that will be partially explored later in the book.

Required supplies: Completed digital customer profile and mood board

What Is a Fashion Color Forecast?

Fashion color forecasting is the art of guesstimating when particular hues will be appropriate for various target markets for specific seasons. The logic behind these predictions is based on what was presented in higher markets up to two seasons before. Naturally, each fashion designer can develop their own color stories, but most manufacturers will find some means of coordinating color because it is an essential element of design.

In high-end markets, color is communicated like fine art. A couture house will not necessarily consult trend forecasting, but will instead wield color at the whim of its creative director.

The fashion media and celebrities also contribute to developing fashion color trends. Fashion magazines help to guide the trends through their editorial pages as well as through their reporting of worldwide fashion events. Photographs of prominent fashion figures and other celebrities in magazines and on the Internet connect consumers to fashion trends long before they ever reach retail stores. The average consumer is well educated and most know exactly what items and in which colors they want to purchase, before they walk through shop doors.

Design teams need to be organized, remain targeted, and communicate effectively with fashion merchandisers and company officials. Before decisions are made to create samples, color stories are presented in merchandise meetings. Generally speaking, it is the retailer who will make the decision as to the color assortment they will market. Store buyers will either approve or reject certain colors.

Step 1: Conduct Color Research

Spend some time looking through online collections to discover color trends from various upscale designers and/or fashion color forecasting services. Go back as far as two to three seasons, keeping notes on how many designers used a particular color story in the couture market. Next, research the designer market that followed the trend the next season, and you will observe that at least four to six colors, which began in the highest level of fashion, influenced lower markets. In addition, pay attention to the wardrobe choices of high-profile celebrities. All of the major fashion magazines keep tabs on what they are wearing, but the most comprehensive information will come from *Women's Wear Daily*, *Vogue*, *Details*, and style.com. Pick twenty popular colors, then narrow your choices to just six to eight distinct hues. Save two to six good photo resources representing the development of key color trends to use on your color forecast storyboard.

Step 2: Locate an Inspiration Photo

Look for a nonfashion image that contains the hues of your color story and personifies the concept of your theme. Some good sources include the following: fine art, ethnic culture, interiors, wildlife, artifacts, travel images, and historical landmarks. You can even select one of the photos from your mood board.

Step 3: Prepare a New Photoshop® Document

Use the same document setup specifications as in the previous storyboard digital tutorials, but change the title to include the words "color forecast," and then add your initials.

Step 4: Fill the Background and Add the Inspiration Photo

Press *Cmd+A / Ctrl+A* to select the background. Go to *Menu Bar > Edit > Fill*, then choose *Color* from the contents menu, and the Color Picker will appear. You can choose the Background fill from the Color Picker by moving the slider on the Spectrum Bar at the right, then select a hue from the larger space by clicking on it. The color that you choose should be one that complements your chosen images and inspiration photo. You can always change the color later. Afterward, click OK and place your inspiration photo into the file on a separate layer (Figure 7.30).

Step 5: Create Selections

The digital color storyboard may require some evidence that the forecast is properly targeted. In higher markets, this is unnecessary. It is acceptable to use a

Figure 7.30

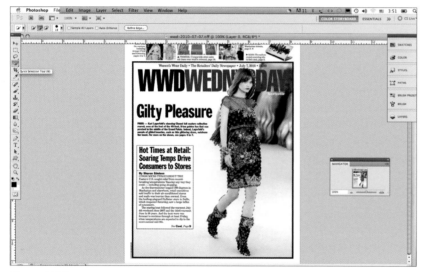

Figure 7.31

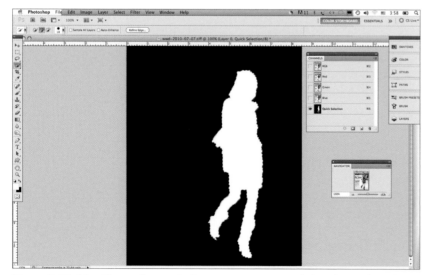

Figure 7.32 **The Channels panel allows you to create Alpha Channel masks like this one.**

few images from current fashions in order to substantiate your predictions, but just be very selective and limit them to six or less.

Something to consider for color forecasting in markets below the designer level is the images of models strutting on runways. They can carry a powerful impact, but you will need to remove the background imagery. To do this, use the Quick Selection Tool (W); it acts like a brush to find color pixels that cluster into shapes. You will be able to generate a general selection of any model on a runway like those who appear on the covers of *Women's Wear Daily* (Figure 7.31). Once you select an area, marching ants will surround it.

Step 6: Create and Reload Alpha Channel Masks to Save Selections

The Quick Selection Tool (W) is easy to use, but it will not always yield ideal results. In addition, perfecting selected areas can be an arduous task. You may need to step away from your desk or stop at the end of a long day before you have finished. To avoid losing your selections, save **Alpha Channels**. This time-saving production technique allows you or a team member to pick up where you left off in the selection process. To save an Alpha Channel, follow these instructions:

1. Go to *Menu Bar > Window > Channels*.

2. Pull the Channels panel fully open to reveal its color composition layers, which are in the Photoshop® default RGB color mode.

3. The top layer is the full-color layer, which can be accessed by pressing *Cmd+2 / Ctrl+2.* At the bottom of the panel is an icon that looks like a gray box with a white circle inside it. It is called the **Save Selection as Channel** button. With your marching ants flashing, click it to create the Alpha 1 channel.

4. Name the channel by clicking on its name. The first selection could be named *General* or *Quick Selection*.

5. When you create the Alpha Channel, the mask will show as a white background with a black silhouette of the **Selected Areas**. To treat the selection as a mask, double-click on the Alpha Channel and select the **Masked Areas** button in the *Color Indicates* field (Figure 7.32). Once you have made your general selection and created an Alpha Channel, save your work. This allows you to save the channel in that file as well.

6. Click the **RGB Channel** to return to the color image.

Loading Channels as Selections

7. If you deselect from an Alpha Channel or you have closed the file, you can restore your selected areas as long as you have properly saved your file in the Photoshop® (.PSD) format. Click the **Load Channel as Selection** button at the bottom of the Channels panel, and your marching ants will reappear.

8. You can perfect the first Alpha Channel by repeating the instructions for saving an Alpha Channel.

9. To help you to stay organized, label each new Alpha Channel with a date or time to mark the change, then save and back up your work.

Step 7: Use the Lasso Tool

The purpose of saving Alpha Channels is to work on selected areas in stages. To perfect a selection, you will need to use additional tools and save new channels. The Lasso Tool (L) is a freehand selection tool. Figure 7.33 reveals an area that the Quick Selection Tool (W) missed. Use the Lasso Tool (L) to add to a selection by holding the Shift key and creating a shape up to the edge. In Figure 7.34, a zoomed view shows a portion of the selection that has overshot the boundary of the model's head. Use the Lasso Tool (L) and hold the Option key (Mac) or the Alt key (PC) to subtract it from selected areas. Just encapsulate the overflow and bring the selection to the edge of the intended target. When you have made a few adjustments, save a new Alpha Channel (Figure 7.35).

Step 8: Refine the Edges

A feature of Photoshop® CS5 and CS6 is its ability to refine the edges of selections. To access this feature, go to *Menu Bar > Select > Refine Edge* or press *Option+Cmd+R / Alt+Ctrl+R* while the marching ants are showing. The Refine Edge dialog box appears, allowing you to change the View Mode, Edge Detection, Adjust Edge, and Output. The most important of these are the *View Mode* and the *Adjust Edge* sections. The *View Mode* allows you to see a preview of what the edges look like against a certain type of background, such as a mask, marching ants, etc. The *Adjust Edge* section has slider options to help you create the edge you want as to smoothness, feathered softness, contrast, and/or shifting. The zoomed view of Figure 7.36 shows adjustments made to the selected image via the new Photoshop® Refine Edge features.

Step 9: Adjust Alpha Channel Masks in Quick Mask Mode

For some users the Lasso Tool (L) is difficult to use when adjusting selections. You can also refine them by using the Edit in Quick Mask Mode (Q) located at the bottom of the Tools panel.

Figure 7.33

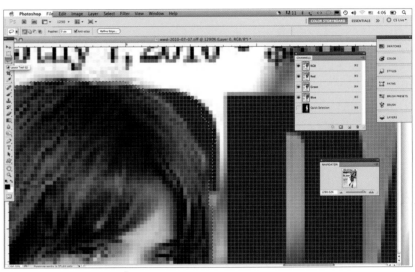

Figure 7.34

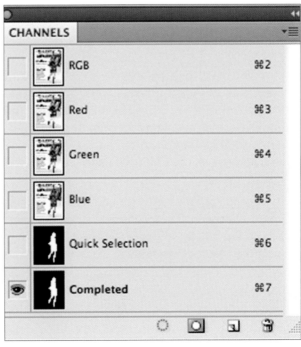

Figure 7.35

Figure 7.36

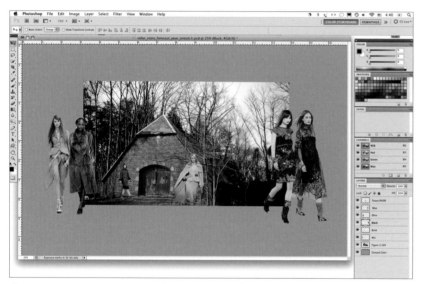

Figure 7.37

- After you have created a general selection and saved it as an Alpha Channel, click on the Load Channel as Selection button at the bottom of the Channels panel, and then click on the *Edit in Quick Mask Mode (Q)* button. A temporary Quick Mask layer appears in the Channels panel beneath the Alpha Channel.

- On the image, the areas around your selection should appear in translucent red. If not, double-click on the button. In the Quick Mask dialog box, select the Masked Areas Edit in Quick Mask Mode (Q) button in the *Color Indicates* section.

- Afterward, select the Brush Tool (B). Use the Hard Round brush in the Brush Preset panel at 100% *Opacity* and 100% *Flow* in the Options Bar. Adjust

the brush size at the top of the Brush Preset panel to fit the area that you need to adjust.

- Press (D) to return to the Default Foreground and Background colors, which are white and black.

- Use the Brush Tool (B) to refine the selection. If you want to add to the selection, the Foreground Color Box must contain black. Press X to switch the Foreground and Background color. To subtract from the selection, switch the Foreground color to white using the double-sided arrow icon in the Tools panel.

- Once you have made your adjustments to the red area, press the Edit in Quick Mask Mode button (Q) again, create a new Alpha Channel, and then save your work.

Step 10: Repeat Steps Five through Eight for all of the Runway Images

Repeat the steps that you followed in Steps Five through Eight for each of the runway models' images that you use in your presentation.

Step 11: Place the Runway Images

Place the images and name the layers to reflect the hues (Figure 7.37).

Step 12: Create Shapes and Fill with Fashion Colors

1. Use the Rectangle Tool (U) or any simple shape tool to create a color shape.

2. To create a square, hold the Shift key.

3. Select the layer and click the Create a New Layer icon. Make as many copies as you need for your color standards.

4. Use the Move Tool (V) to pull the shapes into position.

5. Select all the layers where you have shapes by holding the Shift key.

6. Use the Photoshop® Align panel or the Align Options in the Options Bar to *Distribute Horizontal Centers*.

7. Click *Align Bottom Edges* and rasterize all the layers.

Color Fills

8. Use the Magic Wand Tool (W) to select each shape.

9. Use the Eyedropper Tool (I) to select colors from your runway or inspiration photo(s).

10. Go to *Menu Bar > Edit > Fill > Foreground Color*. Fill each shape with a different color, then save and back up your work (Figure 7.38).

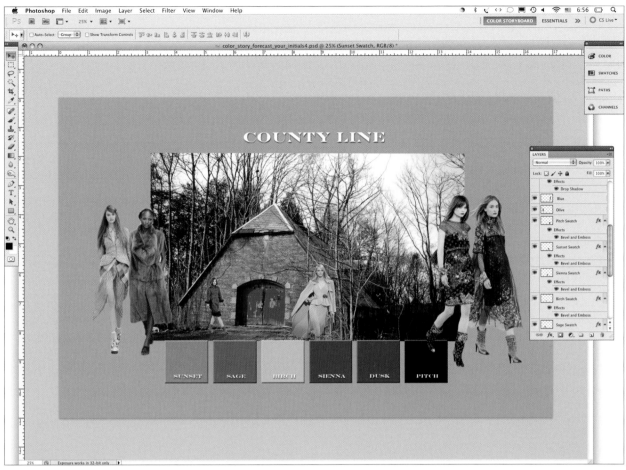

Figure 7.38

Gamut Warning and Color Libraries

Check your Gamut Warning for any colors that may not print to the specified standard. Select and replace them with colors from the Pantone Process Uncoated Color Library. Select the color with the Magic Wand Tool (W), then select the Set Foreground Box to obtain the Color Picker. Click the button labeled Color Libraries located on the right. Select an exact hue from the Library and click OK. Afterward, go back and fill the standard again with the Pantone color. Even if it does not print to standard, you will be able to specify the color when communicating with others. You could do this for each swatch, if needed.

 **Ruler Tool Placement**

Use the Ruler Tool (I) to check the placement of objects and signage in relationship to your inspiration photo. Just click and drag from the corners of the shape to the ends of the signage. Pay attention to the measurements in the Options Bar. You will be able to tell if the signage is off-center.

TIP: Photoshop® Color Libraries

Look through all the Photoshop® Color Libraries by clicking first on the Set Foreground Box and then on the Color Libraries button within the Color Picker dialog box. Having familiarity with these actual color standards will better prepare you for mixing colors and specifying them to outside sources.

Step 13: Add Fashion Color Titles

Assigning fashion titles to the hues in your color story may seem easy, but it will take careful consideration. Think carefully about the association of the images to the colors, then search for the meaning. Be poetic.

To begin, give the color story a name using the inspiration photo, as was done with the tutorial example called *County Line*. This title complements the *Refuge Revisited* mood board. Possible harmonious fashion color titles include sunset, sage, birch, sienna, dusk, and pitch.

Adding Signage

Select the Horizontal Type Tool (T), then click on the canvas near the color shapes. Both a flashing cursor and a type layer appear. The Options Bar displays type character attributes. You can also show the Character panel by going to *Menu Bar > Window > Character*. Choose a simple font that does not distract from your images. Some font sets will offer bold or italic. Click on the color sampler to change the color of your words, but keep in mind that you should be consistent with the font and the color that you used for the mood board. When you type onto the flashing cursor, what you write will be entered on the type layer. After you create a title for each color standard, select the layers. Use the Align attributes that appear in the Options Bar to even up the character sets (Figure 7.39).

Note: Layer Styles can also be added to type set in Photoshop®.

Step 14: Add a Border

In presentations where various objects surround a common geometric shape, as is the case in the tuto-rial example, borders help to maintain visual focus. There are many ways to create a border, but the most common and useful is to simply create the shape with a selection tool.

1. Create a new layer right above the inspiration photo and name it *Border*.

2. Pull Guides to assist your placement of the selection that you will make with the Rectangular Marquee Tool (M). In the tutorial example, Guides were pulled and placed a half an inch from each edge.

3. Make your selection, then go to *Menu Bar > Edit > Stroke*. The Stroke dialog box allows you to choose the *Width* (in pixels), the color, location, and blending. Twenty pixels was used in this example.

The border in Figure 7.39 was filled with a stroke of the background color selected with the Eyedropper Tool (I) that appears when you press the color sampler and move your cursor outside the Color Picker. Layer Styles were added.

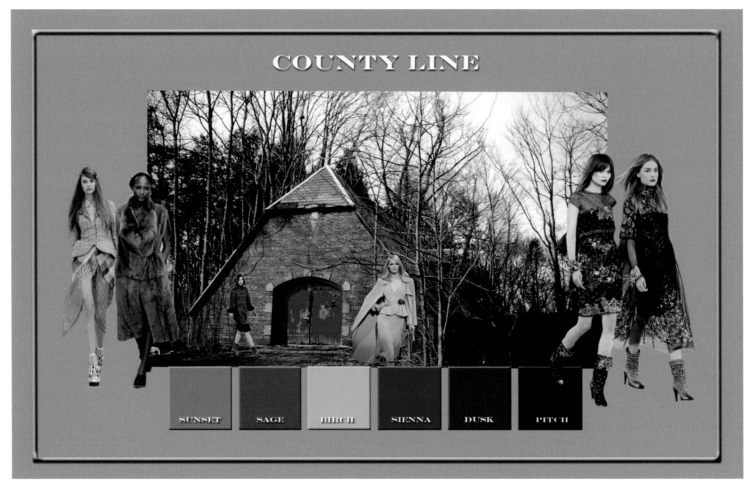

Figure 7.39 **Illustration by Stacy Stewart Smith.**

Tutorial 7.3
DIGITAL FASHION DESIGN
SKETCHING AND PAINTING

Everything in fashion begins with an idea, but conveying these ideas becomes a problem for many who do not sketch well freehand. This tutorial acquaints you with most of the Photoshop® drawing and painting techniques that will allow you to communicate your ideas via digital means. To complete this tutorial, you are free to scan and use either your own croquis or the runway photos of models from ① Digital Duo Modeling Agency. The poses provide a template upon which you can render your digital design sketches. While drawing the full croquis might be ideal, we will focus on the clothing to make action thumbnail sketches.

Figure 7.40

Designing with Computers

The fashion industry is always pressed for time. The need to keep production time schedules and meet the seasonal demands of retailers remains the motivating factor for this frenzy. The objective of design is to keep a focus on the needs of the consumer while creating fresh ideas, maintaining cost efficiency, and fulfilling the needs of marketing.

Freehand drawings are an excellent source for generating the initial design sketches. They allow the talent of the fashion designer as an artist to govern the direction of a particular manufacturer or house. In high-end markets, freehand sketches may remain absolutely essential, but things are changing. Thanks to programs like Illustrator® and Photoshop®, digital fashion sketches can offer the same benefits to the design process as their freehand counterparts.

Note: *Before you begin the tutorial, consider planning your design concepts, silhouettes, and details by drawing freehand in a sketchbook.*

Step 1: Create a New Document

Create a new document in Photoshop® using the same specifications as the other tutorials in this chapter.

Step 2: Place Images

Place multiple full-length photos of the models from ① Digital Duo Modeling Agency and lock the layers. In Figure 7.40, four runway poses of Jade were placed into a file on various layers.

Step 3: Set Up the Workspace as Previously Instructed

Set up your Workspace and include the Brush and the Brush Presets panels.

Step 4: Open the Previously Completed Digital Boards

Open the completed digital customer profile, mood, and color boards. Use them to keep your focus upon the target market and seasonal trend(s). You may also elect to print and post the boards.

Note: *To maintain classicism and add a vintage mystique, The Private Collections, which includes catalogs of select items from the Duke and Duchess of Windsor, served as a source of inspiration for the designs in this tutorial. (Sotheby's. The Duke & Duchess of Windsor, 4 vols. [New York: Sotheby's, September 9–11, 1997].)*

Step 5: Add the Color Story to the Swatches Panel

With the digital color storyboard also open, use the Eyedropper Tool (I) to select the color swatches. Click in your Swatches panel to add the hues. In the Color Swatch Name dialog box, give each swatch the same title that appears on the storyboard (Figure 7.41). Add additional hues that you may need by selecting them from the inspiration photo.

Step 6: Create a Silhouettes Layer

Create a new layer above the others and name it *Silhouettes*.

Step 7: Add a Fill Layer

Create a *Fill Adjustments* layer below the others.

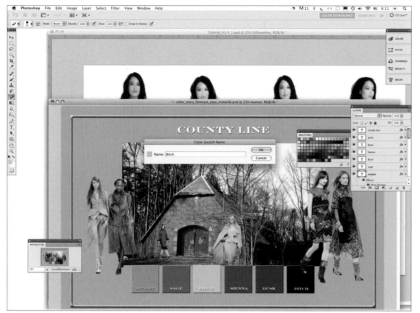

Figure 7.41

Figure 7.42

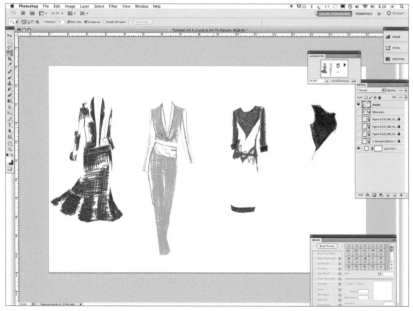

Figure 7.43

Step 8: Use the Brush Panel to Paint Digitally

1. With all the other layers locked, select the Brush Tool (B) or the Pencil Tool (B) and use a 15 to 30 pt brush, at 100% *Opacity*, to quickly outline the silhouette of your designs in the hues you added from the color storyboard.

2. Afterward, select the Flat Blunt Brush or the Round Angle Brush to fill in shadow areas at 100% *Opacity*.

3. Switch to 30% *Opacity* and gradually layer the color onto the unpainted spaces.

4. Work quickly. Rapid strokes usually generate powerful drawings. It will also prevent you from breaking a mark and doubling over your markings.

5. Try the other settings in the Brush panel, such as Shape Dynamics, Wet Edges, and Smoothing to add digital brush versatility, translucency, and layered fluidity.

6. Use the Eraser Tool (E) to clean up the edges. To add more shadow and to indicate lines, click on the Set Foreground Color box and select a color shade, then add it to the Swatches panel. Use different brushes. You can also select tools from the Brush Presets panel.

When you select new fine art brushes, they appear in the upper left corner of your window. Do not cover everything; leave some open spaces and/or translucent areas. Toggle on and off the visibility of the models' images to get a view of your developing digital sketches. Work in segments and save your work periodically. Your silhouettes should look like a freehand sketch when you have completed this stage of the rendering process (Figure 7.42). When you are finished, lock the layer.

Step 9: Add Garment Details and Highlights

Create a new layer above the *Silhouettes* layer and name it *Details*. Use the Photoshop® Pencil Tool (B) and Brush Tool (B) to create the fine details in your designs. Click on the Set Foreground box to select a tint of the color from the Color Picker. Use the tools with a reduced diameter to draw the details, such as collars, cuffs, stitches, seams, etc. To add precise highlights, use white as an accent (Figure 7.43). The completed look is displayed in Figure 7.44.

Step 10: Add Filters and Layer Styles

The tutorials in this and previous chapters have demonstrated using the Filter Gallery and Layer Styles. You can experiment with different filters and styles to enhance the look of your digital fashion sketches. The

Layer Style Bevel and Emboss was used with the Rough Pastels filter, the **Wind filter**, and the Gaussian Blur filter to achieve the freehand look shown in Figure 7.45.

Step 11: Apply Burn and Dodge Tool Effects

Use the Burn Tool (O) to add shadows and the Dodge Tool (O) to add highlights, if needed.

Step 12: Merge Layers

Merge the *Details* layer with the *Silhouettes* layer by holding the Shift key and selecting them. Click the hidden menu icon at the upper right corner of the Layers panel and scroll to Merge Layers. You can also press *Cmd+E / Ctrl+E* to perform this function on selected layers. This will make the two layers into one. The newly merged layer will retain the title of the original layer that was at the top; rename it.

Note: Layers to be merged must be directly next to each other; otherwise, the layers between them will also be combined.

Step 13: Select Items to Copy, Cut, and Paste

Part of the fashion design/merchandising process is finding out how certain items will look in different colors, textiles, etc. In Photoshop® you can select items with any selection tool, then copy them to the clipboard by pressing *Cmd+C / Ctrl+C* and paste them by pressing *Cmd+V / Ctrl+V* to place the copy automatically on a separate layer. You can press *Cmd+X / Ctrl+X* to cut an item from one layer altogether, and then paste it into another one. You can also duplicate an entire layer by pulling it to the Create New Layer icon at the bottom of the panel. Use the Eraser Tool (E) to delete anything that you do not want to appear on the layer. Duplicate items of the same designs as tops and bottoms are shown on separate layers in Figure 7.46. The dresses have been made into tops and skirts by erasing. Once you've done this, zoom in and refine the edges.

Step 14: Adjust and Change the Color of Objects

To recolor an object there are many options, but the simplest of these is to go to *Menu Bar > Image > Adjust > Hue/Saturation*. Use the *Master Channel* to change all the colors on a layer, or choose specific color channels to change only those hues. For more precise results, select, cut, and paste all the objects on separate layers. Make the needed changes to the sliders in the Hue/Saturation dialog box. Try to stay within your color story, but you may also use accent hues, especially neutrals. The hues of the bottoms have been changed in Figure 7.47.

Figure 7.44

Figure 7.45

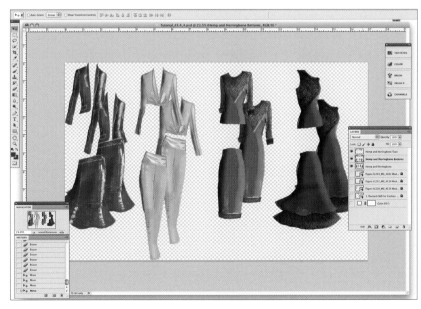

Figure 7.46

Figure 7.47

Selective Color

To add greater depth to a hue and to alter its intensity by blending it with cyan, magenta, yellow, and/or black (the CMYK color mode), go to *Menu Bar > Image Adjustments > Selective Color*. Choose the most relevant color and adjust or mix the hue by moving the sliders.

Color Balance

To adjust the shadows, midtones, and highlights of a hue, go to *Menu Bar > Image > Adjustments > Color Balance*. Move the various sliders to blend the hue with red, green, or blue (the RGB color mode) and the CMYK color mode.

Other Color and Tone Adjustments

Many of the filters under the *Image* and *Image > Adjustments* categories of the Menu Bar will help you to tweak colors. Because the outcomes of these filters will vary from one monitor to the next, it is impossible to predict them for each user. The best way to learn about the filters is to experiment. The following is a short review of those filters not covered previously:

Auto Tone: This setting allows Photoshop® to make adjustments to the tone of colors.

Auto Contrast: Photoshop® automatically adjusts the difference between tones.

Auto Color: This automatically adjusts the color based on the calibration of your monitor.

Brightness/Contrast: This setting is used to adjust the balance between shadows and highlights, and the difference between tones in a color.

Exposure: This setting is used to increase the amount of light in an image.

Vibrance: This filter setting intensifies color tone at various levels of color saturation.

Black & White: To desaturate objects within a color group, use this setting to adjust the balance of the grayscale in various presets or customized color balance.

Photo Filter: Use this filter to cast a color over another, similar to the way photographers alter the mood of a composition by covering lights or lenses with color filters.

Channel Mixer: This adjusts the intensity of the color modes by channels.

Posterize: This decreases the tonal range of an image, with an adjusting slider in the Posterize dialog box.

Shadows/Highlights: These settings intensify and/or tone the balance of the exposure between areas within an image by adding or decreasing the amount of grayscale in shadows, highlights, and/or hue(s).

Desaturate: This setting changes the color mode of a file to grayscale.

Match Color: This setting allows you to match the color in another open file on a specific layer. This filter is especially vital to recoloring because you can locate the swatches on your digital color storyboard and balance the *Luminance*, *Color Intensity*, and *Fade* to convert hues more easily than you can with Hue/Saturation.

Replace Color: Replace Color picks up where Match Color leaves off. Provided in the dialog box is the ability to sample specific hues within an object, via an Eyedropper, and replace them with another color(s). You can add or subtract the amount of various tints, tones, and shades to the selection by selecting the correct eyedropper. In the *Replacement* section, you can also adjust the *Saturation* and *Lightness* of colors. The *Fuzziness* slider allows you to adjust the texture and/or noise of selections.

Equalize: To automatically adjust the color saturation and contrast, select this setting.

Step 15: Use Pattern Fills

Try filling some items with patterns that you define from actual swatches. Follow these steps:

1. Reduce the Tolerance of the Photoshop® Magic Wand Tool (W), then select areas in the object.

2. Go to *Menu Bar > Select > Grow* to increase the immediate areas of the selection or *Menu Bar > Select > Similar* to increase the amount of color pixels selected.

3. By selecting parts of a digital sketch and leaving some of the rendering information, the pattern will take on a natural look when you fill it into the space as instructed in Tutorial 7.2.

4. Use the tools, brushes, and filters to enhance the look. The Mixer Brush Tool (B) was used with a Round Fan brush in size 17 in the tutorial example. Set the Useful Blending and Brush Combinations menu in the Options Bar to Wet, then adjust the settings to the right to add nice blending effects.

5. Add the Wind and the Noise filters for even greater freehand-like enhancements.

Figure 7.48

Keep in mind that these are preliminary digital design sketches similar to presentation floats. Actual presentation flats will be demonstrated later. Figure 7.48 shows a skirt that has been filled with a buffalo-check pattern.

Note: *The skirt was flipped by going to Menu Bar > Edit > Transform > Flip Horizontal. Spend some time exploring the other Transform options in this menu.*

Step 16: Add Layers and Sketch Additional Sportswear Items

Create a layer below the *Silhouettes* layer and render a few blouses or tops that will coordinate with the sportswear items. On a layer above this, render a few coats or outerwear items. Create as many layers as needed until you have designed at least twenty different items.

Step 17: Make a Digital Thumbnail Board

When you have completed the renderings, copy and paste them into a file(s) with a solid background like the one in Figure 7.49 that shows a digital concept board layout of thumbnail sketches.

Note: *The inside necklines were purposefully left out of the digital floats in Figure 7.49 because they will be used to dress the figures in Tutorial 7.4; however, you should always render the inside of garments if you plan to use them as presentation floats.*

Figure 7.49 **Floats can be used to dress croquis.**

At one point or another, every fashion designer and merchandiser is involved with a fashion runway event. Although the event may be rehearsed, visualizing everything far in advance of the event can be difficult and expensive. In the following tutorial, fashion merchandisers and designers can come together to stage a full-scale runway presentation that features the garments you created in Tutorial 7.3. Everything that you need to stage the look of the event has been provided on ① Ch07\Tutorial 7.4. Since you'll be dressing the models in the designs you created in Tutorial 7.3, it is recommended that you reuse the same runway poses you chose for that tutorial.

Step 1: Open a Digital Duo Stage File from DVD One

Locate one of four prepared files showcasing fashion show runways: Ana_Pink_Show.pdf, Carl_Navy_Show.pdf, Navy_Flashes_Show.pdf, Amber_Flashes_Show.pdf.

Use the files with or without the images of the models. You can select and delete, replace, or recolor anything in either of the files. They are all editable by opening them in Photoshop® and selecting the layers.

Step 2: Paste Model Images into the File

In the tutorial example, Carl was removed from Carl_Navy_Show.pdf, and several previously used runway poses of Jade have been placed into the file (Figure 7.50). These poses will accept the apparel designs that were rendered in Tutorial 7.3.

Step 3: Select and Delete the Background

Select the background of each of the photos, then press Delete. If necessary, clean up the white area with the Eraser Tool (E). In Figure 7.51, the Dark Strokes filter was added to blend the edges left over from the backgrounds to create a dramatic effect.

Step 4: Free Transform and Scale

Scale some of the models' photos using the Transform features by pressing *Cmd+T / Ctrl+T* to Free Transform them while holding the Shift key. If you want, create duplicates of the same image by pulling the layer to the Create New Layer icon at the bottom of the Layers panel. Position images on the runway, similar to what is shown in Figure 7.51.

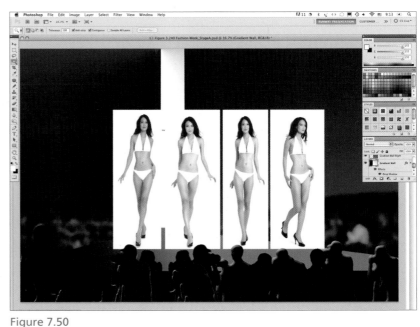

Figure 7.50

Figure 7.51

Step 5: Drag, Drop, and Arrange the Apparel Drawings

Drag, drop, and arrange the digital apparel renderings from the thumbnails board you created in Tutorial 7.3 onto the stage file. Start with the bottoms. Position and transform each item to cover a model's photo. Rearrange the layers and coordinate the looks to create optimal merchandising. Because floats were created, most of the items can be easily adjusted, flipped, and reshaped. Use the Transform Perspective *Menu Bar > Edit > Transform > Perspective* and distort the image to fit the renderings onto the photos if needed. The Warp feature can adjust the apparel renderings to fit the models' images.

Puppet Warp

A Photoshop® CS5 and CS6 feature is the **Puppet Warp**. You can use it to change the position of images with controlled mapping. To activate this feature on a specific object, select the layer, unlink it, and then go to *Menu Bar > Edit > Puppet Warp*. In order to control the mapping, you must click on it at strategic points to add pins. These pinned areas either activate movement or otherwise stabilize the position. Select the pins to reposition the area as if it were actually jointed. In Figure 7.52, the jacket has been repositioned with the Puppet Warp feature. To accept the changes, select any tool in the Tools panel or click on the Commit transform check icon in the Options Bar.

Step 6: Add Finishing Touches to Drawings

Render your own accessories or select, drag, and drop accessories from ① Digital Duo Modeling Agency, which includes a variety of images of Jade, Ana, and Carl wearing hats, sunglasses, and other items. The completely dressed models are shown in Figure 7.53. A men's wear example is shown in Figure 7.54.

Step 7: Change the Backdrop or the Runway

If you want to change the backdrop or the runway, locate the specific layer(s), select the object, and change the look with a pattern, color, and/or filters.

Step 8: Add Images

You can take your project to the next level and add the faces of celebrities, family members, friends, and yourself to the runway, paparazzi, and fashion crowd. You have already learned enough to try this on your own. If you created your own backdrop for the digital fashion show, do not forget to add the Lens Flare filter to the *Runway*, *Fashion Crowd*, and the *Wall* layers by going to *Menu Bar > Filter > Render > Lens Flare*. It will bring the entire scene alive and add a realistic touch.

Note: *If you choose to use the Digital Duo Fashion Week presentation in a portfolio, do not add images of yourself. In addition, make your presentation unique by changing the background elements and use your own freehand or digital figures in place of the models' photos. Be as creative as possible, but keep your target market at the center of everything you do.*

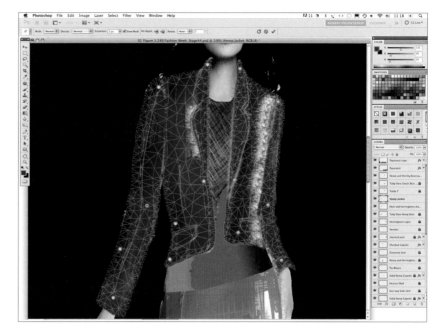

Figure 7.52

Figure 7.53 **Illustration by Stacy Stewart Smith.**

Figure 7.54 **Illustration by Stacy Stewart Smith.**

Contrary to what some designers believe, elegant fashion illustration can be created solely with the use of digital software. Digital software allows the user to interface in multiple ways, but it's important to have the right input devices. Many of these are often outdated. Trying to use a mouse to do the job of a paintbrush is difficult, but a graphic tablet and stylus can provide the type of dexterity needed to render fashion illustration in Photoshop®.

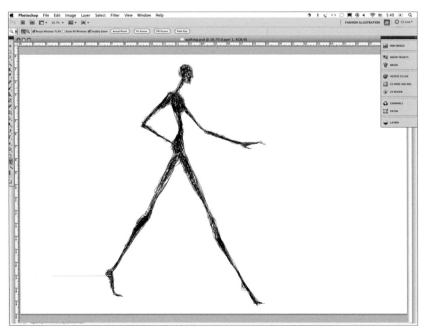

Figure 7.55

Figure 7.56

Step 1: Create a New Document with a White Background

Load Photoshop® and create a new document by using the stats in the New Document dialog box shown in Figure 7.55.

Step 2: Render a Quick Digital Sketch

On a new layer make quick circular motions using a stylus and the Photoshop® Pencil Tool (B) to create a 1-minute action pose on a drawing tablet (Figure 7.56). Use a photo reference to style the pose if needed. This is a good exercise to loosen your freehand dexterity. The practice will help to produce relaxed elegantly posed croquis.

Note: *If you do not have a stylus tablet, scan a freehand sketch and continue in Photoshop® with the mouse.*

Step 3: Create a Quick Outline with the Pencil Tool

Use the Photoshop® Pencil Tool (B) to make an outline of the moving croquis on a new layer (Figure 7.57).

Figure 7.57

Step 4: Render Brush Washes for Flesh Tones

Select any soft brush from the Brush panel and reduce the *Opacity* in the Brushes panel. Create a new layer and apply quick translucent digital washes, but try to cover entire areas and leave spaces in the manner that real watercolor might be applied on paper. This will prevent the overlap shading (Figure 7.58).

Step 5: Smooth with the Gaussian Blur Filter

Select the layer with the skintone-colored digital brush wash, then go to *Menu Bar > Filter > Blur > Gaussian Blur*. Move the sliders to soften the color (Figure 7.59).

Step 6: Paint Accessories

You have rendered stockings and shoes before, but this time, create a new layer and use a digital paintbrush. The soft brushes will do the trick— just reduce the *Opacity* and draw the stockings in one movement (Figure 7.60). Do not lift the stylus until you have made the shape. Use the Photoshop® Eraser Tool (E) to clean up the area.

Step 7: Make a Quick Digital Apparel Line Sketch with the Pencil Tool

Use the Photoshop® Pencil Tool (B) to render a quick digital sketch of our design on a separate layer from the others. Remember, quick motions often result in the most impressive freehand looks that you will be able to produce digitally (Figure 7.61).

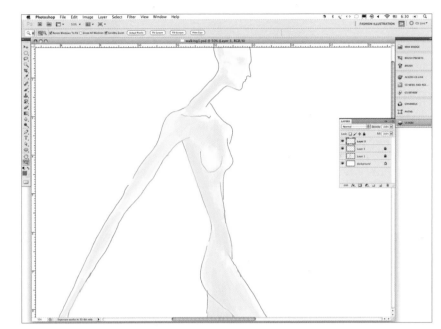

Figure 7.58

Figure 7.59

Figure 7.60

Figure 7.61

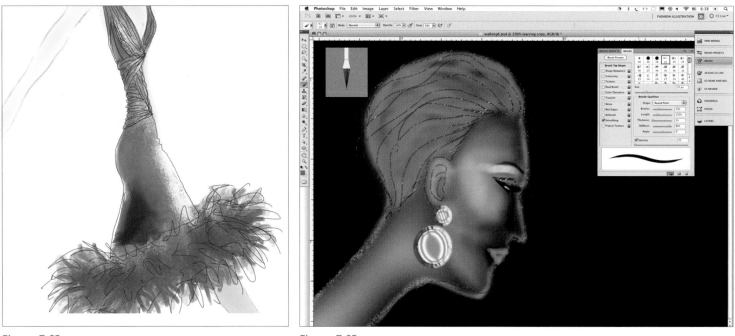

Figure 7.62

Figure 7.63

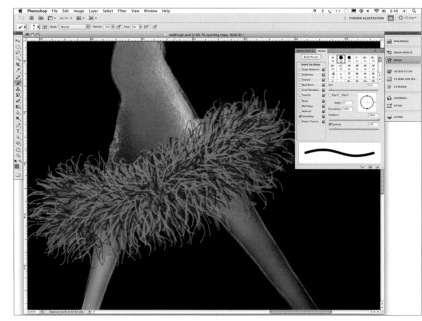

Figure 7.64

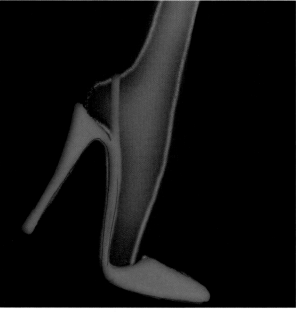

Figure 7.65

Step 8: Add Shadows and Artistic Filters

Create a new layer, then use the art paintbrushes to lay down the digital color inside the lines that you made in Step Seven. Vary the *Opacity* of the paint and change the hue using the Color Picker. Create shadows and highlights. Use the Mixer Brush Tool (B) to blend the various hues. Add an **Artistic filter** to create depth and texture (Figure 7.62).

Step 9: Take Advantage of Working in Translucent Layering

A benefit of working with layers of translucent color is that the effects can be gradually intensified. In Figure 7.63, an Adjustment layer was added to reveal the structure of the digital fashion illustration. The earrings were created from shapes filled with color, and then Layer Styles were added.

Step 10: Render Ostrich Feathers

Try a combination of hues and Photoshop® tools to create ostrich feathers. The look shown in Figure 7.64 was made by combining strokes of the Brush Tool (B) and the Smudge Tool.

Step 11: Quick Fill Strokes

Zoom in on areas and use various digital brushes and tools to perfect your illustration (Figure 7.65).

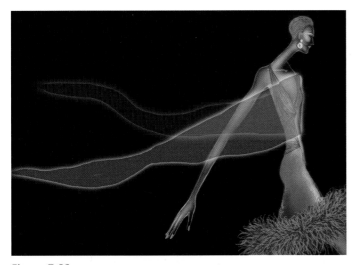

Figure 7.66

Figure 7.67 Photo by Stacy Stewart Smith.

Figure 7.68

Step 12: Use the Liquify Filter to Create Chiffon

Use the Liquify filter to create fluidity and then add the Outer Glow Layer Style (Figure 7.66). The scarf was rendered on a layer above the figure and another one below to achieve this effect.

Step 13: Add a Background Photo

Setting fashion illustrations into environments via photographs is becoming a trend in design presentations. Select one that suits yours. A photo taken of New York's Manhattan Bridge makes for a compelling image. It magnifies the motion pose of the croquis in the tutorial example (Figure 7.67).

Step 14: Stack the Image to Create Opacity

Drag and drop your digital croquis onto the file with the background image, then rasterize all the layers. Pull the layer containing the image of the croquis to the Create a New Layer icon at the bottom of the Layers panel. Repeat this at least twice to increase the *Opacity* of the croquis if desired (Figure 7.68).

Figure 7.69

Figure 7.70 Illustration by Stacy Stewart Smith.

Step 15: Mimic the Art of Futurism

An early modern art movement known as futurism featured the concept of movement. In the tutorial example, additional copies of the croquis layer were created and separated in distance to begin the illusion of dynamism (Figure 7.69).

Step 16: Reduce Opacity to Simulate Motion

Reduce the *Opacity* on each layer to further enhance the mystery of motion (Figure 7.70).

Tutorial 7.6
IMPROVING A FREEHAND PORTFOLIO PRESENTATION WITH DIGITAL PAINTING TECHNIQUES

This tutorial will help you learn to use digital means to improve hand-rendered and assembled portfolio presentations. Afterward, create your own finished digital plates by using scanned fashion sketches with files from ① Ch07\Tutorial 7.6 and/or your own research materials.

Step 1: Scan a Hand-Assembled Mood Board

The components of a hand-assembled mood board may be useful when scanned and separated into parts. In Figures 7.71 and 7.72, the parts have shifted, making for a sloppy presentation.

Step 2: Select, Copy, and Paste the Parts

To improve the board, select, copy, and paste the parts in Photoshop® so they appear on separate layers.

Step 3: Create Digital Color and Mood Boards Using the DVD Files or Your Own

Use the Transform functions, tools, filters, etc. to improve the overall look of the board(s). Use the inspiration photos, textiles, and color standards files from ① Ch07\Tutorial 7.6 to help you create a digital color board and a digital mood board.

Note: *A completed digital example has not been shown in order to allow you creative freedom.*

Step 4: Scan Freehand Sketches

Scan your own freehand sketches. Use what you have learned in previous tutorials to clean up the background. Crop the image if needed (Figure 7.73).

Figure 7.71

Figure 7.72 Some of the elements in this storyboard have shifted.

Figure 7.73

Figure 7.74

Figure 7.75 Illustration by Stacy Stewart Smith.

Step 5: Select the Parts and Improve the Faces and Apparel with Photoshop® Tools

By now you have a general command of the Photoshop® tools, panels, filters, and settings. Use what you have learned to paint and improve the look of your freehand work in color. This is similar to what you accomplished in Tutorial 5.3. This time, go beyond what you were able to achieve before. Figure 7.73 shows what the original drawing

looked like before digital enhancements. The fur was improved with a Spatter brush and the settings shown in Figure 7.74.

Step 6: Print, Draw, then Scan

If you prefer, print Metallic_Cave_Group.jpg (Figure 7.75) from ① Ch07\Tutorial 7.6, draw your own fashion faces, scan the drawing, and then work on improving the presentation in Photoshop®.

Chapter 7 Summary

If you completed all the tutorials in this chapter and have studied the Photoshop® tools, panels, filters, layers, and functions, then you are ready to proceed to Chapter 8. Below are a few questions that you should ask yourself before moving on.

Chapter 7 Self-Assessment

1. Am I familiar with the function of the Puppet Warp and Warp features of Photoshop®, and can I use them effectively to enhance my presentations?

2. Can I develop presentations from a combination of photo images and use the painting aspects of Photoshop®?

3. Can I create and use Alpha Channels to save selections?

4. Do I understand the function of Layer Styles, and am I able to use them appropriately?

5. Can I drag and drop files from window to window, and can I scale and transform objects?

6. Can I use Photoshop® to create comprehensive and compelling storyboard presentations, including mood, color, design concept, and other presentation boards?

7. Do I understand the difference between the Transform and Free Transform functions?

8. Am I comfortable using the Photoshop® Brush panel, and have I learned to draw with a tablet and a stylus to create the look of freehand drawings?

9. Am I comfortable with making adjustments to the colors in my work using the Photoshop® color filters and Adjustment menu options?

10. Can I improve the beauty and poses of my freehand croquis using Photoshop®?

Chapter 7 DVD Extra

Expand your fashion presentation skills with Photoshop® by completing the following DVD Extra tutorial. This tutorial can be found on ① Ch7\DVD Extra 7.1.

DVD Extra 7.1
Photoshop® Painting
Exaggerated Aesthetics in Fashion Presentation

Scanning freehand illustrations, then enhancing them in Photoshop® can create dynamic presentations. This tutorial teaches you how to produce dynamic digital results by rendering your original illustrations in part color or monochromatic color schemes, then inverting those colors digitally (Figure 7.77).

Figure 7.77

Defining Prints
and Patterns

8

Objectives

The subject of defining patterns is discussed and demonstrated throughout this book and is the focus of this chapter. In later chapters, even more textiles, treatments, and finishes will be covered.

This chapter is not a total resource for textile science, digital or otherwise. Although you will learn to create a few classic motifs, the goal of this chapter is not to teach you how to make every type of digital repeat. The objective is to teach you how to use Illustrator® and Photoshop® individually or combined in near endless possibilities to design and define your own textile ideas. In this chapter, you will learn to:

◉ Design, then define seamless Illustrator® patterns with horizontal repeats, vertical repeats, and combinations of horizontal and vertical repeats

◉ Use the Illustrator® Pattern Libraries effectively and learn how to manage pattern swatches

◉ Use the Illustrator® Mesh Tool (U) to create and define tie-dye patterns

◉ Define perfect stripes and plaids in Photoshop® and in Illustrator®

◉ Use the Illustrator® Pattern Libraries to define patterns in Photoshop®

◉ Create and define patterns from fine art in Photoshop®

◉ Use Photoshop® filters to create luxury novelty textiles and manipulate patterns for apparel presentations

◉ Use the ② Textiles and Novelties Library

A digital **repeat** consists of a **motif** (artistic design) placed on a **tile** (square or rectangle). The repeat becomes a defined pattern in Illustrator® when the program is told how to use the tile and the motif repeatedly in directions from all sides of the tile. The tile beneath a motif in a defined pattern is referred to in this book as a ground tile (also Bounding Box). This tile can be filled with a color or have a Fill of None.

A motif can be contained within the tile (tile repeat) or extend in any direction. Motifs that extend the tile on the top and repeat on the bottom are called **vertical repeats.** A **horizontal repeat** is created when a tile has a motif that only extends and repeats from one side to the next. However, some of

the finest repeat patterns contain motifs that repeat both horizontally and vertically. In this tutorial, you will learn to create and define your own vertical pattern repeats, horizontal pattern repeats, and patterns that repeat in both directions.

You will develop three types of pattern repeats simultaneously. Instructions to create each step of the vertical repeat and the horizontal repeat will help you construct the combined vertical and horizontal one, which will follow. A set of instructions is given for each type of repeat at each stage, and then the next step is given to develop all three further. This will continue until you have created the repeats, then the combined repeat will be the example for you to define the patterns for the others. Follow the tutorial instructions, but create your own motifs by using the tools. Practice this tutorial repeatedly until you have mastered the lessons before moving on to the next tutorial in this chapter.

Note: This tutorial is suitable for Illustrator® CS5.5 and earlier versions. For simple instructions about how this works in CS6, watch the movie CS6_Pattern_Editor.m4v on ① Ch03.

Step 1: Load Illustrator® and Open a Letter Size Document with Four Artboards

Because you will learn to create and define three types of repeats in this tutorial, open a letter-size document in Illustrator® with four Artboards in landscape orientation (Figure 8.1). Save your file as previously instructed. In Figure 8.2 the four Artboards are labeled in Green to indicate order and number to help you navigate the tutorial instructions.

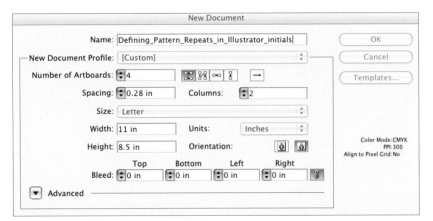

Figure 8.1

The Status Bar

The **Status Bar** is located in the lower-left corner of the Illustrator® window. Use it to show and manage various functions of the program and those that will assist your workflow. For this tutorial you will need to use the **navigation controls for multiple Artboards** (red arrow), which will allow you to switch Artboards throughout the tutorial (Figure 8.2).

1. Click on the arrow pointers in the Status Bar to access the hidden menus. If you need a full view of all four Artboards in a window, use the manual zoom section in the lower left corner. Set it to approximately 58 to 70% (Figure 8.2).

2. Select the **current tool** (cyan arrow) from the *Show* menu to reveal that tool's functions as you use it in relationship to a selected object or feature option (Figure 8.2).

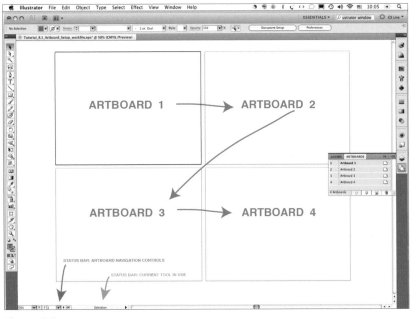

Figure 8.2

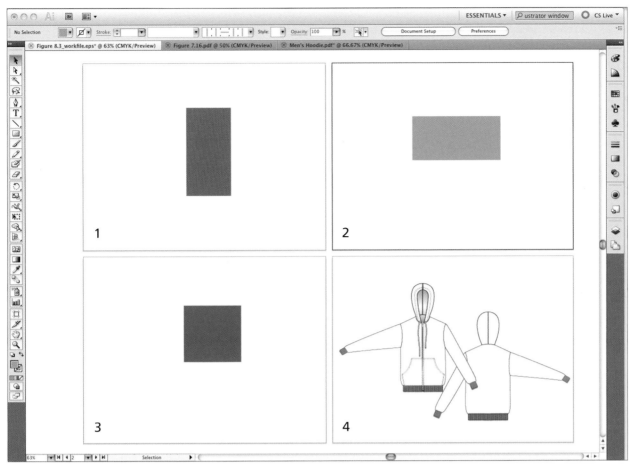

Figure 8.3 Artboard 1 contains a vertical rust-colored rectangle at the upper left.

Step 2: Turn On Smart Guides and Set Snap to Point

For this tutorial, you need to set up a few things to begin creating your pattern:

1. Toggle on your Smart Guides by pressing *Cmd+U / Ctrl+U*. The tool tips will help you with this tutorial.

2. Go to *Menu Bar > View > Snap to Point*. This allows you to see an indicator in the Status Bar current tool when you have your repeat in the right position.

Step 3: Create the Ground Tile for a Vertical Repeat Pattern on Artboard 1

1. Select Artboard 1 in the Artboard panel.

2. Select the Rectangle Tool (M) and use it in conjunction with the Transform panel options to create a rectangle with a width of 2 inches and a height of 4 inches, and then press Enter. Fill the rectangle with a color and a Stroke of None. This shape will represent your ground tile (Figure 8.3).

Step 4: Create the Ground Tile for a Horizontal Repeat Pattern on Artboard 2

1. Select and copy the ground tile that you just made in Step Three.

2. Click on Artboard 2 in the Artboard panel.

3. Paste the copy onto Artboard 2.

4. With the copy rectangle selected, change the width to 4 inches and the height to 2 inches using the Transform panel options, and then press the Enter key on your keyboard. Also fill this rectangle with a color and a Stroke of None (Figure 8.3).

Step 5: Create the Ground Tile for a Horizontal and Vertical Repeat Pattern on Artboard 3

1. Click on Artboard 3 in the Artboard panel.

2. Paste the ground tile that you made in Step Three onto Artboard 3.

3. With the copy rectangle selected, change the width to 2.5 inches and the height to 2.5 inches using the Transform panel options, and then press Enter to create a perfect tile. Also fill this tile with a color and a Stroke of None (Figure 8.3).

Figure 8.5

Figure 8.4

Figure 8.6

Step 6: Select, Copy, and Paste any Vector Sketch on Artboard 4

1. Click on Artboard 4 in the Artboard panel.

2. Select any completed sketch that you rendered in Illustrator® that contains Fills of white with Strokes in black. You can also use files from ② Extra Flats.

3. Paste the sketch onto Artboard 4 (Figure 8.3).

Step 7: Create and Arrange a Vertical Pattern Repeat on Artboard 1

Arrange any shapes inside the ground tile for the vertical repeat on Artboard 1 to create a motif, but place a few extending over the top. Try and imagine how the motif will repeat on the bottom (Figure 8.4).

Step 8: Create and Arrange a Horizontal Pattern Repeat on Artboard 2

Arrange any shapes inside the ground tile for the horizontal repeat on Artboard 2 to create a motif, but place a few extending over the left side. Try and imagine the motif repeating on the right side (Figure 8.5).

Step 9: Create and Arrange a Repeat with Vertical and Horizontal Motifs on Artboard 3

Arrange any shapes inside the ground tile for the vertical and horizontal repeat on Artboard 3 to create a motif, but place a few extending over the top and the left side. For this lesson, avoid placing shapes on the corners of the ground tile because it may cause problems for you later when the pattern is defined. Try and imagine the print repeating on the right side and the bottom (Figure 8.6).

Step 10: Select, Copy, and Paste the Ground Tiles

Select, copy, and paste the ground tiles (Figure 8.7). These copies will later become your Repeat Bounding Boxes. They are used to tell Illustrator® how to replicate the ground tile and motif. Later in this tutorial, you will remove the color from these Repeat Bounding Boxes, align them with the ground tiles, and then send them to the back.

Step 11: Lock the Ground Tiles

Use the Selection Tool (V) to select just the ground tiles, and then press *Cmd+2 / Ctrl+2* to lock them temporarily on the layer.

Step 12: Group the Pattern Motifs and Ground Tiles

1. Use the Selection Tool to marquee over each pattern motif that you created, and then press *Cmd+G / Ctrl+G* to group them individually.

2. Ungroup the ground tiles by pressing *Option+Cmd+2 / Option+Ctrl+2*.

3. Marquee with the Selection Tool (V) around the ground tile and the motifs individually, group all selections, and then reposition them away from the copies that you made of the ground tiles. You will need the space to create the repeats.

Note: Do not cause the repeat motifs and/or the ground tiles to shift positions; this may change your repeat. If they do shift, press Cmd+Z / Ctrl+Z to undo the move(s) and repeat Steps Eleven and/or Twelve.

Step 13: Adjust the Snap to Point in the Selection and Anchor Display Preferences

Go to the Illustrator® Preferences menu and choose Selection & Anchor Display. Check and change the **Snap to Point** to 1 px. This will allow your repeat to be positioned flush to the original (Figure 8.8). In addition, go to *Menu Bar > View > Snap to Point* to toggle on the function. You should see a check next to it.

Step 14: Copy and Align Bottom the Vertical Repeat on Artboard 1

The following instructions will help you to create any vertical repeat pattern:

1. Use the Illustrator® Selection Tool (V) to select the grouped vertical repeat on Artboard 1.

2. On a PC, hold the Alt key (hold the Option key on a Mac).

3. Click into the upper left corner of the ground tile (now grouped with the motif) until you see double pointers of black and white.

4. Drag the ghost copy of your grouped ground tile and motifs from the upper left anchor to the bottom of your ground tile until you position it in alignment with the bottom left anchor of the ground tile. Do not let go of the mouse clicker until you see the double pointers of black and white turn completely white. The words *Snap to and copy* should also appear in the Status Bar's current tool in use indicator, as shown in Figure 8.9.

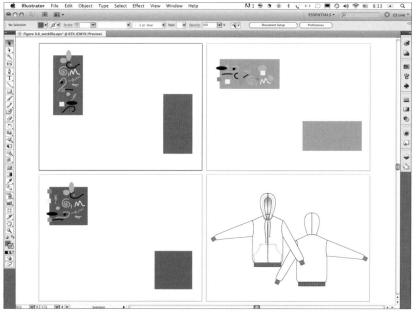

Figure 8.7 Copies of the ground tiles appear to the right of each motif.

Figure 8.8

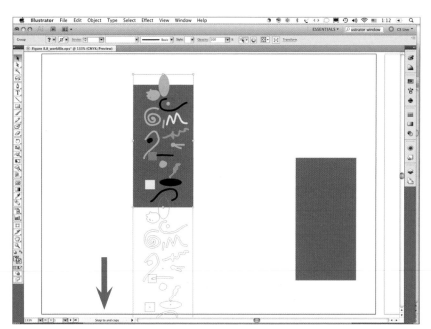

Figure 8.9

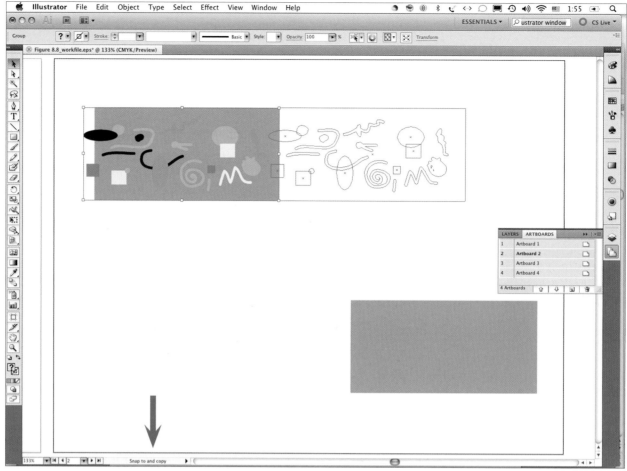

Figure 8.10

5. When you let go of the mouse clicker, the color will be restored. Ungroup the motifs and ground tile.

6. Use the Selection Tool (V) to select and delete the copied motif shapes and the copy of the ground tile that are not a part of the repeat information (those that do not overlap the original ground tile).

Step 15: Copy and Align Right the Horizontal Repeat on Artboard 2

The following instructions will help you create any horizontal repeat:

1. Use the Illustrator® Selection Tool (V) to select the grouped horizontal repeat on Artboard 2.

2. On a PC, hold the Alt key (hold the Option key on a Mac).

3. Click into the upper left corner of the ground tile (now grouped with the motif) until you see double pointers of black and white.

4. Drag the ghost copy of your grouped ground tile and motifs from the upper left anchor to the right of your ground tile until you position it in alignment with the upper right anchor of the ground

tile. Do not let go of the mouse clicker until you see the double pointers of black and white turn completely white. The words *Snap to and copy* should also appear in the Status Bar's current tool in use indicator as shown in Figure 8.10.

5. When you let go of the mouse clicker, the color will be restored. Ungroup the motifs and ground tile.

6. Use the Selection Tool (V) to select and delete the copied motif shapes and the copy of the ground tile that are not a part of the repeat information (those that do not overlap the original ground tile).

Step 16: Copy and Align Right and Bottom the Combined Vertical and Horizontal Repeat on Artboard 3

The following instructions will help you create any pattern motif that repeats both vertically and horizontally:

1. Use the Illustrator® Selection Tool (V) to select the grouped combined vertical and horizontal repeat on Artboard 3.

2. On a PC, hold the Alt key (hold the Option key on a Mac).

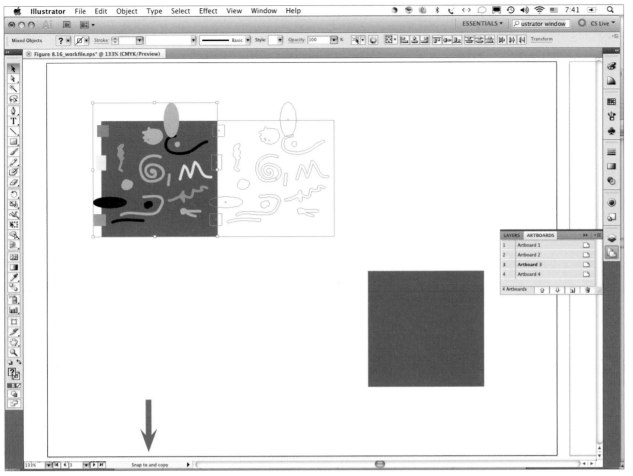

Figure 8.11

3. Click into the upper left corner of the ground tile (now grouped with the motif) until you see double pointers of black and white.

4. Drag the ghost copy of your grouped ground tile and motifs to the right of your ground tile, but do not let go of the mouse clicker until you see the double pointers of black and white turn completely white. The phrase *Snap to and copy* should also appear in the current tool in use indicator of the Status Bar.

5. Marquee to select the original and the newly placed repeat copy, and then group them. Be careful not to move any of the parts.

6. Use the Selection Tool (V) to click again into the upper left corner of the original ground tile until you see double pointers of black and white (Figure 8.11).

7. Drag the ghost copy of your two grouped repeats to the bottom and position the ghost copy over the lower left anchor of the original ground tile that you selected. Do not let go of the mouse clicker until you see the double pointers of black and white turn completely white. The words *Snap to and copy* should also appear in the Status Bar's current tool in use indicator as shown in Figure 8.12.

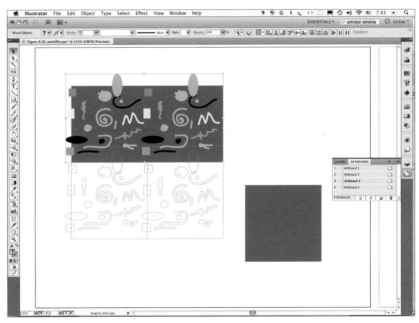

Figure 8.12

8. When you let go of the mouse clicker, the color will be restored. One of the copied sections will now have all the components of a finished repeat on all sides. In the tutorial example, the lower left segment is a **perfect repeat** because it contains all the necessary motifs (Figure 8.13).

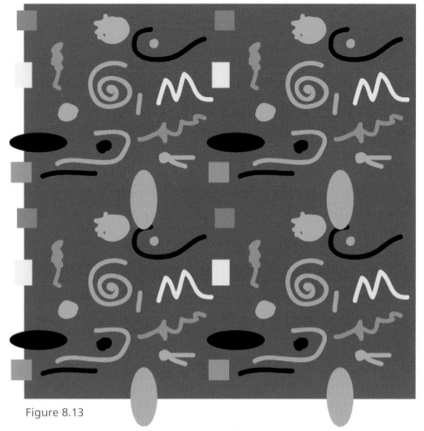

Figure 8.13

9. When you let go of the mouse clicker, the color will be restored. Ungroup the motifs and ground tile.

10. Use the Selection Tool (V) to select and delete the copied motif shapes and the copy of the ground tile that are not a part of the repeat information (those that do not overlap the original ground tile).

11. Select the entire perfected repeat, group it, then go to *Menu Bar > Object > Arrange > Send to Back* or press *Shift+Cmd+[(left bracket) / Shift+Ctrl+[(left bracket)*. Figure 8.14 shows the perfected vertical repeat, horizontal repeat, and the combined vertical and horizontal repeat.

Step 17: Align the Ground Tile and the Repeat Bounding Box

In Step Ten, you pasted copies of the ground tiles in each Artboard. These will become the repeat bounding boxes. Follow these steps for each repeat:

1. Select the shape and bring it to the front.

2. On a PC, hold the Alt key (hold the Option key on a Mac).

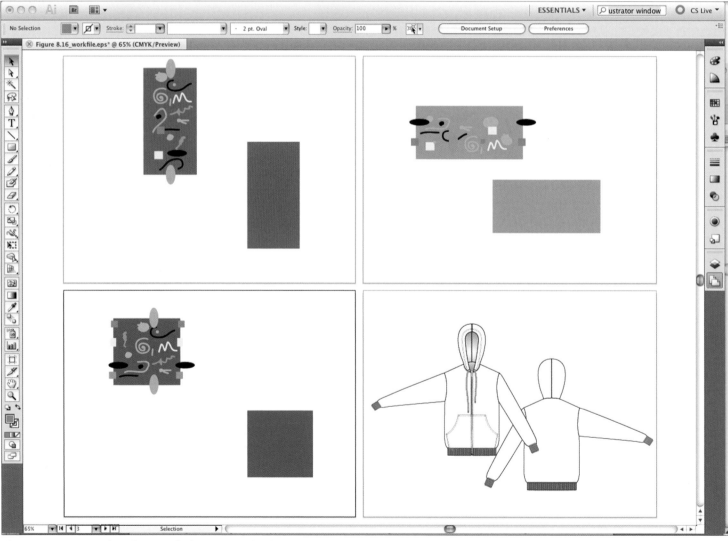

Figure 8.14 Notice that the motifs that are inside the ground tiles are completed on the opposite side within each shape.

3. Click into the upper left corner of the repeat bounding box until you see double pointers of black and white.

4. Drag the ghost copy of your repeat bounding box to the upper right corner anchor of your grouped ground tile, but do not let go of the mouse clicker until you see the double pointers of black and white turn completely white. The phrase *Snap to and copy* should also appear in the current tool in use indicator of the Status Bar.

5. With the repeat bounding box still selected, click the None icon button in the Tools panel. The Stroke should also be None.

6. Then go to *Menu Bar > Object > Arrange > Send to Back*.

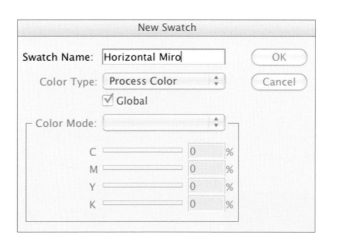

Figure 8.15

TIP: Alignment

It is very important that the repeat box and the ground tile are properly aligned to prevent the presence of fine white lines in the defined pattern. Do not move any of the shapes in your ground tile.

Step 18: Define and Name the Patterns in Illustrator®

Select each repeat and define a pattern by going to *Menu Bar > Edit > Define Pattern*. In the dialog box, give the pattern an appropriate name and use the new pattern swatch in conjunction with the Fill box in the Tools panel (Figure 8.15). Save the file.

Step 19: Investigate the White Lines

If you see breaks in your pattern (fine lines), repeat the previous steps. It is possible that you have not properly aligned something. You should also check for stray objects and anchor points. Zoom in close, investigate, and repeat the steps until you discover the problem (Figure 8.16). Again, this is an advanced technique and will require some practice.

Note: Sometimes your monitor may show a problem that does not exist. Print a copy to see if you need to make further adjustments.

Step 20: Recolor the Pattern

The *Vertical Miro*, *Horizontal Miro,* and the *Vertical and Horizontal Miro* patterns have been defined (Figure 8.17). Recolor your patterns by using the Color

Figure 8.16

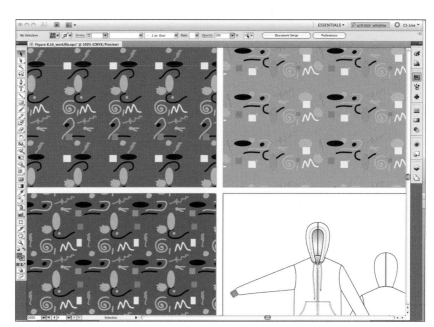

Figure 8.17

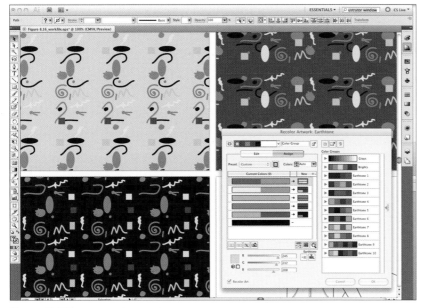

Figure 8.18

Guide panel (Figure 8.18). You learned about the Color Guide panel in Tutorial 3.2. Save your work, and back up a copy to retain the pattern in the file each time you open it.

Quick Pattern-Shifting Shortcut Reminder

When actual garments are cut and assembled in patterns or printed textiles, the repeat will likely shift in each part, i.e., front, sleeves, pockets, etc. This is universally acceptable, although in better garments some matching of patterns is mandatory, especially with plaids, checks, and stripes. One disadvantage of working with pattern fills in Illustrator® is the flat appearance that it gives multiple shapes. To improve digital vector renderings of apparel, select each shape, then press and hold *Cmd+~(tilde)* / *Ctrl+~(tilde)*. The program will allow you to shift the print within the selected area by clicking and dragging.

Note: When digital patterns are shifted, fine lines may appear again. Always investigate and print a copy to discover if your pattern repeats need correction. The pattern was used to design the hoodie in Figure 8.19.

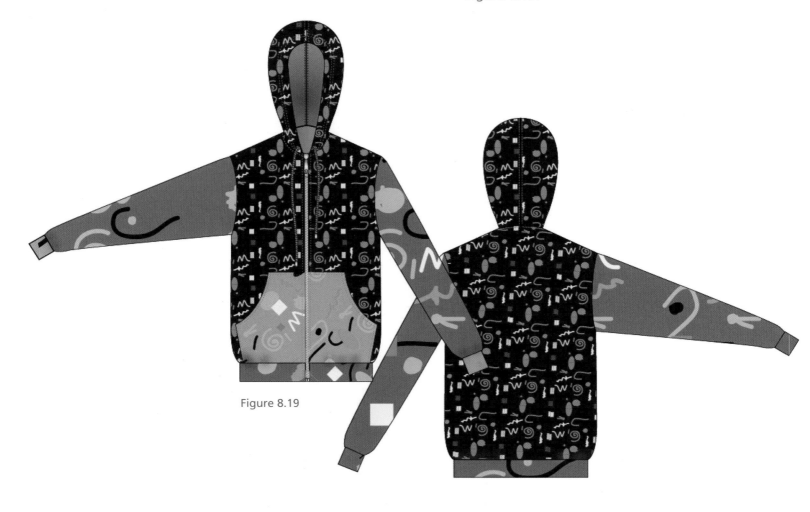

Figure 8.19

Tutorial 8.2
DEFINE A TILE PATTERN REPEAT
IN PHOTOSHOP®

Defining patterns in Photoshop® differs from the process in Illustrator®. In this tutorial, you will learn to use Photoshop® to create a tile pattern repeat from an image of the masterpiece *Harmony in Red*, 1908, by Henri Matisse (Figure 8.20). Tile prints differ from the full pattern repeat that you learned to define in Tutorial 8.1 only in respect to placement of the objects. In this type of pattern, the repeat is engineered inside the boundary of the ground tile (background color of the print). What you learn in this tutorial can also be applied to the principles of defining patterns in any version of Illustrator®. See also the movie CS6_Pattern_Editor.m4v on ① Ch03.

Step 1: Open the Image of *Harmony in Red*, 1908, by Henri Matisse in Photoshop®

Insert ①, then go to *Menu Bar > File > Open* and locate Harmony_in_Red.jpg in the Tutorial 8.2 folder. Open it in Photoshop®. Double-click on the *Background* layer, and change the name to *Matisse Painting*. Save the file as Matisse_Print.psd (using the Photoshop® format to retain the layer compositing), but add your name or initials to this title as a suffix.

Step 2: Select, Copy, and Paste Various Images in the File

1. Go to *Menu Bar > Image > Canvas Size*. In the Canvas Size dialog box, change the *Width* to 12 inches and the *Height* to 12 inches. The **Canvas Size** is the size of your work area in Photoshop®.

2. Use any selection tool or a combination thereof to select the images in the painting. The Quick Selection Tool (W) will be useful, but you can use the Lasso Tool (L) to perfect your selections.

3. Save Alpha Channels if you will be working on this tutorial over a period of time (Tutorial 7.2, Step Six). This will allow you to save, update, and reload your selections.

4. Copy and paste the selections.

5. Label each layer appropriately as shown in Figure 8.21. Toggle off the visibility of the painting's layer or drag it to the Trash icon at the bottom of the Layers panel.

Step 3: Arrange the Images

1. Position the parts on the canvas in an interesting manner with the Move Tool (V). Some will need to be placed near to the edge to keep the tile print even and devoid of gaps.

Figure 8.20 *Harmony in Red*, 1908, by Henri Matisse. © The Art Archive/Hermitage Museum Saint Petersburg.

Figure 8.21

2. Duplicate a few parts by pulling the layers to the New Layer icon at the bottom of the Layers panel. This will make the repeat more compelling.

When you create the duplicate layers, the object will be hidden behind the view of the original. You will need to use the Move Tool (V) and reposition the motifs. Use the Free Transform options to rotate or scale the copies by pressing *Cmd+T / Ctrl+T*.

3. To make a pattern that repeats in both directions, place and/or rotate copies of all the parts that have a distinct appearance. In the tutorial example, the image of the woman would be a perfect example. This is optional. It is important to remember that some patterns and prints only

work in one direction—that is, they have an up and down—while others are called two-way patterns, allowing garment parts to be cut in both directions.

4. Add a layer beneath the current layers, then press *Cmd+A / Ctrl+A* to Select All. Fill this layer with a color (Figure 8.22).

Note: *Images at the sides of the ground tile will mirror when the pattern is defined. Carefully consider the placement.*

Step 4: Save a Copy of the File

Save a copy of the file as a backup.

TIP: Two-Way Patterns

This is a good stage to alternate the direction of the tiles and make a two-way pattern. Save another copy of your file at this stage of development.

Step 5: Check the Photoshop® Repeat

1. Merge all visible layers by pressing *Shift+Cmd+E / Shift+Ctrl+E*.

2. Scale the tile to 3 inches tiled with the Photoshop® Transform options.

3. Reposition the Zero Point to the upper left corner of the page, then pull horizontal and vertical Guides at every 3-inch interval.

4. Copy the tile layer by pulling it to the New Layer icon at the bottom of the Layers panel. You will need a total of 16 tiles to fill the Guide areas (Figure 8.23).

5. Position each tile with the Move Tool (W).

6. Zoom in close to inspect the positions and look for gaps.

7. When you have each of the tiles in place, save your work.

Step 6: Flatten the Image

1. Clear the Guides by going to *Menu Bar > View > Clear Guides*.

2. Inspect for and fix any gaps by repositioning the tiles with the Move Tool (V).

3. Toggle off the visibility of layers to locate them.

4. Flatten the artwork by going to *Menu Bar > Layer > Flatten Image*.

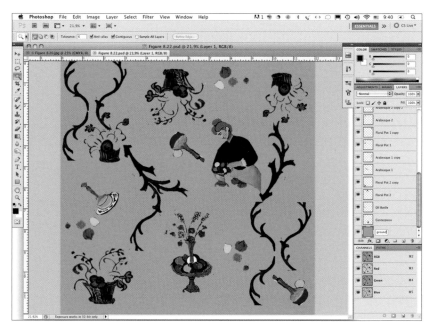

Figure 8.22

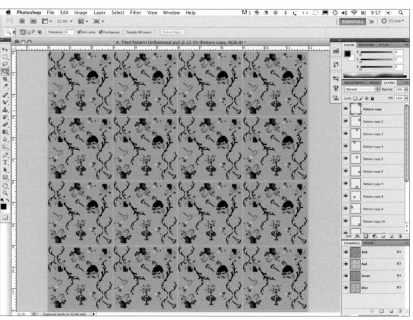

Figure 8.23

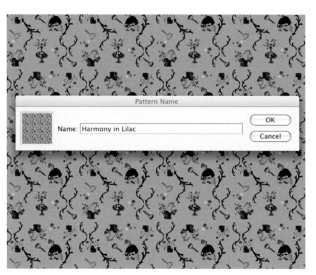

Figure 8.24

Figure 8.25 Hand-rendered fashion drawings can be painted in Photoshop® (see Tutorials 7.3 and 7.5). You can also digitally paint a defined pattern onto your designs with the Photoshop® Pattern Stamp Tool (see Tutorial 8.10). Illustration by Stacy Stewart Smith.

TIP: Scale Proportions

To ensure that there are no gaps, create a layer below the tile, and then select and fill it with the same color of the ground that you used. Flatten the artwork again.

Step 7: Define the Pattern

Press *Cmd+A / Ctrl+A* to Select All, then go to *Menu Bar > Edit > Define Pattern*. In the Pattern Name dialog box, click into the field and type a name for the new pattern (Figure 8.24).

Note: When you define and save a pattern, it will be available for use with that file and for any Photoshop® file on your computer.

Step 8: Fill an Object with the New Tile Pattern

As an exercise, use what you have learned to create a design presentation using the tile print from this tutorial. The completed presentation in Figure 8.25 is an example of "Digital Duo" processes. The figures were hand rendered and then digitized. The dresses and other parts were painted with Photoshop® brushes, including the Matisse prints.

The mystery behind defining patterns has been unraveled in Illustrator® CS4 and later upgrades. The program now has its own extensive library of pattern swatches. In fact, they are so universal that you could use them without having to make your own. The Pattern Libraries cover the essential textile categories, including plaids, stripes, dots, floral, etc. Use the libraries to study how it is done, and then make your own original repeats. Because there are plenty of books and online resources that explain how to create basics textile repeats, there is no need to elaborate on this information here.

Patterns with dots are a staple of design. Illustrator® has a library of them that will satisfy the taste of any fashion designer or merchandiser. The best way to study how to create a pattern is to pull the repeat onto the Artboard. Go to *Menu Bar > Window > Swatch Libraries > Patterns > Basic Graphics > Basic Graphics_Dots*. Each of the patterns was created using the principles of Tutorial 8.1. To create a dot pattern, simply decide on the size of the dot motif and spacing of the ground tile. With this method, no repeat box is needed because the motif is contained within the ground tile.

TIP: 45° Dots

Dots always look their best when rotated 45°. Select the object that you filled, and then double-click on the Rotate Tool (R). In the dialog box, enter 45° and uncheck Objects at the bottom, but leave the Pattern box checked.

Step 1: Load Illustrator® and Open a Letter-Size Document

Step 2: Create the Ground Tile

Use the Illustrator® Rectangle Tool (M) to create a tile or a rectangle as you did in Tutorial 8.1.

Step 3: Use the Illustrator® Ellipse Tool (L) to Create a Circle

To create a perfect circle, use the Ellipse Tool (L) and hold the Shift key.

Step 4: Select and Position the Tile and the Circle

Place the circle on top of the ground tile.

Step 5: Align the Objects from Centers

Use the Align panel to center the objects using both Vertical Align Center and Horizontal Align Center. The repeats are shown at the top right of Figure 8.26. Below them is a messenger bag design created in Illustrator® using the Polka Dotted patterns. The Basic Graphics_Dots Library is shown at the upper left of the page. The repeats shown below it were pulled from the panel. A larger view of dot patterns available from this library is pictured at the bottom.

Figure 8.26

Basic plaids, checks, and striped patterns can be created in Illustrator® by using the Rectangle Tool (M) and making, then placing horizontal/vertical shapes in a rectilinear special arrangement. Usually, these are placed on top of a ground tile; however, patterns can be defined without a ground color, leaving the fallout space empty. Such patterns can be used to create openwork or lace, or positioned over objects with a solid fill color for a different look.

To define a plaid or a stripe, follow the procedures previously outlined in Tutorial 8.1. You will need a Repeat Bounding Box for this type of pattern, and the Align panel will come in handy. Go to *Menu Bar > Window > Swatch Libraries > Patterns > Decorative > Classic Decorative* to study the plaids and checks that come with the program. Then go to *Menu Bar > Window > Swatch Libraries > Patterns > Basic Graphics > Basic Graphics_Lines* to observe the stripe patterns.

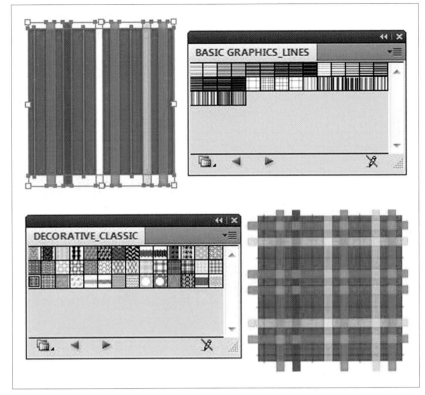

Figure 8.27

Studying Illustrator® Basic Graphics Pattern Repeats

The Basic Graphics Libraries are filled with patterns that have no ground tile; they are contained in transparency. To view the workings of these repeats, select them, and go to *Menu Bar > Object > Flatten Transparency*. In the Flatten Transparency dialog box, check the boxes for *Convert All Strokes to Outlines* and *Clip Complex Regions* in the Preset menu. Afterward, select the repeat and press *Shift+Cmd+G / Shift+Ctrl+G* to unlock it.

Step 1: Load Illustrator® and Open a Letter-Size Document

Step 2: Create the Ground Tile and Lock it on the Layer

Step 3: Use the Rectangle Tool to Create Horizontal Bars Slightly Longer Than the Ground Tile

Create a marquee with the Illustrator® Rectangle Tool (M) to create bars (stripe shapes) that overlap the ground tile slightly.

Step 4: Copy and Paste the Horizontal Bars

Copy and paste the bars that you made, and position them with the desired spacing from each other.

Note: If you are making stripes, you may work with pasted horizontal or vertical bars and skip to Step Seven.

Step 5: Select, Align, Distribute, and Group the Bars

Figure 8.27 shows the Illustrator® Basic Graphics_Lines Library and the Decorative_Classic Library. Next to each are sample repeats. When you define the repeats, they will appear in your Swatches panel.

Step 6: Make Cross Bars for Plaids and Checks

If you are making a plaid or checked pattern, select, copy, paste, and then rotate the horizontal bars 90°. Group the vertical bars.

Step 7: Select and Align the Crossing Bars from the Center

Select both the vertical and horizontal cross bars, and then use the *Horizontal Align Center* and the *Vertical Align Center* options to position the plaid or check properly.

Step 8: Position the Bars on Top of the Ground Tile

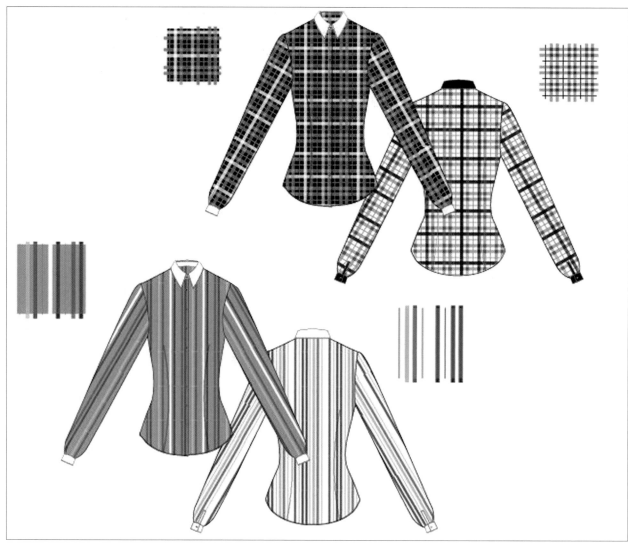

Figure 8.28 Illustration by Stacy Stewart Smith.

TIP: Reduce Opacity of Bars

If you want to create the look of a yarn dye check such as a buffalo, madras, or gingham, select some of the bars and reduce the *Opacity* with the Transparency panel. You learned to do this in Tutorial 3.2, Step Thirteen.

Step 9: Unlock the Ground Tile and Center Align It with the Bars

Step 10: Ungroup, Reposition, Scale, or Resize the Bars to Create a Pattern Repeat

Step 11: Select, Copy, and Paste the Ground Tile to Create a Repeat Bounding Box

Note: *At this point, you can follow the instructions of Tutorial 8.1, Step Seventeen.*

Step 12: Define the Pattern as Instructed Previously

Once you have properly defined a pattern, you can use it to fill objects like the digital flat shirt designs in Figure 8.28. Patterns can be rotated and scaled with the Illustrator® tools. The fill was rotated -30° on the left-sleeve shapes. It was then rotated 30° on the right-sleeve shapes.

The basic principles behind defining a plaid or a stripe in Photoshop® are similar to those detailed in Tutorial 8.4, except in Photoshop®, layers need to be employed to keep things organized. Technically, you could start a pattern repeat in Illustrator® and export it to Photoshop® for further image editing outside of the filters shared by the programs (see Tutorial 5.3, Step Sixteen). However, there are some things that you can only do in Photoshop®, like creating patterns made from patterns and/or gradients. Also, because some users own or favor Photoshop®, but do not have access to Illustrator®, it important to learn to define a plaid or stripe in Photoshop® as well. The full benefit will be seen at the conclusion of this tutorial when the best of both programs are put to use in a "Digital Duo" finished plate. While a Rothesay tartan plaid is demonstrated in the tutorial example, you can research any Scottish clan and re-create their signature cloth or make up your own.

Note: Photoshop® currently does not have the immediate ability to scale patterns or rotate with ease, at least not for the needs of fashion professionals. You will have to scale repeats to acceptable sizes before you define them. Other factors are involved concerning working with raster patterns when you are creating digital apparel presentations. You will learn more about this later in the book.

Step 1: Load Photoshop® and Open a New Document

The size that you begin with depends on how much of the pattern repeat you want to make. Generally speaking, you should create larger repeats in Photoshop® because the margin for error will be reduced by the ability to select the actual repeat from a substantial area (Figure 8.29).

Note: Increase the number of History States in the Performance section of the Preferences menu for this tutorial (see Chapter 5 for instructions).

Step 2: Use the Rectangular Marquee Tool to Make a Shape

Select the Rectangular Marquee Tool (M) from the Tools panel, create a vertical bar, and then fill it with color.

Step 3: Copy the Layer

Copy the layer by pulling it to the New Layer icon at the bottom of the Layers panel. Repeat this process until you have the vertical bars that you need.

Step 4: Distribute the Shapes

Pull vertical Guides from the y-axis to help you evenly space the shapes. Another option is to move the shapes into place, select all the layers that you created with the vertical shapes, then use the Align panel distribute options in the Options Bar to position them evenly (Figure 8.30).

Step 5: Repeat Steps Two through Four for Horizontal Shapes

Figure 8.31 shows the horizontal shapes in complete alignment.

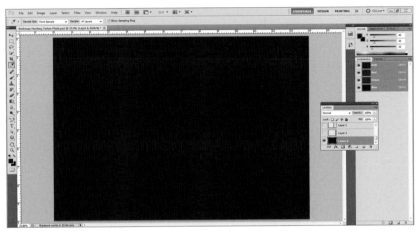

Figure 8.29

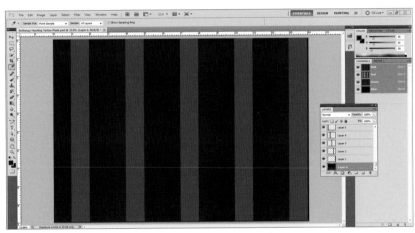

Figure 8.30 Use bars for striped repeats.

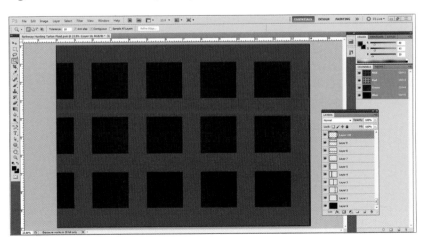

Figure 8.31

Note: If you are creating a simple horizontal or vertical stripe, skip to Step Twelve.

Step 6: Add Additional Horizontal Shapes

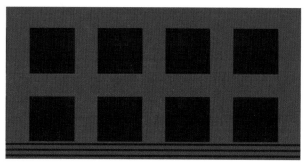

Figure 8.32

Step 7: Merge Layers of Grouped Horizontal Shapes and Repeat Steps Two through Four

Figure 8.33

Step 8: Add More Texture

Some tartan plaids have densely placed lines in certain areas. This gives the plaid character and depth (Figure 8.34).

Figure 8.34

Step 9: Add More Vertical Shapes

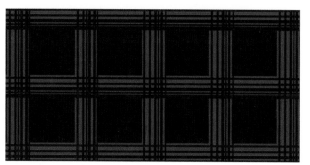

Figure 8.35

Step 10: Add More Texture with Horizontal Shapes in an Accent Color

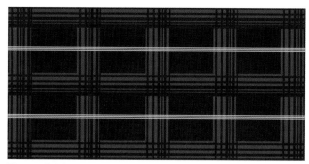

Figure 8.36

Step 11: Add More Texture with Vertical Shapes in an Accent Color

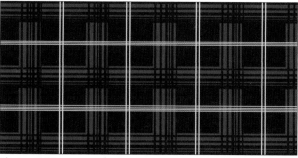

Figure 8.37

Step 12: Flatten and Scale the Image

Save a copy of the file in the Photoshop® .PSD format to preserve the layer compositing. Flatten the image of the original file and save the file again with a different name. Press *Cmd+T / Ctrl+T* to use the Options Bar's Transform options. Scale the repeat in *Width* and *Height* fields to suit your objectives. Locate the repeat, and use the Rectangular Marquee Tool (M) to select the area. Copy and paste the selection, then delete the original layer (Figure 8.38).

Step 13: Add a Filter to Simulate Fabric Texture

Go to *Menu Bar > Filter > Filter Gallery > Underpainting*. The **Underpainting filter** will add texture that will simulate fabric grain, if so desired (Figure 8.39).

Step 14: Scale the Repeat Again

If the repeat is still too large, scale it again using the instructions from Step Twelve (Figure 8.40).

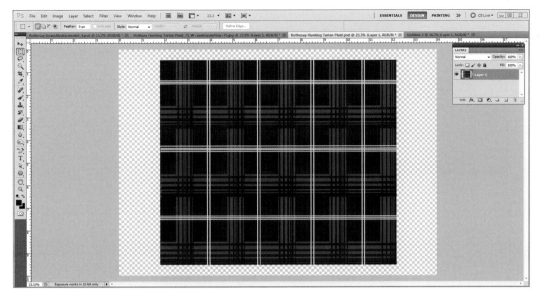

Figure 8.38

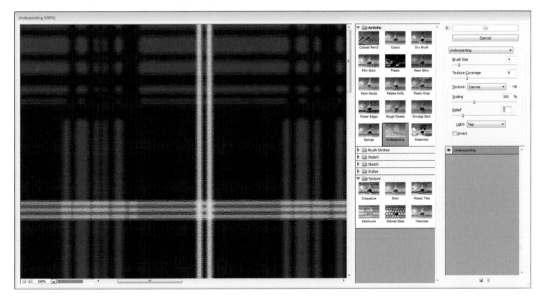

Figure 8.39

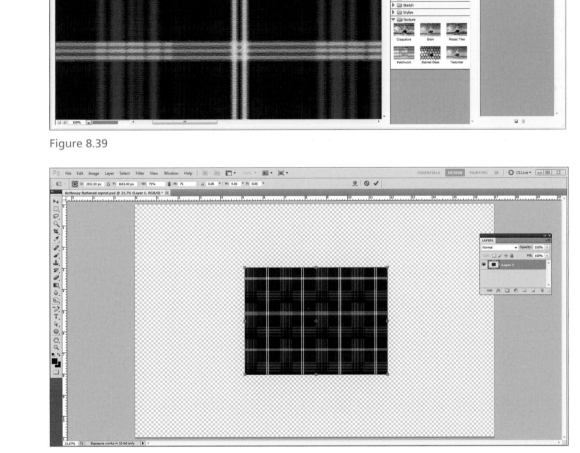

Figure 8.40

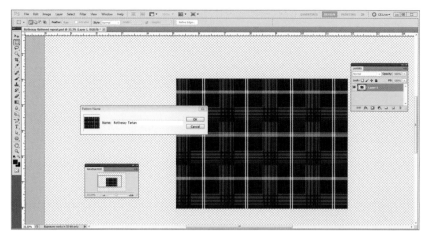

Figure 8.41

Step 15: Define the Pattern

Use the Magic Wand Tool (W) to select the transparent pixels of the background, and then press *Shift+Cmd+I / Shift+Ctrl+I* to Inverse the selection. Go to *Menu Bar > Edit > Define Pattern*, and then give the pattern a name in the Pattern Name dialog box. Click OK (Figure 8.41). In Figure 8.42, a total digital fashion abstractrealist environment has been assembled to showcase the plaid pattern.

Figure 8.42 Illustration by Stacy Stewart Smith.

Tutorial 8.6
DEFINE A MOIRÉ PATTERN IN PHOTOSHOP®

Known for their noble appearance, moiré patterns on silk, rayon, and other textiles are created from a process known as calendering. Authentic moiré has a watery motif, which is made by wetting the fabric, folding it with the selvages facing together, then running it through heat and ribbed moiré rollers. There are also other techniques commonly used to create this finish, including printing moiré patterns.

Moiré taffeta patterned yard goods and ribbons have been used for centuries; they are a staple of eveningwear (Figure 8.43). There are periods when moiré, and other motifs like it, may not be in style, but they do return. In this tutorial, the Photoshop® Liquify filter will be used to create the moiré pattern from stripes.

Step 1: Load Photoshop® and Create a New Document

In the New dialog box, set both the *Width* and *Height* to 20 inches. The *Resolution* should be 300 pixels/inch, and the document should be in the RGB *Color Mode* on a transparent background (Figure 8.44).

Step 2: Create a Background

Press *Cmd+A / Ctrl+A* to Select All. Go *to Menu Bar > Edit > Fill*, select Color from the Fill dialog box's pull-down menu, then use the Color Picker to choose a hue. Shocking Pink is the hue of choice in the tutorial example for the ground color (Figure 8.45).

Step 3: Create Stripes from Tints

Create a new layer and use the Rectangular Marquee Tool (M) to make stripes, and fill them with a tint of the ground color. Simply click on the Set Foreground Color box, which should still contain the hue that you selected for your ground, and when the Color

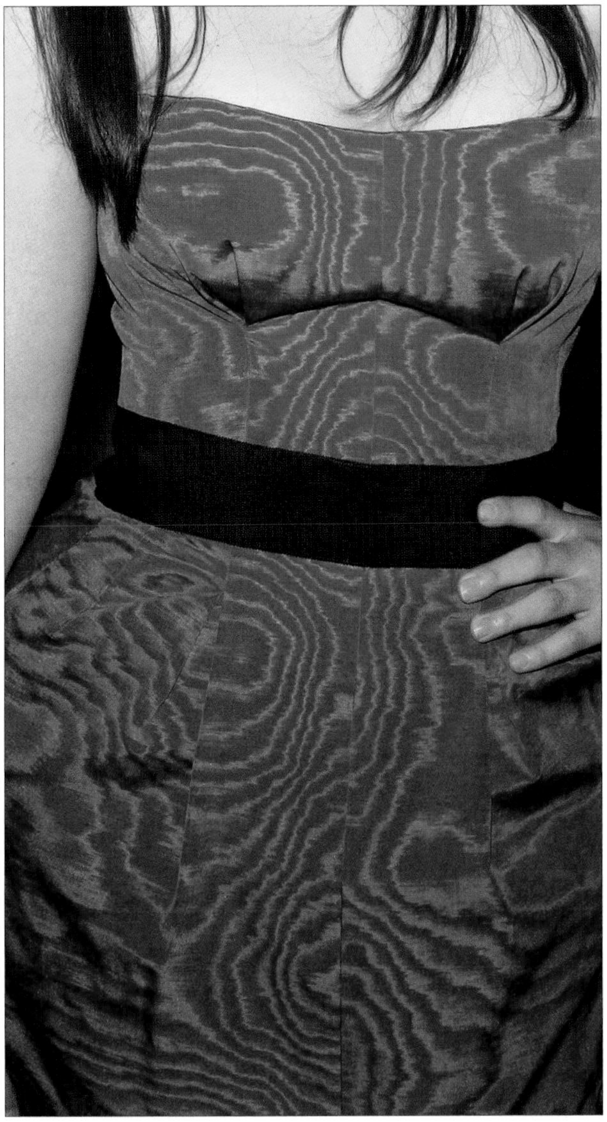

Figure 8.44

Figure 8.43 **Based on image from © Everett Collection Inc./Alamy.**

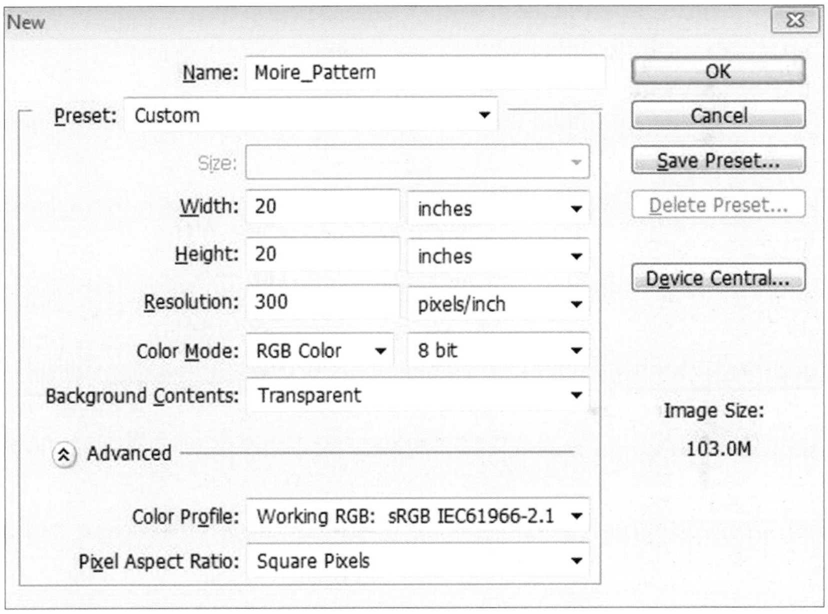

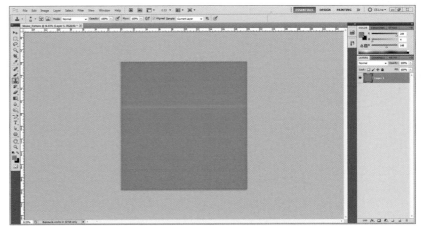

Figure 8.45

Picker appears, click along the top until you find a tint. Click OK, then fill the selection(s) you created with the Photoshop® Paint Bucket Tool (G). Repeat these steps, creating stripes of various narrow to medium widths. Some of them may vary in Opacity or overlap like those exampled in Figure 8.46. Continue to make additional stripes from the ones you already created by pulling layers to the Create New Layer icon at the bottom of the Layers panel. Position the stripes in an uneven manner, but do not leave huge gaps. Select all the layers, then use the Align panel options in the Options Bar to position them evenly at the top (Figure 8.47).

TIP: Jacquards and Damasks

You can also use the techniques demonstrated in this tutorial to engineer digital jacquards or damask patterns.

Step 4: Save a Copy of the File

Save a copy of the file with the layers in the Photoshop® format. You may need to return to this file later.

Step 5: Use the Liquify Filter to Make a Moiré Repeat

1. Flatten the file by going to *Menu Bar > Layer > Flatten > Image*, then save the file with another name. This will ensure that you do not overwrite and lose the original file. You can also merge the layers containing the stripe shapes by selecting them and pressing *Cmd+E / Ctrl+E*.

2. Go to *Menu Bar > Filter > Liquify*.

3. When the Liquify window appears, use the **Forward Warp Tool (W)**, the **Twirl Clockwise Tool (C)**, the **Turbulence Tool (T)**, and others to create a watery moiré pattern.

4. Adjust the brush size, density, and pressure for each tool and action.

5. Click and pull along from side to side with the Forward Warp Tool (W); then use the Twirl Clockwise Tool (C) to generate various radial formations. However, do not change the top and bottom of the repeat.

6. Go back over some of the areas that you have created with the Turbulence Tool (T). Leave the top and bottom edges untouched; they will accommodate a smooth repeat when you define the pattern again later (Figure 8.48).

Note: Be patient with the Liquify filter; it may take time to generate the movements you make with the tools. Do not click too many times, as this may cause your computer to crash. Allow one movement to complete its cycle before you begin another. When you click OK, the Liquify filter may take a few moments to return the results (CS6 works faster).

Step 6: Scale the Repeat

1. Press *Cmd+T / Ctrl+T* to scale your moiré repeat.

2. When the Bounding Box appears, pull it from the sides toward the center (Figure 8.49).

3. Select the repeat layer and pull it to the Create New Layer icon at the bottom of the panel several times; then reposition the copies (Figure 8.50).

Step 7: Liquify, Again

It may be necessary to adjust some of the repeat lines again with the Liquify filter, if striping occurs (Figure 8.51).

Figure 8.46

Figure 8.47

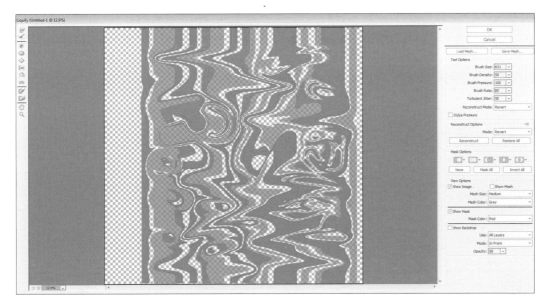

Figure 8.48

Figure 8.49

Figure 8.50

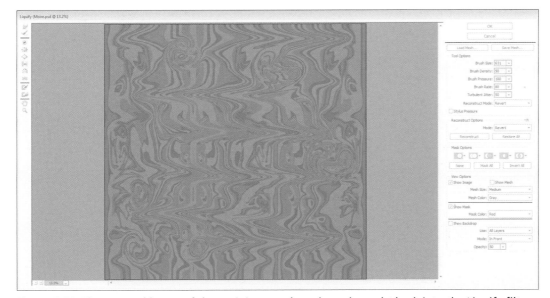

Figure 8.51 The merged layers of the moiré repeat have been brought back into the Liquify filter to add more interesting detail.

Step 8: Define the Moiré

1. Scale the repeat to a size close to the end use for your presentation.

2. Go to *Menu Bar > Edit > Define Pattern*. Give the pattern a proper name.

3. Use the pattern to fill apparel items and other objects that you create, like the fashion abstractrealist environment shown in Figure 8.52.

Figure 8.52 Illustration by Stacy Stewart Smith.

photos of your favorite creatures and use the animal's skin or fur to help you. The Illustrator® Nature_ Animal Skins Pattern Library contains some of the most popular skin prints (Figure 8.53). Select the swatches and pull them onto the Artboard to discover how the repeats work so that you can create your own animal skin prints.

The best way to create prints and patterns that look like the skins of animals is to study them. Locate

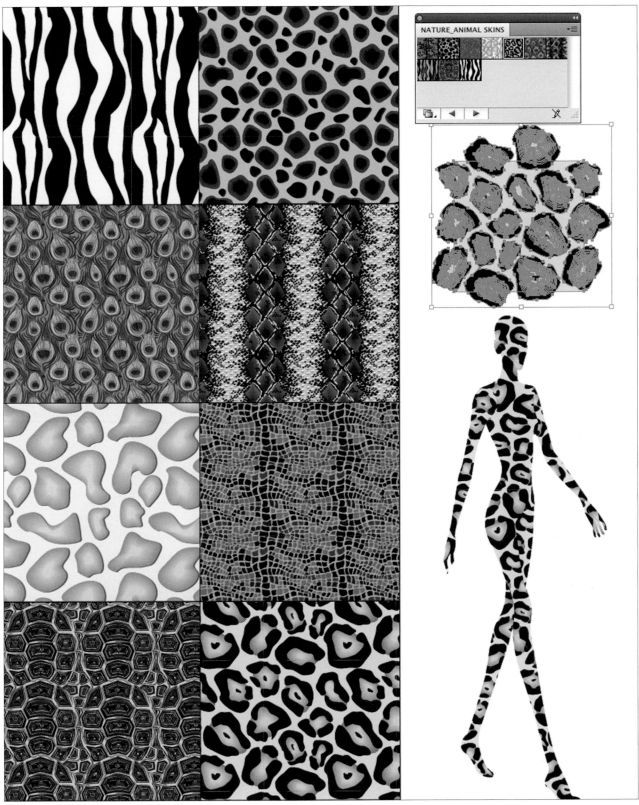

Figure 8.53 Illustration by Stacy Stewart Smith.

Tutorial 8.8
ILLUSTRATOR®
FLORAL PATTERNS

Illustrator® has a Flowers Symbols Library that you can locate by going to *Menu Bar > Window > Symbols Libraries > Flowers*. Follow the steps outlined in Tutorial 5.3, Step Nine, to release the various Flowers symbols from their transparencies, then place them on a ground tile as detailed in Tutorial 8.1 (Figure 8.54). Follow the full instructions to define the pattern. Try creating your own flowers with any of the rendering tools. In Figure 8.55 images from the Flowers Symbols Library were used to create a pattern and the digital fashion abstractrealist presentation. The Illustrator® Pen Tool (P) was used to create the illustration and the floral pattern in Figure 8.56.

Figure 8.54

Figure 8.55 Illustration by Stacy Stewart Smith.

Figure 8.56

By using the Illustrator® **Mesh Tool (U)** and a few special techniques, you can make your own digital tie-dye repeats. Naturally, the Photoshop® **Clouds filter**, Liquify filter, Mixer Paint Brush (B), and painting capabilities can also generate tie-dye effects, but not every one works on both programs.

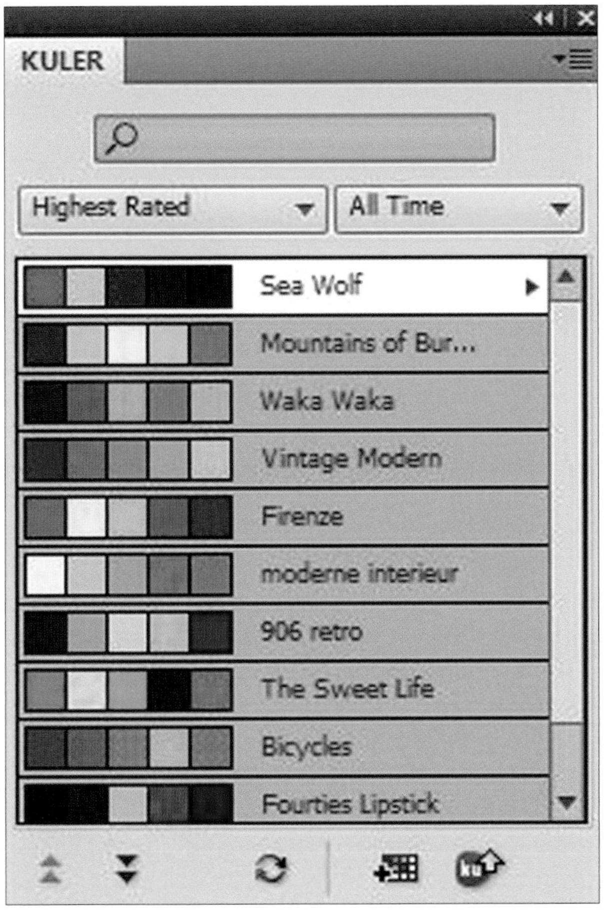

Figure 8.57

Step 1: Load Illustrator® and Create a New Letter-Size Document

Step 2: Use the Rectangle Tool to Make a Large Shape

Step 3: Add a Color Fill with a Stroke of None

Step 4: Select the Mesh Tool (U), Click on the Shape, Then Select a New Color

The Mesh Tool (U) creates gradients based on a grid. With it you can randomly position color blends.

1. With the shape selected, click on the Mesh Tool (U), and click on the shape to build a mesh section.

2. Select a new color from the Color Libraries or double-click on the Fill box and pick a spot color from the Color Picker or from the Kuler panel (Figure 8.57).

To access the Illustrator® Color Libraries, go to *Menu Bar > Window > Swatch Libraries*, then choose any of the Color Libraries. To access the Illustrator® Kuler panel, go to *Menu Bar > Window > Extensions > Kuler*.

Note: *See Chapter 9 for more information on color mixing and the Illustrator® Kuler panel. Both Illustrator® and Photoshop® have Kuler panels.*

3. Once you select a new color, it will immediately create a color blend based on the mesh (Figure 8.58).

4. Use the Mesh Tool (U) to add another grid division, then select another color (Figure 8.59), but keep the color blends away from the sides to avoid the pattern that you defining having a checked effect.

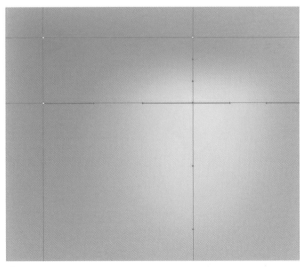

Figure 8.58

Figure 8.59

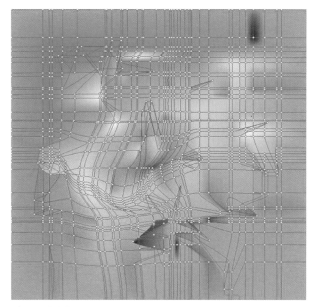

Figure 8.60

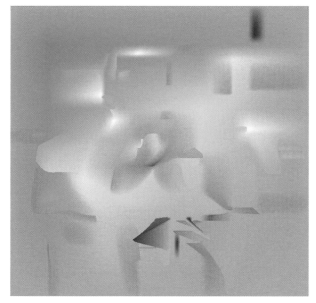

Figure 8.61

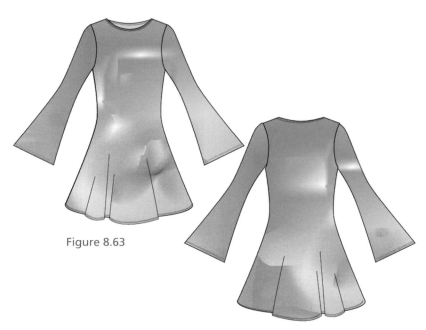

Figure 8.62

Figure 8.63

By clicking on the grid divisions with the Mesh Tool (U) or moving the handles (Figure 8.60), you can manually reposition them. As you add mesh divisions, it may become difficult for you to see the changes you make, so periodically deselect to obtain a better view. Figure 8.61 shows the results of adding several colors and repositioning.

Step 5: Rasterize the Shape

A gradient mesh should not be defined as a pattern unless it is rasterized. Because the shape we began with is rectilinear, Illustrator® can tile a repeat. Before going to the next step, be sure that your colors are not blending into the edges of the shape. If there are issues, use the Mesh Tool (U) to readjust the grid divisions. The ground color should be pure on all sides. This will prevent a checked pattern from repeating in the defined pattern. After you have inspected for any major problems at the edges, select the shape, then go to *Menu Bar > Object > Rasterize*. In the Rasterize dialog box (Figure 8.62), check *High* (300 ppi) in the *Resolution* section, and *Transparent* in the *Background* area of the panel.

Step 6: Define and Use the Tie-Dye Pattern as a Fill

When you have rasterized the shape, go to *Menu Bar > Edit > Define Pattern*. Give the pattern a name, and use it to fill your apparel design(s). The tunic pictured in Figure 8.63 contains the tie-dye pattern created in the tutorial.

Tutorial 8.10
DEFINE AN ILLUSTRATOR® PATTERN
IN PHOTOSHOP®

Adobe Systems Inc. has provided some great patterns for its Illustrator® users, but Photoshop® has none. In this tutorial, you will learn to use "Digital Duo" processes to define pattern repeats created in Illustrator® in Photoshop®. The combined strengths of both software programs will generate unlimited possibilities.

To complete this tutorial, you'll use defined digital pattern repeat(s) from the Illustrator® Pattern libraries. It is highly recommended that you complete the tutorials from Chapters 3, 5, and 6 before starting this tutorial.

Step 1: Load Photoshop® and Create a New Document

Create a new document in Photoshop® large enough to accommodate a fashion croquis, which we will use in the second part of this tutorial. Depending on the pattern that you choose, add a black or color adjustment layer. The icon is located at the bottom of the Layers panel.

Step 2: Load Illustrator® and Create a New Document

Step 3: Select a Pattern with a Ground Tile from the Illustrator® Pattern Library

Select and drag a pattern repeat from the Illustrator® Pattern Library to the Artboard. The pattern that you choose must have a solid-colored ground tile. Use one of your own patterns if you prefer, but an animal print will work best with the steps of this tutorial (Figure 8.64).

Step 4: Drag and Drop the Repeat from Illustrator® into the Photoshop® Document

Step 5: Scale, then Pull Guides to the Edges of the Ground Tile in Photoshop®

Once you have the repeat in Photoshop®, use the Bounding Box that appears to scale the repeat to a size close to the end use, and then double-click on it to accept it. Place horizontal and vertical Guides at the edges of the ground tile (Figure 8.65).

Step 6: Select the Area of the Ground Tile with the Rectangular Marquee Tool

Rasterize the Smart Object, then select the ground tile with the Rectangular Marquee Tool (M) (Figure 8.66).

Figure 8.64

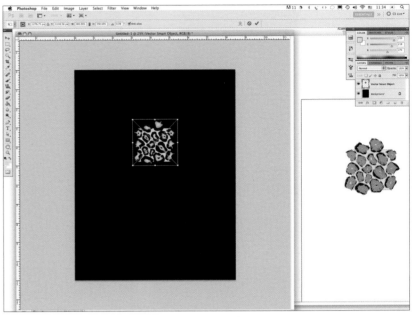

Figure 8.65

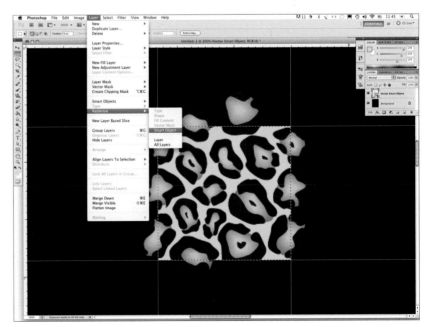

Figure 8.66

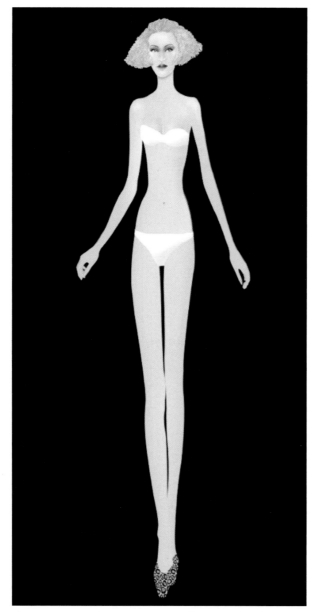

Figure 8.67

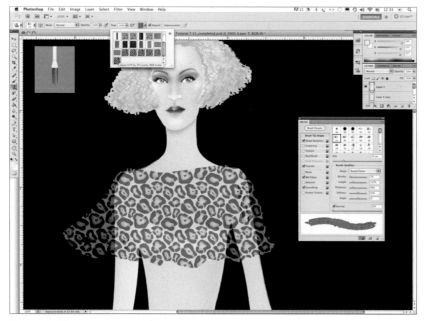

Figure 8.68

Step 7: Define the Pattern Repeat

Go to *Menu Bar > Edit > Define Pattern*, and then name the pattern when the dialog box appears.

Digital Painting with the Pattern Stamp Tool and the Brushes Panel

One of the greatest improvements to Photoshop® is in the area of digital painting. In several tutorials, you have learned to use the Photoshop® Brush panel; however, in the second part of this tutorial you will learn to use the Pattern Stamp Tool (S) along with the brush attributes to paint with patterns.

Step 8: Place a Fashion Croquis into the Photoshop® File

Scan and use your own croquis or follow the tutorial example with Ines.pdf from ① CH08\Tutorial 8.10. The croquis in **Figure 8.67** will be used in the tutorial example.

Step 9: Select the Pattern Stamp Tool and Adjust the Brush Panel Settings

Click on the Pattern Stamp Tool (S) in the Photoshop® Tools panel. Show the Brush panel, and select a brush like the Round Curve. Increase the *Thickness*, and set the size. Check *Shape Dynamics*, *Transfer*, *Wet Edges*, and *Smoothing* in the **Brush Tip Shape** section of the panel. These settings will allow you to paint digitally with fluidity.

Note: *For best results use a stylus tablet.*

Step 10: Work on a New Layer

Before you begin to paint, create a new layer. You can also lock the other layers.

Step 11: Print Painting Techniques

Depending on your goal, the settings in the Brush panel may need to be adjusted.

1. Toggle on the **Bristle Brush Preview** at the bottom of the panel.

2. When you selected the Pattern Stamp Tool (S), the defined patterns pull-down menu appeared in the Options Bar. Select the pattern that you defined, then use the paintbrush as you would freehand but do not let go of your clicker until you render an entire area (**Figure 8.68**). If you let go, the pattern will double over itself and create a darker area.

3. If you want to avoid this watercolor-like technique, uncheck *Wet Edges* in the Brush panel.

4. Using Wet Edges will help build a 3-D effect, especially when rendering sheer textiles.

Figure 8.69

5. After you create the first shape, release the clicker and add on additional shapes to make darkened areas (Figure 8.69). Reduce the brush size if necessary.

Step 12: Clean Up Your Presentation and Add Layer Styles

Clean up the edges of your painting with the Photoshop® Eraser Tool (E). Reshape the object you painted with Transform options, Puppet Warp, Liquify filter, etc., and then add a Layer Style(s), such as Inner Shadow (Figure 8.70).

Brocade and Metallic Textile Effects

Although you could probably attempt to create and define a repeat to simulate elegant textiles like brocades and lamé, it may be easier to work with multiple filters, Layer Styles, and a series of converting Smart Objects to rasterized objects within garment shapes. In this portion of the tutorial, you will learn to build filters in Photoshop® to achieve "Digital Duo" effects.

Step 13: Paint on an Apparel Design with a Defined Print

Use a round soft brush to paint on a defined pattern (Figure 8.71).

Step 14: Add the Smudge Stick Filter

1. With the apparel item selected, go to *Menu Bar > Filter > Filter Gallery.*

2. Tip the Artistic folder and select the Smudge Stick filter.

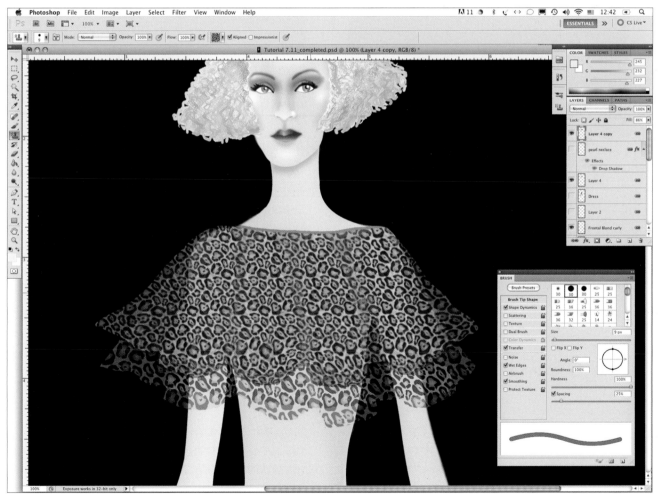

Figure 8.70 The completed flounces show depth even though they represent a skin-patterned chiffon.

Figure 8.71

Figure 8.72

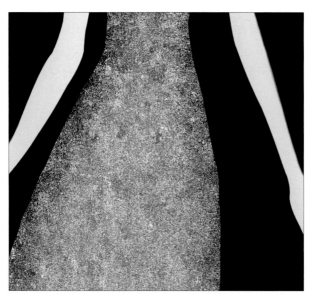

Figure 8.73

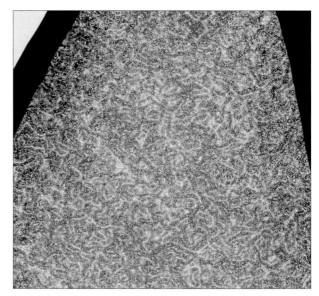

Figure 8.74

3. Set the *Stroke Length* to 3, the *Highlight Area* to 4, and the *Intensity* to 0.

4. To add the Spatter filter to the Smudge Stick, select the New Filter icon at the bottom of the Filter Gallery window. This will create a duplicate Smudge Stick layer at the right.

5. Tip the Brush Strokes folder (left) and select the Spatter filter.

6. Change the *Spray Radius* to 25 and the *Smoothness* to 3, and press OK. The results of this action are dramatic, and may look slightly different from what is shown in Figure 8.72.

Step 15: Add the Inner Glow Layer Style, and Adjust the Color with Vibrance

By now, you have used the Photoshop® Layer Styles to assist your own projects. You created a customer profile storyboard in Tutorial 5.1 that made great use of them.

Add the Inner Glow layer style to the dress. Then, go to *Menu Bar > Image > Adjustments > Vibrance* to intensify the color saturation (Figure 8.73).

Step 16: Transform the Object Layer into a Smart Object, then Rasterize the Layer

In order to add additional filters, transform the selected layer into a Smart Object by going to the hidden menu at the right of the Layers panel and scrolling to the option. This will flatten the Layer Style you added in Step Fifteen. Afterward, return to the hidden menu and rasterize the Smart Object to restore the layer's full editing capability. Save your work.

Step 17: Add the Plastic Wrap Filter

The Photoshop® filter gallery's **Plastic Wrap filter** will simulate the dobby effect observed in most opulent brocades (Figure 8.74). The raised pattern effect is generated from certain elements of the pattern.

Figure 8.75

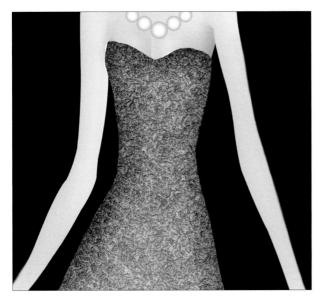

Figure 8.76

Step 18: Repeat Step Fifteen, Add Inner Shadow, and then Repeat Step Sixteen

Figure 8.75 shows the effects of adding the Inner Glow Layer Style again with further adjustments to the color and unchecked, then manually adjusted *Global Light*. In Figure 8.76 the Inner Shadow was added.

Step 19: Add the Lighting Effects Filter

If you are on a 64-bit Mac computer operating earlier versions of Photoshop®, then you will need to run the program in the 32-bit mode in order to add the **Lighting Effects filter**. Before you begin, save and back up your work.

Lighting Effects for Macintosh

- On a Mac, go to the applications folder through the Finder or select the desktop.
- Then go to *Menu Bar > Go > Applications > Photoshop® folder*.
- Right-click the Photoshop® application icon.
- Choose *Get Info*.
- Go to *General* and select *Open in 32-bit mode*.
- Restart your computer.

Lighting Effects for PC

- On a PC the 64-bit settings should work fine without adjustments.

The Lighting Effects filter only works in RGB mode. If you are in the CMYK mode or if you do not know, go to *Menu Bar > Image > Mode > RGB*. Then follow these instructions to create a moody glow on your digital drawing with the Lighting Effect filter:

1. Select the layer with the part of your drawing where you want to apply the filter.
2. Go to *Menu Bar > Filter > Render > Lighting Effects*.
3. When the Lighting Effects dialog box appears, choose a Style. The Soft Spotlight was used in the tutorial example.
4. Choose a Light Type, such as *Spotlight, Omni,* or *Directional*. You will need to try them all in order to decide what works best.
5. Adjust the *Properties* to affect the intensity of the filter.

Note: *Photoshop® CS6 offers an all-inclusive, streamlined interface for the Lighting Effects filter, which includes an entire window of settings, including the Lights panel, which works in conjunction with the pull-down menus in the Options Bar, and the Properties panel, which allows you to adjust settings. This is a great improvement above the smaller Lighting Effects window that appears in CS5.5 and earlier versions. An image of the CS6 Lighting Effects filter appears in Chapter 9.*

Step 20: Complete the Look with Accessories

The completed tutorial example has been adjusted with the Transform options and Layer Styles, showing added accessories (Figure 8.77).

Figure 8.77 **Illustration by Stacy Stewart Smith.**

Chapter 8 Summary

There are millions of textile prints and patterns, but even more can be achieved through your imagination. The goal of Chapter 8 was to acquaint you with procedures for creating pattern repeats in Illustrator®, Photoshop®, and the combined use of both programs. The tutorials in this chapter amplify digital pattern defining techniques presented in previous chapters. If you worked through each of the tutorials, then you should have a general grasp of how to create your own textile designs. Before you venture into Chapter 9, take the following quiz.

Chapter 8 Self-Assessment

1. Can I create a proper repeat in Illustrator® and define it without breaks in the ground tiles?

2. Basic pattern repeats are provided in the Illustrator® Pattern Libraries, but can I use them to define new patterns by manipulating their repeats?

3. Can I create moiré taffeta using Photoshop®?

4. Can I create stripe and plaid repeats in both Illustrator® and Photoshop®?

5. Am I able to use "Digital Duo" procedures to enhance the patterns that I have created in Illustrator® by rasterizing them in Photoshop®, and using the tools, panels, and filters to give them more character?

6. Do I understand the purpose of a Repeat Bounding Box?

7. Do I know how to rotate objects in both Illustrator® and Photoshop®?

8. Can I digitally simulate couture-quality textiles like brocade, and metallic finishes, using the Photoshop® filters?

9. Do I know how to access and edit patterns in both Illustrator® and Photoshop®?

10. Do I understand how to access and use Photoshop® filters?

Digital Color Theory

Objectives

Both Illustrator® and Photoshop® have many ways to choose and use colors. Some of these were discussed in previous chapters; however, the information and tutorials in this chapter will increase your understanding. Because the science of color is vitally important to digital fashion design, merchandising, and illustration, Chapter 9 is devoted to helping you to understand how to choose, mix, and apply color using the simplest forms in Illustrator® and Photoshop®. The entire subject of color is exhaustive, so our objective is limited to only those areas that are essential to digital fashion design art. The chief goal is to explain the fundamentals of color theory. In the tutorials, you will learn about color groups as well as classic color harmonies and schemes. In this chapter, you will:

- Mix digital color in the CMYK and RGB color modes

- Create various color wheels as a means to help you understand color science

- Explore color through the mixing of gradients in both Illustrator® and Photoshop®

- Learn about the Illustrator® Kuler panel

- Apply Photoshop® Lighting Effects filters in the RGB color mode

- Work with color panels and pickers in Illustrator® and Photoshop®

- Discover basic color terms

Basic Color Modes

A color mode (also color model) is a printing process. There are two color modes that concern the digital fashion artist: CMYK (a four-color subtractive printing process) and RGB (a three-color additive printing process). When we discuss color throughout this chapter, we will refer to how it is applied by using one of the two color modes.

The CMYK Color Mode

CMYK is an acronym that stands for cyan (a turquoise hue), magenta (similar to fuchsia), yellow, and black (represented by K). It is the default color mode for Illustrator®. CMYK is a subtractive color mode, meaning that each color added masks or changes the one previously applied upon a white or light-colored surface. The masking continues from cyan to black. In some cases the surface is completely covered (saturated), and the colors subtract the brightness; however, translucency is also essential in the CMYK color mode.

The CMYK color mode is used to blend color and is reliant on a white surface to interpret some hues, especially those that are lighter tints. The screen print in Figure 9.1 reveals the subtractive process of CMYK.

Figure 9.1 **Illustration by Stacy Stewart Smith.**

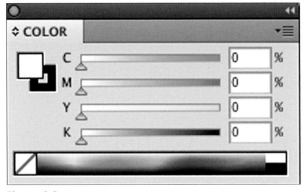

Figure 9.2

Only a few spaces of the white paper remain unmasked by separate screen applications of cyan, magenta, yellow, and black. You can see where each of the colors blended when it was applied on top of others; however, the black in the print remains dominant.

The CMYK Color Panel

The Illustrator® Color panel (Figure 9.2) further demonstrates the subtractive color concept. In the CMYK color mode, all the color sliders begin at the left in pure white; however, gradually move them all to the right side and you'll see that they eventually produce black.

The RGB Color Mode

The default color mode of Photoshop® is RGB. This is a three-color additive printing process, whereby red, green, and blue light are mixed to produce various colors and illuminate darkness. The RGB Photoshop® Lights Preset of the Lighting Effects filter in Figure 9.3 exemplifies the digital color model when the red, green, and blue spots, or chroma colors, cross each other in darkness (black). They blend to create cyan, magenta, yellow, and a brilliant near-white center, depending on the settings of the Properties panel, which only appears in the CS6 Lighting Effects window. The earlier versions of Photoshop® have a Lighting Effects dialog box. The colorful fine art oil painting in Figure 9.4 was digitized and then combined with digital color in the RGB mode. RGB color lights were used to illuminate the digital female form on the left by tinting.

Devices such as monitors, televisions, projectors, etc. use this color mode. RGB is the color mode that you see on your computer display, so images that are shown in this model can possess an animated luminescence. However, each device will vary in its ability to produce color via the RGB mode. In addition, over time, computer displays may gradually lose light intensity. This variation in color can be observed when you are viewing files from one device to the next. This is why calibration is needed. Each device will come with its own set of instructions to assist calibration. Keep in mind that the color as it appears on a monitor, may vary when compared to printed color depending on devices, software, and the media that you select. Most printers allow you to choose how to color manage your files; however, each situation will be different.

The RGB Color Panel

The Photoshop® RGB Color panel demonstrates the additive color concept (Figure 9.5). It appears when you click the hidden menu icon at the top right of the Color panel. In RGB color mode, all the color sliders begin at the left in black (darkness). Gradually move them to the right to mix colors or to produce white.

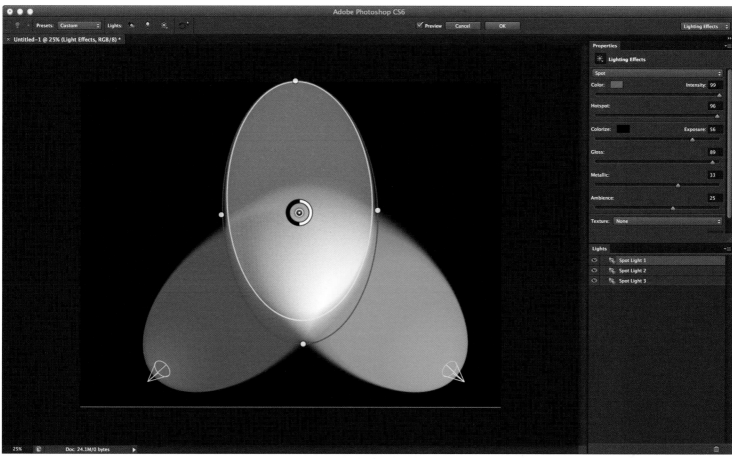

Figure 9.3 The Photoshop® CS6 Lighting Effects filter window with RGB Lights.

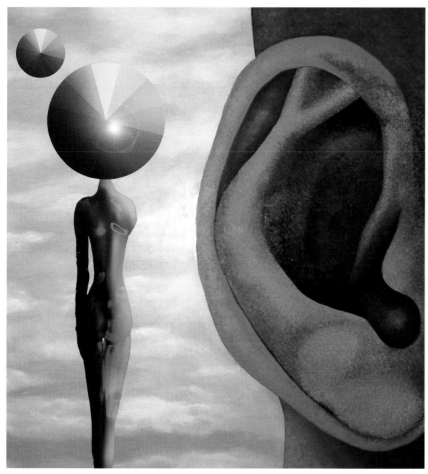

Figure 9.4 Illustration by Stacy Stewart Smith.

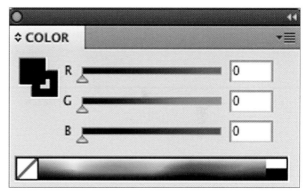

Figure 9.5

The following exercise is devoted to helping you understand how to choose, mix, and apply digital color in the CMYK color mode. In order to complete this exercise, you will need to import the file Radial_Structure.pdf into Illustrator®. The file is located on ① Ch09\Tutorial 9.1.

The Traditional Color Wheel

A traditional color wheel is a type of chart that shows primary colors, secondary colors, tertiary colors (intermediate colors), and their complements around an axis. This simple method of expressing color is more commonly associated with fine art painting, but Illustrator® is a good place to start experimenting with digital color. By creating digital color wheel(s), you will learn to mix color gradients, use the Illustrator® Live Paint Bucket Tool (K), and save swatches. In this exercise, you will learn about color groups as well as classic color harmonies and schemes.

Step 1: Load Illustrator® and Create a Letter-Size Document

Load Illustrator® and create a letter-size document in landscape orientation using the specifications of Figure 9.6.

Step 2: Open or Create the Radial Structure

Import the file Radial_Structure.pdf from ① Ch09\Tutorial 9.1 into Illustrator® by going to *Menu Bar > File > Open*. In the Open dialog box, locate the file on the disk from the menu options, then click the Open button (Figure 9.7).

Note: *Do not Place the file into the program.*

Step 3: Rotate the Radial Structure

No matter if you use the provided file or one that you make, select and group the parts, and then rotate your radial structure 15° by selecting it and double-clicking on the Rotate Tool (R) as shown in Figure 9.8. A segment of the structure should be centered at both the top and the bottom.

TIP: Create Your Own

For more practice, instead of using the provided file, create your own radial structure by following Steps Ten through Fourteen of Tutorial 4.1. Make the structure approximately 6 inches in circumference (6 inches within a Bounding Box) with a 1 pt Stroke of black and a Fill of None.

Figure 9.6

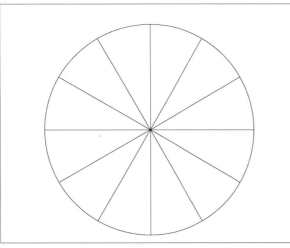

Figure 9.7

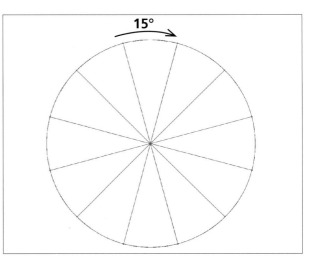

Figure 9.8

Step 4: Identify Primary and Secondary Colors from the CMYK Swatches panel

Go to *Menu Bar > Window > Swatch Libraries > Default Swatches > Basic CMYK* to show the Illustrator® Basic CMYK Swatches panel (Figure 9.9). Use the cursor to identify the color names and formulas; they will highlight as you touch each swatch.

The primary colors are red, yellow, and blue. The color standards for red, yellow, and blue are universally fixed because they are considered to be pure colors from the color spectrum. Secondary colors are created directly from combinations of the primary colors. Mixing red and yellow will make orange. Mixing red and blue will make violet. Blue and yellow can be combined to produce green.

Step 5: Open the Primary and Secondary Color Chart

Open the file Color_Standards.pdf on ① Ch09\ Tutorial 9.1 to view a chart of primary and secondary colors with their highlight formulas from the Basic CMYK panel. You will also find the positions where you will place each of these colors on the radial structure (Figure 9.10).

TIP: Adding Swatch Groups

To add a group of swatches to the Swatches panel, hold the Shift key and select each swatch. Then click on the hidden menu icon at the upper right of the panel and scroll to Add to Swatches. Once you have saved your file, the swatches will appear each time you open it. The Swatches panel is comprehensive and should be used to organize color, patterns, gradients, groups, etc. See Chapter 2 for more information on the Swatches panel.

Step 6: Use the Live Paint Bucket Tool to Fill Color

Unlock the layer, select the structure, and then go to *Menu Bar > Object > Live Paint > Make*. With the structure selected, choose the Illustrator® Live Paint Bucket Tool (K). Click on the structure and highlighted outlines will appear as your cursor passes over the Faces and Edges of each segment that was generated through Live Trace. The same will happen for the Fill and Stroke of a selected object. The Live

TIP: Choose Methods Wisely

Always consider the end use of the project. When you fill areas with the Live Paint Bucket Tool (K) rather than creating actual shapes and filling them, you limit your ability to use the drawing in Illustrator® and Photoshop®. Creating shapes and using layer compositing gives you greater editing capabilities.

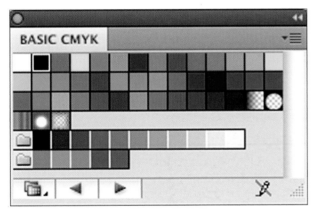

Figure 9.9

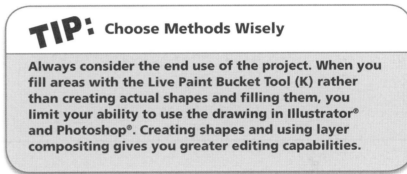

PRIMARY AND SECONDARY COLOR STANDARDS FROM THE ILLUSTRATOR® BASIC CMYK SWATCHES PANEL

YELLOW	ORANGE	RED	VIOLET	BLUE	GREEN
primary color	secondary color	primary color	secondary color	primary color	secondary color
Radial Structure Segment 12	Radial Structure Segment 10	Radial Structure Segment 8	Radial Structure Segment 6	Radial Structure Segment 4	Radial Structure Segment 2
CMYK Yellow	C=0 M=80 Y=95 K=0	CMYK Red	C=75 M=100 Y=0 K=0	CMYK Blue	CMYK Green

Figure 9.10

Paint Bucket Tool (K) allows you to fill areas even if actual shapes have not been created (Figure 9.11).

The Live Paint Bucket Tool (K) is useful when filling multiple areas with the color, gradients, or patterns that are next to one another in the Swatches panel (see Tutorial 6.1, Step Thirteen). The primary and the secondary colors are already in the Swatches panel; filling the appropriate segment is as easy as selecting the swatches, highlighting an area, and then clicking. In the tutorial example, each segment has been given a number. Numbers 12, 8, and 4 represent primary colors, and numbers 10, 6, and 2 are secondary colors. Use the Live Paint Bucket Tool (K) to fill each of these segments with the appropriate colors from the Basic CMYK Color panel (Figure 9.12).

Step 7: Identify Simple Color Schemes

A color scheme is a group of colors that pair well together. They can be seasonal or market based; however, today many designers ignore tradition and develop color schemes as a means of artistic expression. You will learn more about this later when the Illustrator® Kuler panel is discussed. Because the color wheel chart is devoted to the basics, any color schemes developed from it may be considered elementary. Many children's wear lines are available in assortments of these color combinations. The following represent a few simple color schemes that can be observed from the color wheel.

Complementary Colors

A complementary color is the one opposite another on the color wheel. The secondary color green is the complement of red, and the complement of violet is yellow. Complementary color schemes are popular in active sportswear, especially for sports team uniforms. Red and green are popular complementary holiday colors. Combinations of these colors are observed in the official flags of nations, too.

The complement of a color is also the hue that can diffuse its purity. Artists using paint mix complementary colors to develop muted tones of a color. When more than 40% of a complement is mixed into a color, the result is likely to be a muddy brown or gray. Colors are considered pure when closest to their intended chromacity without any discernable tainting by other color(s) or color absences such as black, white, and grays.

Triadic Color Harmonies

Triadic color harmonies form a triangle on the color wheel in any combination of three colors (Figure 9.13).

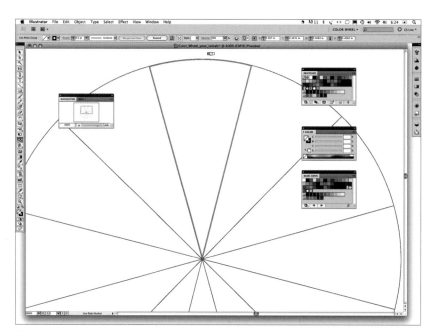

Figure 9.11

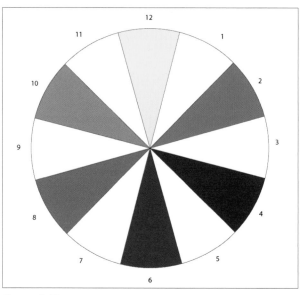

Figure 9.12

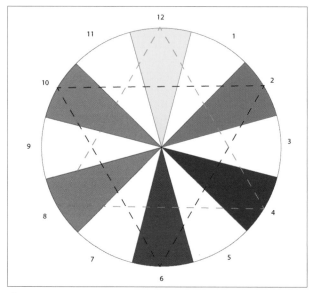

Figure 9.13

Tertiary Colors

A tertiary color is made by mixing one primary and one secondary color. In traditional color mixing associated with fine art painting, the tertiary colors are often given names like blue-violet, red-orange, yellow-green, etc. However, digital references for tertiary colors are usually specific names and refer to a hue (a specific tint, tone, or shade of a color). For example, yellow-green can also be referred to as chartreuse and red-violet is sometimes called plum. Every color wheel and the names associated with the tertiary colors will vary depending on the color mode.

Step 8: Create Color Wheel Segments

The tertiary colors appear in the default Swatches panel, but instead of using them, you will mix gradients in the segments where they would normally be placed. The white segments should be filled with gradients mixed from the primary and secondary colors adjacent to them. To do this, continue the practice exercise by following these steps:

1. Lock the layers, then create a new layer.
2. Select the Pen Tool (P), and carefully render a segment with a Fill of white with a Stroke of None.
3. Use the color wheel as a template. Copy and paste the segment. Select the copy, and double-click on the Rotate Tool (R) to turn it 60°. Select and position the copy.
4. Repeat the process until you have all the segments for spaces 11, 9, 7, 5, 3, and 1.

Step 9: Fill the Segment with Gradients

1. Hold the Shift key and select each segment that you created with the Selection Tool (V).
2. Show the Gradient panel by double-clicking its icon in the Tools panel or press > (greater than).
3. Hold the Shift key and use the Selection Tool (V) to select all of the segments that you just created.
4. Select *Fade to Black* from the pull-down menu in the Gradient Fill selector at the upper left of the Gradient panel. The segments will be filled with a fade of black and transparent pixels, revealing the Artboard (**Figure 9.14**).
5. Deselect, by clicking on the Artboard, and then select each segment individually to fill them with gradients made from blends of the colors in the two adjacent segments.
6. Pull the Swatches panel and the Gradient panel from their docks to float them on the Artboard.
7. Drag a primary color swatch from the Swatches panel and drop it over the black slider on the Gradient Bar in the Gradient panel.

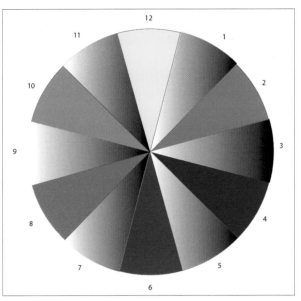

Figure 9.14

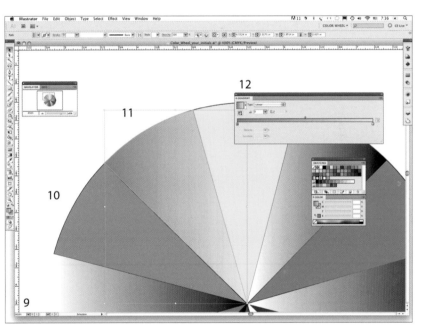

Figure 9.15

8. Select the next secondary color swatch and drop it next to the Transparency slider.
9. Pull the Transparency slider off the Gradient Bar to create a gradient from the fade. All the color standards that you need, shown in **Figure 9.10** on page 271, are on the color wheel. For example, in **Figure 9.15**, a gradient blend of primary yellow and secondary orange creates yellow-orange (segment 11).
10. With the gradient segment selected, simply replace the Black and White sliders on the Gradient Bar with the colors (one primary and one secondary color) to create gradients representing tertiary (also called intermediate) colors.

Step 10: Redistribute the Gradients

Select the segment where you have the gradient. Use the Gradient Tool (G) to redistribute the gradient by clicking and dragging across the widest part of the three segments. The gradient should have the illusion of a mostly even tone of both the primary and the secondary colors (Figure 9.15).

Step 11: Add the Tertiary Gradients to the Swatches Panel

Select each segment, then click the New Swatch icon at the bottom of the Swatches panel. In the New Swatch dialog box, type the appropriate tertiary title in the Swatch Name field. Do this for each of the six tertiary colors, which include:

- 1: yellow-green
- 3: blue-green
- 5: blue-violet
- 7: red-violet

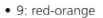

- 9: red-orange
- 11: yellow-orange

Follow these instructions for each segment to create all the tertiary hues. The completed tutorial example is shown in Figure 9.16. Add your gradients to the Swatches panel. Save your work to retain them in the file.

More Color Schemes and Ways to Mix Color

Naturally, color science goes beyond the basics, but when you develop color stories for your apparel designs and presentations, you will need to understand the basic color harmonies and schemes. A color scheme is one that you make up to project a particular ideal. A color harmony is a group of colors that share some commonality. Keep the following concepts in mind, and you will be able to create compelling color stories of your own.

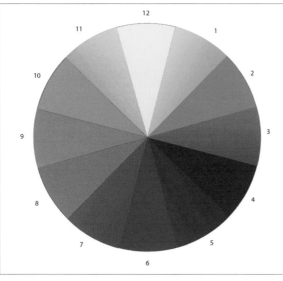

Figure 9.16

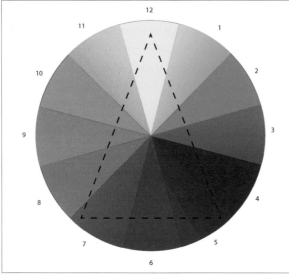

Figure 9.17

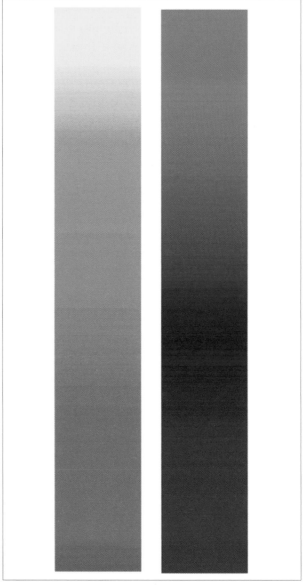

Figure 9.18

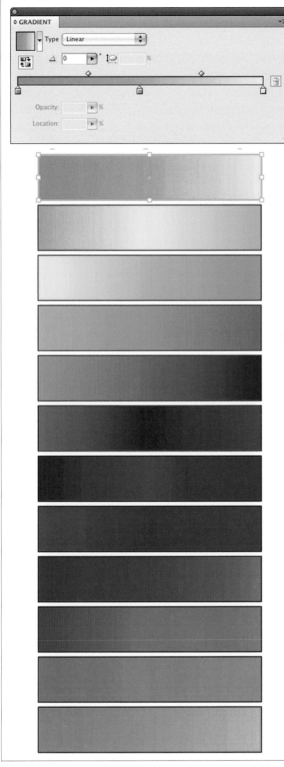

Figure 9.19

Split Complementary Color Schemes

A split complementary color scheme is composed of a color and two colors adjacent to its complement (Figure 9.17). Because tints, tones, and shades can be developed from all the colors in the spectrum, each can have its own split complementary scheme.

Warm Colors

Warm colors are those associated with the sun, like yellow, yellow-orange, orange, red-orange, and red (Figure 9.18). You can take this concept further with muted tones or pastels of warm hues.

Cool Colors

Cool colors are those associated with the water and plant life, like blue, blue-green, and green (Figure 9.18). The warm colors are on the left of the color wheel, and the cool colors are on the right. Create and save your own warm and cool gradients.

Analogous Color Schemes

Colors and those immediately adjacent to them on the color wheel are considered to be an analogous color scheme. These schemes are usually made of three colors. Twelve possible analogous colors schemes are on the color wheel. Follow these steps to create your own chart:

1. Use the Illustrator® Rectangle Tool (M) to create a shape.

2. Copy and paste it 11 times.

3. Select all the objects.

4. Use the Align panel to juxtapose and distribute the shapes in a column.

5. As an exercise, create linear gradients for each analogous color scheme that can be achieved from the colors on the color wheel. Start by selecting the top shape, and then select the yellow-orange gradient that you saved.

6. Click in the middle of the Gradient Bar to add a slider.

7. You can replace this slider with a solid color from the Swatches panel representing the yellow-orange hue.

8. Select the next box, and fill it with the gradient that you just made.

9. Pull off the left slider below the Gradient Bar in the Gradient panel, move the sliders over, and add the next color on the wheel to the right side.

10. Repeat the process until you have filled all the boxes with analogous color gradients from the traditional color wheel.

Note: You will need to use some of the default colors in the Swatches panel; however, they may not be the exact hue of those in your color wheel.

The completed exercise should look similar to the sample shown in Figure 9.19.

The Illustrator® Kuler Panel

Learning how to mix color is something that takes time and effort. Each person sees color differently, but at particular times, a majority will favor certain groups of colors. The **Kuler panel** (Figure 9.20) is a way for you to study and use color stories that millions of people like. You can even upload your own colors stories to the panel. The Kuler panel is available in both Illustrator® and Photoshop®. To access the Kuler panel in either program, go to *Menu Bar > Window > Extensions > Kuler.*

At the top of the panel is a search window. Use it to locate your own uploads or those of your favorite digital colorists. The buttons below this offer category options. The controls at the bottom of the panel help you to interface with the panel, refresh it, add the swatches to your panel, and share with the Adobe online community. You can also click on the color stories to obtain a pop-out menu.

Spot Colors and the Kuler Color Panel

Spot colors selected from the Color Picker or from the Kuler panel may run outside of the color gamut, causing printing and/or Web standard issues. When you select a color, the Color panel appears. Below the Fill box in the Color panel, one of two icons may appear to warn you about problems with color. The first warning is a box-shaped icon that signals that you have chosen a hue that is out of the Web color range. If you are communicating presentations for websites, click on the icon to convert the color to one that will work for your needs. The second type of warning is a Gamut Warning that looks like a triangle with an exclamation mark inside. Click on this icon to correct colors for printing.

Pantone Color Libraries

Each person has a different interpretation of color. This could be based on the light in a room or the calibration of a computer monitor. If you want to be more exact about color, you need to convert spot colors that you create to universal systems of color. Illustrator® and Photoshop® contain **Pantone Color Libraries**. When you use universal standards for color, you decrease the margin for error when communicating with outside sources.

In Illustrator® you can go to *Menu Bar > Window > Swatch Libraries > Color Books* to locate a number of Pantone Color Libraries. In Photoshop® click on the Set Foreground or Set Background Color

boxes. Click on the Color Libraries button on the right to access a dialog box, then select the library of choice from the pull-down menu. The Pantone Color Libraries are generally divided between coated colors (shiny) and uncoated colors (matte). You will learn to use the appropriate library based on your needs for communication. For example, if you're communicating color for raincoats, then a coated library would be apropos, and if the color standard were for velveteen jackets, then an uncoated library would be suitable. The best way to convert your spot colors is through the Color Picker, which will be covered later in this chapter.

Note: *Pantone colors within computer programs are not a foolproof method of communication. Printed standards and/or lab dips (dyed color swatches) should always be sent with tech-packs to outside apparel production resources in order to coordinate and ensure quality control.*

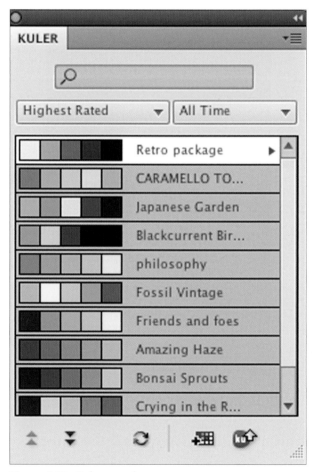

Figure 9.20 Kuler panel.

This exercise prepares you for advanced tutorials and teaches you the foundations for digitally rendering the face and blending flesh tone gradients. In addition, this exercise strengthens your ability to see complex color combinations and choose comprehensive blending solutions with the Illustrator® Gradient panel, Gradient Swatch Libraries, and Gradient Tool (G). The best way to accomplish this is to start with a good photo of you or someone you know. If you can successfully blend brilliant color combinations, then you will also be able to convert them to more realistic hues.

Step 1: Load Illustrator® and Create a New Document

Load Illustrator®, create a letter-size document, and go to *Menu Bar > File > Place*. In the Place dialog box, locate and select the photo's file, then click Place (Figure 9.21). When the photo appears in the window, click the Embed button in the Control Panel to keep the photo attached to the file. If you do not have a photo of your own, use one from ① Digital Duo Modeling Agency.

Note: The photo that you use for this tutorial needs to be in a high resolution of at least 150 to 300 dpi from the original scan in order to work.

Step 2: Outline Shapes in the Photo with the Pen Tool (P)

Use the Illustrator® Pen Tool (P) or the Pencil Tool (N) to outline as many details that you can find in the photo. Create one layer for each shape that you make. To stay organized, you should label the layers such as *Face Shape*, *Eyes*, *Mouth*, etc. Shapes can even be shadows or highlights in the image. The best digital drawings contain many shapes. Try to be precise, but it is not mandatory. Label each layer. Figure 9.22 shows the various shapes and the layer compositing associated with them. Certain layers need to be on top of others to remain visible.

Figure 9.21

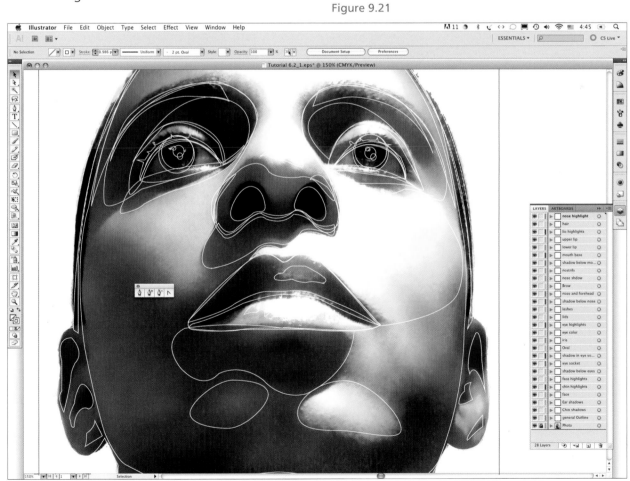

Figure 9.22

Figure 9.23

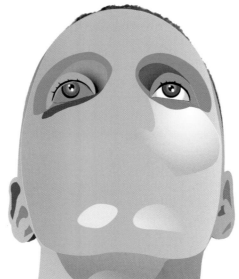

Figure 9.24

Figure 9.25

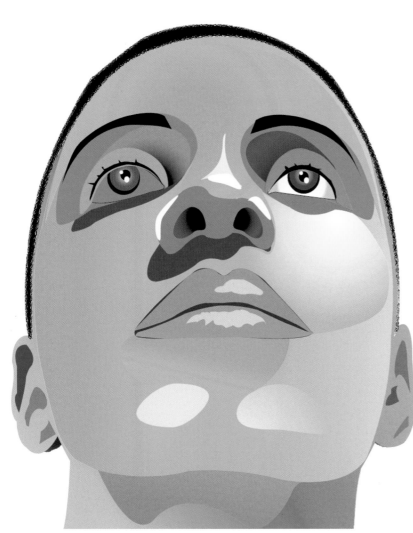

Figure 9.26 Illustration by Stacy Stewart Smith.

Step 3: Create Gradients from Bright Colors in the Swatches Panel

Use what you learned in Tutorial 9.1 to mix gradients from the colors in the Illustrator® CMYK Swatches panel to create colorful artistic interpretation of the photos. Do not use natural colors. Try and colorize the portrait using the colors from Tutorial 9.1 plus black and white. Some shapes could be filled with solid color. Areas beneath the eyes were filled with solid bright colors to create the illusion of strong shadows (Figure 9.23). Highlights in the chin and cheeks were created with gradient blends.

Use the Gradient panel and the Gradient Tool (G) to blend the colors to mimic the highlights, midtones, and shadows in the photo that you scanned. In Figure 9.24 a combination of solid hues and gradient filled shapes adds depth to the midtones. Figure 9.25 shows how you can add even greater convincing effects by choosing strong contrast with color complements. The mouth and nostrils should receive some concentration, so add highlights and shadows (Figure 9.26). As you are completing your portrait, try and imagine the colors blending, even though Illustrator® paths are visible. Do not stroke the shapes that you create unless they require one. The objective is to see the natural color as an unnatural yet convincing color blend. Your subject may look like an alien, but that's the objective.

Step 4: Add Filters

The hair was enhanced with the Glass filter (Figure 9.26). Try other Illustrator® filters to complete your project by selecting a layer, then going to *Menu Bar > Effect > Effect Gallery.*

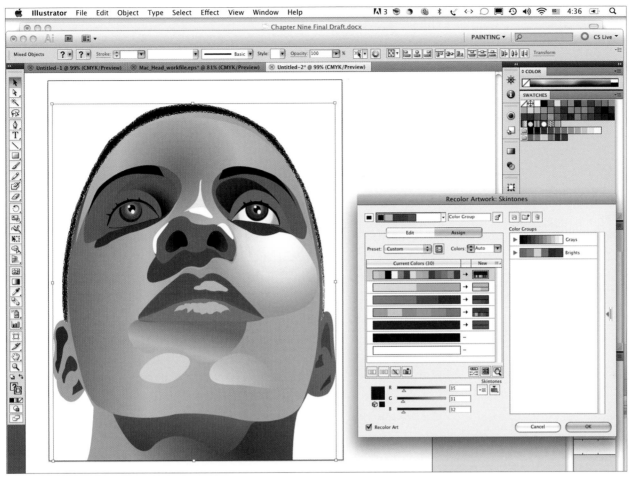

Figure 9.27

Step 5: Test Your Color Sense with the Color Guide Panel

If you have developed a good eye for color and color mixing (digital blends), the Illustrator® Color Guide panel will put it to the test with the Skintones Library. If needed, refresh your memory concerning the Color Guide panel by revisiting Tutorial 3.2, Step Eleven. Follow these steps:

1. Select all the parts that you want to affect. Try selecting everything except the shapes for the hair, lashes, and brows.

2. Show the Color Guide panel. Limit your colors by selecting the Skintones Library via the button at the lower left corner of the panel.

3. Use the Harmony Rules selector menu to scroll to a range of colors that suits the image of your subject.

4. Click the Edit Colors button (Color Wheel) in the lower middle section of the panel.

5. In the Edit Colors: Skintones dialog box, use what you have learned in previous tutorials (see Tutorial 3.2, Step Eleven) about the settings to change the color harmonies (Figure 9.27).

Step 6: Add Gaussian Blur and Other Effects

If you would like to make your image look more blended, select some of the skin areas and then try the Gaussian Blur filter as previously instructed. Experiment with other filters, and make a few changes for a polished finish (Figure 9.28).

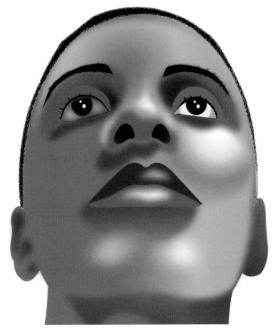

Figure 9.28 Illustration by Stacy Stewart Smith.

The color wheel that you constructed in Tutorial 9.1 is useful to get you acquainted with the subject of color using the CMYK color mode in Illustrator®, and it strengthens some of your digital color mixing skills. However, the concept of digital color models has a few fixed hues that keep it distinct from traditional fine art theory. To enhance your ability to mix color in Photoshop®, you will create a color wheel in the RGB mode, select colors from a spectrum of light, and add them to the Swatches panel.

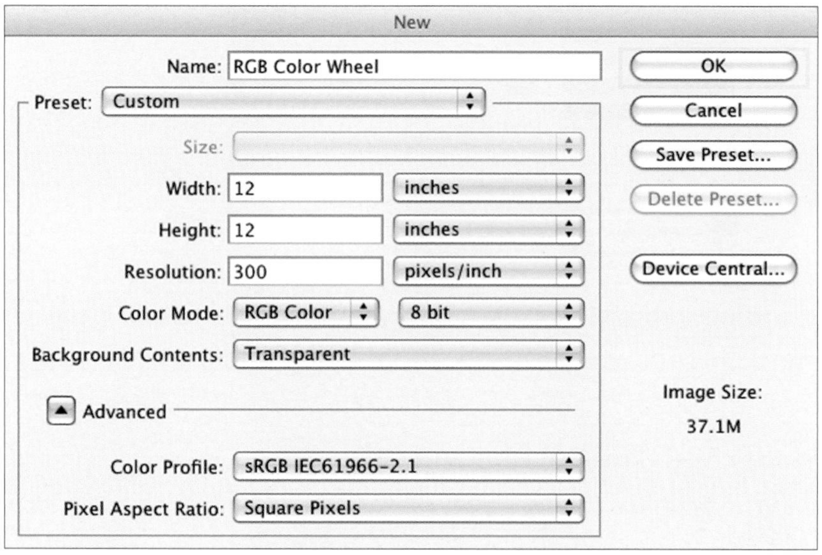

Figure 9.29

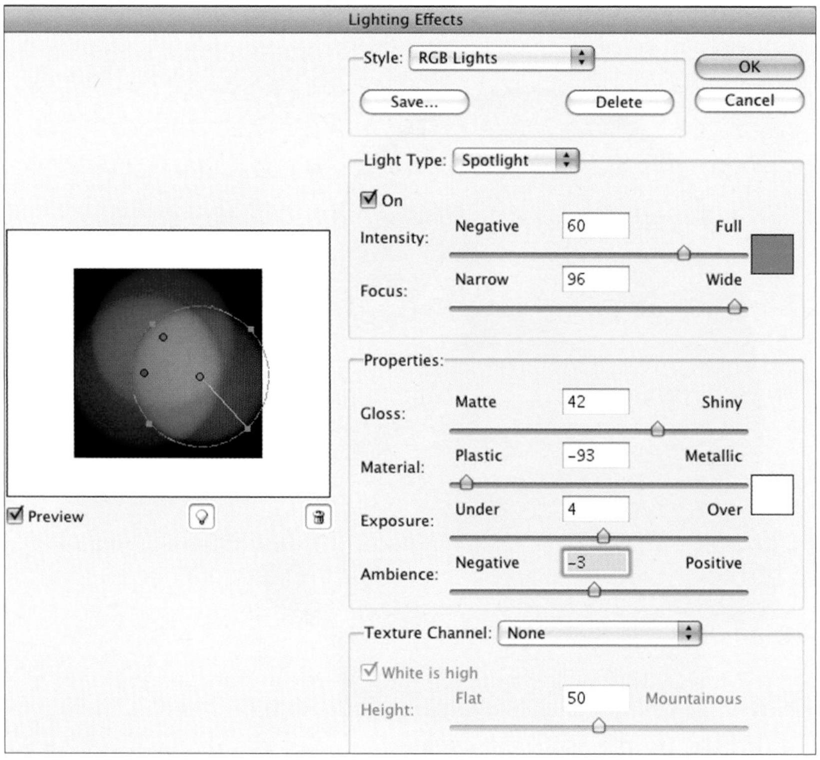

Figure 9.30

Required Filter: If you are using a 64-bit Macintosh computer, follow the instructions given in Tutorial 8.10, Step Nineteen. You will need to run Photoshop® in the 32-bit mode in order to add the **Lighting Effects filter**. You must also use Illustrator® in RGB by going to *Menu Bar > Image > Mode > RGB Color*, or specify this mode when you open the document. (Users of CS6 do not need to do this.)

Step 1: Create a New Document in Photoshop® in RGB

Create a new 12×12-inch document in Photoshop® with a transparent background at 300 dpi (Figure 9.29).

Step 2: Fill the Background with Black

Select the new layer, and then click on the canvas with the Photoshop® Magic Wand Tool (W) to select the entire area. Go to *Menu Bar > Edit > Fill*, and then choose black in the Fill dialog box. Deselect by pressing *Cmd+D / Ctrl+D*. Black is being used to illustrate the additive attributes of the RGB color mode. Save your file again, and then back up the file in a separate location.

Step 3: Add the RGB Lighting Effects Filter

1. Go to *Menu Bar > Effects > Render > Lighting Effects*, then choose the **RGB Lights** in the *Style* section within the Lighting Effects dialog box (CS6 Options Bar). This setting will simulate what happens in the RGB additive color mode.

2. Because the RGB color mode requires light to process its color, we also need to choose an intense light illusion. Spotlights are perfect because they project a beam. In the *Light Type* section choose **Spotlight** (or Spot in the CS6 Properties panel pull-down menu).

3. Rearrange the red, green, and blue spotlights in the Preview by selecting the color circles in the center of the bounding oval shapes. Overlap them as shown in Figure 9.30.

Note: The Photoshop® CS6 Lighting Effects window is shown in Figure 9.3. The settings in this tutorial are all available in the new window interface.

4. To scale the shapes, pull the bounding oval area by the flanking anchors.

5. In the *Light Type* section adjust the **Intensity** to create the illusion of bright light as if it were beaming onto an object or surface.

6. The **Gloss** settings will saturate each color separately, giving the appearance that there is light in the color.

Even though the illusion of light is translucent, the spectrum was created from the crossing sections of the red, green, and blue lights. The RGB additive color has illuminated the black background in Figure 9.31. Save and back up your work.

Note: *If the Lighting Effects filter does not show, try closing the program, open your Applications folder, select the program, then press Cmd+I / Ctrl+I to show the Information window. Select Open in 32-bit mode. Restart the program and repeat the previous steps. If you are using a computer in a college lab, consult with the IT department personnel.*

Step 4: Increase the Exposure in Photoshop®

To view all the colors in the RGB spectrum, you may need to boost the **Exposure**. Go to *Menu Bar > Image > Adjustments > Exposure*, then move the *Exposure* slider right. Click OK to view the results. Repeat the process until you can see primary yellow and cyan, and the center begins to turn into white light (Figure 9.32).

Step 5: Picking and Saving Hues in Photoshop®

Select the Eyedropper Tool (I) from the Tools panel and click to select a color that looks like primary red from the RGB spectrum of light. Then click into the Swatches panel to add the hue. In the Color Swatch name dialog box, name it *primary red*. Repeat this process for the following colors: *rose, magenta, violet, blue, azure, cyan, spring green, green, chartreuse, primary yellow,* and *orange* as shown in Figure 9.33. If you cannot locate the hues in the RGB spectrum, readjust it with the Hue/Saturation filter and others to assist the process.

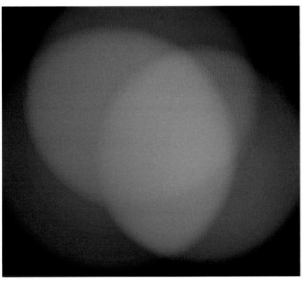

Figure 9.31

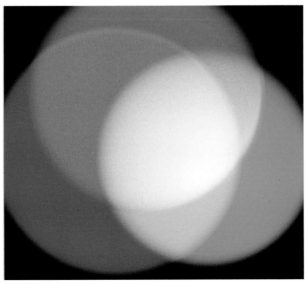

Figure 9.32

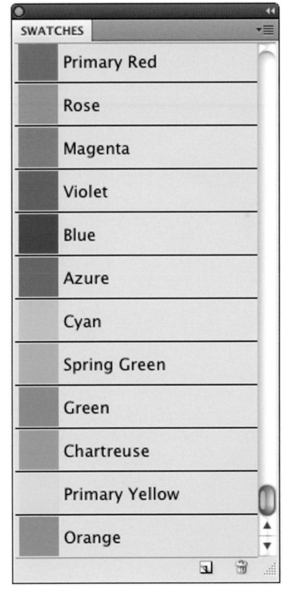

SWATCHES

Primary Red

Rose

Magenta

Violet

Blue

Azure

Cyan

Spring Green

Green

Chartreuse

Primary Yellow

Orange

Figure 9.33

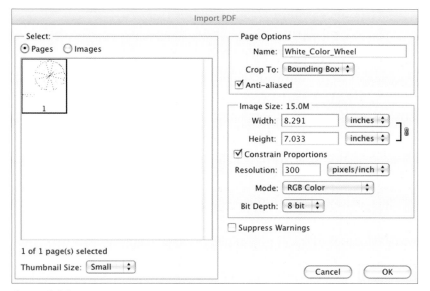

Figure 9.34

Step 6: Import the White Color Wheel in Photoshop®

Press *Cmd+O / Ctrl+O* to import the required file White_Color_Wheel.pdf from ① Ch09\Tutorial 9.3. An Import PDF dialog box appears. The settings shown are fine for this tutorial (Figure 9.34). When the file is imported, use the Move Tool (V) to center the wheel on the canvas (Figure 9.35). You can also place this file into the document, but if you do, rasterize the layer. Save your file.

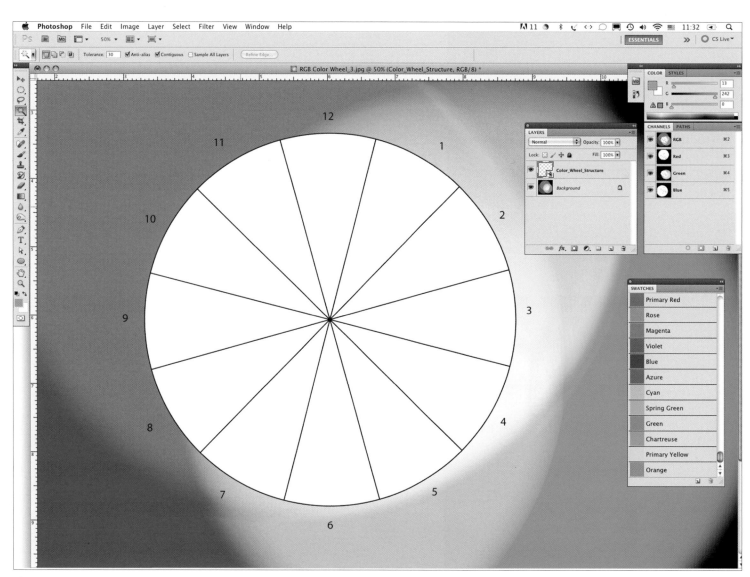

Figure 9.35

Step 7: Select and Fill the Segments

Select the layer containing the wheel. Beginning at the top, select RGB swatches that you saved to the Swatches panel, then use the Photoshop® Paint Bucket Tool (G) to fill each segment (Figure 9.36).

Step 8: Digital Light

The hues of the RGB color wheel are closer to the digital interface than the color wheel that you created in Tutorial 9.1. The RGB color mode is additive; the colors are created with light. Add this concept to your structure by placing a Lens Flare at the center of the wheel. Go to *Menu Bar > Filter > Render > Lens Flare* (Figure 9.37).

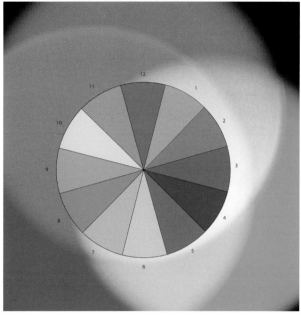

Figure 9.36

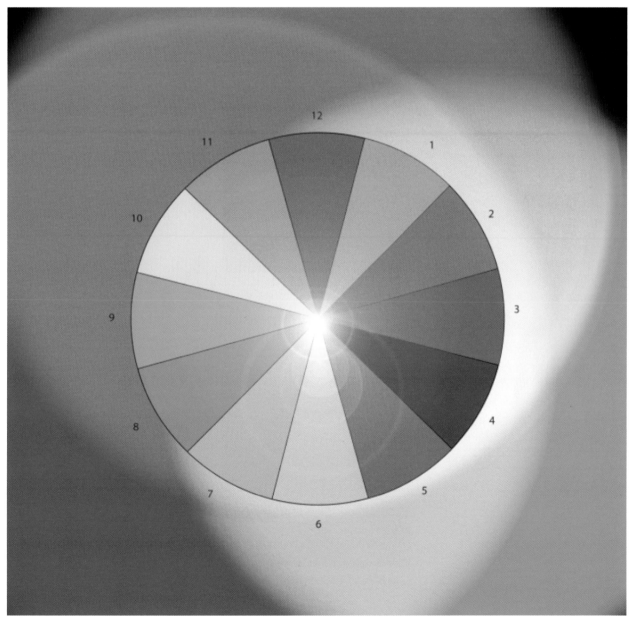

Figure 9.37

Throughout the tutorials in this book, you have used the Color Picker and it will continue to be used to select color in both Illustrator® and Photoshop®. The Color Picker can be used to specify random color selected from a field. It is a square area that appears, within a dialog box, when you click on the Fill or the Stroke in Illustrator® or the Set Foreground Color box and Set Background Color box in Photoshop®. This field reveals the preselected hue in various degrees of saturation (chromacity), and value (lightness and darkness). This tutorial serves as a brief explanation of the Color Picker for the needs of fashion designers and merchandisers. The tutorial is for educational purposes only.

Step 1: Load Both Illustrator® and Photoshop®

Step 2: Open a Letter-Size Document in Each Program in Order to Access the Color Pickers

Step 3: Show the Color Pickers

To reveal the Color Pickers, double-click on the Illustrator® Fill box, and then double-click on the Photoshop® Set Foreground Color box.

Step 4: Make Comparisons Between the Color Pickers

The Illustrator® Color Picker is shown in Figure 9.38, and the Photoshop® version appears in Figure 9.39. The Color Picker dialog boxes in both programs are nearly identical. They include a square color field (left), a spectrum bar (center), a new color sample, the current color sample, and color mode selections (lower right). Access to the Color Libraries and swatch panels is slightly different in each Color Picker dialog box.

Focus your attention on several fields and small buttons at the lower right. These are mode options that can be used for choosing color. A different color field will appear if you select each of the buttons. Fields that display the CMYK equivalents for the current color pick are located at the lower right of each dialog box. In both Color Pickers you have the ability to convert spot colors to CMYK and RGB model equivalents.

When you select an area within the field, you are actually choosing a blend of a spot color. It will appear in the new color sample box in the mid top of the dialog box. The *current* sample is the one that was in the Tools panel when you first accessed the

Color Picker. To convert spot colors to actual color standards, including Pantone colors, click on the Color Libraries button. In the Color Libraries dialog box, the new color will be highlighted in the scrolling menu in whichever color book that you choose from the pull-down menu at the top.

TIP: Locating Pantone® Colors

If you are looking for a specific color, especially the basics, just type a name. The program will take you to that color in the library.

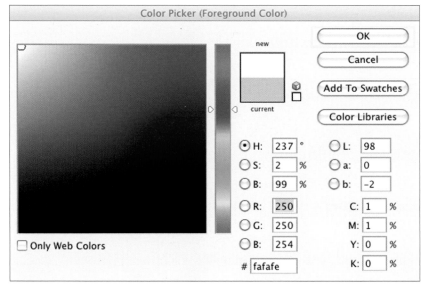

Figure 9.38 Illustrator® Color Picker.

Figure 9.39 Photoshop® Color Picker.

Step 5: Picking Color by Hue

The first and default (H) button allows you to pick color by hue. Hue is a word that is used to describe a specific color, such as canary yellow or tangerine. By selecting the (H) button, you can change the value of the color from 0° to 359°. This is a full circular rotation that will change the hue to various positions around the color wheel.

Starting on the Right with Chroma Color

A good understanding of the **Color Picker field** begins at the upper right corner. Use your cursor to click into this space. This corner would be considered *chroma color*. It contains the pure standard of the specific hue that was in the Fill box in Illustrator® or Set Foreground Color box in Photoshop®. You can also use the Spectrum Bar slider in the middle to choose a different hue. A new color can be chosen by clicking anywhere on the bar. Once you have chosen a hue, clicks in either direction, from the upper right position at the edge of the field, will desaturate the color with either light (white) or darkness (black). When a hue is tainted with white, black, or gray (noncolor grayscale), it is considered to be a tint, or tone, or a shade.

Note: The term "taint" is used to describe the action of making chroma color(s) impure. In the RGB color model, impure colors are sometimes referred to as achromatic.

Grayscale

When you select a color model, you are actually communicating everything in color, including black, white and gray. Grayscale is a range of shades in different values from black to white. You can locate grayscale by clicking along the left side of the Color Picker.

Note: A grayscale color group of swatches is part of the Basic CMYK Swatches panel in Illustrator® CS5 (Figure 9.9 on page 271).

Monochromatic

A monochromatic color scheme uses grayscale and tints, tones, or shades of a specific hue. The Color Picker appears in a monochrome gradient field.

Tints and Pastels

In fashion, a hue mixed with white or light is called a tint. Pastels are representative of white tinted with a hue and can be found at the top of the **Hue Color Picker** by clicking away from the top left of the Hue Color Picker toward the center. As you click, you will notice that the color in the *current sample* will change. Figure 9.40 displays tints of an azure hue.

Tones

Muted colors are those hues that have been tainted with gray. A true representation of these hues can be found by clicking diagonally from the central area of the Hue Color Picker toward the lower left corner. Tones of an azure hue are shown in Figure 9.41.

Shades

Shaded hues are those that have been gradually mixed with black or made impure by darkness. Locate these hues by clicking away from the center right edge of the Hue Color Picker toward the lower right corner. Shades of an azure hue can be observed in Figure 9.42.

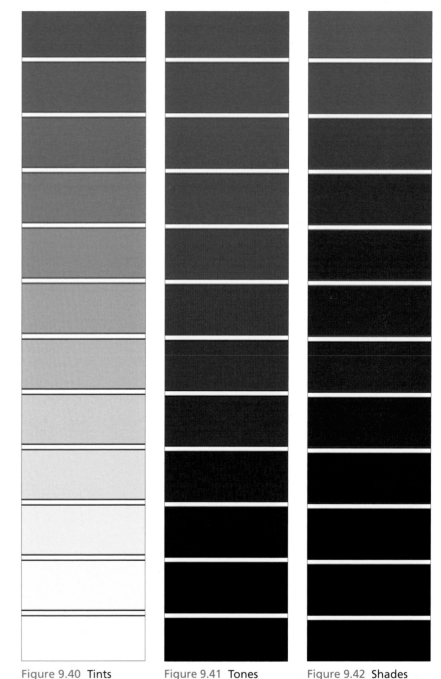

Figure 9.40 **Tints**   Figure 9.41 **Tones**   Figure 9.42 **Shades**

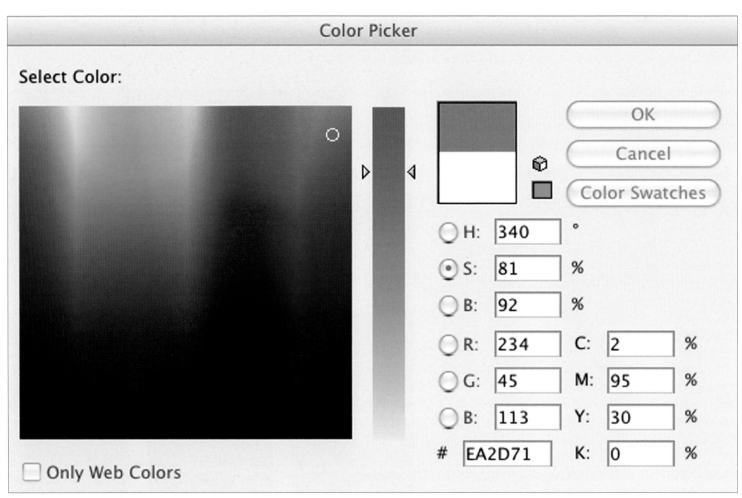

Figure 9.43 Illustrator® Saturation Color Picker.

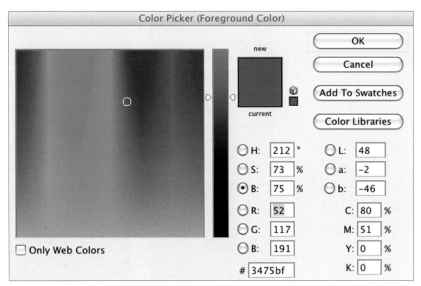

Figure 9.44 Illustrator® Brightness Color Picker.

Step 6: Picking Color by Saturation

If you desire to pick colors based on their intensity, select the "S" button in the Color Picker dialog box. The Saturation Color Picker is useful when you need to see the spectrum and the intensity level of all the hues (Figure 9.43). The Spectrum Bar in this Color Picker acts as a sample of how far you can push the hues from grayscale (0%) to chroma color (100%).

Step 7: Picking Color by Brightness

To show the **Brightness Color Picker**, select the "B" button on the Color Picker to choose colors by the amount of light you allow to enter into them from 0% to 100% (Figure 9.44).

The red, green, and blue Color Pickers allow you to choose colors based on the three hues in the RGB color model. The rest of the Color Picker information goes beyond the scope of the basic needs of fashion designers and merchandisers.

Create color illuminations from grayscale art and fashion in this tutorial that further demonstrates the additive RGB color mode.

Required Filter: If you are using a 64-bit Macintosh computer, follow the instructions given in Tutorial 8.10, Step Nineteen. You will need to run Photoshop® in the 32-bit mode in order to add the Lighting Effects filter. You must also use Illustrator® in RGB by going to Menu *Bar > Image > Mode > RGB Color* or specify this mode when you open the document. (Users of CS6 do not need to do this.)

Step 1: Load Photoshop®

Step 2: Open the Club

In Photoshop®, go to *Menu Bar > File > Open* to import the file Club_Gallery.pdf from ① Ch09\Tutorial 9.5. In the Open dialog box, locate and select the file. Then click the Open button. The image reveals an opulent gallery at a fashionable nightclub (**Figure 9.45**). The club's gallery is currently empty, but you have the opportunity to create objects of art, furnishings, and fashion on models to make it come to life.

Step 3: Curate the Exhibition

The gallery is hosting an exhibit of works by the author. Files containing images to install the exhibition are located on ① Ch09\Tutorial 9.5.

Import the images of the wall art, or scan and use your own grayscale images (**Figure 9.46**). Use the Move Tool (V) to position the images on the page.

Step 4: Add Furniture

Add the special club seating, Patience_Seat.pdf, and position it with the Move Tool (V) as exhibited in **Figure 9.47**. Also try using scans of furniture from magazines.

Step 5: Add Sculptures

Figurative sculptures were commissioned for the club. Import At_Last.pdf and Shadow.pdf into the file. If you would like to flip the image, select the layer, then go to *Menu Bar > Edit > Transform > Flip Horizontal*. Use the Free Transform options to scale object(s) on their respective layers (**Figure 9.48**).

Step 6: Add a Fashion Mannequin

Drag and drop the fully dressed fashion mannequin Coutura.pdf (**Figure 9.49**). This is a good place to add one of your own scanned illustrations (see Tutorials 4.5, 5.3, and 7.4.)

Figure 9.45

Figure 9.46

Figure 9.47

Figure 9.48

Figure 9.49

Step 7: Illuminate the Sculptures and Other Objects with RGB Lighting Effects

Select the layer containing the image of the male model sculpture, then go to *Menu Bar > Filter > Render > Lighting Effects*. Use what you learned in Tutorial 9.3 to illuminate and colorize the image using the RGB spotlights (Figure 9.50).

Step 8: Use the Five Lights Down Lighting Effects

Select the layer where you placed the file Club_Gallery. pdf, then go to *Menu Bar > Filter > Render > Light-*

ing Effects. In the *Style* section choose *Five Lights Down* or any other Lighting Effect filter, then adjust the properties and the light positions (Figure 9.51).

Step 9: Add Additional Filters and Layer Styles

Now that you have learned how to apply RGB Lighting Effects to images, experiment with the file and add other filters and/or Layer Styles, etc., like those added to the sculpture in the rear. Use Bevel and Emboss, Inner Shadow, Drop Shadow, and more (Figure 9.52).

Figure 9.50

Figure 9.51

Figure 9.52 Illustration by Stacy Stewart Smith.

Use what you have learned in the tutorials of this chapter to create a colorful Hawaiian beach scene and design swimwear for men and women. To complete this tutorial, you can use files from the ② Avatar Modeling Agency or your own scanned fashion croquis. You can also choose to create your own background scene, create gradients, and add filter combinations in Photoshop®, or you can use the file Fashion_Beach_Scene.pdf that is provided on ① Ch09\Tutorial 9.6.

Step 1: Load Photoshop® and Create a 17x11-Inch Document

Step 2: Fill a Layer with a Photoshop® Linear Gradient

To make a gradient in Photoshop®, follow these instructions:

1. Select the layer that you want to affect, and then press *Cmd+A / Ctrl+A* to Select All.

2. Select the Photoshop® Gradient Tool (G). The **Gradient Picker** will appear on the left side of the Options Bar.

3. Select a gradient from the Gradient Picker by clicking the arrow pointer and scrolling to one of the options. This selection will now appear in the Gradient Picker.

4. Double-click on the Gradient Picker to access the Gradient Editor dialog box (**Figure 9.53**).

5. In the middle of the Gradient Editor dialog box is a Gradient Spectrum Bar flanked by Opacity Stops and Color Stops that can be moved by clicking and dragging. If you want to rearrange the distribution of color in the Gradient Spectrum Bar, move the Opacity Stops and Color Stops.

6. To change the hues of the Color Stops, double-click on their color section and a Select Color dialog box containing a Color Picker appears. Select a new hue from the Color Picker or the Color Libraries (see Tutorial 9.1), and then click OK (**Figure 9.54**).

Note: *If you are having difficulties, review Tutorial 4.1, Steps Seven and Twenty-One, and Tutorial 9.1.*

7. To add a Color Stop, click on the Gradient Spectrum Bar. To delete one, pull it off the Gradient Spectrum Bar. Remember to reposition the Opacity Stops and the Color Stops if needed to create a specific type of color blend in your new gradient. Copy the placement of the Stops in **Figure 9.53** to create a

Figure 9.53 The Opacity Stops are smaller than the Color Stops.

Figure 9.54

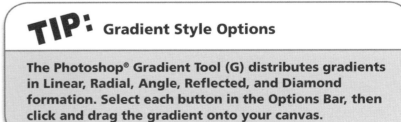

TIP: **Gradient Style Options**

The Photoshop® Gradient Tool (G) distributes gradients in Linear, Radial, Angle, Reflected, and Diamond formation. Select each button in the Options Bar, then click and drag the gradient onto your canvas.

Figure 9.55

Figure 9.56

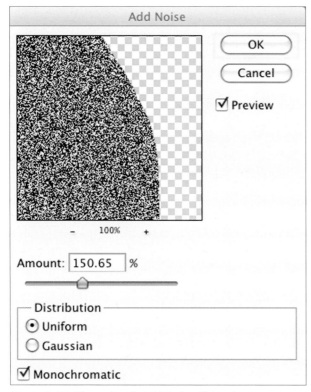

Figure 9.57 Photoshop® Add Noise dialog box.

striped effect that will translate into a sky and beach.

8. Name the gradient, and then click the *New* button to add the gradient to the *Presets* menu. Click the OK button to return to your Workspace.

9. Select the Photoshop® Gradient Tool (G), and then click and drag from the top to bottom in the middle of the canvas (Figure 9.55).

Step 3: The Lasso Tool and Sand Dunes

Create a new layer. Select the Lasso Tool (L) and use it to create a selection at the bottom of the screen. Start on the left side and click on the canvas; keep holding the clicker and move the Lasso Tool (L) up and down to create shapes similar to sand dunes or rocks (Figure 9.56). Do not let go of the clicker. Move toward the right of the screen at the bottom. Continue to hold the clicker and drag the Lasso Tool (L) around the bottom of the window to the position where you first began your selection on the left. Let go of the clicker to create a closed selection. If you did not develop the entire selection for the sand dune, repeat the procedure until you do, and then create an Alpha Channel to preserve your marching ants (see Tutorial 7.2, Step Six). Save and back up your file.

Step 4: Add the Noise Filter

The **Add Noise** filter converts selected areas into tiny particles. The Add Noise dialog box has a preview area that shows you an area of canvas that you click on (Figure 9.57). You can choose the *Amount* of noise that you want to add by pushing the slider. If *Monochromatic* is checked, the color will be mixed with its tints, tones and shades plus black, white, and gray. When this box is not checked, Add Noise will add an array of colors to the color of your selection. In the distribution section, *Uniform* will arrange the particles in a repeat formation, and *Gaussian* will do the opposite (Figure 9.58).

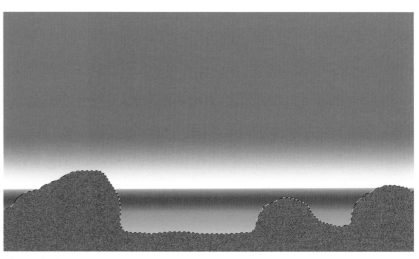

Figure 9.58

Step 5: Add Combinations of Layer Styles and Filters

To achieve the results shown in Figure 9.59, try the following combinations:

1. Reload your marching ants.

2. Apply the Inner Shadow Layer Style, but change the color of the shadow to something that matches the selected object. To do this, click the color field, and then use the Color Picker that appears to make a selection.

3. Click OK and return to the Layer Style dialog box.

4. Adjust the *Size* and *Distance* in the *Structure* Section.

5. Use the Burn Tool (O) to add shadows on one side of any protrusions. Adjust the *Range* and *Exposure* in the Options Bar.

6. Use the Dodge Tool (O) to add light to the opposite side of protrusions. Adjust the *Range* and *Exposure* in the Options Bar.

7. Select a Spatter Brush from the Brush panel menu, reduce the *Strength* to 87% in the Options Bar, and then select the Smudge Tool. With the marching ants still going, use the Smudge Tool to move around some of the particles made by the Add Noise filter.

8. Select the Photoshop® Brush Tool (B), and then click on the Set Foreground Color box to select a green color. Use the same spatter brush to stipple areas of the sand dune that you created.

9. Choose the Smudge Tool with the same brush to lightly sweep away some of the green color by stippling with the clicker.

Step 6: Copy and Use Transform Flip Horizontal

Select the layer containing the sand dune shape, and then pull it to the New Layer icon at the bottom of the panel. When it highlights, let go of the clicker, and a copy layer will appear. Select the copy layer and go to *Menu Bar > Edit > Transform > Flip Horizontal*. Then, press *Cmd+T / Ctrl+T* to Free Transform the shape by stretching out the Bounding Box. Position the copy to complement the original (Figure 9.60).

Step 7: Draw Plants

Use your imagination and the Lasso Tool (L) or the brushes to render plants on various layers above those containing the sand dunes. The Smudge Tool can pull out spiky areas (Figure 9.61).

Step 8: Simulate Water

Create another layer above the others. Make a freehand selection with the Lasso Tool (L). Fill the selected

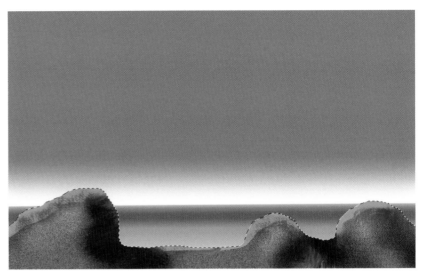

Figure 9.59

Figure 9.60

Figure 9.61

area with a blue hue, and then reduce the Opacity on the layer to simulate water. Add the Ocean Ripple filter by going to *Menu Bar > Filter > Artistic > Distort > Ocean Ripple* (Figure 9.62).

Figure 9.62

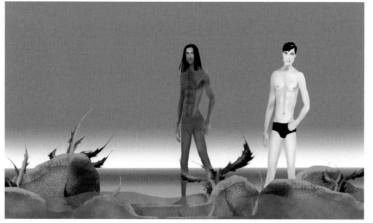

Figure 9.63

Step 9: Add the Men and Women from ② Avatar Modeling Agency

Import the figures into Photoshop®. Select the layers containing all the body parts, but not the swimwear (Figures 9.63 and 9.64). Merge the layers, and then drag and drop the figure(s) into the beach scene. Reorder the layers to place the figures behind certain dunes. Some of the avatars should be scaled smaller and others larger to produce the illusion of perspective. Use the Liquify filter to create waves in the water shape. Clouds can be made with Strokes of white on a layer right above the background; then use the Gaussian Blur filter. Illuminate the background layer with an Omni spotlight from the Lighting Effects filter.

Step 10: Design New Swimwear Using Illustrator® and Photoshop®

Creating the backdrop fashion beach scene was a good way to introduce you to a few Photoshop® filters and color interfaces, especially creating gradients. Now that you have everyone in place, redesign the colorful swimwear by using everything that you have learned in this chapter about color. Replace the swimwear with your own in colorful prints, color blocking, textures, embellishments, etc. Add different accessories and more.

Figure 9.64 Illustration by Stacy Stewart Smith.

Chapter 9 Summary

The science of color is an exhaustive subject, and the information covered in Chapter 9 is just a good start in the right direction for fashion techies. The tutorials in this chapter were designed so that you can create a variety of color solutions and use them to develop your skills independently. Although it may have seemed that spending the time to create some of the environments was not related to fashion, it was actually well worth the effort. It introduced you to various tools, panels, and filters that you can now use in your own creative way. Study and commit the color modes, digital mixing procedures, and harmonies to memory, and then answer the self-assessment questions before moving on to the next chapter exercises.

Chapter 9 Self-Assessment

1. Can I explain and make appropriate use of both the RGB and CMYK color modes?

2. There are 12 colors in the traditional and the digital color wheels. Can I name the colors and mix them using both Illustrator® and Photoshop®?

3. Do I know how to use the Live Paint Bucket Tool, the Color Picker, the Color panel, and the Swatches panel to select and save various hues in both Illustrator® and Photoshop®?

4. Each color mode mixes spot colors by formulas. Can I mix the exact standards of primary and secondary colors?

5. Can I identify complementary, split complementary, warm, cool, analogous, triadic, and tertiary color harmonies?

6. Can I use the Color Picker to identify a value scale, as well as tints, tones, and shades of a particular hue?

7. Can I mix gradients to create the illusion of facial volume, shadows, highlights, and contours?

8. Can I use the Lighting Effects filter to illuminate an object on a layer in RGB display colors?

9. Can I digitally create the delicate color balance between the sand, water, and sky? Can I use digital colors to create exciting apparel items, such as swimwear?

10. Can I mix and save color and gradient swatches in both Illustrator® and Photoshop®?

Fashion Color Correction and Photo Retouching with Photoshop®

10

Objectives

Photography is a key element of fashion merchandising and promotion, but what you see on the Internet and in fashion magazines has to pass through many hands before it can be introduced to the public. Images must be re-touched and color corrected. For this reason, fashion techies who know how to multitask are always in demand.

This chapter will teach you how to manipulate fashion photography with Photoshop®. By completing the tutorials, you will learn to use digital photo retouching and painting techniques in order to:

◉ Repair torn images and refresh vintage photos

◉ Color correct photos

◉ Enhance and replace figure parts

◉ Change fashion figure poses with the Puppet Warp filter

◉ Remove signs of aging through the HDR Toning filter

◉ Photo retouch images using the Spot Healing Tool (J), the Clone Stamp Tool (S), and other Photoshop® image-editing tools and filters

◉ Make use of both photography and Photoshop® painting capabilities to colorize black-and-white photos

Repairing torn photos is a unique skill that can be an asset when you are interviewing for jobs where fashion photography is used to promote products and services. This tutorial will teach you how to repair a photograph by using the Content-Aware feature of Photoshop®, along with the Clone Stamp Tool (S), Color Replacement Tool (B), and other settings. The skills you learn can also be used to repair vintage photos, which are often used on mood and concept storyboards.

Figure 10.1

Figure 10.2

To help you complete this tutorial, four files have been provided on ① Ch10\Tutorial 10.1. You may also choose to use your own damaged photo if you have access to a scanner.

Note: *Because the Photoshop® Content-Aware feature is only available in CS5 and higher, users of lower versions will not be able to complete this tutorial.*

Step 1: Scan Your Own Damaged Photo in Photoshop®

Scan the damaged photo at 300 dpi. If the photo has been torn into pieces, scan them together, if possible, to avoid excessive light distortion.

Step 2: Place the Photo Parts

Place your scanned images into a Photoshop® document. The file size should be the same as the composite of the parts. For example, if the original image was 8×10 inches, then open a new document in Photoshop® in the same size. If you're using the files on ①, place them into a Photoshop® document that is 11×17 inches on a transparent background (Figure 10.1).

Step 3: Rasterize all Layers

When you place the torn images into the file, they appear as Smart Objects in the Layers panel. This means that they are not fully rasterized. In order to modify the images follow these steps:

1. Go to *Menu Bar > Layers > Rasterize > All Layers*.
2. Work on one layer at a time and toggle off the visibility of the others.
3. Use the Quick Selection Tool (W) or any selection tool to produce marching ants around the subject area.
4. Press the Delete key. If your selection overruns the edge, subtract from the selection by holding the Option key (Mac) or the Alt key (PC).
5. To add to the selection, hold the Shift key and, using a selection tool, deselect by pressing *Cmd+D / Ctrl+D*.

Figure 10.2 shows the portion of the background area that was erased and the marching ant selection that was made with the Quick Selection Tool (W). Repeat this procedure for each section of the torn image.

Step 4: Reposition the Parts

Use the Move Tool (V) to reposition the sections and assemble your composite image. Check the surface of each section for parts of the background that were not removed on each layer. Use the tools to make changes and reorder the layers, if necessary.

Figure 10.3

Because the images were placed by hand on a flat-bed scanner, they may need to be rotated into position. Press *Cmd+T / Ctrl+T* to Free Transform them. Bring your cursor to the corner of the Bounding Box until you see the double-sided arrow, and then rotate the object. Figure 10.3 shows the separate parts, and Figure 10.4 reveals the reassembly.

Note: *You may notice some slight color differences. This is due to the nature of scanning objects and reflected light.*

Step 5: Save a Copy of the File

Go to *Menu Bar > File > Save As*. In the Save As dialog box, check the box at the bottom labeled *Copy*. The copy is a backup in case you need to start over again.

Figure 10.4

Step 6: Merge the Layers

Select the layers by holding the Shift key, then press *Cmd+E / Ctrl+E* to merge them in the *Photoshop®* format. This will preserve the surrounding transparency and allow you more freedom to work.

Step 7: Select and Fill Using Photoshop® Content-Aware

1. Use the Lasso Tool (L) to select torn edges that have been placed back into their original positions.

2. Go to *Menu Bar > Edit > Fill or press* Shift+F5.

3. In the *Contents* area, select Content-Aware from the pull-down menu. Figure 10.5 shows the look of one of the tears before, and the after-effects of the Content-Aware filter can be observed in Figure 10.6.

4. Make the selections as close to the seams as possible and work in sections.

5. If a poor Content-Aware fill occurs, simply reselect a smaller area until you can make a selection that is compatible with the filter's capacity.

Note: *Content-Aware does not work well on edge transitions. Keep the selections as close as possible to them. With practice, you will be able to perform this action flawlessly. The CS6 upgrade of Photoshop® offers improved Content-Aware functions.*

Step 8: Eliminate Discoloration and Line Creases

The Content-Aware Tool is only the first step to preparing the finished file. However, it will leave some discoloration and line creases. To eliminate them, use the Clone Stamp Tool (S).

1. Adjust the Opacity to less than 20% using a brush in an appropriate size.

2. This tool works by taking a sample of pixels from one area and placing them in another with a click. Sample an area by holding the Option key (Mac) or the Alt key (PC) and clicking.

3. Click onto the areas that have creases or discolorations.

Mastering the Clone Stamp Tool (S) will take some practice. If you make mistakes, undo them and reduce the settings to assist the outcome. Figure 10.7 shows the development of the tutorial example, using the Clone Stamp Tool (S).

TIP: Practice Advice

A gradual approach is required, so take your time on the first project. Practice by repeating this stage of the tutorial until a desired outcome is achieved.

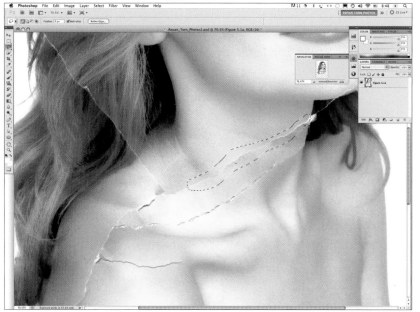

Figure 10.5

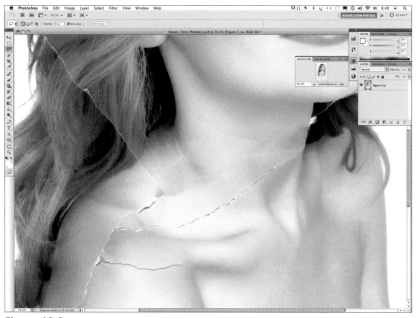

Figure 10.6

Figure 10.7

Step 9: Use the Color Replacement Tool

As discussed in Chapter 3, one of the attributes of the Photoshop® Color Replacement Tool (B) is its ability to replace one color with another from the Set Foreground Color box. In the tutorial example, you may have noticed shading in the hair (Figure 10.8). The section that was reconnected to the lower back is slightly saturated. To rectify this, adjust the tool setting in the Options Bar.

1. Change the *Mode* to *Color*; select the *Sampling Contiguous* icon, as well as the *Contiguous* setting in the Limit pull-down menu.

2. Position the *Tolerance* slider at 72%. These settings may need to be changed depending upon your monitor's calibration; modify them if needed.

3. Zoom in on the area and use a brush between size 50 and 100 to apply the color attributes of the selected hue to the top portion of the hair.

4. Resample the color if it appears too even. Leave some highlights. You may find the coloration of the hair to be too brassy, but we will correct that later (Figure 10.9).

Step 10: Color Correction with Selective Color

The benefit of using the Photoshop® Selective Color filter is that you can adjust the effect of hues in a color mode based upon some basic colors within any image plus black, white, and gray. In the tutorial example, both the reds and yellows need adjusting. To show the Selective Color dialog box, go to *Menu Bar > Image > Adjustments > Selective Color*.

1. The first set of color sliders to appear affect the red hues in the image. The color sliders represent the hues in the CMYK color mode. The red in the image is fine, but there is too much yellow in it, and there is not enough green to balance it. Try moving the yellow slider to the left to diminish it at −41%, and then move the cyan slider to the right at +55%.

2. To remove some of the darkness from the reds, move the black slider to −12% (Figure 10.10).

3. Afterward, switch the *Colors* to yellows in the pull-down menu and position the cyan slider to +75%, the magenta slider to +15%, the yellow slider to −18%, and the black slider to −26% (Figure 10.11).

Note: *The settings are suggested; they may need to be adjusted differently on your computer. Users of CS6 may benefit from the default darkroom interface.*

Figure 10.8

Figure 10.9

Figure 10.10 Selective color dialog box (L).

Figure 10.11

Step 11: Correct Overexposure

Often the last person to recognize that an image has been overexposed is the one restoring it. The combination of filters can cause the image to lose tones.

To correct the amount of light in a photo file, go to *Menu Bar > Image > Exposure* and move the *Exposure* slider left to reduce the white point in the image. This may affect any white in the background or clothing. To prevent the graying of these areas, select only the object you wish to modify before you reduce the Exposure. You can also restore the white after you correct the Exposure, which we will explore later. In Figure 10.12, the Exposure was reduced to –0.52. To intensify the color contrast, the *Gamma* slider was set to 0.91. Remember that your settings may vary; each monitor is different, and it is always best to correct color in a dimly lit room.

Step 12: Restore White

To restore the white in a photo after you have reduced the exposure, follow these steps:

1. Go to *Menu Bar > Image > Adjustments > Replace Color*.

2. In the Replace Color dialog box, select the Eyedropper Tool (I) to increase the *Fuzziness* and then check *Preview*.

3. Then click on the *Result* color sample box to obtain the Color Picker.

Figure 10.12

4. When it appears, select the white space and click OK (Figure 10.13).

5. You can also enter all zeros in the CMYK fields.

6. Use the Crop Tool (C) to crop the image.

7. To add more contrast, use the Curves controls as demonstrated in Tutorial 5.3, Step Seventeen.

The completed Tutorial 10.1 example is shown in Figure 10.14. A good way to evaluate the corrections that you have made is to view it in Full Screen Mode. Go to *Menu Bar > View > Screen Mode > Full Screen Mode*. In the dialog box, follow the Photoshop® instructions, and then click OK. You will see the image on a black background.

Figure 10.13

Figure 10.14

Tutorial 10.2
CHOOSING LIMBS FOR DIFFERENT POSES

The ① Digital Duo Modeling Agency includes photos that can be used to stage various merchandising presentations or to create croquis for fashion design. Within the Anatomical Poses folder, you'll find images of arm, leg, and hand poses that were staged to work with the various full-length images of the models Ana, Carl, and Jade. This tutorial will teach you how to create variations of these full-length images by adding alternative anatomical poses to them. The adjusted poses that you create from what you learn in this tutorial can be used to model freehand croquis. The tutorial example makes use of the file Ana_3Q_heels.jpg on ① Digital Duo Modeling Agency\Ana\Basic Poses in Heels, but feel free to use any of the other full-length poses of Ana, Carl, or Jade and corresponding anatomical poses.

Step 1: Create a New Photoshop® Document

Create a new Photoshop® document of approximately 14×17 inches. It should be large enough to accommodate four or five figures.

Step 2: Paste a Figure into the Document

Select a full-length figure from ① Digital Duo Modeling Agency and place it in the new document. Rasterize the layers by going to *Menu Bar > Layer > Rasterize > All Layers*, then select the background and press the Delete key to remove it.

Step 3: Copy the Figure

Copy the figure several times by pulling its layer to the new layer icon at the bottom of the Layers panel (Figure 10.15). Rename each layer.

Step 4: Pull Guides and Erase the Unwanted Areas

1. Pull Guides to indicate the hip level of the figures.
2. Use the Photoshop® Eraser Tool (E) to remove the lower portion of the legs of the copied figure(s).
3. Select the layers of each figure and use the *Align* and *Distribute* options in the Options Bar to juxtapose the placement of the images in relation to one another.
4. Select the Rectangular Marquee Tool (M), marquee to encapsulate the lower portion of the figures, and then press the Delete key. This will make a straight edge on the bottom (Figure 10.16).

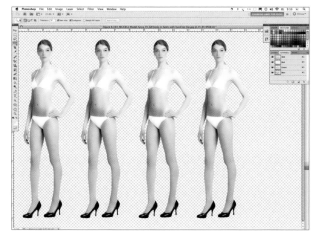

Figure 10.15

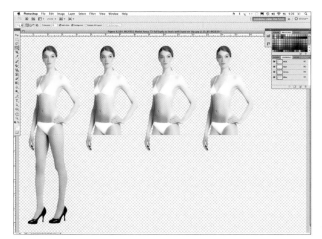

Figure 10.16

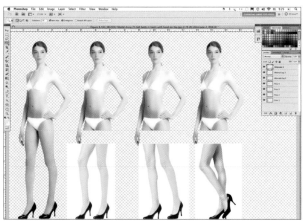

Figure 10.17

Step 5: Place Images of Leg Poses

Pull a horizontal guide from the x-axis and drag it to the knee position. Place appropriate files from the ① Digital Duo Modeling Agency\Anatomical Poses. Use the Move Tool (V) to position them (Figure 10.17).

Step 6: Add Apparel

Add apparel shapes to determine if the poses actually work. Use the Photoshop® Pen Tool (P) or the Lasso Tool (L) to digitally render a dress.

Figure 10.18

Figure 10.19

Figure 10.20

Note: *If you experience difficulty using the Pen Tool (P), revisit the Chapter 3 tutorials, especially Tutorial 3.3. The Photoshop® Pen Tool (P) works just like the one in Illustrator®. Convert the shapes to marching ants and select the buttons at the bottom of the Paths panel to make further adjustments to the Path (see Using the Paths Panel in Chapter 5).*

Afterward, rasterize the layers by going to *Menu Bar > Layer > Rasterize > All Layers*, then select the backgrounds and press Delete to remove them. If needed, use the Puppet Warp filter (See Tutorial 10.3, Step Nine) or the Transform features (See Tutorial 10.3, Step Six) to modify the leg and/or torso poses (**Figure 10.18**).

For more help using the Photoshop® Puppet Warp filter, see Tutorials 7.4, Step Five, and 12.2, Step Seven.

Step 7: Move a Limb Forward

You may have noticed that in the tutorial example file, the apparel covers the model's hand (**Figure 10.18**). To bring the image of the hand forward, copy the figure, then use the Photoshop® Eraser Tool (E) to expunge the image of the body up to the edge of the garment. In the tutorial example, the full arm and a portion of the shoulder and front were retained (**Figure 10.19**). These copies were positioned on layers above the original image and the apparel layers in the completed file (**Figure 10.20**).

Often in fashion photography only a portion of an image is desirable. A particular head pose from one shot might look better on a body from another. Moreover, the entire figure and/or the color may also need serious modifications to suit the needs of a particular project. This tutorial will teach you how to enhance photos by using action shots of Carl from ① Digital Duo Modeling Agency\Carl\Basketball Action Shots.

Note: *This tutorial makes use of features that are only available in Photoshop® CS5 and higher.*

Step 1: Open the Image Files in Photoshop®

Open two full-length action figure files of Carl similar to those pictured in Figure 10.21.

Step 2: Create a New Photoshop® CS5 Document

Create a new Photoshop® document of approximately 14×17 inches on a transparent background. The resolution should be 300 dpi.

Step 3: Prepare the Files

Double-click on the background layer, and in the New Layer dialog box, click OK. The layer will be renamed *Layer 0.*

Step 4: Remove the Background

1. Select the Photoshop® Magic Wand Tool (W), and then reduce its *Tolerance* to 10 in the Options Bar.

2. Click on the background of an image of Carl to select it. Marching ants will appear. Hold the Shift key if you need to select other background areas.

3. Press the Delete key to remove the white spaces; your background will now be transparent (Figure 10.21).

Step 5: Drag and Drop the Images

Use the Move Tool (V) to drag and drop the full-length figures into the new file. They will appear on separate layers. Give the layers titles to help you recognize them.

Step 6: Transform the Images

Use the Transform features by going to *Menu Bar > Edit > Transform* to scale, distort, and/or alter the perspective of the images. In Figure 10.22, the images of Carl were scaled to fit the canvas size.

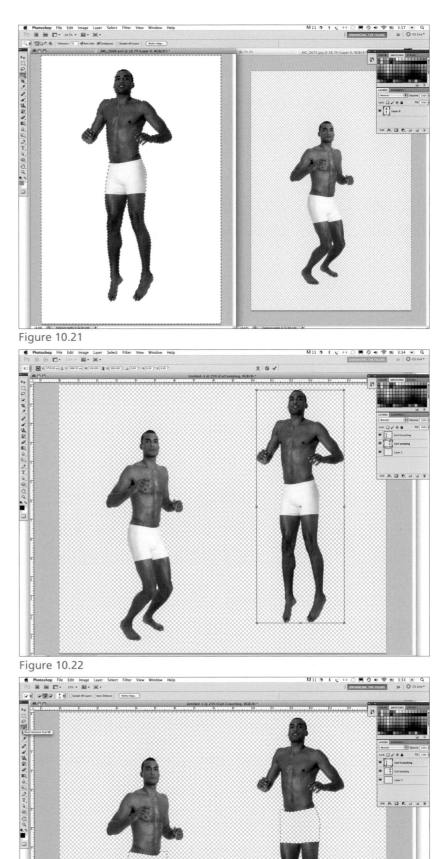

Figure 10.21

Figure 10.22

Figure 10.23

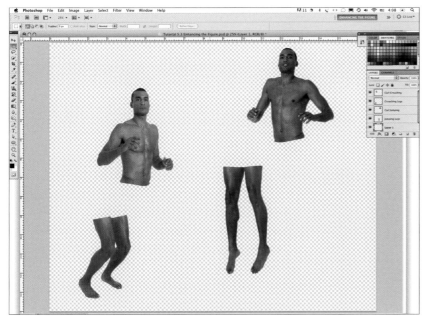

Figure 10.24

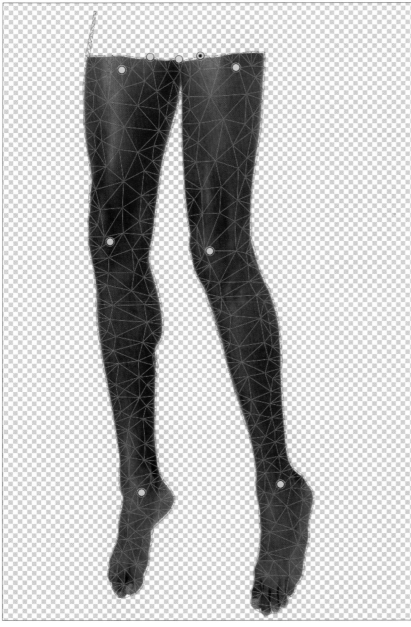

Figure 10.25 Puppet Warp pins may be different colors in CS6.

Step 7: Delete the Middle

Because we are about to completely alter the images of Carl, we will need to delete the briefs that he is wearing. Use the Quick Selection Tool (W) to surround the area with marching ants, and then press the Delete key (Figure 10.23).

Step 8: Separate the Torso from the Legs

1. Select the Rectangular Marquee Tool (M) and perform a marquee around the image of Carl's legs.

2. Press *Cmd+X / Ctrl+X*, then press *Cmd+V / Ctrl+V*, to cut and paste them into new layers.

3. Rename these layers and pull them below the figure layers that now contain just the torsos (Figure 10.24).

Step 9: Lengthen the Legs with Puppet Warp

1. Toggle on your Rulers by pressing *Cmd+R / Ctrl+R*.

2. Pull a horizontal Guide from the x-axis at the hip level.

3. Afterward, pull another about .75 inches below the frontal knee and another .75 inches below the frontal ankle.

4. Use the **Puppet Warp filter** to modify the leg pose by selecting the leg layer and going to *Menu Bar > Edit > Puppet Warp*.

5. When the Puppet Warp mesh appears, place the yellow pins at the top of both sides of the subject with a click. The number of pins you use is arbitrary. The goal is to lengthen the image to that of a well-proportioned croquis. In the case of the tutorial example, Carl's images are suitable for active sports, particularly basketball. The longer legs will make this more convincing.

6. Also place pins at the knees and ankles.

7. First, carefully pull the knee pins slightly downward.

8. Pull the ankle down proportionately.

9. When you pull the pins, the foot position will change (Figure 10.25). Add additional pins where needed to modify the positions.

TIP: Use Good Photos

The success of these changes depends largely upon the images. If you have an unsatisfactory image, delete it and replace it with one that is 150 to 300 dpi.

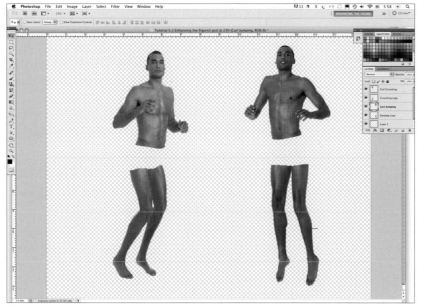

Figure 10.26

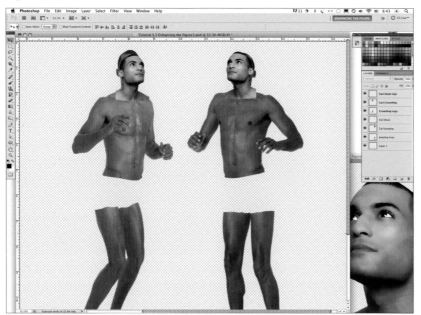

Figure 10.27

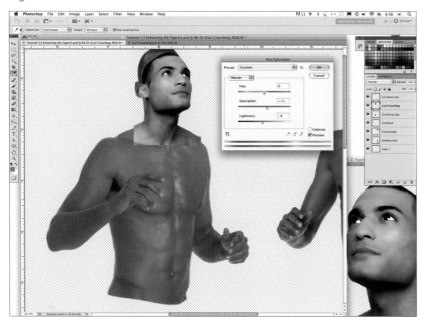

Figure 10.28

The modified legs are shown in Figure 10.26.

Step 10: Change Heads

In the tutorial example, Carl's body looks great, but a different head might look even better on this particular image of his body.

1. Go to *Menu Bar > File > Open* to Import (open) the image Carl_3Q_headshot_looking_up.jpg from ① Digital Duo Modeling Agency\Carl\Basic Headshots into a new Photoshop® file. Locate the file on the DVD and then select it from the menu options of the Open dialog box.

2. Double-click on the background layer in the Layers panel, and in the New Layer dialog box, click OK. The layer will be renamed *Layer 0*.

3. Select the Photoshop® Magic Wand Tool (W), and then reduce its *Tolerance* to 10 in the Options Bar.

4. Click on the background of the images of Carl, to select it. The marching ants will appear.

5. Press the Delete key to remove the white spaces; your background will now be transparent (checkered motif) (Figure 10.27).

6. Use the Move Tool (V) to drag and drop Carl's head into the new file.

7. Pull the layer containing the head to the New Layer icon on the lower right of the Layers panel (next to trash icon) to duplicate it. The two heads will appear on separate layers, but you will need to use the Move Tool (V) to reposition them appropriately. Give the layers titles to help you recognize them.

8. Use the Transform features by going to *Menu Bar > Edit > Transform > Scale* to resize the head. In Figure 10.27, the images of Carl's head were scaled to fit the bodies, and both heads are posed in positions suitable to either torso. The head on the left was flipped by selecting that layer and then going to *Menu Bar > Edit > Transform > Flip Horizontal*.

Step 11: Make Color Adjustments to the Body

The headshot that was dragged and dropped into the new file was retouched using Photoshop® tools and filters available in versions CS5 and higher, which include the **HDR (High Dynamic Range) filter**. This feature of Photoshop® combines various filter features of the program to assist you with generating professional photo retouching and color correction with the adjustment of a few settings. Before you can use that filter, you must attempt to correct the color and connect the head to the body by using the methods demonstrated in Tutorial 10.1.

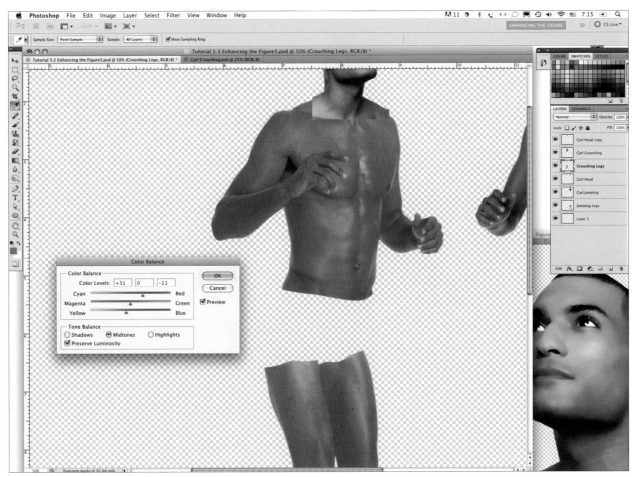

Figure 10.29

Adjust the Hue/Saturation

Zoom in on the area and select the body layer. Go to *Menu Bar > Image > Adjustments > Hue/Saturation*. Adjust the Master sliders to obtain the ranges of hues that come close to those of the head (Figure 10.28). Retain this information so that it can be repeated for the legs.

Modify the Color Balance

Go to *Menu Bar > Image > Adjustments > Color Balance*. Correct the color balance in *Highlights*, *Midtones,* and *Shadows*, as needed. The Highlight and Midtones Color Levels were adjusted in the tutorial example (Figure 10.29). Because each monitor will yield different results, you should gauge how much adjustment is needed. Record the changes you make for each tone balance and then click OK.

Note: *If slight changes to the sliders do not yield acceptable results, click Cancel.*

Step 12: Erase the Unwanted Areas

Use the Photoshop® Eraser Tool (E) to delete the original image of Carl's head, but leave a portion

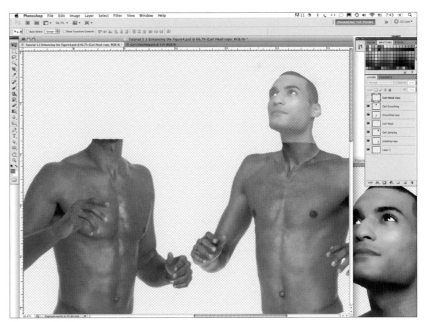

Figure 10.30

of the neck. Erase some of the shoulder area, but leave those portions that appear to match the body. Reduce the layer Opacity on the new head, so that you can see where the parts match. You can restore it later (Figure 10.30).

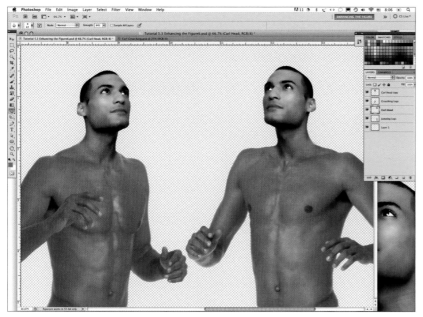

Figure 10.31

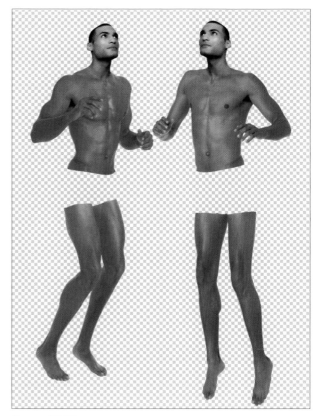

Figure 10.33

Figure 10.32

Step 13: Merge and Content-Aware to Conceal

Hold the Shift key and select the head and torso layers. Press *Cmd+E / Ctrl+E* to merge the layers. Follow the steps outlined in Tutorial 10.1 and use the Content-Aware filter to combine the images (Figure 10.31).

Step 14: Enhance the Image with the Liquify Filter

The Liquify filter can be used not only to make fabric flow, as demonstrated in Chapter 5, but also to enhance the image of the human form. In the tutorial example, photography added some weight to the model Carl. To give him an even better body, select a particular layer and go to *Menu Bar > Filter > Liquify*. Use the Forward Warp Tool (W) with an

appropriate size brush to slightly define muscles and reshape areas like the abdomen (Figure 10.32). Vast improvements to the body made with the Liquify filter can be observed in the image of Carl on the left as compared to the photo on the right (Figure 10.33).

Step 15: Refine and Clean

Some of a background may still be attached to the edges of your images. To remove it, add an adjustment layer filled with black beneath the images. Use the Eraser Tool (E) to remove the obviously unwanted debris and to smooth out some of the rough edges. Figure 10.34 reveals a few areas of concern.

Cleaning Up the Edges

Once you have erased the debris, there may still be problems with the edges. There are many ways to correct this problem, but a simple method is to use the Blur Tool with a small brush at 100% *Opacity* only on the jagged edges. This will make the edges smooth and any debris less visible. If this does not work, try the Refine Edge features discussed in Tutorial 7.2, Step Eight.

Step 16: Transform Distortion

Use the Transform Distort and Rotate options to adjust the poses. The complete tutorial example is shown in Figure 10.35.

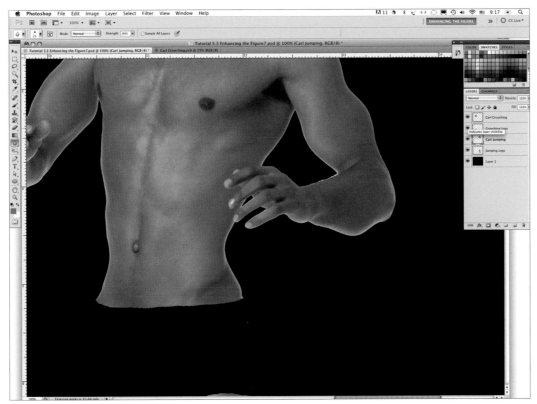

Figure 10.34 Correct the edges of your images.

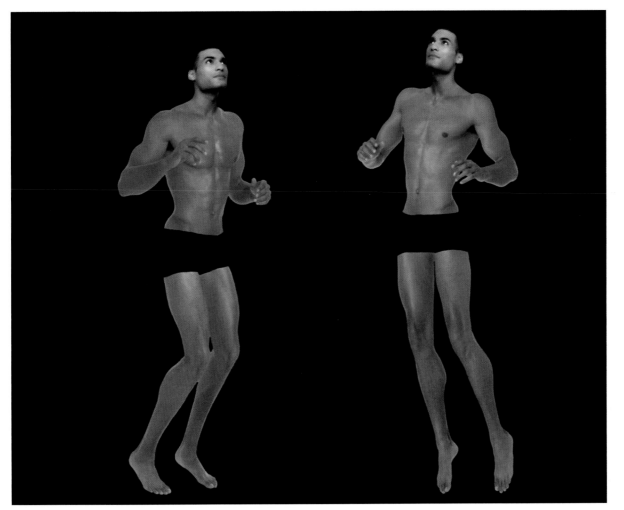

Figure 10.35

Even top models are not perfect; the camera lens reveals many imperfections. Fashion merchandisers and designers may find themselves retouching photos as they prepare images for print or Web hosting. In this tutorial, we will cover some basic procedures used to improve a headshot, including HDR toning. Use your own photo or one of the headshots of Ana located on ① Digital Duo Modeling Agency.

Note: This tutorial makes use of some features that are only available in Photoshop® CS5 and higher.

Figure 10.36

Figure 10.37

Step 1: Scan or Open the Image File in Photoshop®

Figure 10.36 is an image of the model Ana before retouching.

Step 2: Correcting White Space

Often the main problem with a photo is that the white within it needs to be toned. But if you adjust the exposure to modify the whites, the result will be an overexposed image. Follow these steps instead:

1. Go to *Menu Bar > Image > Adjustments > Selective Color*, and then choose the *whites* from the *Colors* pull-down menu.

2. Gradually adjust the sliders to remove the other colors from the white in the image. Typically, *yellow* and *black* will be areas of concern, so you will need to move these sliders left toward the negative percentages.

3. At the bottom of the **Selective Color** dialog box is a *Method* section. If you choose *Relative*, the changes affect the entire image. Clicking on the *Absolute* button results in changes to a specific color within the image. Move the sliders a bit, and then give your eyes a chance to adjust. Make slight modifications; dramatic changes are likely to cause more problems, including white spots in protruding areas when you are using the *Absolute* method. If this occurs, choose *Relative*, then move the sliders to the right toward the positive percentages.

Step 3: Correct Neutral Space

The *Neutrals* in Selective Color govern the midtones; they are generally representative of grays in a color image. Photos sometimes contain so much gray that they give the subject a mottled appearance. Remove some of the black from the *Neutrals* to correct this problem. The corrections made on the tutorial example are shown in Figure 10.37.

Step 4: Remove Imperfections

Zoom in on the image by using the slider on the Navigator panel. Use the Spot Healing Brush Tool (J) to eradicate imperfections. The closeup view in Figure 10.38 reveals fine wrinkles, peach fuzz, skin problems, etc. Sometime the brush can leave marks; adjust its size and hardness in the Options Bar. The type of healing can also be selected in the Options Bar. Content-Aware is desirable for retouching skin texture. Click on *Create Texture* when you are working on areas that should not look completely smooth, such as the eyes. Try using *Proximity Match* where you do not want to change the skin's surface, especially around the mouth (Figure 10.39).

Step 5: Remove Hair

The finest hairs on the human body are usually invisible until the subject is in front of the photographer's lens. You can zoom in close to these areas on images and paint them out with various brushes and sampled colors.

1. Select the Brush Tool (B), and show the Brush panel. Select one of the new Photoshop® painting brushes, such as the Flat Curve.

2. At the bottom of the panel is an icon with an eye on it. Select this to toggle the Bristle Brush Preview, which will appear in the upper left corner of the window.

3. In the Brush panel, you can adjust the size, amount of bristles, length, thickness, softness, and angle of a selected brush. The **Brush Tip Shape** menu allows you to modify the actual color used with the brush. Many of these selections create simulated fine art painting effects, such as the *Wet Edges* selection, which builds color in layers. Experiment with the various selections and their combinations, in order to discover techniques suitable for each project.

4. Sample a color from any area by holding the Option key (Mac) or the Alt key (PC).

5. When the Eyedropper icon appears, click on the desired hue.

6. For better results, reduce the *Opacity* and *Flow* in the Options Bar.

7. Resample colors and change brushes as often as needed.

8. When you have covered all the fine hairs, use the Blur Tool on the area to obscure any slight discolorations or streaking.

9. The Spot Healing Brush Tool (J) will be helpful here, too.

In Figure 10.40, the left nostril shows modifications made using the new Photoshop® brushes. The right nostril is in need of similar retouching.

Note: The appearance of fine hair in certain areas can also be diminished with several strokes of the Blur Tool. This technique is particularly effective on peach fuzz.

Step 6: Apply Finishing Touches

Use the other techniques and tools you have learned to complete the look. In the tutorial example, the mouth was closed by using Content-Aware, then the Liquify filter's Forward Warp Tool was used to reshape it. Afterward, the Burn Tool (O), Dodge Tool (O), and others were applied as accents. The completed example is shown in Figure 10.41.

Figure 10.38

Figure 10.39

Figure 10.40

Figure 10.41 This image does not have HDR toning.

Figure 10.42

Figure 10.43 This image has HDR Toning.

Step 7: Use the Photoshop® HDR Filter to Create Surreal Effects

Some presentations will call for dramatic effects. You can generate a variety of effects—from age modification to surreal and avant-garde effects—using the Photoshop® HDR filter. The filter will flatten your work, so be sure to save a copy if you need to retain your layers.

1. Go to *Menu Bar > Image > Adjustments > HDR Toning*.

2. When the dialog box appears, you may be alarmed at the immediate changes, but do not allow that to deter you. Try slight modifications to each of them by applying *Edge Glow*, *Tone Detail*, and *Color* Sliders.

3. Decrease the amount of *Detail* by moving this slider left, to give the subject a youthful glow.

4. To make more extreme adjustments to the contrast in the image, use the *Toning Curve and Histogram*. Pull the curve down to add more shadows or up to expose more of the image.

There are some presets at the top of the HDR Toning panel that you may also like, or you can create your own. Figure 10.42 shows the HDR toning settings that were applied to the tutorial example to create a couture-quality finish.

Step 8: Correct Eye Problems

To complete the look, paint over any red eye with a soft brush, then do the same for any highlights in the eyes to obscure reflected images. Use the Blur Tool for toning. Darken the eye makeup with the Burn Tool (O) (Figure 10.43).

Photos of men can also be retouched. Most of the procedures discussed in Tutorial 10.4 will apply to them, but a few areas should be treated differently. Try some or all of the techniques in this tutorial to improve the images of men. Use your own photo or one of the headshots of Carl located on ① Digital Duo Modeling Agency.

Note: *This tutorial makes use of features that are only available in Photoshop® CS5 and higher.*

Step 1: Scan or open the Image File in Photoshop®

Figure 10.44 is an image of Carl before retouching.

Step 2: Remove Razor Stubble

Select the Spot Healing Tool (S) from the Tools panel. Using a soft brush, click to sample adjacent areas to skin problems, and then click over the unwanted area. Choose the settings in the Options Bar. Each one of them will help at different stages of retouching. Start with *Proximity Match*. Once you have cleared up most of the problems, select Content-Aware to even the skintone. If you would like to retain more of the skin's surface, use Create Texture. Figure 10.45 shows the results of the Clone Stamp Tool (S) on Carl's shaving problems and new hair growth.

Step 3: Clear Excess Hair

1. Zoom in to identify enlarged pores and stray facial hair.

2. To remove the mustache shadow, decrease the diameter on the Spot Healing Brush Tool (J); work on small spaces, clearing them of the tiny hairs.

3. Select the Clone Stamp Tool (S); copy the good areas by clicking on them while holding the Option key (Mac) or the Alt key (PC).

4. Click on undesirable areas to cover them with the copied image (Figure 10.46).

5. If necessary, resample various areas, and then repeat the procedure.

TIP: **Avoid Masked Faces**

Do not attempt to create a completely flawless appearance, which is usually associated with cosmetics and face-lifts. It may make the subject look artificial.

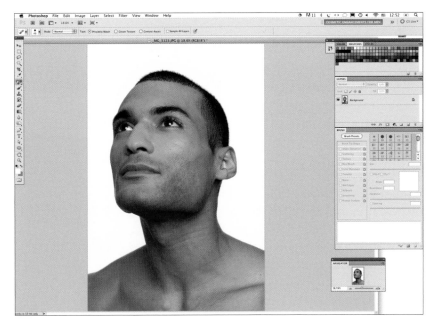
Figure 10.44

Figure 10.45

Figure 10.46

Step 4: Shape the Hair

A key to grooming for men is a good haircut. Unfortunately, the camera lens can intensify the appearance of uneven growth that can occur within hours of sitting in the barber's chair (Figure 10.47). Select the Brush Tool (B), and then change it to one suitable for the type of hair you want to shape up. Because Carl's hair is short and straight with wave formations, the Flat Fan brush was used with white sampled from the background to paint out the protruding strands (Figure 10.48). Do not overdo it; use organic strokes, rather than create a perfect edge, to keep the look natural. If necessary clean up the hairline on the face with the procedures outlined earlier. A stroke or two around the edges with the Blur Tool can also improve the finish.

TIP: Brush Adjustments

Lower the brush *Opacity* and *Flow* in the Options Bar in order to build your modifications.

Step 5: Reconstruct Facial Shapes

Certain poses create unattractive angles. In the tutorial example, Carl's strong jaw is attractive, but the camera angle gave it a bulbous form.

1. Use the Pen Tool (P) to create a new shape above it on another layer with the background fill color (Figure 10.49).

2. Afterward, show the Paths panel and select the *Load Path as Selection* icon at the bottom of the panel.

3. Go to *Menu Bar > Edit > Fill* or press *Shift+F5*.

4. Fill the object with the previously sampled Foreground color.

5. Use the Blur Tool on the edge to restore the natural transition (Figure 10.50). The completed tutorial example appears in Figure 10.51.

Step 6: Create Surreal Effects

Use the HDR filter to remove the fine details and create a youthful appearance. Key settings for men are *Detail* and *Highlight* (Figure 10.52). Try using the HDR filter with Hue Saturation, Liquify, Lens Flare, digital painting, and everything else that you have learned to make an animated character like the one shown in Figure 10.53.

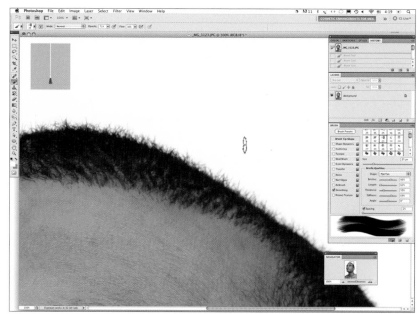

Figure 10.47

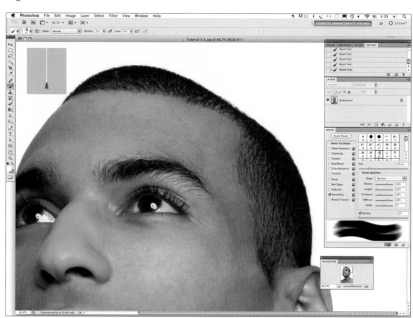

Figure 10.48

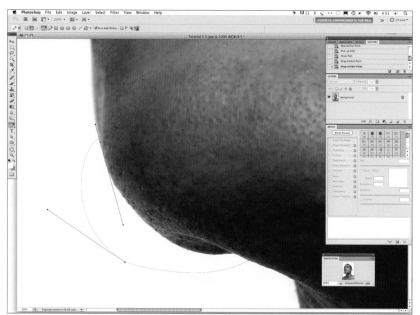

Figure 10.49

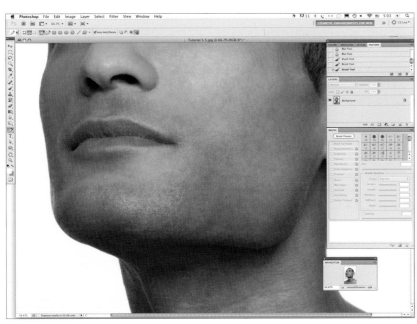

Figure 10.50 A clean jaw line.

Figure 10.51 Image without HDR Toning.

Figure 10.52 Image with HDR Toning.

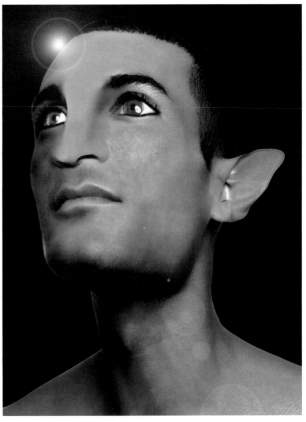

Figure 10.53 A fun alteration of the original image.

Vintage photos are often used in fashion editorials and design storyboard presentations. Because they may have many discolorations, fading, and other problems, you must know how to restore them. black-and-white photos present the greatest problems, so in this lesson we will restore, then colorize, one.

Step 1: Scan or Open the Image File(s) in Photoshop®

Two files are available for this tutorial on ① Ch10\ Tutorial 10.6. The first file June_Chicago.jpg is a vintage black-and-white Polaroid image of a fashionable young woman standing in front of an automobile circa 1952 (Figure 10.54). The photo shows signs of water damage and other surface tears and discoloration, but these problems present an excellent task and you can correct the problems with Photoshop®. This lesson is twofold; first you will restore the image, and then you will colorize it.

You can also use the color file Eartha_Kitt.jpg. This image is also a vintage photo, and it provides the same challenges. If you decide to use it, try and

work in the background, remove spots and shadows, and then colorize the black-and-white photo that appears in the background (Figure 10.55).

Note: *This tutorial makes use of some features that are only available in Photoshop® CS5 and higher.*

Step 2: Crop the Image

Select the Crop Tool (C) from the Tools panel. Perform a marquee only over the full image. To apply the changes to the canvas, double-click on the photo.

Step 3: Adjust a Black-and-White Image in Color Mode

Go to *Menu Bar > Image > Adjustments > Black and White*. When the dialog box appears, it may remove any coloration that is in the black-and-white image. The primary benefit to working on a black-and-white image in a color mode is that it lets you refine the type of gray space you prefer. For example, some black-and-white images are composed of cool blue-grays; others are warm, containing reds. The Photoshop® **Black and White filter** can intensify or decrease the amount of color(s) in the image in order to remove color spots and restore tints, tones, and shades.

The tutorial example needed less blue and cyan to bring back the midtones and shadows, so those

Figure 10.54 **June Chicago.**

Figure 10.55 **Eartha Kitt.**

Figure 10.56 Photoshop® Black and White filter settings.

sliders were pushed toward the left. The red and yellow sliders were pushed right to remove most of the warm discolorations in the image (Figure 10.56).

Step 4: Retouch Freehand

1. Select the Lasso Tool (L) from the Tools panel and encapsulate any spots or tears.

2. Fill the areas with Content-Aware, then use the Spot Healing Brush Tool (J), Clone Stamp Tool, and other options previously discussed to clean the surface of the image.

3. Use the Navigator panel to zoom in and move around the page.

4. Inspect the image closely because spots often masquerade as imagery in vintage photos. The obvious surface problems have been removed in the tutorial example (Figure 10.57).

Figure 10.57

Figure 10.58 **Photoshop® Selective Color Settings.**

Step 5: Remove Cast Shadows

In the photo, the photographer's shadow has been cast on the subject. To remove the shadow, select it with any selection tool, then go to *Menu Bar > Image > Adjustments > Selective Color* and adjust the amount of black in the Blacks (Figure 10.58).

Step 6: Restore Texture

The changes made in Step Five left a marked difference in the texture of the skirt. To add some of it back and cover the mark the filter made, use the Clone Stamp Tool (S).

1. Reduce the tool's *Opacity* to about 70% in the Options Bar.

2. Sample the texture from the good side by holding the Option key and clicking.

3. Release the Option key and click over the flattened area.

4. Work in horizontal sections; resample and apply the tool in rows going across the skirt from left to right.

Figure 10.59 shows progress made on the tutorial example. Use the same method to finish the skirt; correct the problem of the shadow on the top and on the car (Figure 10.60).

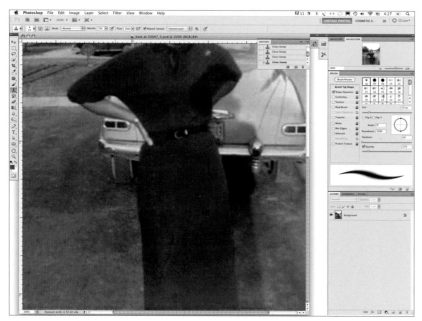

Figure 10.59

Figure 10.60

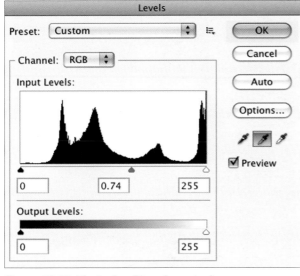

Figure 10.61 Photoshop® Levels controls.

Figure 10.62

Step 7: Correct Levels

The Levels controls can be located by going to *Menu Bar > Image > Adjustments > Levels*. Use it to restore the richness of the shadows by moving the Midtones slider slightly right. Your monitor may require more or less than what is shown in the histogram pictured in **Figure 10.61**.

Step 8: Restore Hair and Jewelry

Use the Burn Tool (O) to restore the luster to dark hair and the Dodge Tool (O) to contrast any sparkling jewelry (**Figure 10.62**). Avoid severe whitening of the teeth, as it will always create an unnatural look in a black-and-white image.

Figure 10.63

Step 9: Reduce Graininess with HDR Toning

The photo used in the tutorial example is somewhat grainy. Try reducing this with the new Photoshop® HDR Toning filter. Go to *Menu Bar > Image > Adjustments > HDR Toning*, and then position the sliders to improve the *Edge Glow* and *Tone and Detail* (Figure 10.63).

Step 10: Colorize Photo

Every photo has grayscale beneath its color (see Tutorial 9.4, Step Five). This makes it easy to colorize black-and-white photos.

1. Show the Brush panel and select a soft brush.

2. Check *Smoothing* in the *Brush Tip Shape* area.

3. Work on a layer above the original and reduce the layer fill.

4. Select colors to represent areas that you would like to paint.

5. Paint over the areas in one motion, reducing the brush size when needed.

6. Use the Photoshop® Eraser Tool (E) to clean up areas where the color went over a boundary. Do not attempt to paint every detail; just tint the color (Figure 10.64).

7. Add new layers each time that you paint an important new object, but do not work on the original.

Figure 10.64

In Figure 10.65, the dolman sleeved angora sweater, silk neck scarf, and skirt were tinted with Navy blue. The Blur Tool was used to take the severe look from the details. The background was painted in on several layers, and then the original's brightness was adjusted to lift the contrast.

TIP: Exercise Restraint

With vintage photos it is best to exercise restraint when colorizing. The images will be more convincing if you stay within historically correct color themes.

Step 11: Slenderizing the Subject

The color process may have added the look of a few extra pounds to your subject. To rectify this, go to *Menu Bar > Edit > Transform > Warp*. Use the Warp grid (Figure 10.66) to slightly pull in and reshape the subject. Marquee with the Crop Tool (C); if the edges become distorted, reshape them by reducing the canvas size. To accept the crop, select any tool in the Tools panel. The completed look is shown in Figure 10.67.

Figure 10.65

Figure 10.66

Figure 10.67

Chapter 10 Summary

In Chapter 10 you were introduced to basic photo retouching techniques. These skills are essential for enhancing and modifying images imported into Photoshop®. Throughout your career this image-editing software program may change, but one objective of fashion presentation will always remain the same, and that is to make everything commercially appealing. That is why a mastery of Photoshop® skills, presented in this chapter, is critical to your progress in the advanced tutorials to come. Review the information covered in Chapter 10, and then answer the following questions before proceeding to Chapter 11.

Chapter 10 Self-Assessment:

1. Can I use the Content-Aware feature of Photoshop® in order to replace sections of imagery with the program's visual calculations?

2. Can I use the Photoshop® Clone Stamp Tool to effectively sample sections of imagery from one area and seamlessly place them over others?

3. Do I have the skill to repair a torn photo, especially one that pictures human subjects?

4. Do I know how to swap images of human limbs and replace them with those from other images in order to alter the pose of a subject?

5. Have I mastered the ability to use the Photoshop® Liquify filter to improve the human figure?

6. Can I use the Photoshop® Puppet Warp controls to modify the length of images, especially the human form?

7. Can I create surreal effects with the Photoshop® HDR filter, especially for the faces of male and female fashion models?

8. Restoring and tinting are terms used when retouching black-and-white images, but can I perform these tasks on a photo myself? Can I adjust black-and-white images in the RGB color mode?

9. Can I use the Photoshop® Spot Healing Tool to mask razor stubble and other skin problems appearing in images?

10. Can I make freehand selections in Photoshop® with the Lasso Tool (L)?

Creating the Fashion Croquis with Illustrator®

Objectives

Illustrator® possesses many features previously available only in Photoshop®. With practice, you can render male and female digital fashion figures that are parallel to or even superior to freehand fashion sketches. The effort might seem arduous at first, but the benefits are incalculable. You can reuse digital fashion figures and alter them in an infinite number of ways. This saves time and money.

A unique feature of this book is its focus on preparing men's wear presentations. While many books model the male croquis from a female perspective, it is the goal of this chapter to make plain the differences in their fashion proportions. By completing the tutorials in this chapter, you will:

◉ Become acquainted with the anatomy of a croquis based on photo images

◉ Use layer compositing to render interactive croquis with movable parts

◉ Add realism to the upper body of male and female croquis using Illustrator® tools, panels, and filters to simulate muscle tone, highlights, and shadows

◉ Render digital croquis templates in proper proportion in frontal, three-quarter, and back views

◉ Make use of the Illustrator® Skintones Library

When it comes to fashion illustration, the proportions have always been dictated by the time in which the artist lives. However, today, there are many acceptable styles, so no one individual can dictate what is appropriate for everyone. Branding is often key to success. Just as fashion houses select specific types of models for runway presentations, the fashion figure, whether hand-rendered or digital, must convey a desired aesthetic. Each fashion house will set its own parameters as to the look of presentations, and a wise designer will give them what they want.

It is nearly impossible to prepare a compelling apparel design presentation without a croquis posed at full frontal view, but using the same pose can be boring and look amateurish. Most fashion professionals will not have time to create a new croquis with a slightly different frontal pose each time that they need one. In this tutorial, you will render the croquis using Illustrator® in a manner that will allow you to make alterations to the leg and/or arm poses with ease. Once you have built the croquis, you will learn how to fill it with skintone gradients and colors to look like light flesh. Use the lessons to help build a library of different croquis and limbs by creating more frontal files with different poses.

Note: To get you started, the completed male and female frontal view croquis from this tutorial have been placed on ② Ch11\Tutorial 11.1. Import them into Illustrator® CS5 or CS6 for further observation and use. The files may also be used with earlier versions of Illustrator®, but flattening of the layers may occur.

Step 1: Create a New Document in Illustrator®

Figure 11.1 shows the New Document dialog box with the specifications for creating an 11×14-inch page. Open this new file for either the male or female croquis tutorials, and title it appropriately.

Step 2: Place and Embed Your Photo on a Layer

In this tutorial you will be working in layers. Choose a full-length frontal image of Ana, Carl, or Jade from ① Digital Duo Modeling Agency and place it on the bottom layer. Double-click on *Layer 1* and rename it *Photo* (Figure 11.2). The same photo will be used to create all the parts of the figure; however, you will need to render each new shape on a separate layer. You will be instructed in the tutorial steps how to create each shape with the Illustrator® Pen Tool (P) and fill them with a color.

Step 3: Compare Normal and Exaggerated Figure Proportions

Figures 11.3 and 11.4 both compare actual proportions of the models (left) with the proportions of fashion illustration (right). The photo on the right was elongated in Photoshop®. The photos on ① Digital Duo Modeling Agency have been adjusted to accommodate some of the required proportion differences, but you will need to use the Bounding Boxes in Illustrator® and your own discretion when adding further distortion.

Figure 11.1

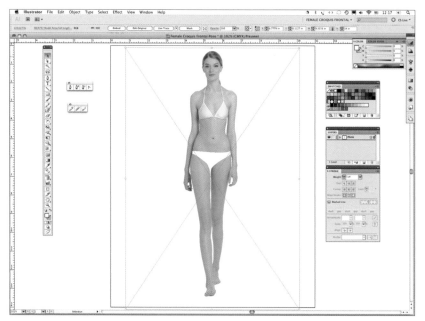

Figure 11.2

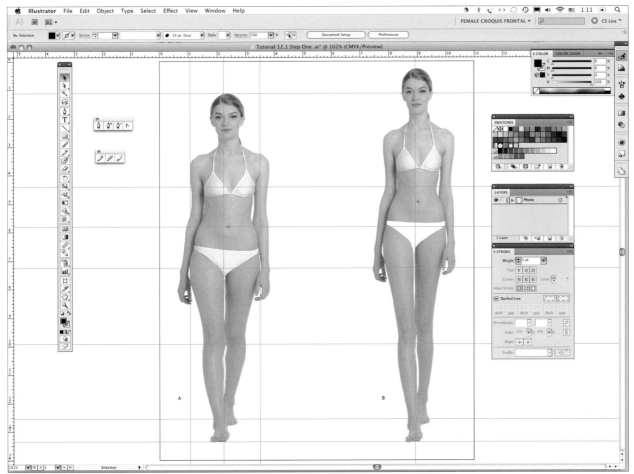

Figure 11.3 Female fashion illustration proportions (right) were created from the original photo (left). The horizontal red lines reference the original height, apex, waist, low hip, and knee levels.

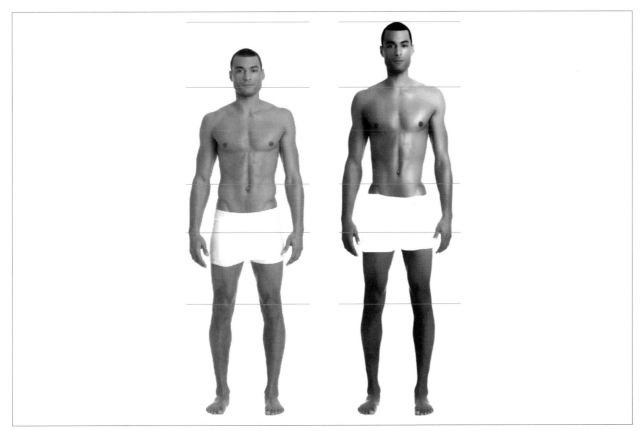

Figure 11.4 Male fashion illustration proportions (right) were created from the original photo (left). The horizontal red lines reference the height, shoulder, waist, low hip, and knee levels of the elongated image.

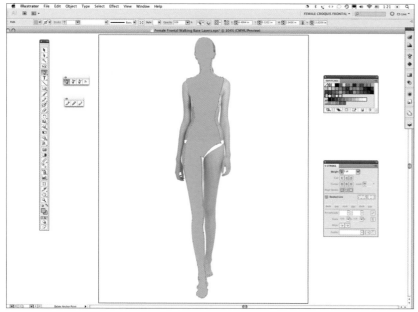

Figure 11.5

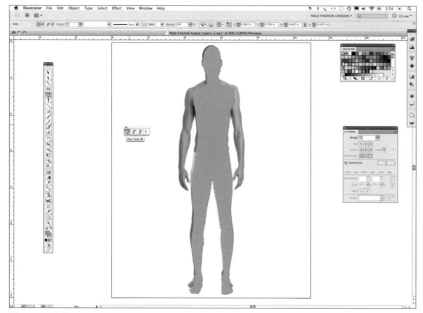

Figure 11.6

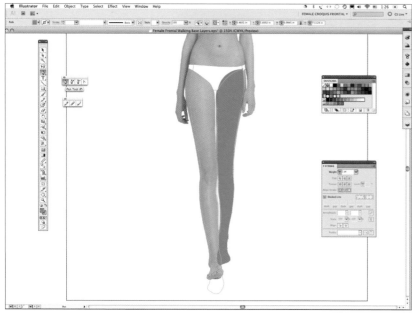

Figure 11.7

Scaling Figurative Photography for Fashion

A general distortion rule that you can follow to convert your own photographs to fashion proportion is to scale the width 90% and the height 110%. But note that when photos are elongated, the head often becomes too long. You will need to make adjustments to it in your rendering. In addition, avoid distorting the arms of poses that are extended from the body. Always reevaluate the arms and legs and consider them separately from the torso.

Step 4: Create the General Outline

The "general outline" here refers to the basic form of the head and the body. In Figure 11.5, the left leg, torso, and head are attached in one shape on the female pose. This will keep the leg behind it separate and movable. Because the male pose is in full frontal view with the model's legs apart, it is unnecessary to render separate legs. Figure 11.6 shows the shape that you should produce with the Illustrator® Pen Tool (P).

Note: *The photo is only a guide. Feel free to interpret the form and make it your own. You may need to scale parts as you continue the rendering(s).*

> # TIP: Scale Proportions
>
> **You will use the Illustrator® Pen Tool (P) for most of the steps to build the croquis figures in this chapter. Always begin rendering with a Stroke of a color, and then with the object selected, swap the Stroke with the Fill by pressing *Cmd+X / Ctrl+X.***

Step 5: Create the Right Leg

In the tutorial examples, some of the appendages should be rendered separately from the general outline, so that you can move them slightly when rendering apparel on the croquis. In some cases, a leg or an arm may need to be placed above a portion of a garment, and having attached parts would prevent this. The right leg of the female croquis is a perfect example (Figure 11.7).

Step 6: Create the Right Arm for the Croquis

Figure 11.8 shows the rendered right arm for the female croquis, and Figure 11.9 shows the rendered right arm for the male croquis.

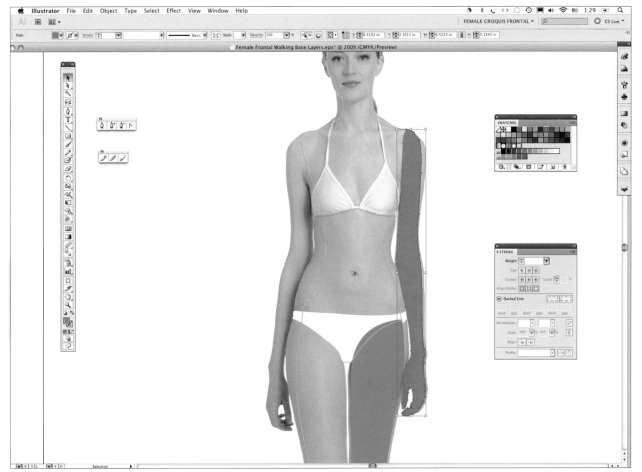

Figure 11.8 Use your judgment for the drawing, as you compare it to the photo.

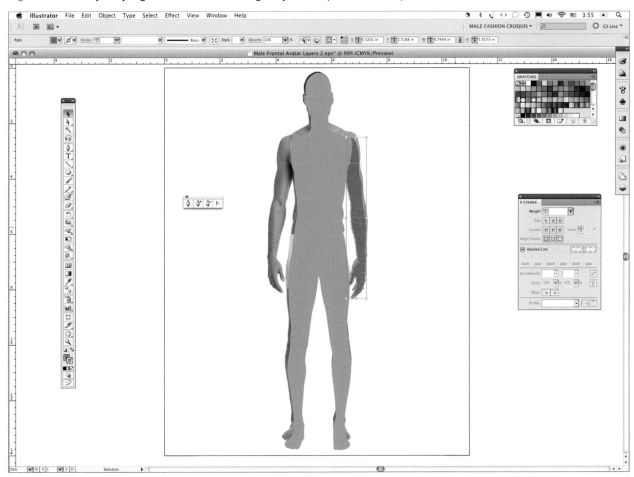

Figure 11.9

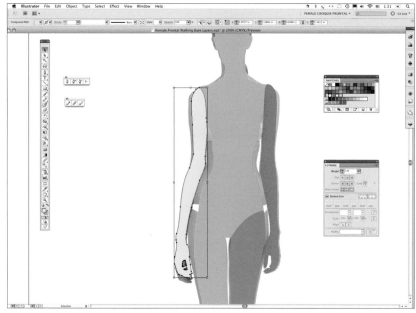

Figure 11.10

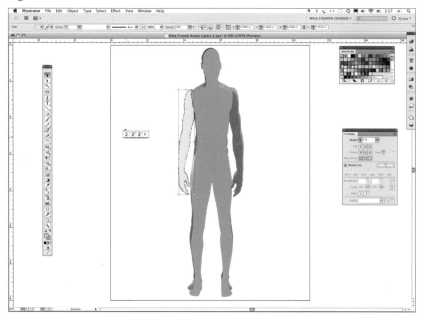

Figure 11.11

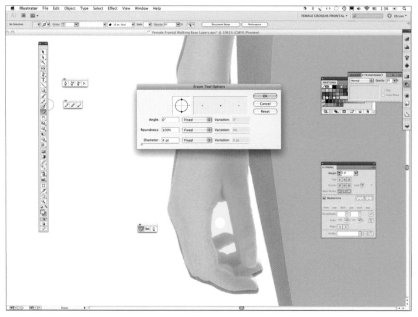

Figure 11.12 Illustrator® Eraser Tool Options.

Step 7: Create the Left Arm

Figure 11.10 shows the rendered left arm for the female croquis and Figure 11.11 shows the rendered left arm for the male croquis.

Step 8: Use the Eraser Tool to Create Small Negative Spaces

The Eraser Tool (E) is useful for creating instant negative spaces. Use the Transparency panel to reduce the Opacity of the object. The diameter of the tool can be adjusted by double-clicking on its icon in the Tools panel (Figure 11.12). The completed frontal views are shown in Figures 11.13 and 11.14.

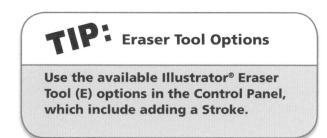

TIP: Eraser Tool Options

Use the available Illustrator® Eraser Tool (E) options in the Control Panel, which include adding a Stroke.

Step 9: Select and Fill the Parts with Gradients

In Figures 11.15 and 11.16 the parts have been filled with a gradient from the Skintones Library. Select the parts of your croquis, and then fill them with any of the Skintones gradients, but use a Stroke of None. Adjust the gradients; some parts will need *Linear* gradients and others will benefit from a *Radial* gradient. Try and match the color ranges in the parts by selecting them, then clicking on the page with the Gradient Tool (G). Move the sliders.

Step 10: Create Graphic Styles

Using raster-like effects in a vector software program is a dynamic plus for those who prefer to work in one program. Some filters, like the Gaussian Blur, were previously available only to Photoshop® users, but were added to Illustrator® CS5 and make it possible to simulate realistic shadows and highlights.

To master the use of the Gaussian Blur, use it in combination with the Graphic Styles panel, which allows you to save a combination of filters in a preset color range and intensity. The cleavage shadow shown in Figure 11.17 was created with the Blob Brush Tool (Shift+B) and a darker gradient from the Illustrator® Skintones Library. The shape was selected, and the Gaussian Blur filter was added to make the blend smooth. Save a Graphic Style by selecting the shape and then clicking the New Style icon at the bottom of the panel, near the Trash icon. You can also scroll to the panel's hidden menu options. The icon for your graphic style will

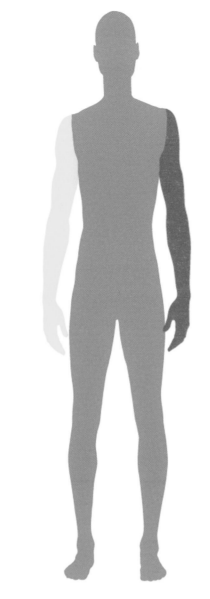

Figure 11.13   Figure 11.14   Figure 11.15   Figure 11.16

appear. Double-click on it to give it an appropriate name, so that you will be able to reapply this combination at the press of a button. When you save your work, the Graphic Style that you made will be saved with it. You can save as many Graphic Styles as needed to represent various shadows, midtones, and highlights in the skin. Use them to cover abrupt lines (see Tutorial 3.2, Step Fifteen). Some of those details were added to the neck and clavicle area.

Note: *Refer to the photos on* *in the Digital Duo Modeling Agency folder if you need help finding correct shadows and highlights.*

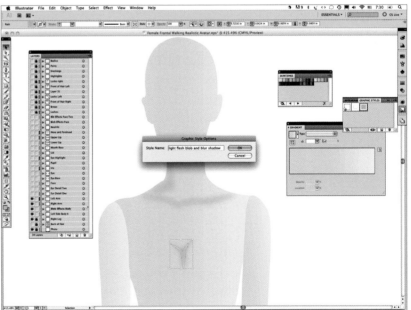

Figure 11.17

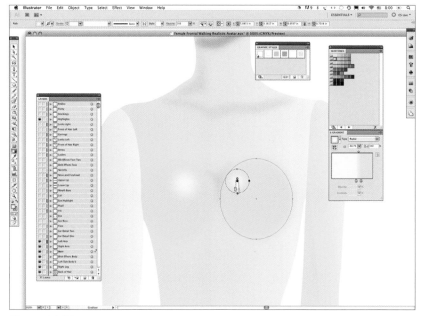

Figure 11.18

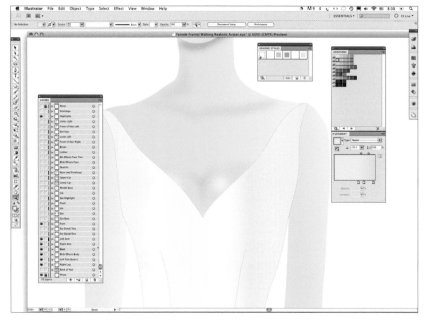

Figure 11.19

Step 11: Use the Ellipse Tool to Make the Bust

Add a layer for each new part that you create. In Figure 11.18, the bust was created with the Ellipse Tool (L) and a radial gradient. Additional colors can be added from the Skintones Library. Drag the swatches to the Gradient panel and drop them on the Gradient Bar. The light source was adjusted, the Gaussian Blur filter was applied, and then a Graphic Style was created.

Step 12: Check the Effect

Add a shape representing an article of clothing to check the effect of your work (Figure 11.19).

Step 13: Add Definition to the Male Chest

Unless you are creating a line of swimwear, the only portion of the male croquis that you should seriously consider giving muscle detail is the chest. Remember that the greatest results will be developed when you export the file to Photoshop®, but you can add shadows and highlights to the figure in Illustrator® by doing the following:

1. Select the Blob Brush Tool (Shift+B) from the Tools panel. If necessary, double-click on it to adjust the size of the brush within the Options dialog box that appears.

2. Use the brush to paint areas on the chest for shadows, midtones, and highlights using appropriate flesh tones. The upper body of Carl in Figure 11.20 makes an excellent study for the placement of these shapes. In Figure 11.21, all of the painted areas have been selected to give you an idea of the free-form shapes that you should strive for.

3. Select the painted shape(s) and blend them with the Gaussian Blur filter or choose various selections from the Additive for Blob Brush Library by going to *Menu Bar > Window > Graphic Style Libraries > Additive* for Blob Brush. The completed look using the airbrushes is shown in Figure 11.22.

The Additive for Blob Brush Library

There are 14 default graphic styles in the Additive for Blob Brush Library, and their effects are displayed in Figure 11.23. Experiment with colored squares to discover which effects will work for you:

1. Select the Rectangle Tool, hold the Shift key, and create squares.

2. Fill each square with a flesh tone.

3. Select each square and then click the preset in the Additive for Blob Brush Library to apply the effect to the square. Not all of the presets will be appropriate for shadows and highlights on your croquis. For example, the presets shown in the top row of Figure 11.23 will create better shadows than those shown in the bottom row.

To save a color and effect for later use, select the square and then click the New Graphic Styles icon on the bottom right of the Graphics Style panel. Double-click on the new Graphics Style that appears and label it. You'll now be able to use that new Graphics Style again and again by clicking on it whenever you select the Blob Brush Tool.

Note: *Save your finished croquis for use in the Chapter 12 tutorials.*

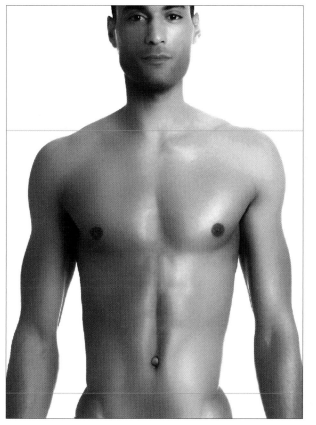

Figure 11.20

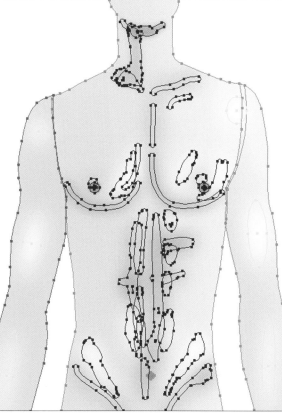

Figure 11.21

Figure 11.22

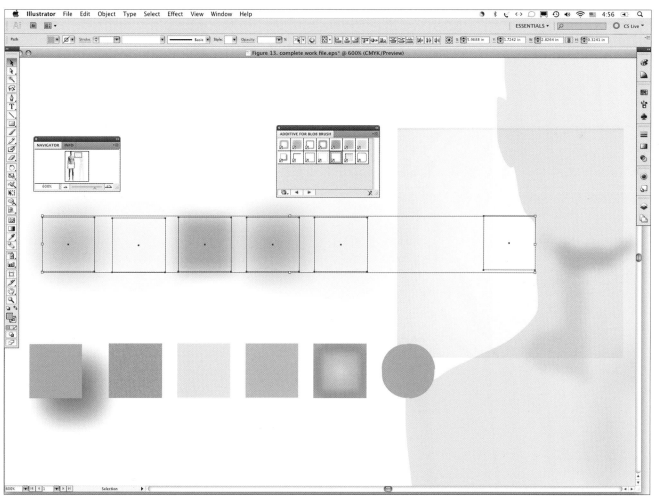

Figure 11.23 The square shapes shown correspond to the effects of the Additive for Blob Brush Library panel (center).

Tutorial 11.2
THE DIGITAL THREE-QUARTER-VIEW POSE

The three-quarter-view pose of a fashion figure can be difficult for some to render freehand. The problem can be magnified in the light of graphics software programs like Illustrator®. The following tutorial takes you through the steps of creating a three-quarter-view fashion croquis from a photograph. Further techniques of creating the illusion of perspective and volume are discussed. Because swatches and gradients for fair skintones were applied in Tutorial 11.1, emphasis is placed on the creation of illusions for darker tones in this tutorial.

Note: Completed male and female three-quarter-view croquis from this tutorial have been placed on

② *Ch11\Tutorial 11.2. Import them into Illustrator® CS5 or CS6 for further observation and use. Opening the files in earlier versions of Illustrator® may cause the layers to become flattened.*

Step 1: Create a New Document in Illustrator® and Place a Three-Quarter Photo Pose

Set up your document as you were instructed in Tutorial 11.1. Choose a full-length three-quarter-view image of Ana, Carl, or Jade from ① Digital Duo Modeling Agency folder and place it on the bottom layer (Figures 11.24 and 11.25).

Step 2: Work from the Distance to the Front

When creating the digital three-quarter view you will need to build the composition starting from the part of the croquis that is farthest in perspective. In this case, the left arm is rendered first (Figures 11.26 and 11.27).

Figure 11.24

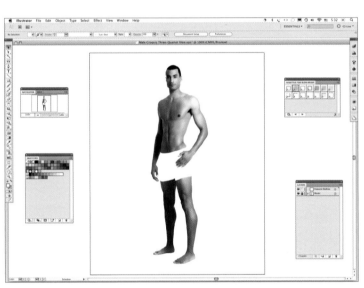

Figure 11.25

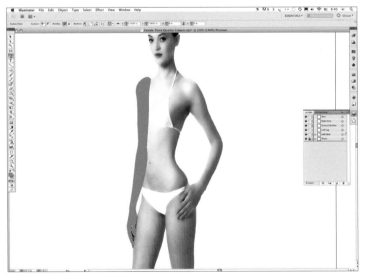

Figure 11.26

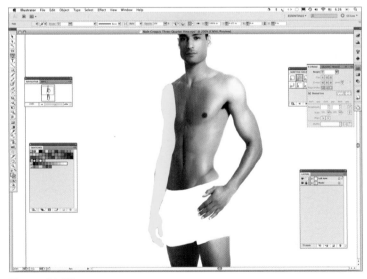

Figure 11.27

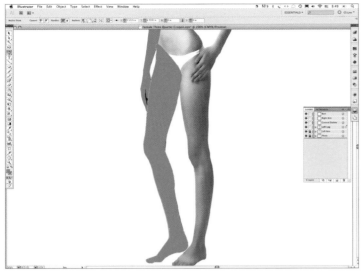

Figure 11.28

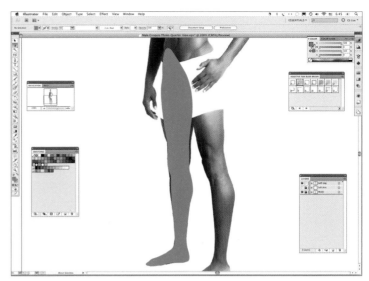

Figure 11.29

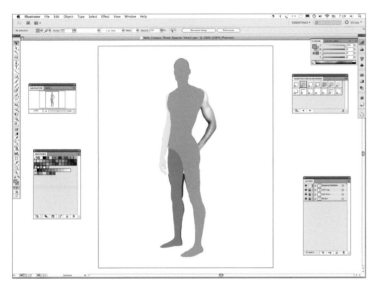

Figure 11.30

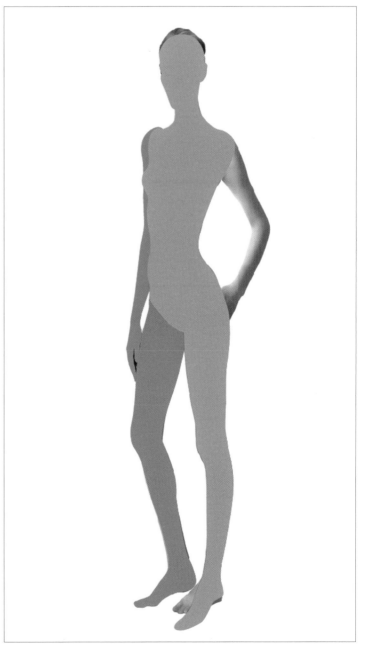

Figure 11.31

Step 3: Render the Leg That Is in the Rear View

Render the leg that is farthest in perspective, but you do not need to draw the entire limb, unless you plan to show the legs and thighs. The poses are designed to allow you to change the position of the feet. If you prefer, choose a set of legs from ① Digital Duo Modeling Agency\Anatomical Poses instead of those in the pose you have chosen.

Because photography adds weight to its subjects, you may want to eliminate some of the muscle structure to create correct illustration proportions Each left leg in the photos is behind the model's torso, so render them on separate layers below the *General Outline* (body) layer (Figures 11.28 and 11.29).

Step 4: Render the Three-Quarter General Outline

The general outline can contain the croquis's head and one of the legs (Figures 11.30 and 11.31).

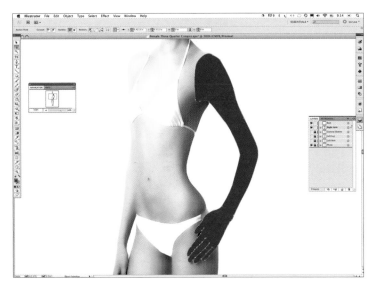

Figure 11.32

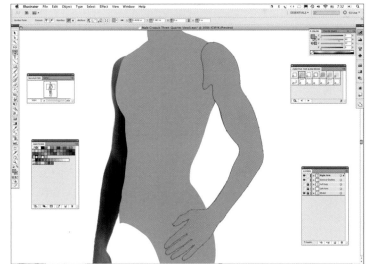

Figure 11.33

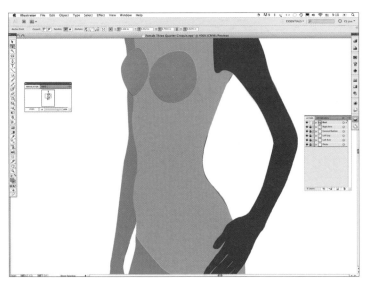

Figure 11.34

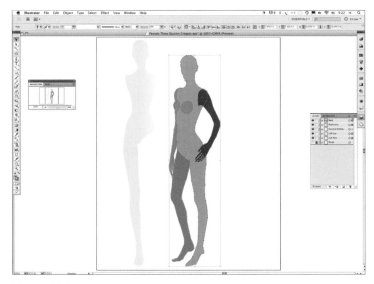

Figure 11.35

Step 5: Render the Frontal Arm

Because the right arm is closest to the viewer, it is rendered last and placed on a layer above the others (Figure 11.32 and 11.33). Give special attention to hand details. Render the fingers and thumbs.

Step 6: Create the Bust on the Female Croquis

Figure 11.34 shows the rendered bust.

Step 7: Place a Figure in the File to Compare the Scale

Even though the photos on ① Digital Duo Modeling Agency have been retouched and adjusted to help you create croquis, the images that you trace from them may still need to be scaled to fashion proportions. Place a croquis with desirable proportions (use the files provided for Tutorial 11.1) temporarily in your file (Figure 11.35). Select your three-quarter croquis and use the Bounding Box to scale the object. In some cases this procedure may cause distortion of certain parts of your croquis. Try pulling the Bounding Box from the bottom or the top only, etc. Whatever you do, try to avoid severe distortion of the shapes.

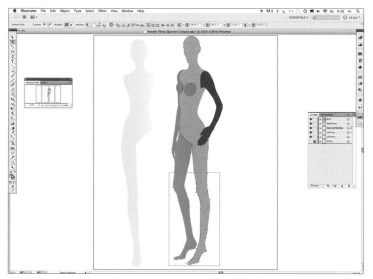

Figure 11.36

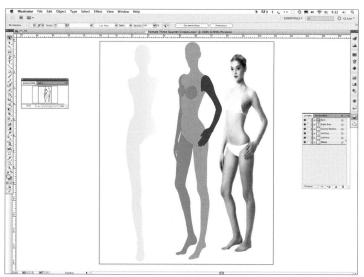

Figure 11.37

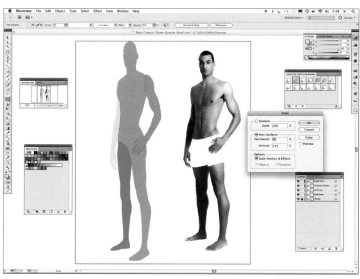

Figure 11.38

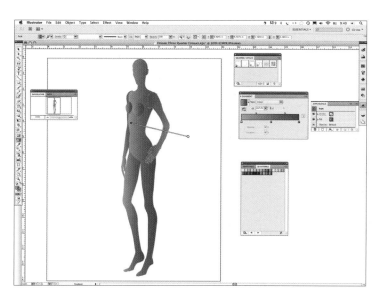

Figure 11.39

Step 8: Elongate Particular Areas of the Croquis

You may need to elongate or shorten particular areas of the croquis. Do so by selecting only the anchors and paths to be affected with a marquee of the Direct Selection Tool (A). Use the direction keys (arrows) to modify just that portion of the croquis (Figure 11.36).

Step 9: Compare Photos and Illustrations

Figure 11.37 shows the vast difference in the digital illustrations and the photo image.

Step 10: Scale the Figure to Fashion Proportions

As an alternative to using a prerendered croquis to compare proportions, try scaling the digital figure instead. A simple way to scale your figure to fashion proportions is to use the *Non-Uniform* option of the Scale Tool (S). Lock the photo, and select the croquis parts by pressing *Cmd+A / Ctrl+A*. Scale the croquis *Horizontal* 90% and *Vertical* 110% (Figure 11.38).

Step 11: Select and Fill the Parts with a Gradient

The fashion croquis in Figures 11.39 and 11.40 have been filled with gradients from the Illustrator®

Gradients Skintones Library. Use the Gradient Tool (G) to readjust the gradient if needed.

Step 12: Add Gaussian Blur and Graphic Styles to a Filled Shape

In Figure 11.41, the outline of the bust was softened with the Gaussian Blur filter. The filter was saved as a Graphic Style so that it could be applied to other shapes.

Step 13: Add Body Shadows with the Blob Brush Tool

1. Select the Blob Brush Tool (Shift+B) from the tools panel. If necessary, double-click on it to adjust the size of the brush within the Options dialog box that appears.

2. Use the brush to paint areas on the figure for shadows, midtones, and highlights using appropriate flesh tones.

3. Adding shapes that represent articles of clothing will help you to check the natural effects of your work (Figure 11.42).

Step 14: Apply Graphic Styles to Affect Multiple Selections

Apply a single Graphic Style to multiple selections and then select certain areas to change the fill. The best results require a combination of variations (Figures 11.43 and 11.44). With practice, you will be able to create convincing 3-D results (Figures 11.45 and 11.46).

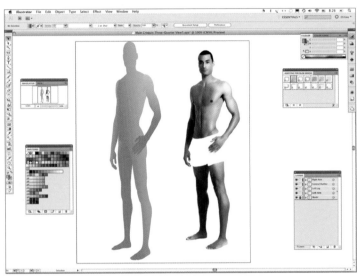

Figure 11.40

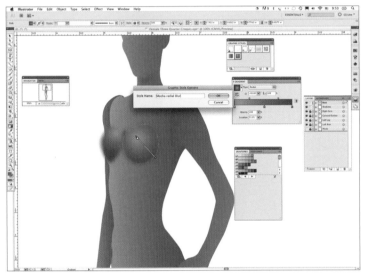

Figure 11.41

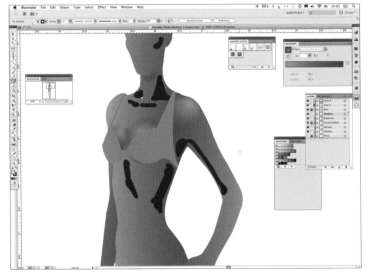

Figure 11.42

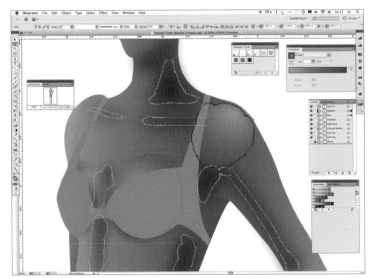

Figure 11.43

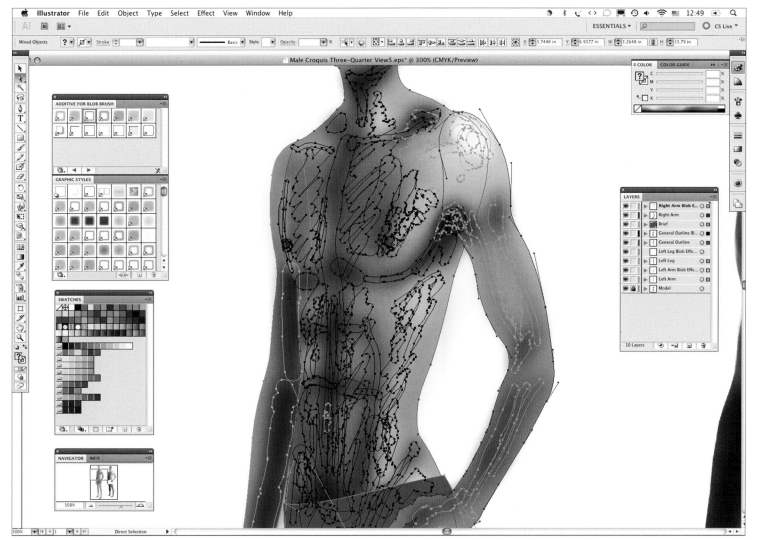

Figure 11.44

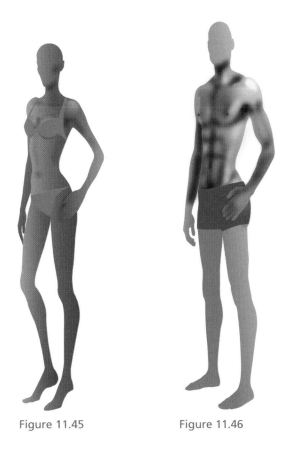

Figure 11.45   Figure 11.46

Chapter 11 Summary

Fashion illustration can be difficult to conquer, if you do not possess a gifted hand. For many fashion novices the techniques for creating female fashion croquis poses demonstrated in this chapter will be a welcomed help; however, they are not intended to be an absolute solution. They are merely suggestions for how you might use Illustrator® to generate fashion figures from photographic references. Extract from them what suits you personally as an artist. If your hand-rendered croquis are a core feature of your style, try combining digitized scans of them with some of the procedures that you have learned in this publication, especially those that modify shadows and highlights. By practicing the tutorials in this chapter, using different poses that you can find from almost any source, you will strengthen your command of Illustrator® and develop a library of croquis that you will be able to use again and again.

This chapter also presented some challenges that are unique to digital rendering of the male croquis. Even if you do not specialize in designing clothing for men, learning to render them is an asset. The tutorials in this chapter made use of poses available on ① Digital Duo Modeling Agency, but you can take the concepts further. Practice will always increase your digital skills and improve the quality of your illustrations. To assist you in the process, extra croquis have been placed on ② Ch11\Extra Croquis. Use the files to help you further understand how to create male and female digital croquis in a variety of poses from photography.

Chapter 11 Self-Assessment

1. Do I know the exact percentages for width and height by which I can scale a photographic image in order to convert it to proportions for fashion illustration?

2. Do I know why the parts of the body need to be rendered in separate parts on various layers in order to construct a digital croquis in Illustrator®?

3. Do I know how to make use of the Adobe Illustrator® Eraser Tool (E) and the Transparency panel in any way when rendering fashion croquis?

4. In reference to the fills used to simulate the color of skin on croquis, do I know where to place *Linear* gradients and *Radial* gradients for optimal effects?

5. Do I know how to make use of the model's photos from the Digital Duo Modeling Agency folder on ① in order to find correct shadows and highlights?

6. Can I make good use of the default graphic styles in the Additive for Blob Brush Library?

7. Do I know how to change the position of the legs and feet using ① Digital Duo Modeling Agency\Anatomical Poses?

8. Can I build the digital three-quarter view in proper perspective?

9. Even though the images have been retouched and adjusted, do I understand how to make further adjustments to the photos in the Digital Duo Modeling Agency folder on ①?

10. Can I elongate or shorten particular areas of a croquis? Do I know which tool(s) and procedures to use in various scenarios?

Chapter 11 DVD Extra

Explore additional poses and details for your digital fashion croquis by completing the following DVD Extra tutorial. This tutorial can be found on ② Ch11\DVD Extra 11.1.

DVD Extra 11.1

This tutorial asks you to apply what you learned in Tutorials 11.1 and 11.2 in order to create the back view of a digital croquis. Using the latest features of Illustrator®, you should be able to re-create the muscular anatomy of the back with near-photographic realness (Figure 11.47).

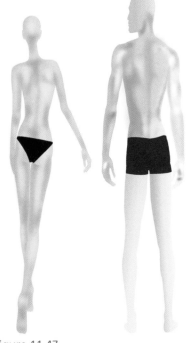

Figure 11.47

Fashion Design Art with Illustrator® and Photoshop®

Objectives

In this chapter, you will add depth and definition to your digital fashion croquis. Several tutorials are devoted to creating and enhancing apparel on male and female fashion figures by combining the effects of both Illustrator® and Photoshop®. After completing each tutorial in this chapter, you will understand how to:

◎ Use the layer compatibility of Illustrator® and Photoshop® to create digital fashion art and 3-D illusions by using style effects, gradient tinting, tools, filters, color correction, and more

◎ Personalize your work by adding digital painting techniques to your exported vector graphics in Photoshop®

◎ Enhance frontal, three-quarter, and back views of male and female fashion croquis using "Digital Duo" techniques

◎ Use Adobe Vector Smart graphics to create and transfer action flats, stitches, and more created in Illustrator® into Photoshop® and back again for further modifications via a temporary folder

◎ Digitally dress the fashion croquis and adjust pattern fills on figures

The "Digital Duo" and New Fashion Design Art

Adobe Systems has gradually added more raster features to Illustrator® to help you produce virtual digital realism. By adding features like the Photoshop® Effects Gallery, Live Trace, and Fades, the program is now more versatile. These upgrades are an asset to anyone who favors vector digital art, but for those who make use of the entire Adobe Creative Suite, even more flexibility is available. Plainly, vector graphics are greatly improved when exported to Photoshop® (a raster-based software program). Inevitably, as technology progresses, these programs and others like them will soon merge.

The strength of combining Illustrator® and Photoshop®, rather than using the programs independently, lies in what makes them different. Vector software has an animated appearance with crisp edges, but this still does not allow you to completely change the composition of the parts that you render. Fortunately, when vector graphics are rasterized, the best features are set, and an ability to affect the converted pixels is accessed. This process allows you to use the filters and painting features of raster-based programs, and produce illusions.

Fashion design and merchandising presentations that are created using vector and raster software programs separately are acceptable, but combining their features portrays realistic idealism through 3-D-looking croquis figures, presentation flats, textiles, and digital fashion sketches. Depending upon your skills, the technique can even blur the lines between fashion illustration and photography as a type of virtual digital realism. E-commerce has already proven that realistic digital images of apparel and accessories, if marketed securely, can result in immediate sales. What more is there to say? This is the "new" fashion design art.

The combination of vector and raster graphics has been referred to throughout this book as the "Digital Duo." These procedures when combined with fashion art/design, fine art, and all-inclusive digital environments form the core of fashion abstractrealism (Figure 12.1).

Note: *Files that originate in Illustrator® must be exported to Photoshop® in the CMYK color mode to prevent merging of the layers. Once exported, convert the file to RGB mode in Photoshop® to use certain raster features, such as the Filter Gallery. Go to Menu Bar > Image > Mode > RGB to change the color mode.*

Figure 12.1 **Illustration by Stacy Stewart Smith.**

The digital frontal-view croquis figures in this tutorial are treated with the care of sculpture. In fact, digital software is more kindred to a 3-D carving or casting than flat disciplines such as freehand fashion illustration on paper. You will discover this as you enhance your own frontal-view croquis figure using the "Digital Duo" techniques of this tutorial.

To complete this tutorial, use the file Eve_Undone. pdf on ① Ch12\Tutorial 12.1.

Note: This tutorial was written to complement CS5 and later upgrades; however, if you are operating earlier versions of Illustrator®, you can still follow the steps.

Step 1: Export Your Completed Croquis

1. Open Eve_Undone.pdf in Illustrator®.

2. Go to *Menu Bar > File > Export*. An Export dialog box appears.

3. Locate the file format pull-down menu, and select Photoshop® (*.psd*).

4. Click *Save (Mac)* or *Export (PC)*. A Photoshop® **Export Options** dialog box appears. The default settings are fine for this tutorial, but the resolution should be at least 150 ppi or higher.

5. Check the **Write Layers** feature to retain the layer compositing.

6. Check **Maximum Editability**, which allows your exported file to be used efficiently by the version of the program that it will be opened in next.

7. Check **Anti-Alias** to prevent your file from having fragmented edges associated with bitmapping and to maintain the vector smoothness.

The program will save your new Photoshop® file in the last location that you saved the Illustrator® file, but if you want to save it in a new location, choose one from the menu. The title will remain the same, but the format identifying extension will be changed to *.psd* (Figure 12.2).

Step 2: Create Shadows with the Burn Tool

1. Select the layer containing the torso of your croquis. In Chapter 11, this layer was named *General Outline*.

2. Lock and toggle off the visibility of the other layers, which will prevent you from writing on them by mistake. The *General Outline* layer has

a few areas that need attention: the neck, the torso, and the legs. In most cases, unless you are designing swimwear, you will not need to improve the entire body of your croquis. However, it is an excellent idea to go ahead and do so, because some garments will require you to show more of the body. This is especially true of sheer garments.

3. Select the Zoom Tool (Z) from the Photoshop® Tools panel and bring up your Navigator panel. Use the Zoom Tool (Z) and perform a marquee around the torso area of the croquis for a closer view of that area.

The Burn Tool (O)

4. Begin by using the Burn Tool (O) to darken the areas on the sides of the torso. Select the Burn Tool (O) in the Tools panel. You will notice that the cursor's icon turns into an empty circle. This circle indicates the brush size. Make additional adjustments to the *Angle* (turn of the brushstroke), *Roundness* (elliptical shape of the brushstroke), and the *Spacing* (stippling of the brushstroke).

5. To temporarily change the brush size, use the menu in the Control Panel. On some laptops, you can hold two fingers on the trackpad and click to access the brush menu. Another way to access the brush menu is to press Option and click or right-click. The brush size will be adjusted several times during this tutorial, but for now the brush diameter (*Size*) should be between 45 px and 80 px.

6. Change the *Hardness* to about 10% to 20%. In addition, adjust the **Range** in the Options Bar to **Shadows**. This will prevent the effect of the Burn Tool (O) from becoming too dark.

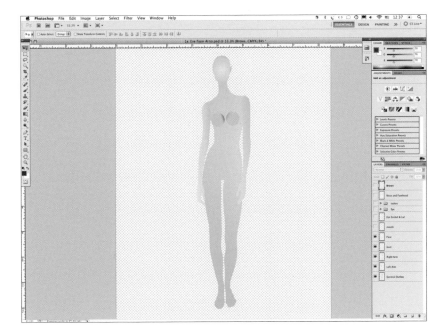

Figure 12.2

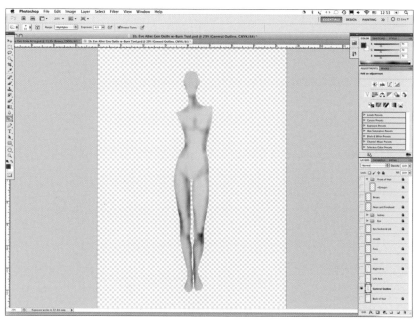

Figure 12.3

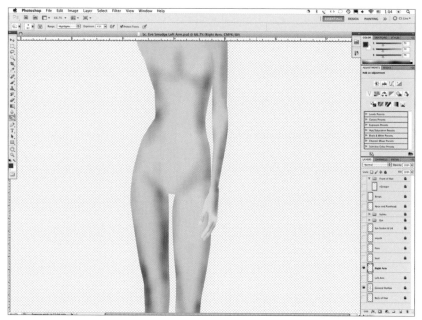

Figure 12.4

Test a Burn Spot

7. With the Burn Tool (O) selected, click anywhere on the croquis figure; this action will leave a round darkened spot.

8. Press *Cmd+Z / Ctrl+Z* to undo this move. This was only a test. Now that you know how the tool works, put it to good use. We can affect the color of the figure with the Burn Tool (O) by clicking and holding the mouse as we move along in a round, sweeping motion. Do not forget to use the Navigator panel to access the areas easily.

9. Start with one side of the torso. Move the cursor to the edge of the figure; click and hold the mouse while you move it along the edge (Figure 12.3). If the impression is too dark, simply undo the move and adjust the *Hardness* in the Brush panel.

How Much Burn?

10. Continue this burn action to create the 3-D illusion all around the figure. Build the muscle tone by mimicking what's in the photograph, but do not overdo it.

11. Shadows should be darker than other areas. The lighter areas are called midtones. The first application will produce midtones.

12. To create shadows, simply go over the darkened midtones with the Burn Tool (O) again. Practice this a few times to create the desired effect.

13. After you complete the *General Outline* layer, work on other parts of the body.

Note: *Photos of models can help with identifying where to place shadows.*

Step 3: Add Definition to the Arms

In this practice tutorial, the layers containing the arms should be left separate from the others because the hands are on them. This layer is also above the *General Outline* layer.

Note: *If the layers with the arms are merged, you will never be able to place them above the clothing later.*

Once you have had ample practice with the Burn Tool (O), you will feel comfortable enough to try it on the rest of the body.

1. Toggle off the visibility of all the layers except for the *Left Arm*.

2. Lock all the other nonvisible layers.

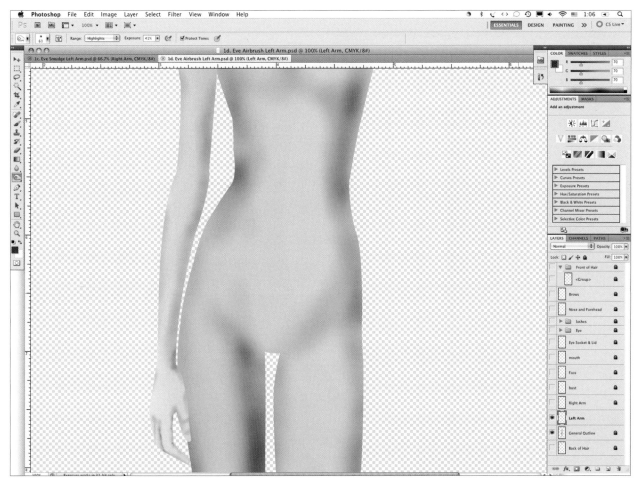

Figure 12.5

3. Use the Burn Tool (O), but begin with a smaller brush size and remember to keep glancing at the original photo for direction as to the placement and the intensity of your shadows and midtones (Figure 12.4).

4. Repeat this process for the right arm (Figure 12.5).

Step 4: Blend the Separated Parts

When you have touched up both arms with the Burn Tool (O), toggle on the visibility of the *General Outline* layer. You may notice that there is a visible difference between the positions where the shoulders meet the torso (Figure 12.6). To remedy this in both the male and female croquis, do the following:

1. Select the Smudge Tool from the Tools panel.

2. Adjust the brush size to a diameter that fits the curve of the arm, and then reduce the *Strength* in the Options Bar to about 50% (or whatever works for you as you experiment).

3. Gently click and drag the Smudge Tool from the arm to spread pixels over the *General Outline* layer (Figure 12.7). This should look like the natural curve over the shoulder. If you make a mistake, press *Cmd+Z / Ctrl+Z* to undo the move.

Step 5: Blend with Bristle Brushes

New features in Photoshop® CS5 and CS6 include bristle brushes that simulate fine art painting techniques. They are a feature of the Brush Tool (B) attributes and appear when you adjust the brush size.

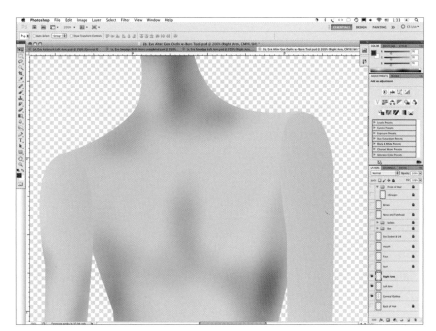

Figure 12.6

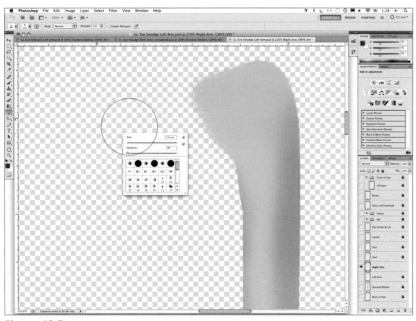
Figure 12.7

Figure 12.8

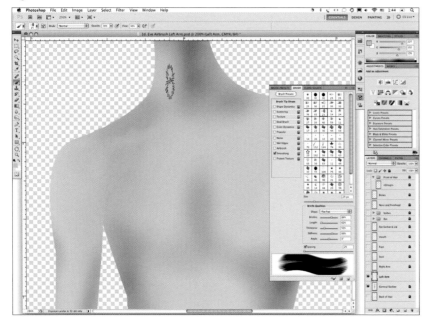
Figure 12.9

There are several ways to do this, including showing the Brush Presets panel, which appears when you select the painting Workspace. Another way to locate the panel is to go to *Menu Bar > Window > Brush Presets*. These new brushes have icons that look and perform like fine art paintbrushes.

1. Select the **Flat Fan High Bristle Count** brush from the Brush Presets panel.

2. In the Options Bar, adjust the size of the brush.

3. Reduce the *Opacity* to about 30% to 40%.

4. Reduce the *Flow* to 80%. This allows you to build the soft effects and make them look seamless, creating the illusion of skin to cover the raw look left by the Smudge Tool (Figures 12.8 and 12.9).

5. Select the appropriate layer and lock the others. Keep the *General Outline* and the *Right Arm* and *Left Arm* layers visible.

TIP: Bristle Brush Preview

To see an animation of any of the art brushes in Photoshop®, toggle the Bristle Brush Preview by clicking the icon at the bottom of the Photoshop® Brush panel. It looks like an eye with a brush beneath it.

Selecting Hues

The term hue refers to a specific color or shade. Flesh tones are composed of many different colors with slightly similar tints, tones, and shades within one range (see Chapter 9.) You need to select appropriate hues to cover and blend certain areas. To select a specific hue from a gradient with the Brush Tool in Photoshop® following these steps:

1. Hold the Option key (Mac) or the Alt key (PC).

2. When the Photoshop® Eyedropper Tool icon appears, click on the portion of the rendering that closely matches the hue space you need to blend. The selected hue will appear in the Set Foreground Color box of the Tools panel.

3. Apply the strokes gently by clicking and dragging with the tool as if you were using real paint on a surface.

4. Use short, sweeping movements, but do not go outside the area of the croquis.

5. Do not overdo it. If you do go outside the boundaries of the figure, you will stain the background. If this happens, simply select the Eraser Tool (E). Use it with a brush of an appropriate size to remove the error.

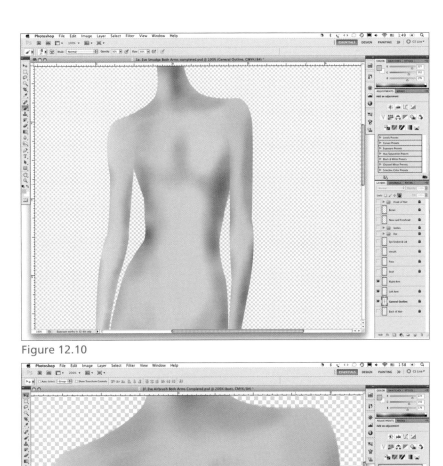

Figure 12.10

6. Work on one arm at a time and then compare one to the other as well as to the coloration of the entire croquis (Figure 12.10).

Step 6: Perfect the Bust

The *Bust* layer contains two elliptical shapes filled with flesh-toned radial gradients. However, some of the features of Illustrator® may have left them looking extremely artificial. This layer was created separately from the *General Outline* for the purpose of teaching the concept of dimension. These two layers will be merged when you have completed work on them.

1. Select the Bust layer and unlock it.

2. Select, hold, and move the *Bust* layer—below the two layers containing the arms. This will keep the illusion anatomically correct because the arms should blend into the bust in the upper chest cavity (*General Outline*).

3. Keep the *General Outline, Left Arm,* and *Right Arm* layers visible but locked.

4. To create a beautiful bust, begin with the Smudge Tool and use an appropriately sized brush to smooth the exported elliptical shapes upward into the chest cavity (Figure 12.11).

5. Use the Burn Tool (O) to delineate the shadows on the underside of the bust, but do not make the shadows too dark (Figure 12.12).

6. Next, use the art brushes with the Brush Tool (B) as we did previously with the arms. Smooth out the transition between the chest and the elliptical shapes. Select samples of different hues as needed by clicking while holding *Option / Alt*.

Step 7: Add Highlights with the Photoshop® Dodge Tool

The Photoshop® Dodge Tool lightens pixels and is located in the same suite as the Burn Tool (O). We will use it to add highlights to those areas of the croquis that are convex, starting with the bust. Continue to glance at the photo in order to properly distribute the highlights.

Figure 12.11

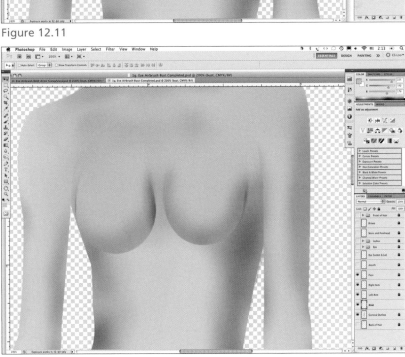

Figure 12.12

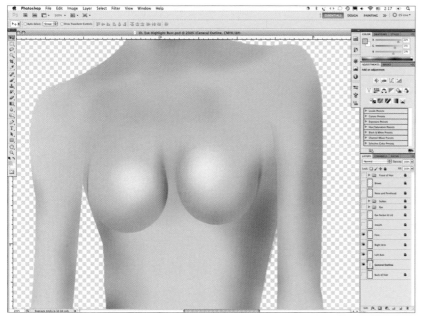

Figure 12.13

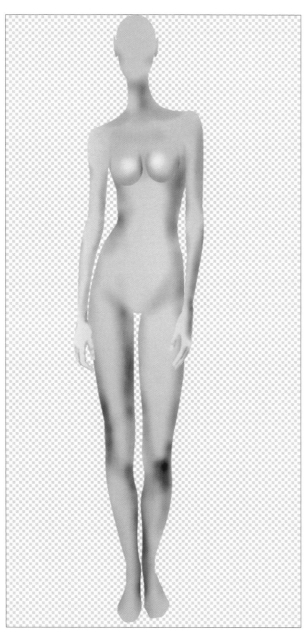

Figure 12.14 Illustration by Stacy Stewart Smith.

1. Select the Dodge Tool (O) in the Tools panel.

2. In the Options Bar menu, reduce the *Exposure* to less than 50% and adjust the *Range* to Midtones.

3. The brush size will also need adjusting.

4. Look at the photo and note the need to add highlights to the bust in the middle portion close to the cleavage.

5. Use the Dodge Tool in short, careful, and rounded stroke motions to add the highlights.

6. If the Exposure is too intense, simply show your History panel by going to *Menu Bar > Window > History*. Go back in your stages by selecting the history levels, with the most recent being at the bottom, to begin again with a lower setting.

The finished product should look somewhat like the example (Figure 12.13).

Step 8: Merge the Bust with the General Outline

As discussed earlier, merge the *Bust* layer with the *General Outline* layer.

1. Unlock the *General Outline* layer, which should be right below the unlocked *Bust* layer.

2. Select both these layers by holding the Shift key.

3. Go to *Menu Bar > Layer > Merge Layers* or Press *Cmd+E / Ctrl+E*.

The completed female frontal view croquis shows extreme enhancements (Figure 12.14) when compared to the original exported file.

Organizing and Merging Hidden Layers

When Illustrator® files are exported to Photoshop®, the filters are often packaged into group folders. This usually happens if you created more than one object on a layer before exporting the file. To reveal the contents of the folder in Photoshop®, click the pointer (arrow) next to it. You may need to reorder the sublayers within the group folder so that the parts and effects can be merged effectively into a single layer. Remember that the filter sublayers need to appear above the parts that they modify.

In this tutorial, you will apply what you learned in Tutorial 12.1 to a three-quarter-view fashion croquis. The Photoshop® Liquify filter and Puppet Warp setting will help you to produce the illusion of agility and to change poses.

To help you complete this tutorial, male and female croquis created in Illustrator® and their photo references have been provided on ② Ch12\Tutorial 12.2. You may also choose to use your own three-quarter-view croquis that you completed for Tutorial 11.2.

Step 1: Export Your Croquis

Follow the steps in Tutorial 12.1 and export the croquis to Photoshop® (Figures 12.15 and 12.16). The Gaussian Blur features will be shown in the Photoshop® Layers panel. Merge them with the layers that they modify.

Note: Often Photoshop® will package objects that were created on one layer in Illustrator® into a group

folder. If the filters that you created have been packaged, simply tip the pointer on that layer to open the folder, then select the layers and pull them above the body part layer. Merge the layers by selecting them and pressing *Cmd+E / Ctrl+E.*

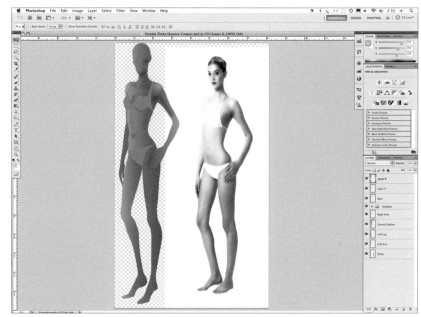

Figure 12.15

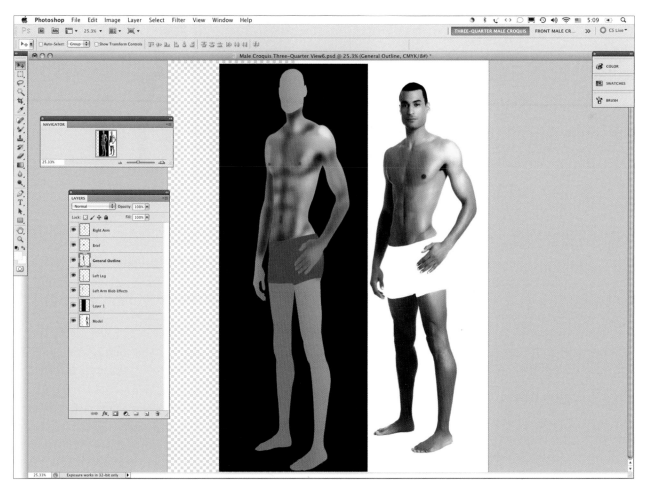

Figure 12.16

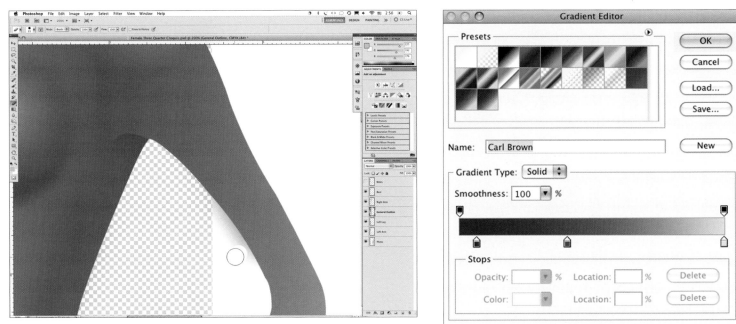

Figure 12.17

Figure 12.18 Photoshop® Gradient Editor.

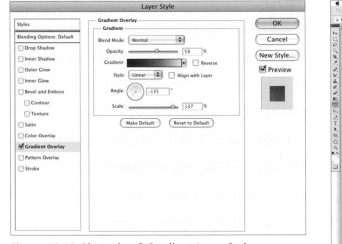

Figure 12.19 Photoshop® Gradient Layer Style.

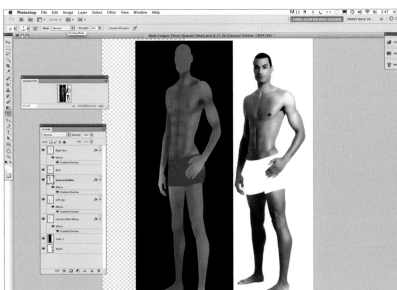

Figure 12.20

Step 2: Erase Excess Blur

The Gaussian Blur filter may have stained the area around the figure (Figure 12.17). Locate the layer(s) containing the problems, and use the Photoshop® Eraser Tool (E) to remove the stained edges. Be careful not to erase portions of your croquis's form. Remove only the misty parts, and then use the Blur Tool to reduce the fragments.

Step 3: Add a Gradient Overlay Layer Style

The high contrast of the Illustrator® filter effects can give your croquis an almost plastic look. To tone the filter effects in Photoshop®, add the Gradient Overlay Layer Style.

1. Prepare a flesh-toned gradient (see Tutorial 9.6, Step Two). The Gradient Editor is shown in Figure 12.18.

2. Select the *General Outline* layer, and then click on the *fx* icon at the bottom of the Layers panel. Scroll to the Gradient Overlay Layer Style.

3. In the Layer Style dialog box, click on the Gradient Bar and choose the gradient that you created.

4. Move the slider to reduce the *Opacity* of the gradient to 58%. This reveals the croquis's definition yet reduces its contrast (Figure 12.19). Adjust the *Scale* and *Angle* to change the gradient's position. Record the information and repeat the procedure for the arm and leg layers (Figure 12.20).

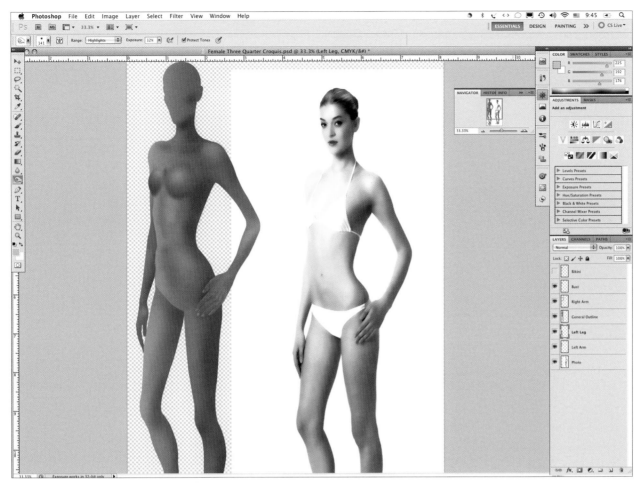

Figure 12.21

Step 4: Continue to Add Shadows and Highlights

Continue to use the photo reference to add shadows with the Burn Tool (O) and highlights with the Dodge Tool (O) as previously instructed. Remember to reduce the settings in the Options Bar to obtain the best results. Periodically save and back up your file. Figure 12.21 shows the effect of the tools on the female croquis as they were observed in the photo.

Step 5: Link the Layers

Select all the layers, and click the Link Layers icon at the bottom left of the panel. This allows you to move the entire croquis around the page. When you have done this, chain icons appear on each layer.

Step 6: Relax and Trim with the Photoshop® Liquify Filter

You can use the Liquify filter to move segments of parts and trim the overall form.

1. Select a layer that you want to modify and go to *Menu Bar > Filter > Liquify*.

2. Use the tools to slightly adjust the pose and the dimensions of your croquis when the Liquify window opens (Figure 12.22).

3. Readjust the other parts accordingly (Figure 12.23).

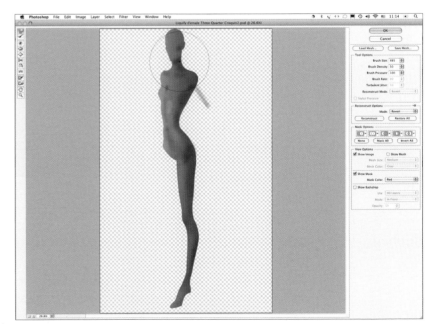

Figure 12.22

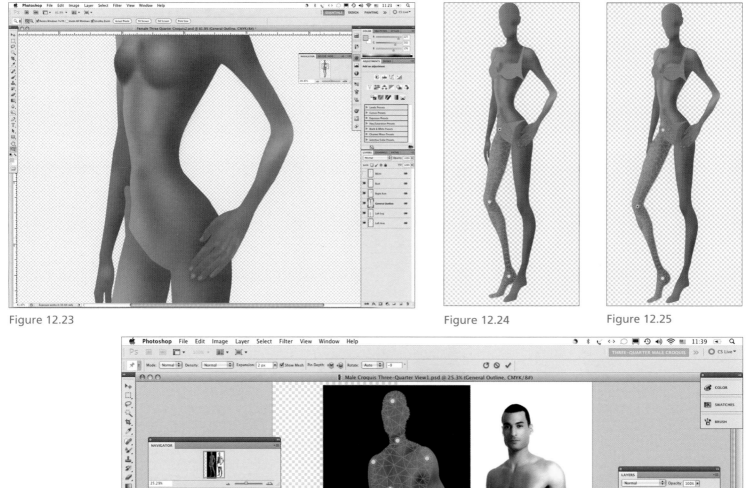

Figure 12.23

Figure 12.24   Figure 12.25

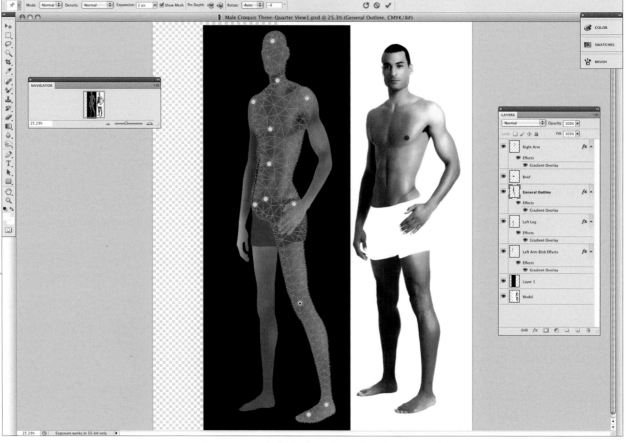

Figure 12.26 Puppet Warp pins are yellow in CS5 default, but the color changes in later versions.

Step 7: Use Photoshop® Puppet Warp to Adjust the Pose

You can use the Photoshop® Puppet Warp to change the position of parts with controlled mapping (see Tutorial 7.4, Step Five.) In order to control the mapping, you must click on it at strategic points to add yellow pins (Figures 12.24–12.26). Experiment with creating different poses by clicking on the pins.

Before moving on to the next tutorial, take a moment to review the tips for working in Photoshop® that are listed in Box 12.1.

Box 12.1: "Digital Duo" Tips for Photoshop®

1. Continue to make photo comparisons, but take into consideration that an illustration, even a digital one, is not a photograph.

2. Use Hue/Saturation and other filters to adjust the color of your image if the effects of the Burn Tool (O) are too dark even at a low *Exposure*. Use the *Range* switcher in the Options Bar to affect the highlights, midtones, or shadows on each layer.

3. The filters you used may have caused some separating issues that cannot be seen on a white or transparent ground. Add an adjustment layer below the others and fill it with black. Zoom in to examine the figure and fix any problems by using painting techniques, the Clone Stamp Tool (S), and others.

4. You must develop your digital painting skills with practice. Correct mistakes rather than start over. The process will strengthen you even if you do not use the outcome of the effort in the tutorial steps.

5. Give your eyes a rest at intervals. Periodically, when working on a lengthy project, step away from it and do something else. When you do come back to the work, your creative eye will have been refreshed and you will see clearly what corrections need to be made.

6. Make copies of your work in stages, so you can go back a few steps if needed after saving a file.

7. Practice drawing freehand and take fine art and fashion figure drawing courses repeatedly. The experience will challenge you and improve your critical analysis of digital renderings.

8. Do not flatten the croquis files. Keep your figure in parts, because it will help you to reorder them properly when rendering clothing on the pose. Besides, you can open the files again in Illustrator® to work on them in the same layers. You can even create new croquis figures from these parts.

This tutorial teaches you how to add clothing to the figure by using vector tools. It begins with instructions for placing Photoshop® (raster) objects in Illustrator® files without a white background. You will then learn to draw a knife-pleated skirt and place it on a back-view croquis. You will also use the Warp features to adjust apparel and accessory items.

To help you complete this tutorial, the file Female_backview.pdf has been provided on ② Ch12\Tutorial 12.3. You may also choose to use your own back-view croquis if you completed the DVD Extra in Chapter 11.

Step 1: Place a Completed Back-View Croquis in Illustrator®

1. Open your file in Photoshop®, and then select the image by pressing *Cmd+A / Ctrl+A*.

2. Save the file in the Photoshop® format.

3. Cut the image (copy it to the clipboard) by pressing *Cmd+X / Ctrl+X*.

4. Load Illustrator® and create a file.

5. Go to *Menu Bar > File > Place*.

6. Use the Place menu to locate the file that you saved in Photoshop®.

7. Select the file from the menu, and then click OK. A **Photoshop Import Options** dialog box appears the first time you do this (Figure 12.27).

8. Check *Convert Layers to Objects* in order to prevent flattening the image (Mac), and then click

OK. When the file is placed in Photoshop® it will not have a background.

9. Click the Embed button in the Control Panel to make the file a permanent part of your Illustrator® file.

10. Save your file.

Note: *When you import your croquis or apparel design files back to Illustrator®, they will not be editable. If you discover problems, you can start over with the original Photoshop® file and save a copy. Another option is to export them again to Photoshop®, after you have finished in Illustrator®, to clean up the file.*

Step 2: Add a Layer for Clothing

Step 3: Render One Item of Clothing on Each Layer

In this tutorial, we are examining the back view of a pleated skirt on the body in motion. The first step would be to create an overall silhouette of the skirt with any rendering tool. Consider the action that is taking place in the figure. This will tell you where the skirt should swing. In the example of Figure 12.28, the skirt is swaying toward the right. Lock all the other layers and render the basic shape of your design on the croquis with a Fill of white and a Stroke of black.

Step 4: Create the Pleat Sections

You will need to decide what type of pleats that you wish to create. Knife pleats have one direction, and box pleats face one another. In this example we will create both types. A copy of the skirt was cut into halves at the centers with the Scissors Tool (C), and

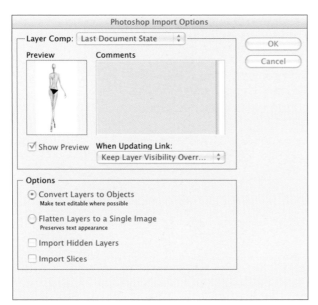

Figure 12.27

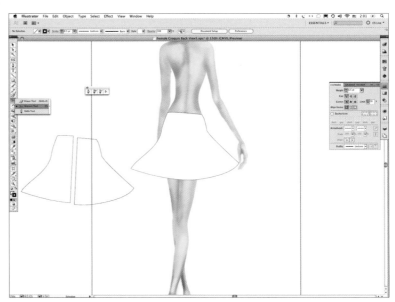

Figure 12.28

then closed at the middle with the Pen Tool (P) (Figure 12.28).

Step 5: Create the Box Pleat

Place the two halves over the original. Add anchor points at the position where you imagine the pleat closing. Place the parts into positions similar to those in Figure 12.29. Adjust the hem to show the depth of the pleats. Copy and paste the two halves, and then lock the other skirt shapes.

Step 6: Create Knife Pleats in Both Directions

Use the Direct Selection Tool (A) to adjust the anchor points on the two halves that you left unlocked from Step Five. Match the shapes on the side seams with the locked copies, but move the other side of each away from the center. Reposition the bottom to create the illusion of your first two knife pleats.

Step 7: Repeat Step Five and Adjust

Copy and paste the last set of shapes that you created, and then lock the others. Repeat the adjustments that you made in Step Six to create another knife pleat. Design your skirt with any amount or type of pleats (Figure 12.30). Add color or patterns, and then create shoes on other layers (see Tutorial 3.2). Try your hand at a top also (Figure 12.31).

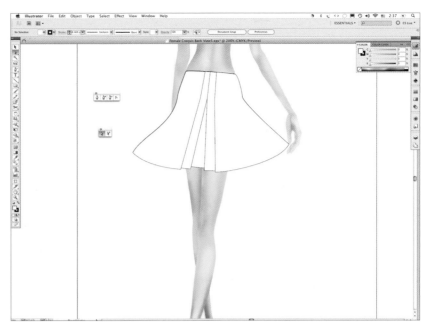

Figure 12.29

Figure 12.31

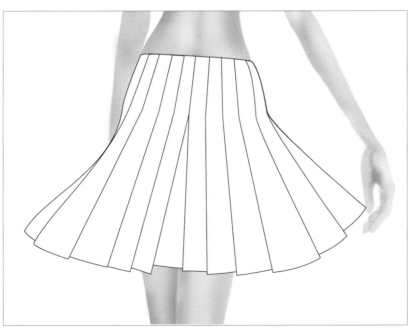

Figure 12.30

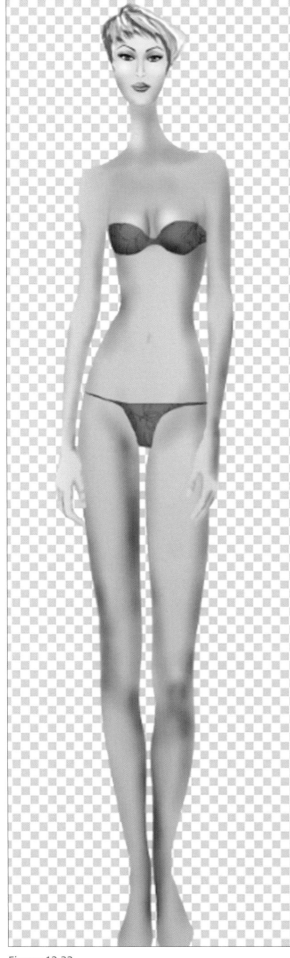

Figure 12.32

In this tutorial, you will learn to use **Vector Smart objects** to make alterations to Photoshop® files in Illustrator®, and then transfer the changes back again. You will also learn how to use Photoshop® filters and layer styles to give apparel a 3-D effect. Attention is given to draping prints created in Illustrator® on the croquis figure in Photoshop®.

Follow the tutorial by using the files provided on ②, then try it with your own croquis figures and digital apparel design concepts.

Note: If you are using Adobe CS4 or lower, the DVD files may be merged upon opening them. This will not prohibit you from following the tutorial.

Step 1: Open the Tutorial DVD Files

In this tutorial you will be working with both Illustrator® and Photoshop®. Open the file Eve_in_Undergarments.pdf (**Figure 12.32**) in Photoshop®, and then open the file Eve's_Dress.pdf, or your own digital sketch, in Illustrator® (**Figure 12.33**).

Step 2: Copy and Paste the Dress from Illustrator® into Photoshop®

1. Select the Illustrator® file and then press *Cmd+A / Ctrl+A* to select the dress.

2. Press *Cmd+C / Ctrl+C* to copy the dress to the clipboard.

3. Select the Photoshop® file, and then select the *Bra* layer.

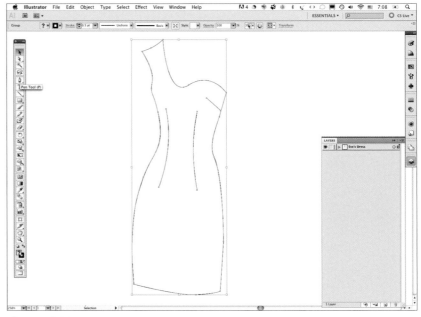

Figure 12.33

Note: *If the file has been merged, you will need to search the sublayers for the right paste position.*

4. Press *Cmd+V / Ctrl+V* to paste Eve's dress into the file.

5. In the Paste dialog box, select the *Smart Object* button, and then click OK (Figure 12.34).

Step 3: Embed the Dress in Photoshop®

When you paste the dress, it will have a Bounding Box with an X formation running through it.

1. Hold the Shift key to constrain the proportions, and generally scale the dress (Figure 12.35).

2. Double-click inside the box to Embed the Smart Object into the Photoshop® file.

3. If needed, Free Transform the shape so that the image of the dress is proportionate to Eve's form.

4. Reposition the shape (Figure 12.36).

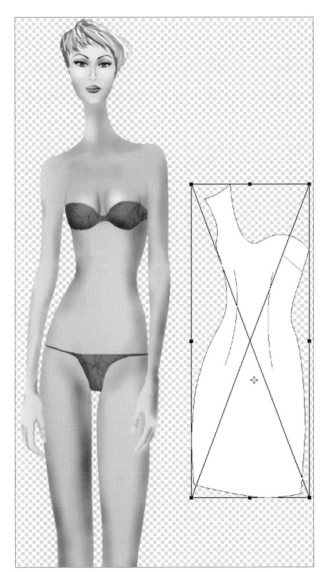

Figure 12.34

Figure 12.35

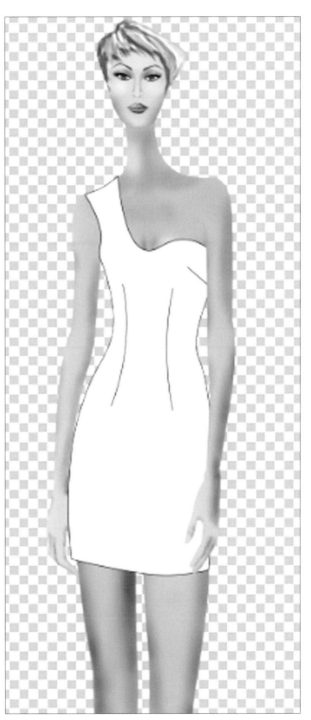

Figure 12.36

Step 4: Rename the Vector Smart Layer in Photoshop®

The layer that is created when you paste the Vector Smart Object will bear that name (Figure 12.37). The Vector Smart layer should be given another name if you plan to paste additional objects (Figure 12.38).

Step 5: Activate Vector Smart Features in Photoshop®

The **Vector Smart icon** on the left side has a small square with a small white square in front of a black one (Figure 12.37).

1. To activate the Vector Smart transfer of your pasted object to a **temporary folder**—and open the dress back in Illustrator®—double-click on this icon.

2. The Photoshop® instructional dialog box that appears explains how to save the document so that the changes you make will be updated in the Photoshop® file, as well (Figure 12.39).

3. Click OK to proceed, and the Illustrator® originating file opens.

Step 6: Make Vector Smart Changes to the Dress in Illustrator®

Refine the bust area or make any other design changes to the file by using Illustrator® tools (Figure 12.40).

Step 7: Save the File in Illustrator® to Update It in Photoshop®

Go to *Menu Bar > File > Save* in Illustrator® (Figure 12.41). Click the Save button to update whatever changes you have made to the Vector Smart Object in the Photoshop® file (Figure 12.42).

Step 8: Fill the Clothing with a Pattern

Fill the dress with a pattern from the Illustrator® Pattern Libraries (Figure 12.43). Patterns such as plaids, checks, stripes, and other repeats tend to appear flat and artificial in a digital environment, but you can rectify this in Photoshop®.

Step 9: Use the Liquify Filter to Align the Pattern

1. With the *Vector Smart Dress* layer selected, go to *Menu Bar > Filter > Liquify*, or press *Shift+Cmd+X / Shift+Ctrl+X*.

2. When the Liquify window appears, use the Zoom Tool (Z) on the left side of this window to zoom in on the transparent pixel grid.

3. Check **Show Backdrop** located on the bottom right, so that you can see the croquis.

Figure 12.37   Figure 12.38

Figure 12.39

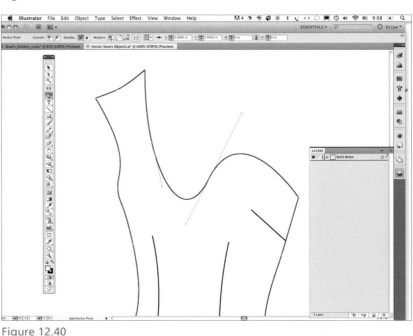

Figure 12.40

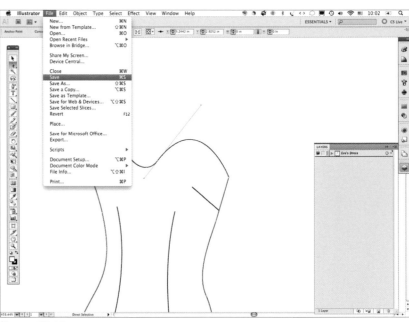

Figure 12.41

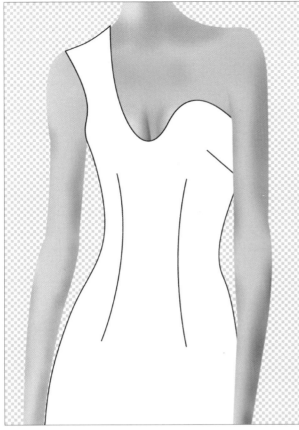

Figure 12.42

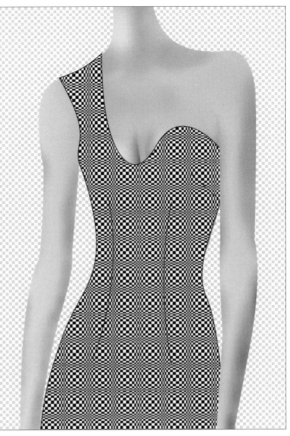

Figure 12.43

4. Choose the Forward Warp Tool and adjust the brush as needed.

5. Reposition the flow of the pattern so that it looks as if it were naturally pulling over the figure beneath. The objective here is to slowly pull the pattern without distorting the silhouette. Therefore, do not place too much pressure on the sides.

6. Slowly pull the horizontal lines into place the way a pattern would flow over the contours of the body (Figure 12.44).

7. Once you are satisfied with the croquis, click OK to return to the file window.

Note: Expect some slight imperfections, which will make the garment more believable as a 3-D illusion.

Step 10: Add a Color Overlay

Apply a few Layer Styles to enhance the 3-D illusion. Access to these are located at the bottom of the Layers panel.

1. Click the *fx* icon and scroll to Bevel and Emboss.

2. A dialog box appears.

3. Adjust the settings according to your preference, but be certain to reduce the *Opacity* of the *Shadow*.

4. Select *Color Overlay* from the menu at the left of the dialog box.

5. When this window appears, click on the *Opacity* slider to reduce the amount of the tint. Click on the Color Swatch on the right in order to change the hue (Figure 12.45).

Note: All of these features can be applied to flats. You will learn more about flats later in the book.

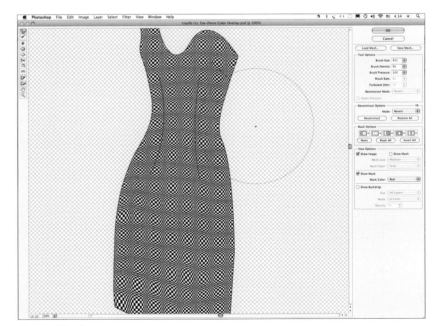

Figure 12.44

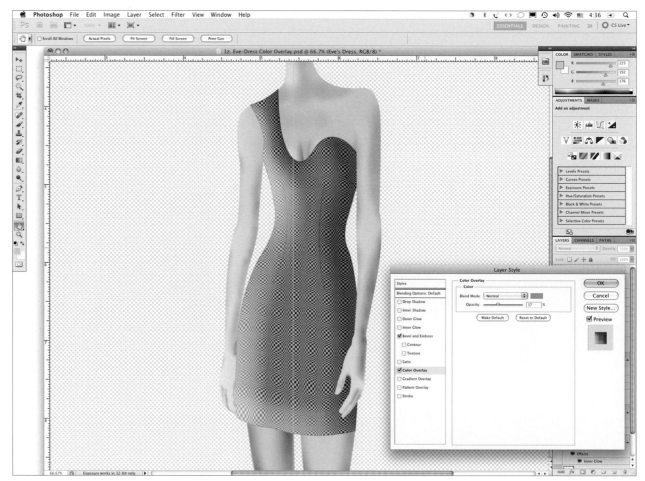

Figure 12.45 Layer Styles Bevel and Emboss and Color Overlay were added to the dress.

Step 11: Finish the Look with Boots

This look would be incomplete without accessories. Follow the steps below to create patent leather boots. You will also be introduced to a new tool: the Magnetic Lasso Tool (L).

1. Create a new layer above the *General Outline* layer and name it *Left Boot*.

2. Select the Magnetic Lasso Tool (L) from the same suite where the Photoshop® Magic Wand Tool is positioned. You may need to scroll to it by holding the pointer.

3. Use the Magnetic Lasso Tool (L) to encapsulate an area of the left leg as if you were creating a sock. The tool will detect the shape of the leg and pin anchors onto its perimeter.

4. In order to lock in the selection, click when you come to the spot where you began to generate the selection.

5. This tool is tricky and can cause problems, so as soon as you have finished and see the marching ants, select the Move Tool (V) to exit. This will prevent you from accidentally creating another selection.

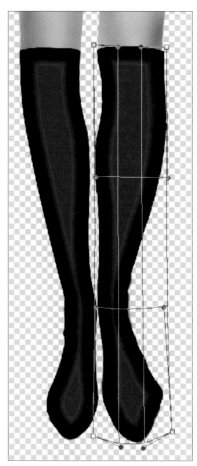

Figure 12.46

6. Fill the selection with black by going to *Menu Bar > Edit > Fill > Black.*

7. Repeat these steps for the other leg after you have created a *Right Boot* layer above this one.

Step 12: Make Wrinkles with the Smudge Tool

To complete the boots, use the Smudge Tool with a hard brush to bring out the shapes. The Eraser Tool (E) will come in handy to clean up the edges.

Step 13: Add Layer Styles to the Boots

If so desired, apply any Layer Style such as Inner Glow, Bevel and Emboss, or Outer Glow to improve the 3-D effect of the boots. Style them to suit your own design aesthetic.

Step 14: Warp the Boots

Form the overall shape of the boots by going to *Menu Bar > Edit > Transform > Warp.* A grid appears around the boot. You can make adjustments to the overall silhouette of the boot by pulling the grid and direction lines. This creates a more realistic shape (Figure 12.46).

Step 15: Finish Your Croquis

To get the most out of the "Digital Duo" procedures, do not be afraid to experiment. All of the tools in each program work together to help you create individual fashion design presentations. To complete this look, use the Warp feature of the Transform menu on the *Dress* layer to further enhance the drapery effect. Use the Burn Tool (O) to add shadows, and the Dodge Tool (O) to add highlights where needed. The "Digital Duo" evolution of Eve, from Illustrator® to Photoshop® and back again, with Vector Smart Objects is shown in Figure 12.47.

Figure 12.47 **Illustration by Stacy Stewart Smith.**

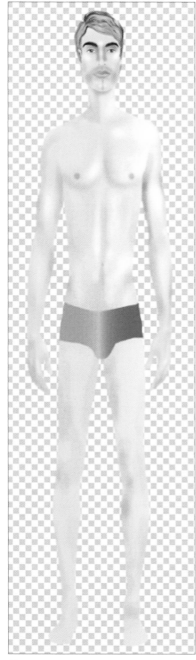

Tutorial 12.5
EXPORT APPAREL DESIGNS FROM ILLUSTRATOR® AND ENHANCE THEM ON CROQUIS IN PHOTOSHOP®

You have already learned how to enhance croquis figures by exporting Illustrator® files to Photoshop®. Because you have a fixed pose, apparel can be designed in Illustrator®, and then modified in Photoshop® through layer compositing.

Follow the tutorial by using the files provided on ② Ch12\Tutorial 12.5, and then try it with your own croquis figure and digital apparel design concepts.

Note: *If you are using Adobe CS4 or lower, the DVD files may be merged upon opening them. This will not prohibit you from following the tutorial.*

Step 1: Open the Tutorial DVD Files

In this tutorial, you will be working with both Illustrator® and Photoshop®. Open Brad_in_Underwear.pdf (**Figure 12.48**) in Photoshop®, and Brad's_Clothes.pdf in Illustrator® (**Figure 12.49**).

Step 2: Study the Layers in Illustrator®

The file Brad's_Clothes.pdf contains everything that you need to follow the tutorial. Show the Layers panel and you will discover that the articles of clothing have been rendered in Illustrator® on various layers. The jacket has been constructed on even more layers. This layer compositing will help you add dimension when you export the file to Photoshop® (**Figure 12.49**).

Step 3: Export the Illustrator® File to Photoshop®

1. Open any frontal-view croquis in Illustrator®.
2. Go to *Menu Bar > File > Export*. The Export dialog box appears.
3. Locate the file format pull-down menu, and Select Photoshop *.psd*.
4. Click *Save (Mac)* or *Export (PC)*. The Photoshop **Export Options** dialog box appears. The default settings are fine for this tutorial, but the resolution should be at least 150 (ppi) or higher.
5. Check the *Write Layers* feature to retain the layer compositing.

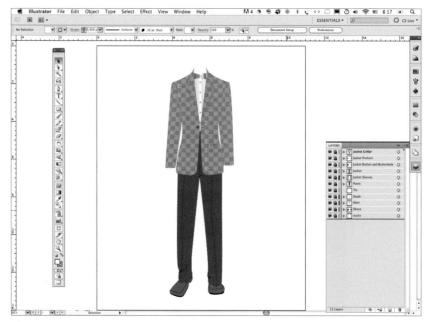

Figure 12.48   Figure 12.49

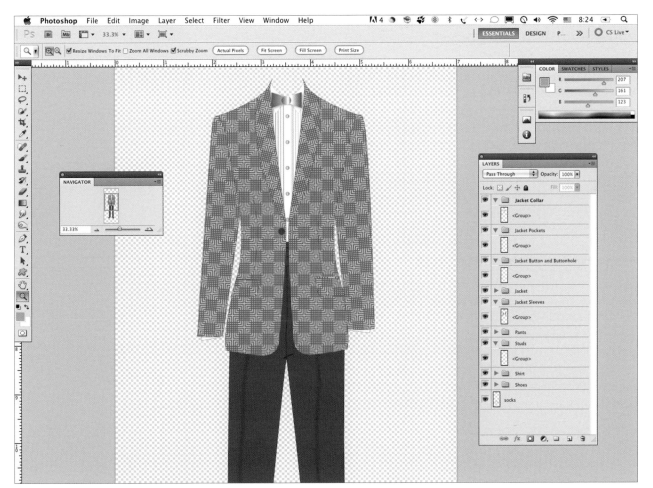

Figure 12.50

6. Check *Maximum Editability*, which allows your exported file to be used efficiently by the version of the program that it will become.

7. Check *Anti-Alias* to prevent your file from having fragmented edges associated with bitmapping and to maintain the vector smoothness (Figure 12.50).

The program will save your new Photoshop® file in the last location that you saved the Illustrator® file, but if you want to save it in a new location, choose one from the menu. The title will remain the same, but the format identifying extension will be changed to *.psd*.

Step 4: Drag and Drop Brad into the Photoshop® File

1. Set up the new Photoshop® file Brad's_Clothes. pdf and the Brad_in_Underwear.pdf file that you opened side by side (Figure 12.51).

2. Hold the Shift key and select all the layers of the Brad_in_Underwear.pdf file.

3. Use the Move Tool (V) to drag and drop the cro- quis into the apparel file.

4. Collect these layers into a Group folder by click- ing the Create a New Group icon at the bottom of the Photoshop® Layers panel.

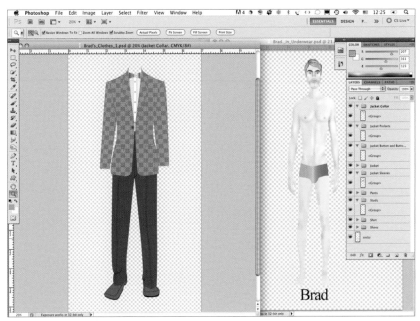

Figure 12.51

5. Hold the Shift key again, and select and drag the croquis layers into the folder. Name it *Croquis*. Select and Align the Croquis Group with the apparel.

Step 5: Enhance the Apparel with Photoshop® Features

In many previous tutorials, you learned to use Photoshop® filters, tools, and panels to enhance the 3-D look of your files. Try a few of these on the apparel layers. The Inner Shadow Layer Style was used on the *Pants* layer; Bevel and Emboss was applied to the *Shoes* layer. The Burn Tool (O) and the Dodge Tool (O) effects were applied to the *Jacket* layers. Adjust the *Range* in the Options Bar to achieve the best results. Certain colors will be affected by switching to *Highlights*, and others will show enhancements with the *Midtones* or *Shadow* settings.

Step 6: Convert the File to RGB

Because the files were exported from Illustrator® in the CMYK color mode, some features of Photoshop® will not work. In order to use the Photoshop® Filter Gallery, you will need to convert the file to the RGB color mode by going to *Menu Bar > Image > Mode > RGB*. The Rough Pastels filter was added to the *Pants* layer to give them the illusion of texture. The completed look is shown in Figure 12.52.

Figure 12.52 Illustration by Stacy Stewart Smith.

When you need to use objects created from paths and fill them with patterns in Photoshop®, you may encounter a few difficulties in manipulating them. Naturally, there are a number of ways to do things, but the goal here is to present a few options that will help you create prints and patterns with a 3-D look.

The end use of your project will always substantiate the logic behind your procedures. For instance, if your objective is to show the general overall look of apparel on the figure in an average page-size view, use the drawing and painting attributes of Photoshop®. However, if you need more precise lines and details (technical flats), creating files in Illustrator®, and then exporting them to Photoshop® is appropriate.

You have already practiced exporting files in the earlier tutorials of this chapter. Now you will use the full Photoshop® method with the Photoshop® Pen Tool Suite and the Paths panel.

To complete this tutorial, use full-length photos of Carl from the ① Digital Duo Modeling Agency.

Step 1: Open a New Document and Place a Photo of Carl

Load Photoshop®. Create a new letter-size document with a white background at 300 ppi (Figure 12.53). The resolution can be reduced later. Place a croquis figure or a photo into the file on a separate layer (Figure 12.54). Save and back up your file on an external disk.

Step 2: Use the Photoshop® Pen Tool and the Paths Panel

The Photoshop® Pen Tool (P) performs differently from the one in Illustrator®, but if you have successfully completed the tutorials prior to this chapter, you should have no difficulty. The tool is used to make paths. The benefit of creating paths in Photoshop® is that you can fill them on a layer, and then create an identical shape by reactivating the path as a selection of marching ants. The controls for these functions are located at the bottom of the Paths panel. In this tutorial, the shapes that you will create need to resemble parts of clothing items, such as pockets, sleeves, etc. You will create them with the Photoshop® Pen Tool Suite (P), the Path Selection Tool (A), and the Photoshop® Direct Selection Tool (A). To begin making your first path, follow these steps:

1. Lock the figure layer, and then create a new layer above it.

2. The layer should be named appropriately for the article of clothing that you intend to render.

3. Show the Paths panel.

4. Create a new Path layer using the Create New Path icon at the lower right of the Paths panel. The first one you create will be labeled *Path 1*.

5. Double-click on the path layer to rename it with the title of the clothing part that you will create. For example, if the layer that you named was *Left Front*, then label the path, *Left Front Path* to help keep you organized.

6. Select the Photoshop® Pen Tool (P).

7. Render any part of the clothing, such as a front or a sleeve, while looking at the photo image or croquis, but close the shape.

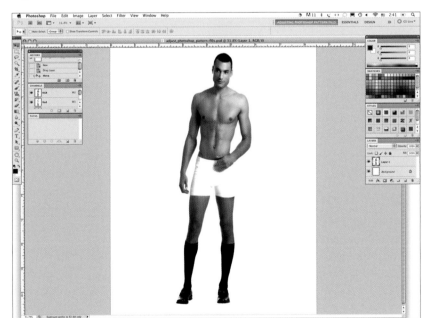

Figure 12.53

Figure 12.54

Work Paths

The paths that you create with the Photoshop® Pen Tool (P) will create **work paths** on the layers where you have loaded them as selections. The marching ants need to be visible by first clicking the **Load Path as Selection button**. Then, click the **Make Work Path from Selection button**, which is next to it on the right. In Photoshop®, a work path can be altered by selecting it with the Photoshop® Direct Selection Tool (A), and by repositioning the handles. Use the Photoshop® Add Anchor Point Tool, Delete Anchor Point Tool, and Convert Point Tool to make additional modifications.

Fill Loaded Selections

When you want to use a work path to create a shape, click the Load Path as Selection button at the bottom of the panel. You can fill them with color, gradients, or patterns on selected or new layers. You can also fill the selection with the contents of the Set Foreground Color box in the Tools panel by clicking the **Fill Path with Foreground Color button**. It is located on the bottom left of the Paths panel.

> ## TIP: Work Path New Layer
>
> **To avoid confusion, create a new layer before you make a new work path or load an existing one. Lock the other layers by selecting them and clicking on the lock icon at the top of the panel.**

Stroke Loaded Selections

When you want to stroke a path, select it and then click the Load Path as Selection button. When the marching ants appear, go to *Menu Bar > Edit > Stroke*. In the Stroke dialog box, increase the *Width* by entering a larger number of pixels in the field. Use the other options to make additional changes such as going to *Menu Bar > Edit > Fade Stroke* to fade one.

Step 3: Fill Paths as Selections

You can use the Photoshop® Paint Bucket Tool (G) to fill selected objects. When the tool is selected, the fill options appear in the Options Bar. Select the *Pattern* option from the pull-down menu, and then scroll to a predefined pattern. Click into the selected area(s) to fill it. You may have noticed that the repeat looks flat on the figure. It will also blend with the other parts, making it difficult to see each one separately (Figure 12.55).

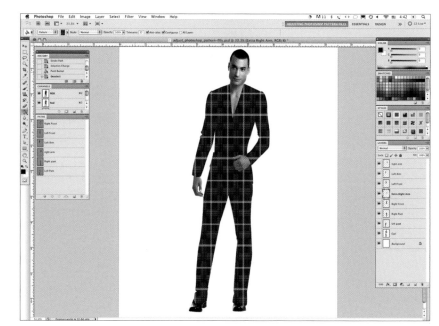

Figure 12.55

Step 4: Scale and Adjust Pattern Fills

There are three primary ways to scale pattern fills in Photoshop®.

Option 1: Pattern Shape Behind a Masked Shape

1. Create a pattern and define it. (See Tutorial 8.5.)
2. Select the repeat.
3. Fill a shape/selection with the pattern (larger than the object) on a layer below it, and then scale the pattern-filled shape by using the Bounding Box in the Free Transform options. (See Tutorial 7.1, Step Four.)
4. Mask the shape, on the same layer by going to *Menu Bar > Layer Mask > Reveal Selection*. Here you have some editing flexibility. For example, you can apply a Layer Style and it will affect just the masked shape. However, you must contend with the shape beneath the mask, and this will increase your file size.

Option 2: Crop, Select, Scale, and Define

Another way to scale a pattern in Photoshop® is to scale it before you define it. Scan a pattern or fill a rectilinear shape with one.

1. Use the Crop Tool (C) to select the repeat within the shape. Double-click to reduce the canvas size.
2. Press *Cmd+T / Ctrl+T* and use the Free Transform Bounding Box to scale the pattern.
3. Hold the Shift key while you increase or decrease the size of the repeat.
4. Select the rectilinear shape with an Inverse of the selected background by pressing *Shift+Cmd+I / Shift+Ctrl+I*.
5. Define the scaled repeat by going to *Menu Bar > Edit > Define Pattern*.

Option 3: Pattern Overlay Layer Style

Patterns can also be scaled and moved within objects by adding a Pattern Overlay Layer Style. To do this:

1. Select the layer where the object is placed.

2. Click and hold the Layer Styles *fx* icon at the bottom of the Layers panel and scroll to Pattern Overlay.

3. Choose the pattern that you defined from the pull-down menu.

4. Use the Scale percentage slider to adjust the pattern size and/or scale.

Remember the percentage that you used to repeat this adjustment for other layers. You can also set the adjustments to make it a default, so that you can repeat them again on additional layers. In Figure 12.56 the digitally simulated Rothesay tartan pattern was scaled to 70%.

Step 5: Adjust the Positions of Multiple Fills

Plaids and stripes look strange when they are not matched in a garment, and the same is true of digital fashion illustration. However, in order to make the digital file more dimensional, you will need to move the pattern slightly inside the contours of each object; certain areas should not match precisely. For example, the pattern repeat in the pants would never be in the exact place as it is on a jacket. The objective is to get rid of the "cookie cutter" look of your digital pattern fills. To do this:

1. Continue to use the Pattern Overlay Layer Style.

2. Move your cursor over the file and manually adjust the position of the pattern by clicking and dragging.

3. Click OK to accept the changes. The Pattern Overlay on each layer was adjusted in Figure 12.57, and the objects are now somewhat visible.

Step 6: Scale and Rotate Patterns in Photoshop®

A good way to rotate a pattern in Photoshop® is to define a pattern repeat at the precise height, scale, and angle needed for the object. If a repeat break shows up in an unwanted position, move the pattern inside the object through the Pattern Overlay Layer Style options described in Step Four.

When placing the position of patterns like plaids, checks, and stripes, often only slight changes to the direction of lines are needed in order to create a convincing flow.

Note: *If you plan to change the angle of a pattern, scale the pattern that you plan to use for the entire garment and define it first.*

To rotate a pattern without having to define additional patterns for each angle, do the following:

1. Select the layer.

2. Click Load Path as a Selection at the bottom of the Paths panel.

3. While the marching ants are flashing, fill the selection with your pattern.

4. Press *Cmd+T / Ctrl+T* to change the angle of the object.

5. Double-click inside the Bounding Box to accept the changes (Figure 12.58).

6. With the marching ants still flashing, fill the object at the angle where you want your pattern to be positioned within it by going to *Menu Bar > Edit > Fill > Pattern*.

7. Press *Cmd+T / Ctrl+T* again to change the angle of the object back to its original position.

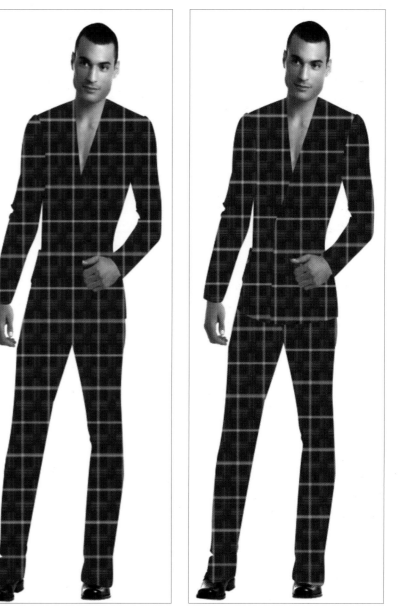

Figure 12.56   Figure 12.57

In Figure 12.59, the left sleeve and pant leg have been rotated using this method.

Note: *Photoshop® will not rotate a pattern fill containing filters. Save a copy of your file as a jpeg, open the copy, and then flatten the layers. Repeat Step Four for each object on separate layers that needs to be scaled, rotated, etc.*

Rotating a Pattern within a Object via Special Paste

Another way to rotate a pattern within an object is achieved by first filling another shape with a pattern that is larger than the object you want to fill.

1. Select and copy the patterned filled object to the clipboard.
2. Afterward, select the object to be filled, and then go to *Menu Bar > Edit > Paste Special >*

Paste Into. The pasted object will appear with a Bounding Box and masked beneath the shape that you selected.

3. Press *Cmd+T / Ctrl+T* to rotate, reposition and scale the pattern within the Bounding Box that appears. This method is most effective for small objects on separate layers, such as sleeves, yokes, and pockets.

Step 7: Render, Rotate, and Fill the Details

Follow the previous steps for creating the pockets, collar, lapel, buttons, cuffs, etc. Add a Stroke of 2 px to any object by loading the paths as selections and then going to *Menu Bar > Edit > Stoke >Width > 2 px.* Add seams and darts as Strokes where needed using the Photoshop® Pencil Tool (B). Figure 12.60 shows this progression.

Figure 12.58

Figure 12.59

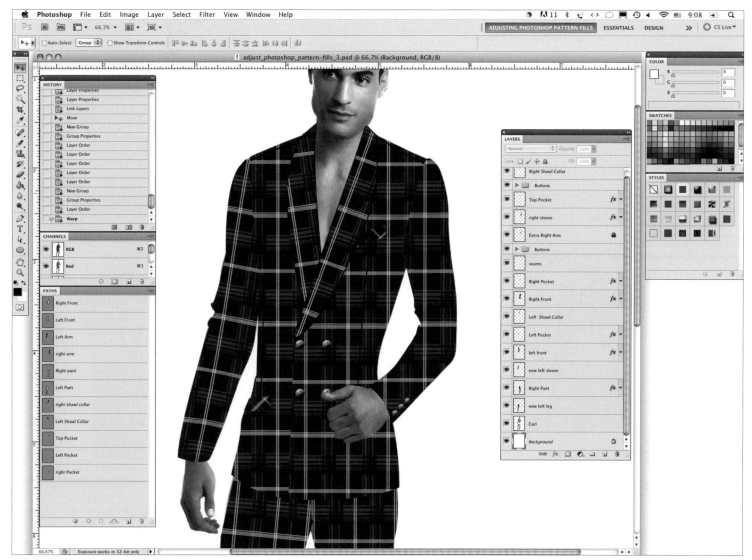

Figure 12.60 The variations of the pattern create a more realistic 3-D illusion.

Step 8: Turn the Textile Grain

Certain areas on a digital rendering need special attention. This is especially true of bends at the elbow on a sleeve. To remedy the problem, create a duplicate sleeve and rotate the angle to get a better position of the pattern at the end of the sleeve. Repeat the procedure for the top angle, then use the Eraser Tool (E) to remove the opposite ends, as shown in Figure 12.61.

Note: Use the Special Paste option to rotate the pattern within the smaller portion of the sleeve.

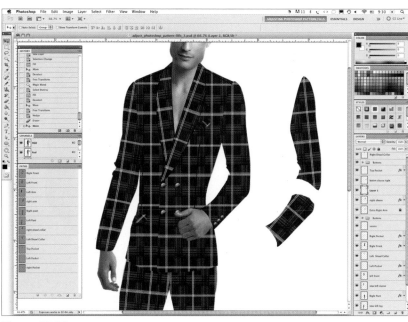

Figure 12.61

Step 9: Simulate Dimension with the Liquify Filter

Use the tools in the Liquify filter to simulate dimension of your patterns on croquis figures or conceptual flats (Figures 12.62 and 12.63).

Step 10: Add Layer Styles and Filters

The completed digital rendering was enhanced with the Inner Shadow, Bevel and Emboss, and Drop Shadow Layer Styles (Figure 12.64). A red mock turtle was added and the Sponge filter was applied.

Figure 12.63

Figure 12.62

Figure 12.64

Figure 12.65

Step 11: Digital Photo and Illustration Combinations

Because the competition is stiff, try new and exciting presentations that combine "Digital Duo" procedures with both photographic and illustration resources. You can use digital drawings with scanned freehand drawings and fashion photography. In Figure 12.65, the photo of Carl is replaced by the fashion avatar Dustin located on ② Avatar Modeling Agency. A vivid red background adds drama to the final presentation.

Note: *The photo was erased, except for the shoes, to which filters were applied. You can also use a photo for your background to add realism to your presentation (Figure 12.66).*

Figure 12.66 Illustration by Stacy Stewart Smith.

By completing this tutorial you will apply everything that you have learned in order to design a mini collection of men's clothing and prepare a group of interactive croquis for a presentation. The figures pictured in the book are for guidance only. Use four or five of your own male croquis and use your creativity to design the apparel and environment of your presentation.

Step 1: Create a New Document in Photoshop®

Load Photoshop®, then press *Cmd+N / Ctrl+N*. In the New dialog box, enter the dimensions to create a tabloid-size file in landscape orientation on a transparent background (Figure 12.67).

Step 2: Open Your Croquis Files in Photoshop®

Step 3: Create Layer Groups, Then Drag and Drop

1. Create a group folder on the Layers panel of each croquis file by clicking the Create a New Group button at the bottom of the panel.
2. Select and drag the layers associated with the croquis into that folder.
3. Afterward, drag and drop the files onto the new file that you created. Each figure will be contained in a folder.
4. Label the folders to identify their contents.
5. Scale the figures with the Free Transform feature by selecting all the layers in the group, then pressing *Cmd+T / Ctrl+T*. Hold the Shift key to constrain the proportions, and then pull the Bounding Box to size (Figure 12.68).

Step 4: Create Interactive Poses with the Photoshop® Puppet Warp Filter

Use the Photoshop® Puppet Warp feature to slightly alter the croquis poses, and make them somewhat interactive (Figure 12.69).

Step 5: Create Apparel for Each Croquis Figure in the Photoshop® Groups Folders

Note: *Textile patterns are available on ② Textile and Novelties Library.*

Figure 12.67

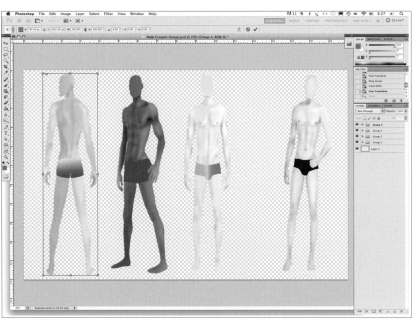

Figure 12.68

Step 6: Add a Background or Create an Environment for Your Presentation

Figure 12.70 shows the completed presentation. After the pants and jeans were created with the Pen Tool (P) as paths and on layers, the Hue/Saturation filter was applied. Layer Styles were added, especially Pattern Overlay, which was used as all-over tattoo designs on the croquis by reducing the *Opacity* in the Pattern Overlay Layer Opacity. Afterward, the Outer Glow Layer Style was added to give the figures a surreal look. An abstractrealist painting was copied, pasted, reflected, and then mirrored to create the perfect background.

For practice creating clothing for the female croquis group, see DVD Extra 12.1. You can also sharpen your skills creating stitch details on clothing by completing DVD Extra 12.2.

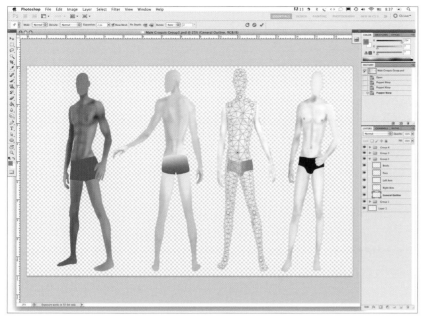

Figure 12.69

Figure 12.70 Illustration by Stacy Stewart Smith.

Chapter 12 Summary

The completion of Chapter 12 should have ushered you into a digital consciousness and showed you why "Digital Duo" procedures are an excellent method for creating fashion presentations. The raster environment of Photoshop® is different from the layer stacking order of Illustrator®. By exporting your vector figures from Illustrator® to Photoshop®, you enable your digital images to be seen in a containment of transparent pixel layers that the human eye will accept as photo imagery. The tutorials in this chapter taught you how to work seamlessly in both programs in order to give your croquis and apparel designs a greater illusion of realism. Depending on your level of computer skill and knowledge of fine art or illustration, you will be able to use these techniques to create avatars that can be used in fashion presentations repeatedly.

Chapter 12 Self-Assessment

1. Can I really add shadows to a selected object or one on a layer in Photoshop®? Do I know several ways to do this?

2. Do I know what a Vector Smart Object is why I should use this feature?

3. Do I know what I must do first before I can use Photoshop® filters on files exported from Illustrator®?

4. Can I name three Photoshop® tools essential to blending objects and flesh tones in Photoshop®?

5. Can I explain how vector and raster graphics software can be combined to produce 3-D presentations?

6. Do I know how to rotate a pattern in Photoshop®?

7. Do I know how to merge, repair, and clean up Graphic Styles that have been exported from Illustrator® documents and appear on separate layers in Photoshop®?

8. Am I able to explain how the Illustrator® Pen Tool (P) differs from the function of the Photoshop® Pen Tool (P)?

9. Can I explain the function of Photoshop® work paths and why they are an essential feature in Photoshop®?

10. Can I modify the sublayer contents of group folders in Photoshop®? Am I able to reorder and rename Photoshop® layers?

Chapter 12 DVD Extras

Explore additional poses and details for your digital fashion croquis by completing the following DVD Extra tutorials. These tutorials can be found on ② Ch12\DVD Extras.

DVD Extra 12.1
Clothing on the Female Croquis Group

In this tutorial, you will learn to render apparel using the Photoshop® Pen Tool (P) and work paths. You will also design and define a print from original artwork and design a group of related sportswear. The tutorial will teach you how to arrange digital group presentations on croquis figures (Figure 12.71). This activity will prepare you for portfolio presentations of your designs and/or merchandise meetings.

DVD Extra 12.2
Vector Smart Digital Stitches

In this short tutorial, you will learn how to use Vector Smart features to add comprehensive stitch details to Photoshop® (CS5 and earlier versions) presentations (Figure 12.72).

Figure 12.71

Figure 12.72

"Digital Duo" Fashion Face and Hair

13

Objectives

Your studies in previous chapters should have helped you to develop a particular balance between the illustrative effects of Illustrator® and Photoshop®. This chapter tests your ability to transition between the programs as you learn to create facial characteristics and hairstyles for male and female fashion croquis.

The first half of this chapter focuses on the digital fashion face. You will use all the tools, filters, and panels detailed in previous chapters to produce different looks and correct imperfections. Special attention is placed on creating various head poses and simulating ethnic features. The remaining tutorials apply the digital rendering process to fashion hair. You will learn to create some styles totally in Illustrator® and Photoshop®; others make use of digitized freehand sketches. By the end of this chapter, you will understand how to use the digital interface to:

◎ Utilize color, shadows, and highlights to transform the fashion face into countless variations

◎ Reproduce current trends in idealized beauty, high-fashion glamour, and cosmetics

◎ Highlight accepted standards of beauty and touch on a variety of ethnic looks

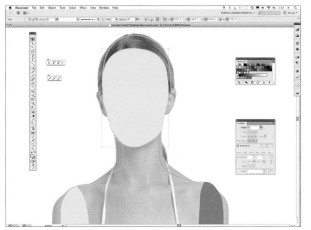
Figure 13.1

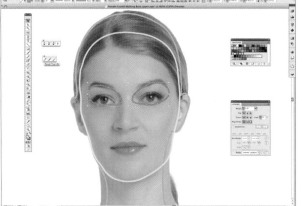
Figure 13.2

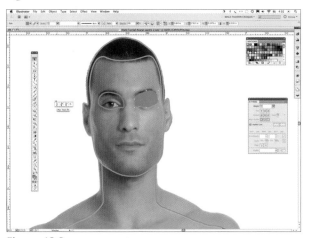
Figure 13.3

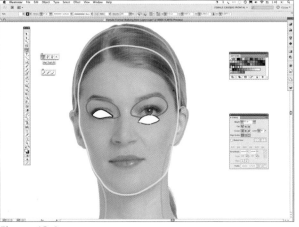
Figure 13.4

In this tutorial, we examine the digital male and female frontal-view face in steps. You will render the facial structure in Illustrator®, fill it with Skintone gradients, add filters, and then export the file(s) to Photoshop® for further cosmetic effects and 3-D enhancements. If you have completed the tutorials in all the previous chapters, you will have no problems following this mostly pictorial tutorial. If you need more clarity, revisit the lessons in Chapter 2 through Chapter 4.

This tutorial utilizes frontal-view headshots from the Digital Duo Modeling Agency. Select and use any Illustrator® rendering tool, such as the Illustrator® Pen Tool (P), to create the shapes in this tutorial. The objects in the steps must be rendered on separate layers in Illustrator® to ensure the best results when you export the file(s) to Photoshop® later. Follow each step as shown in the adjacent figures.

Step 1: Create the Face Shape

Render the face shape as a mask to help maintain symmetry of the feature parts (Figure 13.1). When it's later placed on top of the general outline, it will border the ear shapes. Since the face shape and the general outline will eventually be filled with the same flesh tone gradient, there will not be a visible division at the top. The darker area will be distributed to delineate the neck from the chin.

Step 2: Create an Eye Base

Use the Illustrator® Pen Tool (P) to form a shape that encompasses the eye socket area (Figures 13.2 and 13.3). The other eye parts will eventually be placed on top of this shape. The top of the eye base should form the ridge of the eyebrows. The bottom should not be lower than the bottom of the eye. One side should border the nose, and the other side

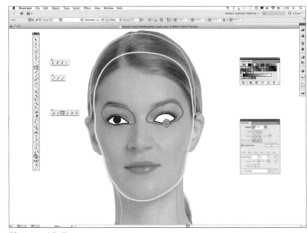
Figure 13.5

should be formed into a curve shape that flows from the bottom of the eye to eyebrow. Use the photo as a reference. If necessary, select objects, and then reduce the *Opacity* settings in the Control Panel, so that you can see the photo beneath. You can restore the Opacity when you have completed your work.

Note: *Do not attempt to create two different eyes. Later, when you have created all the eye shapes, you will group, copy, paste, and reflect them to create the other eye.*

Step 3: Create the Eye Shapes

A great way to create the oval of the eye is to start with the default Fill of white and Stroke of black. Use the Illustrator® Ellipse Tool (L) to marquee an oblong oval. Next, select the Convert Anchor Point Tool (Shift+C), and then click on the left and right anchor points to change them into points. The Direct Selection Tool (A) should be used to shape the fashion eye. Pull the side toward the nose slightly down and the other side slightly up (Figure 13.4). Naturally, the look is up to you and will depend on your presentation objectives.

Step 4: Make the Iris of the Eye

Use the Ellipse Tool (L) to create the shape of the iris (Figures 13.5 and 13.6).

Step 5: Create the Pupil

Place a smaller circle in the center of the iris to create the pupil (Figure 13.7).

Step 6: Add Eye Highlights

Place smaller circles off-center from the pupils to create the illusion of reflecting light (Figure 13.8).

Step 7: Create Eyelids with the Illustrator® Pen Tool

It may not seem important, but without eyelids, your croquis will have a scary stare. The eyelid needs to cover some of the iris (Figure 13.9).

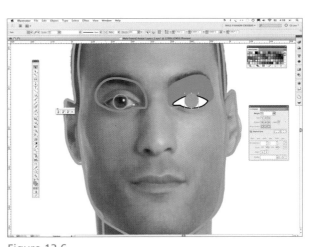
Figure 13.6

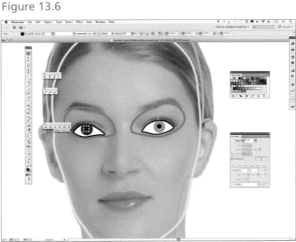
Figure 13.7

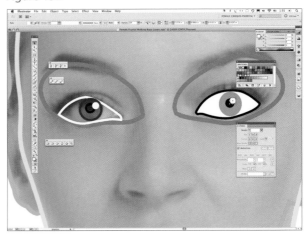
Figure 13.8

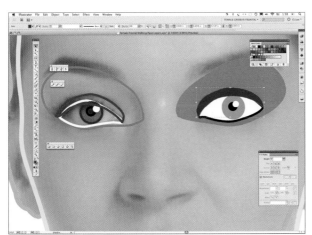
Figure 13.9

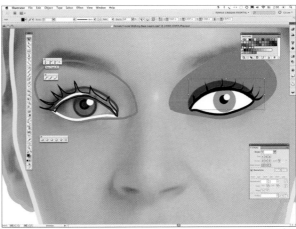
Figure 13.10

Step 8: Create Eyelashes by Making Small Curved Paths

They may seem complicated to make, but digital false eyelashes are a series of curved line segments. There is a large curve on the bottom, and each lash is suggested with two. Create a space between lashes, and then make another (Figure 13.10). Lashes on male croquis should be minimal (Figure 13.11).

Step 9: Render the Whole Shape of the Mouth

Use the photo as a guide to create a shape that covers the entire mouth area. The upper and lower lips will eventually be placed on top of this shape (Figure 13.12).

Step 10: Make the Lower and Upper Lips

Create separate shapes for the lower and upper lips as shown in Figures 13.13 and 13.14.

Note: Ana and Carl have proportionate facial features, so tracing these shapes is optimal for the tutorial. Try to follow what you see the first time that you do this. However, if you want to create a slightly different look, render a second set of features. Try reshaping the mouth shapes to create a pouty expression or add allure, but do not overdo it.

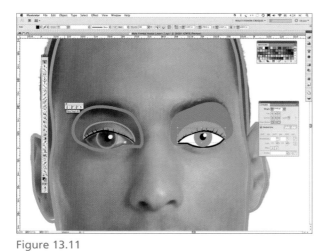

Figure 13.11

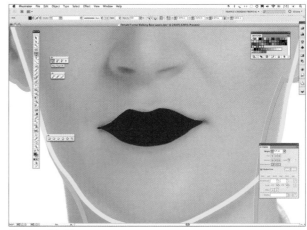

Figure 13.12

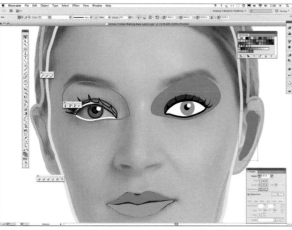

Figure 13.13

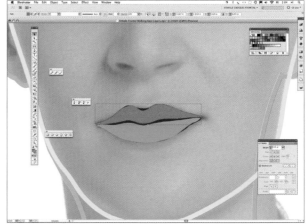

Figure 13.14

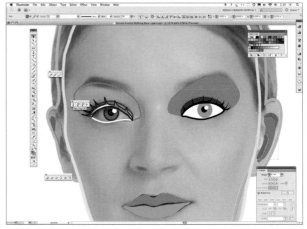

Figure 13.15

Figure 13.16

Step 11: Detail the Inside of the Ear

The earlobe attached to the general outline that you created will look odd if you do not add more definition. Even though this is only a tiny area on the croquis, you never know when you will need to show a closer view in a presentation. Besides, many files are now viewed electronically and areas can be zoomed-in on for closer inspection (Figure 13.15).

Step 12: Make More Ear Shapes

The extra effort is worth it and will make you a better digital fashion illustrator, so render all the shapes that will make the ear look more real (Figures 13.16 and 13.17).

Step 13: Combine the Nose and Forehead in One Shape

Combining the nose and forehead as one shape will help you to conceal the edges of the upper eye shapes and helps you to later apply more dimensions to the face without covering parts with filters (Figures 13.18 and 13.19).

Note: *Sometimes photos are distorted or models may have uneven features. To alleviate a potential problem, render only one side of the nose and forehead, and then copy, paste, and reflect it. Combine the shapes by aligning them. Combine the two halves with the Unite feature or the Pathfinder panel.*

Step 14: Create Eyebrows

Use the Width Tool to shape a Stroke for the brows; or create the shape with the Illustrator® Pen Tool (P) (Figures 13.20 and 13.21).

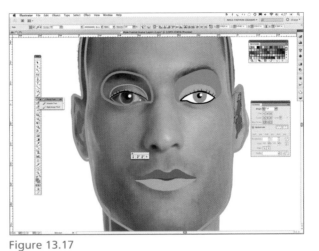

Figure 13.17

Figure 13.18

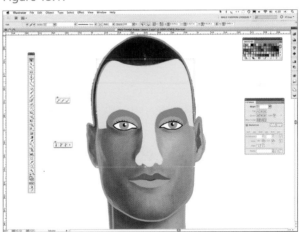

Figure 13.19

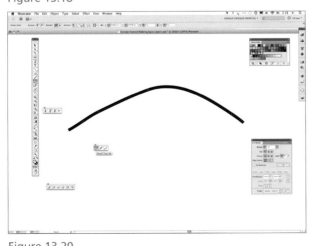

Figure 13.20

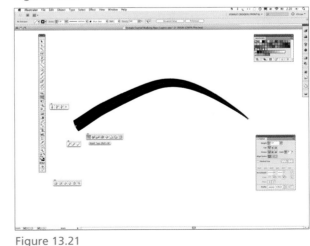

Figure 13.21

Step 15: Use Bounding Boxes to Fit the Brows

Because eyebrows are a fashion statement, you will need to use your own fashion sense to style them. Currently, the size of the brow has more to do with the look that is appropriate for the individual; however, in the 1980s thick brows were all the rage and in the 1930s thin lines were considered fashionable. Follow the current trends to avoid negative comments by viewers (Figures 13.22 and 13.23).

Step 16: Create Nostrils to Complete the Nose

If you trace the shapes shown in the photo, you will have perfect nostrils. Avoid making them too large to prevent an odd look (Figure 13.24).

Figure 13.25 shows the completed rendering of the frontal female face shapes in Illustrator®.

Step 17: Add Realistic Color to the Face

Fill the shapes with Illustrator® Skintone Gradients and use the Gaussian Blur filter on some to create blending. Use a Radial gradient for the face shape and the eye base. Select and adjust the darker areas with the Gradient Tool (G) such that they create convincing depth in the eye sockets and define the chin (Figures 13.26 and 13.27).

Step 18: Add Color to the Iris and Eyelids

Use Radial gradients to fill the iris and eyelids, and then use the Gaussian Blur on the mouth base (Figure 13.28).

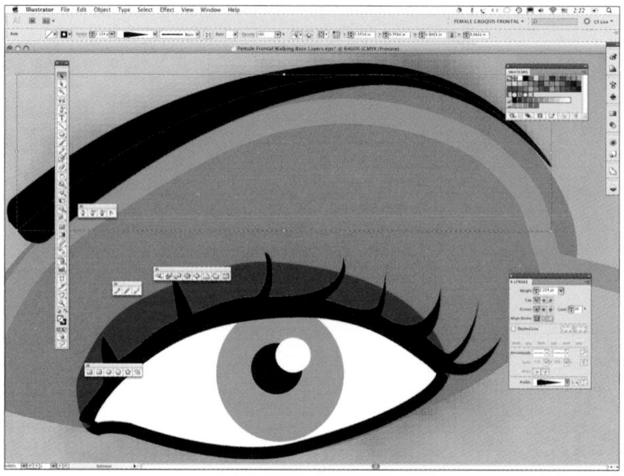

Figure 13.22

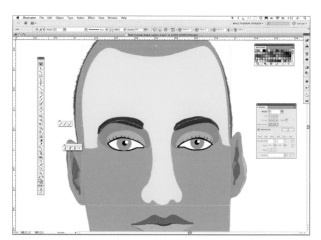

Figure 13.23

Figure 13.24

Figure 13.25

Step 19: Add Color to the Lips

Use Linear Gradient Fills for upper and lower lips (Figures 13.29 and13.30).

Step 20: Create Facial Shadows and Highlights

Apply the Blob Brush Tool and the Gaussian Blur filter to add natural contours and highlights to the face and neck (Figures 13.31 and 13.32).

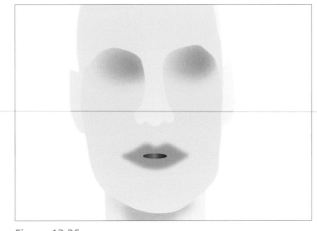

Figure 13.26

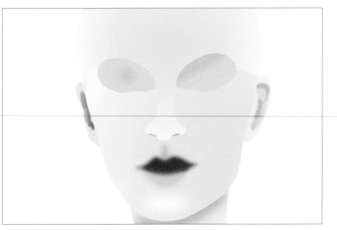

Figure 13.27

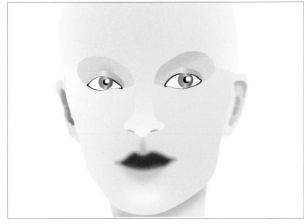

Figure 13.28

Figure 13.29

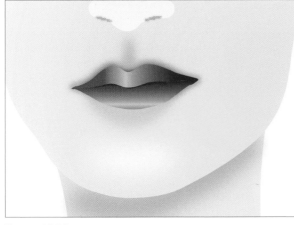

Figure 13.30

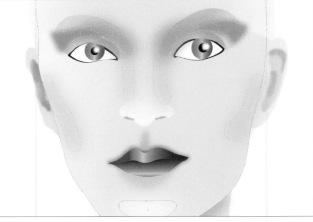

Figure 13.31

Step 21: Complete the Face

Toggle on and off the visibility of the layers to inspect the parts that you have made. Afterward, add finishing touches to make the look your own; you may want to have less or more illusions of glamour. Sometimes a more natural look is stylish, so you may want to remove the lashes and apply simple dark lines as a liner on top of the eyelids. If the presentation calls for drama—well, you can always apply more techniques. Naturally, the male face should be conservative but handsome. The completed tutorial examples appear in Figures 13.33 and 13.34.

Figure 13.32

Note: *Save your file for use in Tutorial 13.2.*

Figure 13.33

Figure 13.34

**Tutorial 13.2
THE "DIGITAL DUO" FACE
USING ILLUSTRATOR®
AND PHOTOSHOP®**

This tutorial picks up where the previous one stopped, but will exclude the Illustrator® Gaussian Blur, so use a copy of your croquis and delete the filters to avoid problems in Photoshop®. You will be taken through more steps to teach you how to enhance the female frontal-view face after you export the parts from Illustrator® to Photoshop®.

Step 1: Export the Illustrator® File Created in Tutorial 13.1 to Photoshop®

For exporting instruction, see Tutorial 12.1, Step One. Sometimes, shapes created from photos come out uneven. Once you have opened your file in Photoshop® (Figure 13.35), follow these steps to correct any problems:

1. Select any layer where there may be uneven parts and make corrections using the Transform options by going to *Menu Bar > Edit Transform > Perspective.*

2. A Bounding Box appears around the entire shape. This perspective-editing feature allows you to reposition areas of the shape without affecting its entire position.

3. Select the anchor beneath the problem area, and pull it slightly.

4. If you so desire, reposition other parts of the face (Figure 13.36). Naturally, there are many things you can do by experimenting with the Transform options. Play around with them and learn by exploring.

5. To exit the Bounding Box, double-click inside it, but not in the center.

Step 2: Add Shadows to the Face in Photoshop®

The original photograph that you used from the ① Digital Duo Modeling Agency provides enough information to proceed with adding shadows to the face with the Burn Tool (O). Because we are creating an illustrated character, you can be imaginative. For this tutorial, we will apply the basics: contours and shadows from a cosmetic perspective as if makeup was being applied for a fashion event. You are encouraged to challenge yourself to create various types of facial features as you make further progress.

Figure 13.35

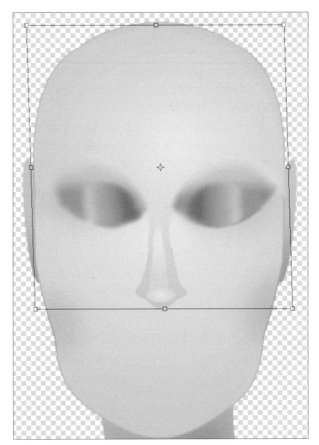

Figure 13.36

Figure 13.37

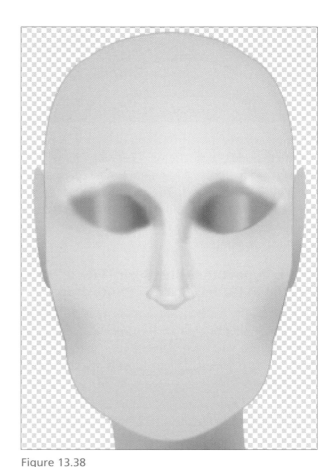

Figure 13.38

Creating Contour Shadows for Chic Cheekbones

While on the unlocked *Face* layer, select the Burn Tool (O) and apply a light shadow to the hollow beneath the cheekbones.

1. In the Options Bar, select *Midtones* in the *Range* field and reduce your exposure to less than 20%. Also select an appropriate brush.

2. Test the brush size and *Exposure*. If the mark is too severe, simply press *Cmd+Z / Ctrl+Z* to undo the move(s), adjust the settings, and repeat this step.

Note: *A soft, large brush with a low exposure will produce elegant tones.*

Building Facial Definition

Toggle on the visibility of the *Nose and Forehead* layer. Adjust the brush size and use the Burn Tool (O) to shadow the area of the eye sockets (Figure 13.37).

Step 3: Blend the Eye Area in Photoshop®

The Photoshop® (CS5 and higher) art brushes located in the Brush Presets panel will help with blending the eyelids, forehead, and face when used with the Brush Tool (B). Select the Brush Tool from the Tools panel, and then show the Brush Presets panel. Because the details of the face are delicate, choose an appropriate brush like the *Round Point Stiff Preset*. Blend the eye area:

1. From the Options Bar, reduce the size appropriately.

2. Also reduce the *Opacity* to 46% and the *Flow* to 34%, or whatever works.

3. A specific color can be sampled from the area; just hold the Option key (Mac) or Alt key (PC) and click.

4. Test the brush.

5. You should apply the brush on top of the eyelids in click strokes, and build translucent color into the objects on the *Eye Socket* layer (Figure 13.38).

Saving Flesh Tones

As you select the various hues of the croquis's flesh tones, save a few for future use, to your Illustrator® Swatches panel (see Tutorial 9.1, Step Eleven).

Step 4: Blur the Parts in Photoshop®

Another tool, which will make blending the parts almost seamless, is the Blur Tool. This tool softens pixels and can render objects out of focus. The face is a perfect place to practice because even digital makeup requires plenty of blending. Set the *Strength* at 50% and use a soft brush size of approximately 40 px.

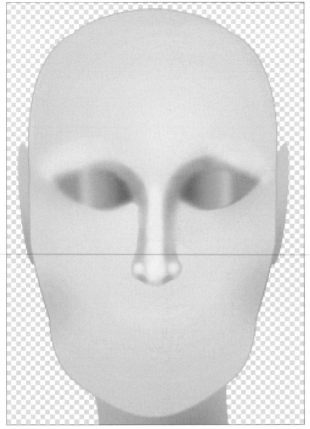

Figure 13.39

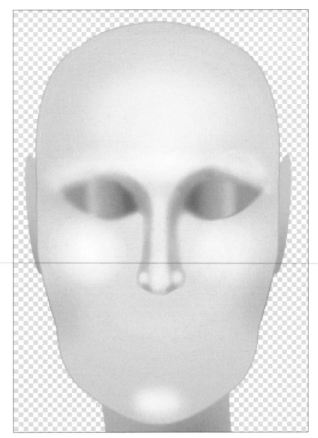

Figure 13.40

The application of the Blur Tool should be smooth and organic, much like the other brush-oriented tools. Try not to use streaky, scratchy, or zigzag motions; use graceful ones instead. Follow the contours of the forehead and allow your strokes to gently smooth in the work. When the eyelids, sockets, and forehead look as if there is a gradual transition between them, you have applied enough (Figure 13.39).

Step 5: Add Highlights to the Face with the Photoshop® Dodge Tool (O)

The Dodge Tool (O) can be effective on the bridge of the forehead, cheeks, and chin area, as shown in Figure 13.40. Use the Blur Tool to blend the highlights. You can tone the blending by alternating between the art brushes and the Burn Tool (O).

Step 6: Refine the Mouth in Photoshop®

Toggle on the visibility of the *Mouth* layer and unlock it. You may want to reposition the mouth relative to the nose with the Move Tool (V). Select it and tap the direction keys (arrow keys) until you have it in place. Now use a small soft brush to work in the highlights with the Dodge Tool (O). Use the Burn Tool (O) for shadows (Figure 13.41).

Figure 13.41

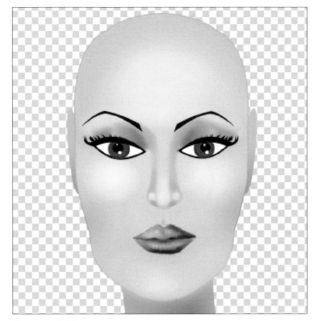

Figure 13.42

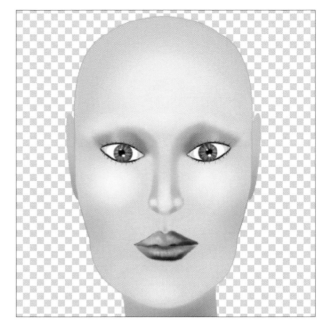

Figure 13.43

Lipstick Color

To change the lipstick color, go to *Menu Bar > Image > Adjustments > Hue/Saturation*. In the dialog box adjust the *Hue* slider to the color of your choice. The *Saturation* slider will either desaturate or intensify the color (Figure 13.42).

Step 7: Adjust the Eyes in Photoshop®

The eyes exported from Illustrator® are now cartoon-like in comparison to the work you have completed on this file. However, making a few adjustments will diminish that contrast. To begin, lock all the other layers, but unlock and toggle on the visibility of the layer that you created for the eyes. If you created the entire eye on one layer, Photoshop® will have packaged the parts in a group folder. Tip the pointer and toggle off the visibility of the sublayers to discover where the parts are located.

Working from the Good Eye

In a frontal pose the eyes are often the same. You can copy and reflect one of them to create a perfect pair. Drag the layer with the eye that you do not favor to the Trash icon at the lower right corner of the Layers panel. Copy the good eye layer, and then flip the eye vertically with the Reflect Tool (O) options. Position it on the opposite side of the face to replace the eye you trashed (Figure 13.43).

Reshaping the Eye

Select the Move Tool (V) and reposition the eye relative to the socket and lid area. To add character and more realism, select the layer where you created the iris of the eye. Use the Brush Tools and others to create lines and add realism (Figure 13.44).

Figure 13.44 The eyeliner in this zoomed-in image looks pixelated because it is actually only a fraction of an inch in size.

TIP: Three Eyes Across

A standard fashion illustration of the face generally has the space of an eye between the eyes, so you should consider resizing the eye as well.

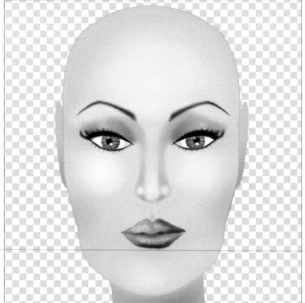

Figure 13.45

Figure 13.46

Highlights in the Eye

Select, lock, and toggle off the visibility of the layer containing the highlights of the eye. If needed, use the Dodge Tool (O) to brighten them.

Eye Realness

Click on the Set Foreground Color box and select a salmon hue from the Color Picker. Use a small brush to color in the corners of the eye. Do the same with a dove gray tone (Figure 13.44). After this, use the Eraser Tool (E) to reshape the eye with a small brush.

Step 8: Create Lash and Brow Detail in Photoshop®

Use a smaller brush with the Smudge Tool to pull out tiny lashes from the black outline. Alternate between tools and create a real fashion eye that you like. Do the same with the eyebrows. Use the Blur Tool on both to diminish their sharpness (Figure 13.45).

Linking Facial Parts on Photoshop® Layers

Because you are keeping the facial features on separate layers, you may want to link them to prevent accidental shifting. To link the layers, hold the Shift key, go to Layer Properties in the hidden menu at the right of the panel, and click the chain icon at the bottom of the panel. This icon will appear on each linked layer, and you will be able to move the parts together without as a group.

Shaping and Toning

You may want to go back to any of the previous steps and make adjustments. Experiment with using the various tools, filters, and effects, especially the Dodge Tool (O) to add highlights. Even out the colors and correct the anatomy of your drawing. A few

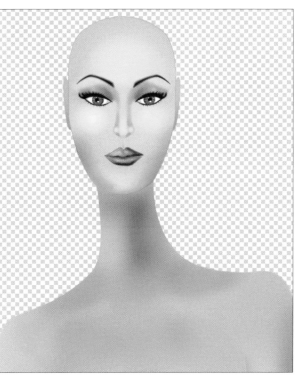

Figure 13.47 **Illustration by Stacy Stewart Smith.**

strokes can change how one perceives the weight, height, and/or age of the illustrated model. In this image, the jaw has been reduced to make the croquis appear slightly younger. The color has also been adjusted to create a beautiful tone (Figure 13.46).

This completed exercise has taken you through the "Digital Duo" process for rendering the female face. These are suggested procedures. You can use all or some of them to suit your taste or those of your clients. The completed example is shown in Figure 13.47.

Note: *Later tutorials will make use of the croquis face, so save it in a location you'll have access to.*

This tutorial teaches you how to use Illustrator® to digitally render the male and female profile from a photo. Later, complete the 3-D look by exporting the file to Photoshop®. To help you complete this tutorial, profile headshots have been provided in ① Digital Duo Modeling Agency.

Note: *Select and use any rendering tool, such as the Illustrator® Pen Tool (P), to create the shapes in this tutorial. The objects in the steps must be on separate layers in Illustrator® for the best results later when exporting the file to Photoshop®. Follow each step as shown in the figures.*

Step 1: Create the Profile Silhouette

Use the Illustrator® Pen Tool (P) to outline the face and head as shown in earlier chapters (Figures 13.48 and 13.49).

Figure 13.48

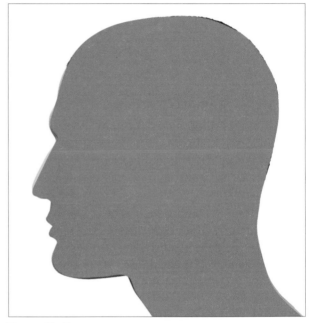

Figure 13.49

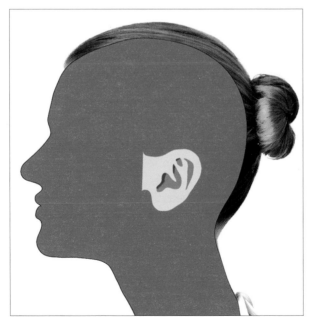

Figure 13.50

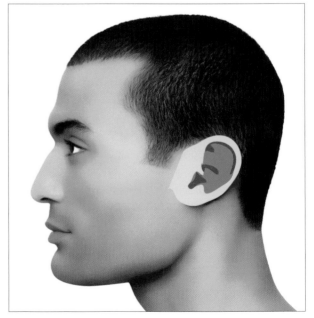

Figure 13.51

Step 2: Render the Earlobe and the Ear Detail Shapes

Create a new layer and use the Pen Tool (P) or the Pencil Tool (N) to draw the shape of the ear (Figures 13.50 and 13.51). Leave an area to hide underneath the face later as shown. Afterward, render the shapes within the ear separately.

Step 3: Create a New Layer and Render the Face

Because the face needs to hide the ear, draw it on a new layer as shown in Figures 13.52 and 13.53.

Step 4: Create the Mouth and Eye Base

Create new layers above the face for both the mouth and the eye base. Render the mouth layer on the lower layer and the eye base on the layer above it (Figure 13.54).

Step 5: Create the Oval of the Eye

The eye can be created on the same layer with the eye base. Lock the base and render the oval of the eye on top of it with the Pen Tool (P) (Figure 13.55).

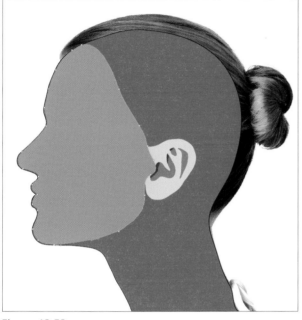

Figure 13.52

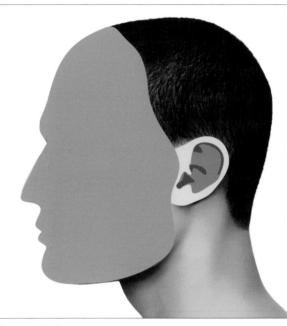

Figure 13.53

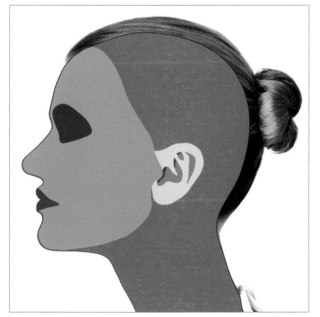

Figure 13.54

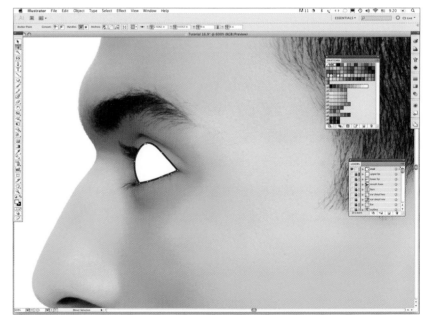

Figure 13.55

Figure 13.56

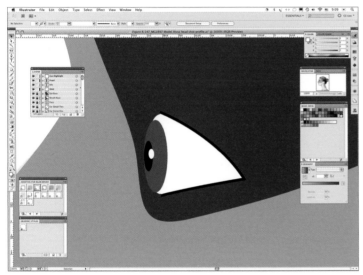
Figure 13.57

Figure 13.58

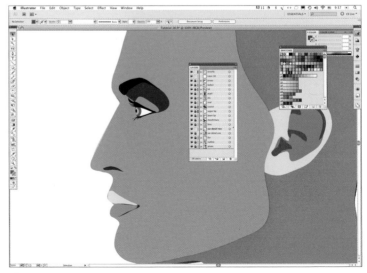
Figure 13.59

Step 6: Create the Iris of the Eye

The Ellipse Tool (L) can create the iris with a click and drag. Use the Bounding Box to shape it (Figure 13.56).

Step 7: Create the Pupil and Eye Highlight(s)

Use the Ellipse Tool (L) to create the tiny pupil shape, as well (Figure 13.57).

Step 8: Eyelids, Lashes, and Mouth

The eyelids and lashes can be rendered on the same layer with the other eye parts (Figure 13.58). Use the Illustrator® Pen Tool (P) to create the upper and lower lips on top of the *Mouth Base* layer (Figure 13.59).

Illustrator® Scissors Tool Alterations

Often what looks excellent in photography will not translate well in fashion illustration. Be your own judge, but consider the look of the work, and if necessary, perform a few digital cosmetic alterations. Use the Direct Selection Tool (A) and marquee over areas, and then press the direction keys to make adjustments. Figure 13.60 shows the differences between the original red profile shape and the altered face in blue. The ear, eye, and mouth were also reshaped and repositioned.

Note: *If you do not need to make this alteration, skip to Step Ten.*

Step 9: Clip the Silhouette with the Illustrator® Scissors Tool

The Illustrator® Scissors Tool (C) can be used to cut into a line segment, but not on an anchor point. If you want to remove a part of the shape, an additional cut must be made in another place. In Figure 13.60,

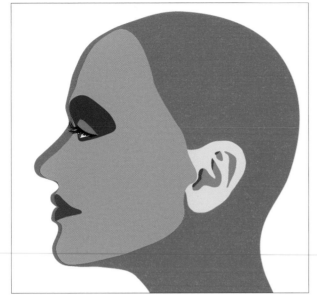

Figure 13.60 **Before digital cosmetic alterations.**　　Figure 13.61 **After digital cosmetic alterations.**

Figure 13.62　　　　　　　　　　　　　　　　　　Figure 13.63

the face was reshaped, but it left the one on the *General Outline* layer protruding. You can use the Illustrator® Eraser Tool (E) to reduce the shape or cut it off with the Scissors Tool (C) by clicking on the two opposite sides of the shape. Pull the shape away and press the Delete key to discard it (Figure 13.61).

Step 10: Add a Separate Nose Shape

On some profiles it is necessary to add a separate nose shape, especially for male croquis (Figure 13.62).

Note: *If you do not need to make this alteration, skip to Step Eleven.*

Step 11: Elongate the Neck and Readjust Parts

Female fashion croquis have long necks. You may also want to change the angle of the eyes and reshape the mouth (Figure 13.63).

Note: *If you do not need to make this alteration, skip it.*

TIP: Face Library

By developing a library of digital fashion faces, you can replace the old with the new easily. Examine the layers of each file on ② Avatar Modeling Agency, and then try replacing the faces with those that you have created. As an exercise, before you go on to Chapter 14, develop your own set of ten fashion croquis with fashion faces.

Step 12: Color the Face

Fill the face with skintone gradients and color facial features with solid colors as shown in Figures 13.64 and 13.65.

Step 13: Check the Symmetry of the Face

Toggle off the visibility of the face and profile outline to examine the relationship of the eyes, ears, and mouth. If the positioning of the parts produces an elegant rendering without the face and neck, then the drawing is good. Adjust the parts if needed (Figure 13.66).

Figure 13.64

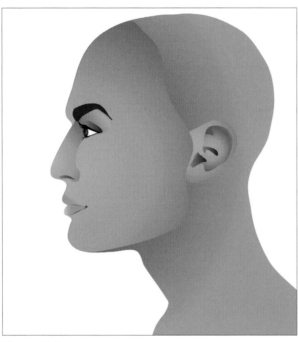

Figure 13.65

Figure 13.66

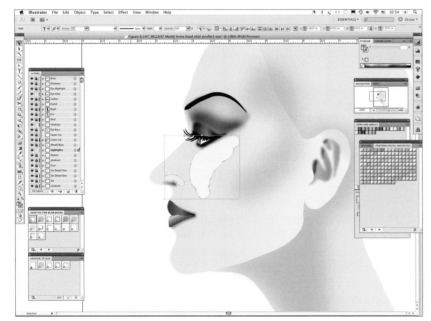

Figure 13.67

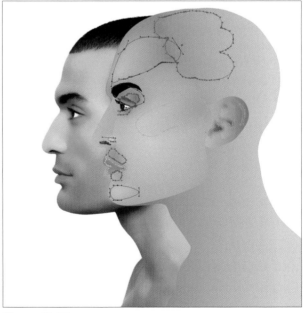

Figure 13.68

Step 14: Add Highlights to the Face

Use Graphic Styles and the Blob Brush Tool (Shift+B) to add highlights to the face (Figures 13.67 and 13.68).

Step 15: Complete the Profile in Photoshop®

The male and female fashion profiles as rendered in Illustrator® are shown in Figures 13.69 and 13.70. Notice the seam that separates the face from the rest of the head. To eliminate this effect, export your file to Photoshop® and use brushes to conceal the seam (Figure 13.71). This was done to the male profile face that appears in Figure 13.72.

Figure 13.69

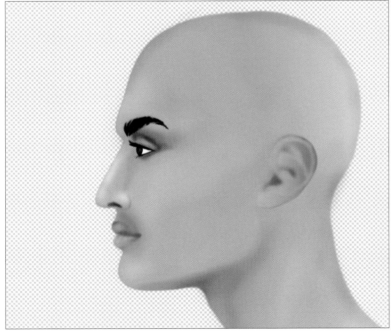

Figure 13.70

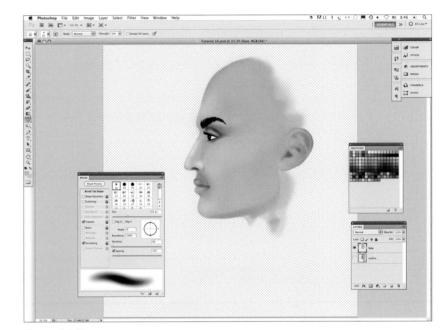

Figure 13.71

Figure 13.72 Illustration by Stacy Stewart Smith.

The three-quarter-view face is another common pose that you will need throughout your career. It does not matter if you are a designer, merchandiser, illustrator, or graphics major—you will need to understand how to arrange this pose digitally. To help you complete this tutorial, three-quarter-view headshots have been provided on ① Digital Duo Modeling Agency. After you create your croquis face in Illustrator®, use what you learned in the tutorials of this chapter to enhance your work in Photoshop®.

Note: *Select and use any Illustrator® rendering tool, such as the Illustrator® Pen Tool (P), to create the shapes in this tutorial. The objects in the steps must be rendered on separate layers in Illustrator® for the best results later when exporting the file to Photoshop®. Follow each step as shown in the adjacent figures.*

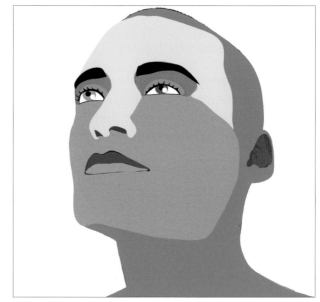

Figure 13.73

Step 1: Create the Face Shapes in Illustrator®

Using the photo as a reference, create face shapes as you were instructed in Tutorials 3.1 and 3.3. A fully shaped face is pictured in Figure 13.73.

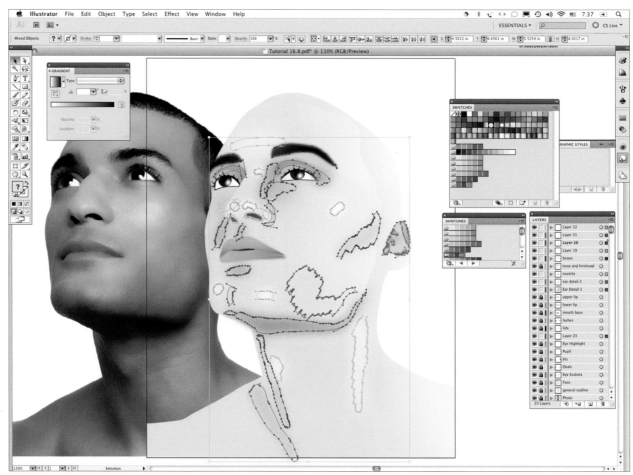

Figure 13.74

Figure 13.75

Step 2: Add Color, Highlights, and Shadows to the Face

Fill the shapes with Illustrator® Skintone Gradients and use the Gaussian Blur filter on some to create blending. Use gradients to add color to facial features like the lips and eyes, and apply the Blob Brush Tool (Shift+B) and the Gaussian Blur filter to add natural contours and highlights to the face and neck (Figure 13.74). The male three-quarter view face as rendered in Illustrator® is shown in Figures 13.75.

Note: Tutorial 3.6 makes use of this completed Illustrator® file, so save it in a location that you'll have access to later.

Step 3: Complete the Face in Photoshop®

The male croquis face needed some character to make it distinguished-looking, so it was exported to Photoshop® and further enhanced with shadows, midtones, and highlights (Figure 13.76).

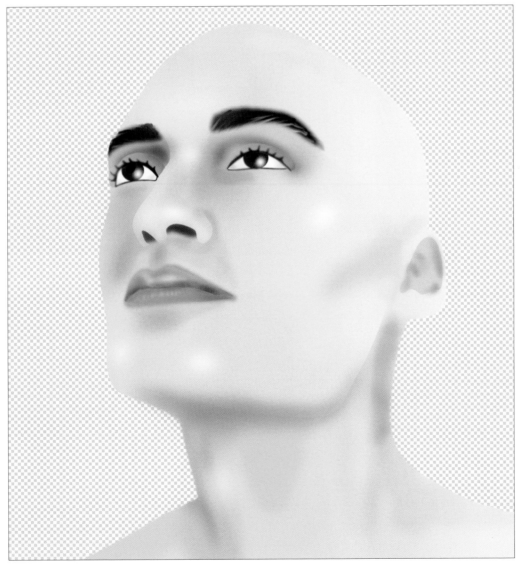

Figure 13.76 **Illustration by Stacy Stewart Smith.**

If you want to create the illusion of dark skin for a presentation without having to generate an entirely new croquis, the solution is simple, but it requires precision.

In this tutorial, you will learn how to change the color of flesh tones and enhance facial features by using Photoshop® to simulate ethnic features.

Note: *Each monitor is calibrated differently and may produce a different outcome. Depending on your computer's monitor, you may have to do some tweaking to get the results you are looking for.*

The goal of this tutorial is to convert male and female croquis rendered with light-colored hues and aquiline features into croquis with dark colors and Afro-ethnic features. We will not attempt the entire body in this exercise because of the various detached layers. However, you may want to do that yourself later.

Step 1: Save a Copy of the File in Photoshop®

Save a copy of the file you completed in Tutorial 13.2 and give it a new relevant name.

Step 2: Lock and Unlink Layers

1. Lock all the other layers on this file except the *Face* layer. Select, unlock, and unlink the *Face* layer if needed.

2. Then, zoom in on the face.

3. With the *Face* layer selected, go to *Menu Bar > Image > Adjustments > Photo Filter*.

4. In the dialog box, select the *Filter* button and change the color to yellow from the pull-down menu. Type in 65% into the field (Figure 13.77).

Step 3: Adjust Exposure

Next, go to *Menu Bar > Image > Adjustments > Exposure* and change the following coordinates.

Exposure: -0.20

Off Set: -0.2390

Gamma Correction: 0.44

Again, you may need to tinker with things to discover whatever works for you and your monitor's calibration (Figure 13.78).

Figure 13.77

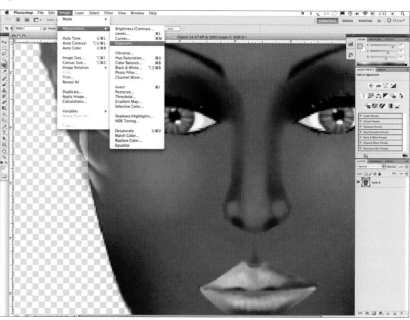

Figure 13.78

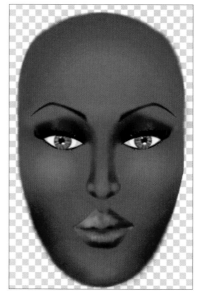

Figure 13.79

Figure 13.80

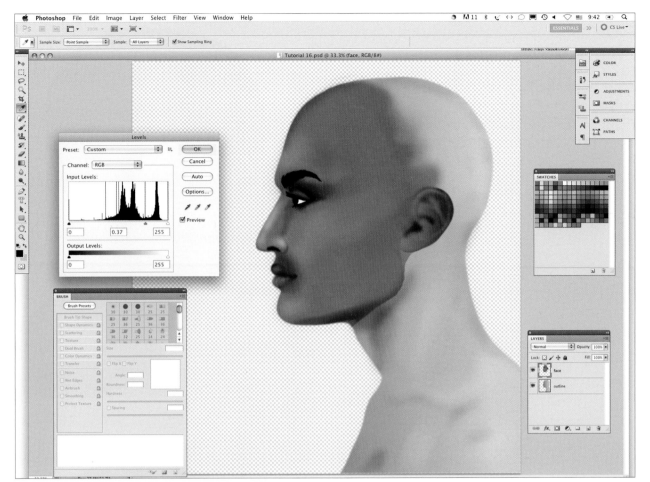

Figure 13.81 The Levels controls will help you correct the tone of the color.

Step 4: Morph Features with Photoshop® Free Transform

Facial features come in all shapes, but there are certain features that you may want to emphasize through the Photoshop® Free Transform options. Press *Cmd+T / Ctrl+T* to scale objects on selected Photoshop® layers (Figures 13.79 and 13.80).

Additional Ways to Morph Facial Features with Photoshop®

The Photoshop® Levels, Warp, and Puppet Warp filter settings can be used to modify the features of your croquis (male or female) and allow you to create a variety of character types. To continue with the tutorial, use the profile-view croquis that you completed for Tutorial 13.3.

Step 5: Save a Copy of the File in Photoshop®

Save a copy of the file you completed in Tutorial 13.3 and give it a new relevant name.

Step 6: Darken the Color of the Face

Select a layer that you want to affect, and then go to *Menu Bar > Image > Adjustments > Levels*, and use the histogram settings to darken the color of your croquis (Figure 13.81).

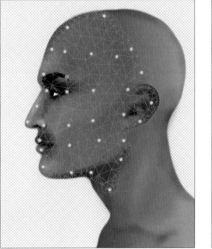

Figure 13.82

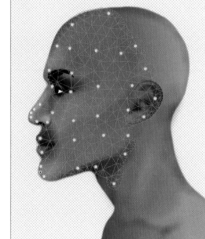

Figure 13.83

Step 7: Place the Photoshop® Puppet Warp

In Photoshop® CS5 and CS6, the Puppet Warp pins can assist in reshaping digital drawings. Select a layer that you want to affect, and then go to *Menu Bar > Edit > Puppet Warp*. Place the pins at strategic reference points as shown in Figure 13.82.

Step 8: Slightly Extend the Nose and Chin

Pull the Photoshop® Puppet Warp pins to slightly extend the nose and chin as shown in Figure 13.83.

Step 9: Darken the Face Again

Use the Levels histogram to darken the color of the face as shown in Figure 13.84.

Step 10: Make Further Adjustments to the Face

Select the layer you want to affect and go to *Menu Bar > Edit > Transform > Warp*. A gridded Bounding Box will appear around your image. Notice how slight adjustments to the grid affect the slope of the nose and forehead in Figure 13.85. The completed Afro-Ethnic male croquis appears in Figure 13.86.

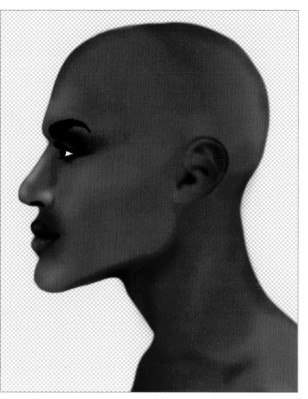

Figure 13.84

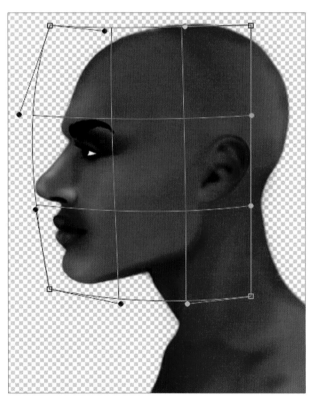

Figure 13.85

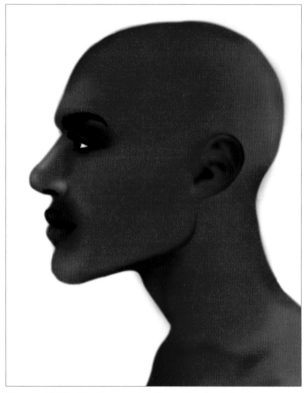

Figure 13.86 Illustration by Stacy Stewart Smith.

TIP: Rendering Asian Faces

A good way to render Asian-ethnic facial features on your fashion croquis is to follow a good photo. However, if one is not available, create the face with a full jaw but a sharp chin. High cheekbones also add strong facial character to this croquis.

To add the Asian aesthetic to your male and female croquis using Photoshop®, try some of the techniques demonstrated in this three-quarter croquis face tutorial. To help you complete this tutorial, three-quarter-view headshots have been provided on ① Digital Duo Modeling Agency.

Note: Select and use any Illustrator® rendering tool, such as the Illustrator® Pen Tool (P), to create the shapes in this tutorial. The objects in the steps must be rendered on separate layers in Illustrator® for the best results later when exporting the file to Photoshop®. Follow each step as shown in the adjacent figures.

Step 1: Create the General Outline of the Head and Ear Parts

Give the face a full jaw but a sharp chin. High cheekbones also add strong facial character to this croquis (Figure 13.87).

Step 2: Render the Face Shapes

Create shapes for the face, ear parts, mouth, and eyes. Keep the bottom of the eye sockets flat. The mouth should be well-shaped (Figures 13.88 and 13.89).

Figure 13.87

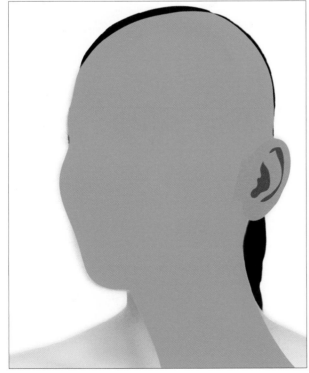

Figure 13.88

Figure 13.89

Step 3: Create the Eyes

Pull a Guide to keep the bottom of the eye flat as shown in Figure 13.90. Add shapes for the iris, pupil, eye highlight, and eyelids on separate layers (Figure 13.91).

Step 4: Render the Upper and Lower Lips

Create separate shapes for the lower and upper lips as shown in Figures 13.92.

Step 5: Check the Symmetry

Use the original photo to check the symmetry of the parts by toggling off the visibility of the face and the outline of the head (Figure 13.93).

Step 6: Draw Lashes, Eyebrows, and Eyeliner

Take some time to study the photo of your human subject. Draw on eyeliner to emphasize the eyes' regal shape (Figure 13.94).

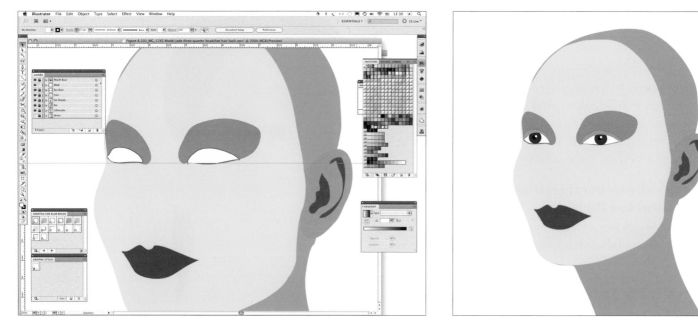

Figure 13.90

Figure 13.91

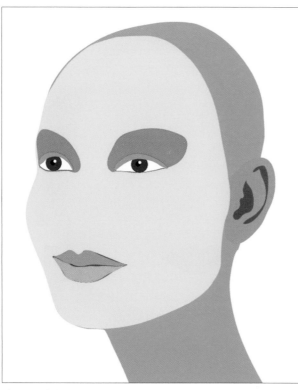

Figure 13.92

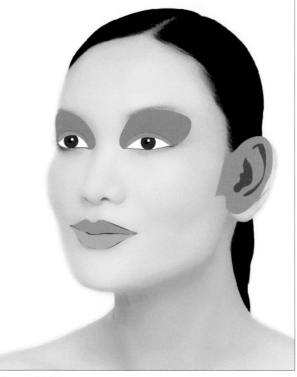

Figure 13.93

Step 7: Apply Color, Gradients, and Filters with Illustrator®

Be creative to generate a presentation that is complementary to the subject. The completed Asian-ethnic female croquis face is shown in Figure 13.95.

Asian-Ethnic Enhancements with Photoshop®

With just a few different Photoshop® settings, you can generate convincing Asian-ethnic features for male croquis from nearly any other croquis with light-colored filled shapes. To complete the next portion of this tutorial, use the three-quarter-view male croquis that you created in Illustrator® for Tutorial 13.4, as long as you filled it with fair to medium hues (Figure 13.96).

Step 8: Export the Croquis from Illustrator® to Photoshop®

Figure 13.94

Figure 13.95

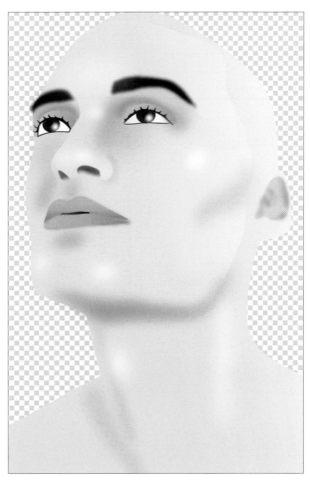

Figure 13.96

Step 9: Add Yellow Tones to the Face

Use the Photoshop® Hue/Saturation filter to add more yellow to the filled facial shapes (Figure 13.97).

Step 10: Adjust the Shape of the Eyes and Narrow the Mouth

Flatten the bottom of the eyes. Remove the eyelid shapes and scale the iris, pupil, etc. Use the Photo-shop® Free Transform feature to narrow the width of the mouth (Figure 13.98).

Step 11: Widen the Nose and Forehead

Use the Photoshop® Free Transform Feature to widen the nose and forehead as shown in Figure 13.99. The completed male croquis with Asian-ethnic features is pictured in Figure 13.100.

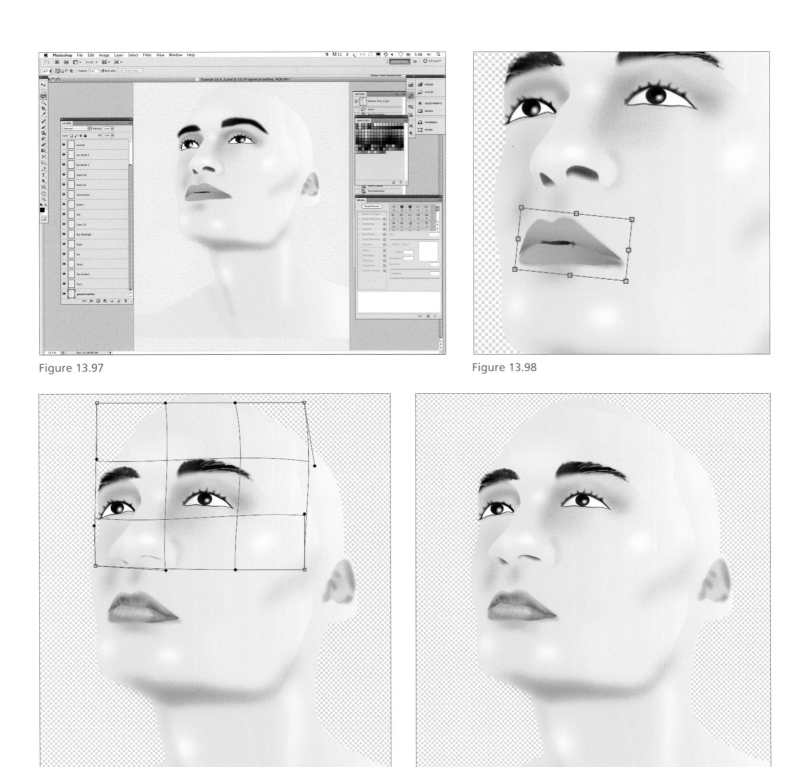

Figure 13.97

Figure 13.98

Figure 13.99

Figure 13.100 Illustration by Stacy Stewart Smith.

Tutorial 13.7
CREATING DIGITAL
BLOND HAIRSTYLES USING
ILLUSTRATOR® GRADIENTS, TOOLS,
AND FILTERS

Being a blond is a fashion aesthetic above mere hair color. Depending on the times, anyone can be a blond, and blond hair is always in style. This tutorial suggests a variety of digital processes to produce classic blond hairstyles by using Illustrator® and Photoshop®. By following the instructions for each exercise in this tutorial, you will create straight, wavy, and curly styles for men and women.

Note: *Some of the exercises in this tutorial require hand-rendered or painted hairstyles.*

Although these procedures feature blond hairstyles, the same techniques will work for almost any hair color. There are three factors to bear in mind when creating digital hair, especially frontal and three-quarter poses:

1. The back of the hairstyle is a shape that begins on a layer beneath the croquis (the body outline and the face) in either program. You need this shape to maintain the look of the hairstyle (Figures 13.101 and 13.102).

2. The front of the hair should be rendered on a layer(s) above the face (Figure 13.103).

3. Hair should be accented to create the illusion of dimension. Highlights and shadows are needed for the best results in both vector and raster programs (Figure 13.104).

Figure 13.101

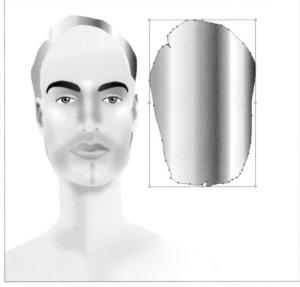

Figure 13.102

Figure 13.103

Figure 13.104

Step 1: Open the Front View Croquis Face in Illustrator®

Open the frontal-view croquis face you created in Tutorial 13.1.

Step 2: Create a Shape for the Back of the Hair

On a layer below the croquis figure, render a hair shape using a Gold or Brass gradient from the Illustrator® Metals Gradients Library. Adjust the fill with the Gradient Tool (G) (Figure 13.102).

Step 3: Create the Front of the Hair

On a new layer, above the face layer, render the hair shape for the right section of the hairstyle. Fill the shape with the same gradient, and then adjust it with the Gradient Tool (G) (Figure 13.103). Afterward, do the same for the left side (Figure 13.104).

Step 4: Add Locks and Strands

Use the Pen Tool (P) to create locks of hair filled with the same or different gradients, and then adjust them in different ways as in Figures 13.105 and Figure 13.106. For even greater definition, use the Pencil Tool (N) to make individual strands as shown in Figure 13.107.

Step 5: Add Details and Highlights

Detail the sides of the hair, and then add highlights with the Blob Brush Tool (Shift+B) and the Gaussian Blur filter (Figures 13.108 and 13.109).

Step 6: Export the File to Photoshop®

Export your Illustrator® file to Photoshop®, and toggle off the visibility of layers except the croquis's outline and the back of the hair (Figure 13.110).

Figure 13.105

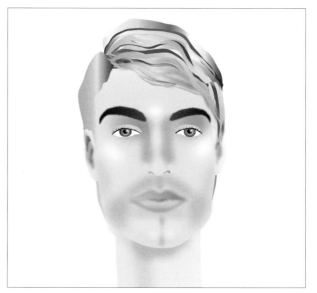
Figure 13.106

Figure 13.107

Figure 13.108

Step 7: Smudge the Hair Locks

Select the Smudge Tool and adjust your brush size appropriately to the locks that you intend to make. For example, if you are going to create strand effects for long hair with lots of volume, then use a large brush diameter. A medium-to-small-size brush will create natural-looking locks as shown in Figure 13.111. Using a smaller brush size with increased *Strength* will be helpful in creating the illusion of hair strands (texture). The larger brush sizes with decreased *Strength* will assist with the overall look of the hairstyle.

You can add additional color to certain areas with the Brush Tool (B). The Burn Tool (O) will come in handy for creating shadows and the Dodge Tool (O) for highlights.

Step 8: Add an Adjustment Layer Filled with Black

Create a temporary Adjustment layer (see Tutorial 7.1, Step Eight) below the *Back of Hair* layer. It will help you to see the shape and texture of the hair as it develops (Figure 13.112).

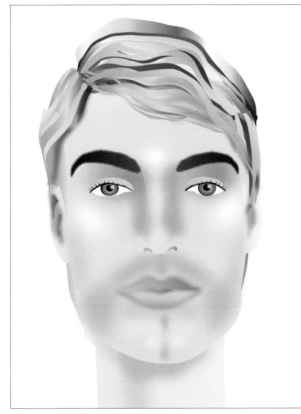

Figure 13.109

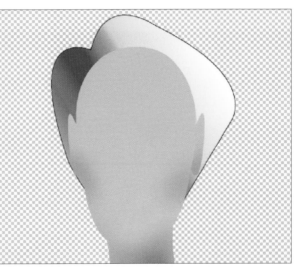

Figure 13.110

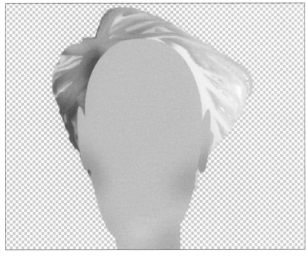

Figure 13.111

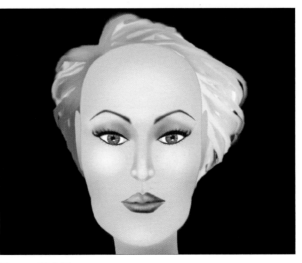

Figure 13.112

Step 9: Make the Front of Hair in Illustrator®

Treat the front hair as you did the back hair, using various tools to accomplish a style in Illustrator®. Add single strands of hair with the Brush Tool (B) or the Pencil Tool (N). Use the Smudge Tool to smooth them into the flow of the locks. Pretend you are actually styling the hair, so click and drag in quick sweeping motions in the direction and flow of the pictured hairstyle. Once you are satisfied with the results, export the file to Photoshop® (Figure 13.113).

TIP: Keep Color Change Records

If you would like to alter the color, go ahead and do so, but keep a written record of whatever you changed on the *Back of the Hair* layer so that you can make the same changes on the *Front of Hair* layer.

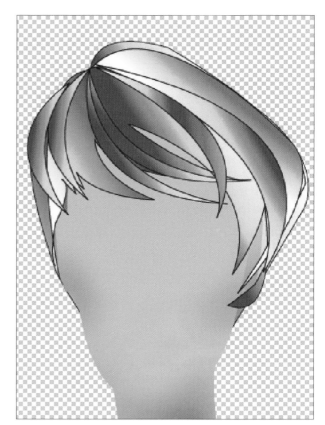

Figure 13.113

Figure 13.114 Illustration by Stacy Stewart Smith.

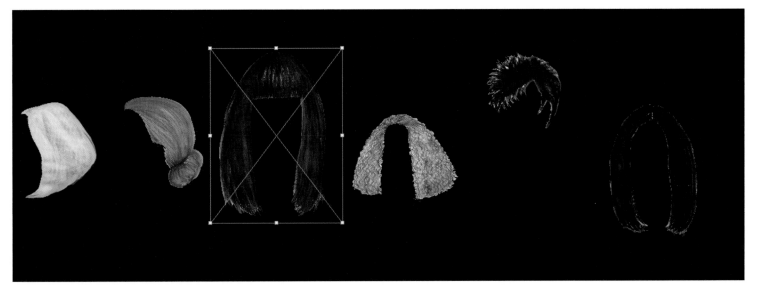

Figure 13.115

Step 10: Add Layer Style(s) in Photoshop®

Layer Styles can add special effects to your work. The *Front of Hair* layer is a good candidate for the Layer Style entitled Bevel and Emboss.

1. Click this Layer Style icon and scroll to Bevel and Emboss.

2. For this exercise, use the following settings: Create an *Inner Bevel*, because it will complement the small strokes you have already created.

3. The *Technique* section should be set to *Smooth* to create a soft effect.

4. Check *Anti-Aliased* to ensure a vector-smooth quality to your exported file.

5. Change the *Highlight Mode* and the *Shadow Mode* color by clicking on the rectangular boxes to the right.

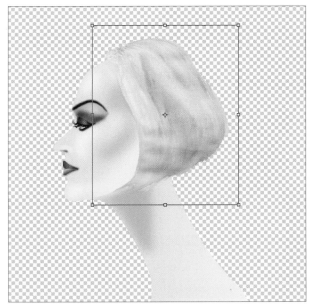

Figure 13.116

In addition, Color Overlay may be useful if you would like to tint the color, but remember to exercise restraint and reduce the *Opacity*. Keep experimenting with the various options to learn the extent of this tool.

Step 11: Erase Some of the Hair

Erase all the hair you do not want with the Photoshop® Eraser Tool (E). Much of the bangs on the *Front of Hair* layer and sides on the *Back of Hair* layer have been eliminated in the example (Figure 13.114).

Step 12: Use the Blur Tool to Complete the Front of the Hair

When you have completed your choices in Bevel and Emboss, use the Blur Tool. Use a large brush with the strength of approximately 34% to complete the look of the front of the hair. Just rub, click, and drag in the flow of the locks until the style looks complete. The finished look appears in Figure 13.114.

Adding Hair with a Placed Painting

Another way to create realistic-looking hair is to paint a style in watercolor or other media on paper, and then scan and place it into a Photoshop® file. The folder Wigs on ② Ch13 contains six hairstyles that have been created in this manner (Figure 13.115). Simply place them into any croquis file and use the Bounding Box to scale them (Figure 13.116). For best results, place them into Photoshop® first, edit the looks and shapes, save copies, and then place them into Illustrator® if needed.

Note: *Do not forget to Embed or rasterize the files if you place them in Illustrator®. (See Tutorial 3.1, Step Eight.)*

Practice placing and adjusting various wig files using the methods described in the following examples.

Figure 13.117

Straight Bob: The "wig" pictured in Figure 13.117 was placed into Photoshop® and scaled using the Free Transform features. Then, the locks were smudged with the Scatter Brush to give the hair a more realistic look (Figure 13.118). Necessary adjustments to the color were made by going to *Menu Bar > Image > Adjustments > Color Balance* and moving the slider controls (Figure 13.119). Finally, the Bevel and Emboss Layer Style was added to give further dimension to the style.

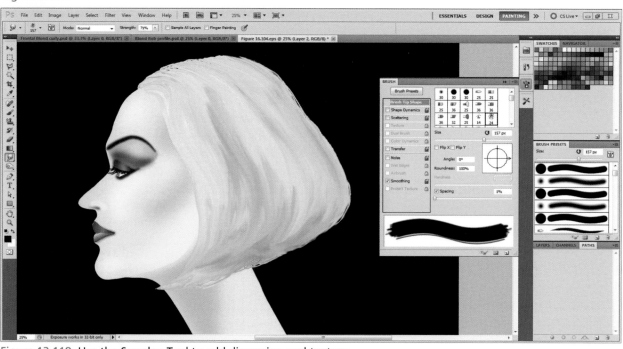

Figure 13.118 Use the Smudge Tool to add dimension and texture.

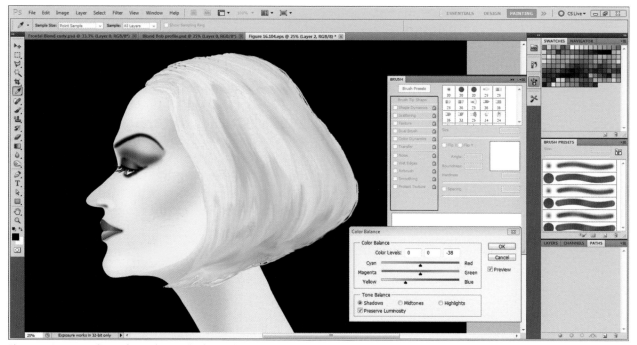

Figure 13.119 Adjust the color with the Color Balance settings.

To achieve the results pictured in **Figure 13.120**, try the following:

1. Add the Bevel and Emboss Layer Style, but uncheck *Global Light* to change the lighting angle manually.

2. Afterward, click on the shadow color and select the new color from a dark portion of the hair in your scanned image.

3. If necessary, choose a darker hue from the Color Picker when it appears and click OK.

4. Tweak the settings to taste, and then click OK in the Layer Style dialog box.

Curly Bob: The same technique can be applied to curly hair using different tools and filters to modify a painted or drawn image in Photoshop® (**Figure 13.121**). This curly hairstyle was stretched and shaped using the Puppet Warp and Transform Warp features (**Figures 13.122** and **13.123**). The texture of the curly hair was enhanced by going to

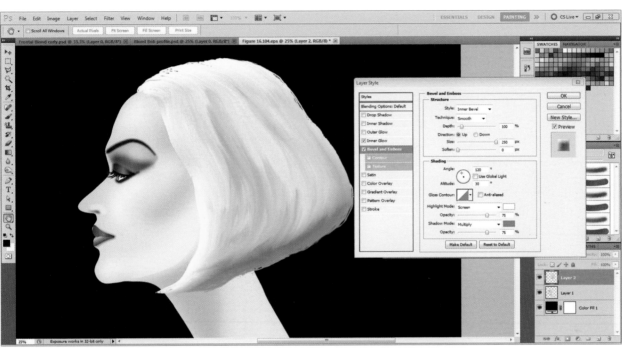

Figure 13.120 Bevel and Emboss can create even greater dimension and perspective.

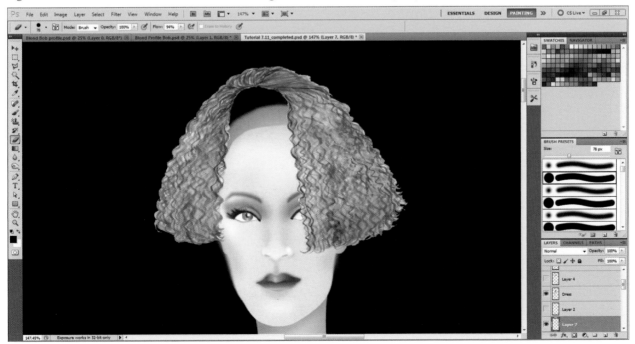

Figure 13.121

Menu Bar > Image > Adjustments > Brightness/Contrast, brightening the overall color, and then altering the variance between light and dark (Figure 13.124). Further enhancements were made by adding the Paint Daubs filter (Figure 13.125). Finally, Paint, Smudge, Burn, Dodge, Erase, Liquify, and Blur tools and filters were used to complete the look (Figure 13.126).

Figure 13.122

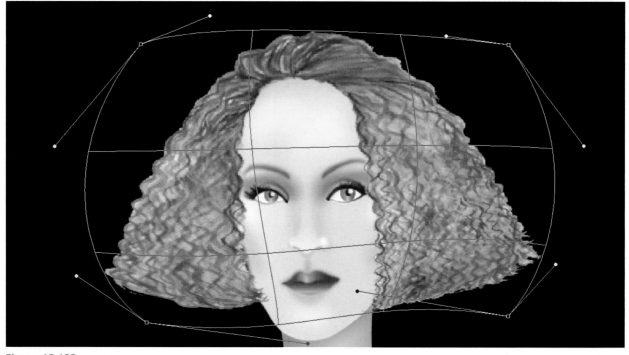

Figure 13.123

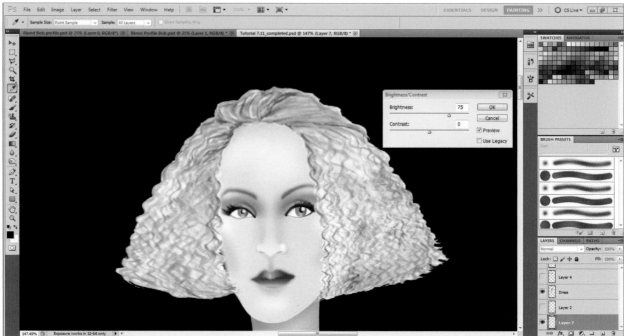

Figure 13.124

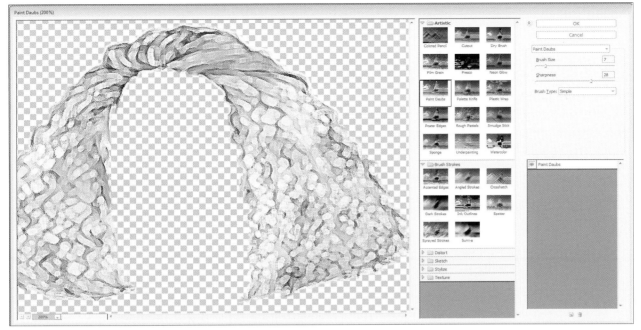

Figure 13.125 Photoshop® Paint Daubs window interface.

Figure 13.126 Illustration by Stacy Stewart Smith.

This tutorial teaches you how to use a photo of long curly hair to complete your croquis's look. You'll learn to use the Photoshop® Warp grid to help add volume and style. To complete this tutorial, use any curly hair headshot of Jade from the ① Digital Duo Modeling Agency and a coordinating croquis file that you completed earlier in the chapter.

Step 1: Open a Curly Hair Headshot in Photoshop®

1. Open a curly hair headshot of Jade (Figure 13.127) from ① Digital Duo Modeling Agency.

2. Rename the Background layer.

3. Select the white background with the Photoshop® Magic Wand Tool (W), and then press the Delete key.

4. If you will be using a white background for your work, you can make a rough selection with the Lasso Tool (L).

5. Afterward, drag and drop the image of the hair into your croquis file (Figure 13.128).

Note: *You may need to adjust the Tolerance in the Options Bar.*

Step 2: Use the Photoshop® Transform Warp Grid to Resize the Hair Image

See Figure 13.129.

Step 3: Use the Photoshop® Rough Pastels and Dark Strokes Filters

1. Go to *Menu Bar > Filter > Artistic > Rough Pastels*. This filter will add texture to the photo and make it look more like a drawing (Figure 13.130).

2. On the right side of the screen you can adjust the *Stroke Length, Stroke Detail, Texture, Scaling Relief,* and *Light*.

3. To add an additional filter to this one, such as *Dark Strokes,* select the *New* icon at the bottom right and then click on the next filter.

4. Select a filter from the menu on the lower right to change the settings or toggle off its visibility icon to see your work without it.

5. Experiment and add a few filters; the choice is yours. Try the Liquify filter too.

6. When you have the filters adjusted, click OK.

Figure 13.127

Figure 13.128

Figure 13.129

Step 4: Add Volume to the Hair

Use the Transform Warp Grid again to add more volume to the hair (Figure 13.131). The completed look is pictured in Figure 13.132.

Figure 13.130

Figure 13.131

Figure 13.132 Illustration by Stacy Stewart Smith.

Try your hand at creating straight dark hair from one of the files on ② Ch13\Wigs (Figure 13.133). Simply place the wig into your Photoshop® croquis file and use the Lasso Tool (L) to separate it into parts by selecting, then pressing *Cmd+X / Ctrl+X* to cut, and pasting the parts into new layers. Flip, rotate, and place the wig parts onto your croquis to create a long hairstyle (Figures 13.134 and 13.135).

Figure 13.133

Figure 13.134

Figure 13.135 Illustration by Stacy Stewart Smith.

Tutorial 13.10
CREATING DIGITAL HAIRSTYLES USING ILLUSTRATOR® GRADIENTS AND SYMBOLS

This tutorial teaches you how to use the Illustrator® Symbols Library to create a dynamic hairstyle. You'll then export the file to Photoshop®, where you'll make the strands come alive with color and more. Use any frontal-view croquis face that you created earlier in this chapter.

Step 1: Open the Croquis File in Illustrator®

Step 2: Create and Fill a Hair Shape

Fill the shape with a gradient as shown in Figure 13.136.

Figure 13.136

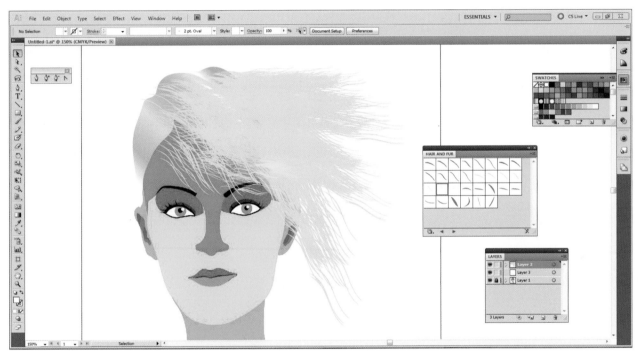

Figure 13.137

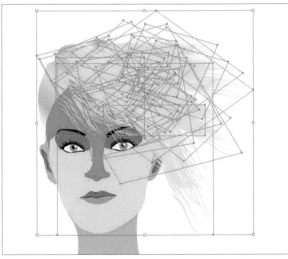

Figure 13.138

Step 3: Create Strands of Hair

1. Show the Illustrator® Hair and Fur Symbols Library and select a symbol.

2. Use the Symbol Sprayer Tool (Shift+S) and others in the suite to adjust the strand(s).

3. Copy, paste, rotate, scale, and group the hair in sections and place them on top of the gradient-filled shape (Figure 13.137).

Step 4: Make Adjustments to the Hair

Select and copy the Hair Symbols parts and use the Symbols Tools to make further adjustments as shown in Figure 13.138.

Step 5: Open Photoshop®

Select, drag, drop, and place the hair parts into Photoshop® as pixels or a Vector Smart Object (Figure 13.139).

Note: *Use a copy of your croquis figure in both programs and apply Vector Smart techniques. See Tutorial 12.4, Steps Five through Seven, for more detailed instructions.*

Step 6: Add Curls and Waves

Use the Liquify filter to add curls and waves to the hairstyle as shown in Figure 13.140.

Step 7: Change the Color of the Hair

Use Hue/Saturation to change the color hair (Figure 13.141). Adjusting the color of the croquis face creates a dramatic presentation, as shown in Figure 13.142.

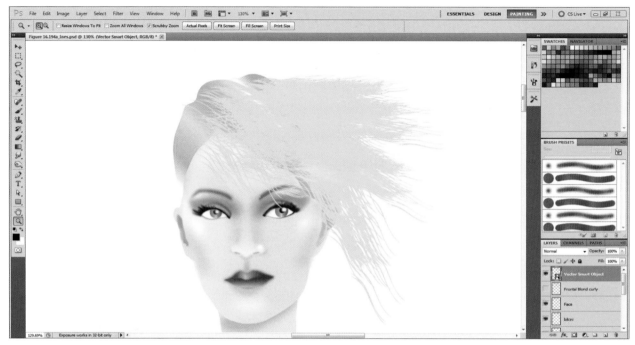

Figure 13.139

Figure 13.140

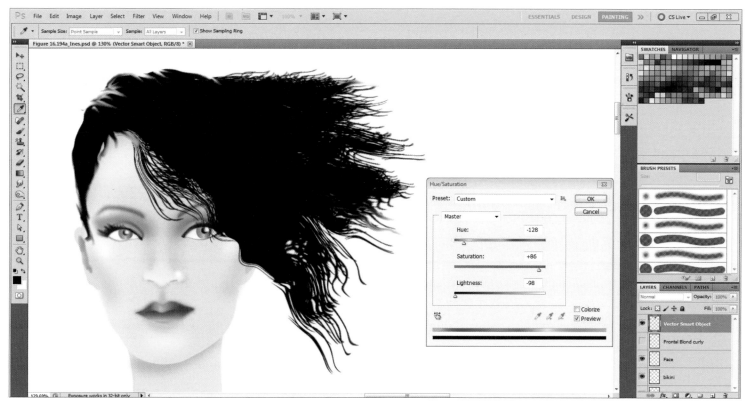

Figure 13.141

Figure 13.142 Illustration by Stacy Stewart Smith.

Chapter 13 Summary

If you are or will be a professional fashion designer, illustrator, or merchandiser, then you will also encounter the need to render or select/style the most current fashion faces. Just as models come into vogue, you will also need to update the look of your croquis. Cosmetic and hair trends date quickly. With digital files you can transform the facial features, the cosmetic effects, and the hairstyles of your croquis at will.

In Chapter 13, you were taken through advanced techniques that combined the functions of both Illustrator® and Photoshop®. Having learned most of these functions in earlier chapters, integrating them in this chapter's tutorials was in itself an examination of how much you have learned. If you did not work through all the tutorials in this chapter, go back and do so, even if you prefer to stay in one gender type. The combined lessons will produce the sharpest skills.

In order to be the best, you must be skilled. Before attempting to move on to the next chapter, ask yourself the following questions. If your answers are not positive, revisit the tutorials in this chapter first.

Chapter 13 Self-Assessment

1. Do I know how to use the Transform Perspective feature of Photoshop® to even out unsymmetrical facial parts?

2. Can I properly use the new Photoshop® art brushes located in the Brush Presets panel to help with blending facial parts exported from Illustrator®?

3. By now saving swatches should be easy, but have I taken out time to mix my own skintone gradients? Have I given them proper titles in the Illustrator® and Photoshop® Swatches panels?

4. Do I understand how to use the Dodge Tool (O) on the bridge of the forehead, cheeks, and chin area to create highlights?

5. Can I change the color of lips, eyelids, and other facial parts? Do I know which filters to use?

6. Can I articulate how to link layers in Photoshop® to prevent accidental shifting of facial parts?

7. Rendering fair skintones is relatively simple, but can I convert them into darker colors using Photoshop® filters in order to make croquis with Afro-ethnic features?

8. Am I familiar with the Photoshop® Levels, Warp, and Puppet Warp filter settings, and can I use them to modify the features of male and female croquis in order to create a variety of character types?

9. Can I apply appropriate Illustrator® Blob Brush Tool (Shift+B) and Graphic Style Shadows and Highlights on faces that I render?

10. Can I simulate Asian-ethnic facial features with Illustrator® and Photoshop®?

11. Do I know how to use the Illustrator® Scissors Tool (C) to cut into a line segment, but not on an anchor point?

12. Do I know the three factors to bear in mind when creating digital hair?

13. Can I properly make use of the files on ② Ch13\ Wigs?

14. Can I effectively use the Photoshop® Warp grid to add volume to a digital hairstyle?

15. The Illustrator® Hair and Fur Symbols Library offers another way for me to create digital hairstyles, but can I use them effectively with the Symbol Sprayer Tool (Shift+S)?

16. Can I create digital Afro-Ethnic hairstyles?

17. Am I comfortable creating digital blond hairstyles in a variety of ways?

Chapter 13 DVD Extras

Master a variety of hairstyles by completing the following DVD Extra tutorials. These tutorials can be found on ② Ch13\DVD Extras.

DVD Extra 13.1
The Basic Digital Chignon from Freehand Paintings and Photographs

One great feature to digital processes for fashion illustration is the ability to blur the lines between drawing, painting, and photography. In this tutorial, you will render a classic hairstyle in the form of a pulled-back chignon using Photoshop® painting techniques and your own freehand drawings or photography from the ① Digital Duo Modeling Agency (Figure 13.143).

Figure 13.143

DVD Extra 13.2
Digital Short and Wispy Hair from a Freehand Painting

A very classic hairstyle comes in the form of the short and wispy boyish cut. Try drawing or painting the style, then digitizing it to use on a variety of croquis. In this tutorial, you will use the Photoshop® Puppet Warp features to adjust the hair onto the three-quarter-view croquis (Figure 13.144).

Figure 13.144

DVD Extra 13.3
Men's Three-Quarter-View Digital Straight Dark Hair from a Freehand Painting

This tutorial will further your ability to digitally render straight hair by manipulating a freehand painting with the Photoshop® Perspective Transform settings (Figure 13.145).

Figure 13.145

DVD Extra 13.4
Frontal, Profile, and Three-Quarter-View Digital Straight Dark Hair with Photoshop® Painting and Filter Features

Having the ability to style hair digitally enables you to create a variety of looks from just one croquis. As you advance, you will want to lean more on total digital croquis and avoid the scanned images of photos and hand-rendered drawings, paintings, etc. In this tutorial, you will learn to use the Photoshop® art brushes and the Brush panel to help turn digital lines and shapes into believable straight and wavy styles for dark hair (Figure 13.146).

Figure 13.147

DVD Extra 13.6
Facial Hair

At various times, facial hair is considered stylish for men, and fashion presentations should reflect this. Photoshop® Brush Tools (B) and the Brush panel attributes can be used to create a mustache, a goatee, and the Mohawk hairstyle. In this tutorial, you will use the techniques previously demonstrated in this chapter to create facial hair (Figure 13.148).

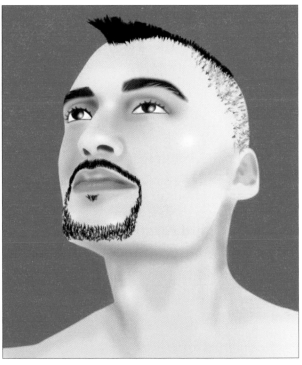

Figure 13.146

DVD Extra 13.5
Afro-Ethnic Hairstyles

Naturally, you could use most of the hairstyles previously discussed on croquis with Afro-ethnic features, but why not try to create a few classic styles that reflect current cultural trends? This tutorial shows you how to use a combination of tools, panels, and filters to generate everything from fades to Afros to locks from a few simple shapes (Figure 13.147).

Figure 13.148

Technical Design with Illustrator®

Objectives

In the apparel market, nearly all digital production flats are created with vector-based software programs like Illustrator®. The need to communicate with global resources and the fast pace of the garment center have nearly eclipsed the use of freehand technical flats for production.

Because the scope of this book is digital fashion design and illustration, the portion of technical design concerned with specifications and grading will not be covered. However, you will learn the following aspects for men's wear and women's wear as components of tech-packs:

◎ Concepts of shape theory and Western tailoring in relationship to the human form

◎ Digital production flat sketches of basic garments using technical design templates and electronic drawing methods

◎ Digital production action-flats (floats)

◎ Digital rendering techniques for apparel details such as pockets, pleats, tucks, and zippers

◎ Using the Illustrator® Stroke panel Arrows menu to help prepare technical schematics details for tech-packs

◎ Placing digital flats into a specification spreadsheet

◎ Preparing a line sheet

◎ Creating a multiple-page Acrobat Pro® (.pdf) file to package all the completed pages of a tech-pack or other fashion presentations

Flats and Floats

Technical flat sketches are digital drawings of apparel items used to assist the creation of patterns for production along with **specifications (specs)**. These specialized drawings appear as if they were laid on a surface. In some cases, **technical action flats (floats)** are used, especially for tailored apparel, because it cannot be positioned comfortably flat. Floats are stylized as if hanging in mid-air. Flats and floats can be used interchangeably for both presentation and production. You will examine and create them in the tutorials in this chapter.

Digital Morphing

Developing good technical flats takes time, but the results can be put to good use. Completed files can be saved and used again. The term digital morphing refers to the process of using a digital flat to create another one. This is a time-saving technical design procedure.

The Illustrator® shape tools, the Pen Tool Suite, and others are used to create basic apparel shapes called technical design templates. With the templates you can create digital technical flats and floats by manipulating them rather than drawing items completely from scratch. Digital morphing relies heavily on the Illustrator® Convert Anchor Point Tool (Shift+C). It is used to convert straight paths into curved line segments and vice versa. With proper organization, this method enables you to respond quickly to requests for the components of tech-packs.

Tech-Packs

A **technical package** contains all the information necessary to produce a particular garment, and the extended needs of production. There are many different ways to prepare a **tech-pack**, so there is no exact science. Every tech-pack will contain the essential components:

• Line sheets for entire groups of styles being sent to factories

• Technical flat sketches

• Specifications (measurements)

• Digital sketches with detailed diagrams of garment areas (schematics)

• Digital sketches of custom hardware (logo buckles, buttons, etc.)

• Production information for fabrications, colorways, notions, trims, hardware, etc.

• A grading worksheet that provides the finished measurements for all the sizes in the production range for a particular style

Fit Model Work Files for Technical Flats

For your convenience, front- and back-view poses of Jade and Carl have been placed in the files Female_Fit_Model_for_Flats.pdf and Male_Fit_Model_for_Flats.pdf on ② Ch14\Tutorial 14.1. To retain the original layers, open the files in Illustrator® CS5 or higher. These files help you work through the chapter tutorials and learn how to develop well-proportioned digital technical flats (**Figures 14.1 and 14.2**).

Note: If you are using Illustrator® CS4 or lower, the layers may be merged when you open the file. However, this will not prevent you from using them. You can also reposition the parts or copy and paste them into new layers.

The layers of the *Fit Model Work Files* and the items on them have been locked to prevent shifting of the parts. You will need to click the *Lock* icons on each layer, and as well *Option+Cmd+2 / Option+Ctrl+2* in order to select, move, or manipulate the objects on them. The *Fit Model Work Files* also contain completed basic apparel templates on separate layers that can be used to digitally morph almost any type of technical apparel flat (**Figures 14.3 and 14.4**). You can toggle off the visibility of the layers to hide the templates that are not in use.

Fit Model File Movable Parts

While you are learning how to navigate the tutorials, avoid unlocking the layers containing the model's images (photographs). However, the color-coded arms or legs may be unlocked, moved, or rotated to help you render specific types of garments and details. You can adjust these parts by using the double-arrow features of the Bounding Boxes that appear when you bring your cursor near the corners.

If you move the photos and discover that the model's proportions have been distorted, simply close the file and reopen it again from the DVD. Once you become familiar with the proportions, you will be able to reposition the files at will. Eventually, you will develop templates and flats of your own and rarely use the fit model files.

Your Work Layer, Line Layers, and the Reference Points Layer

Work on the layer labeled *Your Work Layer* with the others locked. It is positioned below the *Reference Points and Levels* layer. This layer contains the lines corresponding to the *Key* at the bottom of the file. Each reference point has a letter and a line that marks a particular area of the model's body. Use these reference points as you study actual garments to create digital flat sketches.

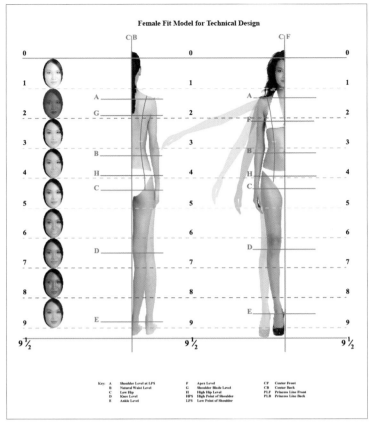

Figure 14.1

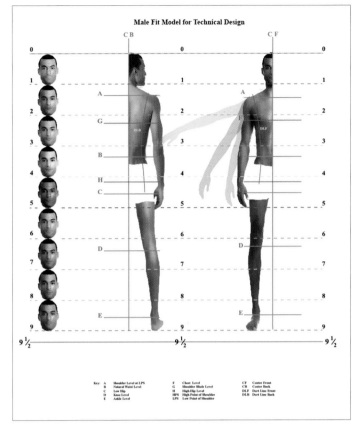

Figure 14.2

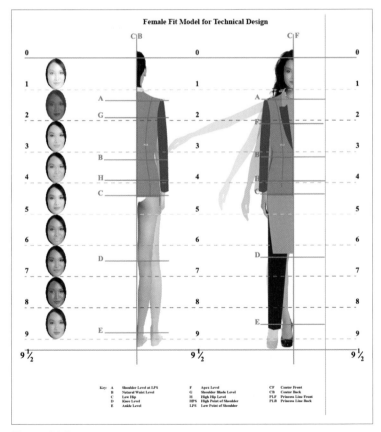

Figure 14.3

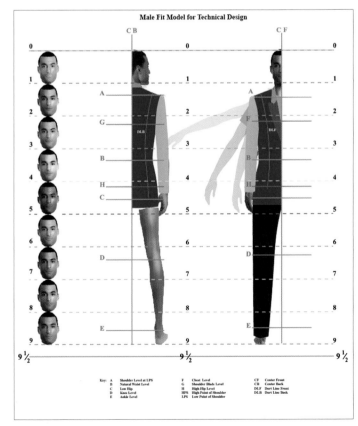

Figure 14.4

You can reposition the *Dart* or *Princess Line* layers above or below the layer labeled *Your Work Layer*. You can use the red vertical curved lines on these layers to help you create and position darts or side yokes. You can also toggle off the visibility of these layers or delete them if they obscure your view (Figure 14.5).

The Blocks Layer

The *Blocks* layer may be used to hide half of the model's image. This enables you to render the digital flat on one side, and then later mirror the drawing with a copy. Toggle on or off the layer as needed (Figure 14.5).

Fit Model Scale Proportions

In fashion drawing, the scale of a croquis is divided by the length of the head. Images of the models' faces have been placed on the left of each file to indicate the scale increments. In the *Fit Model Work Files* a scale of dashed lines marks each proportion level corresponding to numbers on the sides and center. This scale helps you make use of reference points as you are rendering your flats in Illustrator® (Figures 14.1 and 14.2).

Fit Model File Reference Points

A **reference point** is a particular place on the body where spatial relationships are made in order to create well-proportioned technical flats. A Key is located at the bottom of each file (Figures 14.1–14.4). The Key lists the body reference points with their letter codes that appear on the scale.

TIP: Press A and Then Press P

Always select the Direct Selection Tool (A) first and then select the drawing tool of choice, such as the Pen Tool (P), to toggle the two tools. This gives you a greater ability to instantly affect the anchors and paths without having to switch tools.

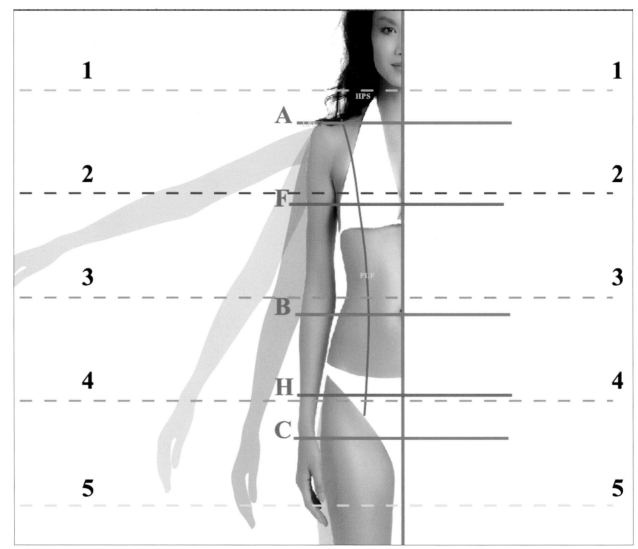

Figure 14.5 The solid white shape to the right is on the Blocks layer.

The practice of creating body coverings from cloth or animal skins cut or torn into ovals and rectangles can be observed in the dress of ancient Eastern civilizations. This shape theory design approach is apparent in some styles that have survived over the centuries, such as the kimono and the kaftan. Today, most clothing is manufactured based on theories of Western tailoring. Contemporary apparel is cut with a combination of sickle shapes and curved and straight lines to tailor garments to the human form.

When most people think about technical sketches, they think of them as being flat, but in reality nothing is totally flat. A good fashion designer is judged on how well his or her technical flats communicate the volume that's needed to produce quality samples and production. To help you develop flat sketches with convincing volume, this tutorial applies concepts of classic apparel shape theory and Western tailoring to the rendering of **technical design templates**. You will learn how to create these templates from basic geometric shapes using Illustrator®.

This tutorial utilizes the file Female_Fit_Model_for_Flats.pdf on ② Ch14\Tutorial 14.1. You'll notice that technical design templates already exist in the files; however, follow the steps of this tutorial to create your own templates with new silhouettes.

Note: This tutorial focuses on creating design templates for women's wear, but the exact same logic applies to men's wear and the steps can be followed using the file Male_Fit_Model_for_Flats.pdf on ② Ch14\Tutorial 14.1.

Step 1: Open a Fit Model File in Illustrator® CS5 or CS6

1. Begin this tutorial with one of the two fit model files.

2. Open the file in Illustrator® and save a copy to your computer.

3. Take a moment and observe the layer compositing.

4. Unlock the Your Work Layer.

5. Move the Zero Point to the Center Front position (see Tutorial 3.1, Step Twelve).

6. Open and watch the movie Steps 1-6.m4v on ② Ch14\Tutorial 14.1.

Note: The reference points needed to help you draw are already in the file, but you may want to pull a few Guides as well to assist the rendering process.

Step 2: Create a Basic Geometric Shape

1. Use the Rectangle Tool (M) to create a rectangle.

2. Fill the rectangle with any color. You do not need to stroke the shape.

3. Place the shape flush against the CF line and use the Bounding Box to pull the width to the low hip level (Figure 14.6).

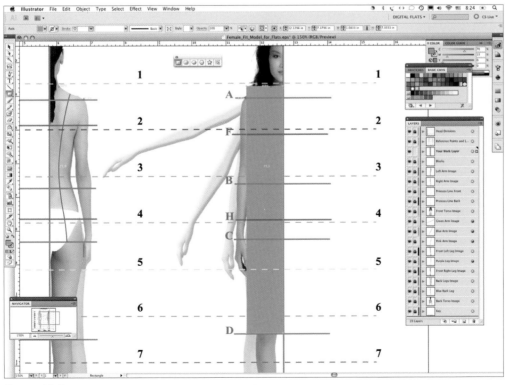

Figure 14.6

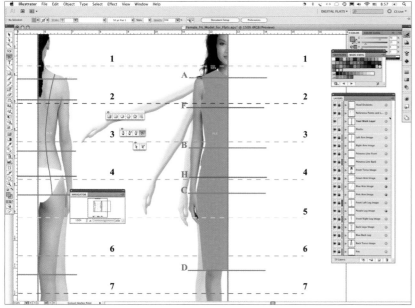

Figure 14.7

Step 3: Reshape the Rectangle into a Shift Dress Template

1. Use the Add Anchor Point Tool (+) to add vectors (also termed anchor points) to the left side of the rectangular shape at the bottom of the fit model's front armhole (Division 2), the front waist (Level B), and the front low hip level (Level C).

2. Add another anchor point between the armhole and the top and still another near the high point of the shoulder at the top.

3. You will also need to add another anchor point at the high hip.

4. Use the Direct Selection Tool (A) to select the anchor points, and then move them with your direction keys (arrows) or manually to create the shape shown in Figure 14.7.

Step 4: Create Curves

1. Use the Convert Anchor Point Tool (Shift+C) to turn the paths shown from straight to curved by clicking on the anchors and manipulating the handles (Figure 14.8).

Note: *Simply click on the anchor point with this tool. Hold the clicker and drag outward in a twist. This will turn the straight paths into curves. You can also view this procedure in the movie (Steps 1–6.m4v located on ② Ch14\Tutorial 14.1).*

Step 5: Copy, Paste, and Reflect

Select, copy, paste, and use the Reflect Tool (R) options to position a copy of the shape on the opposite side (Figure 14.9).

Step 6: Overlap, Align, and Unite

1. Position the copy so that it overlaps the original shape, select both, and then use the Align panel to reposition both shapes at the same level by clicking Vertical Align Top.

2. With both the original and the copy shape selected, click the *Unite* icon on the upper level of the Pathfinder panel, and the two shapes will become one (Figure 14.10).

3. Use the Convert Anchor Point Tool (Shift+C) to curve the anchor at the center and create a jewel neckline by pulling the handles even horizontally.

Step 7: Cut and Paste

1. Select, copy, and paste the developed shape that is now a technical design template into a new layer named *Dress* (Figure 14.11).

2. Toggle off the visibility of this layer and lock it.

3. Save and back up your file.

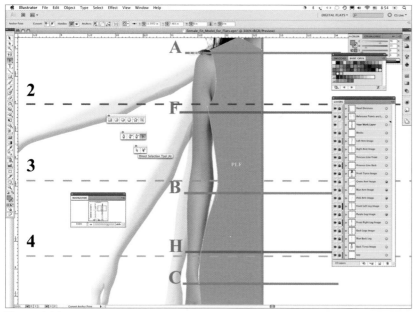

Figure 14.8

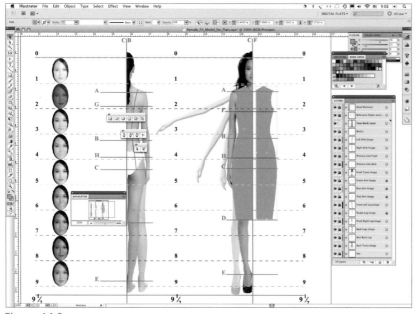

Figure 14.9

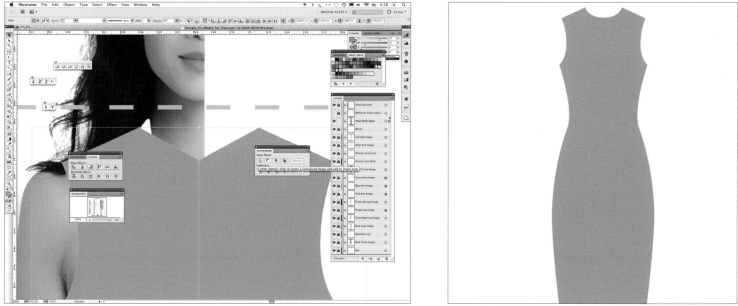

Figure 14.10

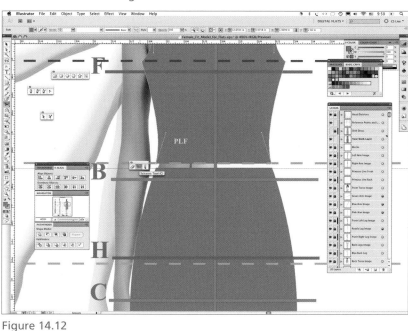

Figure 14.11

Step 8: Morph a Skirt and Bodice

1. Open and watch the movie Steps 8-9.m4v on ② Ch14\Tutorial 14.1.

2. Select, copy, and paste the shift dress technical design template that you just created on the *Your Work Layer*.

3. Fill it with a different color.

4. Pull a Guide to the anchor that you set near the waist level. Use the Scissors Tool (C) to click on both sides just above or below the anchors to cut the shape in two (Figure 14.12).

5. Use the Pen Tool (P) to close the bottom of the bodice shape and the top of the straight shirt shape.

6. Fill the skirt with another color, then cut and paste these into separate layers with appropriate names. Lock the layers.

Step 9: Create a Sleeve Template from a Rectangle

1. Toggle on the visibility of the *Bodice* layer.

2. Create a new layer above it entitled *Basic Sleeve*.

3. Follow the previous steps to create the shape shown in Figure 14.13 using the angle of the pink arm.

4. Add anchor points to the underarm, and at the top between the two corners.

5. Pull the angles to shape and create curved paths as previously instructed using the Convert Anchor Point Tool (Shift+C) (Figure 14.14).

6. The top of the sleeve shape should be positioned at the LPS.

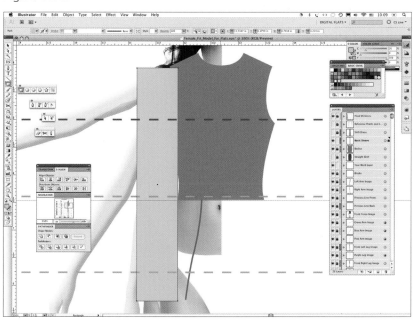

Figure 14.12

Figure 14.13

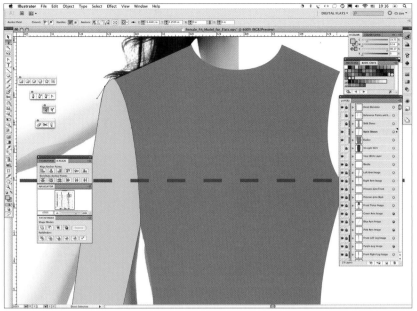

Figure 14.14

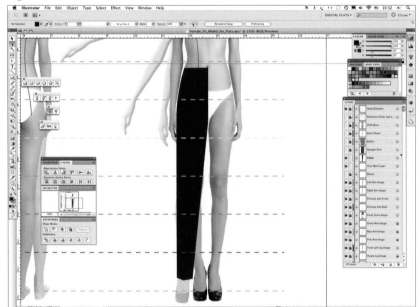

Figure 14.15

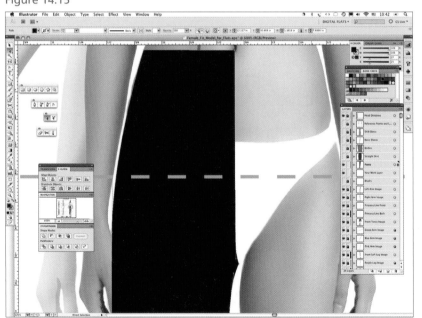

Figure 14.16

7. Pull the underarm anchor to the position of the fit model's arm, which will hang outside of the template. Adjust the bodice armhole on the left side to fit the sleeve.

8. You may add anchors to the center, then select the right side with a marquee of the Direct Selection Tool (A). Remove the opposite side by pressing the Delete key.

9. Select, copy, and paste the left side.

10. Select the copy, and then double-click on the Reflect Tool (P) to flip the shape 90° vertically.

11. Place and overlap the two bodice parts, and then align them as instructed previously.

12. Select both sides.

13. Click the *Unite* icon in the Pathfinder panel to make the two shapes one (Figure 14.14)

Step 10: Create the Pants Template

1. Open and watch the movie Steps 10-11.m4v on ② Ch14\Tutorial 14.1.

2. Create another layer named *Pants.*

3. Use the Rectangle Tool (M) to create an oblong shape from the waist level to just past the ankle level, and as wide as the hips.

4. Use any color Fill; you do not need a Stroke.

5. Place the shape flush against the CF line and use the Bounding Box to make adjustments to the shape (Figure 14.15).

Step 11: Pants Template Details

1. To make the pants template functional, add anchors to both sides at the knee level. You will need them later to develop certain styles.

2. In addition, add anchors on both sides of the inner-rise area.

3. Convert these two to curved paths and manipulate them to develop a shape similar to the one pictured in Figure 14.16.

4. Make adjustments with the Direct Selection Tool (A), but keep the path at the center straight and close to or on the center front (CF).

5. Save and back up your file.

Step 12: Create a Blazer Template

1. Open and watch the movie Steps 12–14.m4v on ② Ch14\Tutorial 14.1.

2. Create a *Blazer* layer.

3. Use the Rectangle Tool (M) to create a rectangle.

4. Add anchor points with the Add Anchor Point Tool (+). Use the Guides and reference points to assist your placement of the anchors.

5. Convert the left side and the armhole to curved line segments with the Convert Anchor Point Tool (Shift+C).

6. Move the anchors with the Direct Selection Tool (A) to create the shape of a panel similar to the one that you see in Figure 14.17. Notice that the example has an extension of an eighth of an inch at the front (x-axis). This has been done to accommodate the jacket closure.

7. The armhole is not as close to the body as the bodice that was created in Step Eight. The LPS was pulled slightly above the shoulder to give the template a somewhat strong signature.

TIP: Morphing

Morphing the shape of a template is a personal creative decision. Always include the concept of ease (room to move in a garment) in your renderings. Do not make them appear as if they were painted onto the fit model's skin (Figure 14.17).

Step 13: Create the Blazer Sleeve

1. With the visibility of the *Blazer* layer on, create yet another layer labeled *Blazer Sleeve*.

2. Use the Rectangle Tool (M) to create a sleeve similar to the one shown in Figure 14.18. This sleeve should fall slightly closer to the body.

3. Notice the pronounced cap at the LPS, the shaped outer sides and bottom. Create them by adding anchors and using the Convert Anchor Point Tool (Shift+C).

Step 14: Add the Blazer Lapel and Top Collar

The lapel and top collar shown in Figure 14.19 were created with the Illustrator® Pen Tool (M). However, you can make them with rectangles, and then just add anchors. Reposition the anchors with the Direct Selection Tool (A) as previously demonstrated. The peaked lapel shape was given a slight curve on the left side. The path at the top near the inner neck was left open. Later this will help to create a 3-D illusion.

Step 15: Create the Blazer Back

1. To create the back of the blazer, begin with the front.

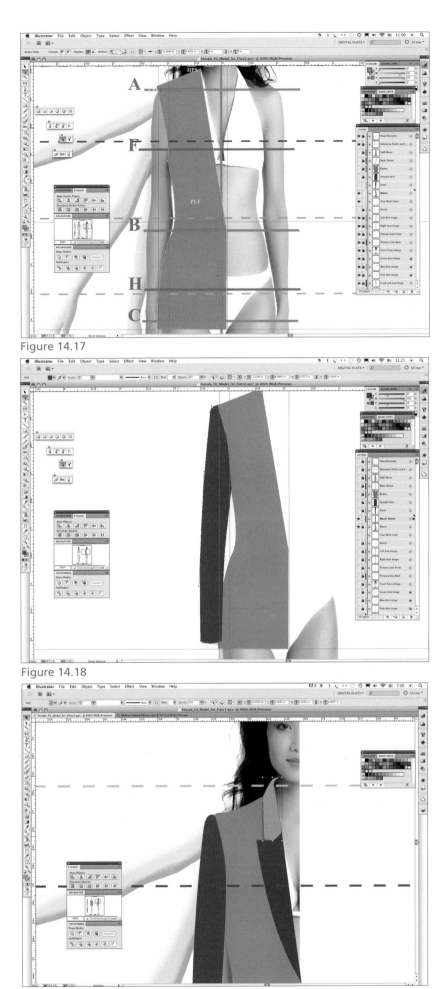

Figure 14.17

Figure 14.18

Figure 14.19

2. Copy the blazer technical design template twice and paste it into a new layer below the *Blazer* layer. Label this layer *Back Blazer*.

3. Reflect one, align both, and then overlap them on the figure to fit with the front. The green copy in Figure 14.20 shows this development.

4. Use the Pathfinder to unite the two parts.

5. Delete the anchor in the center that was left after convergence of the angles. The flat area will do fine for the back view of the neck, because a collar will cover it.

6. Copy the sleeve and adjust the anchors to push the inner curve slightly toward the waist.

7. Select the anchors and narrow the width at the bottom to create a more convincing illusion.

With this movement, you will have created a working set of fashion templates that can be useful in creating a variety of digital flats (Figure 14.20).

Note: *The following tutorials make use of the color technical design templates created in Tutorial 14.1 to morph digital flat sketches. The finished flats should contain a Fill of white and a Stroke of black. In the tutorial examples, the outline Weight of the Stroke will be 1 pt. Design details and dashed lines will be indicated in a Weight of 0.5 pt. The settings may vary depending on the tutorial. Use your own discretion and design sensitivity, but consult your instructor or client for exact academic or production standards.*

In some versions of Illustrator® it may be necessary for you to adjust the Preferences for Stroke Weight from inches to points by going to Menu Bar > Illustrator > Preferences > Units (Mac) or Menu Bar > Edit > Preferences > Units (PC). In the Preferences dialog box, change the Stroke from inches to points in the pull-down menu.

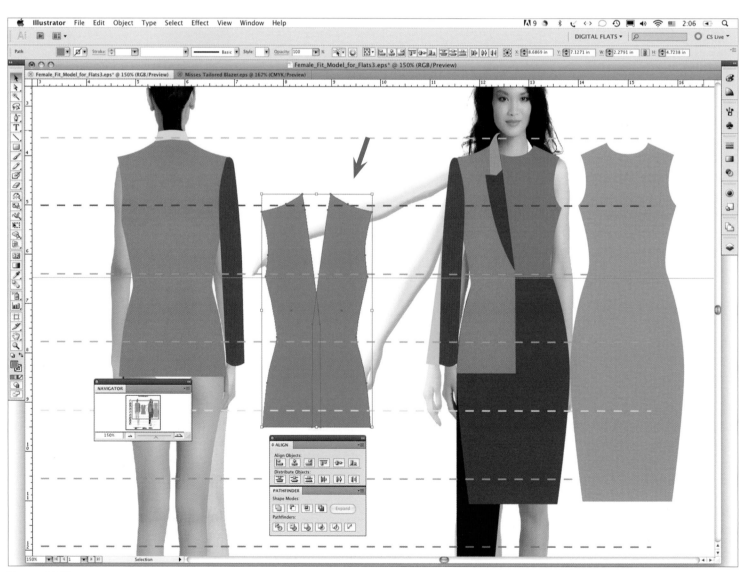

Figure 14.20

Tutorial 14.2
THE MISSES BUTTON-DOWN SHIRT DIGITAL FLAT

The button-down shirt is a quintessential wardrobe component, and it never goes out of style. Nearly every sportswear line will contain this item. Although it might appear simple, creating a proper digital technical flat will pose a challenge.

Note: Study the file *Misses_Button_Down_Shirt.pdf* on ② *Extra Flats\Women's Extra Flats*. Open the file in *Illustrator®*, and select and ungroup the parts to examine the shapes. See also the three movies on ② *Ch 14\Tutorial 14.2*.

Step 1: Create the Shirt Fronts and Back from the Template

1. Copy and paste the bodice and sleeves technical design templates that you created in Tutorial 14.1 into the *Your Work* layer.

2. Use the Illustrator® Direct Selection Tool (A) to reposition the anchors and create a full shirtfront shape, but try to draw what you see from an actual blouse or a photo of a garment.

3. The template is already proportioned, but keep the figure in mind as you style the shape. Pull Guides if necessary to help you with this.

4. You will also need to use the Add Anchor Point Tool (+) and the Convert Anchor Point Tool (Shift+C) to form the fronts.

5. Think of the flat as if it was an actual garment. Perfect one side of the flat, and then create a copy. Separating the parts will help later when you use them to morph other styles.

6. To create the back of the shirt, begin with the fronts. Copy and paste them both, then position them over the back figure.

7. Overlap the two shapes on the figure to fit. With both shapes selected click the Vertical Align Top in the Align panel.

8. Keep the parts selected, then use the Pathfinder panel to make them one shape by clicking *Unite*.

9. Use the Direct Selection Tool (A) to alter the anchor points and paths to fit the back figure. Give special attention to the neck area. Raise it to cover the upper back. You will cover the neckline later with the collar.

Figure 14.21 shows the shapes that were created from the bodice technical flat template. Notice that the armholes are different in front and back. Examine the garment or photo that you are working with to get the shapes right.

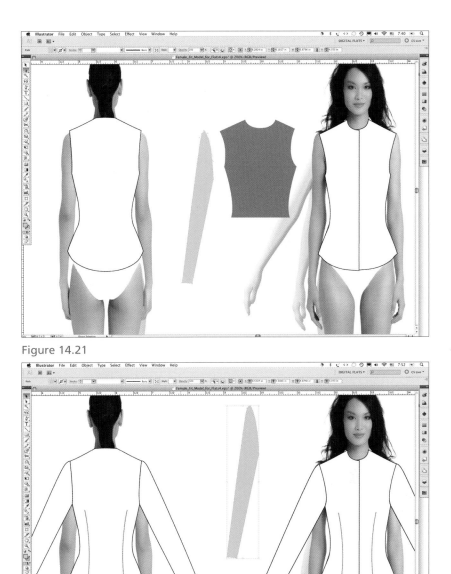

Figure 14.21

Figure 14.22

Step 2: Create the Sleeves and Add Darts

1. Use the bodice sleeve template to generate the sleeve shapes, but rotate the angle corresponding to that of the blue arm or whichever arm position is suitable for your garment. Remember that both the front and back armholes are always slightly different on better garments. Study this on your garment, and do not hide the sleeves behind the fronts.

2. Make the arm curve portion fit the shape that was made on the fronts and backs. Add anchors toward the sleeve ends and pull them out to develop the blouson feature of your shirt or blouse.

3. Use the Convert Anchor Point Tool (Shift+C) to shape the sleeves (Figure 14.22).

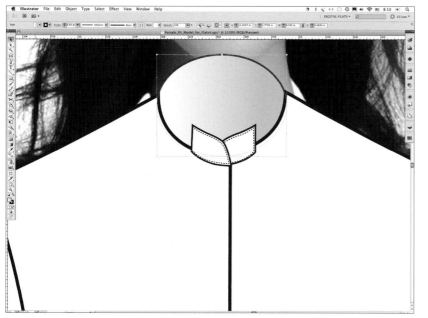

Figure 14.23

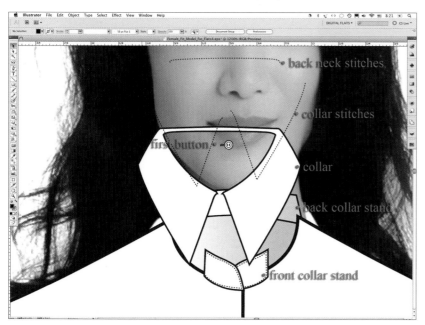

Figure 14.24

3. Convert the anchor to a curved shape with the Convert Anchor Point Tool (Shift+C). Use the Direct Selection Tool (A) to slightly pull the curve downward. The curve at the bottom of the stand should look like the neckline of your shirt/blouse. If you garment does not have a stand, practice making one anyway.

4. Copy and paste the collar stand shape.

5. Remove the fill from the pasted copy and select *Dashed Lines* in the Stroke panel. Use the *dash* and *gaps* to representing stitches. Try a 1 pt dash and a gap with a Stroke *Weight* of .5 pt. Scale the dashed line copy so that it fits inside the Stroke of the original collar stand when placed on top of it. Select and align the two parts by clicking the Vertical Align Center and then the Horizontal Align Center buttons in the Align panel.

6. Group the parts, and then copy, paste, and reflect the copy.

7. With it selected, send the right side of the collar stand to the back by going to *Menu Bar > Object > Arrange > Send to Back*. Position it as shown in Figure 14.23.

Step 4: Draw Inside the Front Neckline

1. Use the Ellipse Tool (L) to make an oval shape filled with the default black-and-white gradient to represent the inside of the front neck.

2. Select it right from the Gradient panel.

3. Use the Gradient Tool (G) to redistribute the value.

4. You can also make the gradient lighter by adding grays and removing the black slider from the Gradient Bar.

5. This shape must be below the back collar stand (Figure 14.24).

Step 5: Morph the Back Collar Stand

Before you make the collar, create the back stand. You can create it with the Rectangle Tool (M) or use the Pen Tool (P) to make a more contoured shape. The collar stand can also be filled with a Radial black-and-white gradient to give the illusion of depth (Figure 14.24).

Step 6: Create the Collar

1. Lock all the parts on the layer, and then create half the collar in one shape (Figure 14.25). To do this, use the Pen Tool (P) and begin at the back of the neck where the top of the collar would sit similar to the way the blazer collar template was created in the movie Steps 12-14.m4v on ② Ch14\Tutorial 14.1. (Also see Tutorial 4.3, Step Seven.)

4. Select and lock the front and/or the back by pressing *Cmd+2 / Ctrl+2*. Add darts to your design if required with a .5 pt *Weight* Stroke of black with a Fill of None.

Step 3: Create the Collar Stand

The digital rendering of woven shirts and blouses with collars and cuffs presents a challenge because of the many shapes needed. Once you render them all, the rest will be easy.

1. To begin, create the collar stand with a marquee of the Rectangle Tool (M).

2. Add an anchor to the bottom with the Add Anchor Point Tool (+).

2. Select, copy, paste, and then reflect the collar shape.

3. Use the Pathfinder *Unite* option to make the two halves one. Notice the stacking order of all the parts (Figure 14.24), as follows.

Shirt Front Stacking Order Front-to-Back:

1. first button	**8.** right collar stand
2. first buttonhole	**9.** left front shirt
3. collar stitches	**10.** right front shirt
4. collar	**11.** back neck stitches
5. left collar stand stitches	**12.** back collar stand
6. left collar stand	**13.** back neck ellipse
7. right collar stand stitches	

4. Copy and paste the full collar shape to create dash lines for topstitched effects but delete the fill (Figure 14.24). Add topstitching details on the hems and/or wherever else you want (Figure 14.25). Buttons and buttonholes are also needed (see Tutorial 4.3, Step Seventeen) (Figure 14.26).

Step 7: Add Contoured Cuffs, Pleats, and Plackets

In Tutorial 4.3, you created a shirt for a groom. For technical flats, you should place more emphasis on the shape of the cuffs. Even though you can make them with simple rectilinear forms, exercise greater effort to shape them by adding anchors and using the Convert Anchor Point Tool (Shift+C).

Creating Simple Released Pleats

The pleats that you see in Figure 14.27 were made with three clicks of the Illustrator® Pen Tool (P). They have been filled with a gray-and-white gradient to create the look of depth.

Creating Sleeve Plackets

Most long-sleeved dress shirts and blouses with cuffs have some kind of sleeve placket. When you have rendered the items you need, position the plackets, and then group the cuffs with the rest of the drawings. To create this effect, do the following:

1. Select the Direct Selection Tool (A), then the Illustrator® Pen Tool (P). You should have a Stroke of black at a Weight of 0.5 pt and a Fill of None.

2. Click and drag from position 1 in Figure 14.27 to position 2. Press and hold *Cmd / Ctrl* to toggle to the Direct Selection Tool (V). Use the Direct Selection Tool (A) to adjust the curved line segment as previously instructed.

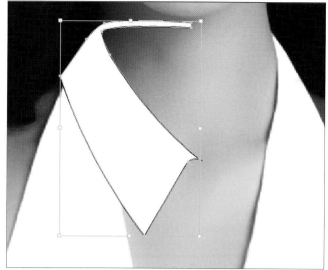

Figure 14.25

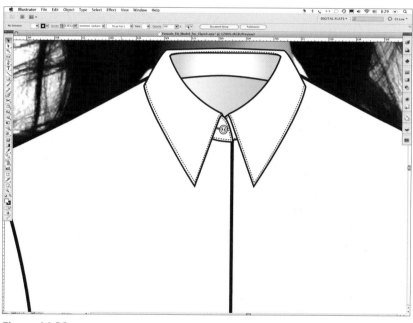

Figure 14.26

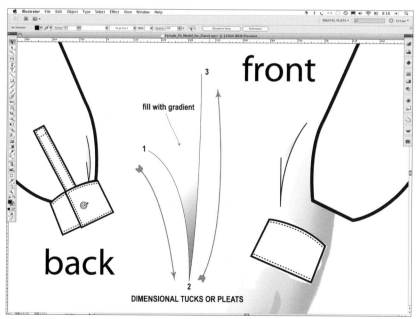

Figure 14.27 With three clicks you can create a pleat in Illustrator®.

3. Release the hold on *Cmd / Ctrl* to revert back to the Pen Tool (P), then click from position 2 to position 3.

4. Select the object with the Selection Tool (V), and then double-click on the Gradient Tool (G). The Gradient panel should appear. If you do not see it go to *Menu Bar > Window > Gradient* to show it.

5. The default gradient is a blend of black and white. The black will be too harsh, so replace it with 50% to 70% gray from the CMYK Swatches panel. Just drag the gray swatch onto the bottom of the Gradient Bar. You could drop it right on top of the black to replace it, but if the black slider still remains, just pull it off. Move the white slider a bit closer to the gray; however, leave a little space between them.

6. With the object still selected, use the Gradient Tool (G) to redistribute the gradient fill by clicking and dragging. You can also redistribute the gradient sliders on the slider that the tool makes. The goal is to make the gradient look like a slight shadow. This is a fine detail that will make your flat look dimensional.

Completed Examples

The completed front and back views of the digital flat for a Misses shirt are displayed in Figure 14.28. Add additional details, such as a pockets, yokes, etc.

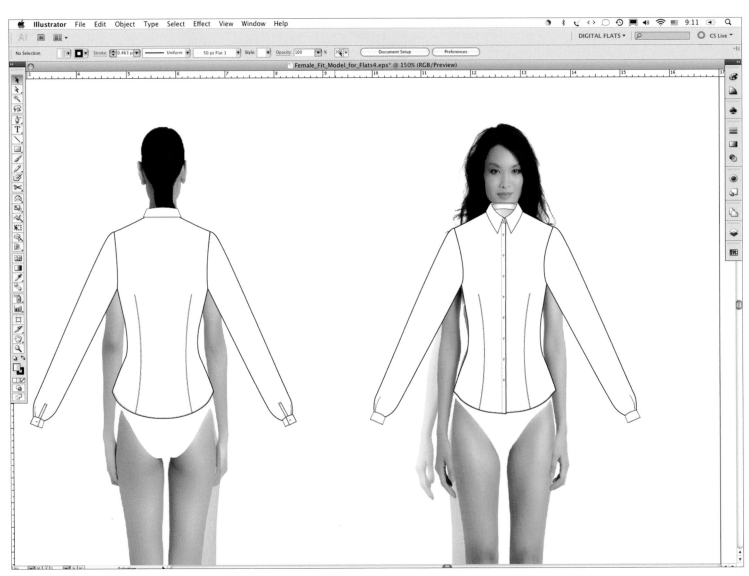

Figure 14.28

Knitwear is a vast subject, and although this book does not give it full focus, there are a few apparel items that require emphasis. In this tutorial you will learn to digitally render the basic crewneck sweater and create a brush to mimic ribbed knit trim.

Note: *Spend some time studying the file* Misses_ Crewneck_Sweater.pdf *on* ② *Extra Flats\Women's Extra Flats. Open the file in Illustrator®, and select and ungroup the parts to examine the shapes.*

Step 1: Copy the Bodice and Bodice Sleeve Template

1. Copy the bodice and the bodice sleeve technical design template and paste them into *Your Work Layer*.

2. Modify the silhouette with the Pen Tool (P) by adding an anchor to the center bottom of the bodice shape.

3. To keep the garment symmetrical, eliminate the side you do not need by performing a marquee over it with the Direct Selection Tool (A), but do not select the center anchors.

4. Press the Delete key to remove the unwanted side.

5. To create the illusion of a sweater knit in the example, an area was created for ribbing at the bottom hem, neck, and sleeves. Anchor points were added and the Convert Anchor Point Tool (Shift + C) was used to suggest a blouson shape above the transfer points at the sides.

6. Use the blue arm to gauge the angle of the sleeve.

7. Encapsulate the bottom area of the anchor points with a marquee, and then use the direction keys to reposition it. You can also use the Rotate Tool (R) options.

8. Adjust the armhole to fit the sleeve shape, but keep the sleeve in front. To reorder a part, select it, and then press *Shift+Cmd+[(left bracket) / Shift+Ctrl+[(left bracket)*.

9. Copy the parts and set them aside for now (Figure 14.29).

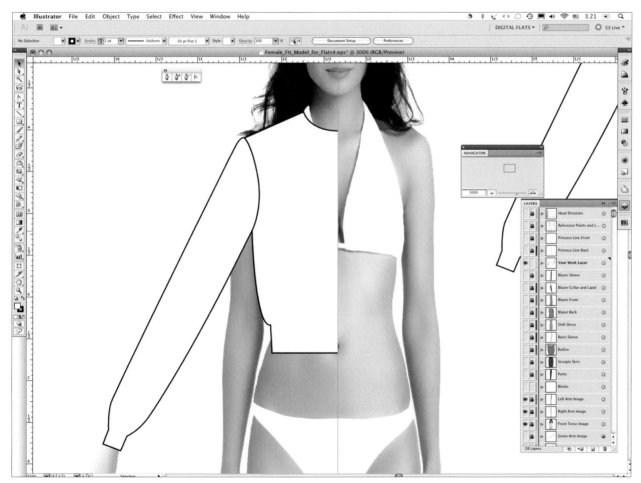

Figure 14.29

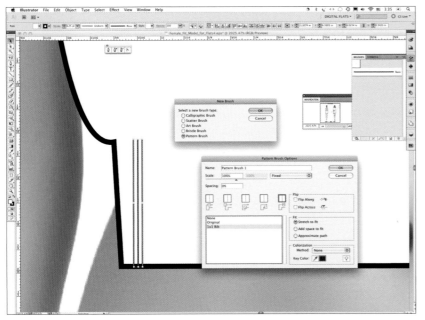

Figure 14.30

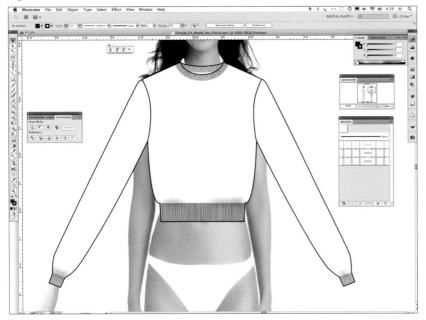

Figure 14.31

Step 2: Create a Ribbed Trim Brush

1. Zoom in close to your transfer points (area where the rib shape begins) at the hems.

2. Lock the shapes on the layer.

3. Use the Pen Tool (P) while holding the Shift key to create one straight line about the length of the bottom in a Stroke of 0.25 pt and a Fill of None.

4. Copy and paste the line a few times.

5. Align and evenly distribute the lines.

6. Select all the lines and go to *Menu Bar > Edit Define Pattern*.

7. Name the pattern *1x1 Rib*.

8. Open the Brushes panel and click the hidden menu options on the right side to access the new pattern brush option.

9. A New Brush dialog box appears. Select *Pattern Brush*, and then click OK.

10. In the Pattern Brush dialog box, select each window, and then choose the 1×1 Rib pattern from the field on the lower left as shown in Figure 14.30, then click OK.

Step 3: Create the Whole Front Design and Add Rib Trim

1. Copy and paste the sweater shapes to create the other side.

2. Reflect one side at 90° vertically, then align and overlap the fronts.

3. Use the Pathfinder panel to unite them, and then add the right sleeve from the copy that you placed aside.

4. Select and lock the objects on the layer.

5. Apply the rib to your design with the Pen Tool (P). This allows you to create a clean flow. Do not forget to create the inside of the back neck.

6. Group the brush trims with their associated shapes, so that they do not shift.

7. Use the Blob Brush Tool (Shift+B) with the Gaussian Blur filter to make shadow effects, and then group them with the entire front (Figure 14.31).

TIP: Retain Rib Brush Effects

If you would like to keep the exact look of this rib for other areas on your technical flat, repeat the procedure at the exact lengths needed; otherwise, you may encounter difficult scaling tasks.

Step 4: Create a Sleeve Bend

When you create flats with long sleeves that are extended, the width of the entire flat is often cumbersome. To maximize space, create a bend in one of the sleeves, but be consistent as to which side throughout your portfolio or presentation. This is only one method of many. To do this:

1. Ungroup the sleeve from the body, and then use the Scissors Tool (C) to cut the sleeve on both sides of the elbow.

2. Rotate the bottom portion with the trim at an angle of -45° or whatever works best. The Pen Tool can be used to reconnect the outer path with a curve.

3. Use the Direct Selection Tool (A) to position the inner paths to touch one another but do not overlap.

4. Add a shadow as shown in Figure 14.32.

Step 5: Create the Sweater Back from the Front

1. Morph the back view from a copy of the front.

2. Flip the back view vertically 90°.

3. Readjust the neckline, fold, and the armholes. The completed sweater digital flat is pictured in Figure 14.33.

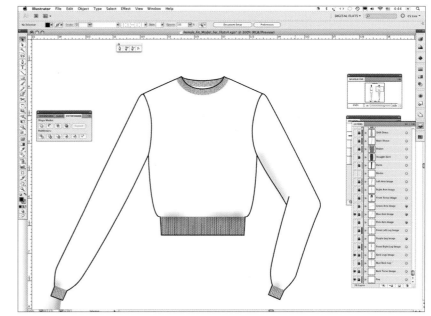

Figure 14.32

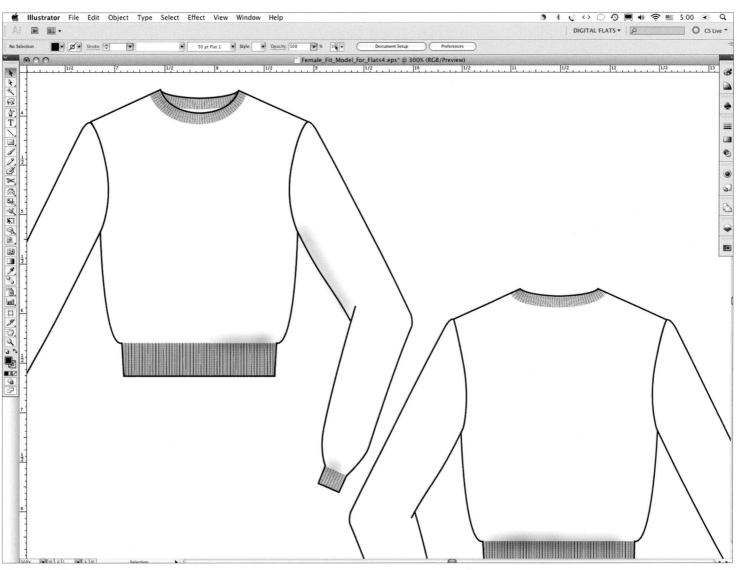

Figure 14.33

The shift or chemise was made popular by French couturiers of the late 1950s, and the look remained popular through the 1960s. The modern shift dress is stylish in almost any fabric and color. Use the shift technical design template from Tutorial 14.1 to create your own design by following the basic steps in this tutorial.

Note: Open the file *Misses_Shift_Dress.pdf* on ② *Extra Flats\Women's Extra Flats in Illustrator®, and select and ungroup the parts to examine the shapes.*

Step 1: Copy the Shift Template and Add Details

1. Copy the shift dress technical design template and paste it into *Your Work Layer.*

2. Convert the shape to the default Fill and Stroke.

3. Morph the silhouette to transform and design the dress; make it your own.

4. Create a copy of the converted shift and place it on the side for stitch details if needed.

5. Lock the shift shape and use the *Princess Line Front* layer to help you design your dart construction (Figure 14.34).

Digital Bust Darts

Both bust darts and French darts work well with this style. French darts begin a little above or below the waist at the side seam and finish on an upward angle, just shy of the apex of the bust. Use a *Weight* of .05 pt on the Stroke for details to create cleaner lines. If you are using Illustrator® CS5 or higher versions, finish darts by selecting the ends that show with the Width Tool (Shift +W). Zoom in, and then pull in the flat edge to make it pointed for a cleaner look.

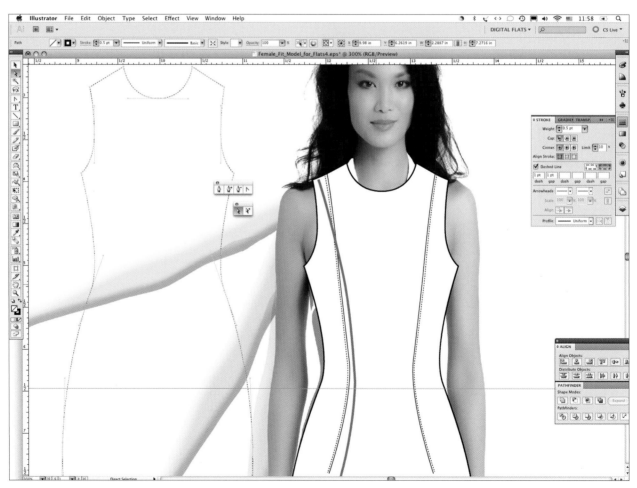

Figure 14.34

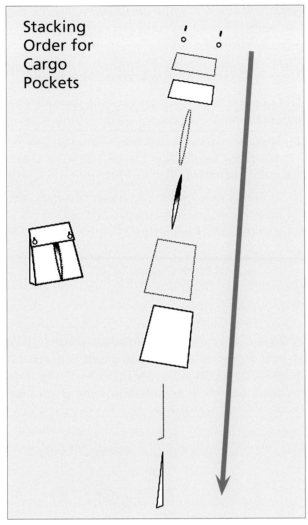

Stacking
Order for
Cargo
Pockets

Figure 14.35 Items appear from top to bottom.

Step 2: Add Construction and Defining Details

The shift dress is a basic item, but you can add special details in the form of pockets, stitch details, and seams to give it a fresh twist. In Figure 14.35, cargo pockets created totally from rectangles, dashed lines, and gradient fills do the trick. Notice the stacking order of the parts. The developing technical shift flat is shown in Figure 14.36.

Step 3: Create the Back Neck Front Detail

Always render the total garment from the front view, including the back of the dress that shows in the front at the neckline.

1. Copy and paste the front.

2. Delete the parts you do not need, and heighten the curve of the neck.

3. Fill the shape with the default gradient.

4. Create the other side from a reflected duplicate.

5. Add stitch details, and then group the entire shape.

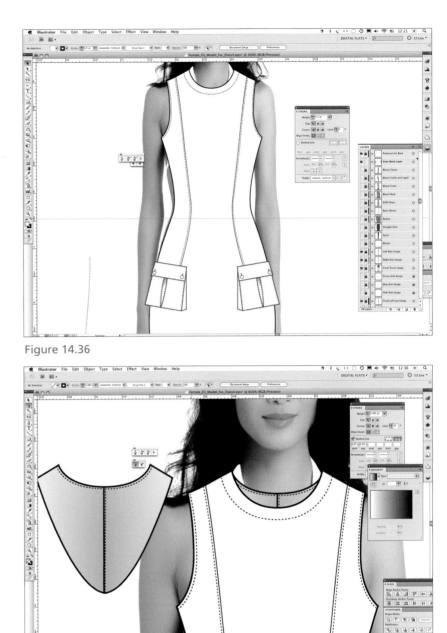

Figure 14.36

Figure 14.37

6. Send this to the back of all the objects by pressing *Shift+Cmd+[(left bracket) / Shift+Ctrl+[(left bracket)*.

7. Select the parts, align, and position them (Figure 14.37).

Step 4: Create a Keyhole with the Eraser Tool

Use the Illustrator® Eraser Tool (E) to make holes in shapes in the form of instant compound masks. To adjust the attributes of this tool, including the brush size, double-click on its icon in the Tools panel. You can make adjustments to the shape with the Pen Tool Suite and the Direct Selection Tool (A). In Figure 14.38, the Eraser Tool (E) was used to make the keyhole neckline.

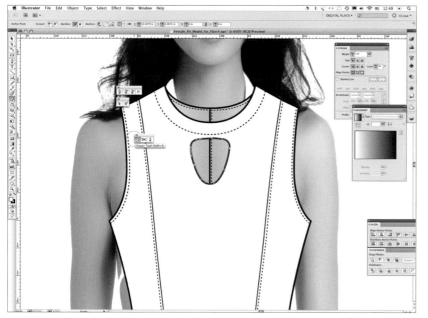

Figure 14.38

Note: *Always lock items underneath an area that you want to erase to prevent erasing portions of them by error with this tool.*

Step 5: Create the Back from the Front

1. Copy and paste the front to create the back view of the shift.

2. Select anchors with the Direct Selection Tool (A) and press Delete. You can also use the Delete Anchor Point Tool (-).

3. To further develop the two halves of a back, add darts, the zipper stitch detail, and vent stitch (if applicable) to your design.

4. Extend the vent a point lower than the hem for a dimensional touch (**Figure 14.39**).

Note: *Back armholes on sleeveless garments should always differ slightly from the front. Usually, the apex of the back armhole's sickle shape is positioned more toward the center back. This is opposite of what is done for garments with set-in sleeves. Finally, darts in back should differ from those in front. These small details in your work will give it a professional touch.*

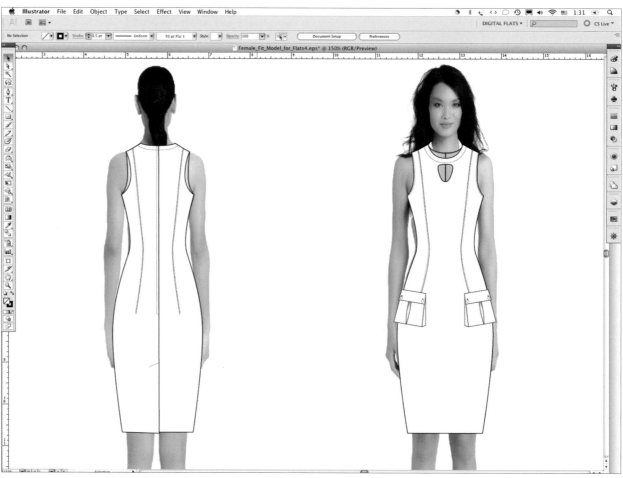

Figure 14.39

Tutorial 14.5
THE MISSES WOVEN VEST DIGITAL FLAT

Although the vest is not always a popular fashion, it takes on universal importance when it is revived. Fashionable women will always have one or more in their closets waiting for the perfect occasion to wear them. The vest, like other modern apparel items for women, borrows much from men's tailoring. However, the female figure requires special attention in design and rendering this technical flat. In this tutorial, you will use the bodice template to digitally morph your own vest design. Try creating the traditional vest in the tutorial, then go on to create another more ostentatious version.

Note: Examine the file Misses_Tailored_Vest.pdf on ② Extra Flats\Women's Extra Flats. Open the file in Illustrator®, and select and ungroup the parts to study the shapes.

Step 1: Create the Vest Shape from the Bodice Template

Use the bodice template to morph the vest front and back on the *Your Work Layer* as previously instructed (Figure 14.40). Do not forget the concept of ease in your design.

Step 2: Add Darts and Seam Details

Use any drawing tool to create your darts, yokes, seam detail, etc. However, if your garment contains any areas that extend from the back, such as forward front shoulder seams or side yokes, render them as separate shapes (Figure 14.41).

Step 3: Add Stitch Details, Lining, and Pockets

If your lining is a different fabric from the vest front, fill it with 10% (CMYK) gray to indicate the combo. Create pockets from rectangles or render them with the Pen Tool (P). Make complicated stitch details from pasted copies of the original shapes rather than attempting to re-create the exact curves. Resize the line segments that represent stitches with the Bounding Box or reposition and shape them with the Direct Selection Tool (A). Remember to keep the concept of ease in the technical flat (Figure 14.42).

Step 4: Create the Other Front from the Original

Select, copy, paste, and use the Reflect Tool (R) options to position a copy of the shape on the opposite side (Figure 14.43). Remember that in women's wear, the left side of buttoned garments overlaps the right.

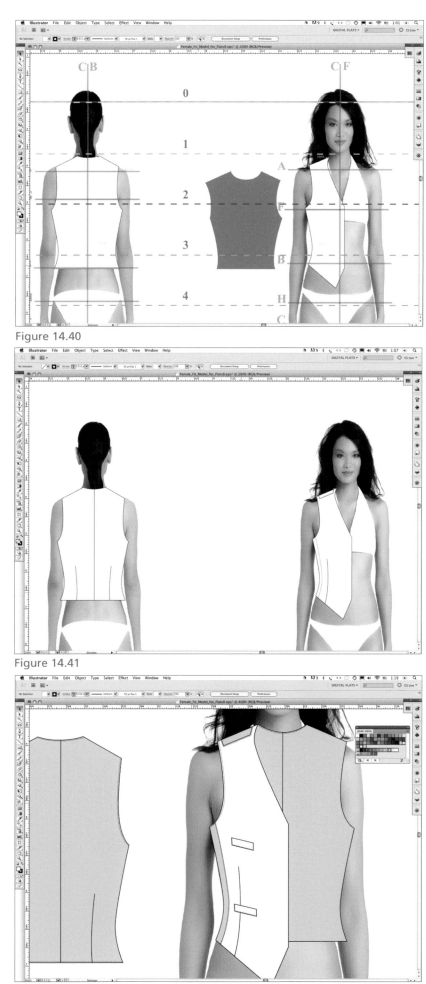

Figure 14.40

Figure 14.41

Figure 14.42

Step 5: Add Button Details and Finishing Touches

It is a good practice to create new layers when you are working on details. This prevents drawing difficulties and confusion of the parts, especially for tiny objects like buttons and buttonholes. Because the button is usually placed on top of the buttonhole, let's begin there. A buttonhole is made simply by using the Rectangle Tool (M) to click and drag a slender rectangle onto the page. Use a Stroke with a *Weight* of 1 pt and a *Dashed Line* of 0.2 pt. Check out the new *Align Dashes to Corners*, *Bevel Join Corner*, and other features in the Stroke panel.

To create buttons, select a shape tool like the Ellipse Tool (L). Hold the Shift key to constrain the proportions as you click and drag to create a perfect circle. Use the Ellipse Tool (L), Pencil Tool (N), Pen Tool (P), and others to create the look of the thread flowing through holes in the button. Group the parts by selecting them, then pressing *Cmd+G / Ctrl+G*. Place the button on top of the buttonhole that you rendered, and then group the two. You can copy and paste as many as you need to complete your vest. Position the buttons according to your needs, select the buttons that you have placed, then select the Vertical Distribute Center option in the Align panel.

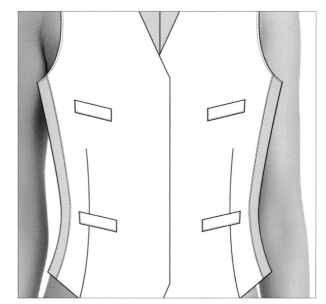

Figure 14.43

This ensures that the grouped buttons and buttonholes are evenly spaced (Figure 14.44).

Use your imagination and what you have learned in previous tutorials to add other details like trims from brushes.

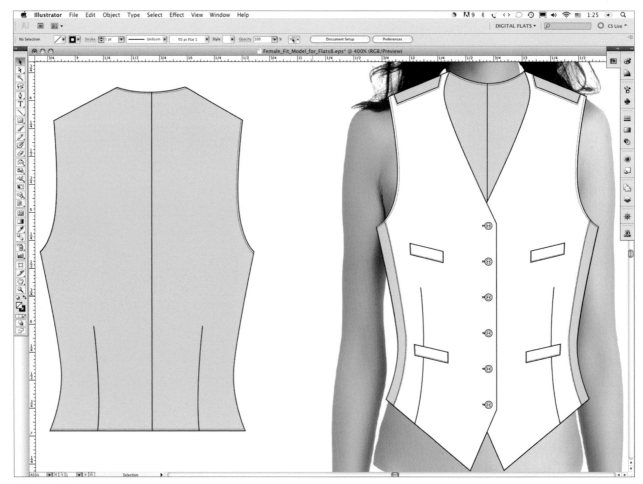

Figure 14.44

Tailored apparel is always in style, and the classic blazer is a staple in every person's wardrobe. Although the silhouette had been around for some time, especially in men's wear, it was French fashion designer Yves Saint Laurent who made it popular in the late 1960s. Nevertheless, every fashion designer should have a full understanding of how to properly render the proportions of this timeless jacket. Follow the suggested steps to create a finished technical flat rendering of a digital blazer by using the templates created in Tutorial 14.1.

Tailored jackets and coats should always be rendered with the sleeves positioned close to the body. Because tailored garments cannot be placed comfortably on a flat surface, the flat should be rendered as if it were floating on an invisible hanger.

Misses Classic Single-Breasted Blazer

Note: Examine the file *Misses_Tailored_Blazer.pdf* on ② *Extra Flats\Women's Extra Flats. Open the file in Illustrator®, and select and ungroup the parts to study the shapes.*

Step 1: Copy the Templates and Add Silhouette Details

1. Copy and paste the blazer template parts into *Your Work Layer*.

2. Select the parts, and then press the D key to fill them with the default Fill and Stroke.

3. Because you are using a technical design template that is already well proportioned, toggle off the visibility and lock the layers that you do not need.

4. Add any style details to the silhouette, such as a rounded front or a curve at the back, etc. (Figure 14.45).

Step 2: Copy Parts, Make Stitches, and Create Darts/Seams

1. Copy and paste anything that requires visible stitching, then lock the originals on the layer.

2. Select the copies and give them a Fill of None and a Stroke of black at 0.5 pt.

3. Select the Dashed Line box in the Stroke panel and use a dash of 1 pt and a gap of 1 pt.

4. Use the Direct Selection Tool (A) to select the parts of the shapes that you do not need for stitches, and then press the Delete key to remove the unwanted paths.

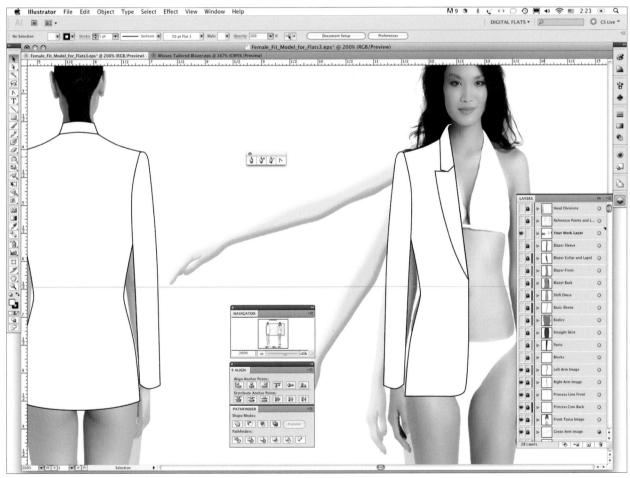

Figure 14.45

For example: If you wanted to create stitches for the front of the blazer from the copy, you would need to delete the armhole, side, and shoulder paths. Select these paths individually with the Direct Selection Tool (A) and then press the Delete key to remove them from the whole shape. You may also need to make adjustments to the remaining paths to suit the style that you are rendering.

Note: *By using this method, you do not need to attempt to redraw curved areas, which can be difficult to repeat.*

5. Use the Bounding Box to reshape or fit the lines in place. You may need to adjust certain paths with the Direct Selection Tool (A) or connect them with the Pen Tool (P).

6. Join any parts such as those between the top collar and lapel by selecting the end point anchors with a marquee of the Direct Selection Tool (A), and place the stitches on top of the original shapes. If you have a difficulty placing the shapes on top of others, check to see that they are on the right layer with the object that you copied them from. Once you have the objects and the stitches in position, select and group them by pressing *Cmd+G / Ctrl+G*. The stages of progression are shown in Figure 14.46.

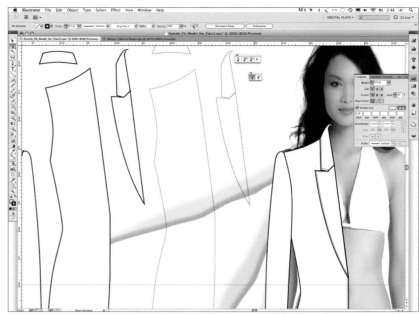

Figure 14.46 Stitch details made from copies have no fill.

> ## TIP: Preferences for Scaling Strokes and Effects
>
> **If you do not want to scale the *Weight* of your strokes, make sure that you uncheck the *Scale Strokes* and *Effects* box by going to *Menu Bar > Illustrator > Preferences > General (Mac)* or *Menu Bar > Edit > Preferences > General (PC)*. This will ensure that your stitches and strokes stay visually uniform.**

Step 3: Add Darts and Seams

You cannot have a well-tailored blazer without darts and/or yokes. If needed, pull the Princess Line Layer above your work and use the curved line to gauge the placement. If you are not looking at an actual garment, darts are a preference, so you can position them at will (Figure 14.47).

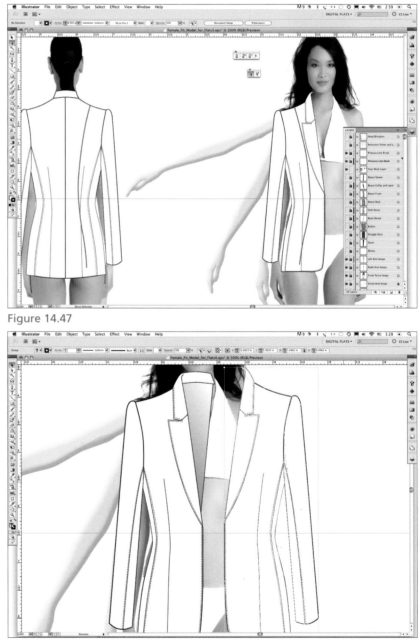

Figure 14.47

Figure 14.48

Step 4: Create the Inside Back Details and the Right Side

1. Use the Pen Tool (P) to create a shape that will cover the back of the garment showing inside the front view.

2. Fill the shape with a default gradient.

3. Send the shape to the back of all the objects by going to *Menu Bar > Object > Arrange > Send to Back*.

4. Copy the collar from the back and place it in the neck beneath the front collar. This may take a little reordering, but if you group the parts that you create on the left side, the process will be simple.

5. Copy and paste the left side and reflect the copy as shown in Figure 14.48 to create the right side. Do not forget that the left side should be on top of the right for Misses apparel.

Step 5: Add Buttons and Finishing Touches

1. If you want, add pockets created from rectangles, or you can render special shapes with the Pen Tool (P).

2. Buttonholes can be created with the Rectangle Tool (M) (see Tutorial 4.3, Step Seventeen).

3. A button is just an ellipse, but you can create them in any shape and style that you prefer. Figure 14.49 exhibits the completed flat.

The Classic Blazer Digital Flat for Men's Wear

This classic jacket exercise will give you the practice you need to develop proper proportion for men's

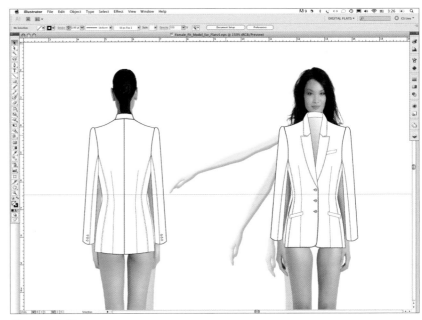

Figure 14.49

tailored jackets and coats. Use the file Male_Fit_ Model_for_Flats.pdf located on ② Ch14\Tutorial 14.1 and the templates that you created to morph your own design concepts, but keep the sleeves close to the torso for this type of apparel item.

Note: *Men's apparel fastens on the opposite side compared with women's clothing.*

A completed example is shown in Figure 14.50.

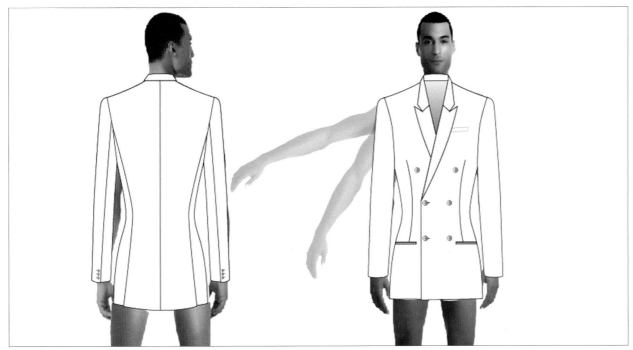

Figure 14.50

Tutorial 14.7
THE MISSES STRAIGHT SKIRT DIGITAL FLAT

The basic straight skirt is always in style. Use this tutorial to help you render a well-proportioned digital flat. Exercise your own creativity by adding elegant details.

Note: The file *Misses_Straight_Skirt_With_Cascade_Flounce.pdf* on ② *Extra Flats\Women's Extra Flats* has been provided for your use with this tutorial. Open the file in Illustrator®, and then select and ungroup the parts to study the shapes.

Step 1: Copy the Straight Skirt Template

1. Copy and paste the straight skirt technical design template into *Your Work Layer*.

2. Select it and press the D key to change the shapes to the default Fill and Stroke.

3. Adjust the silhouette and proportion (Figure 14.51).

Step 2: Add Darts

Use the Pen Tool (P) to create darts. Figure 14.52 displays the difference in the shape of the template in comparison to development of the design.

Step 3: Create a Waistband and Add Some Design Detail

1. Create a waistband from the Rectangle Tool (M) or make a particular shape with the Pen Tool (P).

2. The cascade flounce seen in Figure 14.53 was created with triangles and various curved and angled bottom edges. The selection reveals how the parts were stacked from smallest to largest. A copy of this cascade is available in the file Misses_Straight_Skirt_With_Cascade_Flounce.pdf on ② Extra Flats\Women's Extra Flats.

Step 4: Create the Back from the Front

Copy and paste the front shape to make two halves of the back (Figure 14.54).

Step 5: Add Back View Details to Complete

Add the waistband, button and buttonhole, back zipper detail, dart, and anything else to make the look chic. The completed example is shown in Figure 14.55.

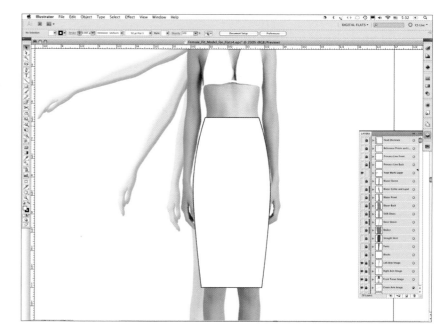

Figure 14.51

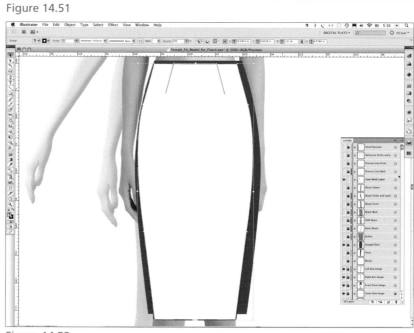

Figure 14.52

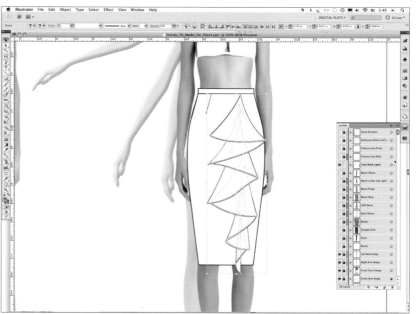

Figure 14.53

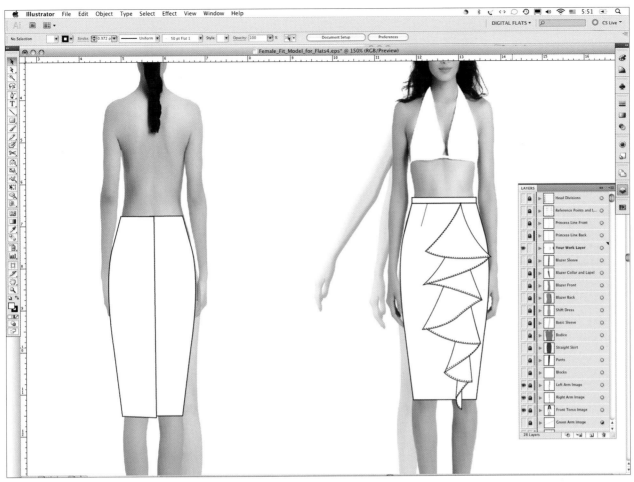

Figure 14.54

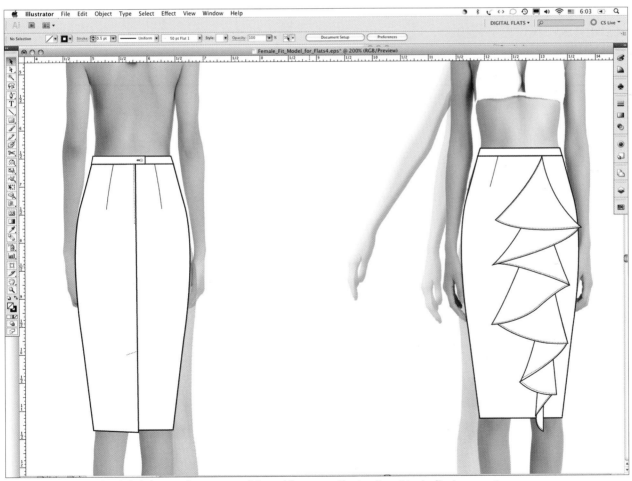

Figure 14.55 The back left hem edge was positioned lower at Center Front to indicate a vent.

In this tutorial, you will be guided in steps to render the front and back views of technical flats for both the A-line and flare skirts. Make them your own by adding a twist; spice them with simulated trims, stitch details, buttons, waistbands, pockets, etc. You can also attempt your hand at rendering an actual skirt.

Note: The file *Misses_Six_Gore_Flare_Skirt.pdf* on *Extra Flats\Women's Extra Flats has been provided for your use with this tutorial. Open the file in Illustrator®, and then select and ungroup the parts to study the shapes.*

Step 1: Begin with the Straight Skirt Template

1. Select each anchor on the bottom sides with the Direct Selection Tool (A).

2. Use the direction keys to move the sides outward. Count out the number of times that you press them, so that you can repeat the same on the opposite side.

3. If the anchor at the low hip becomes a problem, delete it (Figure 14.56). The nature of the shape also necessitates a slightly curved hem, so move the center anchor downward and convert the straight anchor. If you have more than one anchor at the bottom center, delete the others first.

Step 2: Add Seams and Details

Some A-line and flare skirts have panels called gores. The tutorial example has six gores, but you can have many more.

1. For the six-gore model, place the seams at princess line and veer outward as shown in Figure 14.57.

2. Add a waistline and hem finish.

Step 3: Create Flares

In Tutorial 4.2, Step Twelve, you learned how to create cone shapes to simulate the flares in a skirt. This was reinforced in Tutorial 4.5, Steps Nineteen through Twenty-One.

1. To begin, give the A-line shape more width at the sides, as instructed in Step One of this tutorial. You may want to increase the curve (sweep).

2. Create the flare shapes with the Pen Tool (P), but do not close the tops.

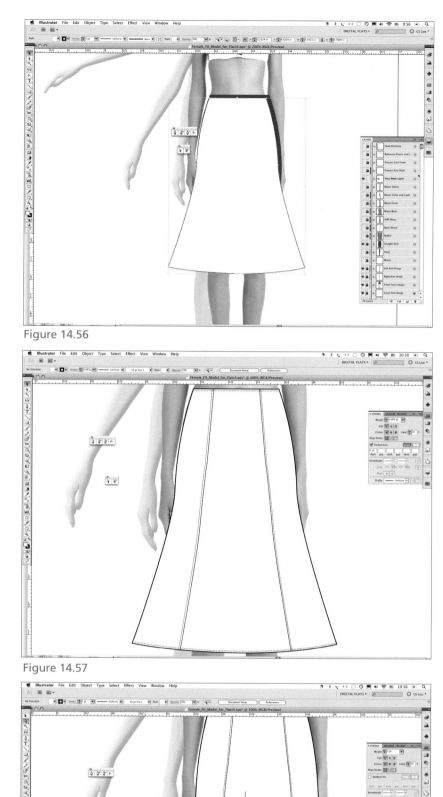

Figure 14.56

Figure 14.57

Figure 14.58

3. Fill the cone shapes with white and place them on top of the skirt shape. If you added a hem detail, render the same on each flare (Figure 14.58).

Step 4: Show a Combination of Fabrics

If a garment is made from two or more different textiles, the technical flat needs to indicate the placement of each combo with a color or texture. Try to use black or gray for the combo fill. For example, in Figure 14.59 the flare skirt has a lace lining that hangs below the self-fabric skirt. The underskirt is a copy of the original.

Step 5: The Back is Complete

Depending on the fit and the fabric, a gore skirt is constructed in equal panels. You should flip the copy and vary the flares to indentify the back view. The back and the front of the skirt are now completed (Figure 14.60).

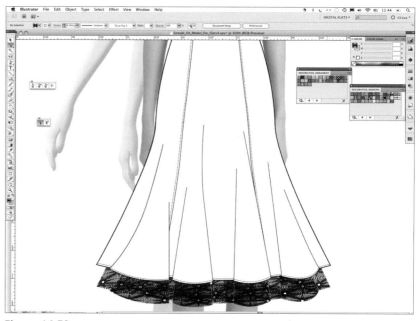

Figure 14.59

Figure 14.60

Can you believe that at one time women were forbidden to wear pants in public establishments such as restaurants in New York City? We again salute Monsieur Yves Saint Laurent for popularizing pants for women in the 1960s and 70s. In this tutorial, you will learn to create a technical flat of a pair of tailored slacks (the term preferred by YSL) by using the pants fashion template. You will also create pleats and welt pockets.

Note: The file *Misses_Tailored_Pleated_Slacks.pdf* on ② *Extra Flats\Women's Extra Flats* has been provided for your use with this tutorial. Open the file in Illustrator®, and then select and ungroup the parts to study the shapes.

Step 1: Copy, Paste, and Adjust the Pant Template

There are too many pants styles to cover each one, but this tutorial will teach the basic concepts associated with a tailored version, including pleats and welt pockets. Use the pant template to develop the front and back silhouette of your pants design on *Your Work Layer*. Notice that the back view in Figure 14.61 has a flat CB line. Decide if you want your pant design to hang from the natural waist (B) or at another position on the body (Figure 14.62). If you are rendering an actual garment, have someone try it on, and take a photo.

Step 2: Create Creases

In Chapter 4 a very basic rendering of pants was demonstrated for the groom of Tutorial 4.3, Steps Ten and Eleven. This pant is similar, except both views will consist of two separate sides. This is being done so that when you are filling the shapes with patterns, particularly stripes, you will be able to move the angle of each side to reflect proper grain in your pattern fills. The hem on the pants has an angle that simulates what happens to tailored pants that have a crease. In the previous flats tutorials, we did not make use of the *Reference Points and Levels* layer because the templates were adequate to proportion. Toggle on these layers if you are not using a pants technical design template. You will use the blue and the purple leg poses for this flat.

1. Lock the pants shapes on the layer.

2. Use any drawing tool to render the creases, but do not start them above the low hip level (C). A Stroke of 0.25 pt is good.

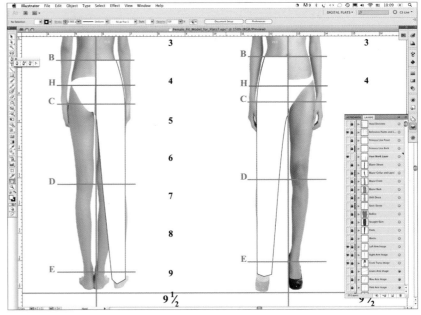

Figure 14.61

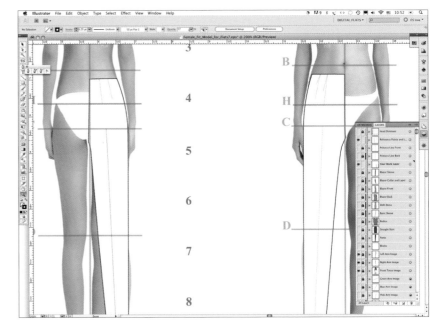

Figure 14.62

3. If you do not desire a crease, round off the pointy shape at the bottom and create a curve with the Convert Anchor Point Tool (Shift+C).

Step 3: Create Welt and Besom Pockets

It is likely easy for you to imagine how to create a design line for a side front pocket by adding a line. Structured western pockets are available for you to view in ② Extra Flats. However, welt and besom pockets need to be given attention.

Digital Welt Pockets

1. The welt pocket can be created from a base rectangular shape of 0.50 pt Stroke *Weight* as a dashed line.

2. Place two similar shapes above the one that you just made, but they should be only half the width with a Stroke of 0.25 pt *Weight*.

3. Fill them with white. Some welt pockets have reinforced stitching and others do not (Figure 14.63).

Besom Pockets

The besom pocket is a rectangular flap covering the workings of what would normally be a welt pocket.

1. Use the Rectangle Tool (M) to create it.

2. Add stitch details to the sides and bottom. This type of pocket is illustrated in the back view of the pants. A slanted welt pocket has been rendered on the front panel (Figure 14.63).

Step 4: Add Digital Darts and Pleats

1. Create darts in back up to the high hip (H) position as previously instructed.

2. Watch the movie Pants_Pleat.m4v on ② Ch14\ Tutorial 14.9.

3. In the front, try to practice making pleats, even if your style does not have them. Use the Illustrator® Pen Tool (P) and a Stroke of black at 0.25 pt *Weight*.

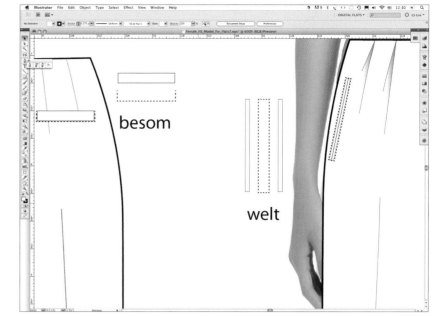

Figure 14.63

4. Start at the bottom of the direction of the pleat, which is usually the lower side of its pick-up.

5. Create a curved path toward the top of the pleat where it would normally be held in place by a seam.

6. Finish the pleat with a longer curve on the opposite side as demonstrated in the short film.

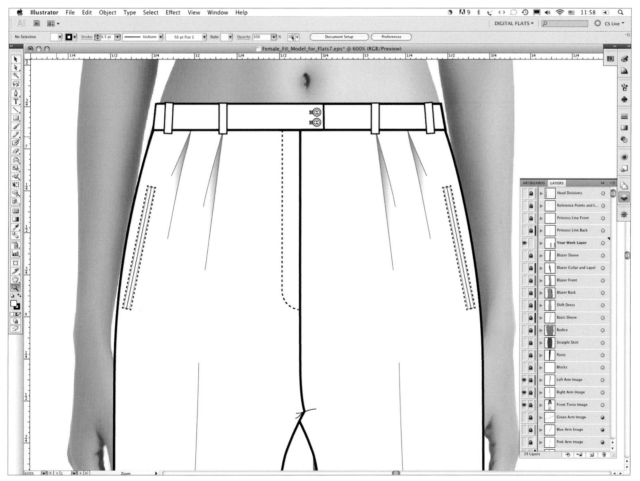

Figure 14.64

In Figure 14.64, the creases, darts, and pleats have been added to both the front and back views.

TIP: Adding Pleat Shadows

Adding a gradient to fill the digital pleat gives it a 3-D effect. To do the same on a garment with color or a fabric fill, use a Fade.

Step 5: Create the Other Sides and Add Details

1. Copy and paste the front and back views.
2. Use the Reflect Tool to position the copies opposite the originals and position them.

3. Add a waistband, buttonholes, buttons, belt loops, etc.
4. Most tailored pants have a fly. The Misses pant fly in slacks (in artwork view) has the left over the right, but jeans are right over left. If you need to change it, just flip the entire work or select the side of concern and go to *Menu Bar > Object > Arrange > Bring to Front.*

A zoomed-in view of the front view in exhibits the details, including an optional **crotch indicator** (Figure 14.64). Certain factories and manufacturers exclude crotch indicators, while others include them to differentiate the back and front views of flat illustrations. A full view of both the front and back views illustrates additional alterations to the proportions of the flats in reference to the fit model's form (Figure 14.65).

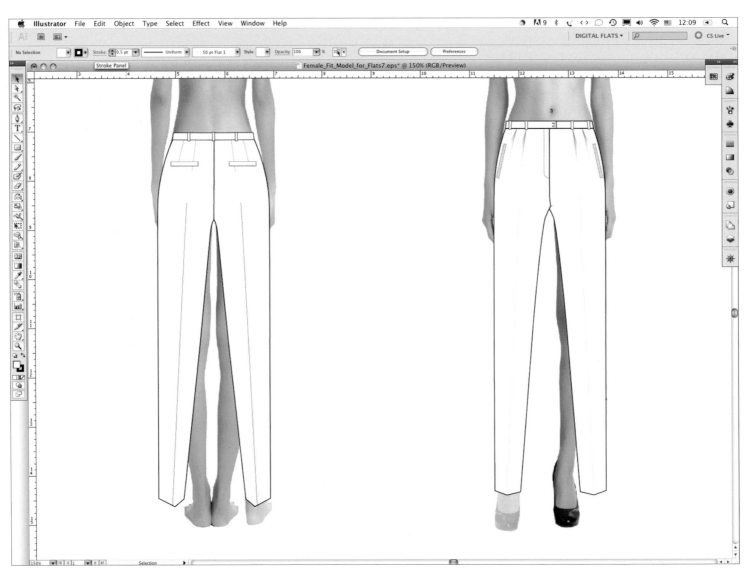

Figure 14.65

Step 1: Place a Runway Photo of Jade

1. Open the file Female_Fit_Model_for_Flats.pdf on ② Ch14\Tutorial 14.1.

2. Place the file Jade_3Q_runway_wide_stride.jpg from ① Digital Duo Modeling Agency\Jade\Runway on a layer above the Key layer (Figure 14.66).

Note: *Photographs of both Jade and Ana work with the Female Fit Model for Digital Flats file.*

Step 2: Work from Left to Right

An action flat is apparel rendered as if floating in a pose.

1. Begin on the farthest side of the perspective. In the case of the example, that is located on the left side.

2. If you prefer, flip the image by selecting it, and using the Reflect Tool (R) options.

3. Use the Illustrator® Pen Tool (P) to render the left sleeve on *Your Work Layer*.

Tutorial 14.10
THE THREE-QUARTER-VIEW SHIRT AS A DIGITAL ACTION FLAT

Rendering three-quarter views of garments is not a requirement by every import manufacturer; however, it becomes important to augment the renderings of certain designs, especially active sportswear. Most often three-quarter and side views are used for pants, but blouses and tops may also need an action-view floating pose to convey fit, proportion, and details that cannot be seen full-frontal. Use this tutorial to practice rendering the three-quarter view of a shirt. Try a few of the other items, too.

Note: *The file Misses_Three_Quarter_View_Shirt_Float.pdf on ② Extra Flats\Women's Extra Flats has been provided for your use with this tutorial. Open the file in Illustrator®, and then select and ungroup the parts to study the shapes.*

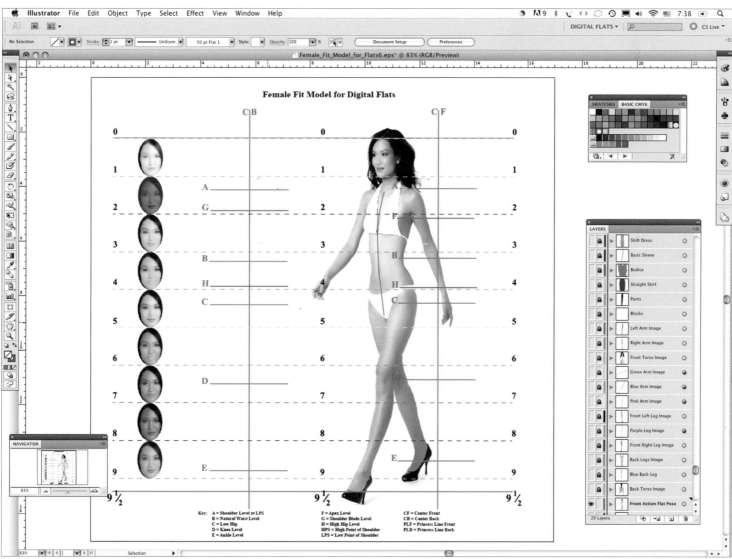

Figure 14.66

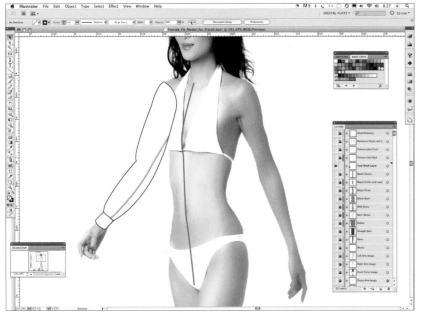

Figure 14.67

Figure 14.68

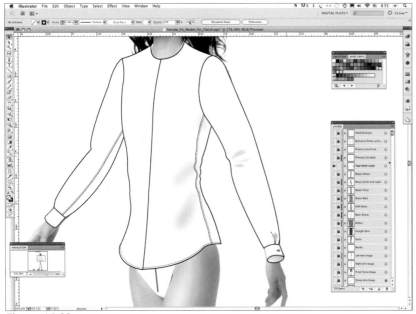

Figure 14.69

4. Add the inside seam and cuff (Figure 14.67). The sleeve will need to protrude into the body, but the left front in the next step will cover it.

Step 3: Create the Left Front

1. Render the left front, but try to imagine what would happen to the drapery of the fabric if you were wearing the garment. Naturally, the front might shift, so do not just simply follow the CF body action line (shown in red) exclusively.

2. The side closest to the sleeve should have some unevenness to impersonate gentle wrinkles.

3. Add topstitching or dart details. Remember, this side needs to be placed on top of the right front, so you need to rearrange the objects by bringing some forward and backward, etc. (Figure 14.68).

Step 4: Create the Right Front

1. The right front should be rendered showing the full curvature of the right side of the body with slight wrinkles (Figure 14.69).

2. The armhole must curve under the arm toward the back to show the full volume of the proposed garment.

On an actual garment the side seam will show under the arm and you would be able to see some of the back panel. Use the Pen Tool (P) to create a full sickle shape that comes down from the low point of the shoulder into the curve of the armhole seam, and then curves up from the bottom toward the back. This will later be covered by the right sleeve.

3. Use the Pen Tool (P) to create a separate side seam and stitching, darts, etc.

Step 5: Add Realistic Effects

For greater realistic effects, try placing a few shadows on the side with the Blob Brush Tool (Shift+B), gray hues, and the Gaussian Blur filter (Figure 14.69). Follow these steps:

1. Select the Blob Brush Tool (Shift+B)

2. Select the Fill color that you want to use. It is suggested that you use 20% gray from the Basic CMYK Swatches panel. You may need to adjust the brush size in the Control Panel, or by double-clicking on the brush's icon in the Tools panel.

3. Lock the shirt objects on the layer by selecting them and pressing *Cmd+2 / Ctrl+2*.

4. Use the Blob Brush Tool (Shift + B) to create highlights or shadows.

5. Select the shapes that you painted with the Selection Tool (V) and go to *Menu Bar > Effects > Blur > Gaussian Blur*.

6. In the Gaussian Blur filter dialog box, move the *Radius* slider to 38.0 px or whatever works for your selection, then click OK.

Step 6: Create the Right Sleeve

1. Carefully render the right sleeve considering the action of the model's arm.

2. Add the cuff details, including the oval shape filled with a gradient to give the appearance of three dimensions.

3. You may need to study the actual file on ② Extra Flats to perfect the illusion.

4. The shadowed wrinkles were created with the Pencil Tool (N). The shapes on top were filled with white and the shapes below them were filled with gray hues, and then completed by applying the Gaussian Blur filter (Figure 14.69).

5. This type of flat needs to reveal what happens with the back views shown from the front. A partially rendered shape representing the back-bibbed hem and construction details have to be rendered, filled with a gradient, and placed underneath what you have already completed (Figure 14.70).

The rest of the finishes were covered in Tutorial 14.2. The only difference here is the angle. An action flat back view is shown next to the completed front view (Figure 14.70). Add finishing shadows to your digital flat to suit your own artistic inclination or your client's needs.

Figure 14.70

An alternative classic men's wear item is found in the silhouette of the bomber jacket. Like many other apparel items, this jacket has origins in the uniforms of World War I. This tutorial makes use of the blazer templates and teaches you to combine rigid textiles with knit trims. This type of jacket has a structured body with a relaxed sleeve, so use an extended arm position to render them. You will also learn to create your own zipper brush.

Note: The file *Men's_Bomber_Jacket.pdf* on ② Extra Flats\Men's Extra Flats has been provided for your use with this tutorial. Open the file in Illustrator®, and then select and ungroup the parts to study the shapes.

Step 1: Create a Bomber Jacket Silhouette

1. Copy the men's blazer template and paste it into *Your Work Layer.*
2. Convert the shape to the default Fill and Stroke.

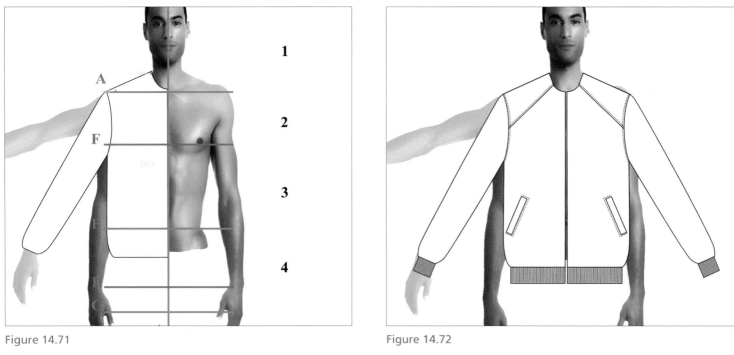

Figure 14.71

Figure 14.72

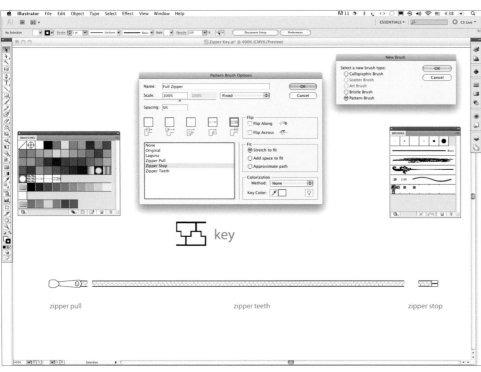

Figure 14.73

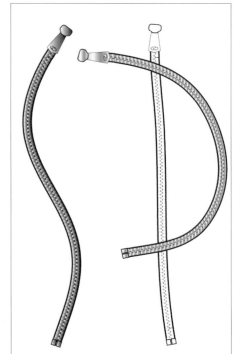

Figure 14.74

3. Rework the silhouette to make a bomber jacket as shown in the completed example in Figure 14.71, but give it your own creative touch. Use the Mid Arm to make the sleeve.

Step 2: Add Construction and Defining Details

1. Add yokes, knit cuffs, banding, and pockets to the jacket front.

2. Use the rib that you created in Tutorial 14.3, Step Two. Drag and drop something created with the rib brush into the file. The brush will appear in the Brushes panel. You can also create a new rib (Figure 14.72).

Step 3: Create a Simple Zipper Brush

1. To make a zipper brush, study the files Zipper_ Key.pdf and Zipper_Key2.pdf on ② Ch14\Tutorial 14.11.

2. Open either file in Illustrator®. Essentially, the key has been constructed from T shapes that interlock, but in order to get the brush to repeat, a portion on the ends need to be left open. Study the key shown in Figure 14.73.

3. In addition to the key, which is a rendering of zipper teeth on a tape, you will need to make a zipper pull and a zipper stop (Figure 14.73).

4. Select the zipper parts separately with the Selection Tool (V), and then define them as patterns by going to *Menu Bar > Edit > Define Pattern*.

5. Give each pattern a recognizable name.

6. The patterns will appear in your Swatches panel. (Figure 14.73).

7. Deselect and show the Brushes panel.

8. Click the New Brush icon at the bottom of the panel.

9. Select the Pattern Brush button, and in the Pattern Brush Options dialog box, assign the brush a name.

10. You will see five tile windows. The first three, from the left, should be selected, then click on the pattern name that you defined for the zipper teeth/ tape. The preview appears in those tile windows.

11. The fourth tile is the **Start Tile window** where the zipper pull should be positioned.

12. Select the **End Tile window** (right), and then click on the zipper stop (Figure 14.73).

13. The zipper brush appears in the Brushes panel. Save your work.

14. Use any rendering tool to create the full zipper.

15. To change the color of the zipper and undo its brush function, select it, and then go to *Menu Bar > Object > Path > Outline Stroke*.

16. Select the parts and fill or stroke them with color, gradients, patterns, etc. (Figure 14.74).

Step 4: Scale the Zipper

If the zipper teeth are not properly sized for your sketch, double-click on the brush in the panel and scale it and click OK. In the Brush Change Alert dialog box, click Apply to strokes. Repeat the process if necessary. Add dashed line strokes along the zipper if so desired. To change the zipper pull and separating clasp, redraw them and then define a new brush. Create the collar, neckline, and back view of the bomber jacket (Figure 14.75).

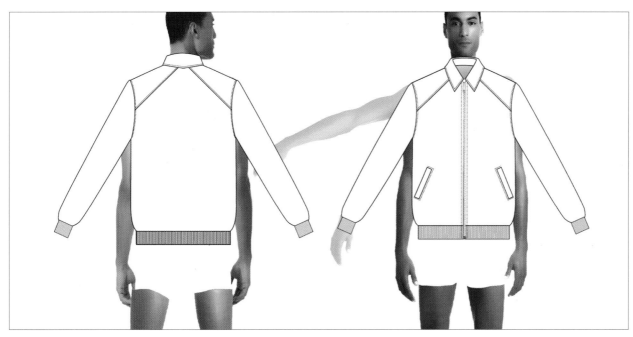

Figure 14.75

Tutorial 14.12
THE TURTLENECK SWEATER
DIGITAL FLAT

The turtleneck sweater or mock turtle can be worn by anyone. Use this tutorial to create one for men's wear, and then design one for a woman. Use what you have learned in the previous tutorials to signify ribbed trim, stitch details, pockets, zippers, etc. The principles of this tutorial will also enable you to render the basic T-shirt.

Note: The file Men's_Mock_Turtleneck_Top.pdf on ② Extra Flats\Men's Extra Flats has been provided for your use with this tutorial. Open the file in Illustrator®, and then select and ungroup the parts to study the shapes.

Step 1: Create the Sweater Silhouette

1. Copy the T-Shirt and Sleeve templates and paste them into *Your Work Layer*.
2. Rework the shapes to make a sweater silhouette as shown in Figure 14.76.

Step 2: Render the Neckline

1. The top of the neckline shape should extend over the chin so that it is aligned with the base of the back of the head (Figure 14.77).
2. Select, copy, and paste the neckline shape to morph the turtleneck fold shape (Figure 14.78).

Step 3: Complete the Flat

Add a gradient-filled ellipse to the neckline and morph the back view (Figure 14.79).

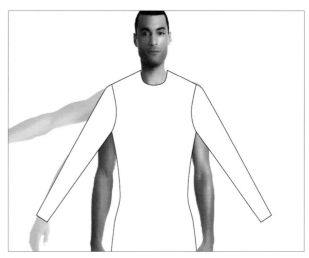

Figure 14.76

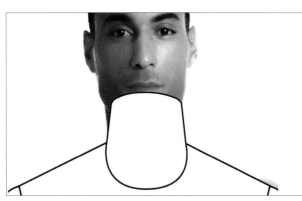

Figure 14.77

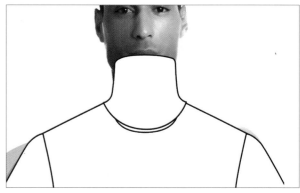

Figure 14.78

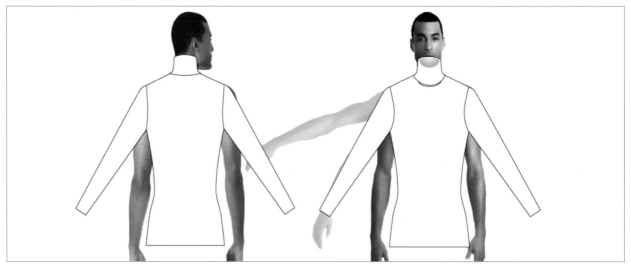

Figure 14.79

Denim apparel comprises a large apparel market sector, and jeans are its key item. Fashion designers and merchandisers who specialize in denim apparel will always have plenty of potential employment opportunities.

Note: *The file Men's_Jeans.pdf on* ② *Extra Flats\ Men's Extra Flats has been provided for your use with this tutorial. Open the file in Illustrator®, and then select and ungroup the parts to study the shapes.*

Step 1: Copy the Pant Template

1. Copy and paste the pant template into *Your Work Layer*.
2. Select it and use the default Fill of white and Stroke of black.
3. Adjust the silhouette and proportion.

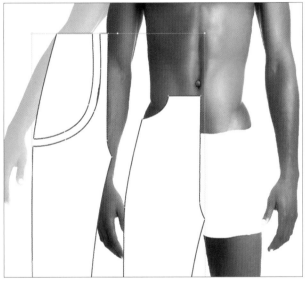

Figure 14.80

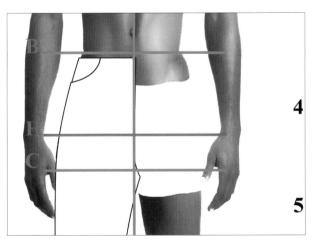

Figure 14.81

Step 2: Use the Eraser Tool to Create Western Pockets

1. Copy and paste the front panel. Select the Illustrator® Eraser Tool (E) from the Tools panel.
2. Use it to remove an area from the side of the pants and make the shape of a western pocket.
3. Select the copy that you made and erase a section for the pocket, then delete the other portion of the pant (Figure 14.80).
4. Send the smaller shape to the back by pressing *Shift+Cmd+[(left bracket) / Shift+Ctrl+[(left bracket).*

Step 3: Lower Distance from the Natural Waist

Perform a marquee with the Direct Selection Tool (A) around the top of the pant with the pocket in place. Press the down arrow key to lower the waist (Figure 14.81).

Step 4: Copy and Paste to Make the Other Side

1. Add stitch details to the pockets.
2. Group the parts by pressing *Cmd+G / Ctrl+G.*
3. Copy and paste the side that you created from the template, to create the other pant leg.
4. Add the fly and pocket stitch details.
5. Adjust the bend of the shape at the rise with the Direct Selection Tool (A), and then use the Illustrator® Pencil Tool (N) to render a **rise indicator**, if desired (Figure 14.82).

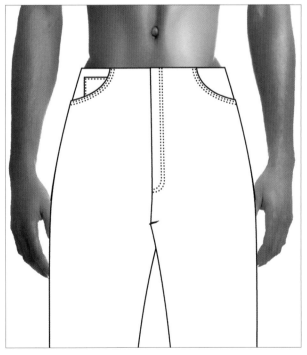

Figure 14.82

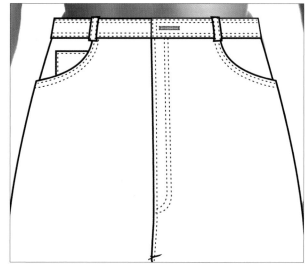

Figure 14.83

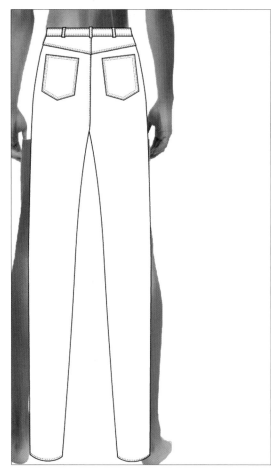

Figure 14.84

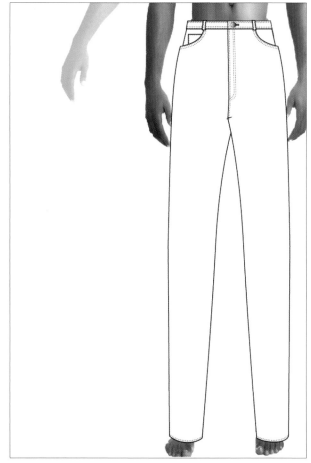

Figure 14.85

Step 5: Make the Waistband

1. Use the Rectangle Tool (M) to make the waistband parts and belt loops.

2. Copy and paste the parts to make the stitches from dashed lines (Figure 14.83).

Note: A Weight of 0.5 pt may have the appearance of actual stitches.

3. Use the Rectangle Tool (M) to make a buttonhole.

4. In the Stroke panel, change the *Weight* to 1 pt and the *Dashed Line* to 0.2 pt (dash and gap).

Step 6: Design the Hem

Most jeans are not creased, so use the Convert Anchor Point Tool (Shift+C) to reshape the hem, and then add stitch details (Figures 14.84 and 14.85).

In this tutorial, you will learn to create a hoodie for men's wear complete with a pull-cord brush, grommets, and ribbed knit trim.

Note: The file *Men's_Hoodie.pdf* on ② *Extra Flats\ Men's Extra Flats* has been provided for your use with this tutorial. Open the file in Illustrator®, and then select and ungroup the parts to study the shapes.

Step 1: Copy the Bomber Jacket from Tutorial 14.3

A "hoodie" is the slang term for a cut and sewn hooded knit top or jacket, usually made of cotton fleece. The style has been around for decades but became popular in the 1980s because of hip-hop culture and streetwear. Today, the term is common. Use the flat that you created in Tutorial 14.12 to help make the shape of the hoodie. Delete the collar, yokes, pockets, etc. Add the shape shown in Figure 14.86 for the back of the hood.

Step 2: Create the Other Side of the Hood

Copy, paste, reflect, and unite the shape you just created to form a complete hood (Figure 14.87).

Step 3: Add Dimension to the Inside of the Hood

Fill the hood shape with a radial gradient (Figure 14.88).

Step 4: Add Details to the Inside of the Hood

Add a center back seam and topstitches to the inside of the hood shape (Figure 14.89).

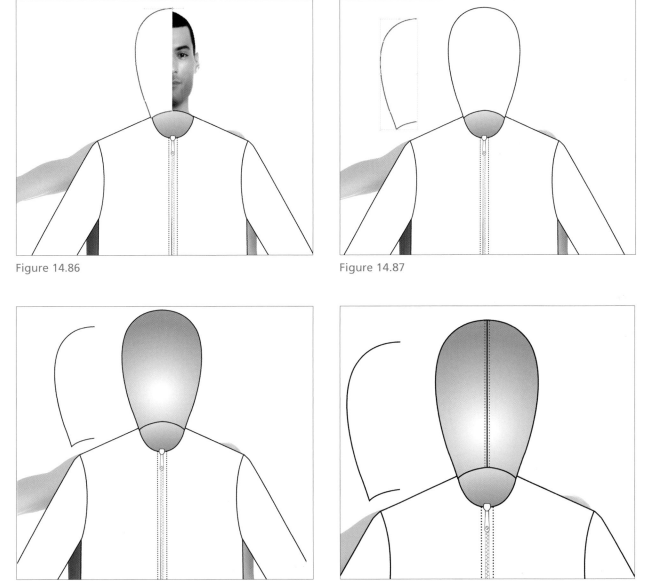

Figure 14.86

Figure 14.87

Figure 14.88

Figure 14.89

Step 5: Create the Front of the Hood

1. Bring the extra shape to the front and align its bottom with the jacket neckline (Figure 14.90).

2. Shape the front opening as shown in Figure 14.91.

3. Copy, paste, and reflect the front shape to create the other side of the hood and add details (Figure 14.92).

Step 6: Make a Pull-Cord Brush

Most hoodie designs come with a pull-cord that adjusts the fit of the hood to the head. To render this, you need to define a pattern for a shape like the one in Figure 14.93, but it must contain a ground box filled with a color (14 Gray) the same size beneath it. See Chapter 4 for detailed instructions for creating pattern brushes.

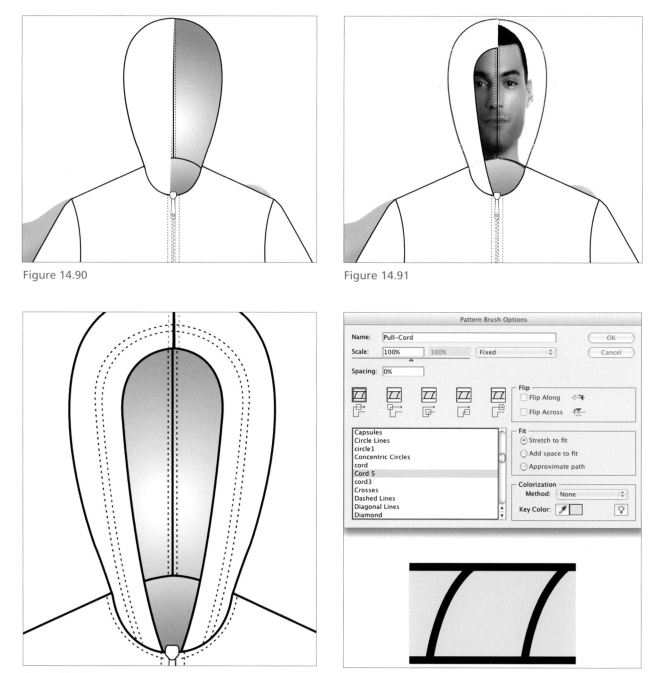

Figure 14.90

Figure 14.91

Figure 14.92

Figure 14.93 Pull-cord brush key and options.

Step 7: Create Eyelets and Brush On the Pull-Cord

1. Hold the Shift key and use the Ellipse Tool (L) to make an eyelet from two centered aligned circles.

2. Fill the inner circle with the gray hue that you used for the pull cord. Group, copy, and paste the shape.

3. Use the Illustrator® Brush Tool (B) to draw the pull-cord on each side as if it were coming from the eyelet (Figure 14.94).

4. Finish the ends of the pull-cord as shown in Figure 14.95 or create your own.

Step 8: Add Pockets to the Front of the Jacket

Kangaroo pockets were added to the jacket in Figure 14.96.

Step 9: Reposition the Left Sleeve

The sleeve on a cut and sewn knit such as a hoodie is usually cut at the high arm position. Marquee

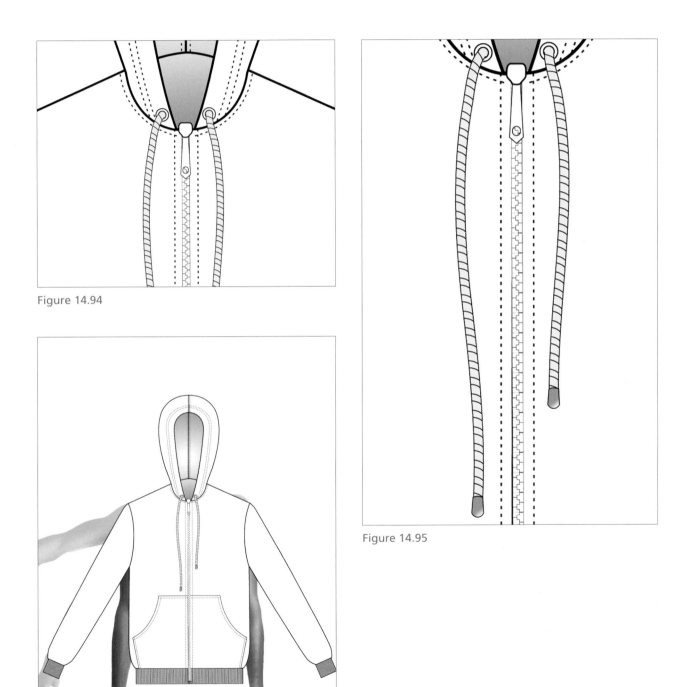

Figure 14.94

Figure 14.95

Figure 14.96

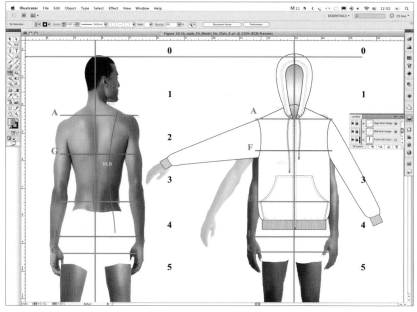

Figure 14.97

around the lower portion of the left sleeve with the Direct Selection Tool (A), then use the arrow keys to move the sleeve upward. Select specific anchor points and reposition them. Use the Rotate Tool (R) to turn the cuff. Leave the right sleeve as is to save space (Figure 14.97).

Step 10: Create the Back View from the Front View

The completed flat is shown in Figure 14.98.

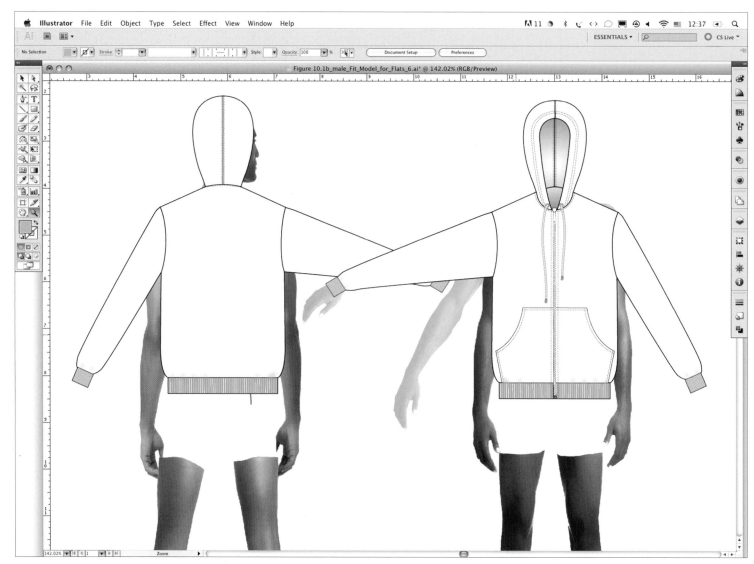

Figure 14.98 Many knit garments with fuller cuts like the hoodie have identical front and back armholes as shown.

The trench coat was originally designed for American soldiers of World War I, but has survived as a fashion classic. In this tutorial, you will learn how to create a digital flat of a men's traditional raglan-sleeved trench coat complete with belt, buckle, and inverted pleat back, using Illustrator®. Use the procedures to design your own version for men's wear or women's wear.

Note: The file *Men's_Trench_Coat.pdf* on ② *Extra Flats\Men's Extra Flats has been provided for your use with this tutorial. Open the file in Illustrator®, and then select and ungroup the parts to study the shapes.*

Step 1: Create the Trench Coat Silhouette

1. Copy the men's blazer template and paste it into *Your Work Layer*.

2. Rework the silhouette to make a trench coat as shown in Figure 14.99.

Step 2: Create a Raglan Sleeve

Use the Direct Selection Tool (A) to reposition anchor points from the arm sickle of the sleeve shape and make a raglan seam (Figure 14.100).

Step 3: Redesign the Collar and Lapel

The blazer template's collar and lapel need to be adjusted to suit the proportions of the trench coat (Figure 14.101).

Figure 14.99

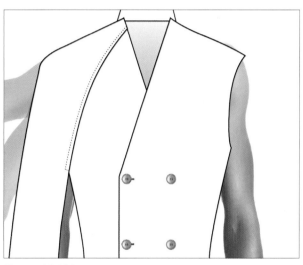

Figure 14.100

Figure 14.101

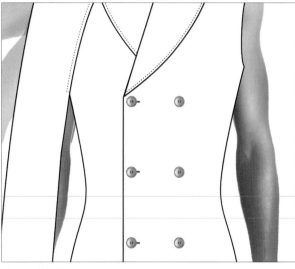

Figure 14.102

Step 4: Prepare the Location of the Belt

1. Pull horizontal Guides to the waist to guide the belt as shown in Figure 14.102.
2. Add anchor points to create a blouson shape as shown in Figure 14.103.
3. Render gathers with the Pencil Tool (N) as shown in Figure 14.104.

Step 5: Add Belting, Buckles, Loops, and Pockets

1. Create the belt base with the Rectangle Tool (M).
2. Use the Rounded Rectangle Tool to make a buckle shape, and modify it with the Direct Selection Tool (A) or the Bounding Box. Copy, paste, and scale the shapes, then select and align the two from their centers. Click on the Pathfinder panel's *Exclude* icon to open the center.
3. Position the buckle at the waist.
4. Render the hanging portion of the belt and the belt loops. Use the forward Warp Tool (Shift+R) to give it a natural wave as if it were windborn.
5. Add besom pockets to accentuate the coat's sporty look and function (Figure 14.105).

Step 6: Make the Back from the Front Flat

The completed flat is shown in Figure 14.106. The inverted pleat was made by separating the back shapes on an angle from the neck and adding shape beneath.

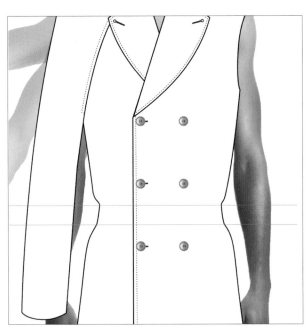

Figure 14.103

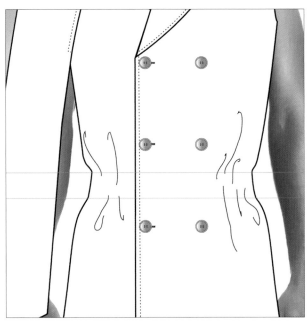

Figure 14.104

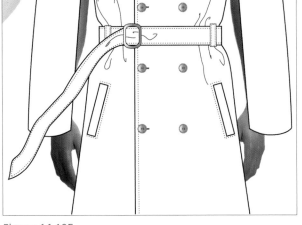

Figure 14.105

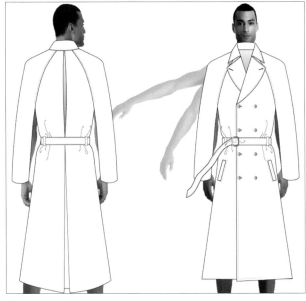

Figure 14.106

During your career, you may be asked to prepare certain types of forms. The most common are line sheets, specification sheets, detail callout sheets, and grading worksheets. In this tutorial, you will become familiar with these forms and learn how to insert your technical sketches in them.

Note: *Microsoft Excel® is required for the exercises in this tutorial.*

Line Sheets

A line sheet is an organized display of associated items being marketed or manufactured that have been grouped by shipping cycle, fabrication, and/or trend. There are generally two types of line sheets: the showroom line sheet and the technical or production line sheet.

Showroom Line Sheets

Some line sheets are used prior to or during a market week to present a collection. They are used primarily as organizational sales forms. This type of line sheet is given to wholesale buyers who visit showrooms.

Written information makes vital connections between the products that are being offered and how they fit with the merchandising concepts of the entire marketplace. A good buyer always remembers key words. In Figure 14.107, styles were selected that have references to the 1940s, but it is the title that makes this point memorable. Each of the styles has a number, so the buyer can reference them when posing questions. The shipping period and some basic fabric information should be stated clearly.

The orientation of the showroom line sheet is up to the company, but landscape orientation works best because it allows the flats to be juxtaposed in a comprehensive manner. Tops and jackets should not be placed beneath pants and skirts. If the market is specialized, such as the dress market or intimate apparel, the arrangement of line sheets may need to fit the space needed to display the items on a page.

The most important thing to remember is not to allow the presentation of the showroom line sheet to eclipse the products being marketed. For this reason black-and-white digital printouts are ideal. Avoid adding extra graphics and enhancing the styles in any

The Fab 40s

"Digital Duo" Boutiques
Spring Shipping January–March 2014

silk crepe de chine
fully lined
prints and solids

Figure 14.107

manner that might cause confusion. The showroom line sheet is simply a reference. Limit your styling to specific fonts, borders, and style names, like those shown on the line sheet in Figure 14.108.

Two sample showroom line sheet files Fab_40s_Line_Sheet.pdf and Boss_Lady_Line_Sheet.pdf on ② Ch14\Tutorial 14.16 are available for you to examine.

Technical Line Sheets

The other type of line sheet is usually created in Microsoft Excel® and sent to a contractor in a tech-pack (Figure 14.109). It can also be e-mailed to buyers or used in showrooms. The information on this line sheet is more detailed, but will be slightly different at each company.

In addition to technical flat sketches, the basic information required for each style on a technical line sheet should include, but is not limited to:

- Style number
- Price
- Description
- Fabrication
- Color assortment

A sample Microsoft Excel® worksheet Blank_Technical_Line_Sheet.xls on ② Ch14\Tutorial 14.16 is available for you to use as a simple exercise.

Preparing and Placing Illustrator® Files into Line Sheets

You need to know how to prepare and insert your technical drawings into line sheets, specification sheets, tech-pack schematics sheets, and grading worksheets created in Microsoft Excel®. The same method works for each type of document. Follow these steps:

1. Open the Microsoft Excel® worksheet Blank_Technical_Line_Sheet.xls on ② Ch14\Tutorial 14.16.

2. Open any technical flat that you have created in Illustrator®. You can also use the files on ② Extra Flats\Women's Extra Flats or ② Extra Flats\Men's Extra Flats.

3. For a simple line sheet you only need to place the front views of the technical sketches. This form gives an overall view of a group of items being placed as a sample request or examples of availability and shipping of items as they are delivered to a manufacturer's warehouse. If your file has a back view on the same page, delete it.

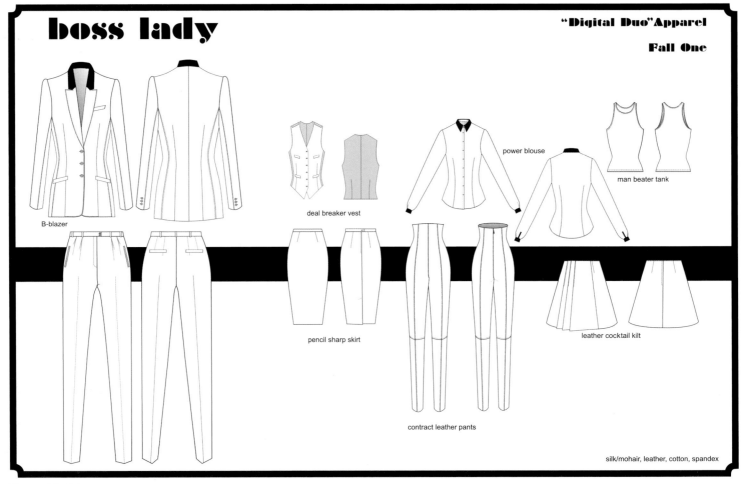

Figure 14.108

Company Name/Address		Tele		Delivery		Fax	
		Email		Rep		Quantity	

Style: Price:	Style: Price:	Style: Price:	Style: Price:	Style: Price:
Description:	Description:	Description:	Description:	Description:
Fabrication:	Fabrication:	Fabrication:	Fabrication:	Fabrication:
Shipping:	Shipping:	Shipping:	Shipping:	Shipping:
Colors:	Colors:	Colors:	Colors:	Colors:
Sizes:	Sizes:	Sizes:	Sizes:	Sizes:
Style: Price:	Style: Price:	Style: Price:	Style: Price:	Style: Price:
Description:	Description:	Description:	Description:	Description:
Fabrication:	Fabrication:	Fabrication:	Fabrication:	Fabrication:
Shipping:	Shipping:	Shipping:	Shipping:	Shipping:
Colors:	Colors:	Colors:	Colors:	Colors:
Sizes:	Sizes:	Sizes:	Sizes:	Sizes:

Figure 14.109

Note: *Microsoft Excel® will not interpret line work as a filled object. Your flats need to be filled with white for the best results.*

4. Select the Illustrator® Artboard Tool (Shift+O). You will see the Artboard flanked with a Bounding Box surrounded by a gray area.

5. Hold the Shift key to constrain the proportions while you resize the Bounding Box to fit your technical flat sketch (**Figure 14.110**).

6. Click one of the tools in Tools panel to accept the adjustment.

7. Save the file in the Adobe EPS (.eps) format.

8. Select the Blank_Technical_Line_Sheet.xls line sheet that you opened.

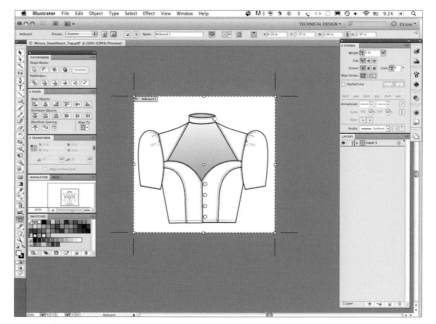

Figure 14.110

Figure 14.111

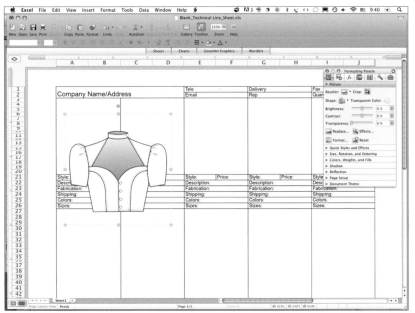

Figure 14.112

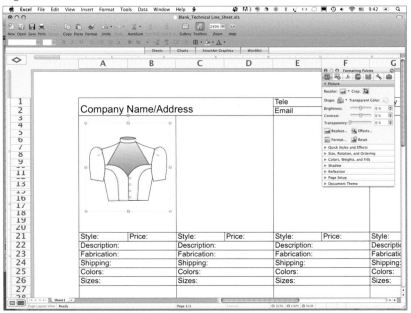

Figure 14.113

9. In Microsoft Excel, go to *Menu Bar > Insert > Picture > From File . . .*

10. Select the adjusted pdf technical flat file in the Choose a Picture dialog box (Figure 14.111). The image of the flat will be placed in a frame within a transparent background (Figure 14.112).

11. Select the frame.

12. Hold the Shift key to constrain the proportions of the image, and pull inward with your mouse to resize it to fit the area (Figure 14.113).

Specification Sheets

A **specification sheet** contains technical flats and all the measurements needed to draft a pattern as a part of a tech-pack. Each style shown on the technical line sheet will have a specification sheet and detailed callouts. Certain garments require many measurements, which will increase the number of pages (Figure 14.114).

A sample Microsoft Excel® specification sheet for a blazer Blank_Blazer_Spec_Sheet.xls on ② Ch14\ Tutorial 14.16 is available for you to use. The specification sheet contains suggested categories and fields for you to enter measurements.

Preparing and Placing Technical Sketches into Specification Sheets

No matter whether you are using Microsoft Excel® or another software program, each apparel specification sheet will contain fields where you can insert technical flats. This is achieved in Microsoft Excel® the same way as demonstrated for the line sheet. However, sometimes you will need to arrange the views so that space is maximized. For example, you may need to insert both the front and back views into one space. To do this, follow these steps:

1. Open the Microsoft Excel® worksheet Blank_Blazer_ Spec_Sheet.xls on ② Ch14\Tutorial 14.16.

2. Open any technical flat that you have created in Illustrator® with front and back views. You can also use the files on ② Extra Flats\Women's Extra Flats or ② Extra Flats\Men's Extra Flats.

3. Arrange the front and back views on the Artboard to fit the space of the target cell in the spreadsheet.

4. Select the Illustrator® Artboard Tool (Shift+O).

5. Hold the Shift key to constrain the proportions while you resize the Bounding Box.

6. Add any instructions or titles, such as *Front View, Back View*, etc. (Figure 14.115).

7. Save the file in the Adobe PDF (.pdf) format.

Season:	Label:	Date:	Fabrication:	
Style:		Accessories:	Sample Size:	Lining:

Description:

Trims:

SAMPLE REQUESITION

SPECIFICATION CATEGORY	Front	Back	Total	SKETCH
1. HPS TO CF NECK DROP				
2. HPS TO CB NECK DROP				
3. NECK OPENING WIDTH			0.00	
4. LENGTH OF SHOULDER				
5. FORWARD FRONT DROP				
6. ACROSS BACK				
7. LENGTH: HPS TO HEM				
8. LENGTH: LPS TO HEM				
9. LENGTH: CF/CB TO HEM				
10. LENGTH: SIDE SEAM TO HEM				
11. CHEST: 1' BELOW ARMHOLE			0.00	
12. DROP: HPS TO UNDERARM				
13. WAIST: 17" FROM HPS			0.00	
14. HIGH HIP: 21" BELOW HPS			0.00	
15. LOW HIP: 24" BELOW HPS			0.00	
16. BOTTOM HEM OPENING (SWEEP)			0.00	
17. HEM DEPTH				
18. SIDE PANEL WIDTH AT BUST			0.00	
19. SIDE PANEL WIDTH AT WAIST			0.00	
20. SIDE PANEL WIDTH AT HIP			0.00	
21. SIDE PANEL WIDTH AT HEM			0.00	
22. DART FROM CF/CB FINISH				
23. DART DROP FROM HPS				
24. DART FROM CF/CB WAIST				
25. DART FROM CF/CB HEM			0.00	
26. COLLAR WIDTH			0.00	
27. COLLAR WIDTH CB				
28. COLLAR STAND HEIGHT CB				
30. COLLAR WIDTH FRONT EDGE TO POINT				
31. LAPEL WIDTH FRONT EDGE TO POINT				DETAIL 1
32. ARMHOLE CIRCUMFERENCE			0.00	
33. SLEEVE LENGTH				
34. OVERARM				
35. UNDERARM				
36. SLEEVE HEM FROM HPS				
37. SLEEVE HEM FROM CB				
38. WIDTH: UPPER SLEEVE 1" BELOW UNDERARM			0.00	
39. WIDTH SLEEVE AT ELBOW			0.00	
40. SLEEVE HEM OPENING				
41. SLEEVE PANEL WIDTH 1" BELOW ARMHOLE			0.00	
42. SLEEVE PANEL WIDTH AT ELBOW				
43. SLEEVE PANEL WIDTH AT HEM			0.00	

44. SLEVE HEM DEPTH				DETAIL 2
45. FRONT POCKET FROM HPS				
46. FRONT POCKET PLACEMENT FROM CF				
47. FRONT POCKET FROM SIDE SEAM				
48. FRONT POCKET WIDTH				
49. FRONT POCKET LENGTH				
50. FRONT POCKET DROP				
51. FLAP WIDTH				
52. FLAP LENGTH				
53. FLAP ANGLE DROP: L/R				
54. BREAST POCKET FROM HPS				
55. BREAST POCKET WIDTH				
56. BREAST POCKET LENGTH				
57. BREST POCKET FROM ARMHOLE SEAM				
58. FIRST FRONT BUTTON PLACEMENT				
59. FRONT BUTTON SPACING				
60. FIRST SLEEVE BUTTON FROM HEM				
61. SLEEVE BUTTON SPACING				

COMMENTS:

FRONT	BACK

Figure 14.114

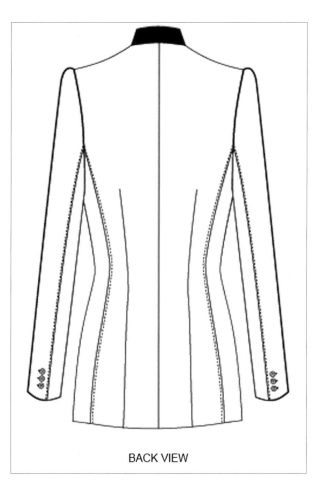

FRONT VIEW   BACK VIEW

Figure 14.115

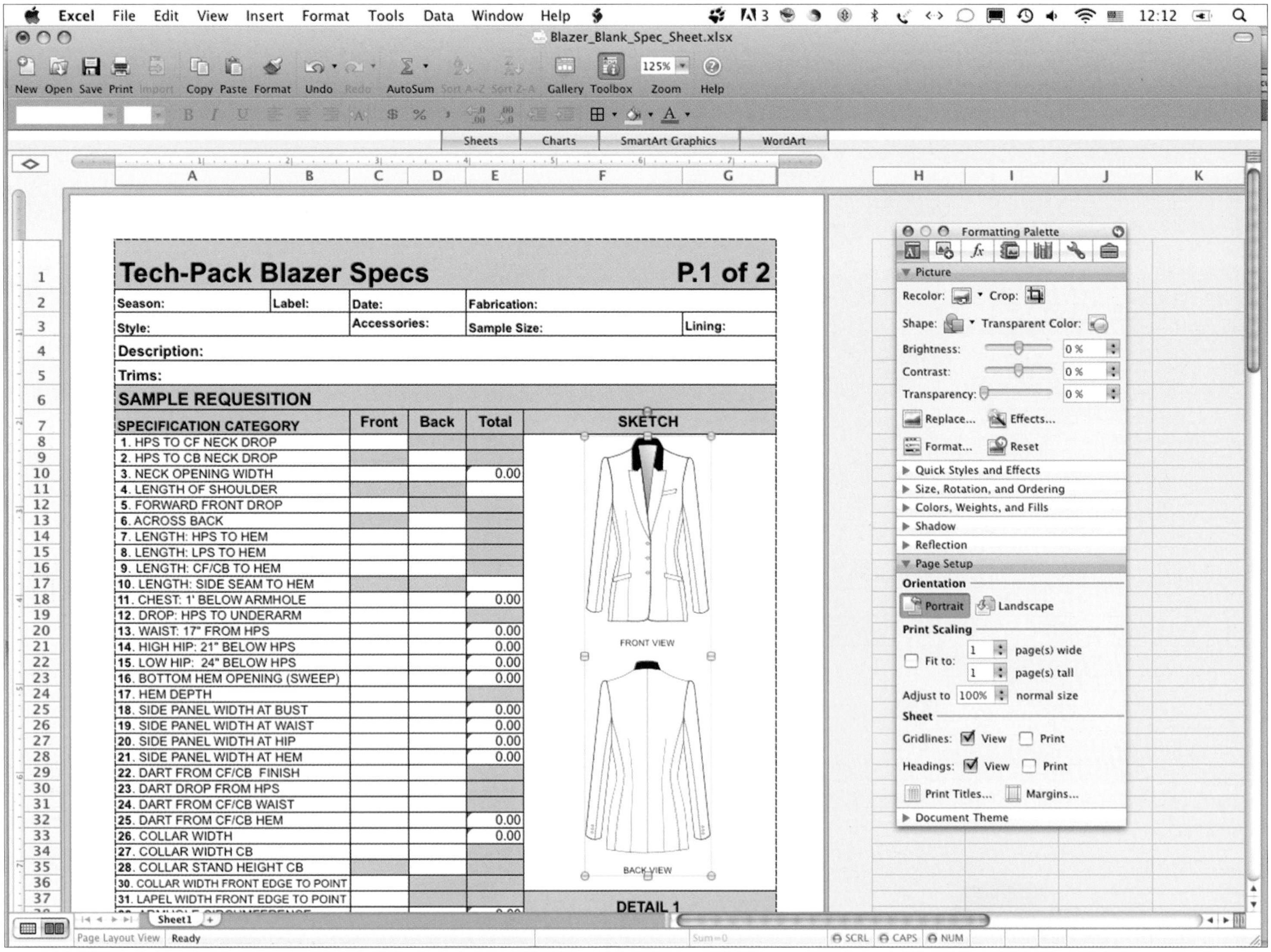

Figure 14.116 The blazer flat has been scaled to fit the sketch area of the spec sheet.

8. Insert the technical sketch into the Microsoft Excel® spreadsheet as previously instructed (Figure 14.116).

Detailed Callouts

In addition to the simple technical sketches that you insert in the specification sheets, you also need to provide detailed areas often referred to as a **callout** (schematic). These are close-ups of the flats containing reference points and diagrams that clarify construction details that cannot be seen in a small technical flat. Specification sheets can contain space for some of the callouts, but you may also need to prepare them on an entire page. Such is the case for contained areas like pockets and closure details.

Creating Callouts

To create the callouts, you need three components: a completed technical flat in Illustrator®, the Stroke panel *Dashed Lines*, and the *Arrowheads* menu options.

Stroke Arrowheads: The Illustrator® Stroke *Arrowheads* are activated when a line segment is created or selected and the Stroke contains a color, but the Fill should be None. With the menu, you can add arrows to either or both sides of a straight or curved path. The *Arrowhead* menus allow you to choose different start and end finishes, and there is an icon on the upper left that swaps them. In addition you can adjust the size of the start or finish arrowheads, and align and lock them with options right on the panel section (Figure 14.117).

Technical designers put the Illustrator® *Arrowheads* menu to good use when creating callouts to point to areas on the technical flat and clarify measurements. Usually, these arrows have numbers of finished specs adjacent to them. The completed specification sheet may need a number of callouts to facilitate the patternmaking for each style in a line. One way to do this is to place all the arrowhead paths on one flat (Figure 14.118).

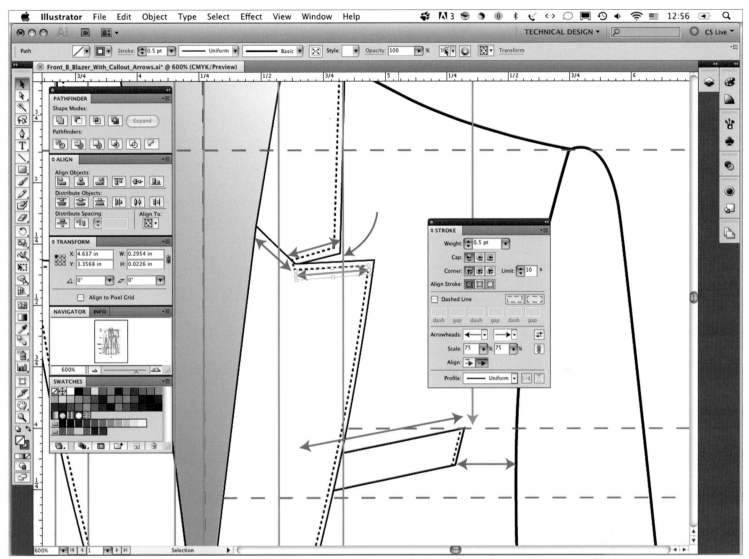

Figure 14.117 The *Arrowheads* shown above indicate actual points of measurements on a spec sheet.

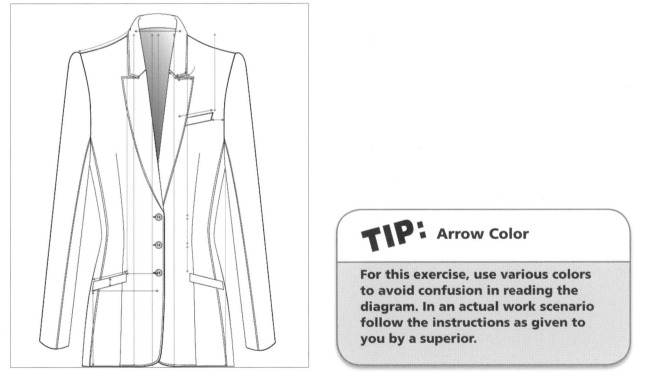

Figure 14.118

TIP: Arrow Color

For this exercise, use various colors to avoid confusion in reading the diagram. In an actual work scenario follow the instructions as given to you by a superior.

Screen Shots on a Mac: Zoom in on an area with a marquee using the Illustrator® Zoom Tool (Z).

1. Press *Shift+Cmd+4*. Your cursor turns into a circle image with cross marks and numbers that change as you move around the page. The image appears on your desktop in a TIFF format. Marquee over the area that you want to feature as a detailed callout.

2. Open the image in Illustrator® or Adobe Acrobat Pro® and save the file in the PDF format.

Screen Shots on a PC: All PCs have screenshot applications that work by selecting areas.

Dashed Lines: In addition to the *Arrowheads*, the Stroke panel *Dashed Lines* is useful for clarifying reference points on your callouts (Figure 14.119).

Measurement Details: Add the actual measurements next to the *Arrowhead* paths. You can also use them to reference an area numbered on the spec sheet (Figure 14.120).

When you have the screen shots that you need, insert them into the detailed cells of your specification sheets as previously instructed or prepare them separately on a page (Figure 14.121).

Note: *Detailed specifications and screenshots are also needed for hardware items such as buckles, grommets, filigrees, etc. Draw the hardware as actual 3-D objects. Use the Metals Swatch Libraries. (See Tutorial 4.1, Step Seven.)*

Grading Worksheets: Grading worksheets are required for each style that is sent to a contractor as part of the tech-pack. This sheet shows all the specifications for the sizes in a range for a particular apparel item. Some contain the technical flats. Insert the image(s) in Microsoft Excel® as previously instructed.

Creating a Multiple-Page PDF Document with Acrobat Pro®

When you have completed all of the components necessary to send to a contractor, including the measurements and other details, follow these steps if you are required to send them via e-mail or other electronic means:

1. Save each file in the same document size and format by going to *Menu Bar > File > Save As*.

2. In the Save As dialog box, choose Illustrator PDF (in Microsoft Excel® choose PDF) in the format section at the bottom of the window, and then click OK.

3. Open Adobe Acrobat Pro®.

4. Go to *Menu Bar > Combine > Merge Files* into a single PDF.

Note: *PC and Mac may have a slight variation in the Menu Bar setup.*

5. When the **Combine Files** dialog box appears, click **Add Files**.

6. Select the files that will be combined, and then press OK. They will appear in your Acrobat® window.

7. To reorder the files, select them, and then click the *Move Up* or *Move Down* buttons at the bottom of the window.

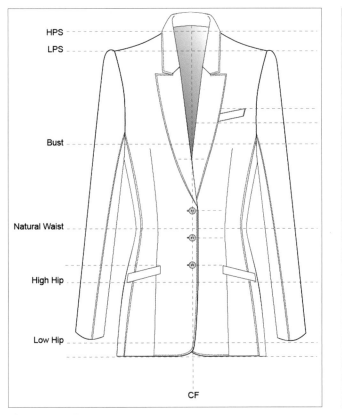

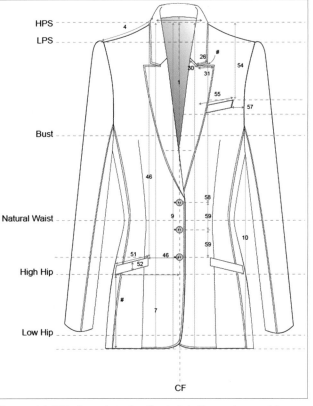

Figure 14.119

Figure 14.120 Completed callout details can be sent to a contractor on a separate sheet of a tech-pack.

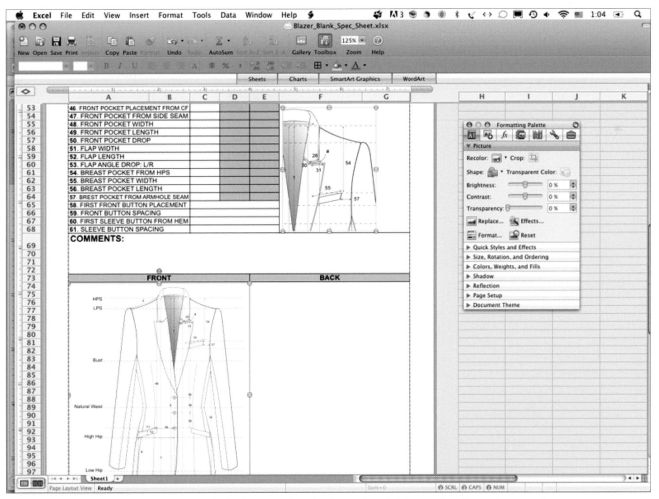

Figure 14.121 Manufacturers often include the completed callouts in addition to details on the spec sheet.

Chapter 14 Summary

In this chapter, you learned to create digital technical flats from templates, which were morphed from basic shapes or rendered with the Illustrator® Pen Tool (P). Included in the classic styles of this chapter were lessons on how to render blouson looks, belted waists, pull-cords, zippers, and more. These methods were designed to help you to create presentations that will open doors to further studies and possible employment opportunities in the fashion industry. However, there are many methods for developing technical flats, and not one of them is right or wrong. The global fashion industry dictates the appropriate methods based on the specific needs of apparel manufacturers communicating with contractors to facilitate production. Each company will establish rules and standards for their employees to follow. Some of these will be simplistic, while others may be more complex than the procedures shown here. In the workplace it is wise to ask questions and apply techniques used by successful coworkers.

Hands-on expertise is key to mastering technical flats. Try generating your own digital fashion designs, using the methods shown throughout the tutorials, several times for various garment categories before proceeding to the tutorials in the final chapter. When you are able to make your flats without the use of the textbook, answer the questions below.

Chapter 14 Self-Assessment

1. Can I name three important components to creating a finished zipper brush?

2. Do I know how to use the Offset Path feature to simulate double-needle topstitching?

3. In Illustrator® am I able to morph the back views from most of the parts that I create for the fronts? Do I know which areas to alter afterward?

4. Can I render a buckle in Illustrator®, and do I know which feature of the Pathfinder panel to use in order to create the hole(s)?

5. Can I name and point out at least ten reference points on the female or male figure/croquis?

6. Tailored apparel items should be rendered as if they are hanging on a coat hanger, but can I do this? Can I make my technical flats look 3-D?

7. Do I know when to change the *Weight* of the Stroke when rendering technical flats in Illustrator®? Do I know how and what adjustments to make to outlines, seams, darts, stitches, etc?

8. Do I know what tool to use in Illustrator® to change an angle into a curve?

9. Can I simulate ribbed-knit trims and edges in Illustrator®?

10. Do I know how to render a sleeve with a bend at the elbow?

"Digital Duo" Color Flats, Floats, Design, and Presentation

Objectives

The primary objective of this chapter is to teach you how to create exceptional 3-D digital color flats and floats from technical drawings. Therefore, the tutorials in Chapters 12, 13, and 14 should be completed before attempting the ones here. In fact, some of the technical flats presented in Chapter 14 will be enhanced in this one. This chapter also culminates all the lessons in the book, and reinforces the skills you will need to create a totally digital fashion portfolio presentation. In this chapter, you will:

- Use techniques previously demonstrated in the tutorials in all the previous chapters

- Render full 3-D color digital designer and couture-quality apparel flats and floats

- Learn interchangeable procedures to create printed and virtual marketing aids for both men's wear and women's wear

- Create digital luxury textiles, faux fur, simulated animal pelts, embroidery, novelties, treatments, and trims

- Use the ② Textiles and Novelties Library

- Style and merchandise a complete wardrobe composed of distinct items

Women's Designer Flats and Floats

The following tutorials magnify the digital skills needed to create fashion designs and presentations for the designer and couture markets. The purpose of this approach is to help you to develop a higher market sensitivity from which it is feasible to adjust to lower markets. In both fashion academia and in the apparel job market, the reverse approach is chiefly implausible.

Although thousands of various textiles and techniques could and should be covered, what is presented here represents the basic essentials. It is recommended that you follow the tutorials precisely, but feel free to make them your own if the outcomes would be more suitable. Change the look, design, colors, fabrics, etc. In addition, make use of ② Textiles and Novelties Library to help you enhance your presentation with images of elegant and definable textiles and novelties.

Note: *Some technical flats files have been provided with the tutorials on the DVD and are ready for immediate use. However, if you use the files on ② Extra Flats\Women's Extra Flats, you will need to ungroup the parts by selecting them and repeatedly pressing Shift+Cmd+G / Shift+Ctrl+G. When the parts are totally ungrouped, you may want to cut and paste them into new layers. You can also scroll the hidden menu on the right side of the Layers panel, and then select Release into Layers (Sequence). This will give you some of the layers that you will need when exporting the files from Illustrator® to Photoshop®.*

This tutorial provides you with simple instructions to digitally simulate leather or vinyl apparel on a pre-rendered technical flat sketch.

Step 1: Open or Create a Technical Flat in Illustrator®

Figure 15.1 shows the file Leather_Jacket.pdf from ② Ch15\Tutorial 15.1, but feel free to use any jacket flat that you created in Chapter 14.

Step 2: Export the File to Photoshop®

Export the file from Illustrator® to Photoshop® in the PSD file format (Figure 15.2). For more instructions for exporting files, see Tutorial 5.3, Step Sixteen.

Step 3: Fill the Image with Gradients

Name the layers, select the sections with the Photoshop® Magic Wand, and fill them with Gradients as shown in Figure 15.3.

Step 4: Add Photoshop® Filters to the Parts

1. The Photoshop® **Dry Brush filter** will add a twill texture to your gradient-filled parts. Select each layer separately, and then go to *Menu Bar > Filter > Artistic > Dry Brush* to access the settings (Figure 15.4).

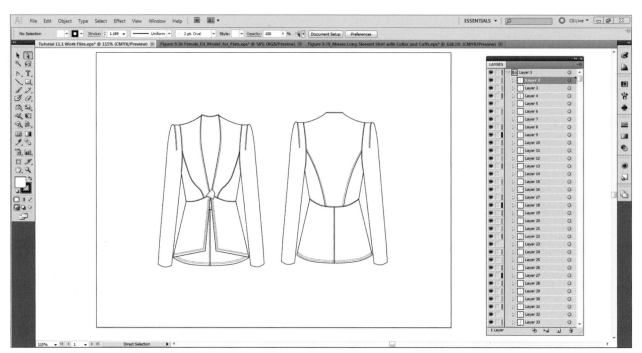

Figure 15.1 Illustrator® file

TIP: Exaggerating Scale

When using digital photo images to signify actual textile textures, the scale should be slightly exaggerated. This will make them visible and immediately communicate the elements of design. If you decide to use the photo images, reduce the resolution in Photoshop® by going to *Menu Bar > Image > Image Size*. Change the Resolution to 150 dpi for printing or to 72 dpi if you plan to e-mail the completed presentation. This will prevent your file size from becoming too large when you define the prints as patterns in earlier versions of Illustrator®. In addition, avoid placing defined prints into Strokes in Illustrator® (CS5 and earlier), which can cause your computer to crash or prevent printing.

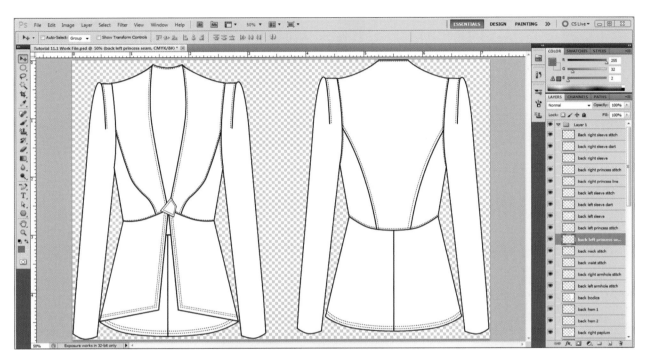

Figure 15.2 Photoshop® file.

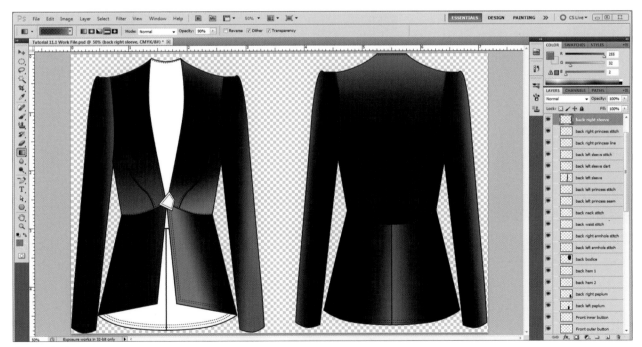

Figure 15.3

2. To simulate the look of leather, add the **Water Paper filter** by going to *Menu Bar > Filter > Sketch > Water Paper* (Figure 15.5).

3. Add the Dry Brush filter to the parts again.

4. Merge the Solid Shape layers, and then add the Photoshop® Noise filter (Figure 15.7).

Step 5: Adjust the Highlights

Use the Photoshop® Forward Warp Tool (W) in the Liquify filter window to adjust areas that represent highlights (Figure 15.8). For further instructions about the Liquify filter, see Tutorial 10.3, Step Fourteen.

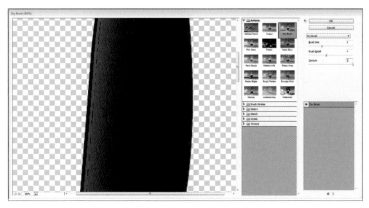

Figure 15.4

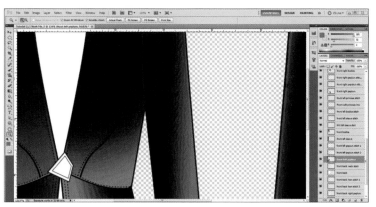

Figure 15.5

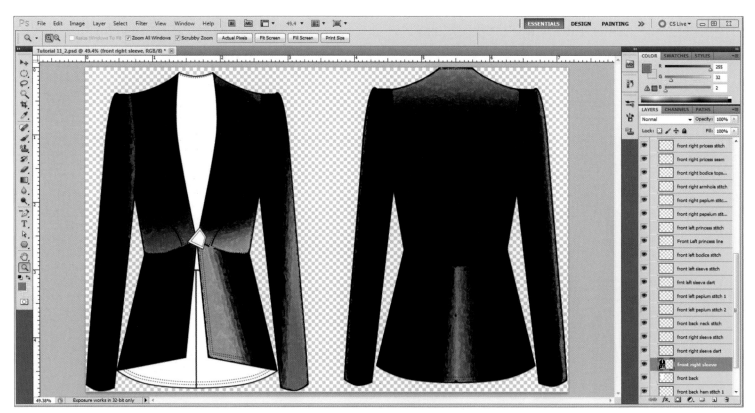

Figure 15.6

Step 6: Add Color to the Lining and the Notions

1. Select the lining with the Photoshop® Magic Wand Tool (W) and change the color.

2. Use gradient fills and the Bevel and Emboss Layer Style to give the button(s) a 3-D effect (Figure 15.9). See Tutorial 5.1, Step Ten for more information about Bevel and Emboss.

Step 7: Create the Effect of Leather

Box 15.1 explains how to create the effect of leather using the Leather photo fill method in Illustrator® and Photoshop®. If you prefer, use the file Black_Leather. jpg from ② Textiles and Novelties Library to define a textural pattern fill.

Figure 15.7

Figure 15.8

Figure 15.9 **Illustration by Stacy Stewart Smith.**

Box 15.1: The Leather Photo Fill Method in Illustrator® and Photoshop®

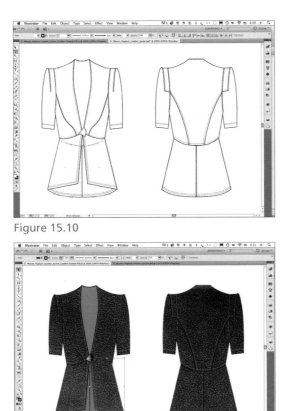

Figure 15.10

Figure 15.11

Figure 15.12

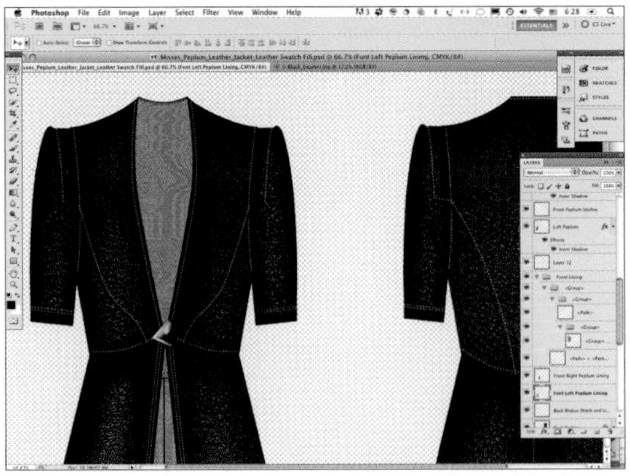

Figure 15.13 **Contrast stitching can be added.**

Figure 15.14

In Illustrator®, after you have filled the shapes with the defined photo images, save a copy, and then select the parts and go to *Menu Bar > Object > Rasterize*. In the Rasterize dialog box, if you have not already reduced the resolution, change it to *Medium* if you plan to print or *Screen* if you are using the file for e-mail. In the *Background* section, check *Transparent*. When you have made these changes to the copy file, follow these steps:

1. Open or create a technical flat in Illustrator®.

2. Replace any gradient fills with white in Illustrator® (**Figure 15.10**).

3. Open the file Black_Leather.jpg file into Photoshop® (**Figure 15.11**).

4. Select the photo image and define a pattern (see Tutorial 3.2, Step Nine).

5. Drag and drop the Black_Leather.jpg file into Illustrator®.

6. Fill the parts with the pattern, and scale the pattern only, approximately 50%, as shown in **Figure 15.12**. (See Tutorial 3.2, Step Ten.)

7. Fill the buttons and color the stroked stitches.

8. Export the file from Illustrator® to Photoshop®.

Note: *If you prefer, use the file Black_Leather.jpg from ② Textiles and Novelties Library to define a textural pattern fill.*

9. The layer compositing will be transferred, but some parts may be grouped. Merge layers if needed.

10. Select each layer and add tool effects, panel options and/or Layer Styles. The Inner Shadow Layer Style was used in the tutorial example (**Figure 15.13**).

11. The completed look in **Figure 15.14** has a moiré patterned lining (see Tutorial 8.6).

There are plenty of ways to simulate novelty fabrics, but when it comes to those with all-over flat French sequins, the originality lies in the repeat. In this tutorial, you will learn to create a sequin repeat using the features of Illustrator®, then further append and define it in Photoshop®. In addition, you will add tool and filter attributes to mimic the brilliance of this popular evening wear specialty textile treatment. To practice this tutorial, use the file Sequined_Dress.pdf from ② Ch15\Tutorial 15.2 or any dress flat that you completed from the Chapter 14 tutorials.

Step 1: Open or Create a Technical Flat in Illustrator®
Figure 15.15 shows the file Sequined_Dress.pdf, but feel free to use any dress flat that you created in Chapter 14.

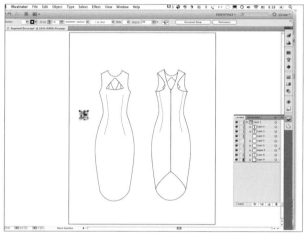

Figure 15.15

Step 2: Create a Sequin Repeat
On a separate layer, create a sequin repeat in a monochromatic color scheme (Figure 15.16). For more information about monochromatic color schemes, see Tutorial 9.4, Step Five.

Step 3: Export the File to Photoshop®

Step 4: Define the Sequin Repeat
After you've exported the file to Photoshop®, investigate the layers and reorder them if needed. Then, select and define the sequin repeat that you created as a pattern (Figure 15.17). See Tutorial 8.10, Steps One through Seven, for more information about defining pattern repeats.

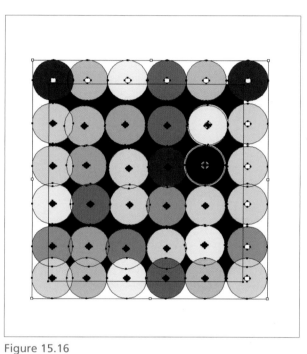

Figure 15.16

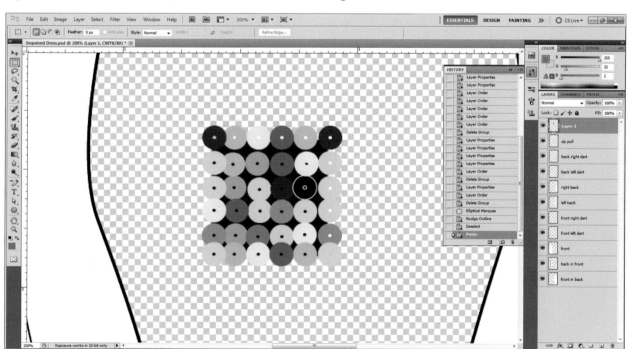

Figure 15.17 In Photoshop® select only the area with the ground square (Rectangle Marquee Tool), and then define the sequin pattern.

Step 5: Fill the Dress Shapes

Fill the dress shapes with the newly defined pattern repeat (Figure 15.18).

Step 6: Add the Illusion of Reflected Light to the Dress

Use the Lighting Effects filter to give the dress the illusion of reflecting light as shown in Figure 15.19.

For more instructions about using the Lighting Effects filter, see Tutorial 8.10, Step Nineteen.

Step 7: Create Dimension and Contour

1. Use the Burn Tool and Dodge Tool to enhance the surface of the dress (see Tutorial 12.1).

2. Add a color lining (Figure 15.20).

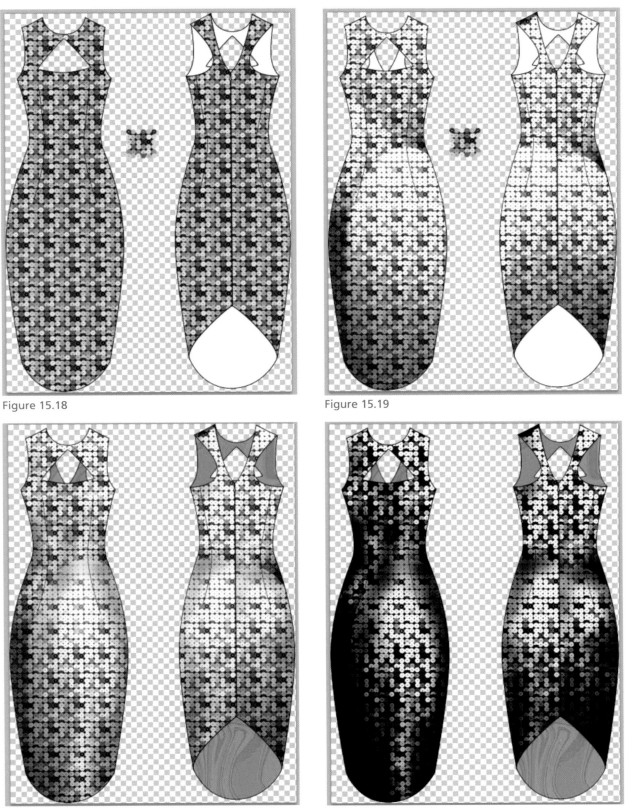

Figure 15.18

Figure 15.19

Figure 15.20

Figure 15.21

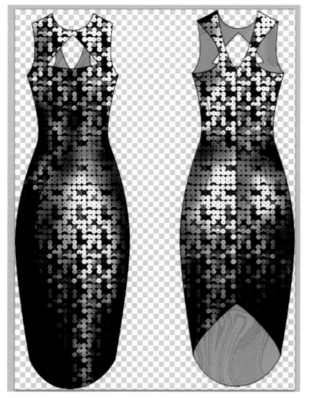

Figure 15.22

Step 8: Add Contrast to the Dress

1. Use the Levels histogram to add contrast to the dress as shown in Figure 15.21. See Tutorial 5.3, Step Twenty, for more information about the Photoshop® Levels feature.

2. Use the **Shadows/Highlights** filter to bring out even more contrast in your monochromatic color scheme (Figure 15.22).

Step 9: Finish the Image with Sparkling Effects and Trim

1. Add Lens Flares to simulate sparkling effects on the dress surface as shown in Figure 15.23.

2. The Exposure filter provides even greater contrast to the finished image (Figure 15.24). Make the dress your own by adding original details like a tassel.

Box 15.2 explains how to use the photo fill method to add sequins to a digital illustration.

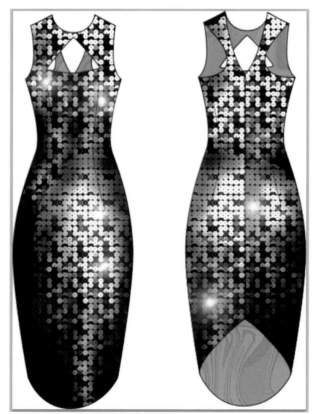

Figure 15.23

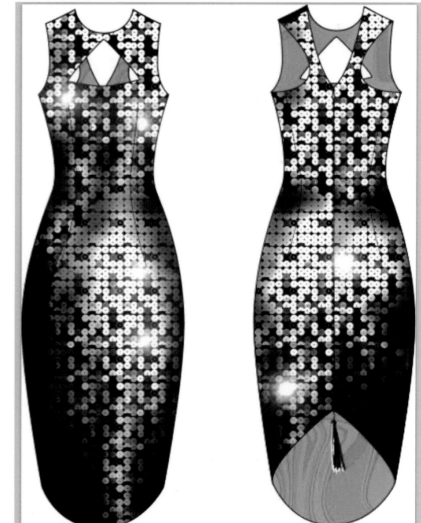

Figure 15.24

Box 15.2: Using the Sequin Photo Fill Method

Once you have filled the shapes with the defined photo images, save a copy, and then select the parts and go to *Menu Bar > Object > Rasterize*. In the Rasterize dialog box, if you have not already reduced the resolution, change it to *Medium* if you plan to print or *Screen* if you are using the file for e-mail. In the *Background* section, check *Transparent*. When you have made these changes to the copy file, follow these steps:

1. Open or create a technical flat in Illustrator®. You may also use the file Sequined_Dress.pdf from ② Ch15\Tutorial 15.2.

2. If your file contains any gradient fills, replace them with white in Illustrator®.

3. Open the photo image Sequins.jpg in Photoshop® from ② Textiles and Novelties Library to define a textual pattern fill in Illustrator® (**Figure 15.25**).

4. Use the Photoshop® Crop Tool (C) to set a long vertical rectilinear area that has a recognizable repeat (see Tutorial 10.6, Step Two).

5. Drag and drop the cropped sequin photo file from Photoshop® into the Illustrator® file containing your technical flat.

6. Select the photo image and define a pattern in Illustrator® (see Tutorial 3.2, Step Nine).

7. Fill the parts with the pattern, and then use the Illustrator® Scale Tool (S) to reduce the pattern (see Tutorial 3.1, Step Fourteen).

8. Export the file from Illustrator® to Photoshop®.

9. Follow Tutorial 15.2, Steps Five through Nine, to obtain compelling results (**Figure 15.26**).

Figure 15.25

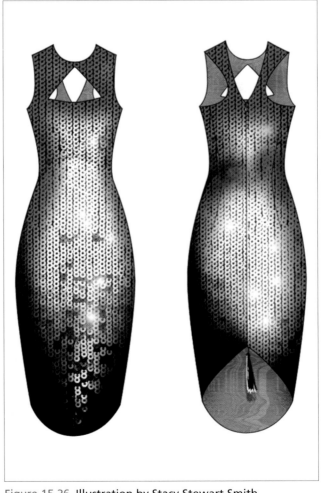

Figure 15.26 Illustration by Stacy Stewart Smith.

The twin sweater set is a fashion that surfaces from time to time as a trend. While many of them feature clean lines made from cut and sewn knits, the most beautiful versions are vintage fine-gauge sweaters from the 1930s–1950s. Use this tutorial to design your own version of the classic pair with Illustrator® and/or Photoshop®.

Step 1: Open or Create a Technical Flat in Illustrator®

Figure 15.27 shows the file Twin_Sweater_Set.pdf from ② Ch15\Tutorial 15.3, but feel free to use any knit flat that you created in Chapter 14.

Step 2: Add Details to the Flat

Use various brushes and symbols to created details on the front and back of the sweater (Figure 15.28). See Tutorials 4.2 and 4.5 for more information about creating surface details with brushes and symbols.

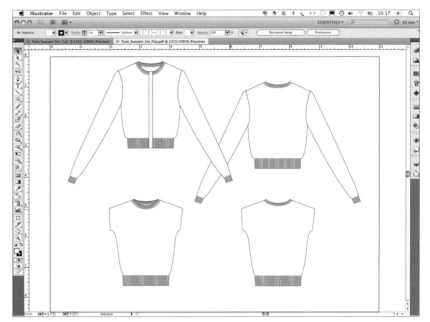

Figure 15.27

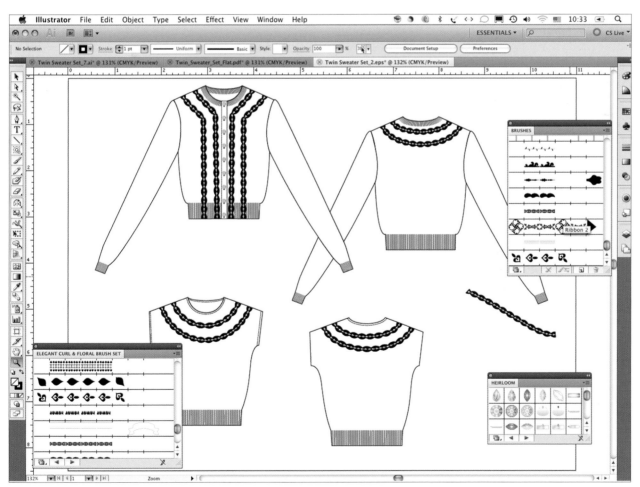

Figure 15.28

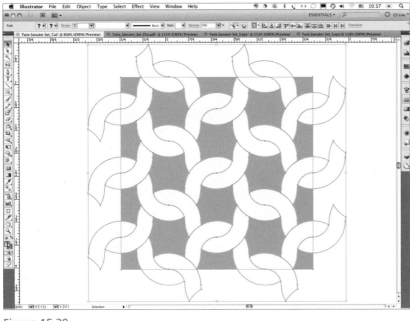

Figure 15.29

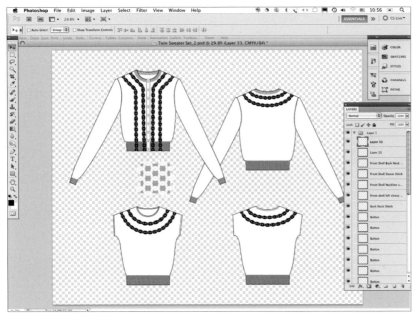

Figure 15.30

Figure 15.31

Step 3: Create a Knit Repeat

Pull the knit repeat from the Illustrator® Pattern Library, fill the ground tile, make a repeat bounding box, and send it to the back (Figure 15.29).

Step 4: Export the File to Photoshop®

Step 5: Define the Knit Pattern

After you export the sweater file to Photoshop®, copy and paste the adjusted repeat into Photoshop®, scale it, and then define it as a pattern (Figure 15.30).

Step 6: Fill the Parts with the Defined Pattern

Select and fill the parts with the defined pattern and use the Inner Shadow Layer Style to add dimension (Figure 15.31).

Step 7: Add the Noise Filter

To diminish the animated look that comes with vector graphics, add the Noise filter (Figure 15.32). The completed knit crepe look is shown in Figure 15.33.

Box 15.3 explains how to use the photo fill method to add a knit effect to a digital illustration.

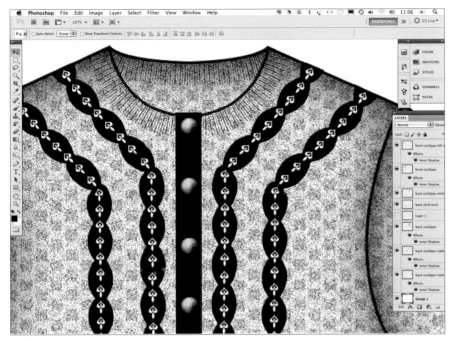

Figure 15.32

TIP: Rasterize Objects

Once you have filled the shapes with the defined photo images, save a copy, and then select the parts and go to *Menu Bar* > *Object* > *Rasterize*. In the Rasterize dialog box, if you have not already reduced the resolution, change it to *Medium* if you plan to print or *Screen* if you are using the file for e-mail. In the *Background* section, check *Transparent*.

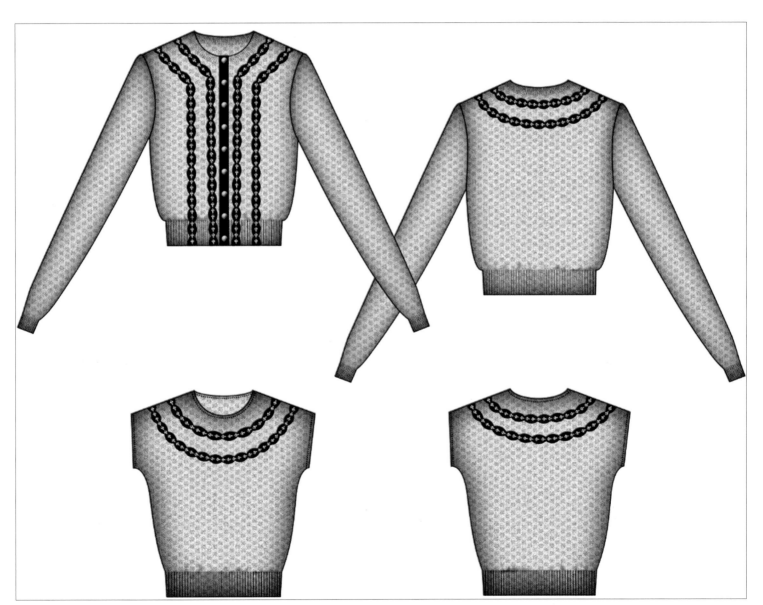

Figure 15.33 Illustration by Stacy Stewart Smith.

Box 15.3: Use the Knit Photo Fill Method

If you prefer, use the file Mauve_Solid_Knit.jpg from ② Textiles and Novelties Library to define a textural pattern fill in Illustrator®.

When you have made these changes to the copy file, follow these steps:

1. Open or create a technical flat in Illustrator®. You may also use the file Twin_Sweater_Set.pdf from ② Ch15\Tutorial 15.3 (Figure 15.27).

2. Open the file Mauve_Solid_Knit.jpg from ② Textiles and Novelties Library (Figure 15.34).

3. Use the Photoshop® Crop Tool (C) to set a long vertical rectilinear area that has a recognizable repeat.

4. Drag and drop the cropped knit photo file from Photoshop® into the Illustrator® file containing your technical flat.

5. Select the photo image and define a pattern in Illustrator.® (See Tutorial 3.2, Step Nine.) Make color adjustments if desired (see Tutorial 7.1, Step Nine).

6. Fill the parts with the pattern, and then use the Illustrator® Scale Tool (S) to reduce the pattern (see Tutorial 3.1, Step Fourteen).

7. Use the Illustrator® Rotate Tool (R) to adjust the pattern to the angle of the sleeves. In the tutorial example the left sleeve pattern was rotated -30° and the right sleeve pattern was rotated 30°.

8. Change the outline color and reduce the Stroke *Weight* in Illustrator®.

9. Create a sequin shape by using the Illustrator® Ellipse Tool (L), and then define it to create a brush. (See Tutorial 4.5, Step Six.) Use the Brush Tool (B) to place the sequin strands artistically (Figure 15.35).

10. Add accents with the Illustrator® Flare Tool (Figure 15.36).

Figure 15.34

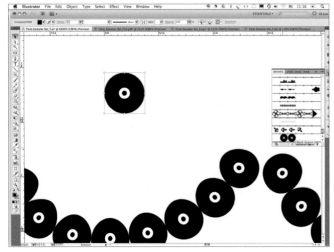

Figure 15.35

Figure 15.36

11. Instead of adding black shadows, try the Illustrator® Inner Glow filter and use a shade of the hue in your work. Select each part. Go to *Menu Bar > Effect > Stylize > Inner Glow*.

12. In the Illustrator® Inner Glow dialog box, check the Preview box, so that you can see how the settings will affect your flat.

13. In the *Mode* option, choose *Screen*.

14. Click on the color box to the right of the *Mode Option*.

15. Select a coordinating shade of the hue in your flat from the Illustrator® Color Picker.

16. Adjust the *Opacity* and the *Blur*. Check the *Edge* button, because that is the area on the flat that will make it look shadowed (Figure 15.36). The completed sweater set knit photo fill finish is shown in Figure 15.37.

Figure 15.37 **Illustration by Stacy Stewart Smith.**

The rendering of digital fox fur and suede present difficulties that can be solved in a variety of ways; however, in this tutorial, you will learn to use "Digital Duo" procedures to reproduce them with ease by using the Photoshop® Clouds filter and Brush panel options.

Step 1: Open or Create a Technical Flat in Illustrator®

Figure 15.38 shows the file Tailored_Blazer.pdf from ② Ch15\Tutorial 15.4, but feel free to use the blazer flat that you created in Chapter 14.

Step 2: Export the File to Photoshop®, and Label the Key Layers

Note: *The file must have proper layer compositing. See Chapter 2 for more information.*

Step 3: Increase the Canvas Size

Go to *Menu Bar > Image > Canvas Size*, and then add 2 inches to each side of the canvas.

Step 4: Create a Suede Look

1. Select a shade and a tone of a color with the Color Picker.
2. Place the darker one in the Set Foreground Box by pressing the X key.
3. Select, and then add the colors to the Swatches panel.
4. Save the file.
5. Select the parts of your flat with the Photoshop® Magic Wand Tool (W), and then fill the areas with the **Clouds filter** by going to *Menu Bar > Filter > Render > Clouds*. The result will look like suede (Figure 15.39).
6. Add the Inner Shadow Layer Style to each part to enhance the effect (Figure 15.40).

TIP: **Suede Photo**

You can also use and colorize the file Gray_Suede.jpg from ② Textiles and Novelties Library as a photo texture fill.

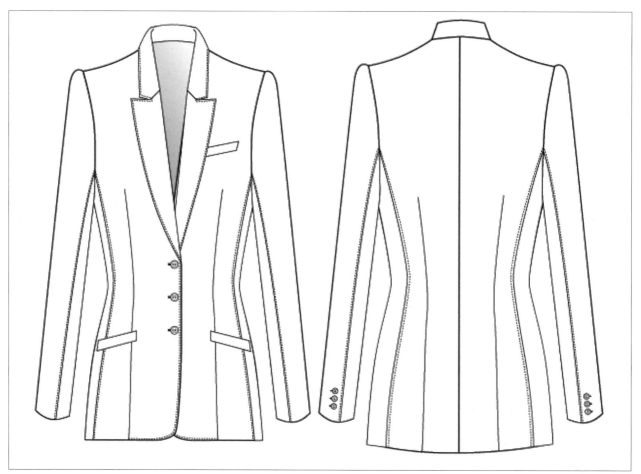

Figure 15.38

Figure 15.39 Photoshop® Clouds filter.

Figure 15.40 Photoshop® Inner Shadow Layer Style.

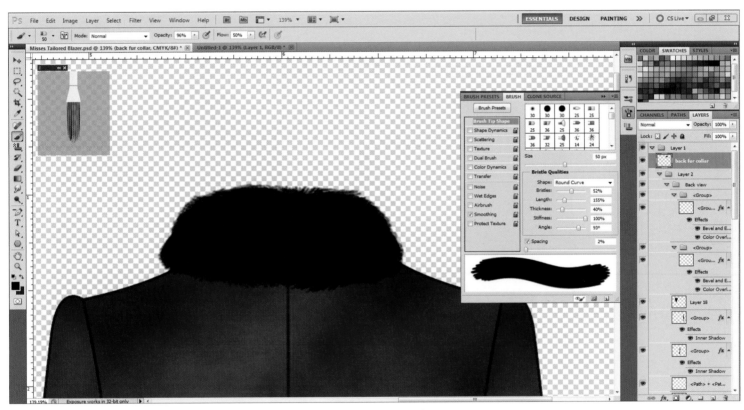

Figure 15.41

Step 5: Paint on Fox Fur Trim(s)

1. Show the Photoshop® Brush panel, and work on a layer above the flats.

2. Use a combination of Photoshop® art brushes to create fur. Start with the Round Curve brush to make the overall shape.

3. Paint one side, and then paint the other.

4. Increase the amount of bristles to 54%, and adjust the *Angle* option slider in the *Bristle Qualities* section to help you manage the strokes when you brush the bristles to the left or the right.

5. The *Smoothing* and *Shape Dynamics* in the *Brush Tip Shapes* should be checked (**Figure 15.41**). This will help you control the viscosity of the digital paint and add a versatile dimension to the brush.

6. Toggle on the Bristle Brush Preview icon at the bottom left of the panel, so you can see the movements. (See Tutorial 7.3 and Tutorial 7.5 for further instruction.)

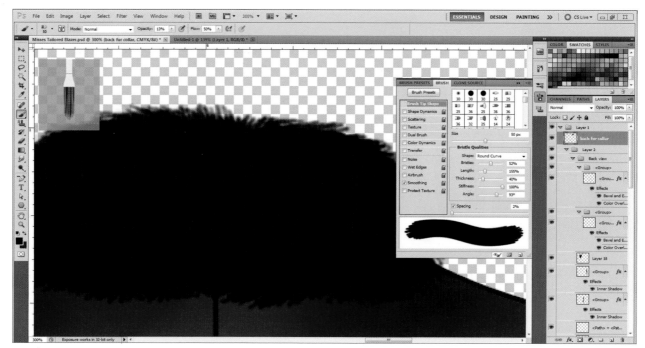

Figure 15.42

Figure 15.43 Illustration by Stacy Stewart Smith.

Step 6: Paint in Highlights

Using the same brush, select a tone of the color and reduce the Opacity to 13% in the Options Bar. Stroke in highlights, but do not over do it. Swap the color back to the original and add more strokes on top to tone down the highlights (Figure 15.42). The completed look is shown in Figure 15.43.

Tutorial 15.5
WOMEN'S COUTURE SILK VELVET, SILK CHIFFON, AND BEADED TANGO DRESS

In recent years, Christian Dior has shown voluminous and colorful skirts in the couture. Although many designers avoid using computers to render these delicate evening wear confections, it is possible to do so by using the concepts taught throughout this book. In this tutorial, you will learn to digitally render velvet, organdy, and bugle beading to create a couture quality tango dress as a digital float.

Step 1: Create a Technical Flat in Illustrator®

The dress pictured in Figure 15.44 serves only as an example for this tutorial. Test your creativity by designing your own style that incorporates velvet, organdy, and bugle beading. For best results, work out your design concept on paper before creating your digital flat in Illustrator®.

Note: The file *Cascades.pdf* on ① *Ch04\Tutorial 4.5* provides instructions for creating cascades similar to those featured on this tutorial's sample dress. Follow the instructions and watch the corresponding movie *Cascade_Demo_1.m4v* if you choose to include this detail in your design.

Step 2: Export the File to Photoshop® and Label the Key Layers

Step 3: Increase the Canvas Size and Convert the File to the Photoshop® RGB Color Mode

Note: Files that originate in Illustrator® must be exported to Photoshop® in the CMYK color mode to prevent merging of the layers. Once exported, convert the file to RGB mode in Photoshop® in order to use certain raster features, such as the Filter Gallery. Go to *Menu Bar > Image > Mode > RGB* to change the color mode.

Figure 15.44

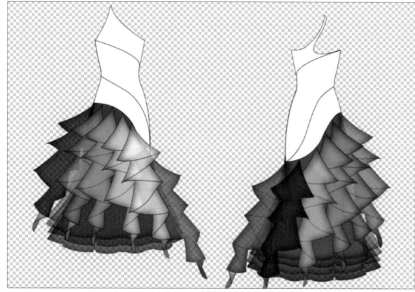

Figure 15.45

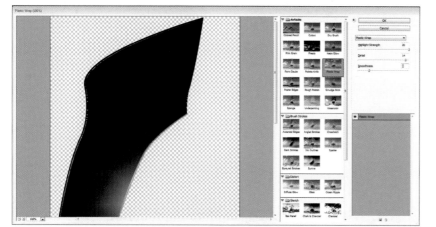

Figure 15.46

Step 4: Create the Illusion of Chiffon

1. Select and fill the parts of the dress that you want to be chiffon.

2. Reduce the *Opacity* fill in the Layers panel by 50% to 90%.

3. Add the Inner Shadow Layer Style (Figure 15.45). For more information about layer styles, see Tutorial 5.1.

Step 5: Create the Illusion of Velvet

1. Select and fill the parts of the dress that you want to be velvet.

2. Add the Photoshop® Plastic Wrap filter by going to *Menu Bar > Filter > Filter Gallery > Plastic Wrap* (Figure 15.46).

3. Add the Inner Glow Layer Style (Figure 15.47).

Step 6: Create the Illusion of Beading

1. Create a repeat for the beading from shapes and gradients as pictured in Figure 15.48, and then define it as a pattern.

2. Create a new layer and fill a large rectangle with the beading pattern as pictured in Figure 15.49, and then define it as a pattern.

3. After selecting the area of the dress to be filled with the beading pattern, select the pattern and use the Layer Style Pattern Overlay to fill the area. See Tutorial 5.1, Step Fourteen, for more information about applying a pattern overlay.

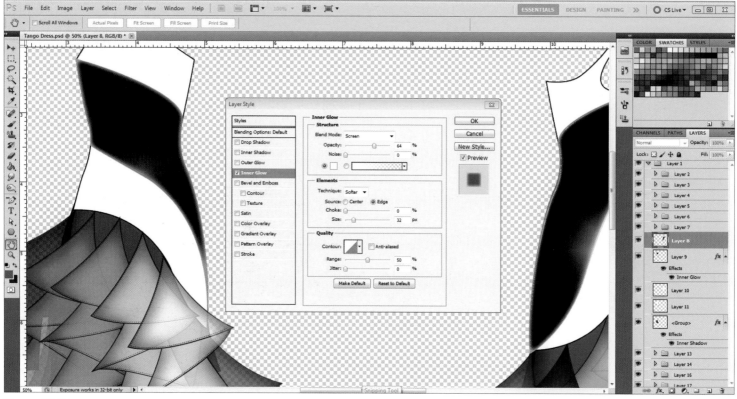

Figure 15.47

4. Scale and change the position of the beading pattern as needed within the Layer Style Dialog box.

5. Convert the layer to a Smart Object and then rasterize it.

Step 7: Finish the Image with Light Effects

Use the filters and tools as described in Tutorial 15.2 to add the illusion of reflected light to the beading on the dress. The completed tutorial example appears in Figure 15.50.

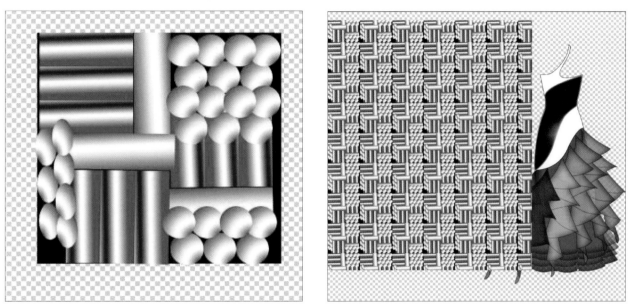

Figure 15.48

Figure 15.49

Figure 15.50 **Illustration by Stacy Stewart Smith.**

"Digital Duo" processes make it easy for you to design fox fur, as you learned in Tutorial 15.4; however, mink and sable require a few tricks that you will learn in this tutorial. Once you have mastered them, you will be able to generate almost any fur imaginable.

Step 1: Create a Technical Flat in Illustrator®

The coat pictured in Figure 15.51 serves only as an example for this tutorial. Test your creativity by designing your own style. For best results, work out your design concept on paper before creating your digital flat in Illustrator®.

Step 2: Apply a Textured Outline to the Coat Parts

Use the Illustrator® Sprayed Strokes filter by going to *Menu Bar > Effect > Brush Strokes > Sprayed Strokes* (Figures 15.52 and 15.53). Change the *Brush Length* to 17 and the *Spray Radius* to 20. The *Stroke Direction* can be right directional or whatever works for your design.

Figure 15.51

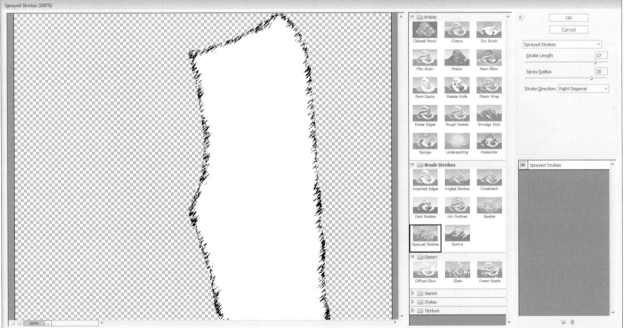

Figure 15.52

Figure 15.53

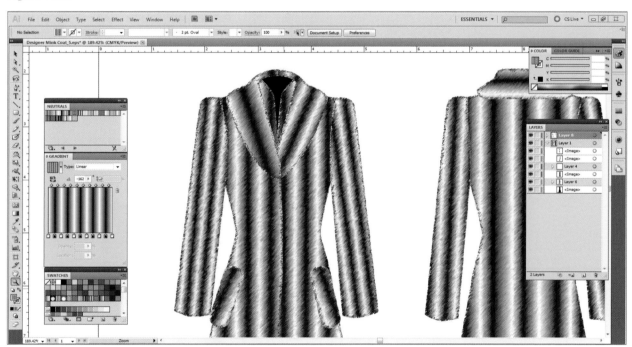

Figure 15.54

Step 3: Create the Illusion of Fur

Select gradients from the Gradients Neutrals Library for a Fill and use the Illustrator® Gradient Tool (G) to adjust the pattern for each part (Figure 15.54).

Note: *You can also use the file Fur_Seamless.jpg on* ② *Textiles and Novelties Library as a photo texture fill.*

Step 4: Rasterize the Parts on Each Layer

Step 5: Copy and Paste the Parts into Photoshop® as Pixels on Separate Layers

This file may be too large to export. If applicable, copy and paste each part into Photoshop®, then add the Inner Shadow Layer Style (Figure 15.55).

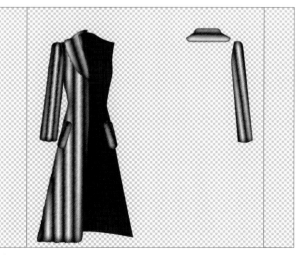

Figure 15.55

Step 6: Paint the Edges

Use the Brush panel and the Mixer Brush Tool (B) to enhance the edges of the parts. Add the Drop Shadow Layer Style on the collars and/or other parts (Figure 15.56). The completed tutorial example is shown in Figure 15.57.

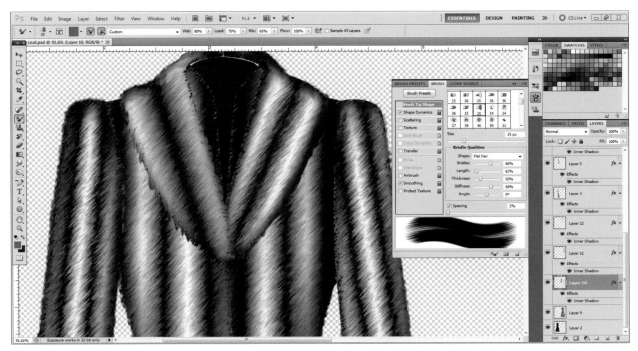

Figure 15.56

Figure 15.57 Illustration by Stacy Stewart Smith.

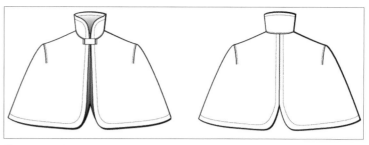

Figure 15.58

This short tutorial will take you through a few techniques that you can use to simulate marabou feathers in Illustrator®. Learn the techniques by following the tutorial, and then add your own design concept.

Step 1: Open or Create the Flat Template or Design in Illustrator®

At this point, you should be able to create your own flats for original design concepts; however, you can use the files located on ② Extra Flats\Women's Extra Flats to complete this exercise. The cape pictured in Figure 15.58 is the file Misses_Abbreviated_Cape. pdf. If you choose to use the files in this folder, just Import them into Illustrator® by going to *Menu Bar > File > Open*, then locate the file on the disk in the Open menu. You need to delete areas of the file(s) that you do not want by selecting them with the Direct Selection Tool (A), then pressing the Delete key.

Step 2: Create Marabou Boa Rows

Create a new layer above the flat that you imported into Illustrator®. The Blob Brush Tool (Shift+B) Options dialog box shown in Figure 15.59 shows the suggested settings for this step. Use the Blob Brush Tool (Shift+B) to create rows of simulated feather boas that have been sewn onto a cape flat or another apparel item (Figure 15.60).

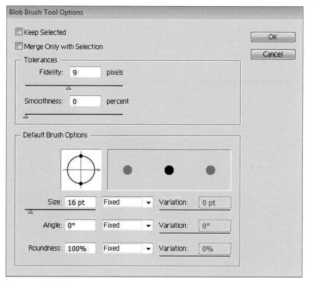

Figure 15.59

Step 3: Create Texture

Double-click on the Illustrator® Wrinkle Tool to access the Options dialog box (Figure 15.61). Working on one section at a time, with the others locked on the layer, use the Wrinkle Tool to make marabou edges (Figure 15.62).

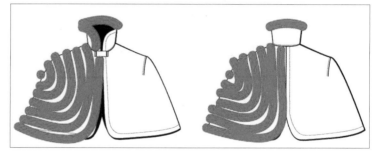

Figure 15.60

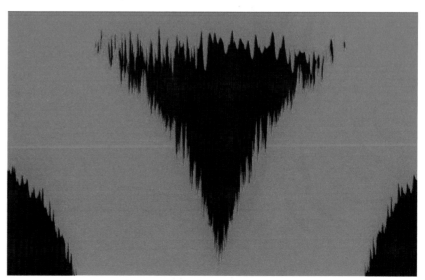

Figure 15.61

Figure 15.62

Step 4: Fill the Marabou with Solids and/or Gradients

Step 5: Add a Jewel and Passementerie Closure

Use the Pen Tool (P) or any other drawing tool to create a passementerie frog closure (Figure 15.63) and then add a simulated gemstone. (See Tutorial 4.1.) The completed opera cape is shown in Figure 15.64.

TIP: White Diamond

You can also use the file White_ Diamond.jpg from ② Textiles and Novelties Library. Select the photo image in Photoshop®. Follow the steps of Tutorial 12.3 to place the image of the gemstone in the Illustrator® file without the white raster background from Photoshop®.

Figure 15.63

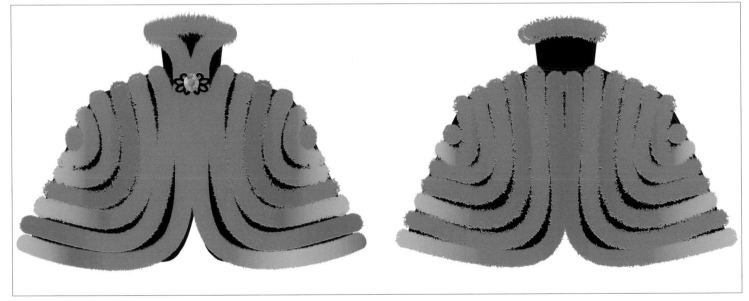

Figure 15.64 Illustration by Stacy Stewart Smith.

In this tutorial you will design a beaded sleeveless shell top. You will apply what you've learned about rendering beading and learn new techniques for defining drapes and cowls.

Step 1: Open or Create a Technical Flat in Illustrator®

Figure 15.65 shows the file Misses_Tank_Top.pdf from ② Extra Flats\Women's Extra Flats, but feel free to design your own.

Step 2: Create a New Design from the Flat

Manipulate the anchor points and paths with the Pen Tool Suite and the Direct Selection Tool (A) to create a new design from the tank top flat (Figure 15.66).

Step 3: Export the File to Photoshop®

Increase the Canvas Size by 2 inches and inspect the layers in Photoshop® (Figure 15.67).

Note: *Files that originate in Illustrator® must be exported to Photoshop® in the CMYK color mode to prevent merging of the layers. Once exported, convert the file to RGB mode in Photoshop® in order to use certain raster features, such as the Filter Gallery. Go to Menu Bar > Image > Mode > RGB to change the color mode.*

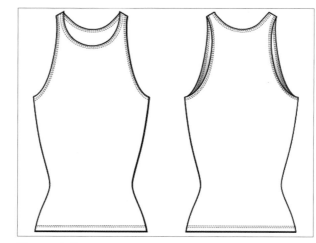

Figure 15.65

Figure 15.66

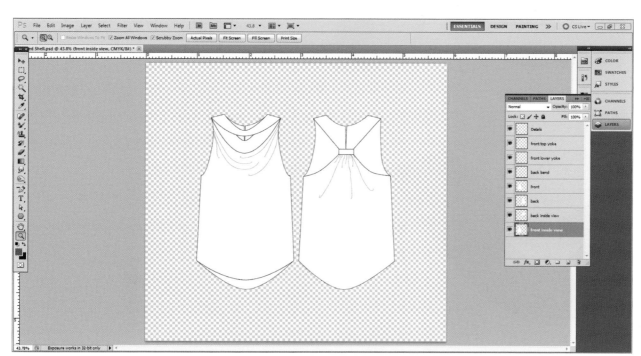

Figure 15.67

Step 4: Fill an Area with a Beaded Pattern and Desaturate the Color

Use the beaded pattern you created in Tutorial 15.5. Press *Option+Shift+Cmd+B* / *Alt+Shift+Ctrl+B*, then move the color slider to desaturate the color (Figure 15.68).

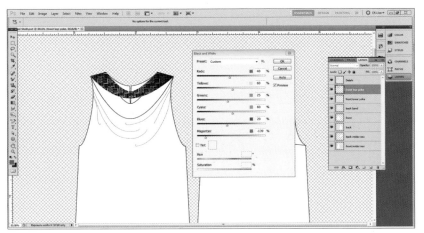

Figure 15.68

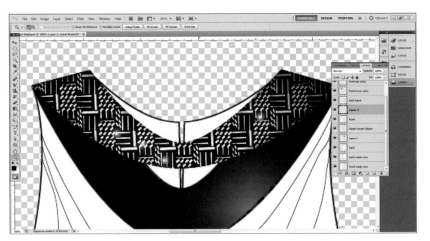

Figure 15.69

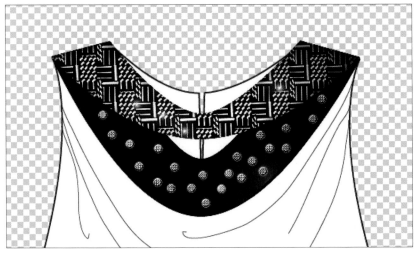

Figure 15.70

Step 5: Add Light Effects to the Beading

Use the filters and tools as described in Steps Six though Nine of Tutorial 15.2 to add the illusion of reflected light to the beading (Figure 15.69).

> ## TIP: Applying Multiple Photoshop® Filters
>
> In Photoshop® some filters cannot be added on top of others. If needed, convert the layer to a Smart Object through the option in the hidden menu of the Layers panel, and then rasterize it by going to *Menu Bar > Layer > Rasterize > Layer*.

Step 6: Add Detail Beaded Motifs to Another Part of the Top

1. Select the layer where you have created the beaded yoke.
2. Select the Photoshop® Clone Stamp Tool (S).
3. Select a solid brush like the Hard Round 30 from the Photoshop® Brush panel. Adjust the size of the brush to about 12 px.
4. Sample a luminous area of the beaded motif with the Photoshop® Clone Stamp Tool (S) by clicking on the area.
5. Create a new layer above the beaded yoke.
6. Click to place the round motif on the layer.
7. Resize it with the Photoshop® Transform options.
8. Add Layer Styles to give the shape dimension.
9. Copy and paste the beaded shape to create several ornaments, and then position them randomly (Figure 15.70).

Step 7: Generate a Speckled Pattern on the Rest of the Shell

Select the shell parts and add the Reticulation filter to add an instant speckled pattern (Figure 15.71).

Step 8: Add Dimension to the Back of the Shell

Select the back parts and add the Inner Shadow Layer Style to create dimension as shown in Figure 15.72.

Step 9: Create the Illusion of Drapes and Cowls

Use the Burn Tool to darken areas and the Dodge Tool to lighted areas to achieve effects similar to those pictured in Figure 15.73. The completed tutorial example appears in Figure 15.74.

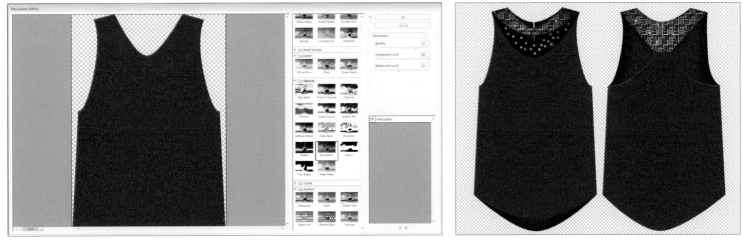

Figure 15.71

Figure 15.72

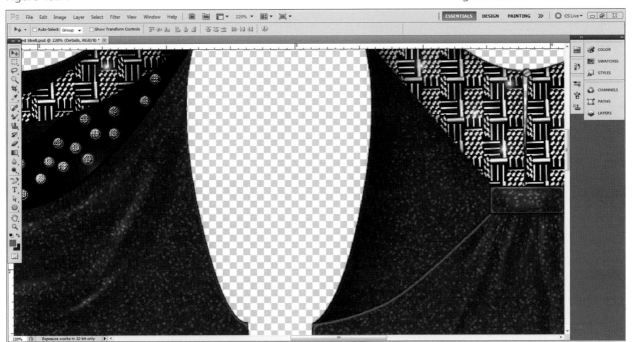

Figure 15.73

Figure 15.74 Illustration by Stacy Stewart Smith.

Tutorial 15.9
WOMEN'S DESIGNER TUXEDO PANTS

Yves Saint Laurent is credited with perfecting the traditional men's tuxedo for women, and this tuxedo look is as classic today as it was in the 1960s and 1970s. This tutorial has a few quick techniques that you can use to design black-on-black apparel items using Illustrator® and Photoshop®.

Step 1: Open or Create a Technical Flat in Illustrator®

Figure 15.75 shows the file Misses_Corset_Waist_Tailored_Slacks.pdf from ② ExtraFlats\Women's Extra Flats, but feel free to design your own.

Step 2: Create a New Design from the Flat

Manipulate the Anchor Points and Paths with the Pen Tool Suite and the Direct Selection Tool (A) to create a new design from the pants flat (Figure 15.76).

Step 3: Export the File to Photoshop®

Increase the Canvas Size by 2 inches and inspect the layers in Photoshop®.

Note: *Files that originate in Illustrator® must be exported to Photoshop® in the CMYK color mode to prevent merging of the layers. Once exported, convert the file to RGB mode in Photoshop® in order to use certain raster features, such as the Filter Gallery. Go to Menu Bar > Image > Mode > RGB to change the color mode.*

Step 4: Give the Pants a Tuxedo Look

Use the Magic Wand Tool (W) to select and fill the satin parts with a gradient, and then select and fill the remaining parts with black. The completed tutorial example appears in Figure 15.77.

Figure 15.75

Figure 15.76

Figure 15.77 Illustration by Stacy Stewart Smith.

This tutorial will help you strengthen your ability to render and define lace patterns in Illustrator®. You will also use the repeat in Photoshop® to create a flare skirt design. The flare skirt flat in this tutorial is available for practice in Extra Flats\Women's Extra Flats folder on ②.

Step 1: Open or Create a Technical Flat in Illustrator®

Figure 15.78 shows the file Misses_Six_Gore_Flare_Skirt.pdf from ② Extra Flats\Women's Extra Flats, but feel free to design your own.

Step 2: Export File to Photoshop®

Increase the Canvas Size by 2 inches and inspect the layers in Photoshop®.

Step 3: Create a Lace Repeat in Illustrator®

The lace in the tutorial example was created from the Illustrator® Optical Illusion 1 pattern located in the Decorative_Modern Pattern Library (Figure 15.79).

Step 4: Copy and Paste the Lace Pattern Repeat into the Photoshop® File

When you see the Paste dialog box, select *Pixels*. This will prevent the motif from having a white background that covers whatever is beneath it. Afterward, scale, Sharpen (filter gallery), and then define the repeat.

Box 15.4 explains how you can define a pattern from a textile swatch in Photoshop®.

Step 5: Create a Lace Overlay for the Skirt

If you would like to create the lace overlay shown in the tutorial example, you need to work in layers. To keep everything organized, create group folders in the Layers panel for the skirt fronts and then the backs.

1. Hold the Shift key and select the *Front* layer.

2. Copy the layer by pulling it to the Create New Layer icon at the bottom of the Layers panel near the Trash icon. Use the Move Tool (V) to reposition the copy of the front view, so that you can see it (Figure 15.80).

3. Select the two layers, and then collect them into a Group folder by clicking the Create a New Group icon at the bottom of the Photoshop® Layers panel. The icon looks like a folder. You can also label the layer *Front*.

4. Repeat these steps for the back view of the skirt.

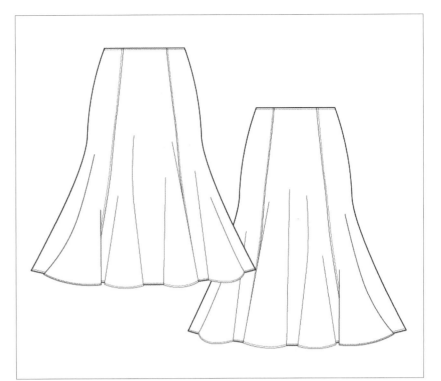

Figure 15.78

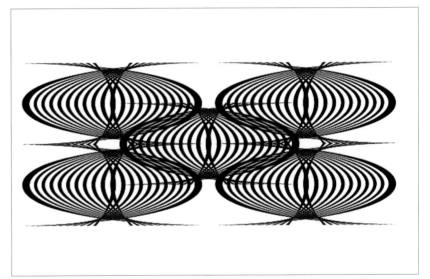

Figure 15.79

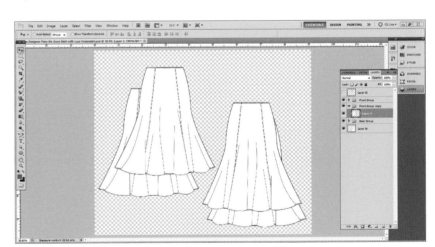

Figure 15.80

Box 15.4: Defining a Pattern in Photoshop® from a Textile Swatch

As an alternative you can use the file Black_Lace_White_Ground.jpg from Textile and Novelties Swatch Library folder ② (Figure 15.81). If you decide to use this file or any other lace textile scan, follow these steps:

1. Select and delete the white background.

2. Afterward, locate a repeat in the lace pattern image, and crop the area with the Photoshop® Crop Tool (C).

3. Increase the canvas size if you would like to create a larger repeat from copies of the motif (cropped area).

4. Copy and paste the motif, then place the copies where they should repeat on the sides, top or bottom. Generally, you will need five copies to increase the repeat. They will be lined up in rows of three and in two columns. If you discover that you need to overlap the motifs, use the Photoshop® Rectangular Marquee Tool (M) to encapsulate the part that you do not need and press the Delete key.

5. Merge the parts into one layer by selecting these layers and pressing *Cmd+E / Ctrl+E*.

6. Repeat Steps Four and Five if needed to create a larger repeat. Essentially all you are doing here is creating the motif that will ultimately become your defined pattern. The important thing to remember is that the parts must match. The edge of the top must flow into whatever is on the bottom edge. The same thing applies to the left and right sides. If you own Illustrator® CS6, you can test the repeat and make adjustments with the Pattern Editor.

7. Select all the motif layers, and then press *Cmd+E / Ctrl+E* to make one motif.

8. Select the ground color of the lace motif with the Photoshop® Magic Wand Tool (W). If all of the background is not selected go to *Menu Bar > Select > Similar*. Press the Delete button to remove the white background.

9. If you would like to change the color of the lace, go to *Menu Bar > Select > Inverse* to select the actual motif. Fill the selection with a color, then deselect.

10. Crop and scale the repeat to an acceptable size before defining it in Photoshop®. (See Tutorial 8.2.)

Figure 15.81

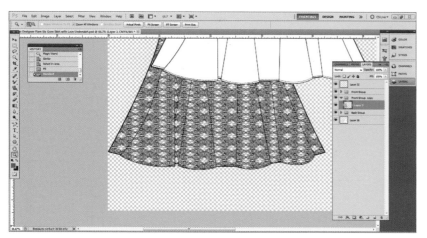

Figure 15.82

Step 6: Add Pattern and Color to the Skirt

Select the white fill with the Photoshop® Magic Wand Tool (W) and then fill the skirt copies with the defined lace pattern (Figure 15.82). Select and fill the original skirt shape with a solid color (Figure 15.83).

Optional: Copy and recolor the lace skirt and then place the layers above the solid skirt to achieve the look pictured in Figure 15.84.

Step 7: Finish the Image

Use the Liquify filter to readjust the sweep of the skirt. The completed tutorial example appears in Figure 15.85.

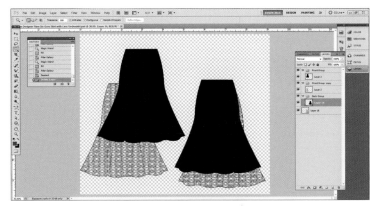

Figure 15.83   Figure 15.84

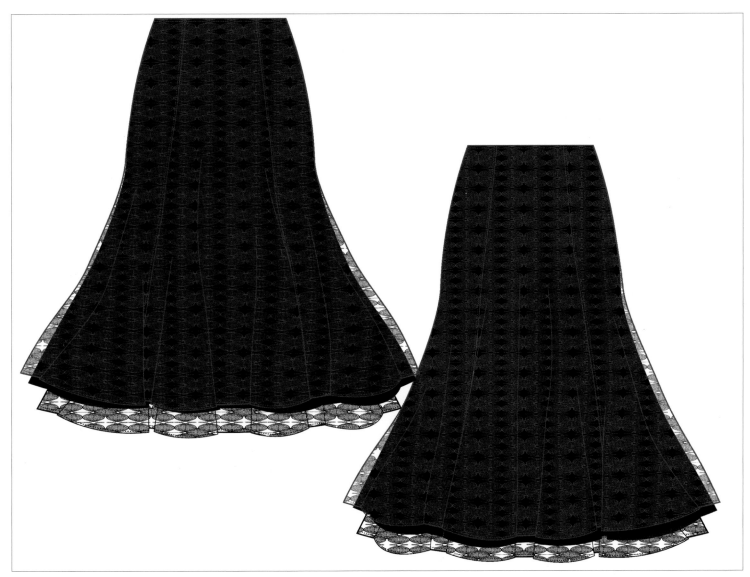

Figure 15.85 Illustration by Stacy Stewart Smith.

The classic men's trench coat can be refined with a few changes in fabrication. In this tutorial, you will learn to use gradients to simulate water-repellent textiles and fur trim by using "Digital Duo" processes.

Step 1: Open or Create a Technical Flat in Illustrator®

Figure 15.86 shows the file Men's_Trench_Coat.pdf from ② Extra Flats\Men's Extra Flats, but feel free to design your own.

Step 2: Create a Fur Collar

Use what you learned in Tutorial 15.6 to create a fur collar with the Sprayed Strokes filter (Figure 15.87).

Step 3: Export File to Photoshop®

Increase the Canvas Size by 2 inches, and then copy and paste the collar into the file. Remember to convert the file to RGB color mode and inspect the layers.

Step 4: Color the Coat

Select and fill the coat parts with a gradient (Figure 15.88).

Note: *As an alternative, you can use any of the files from the* ② *Textiles and Novelties Library to add fabrication to the coat.*

Step 5: Color the Collar

Select and fill the collar with a gradient, and then add the Sprayed Strokes and Film Grain filters as you did in Tutorial 15.6 (Figure 15.89).

Note: *As an alternative, you can use the file Fur_Seamless.jpg from the* ② *Textiles and Novelties Library to simulate the fur collar.*

Step 6: Complete the Look

Use Inner Shadow, Bevel and Emboss, and Drop Shadow Layer Styles to add dimension to the coat. The completed tutorial example appears in Figure 15.90. (See Box 15.4.)

TIP: **Blazer Template**

Use the blazer template to morph this trench coat in Illustrator® using the Direct Selection Tool (A) and others.

Figure 15.86

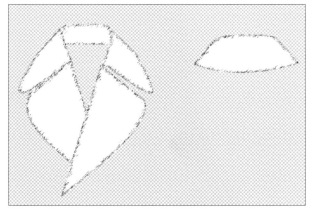

Figure 15.87

Figure 15.88

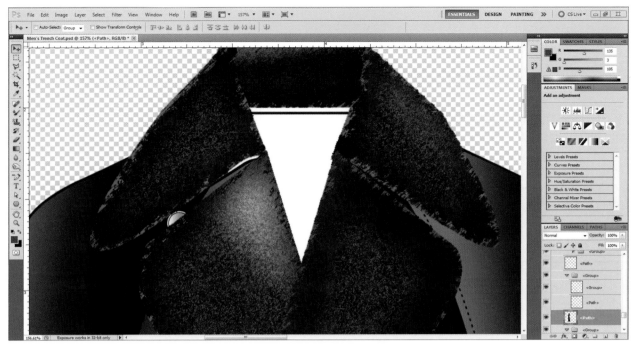

Figure 15.89

Figure 15.90 Illustration by Stacy Stewart Smith.

Photoshop® has a Fibers filter. Use it to simulate textiles with nap as in the case of wool camelhair. After completing this men's wear tutorial, experiment with the settings. You can render textiles like mohair by using the Smudge Tool and others for men's wear and women's wear. Just select a Spatter Brush from the Photoshop® Brush Presets panel and slightly pull out the fiber images.

Step 1: Open or Create a Technical Flat in Illustrator®

Figure 15.91 shows the file Men's_Double_ Breasted_Blazer.pdf from ② Extra Flats\Men's Extra Flats, but feel free to design your own.

Step 2: Create a New Design from the Flat

Use Illustrator® tools such as the Direct Selection Tool (A), the Pen Tool (P), and others to morph the template into your own blazer design (Figure 15.92).

Step 3: Export the File to Photoshop®

Increase the Canvas Size by 2 inches. Remember to convert the file to RGB color mode and inspect the layers.

Step 4: Color the Blazer

Select a set foreground and background color, then select the blazer parts and fill them with the fibers filter by going to *Menu Bar > Render > Fibers* (Figure 15.93).

Step 5: Add Layer Styles and Accent Color Features to make the Flat Look 3-D

The Photoshop® Layer Styles were featured in previous chapters. Here is your chance to test what you have learned to make the blazer look more dimensional (Figure 15.94). The Inner Shadow layer style is essential; try others, too.

Figure 15.91

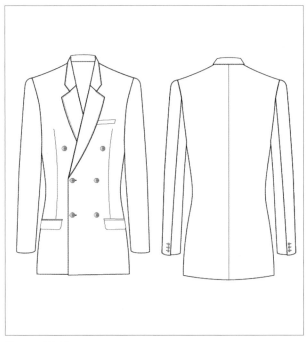

Figure 15.92

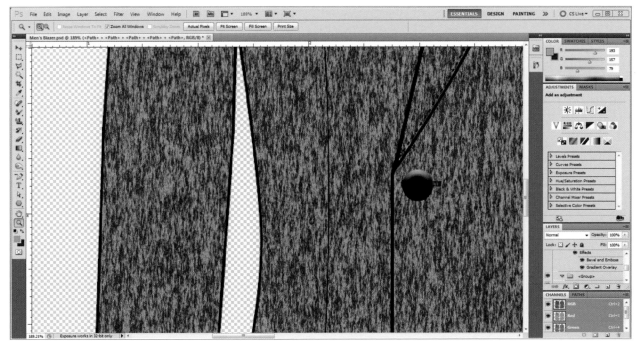

Figure 15.93

Figure 15.94 Illustration by Stacy Stewart Smith.

Tutorial 15.13
MEN'S DESIGNER
PINSTRIPE WOOL SUIT

The pinstripe suit is a men's wardrobe staple. This tutorial challenges you to use what you've learned about striped pattern repeats to simulate these classic lines.

Step 1: Open or Create a Technical Flat in Illustrator®

Use the flat template you created in Tutorial 14.11 or use the blazer and pants files provided on ② Extra Flats\Men's Extra Flats.

Step 2: Create a New Design from the Flat

Manipulate the anchor points and paths with the Pen Tool Suite and the Direct Selection Tool (A) to create a new design from the blazer and pants flats (Figure 15.95).

Step 3: Export the File to Photoshop®

Increase the Canvas Size by 2 inches. Remember to convert the file to RGB color mode, but don't merge the layers.

Step 4: Create a Pinstripe Repeat and Define the Pattern

If you need to, review Tutorial 8.4 for more information about defining a stripe pattern in Photoshop®.

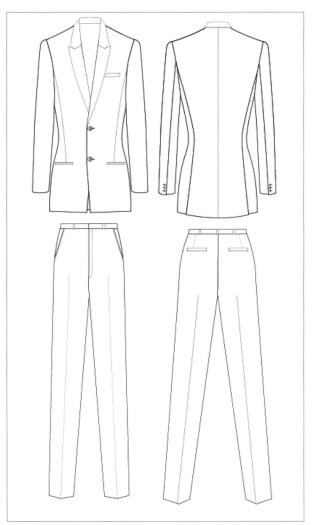

Figure 15.95

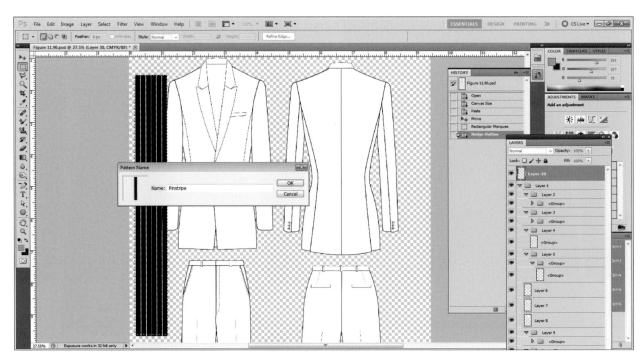

Figure 15.96 The Pattern Name dialog box appears when you define a new swatch in Photoshop® like the one shown here.

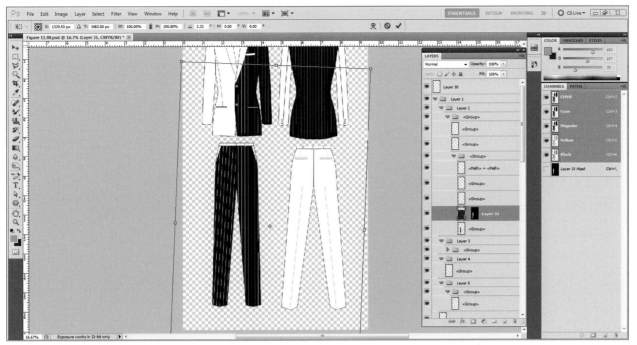

Figure 15.97 Always rotate patterns to simulate fabric grain.

Step 5: Color the Blazer and Pants

1. Fill the blazer and pants parts with the Pattern Overlay Layer Style and the Inner Shadow Layer Style. Some parts may need to be filled with the *Menu Bar > Edit > Fill* option.

2. Fill the blazer and pants parts with the defined pinstripe pattern (Figure 15.96).

Step 6: Angle the Pinstripes on the Pants

Turning the pinstripes on an angle gives the pants realistic contours. To do this, create and copy a large swatch, then go to *Menu Bar > Edit > Paste Special > Paste Info*. Press *Cmd+T / Ctrl+T* in order to rotate and/or scale the print as shown in Figure 15.97.

Step 7: Simulate Texture on the Suit

Add Layer Styles and the Smudge Stick filter to simulate texture. The completed tutorial example appears in Figure 15.98.

Figure 15.98 Illustration by Stacy Stewart Smith.

Tutorial 15.14
MEN'S DESIGNER CASHMERE ARGYLE SWEATER

As demonstrated previously, Illustrator® has a comprehensive Pattern Library that can be used to generate classic knits such as the argyle as well as geometric patterns. In this tutorial, you'll morph a new style for a sweater from an existing flat. Once you have competed the exercise, export the file to Photoshop® and apply further tool and panel features.

Step 1: Open or Create a Technical Flat in Illustrator®

Figure 15.99 shows the file Men's_Hoodie.pdf from ② Extra Flats\Men's Extra Flats, but feel free to use any flat that you've created in Chapters 14 or 15.

Step 2: Create a New Design from the Flat

Manipulate the anchor points and paths with the Pen Tool Suite and the Direct Selection Tool (A) to create a new sweater design from the flat (Figure 15.100).

Step 3: Add a Knit Pattern to the Sweater

1. Pull the Diamond Harlequin Color Repeat from the Illustrator® Decorative_Geometric 1 Pattern Library to create an argyle pattern.

Note: You may also use another pattern or render your own design motif.

2. Resize the motif with the Bounding Box to fit the front of the sweater as shown in Figure 15.101.
3. Fill the sleeves with the pattern as shown in Figure 15.102.
4. Copy the motif on the front of the sweater and place it on the back.

Step 4: Rotate the Sleeve Pattern Fills

Double-click on the Rotate Tool (R) to turn the pattern fills 30° (Figure 15.103).

Note: The left sleeves require negative integers.

Step 5: Add Color to the Sweater

1. Fill the trim with a color as shown in Figure 15.104.
2. Add a background color to the sleeves by copying, pasting, and filling them with a solid color (Figure 15.105).

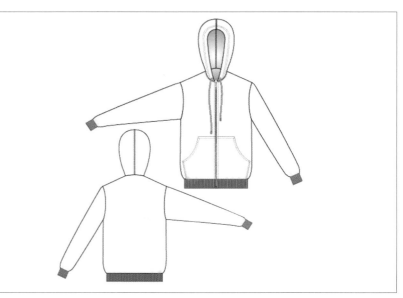

Figure 15.99

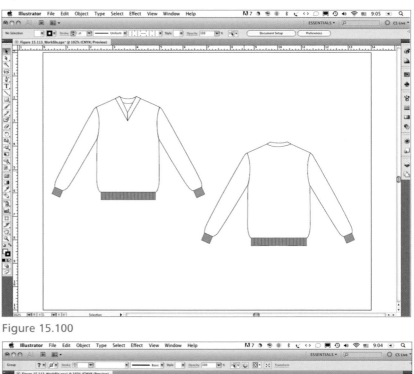

Figure 15.100

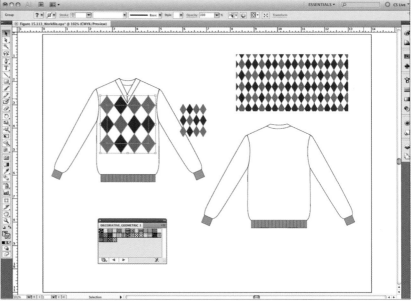

Figure 15.101

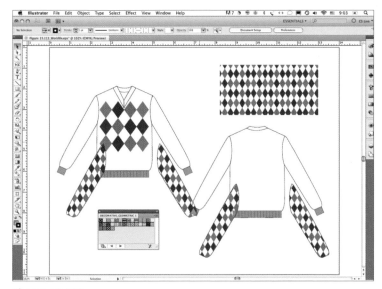

Figure 15.102

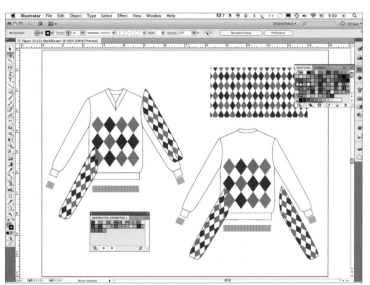

Figure 15.103

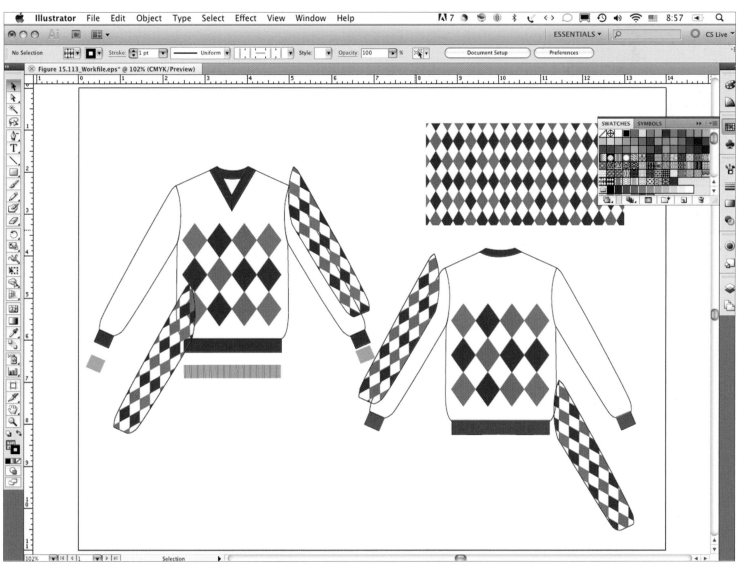

Figure 15.104

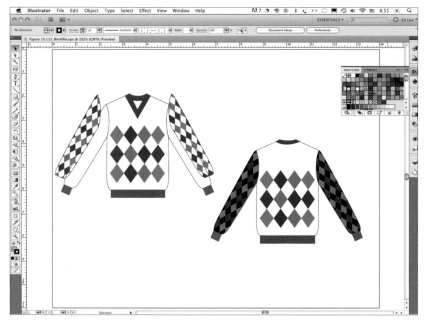

Figure 15.105

Step 6: Add Another Design Motif to the Sweater

Create a central motif, then place it beneath the repeat as shown in Figure 15.106.

Step 7: Apply Texture to the Sweater

To add interesting texture to the sweater flat, select the parts, then go to *Menu Bar > Effect > Texture > Patchwork*. Change the *Square Size* to 1 and the *Relief* to 4 or make suitable adjustments, and then click OK. The results will be similar to what's shown in Figure 15.107. The Opacity of the argyle intarsia motif in Figure 15.108 was reduced to 80% to allow the texture of the pattern used on the body of the sweater to show.

Step 8: Export the File to Photoshop®

Once you export the file to Photoshop®, add features to enhance the realness of the flat. In this case, it would be the texture of the simulated knit. Try the Layer Styles, Inner Shadow, Bevel and Emboss, and/or Color Overlay to get the effects shown in Figure 15.109. Remember to uncheck the *Global Light* box in the Layer Styles dialog box if you do not want the changes that you made on one part to be affected by what you do to another. In the completed tutorial example, the Add Noise filter gives the sleeve a speckled yarn effect (Figure 15.110).

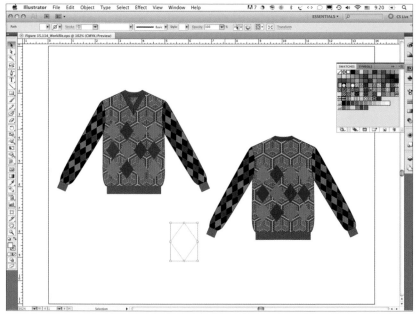

Figure 15.106

Figure 15.107

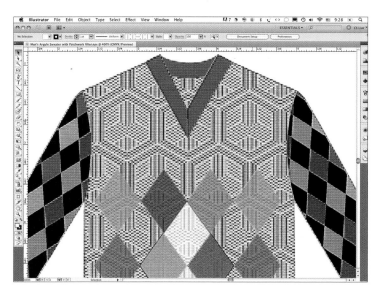

Figure 15.108

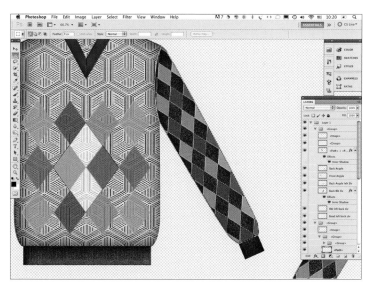

Figure 15.109

Figure 15.110 Illustration by Stacy Stewart Smith.

Exercise 15.1: Conceptual 3-D Flats Storyboard

Now that you have completed the tutorials, design a mini collection of your own using the procedures that you have learned in this chapter. Prepare a digital storyboard presentation of 3-D conceptual flats for a particular market and season. Incorporate everything that you have learned in the previous chapters, but try to do this without looking through the chapters for help. If you find yourself needing the book, go back and repeat the tutorials and/or read the chapters until you can create digitally without referencing. It is only by practicing that you will learn and remember the procedures and terminology.

Note: The conceptual flats created in this chapter are available on ② Ch15\Conceptual Color Flats. Use them to practice, but always present your own designs to potential employers and for academic projects.

As an exercise to provide practice dressing the digital figure (see Chapter 7 and Chapter 12), use everything that you have learned to create an opera opening night gala and/or a runway fashion show. Use the color 3-D flats that you have created in this chapter to dress the croquis that you have rendered to make your own digital presentation storyboards. (See Tutorial 7.4 and Chapters 11 through 13.)

Use the backgrounds from the files Ana_Pink_Show.pdf or others from ① Ch07/Tutorial 7.4 (Figure 15.111). Another file that you can use is Club_Gallery.pdf from ① Ch09\Tutorial 9.5 (Figure 15.112). If you prefer, challenge yourself and create your own background or leave it plain.

Note: *The fully dressed fashion avatars shown in Figures 15.111 and 15.112 are available for use and study on ② Avatar Modeling Agency. Use them to practice, but always present your own figures and designs to potential employers and for academic projects.*

Figure 15.111 Illustration by Stacy Stewart Smith.

Exercise 15.2: Merchandise Window Display for Eveningwear

If you are taking courses in fashion merchandising, marketing, and management, use everything that you have learned to create a fabulous eveningwear window display. Imagine that you are working for a retailer, such as Bergdorf Goodman, Barneys, or Bloomingdale's. Make use of the fully dressed avatars or create and design your own croquis and apparel. Add props, lighting, etc.

Figure 15.112 Illustration by Stacy Stewart Smith.

Exercise 15.3: Design Your Own Fashion Show

In Chapter 7 you learned how to stage a fashion exhibition using photos. You also have a predesigned backdrop and runway. Use what you have learned to create your own runway layout, including the stage platform, lighting, backdrop, and fashion crowd. Study the four files on ① Ch07\Tutorial 7.4 if you need references. Afterward, design an entire collection of digital or scanned croquis for a compelling presentation. Finish the work by designing your own company logo or title branding.

Chapter 15 Summary

This chapter proposed one huge test of what you have learned in previous chapters. Although you focused on luxury markets, the tutorials should have helped you to increase your digital rendering skills and prepared you for almost any imaginable task in lower markets. If you are required to create conceptual color flats and floats, the ideas presented in this chapter offered a bevy of options. You were taught a few essential and some unique tricks. These can be used to simulate classic or novelty textiles, leather, fur, feathers, knits, and apparel construction details on conceptual flats presentations for the designer and couture-level apparel.

If you have a preference for realistic presentations, you may have found the use of the files from ② Textiles and Novelties Library to be an asset. On the other hand, simple combinations of Illustrator® and Photoshop® tools, panel options, and filter features may have been sufficient.

Chapter 15 Self-Assessment

1. Can I digitally simulate leather or vinyl apparel in Photoshop® using a prerendered technical flat sketch exported from Illustrator®?

2. Am I able to experiment with multiple filters to generate textiles and/or rendering effects?

3. There are plenty of ways to simulate novelty fabrics, but when it comes to those with all-over flat French sequins, am I able to create them in at least two different ways digitally?

4. Do I know how to add contrast to my digital renderings with the Photoshop® Levels histogram?

5. Do I possess the ability to use the Photoshop® Crop Tool (C) to set a long vertical rectilinear area that has a recognizable repeat in order to define a pattern from a photo image?

6. I know how to use the Photoshop® Burn Tool (O), but can I also use the Inner Shadow Layer Style to add dimension to my digital drawings?

7. Have I mastered the use of the Illustrator® Inner Glow filter in a shade of a hue in my work instead of adding black shadows to create 3-D illusions?

8. Can I digitally simulate fox fur and suede by using the Photoshop® Clouds filter and Brush panel options?

9. Have I experimented with the Photoshop® Brush Preset panel's *Smoothing* and *Shape Dynamics*

settings located in the in the *Brush Tip Shapes* section? Can I control the viscosity of digital paint and add versatile dimension to the Photoshop® brush that I choose?

10. Do I really understand how to create a repeat for beading from shapes and gradients, and can I define them as patterns in Illustrator® and Photoshop®?

11. Can I simulate marabou feathers with the Illustrator® Blob Brush Tool (Shift+B)?

12. Do I know how to use the Photoshop® tools and filters to digitally mold drapes and cowls from flat areas?

13. The ability to differentiate various shades of black is an advanced technique. Can I design black-on-black apparel items using Illustrator® and Photoshop®?

14. Photoshop® has a Fibers filter, but can I use it to simulate textiles like camelhair?

15. Illustrator® has a comprehensive Pattern Library that can be used to generate classic knits such as the argyle and geometric patterns, but am I comfortable using the combinations to simulate knitted and other patterns?

16. Do I know why I must uncheck the Global Light box in the Photoshop® Layer Styles dialog box?

DVD Extra 15.1:
Men's Designer Linen Paisley Vest

You learned to define patterns using Illustrator® in Chapter 8, but the classic paisley was not covered. This tutorial will give you insights on how to create this textile motif using the Illustrator® CS6 Pattern Editor (Figure 15.113).

Figure 15.113

Appendix:
The e-Portfolio for Fashion
Designers and Merchandisers

Throughout your fashion career you will need to prepare various portfolios. The first one will probably be an academic version, which will be greatly influenced by your instructors. That is a good start, but update your portfolio often to keep it current and to appeal to various types of clients.

One way to refresh your existing portfolio is to augment the presentation with an **e-Portfolio**. Everything that you have learned about fashion presentation can be placed into multiple page files. In an e-portfolio, individual groups or collections can be assembled at random to target specific manufacturers in the job market.

Formatting the e-Portfolio

There are a few factors to think about before you begin to assemble the e-Portfolio. Consider the following points:

Who Will View the e-Portfolio?

If you are preparing your e-Portfolio for a potential employer, first find out if the recipient will view it before, during, or after your formal interview. If the e-Portfolio is a pre-interview presentation, you will need to inform the recipient of your intent to send the file to them with a request for more instructions. Ask the client about their hardware for viewing files. Are they working with a Mac, PC, or both, and should you e-mail the file, use a server, or mail it through the Post Office, UPS, etc? If you will bring the e-Portfolio to an interview, do not rely upon it as your only source. Always show your work in the formal printed book first, and then depending on how the interview goes, offer to show some additional ideas.

How Can Clients View an e-Portfolio?

A very important factor to consider is how others will actually view your e-Portfolio. If the interviewer is open to viewing your e-Portfolio, be prepared to quickly open the file on your own hardware, unless they would prefer to use their computer. Your system should be ready to present the files as a slideshow presentation without waiting for your computer to start and software programs to load. In the case that the interviewer runs out of time, be prepared to leave a copy of the e-portfolio on a DVD in professional packaging containing a printed cover to identify yourself.

What Format Should You Use?

There are several software programs that offer the ability for you to prepare a multipage layout, including Microsoft Power Point® and InDesign®. Acrobat Pro® (versions 9 and higher) is the program that offers the simplest solution because it creates cross-platform PDF files that are easy for most computers to read, and the files maintain their original integrity. Most computers come installed with Adobe Reader®. This application is also a free download on the official Adobe website.

How to Identify Yourself as the Creator of an e-Portfolio

If you decide to use Acrobat Pro®, you can add a cover page to your presentation. The cover page should be simple in design and free from any images that are subject to copyright laws. The best cover pages stick to the basics, so include your full name, the season of the collection that you are showing, and a theme. Think of this page as a backdrop for your first fashion show. Maintain a clean look, and be consistent throughout the pages. On the last page of the presentation, prepare a conclusion page with your contact information, which would again state your full name, e-mail address, telephone number, website, etc.

How to Protect Your Ideas

A portfolio of any type is just for viewing. You should be prepared to show it to anyone who can help you secure employment in fashion. If you are concerned about protecting your ideas, then you may want to reconsider what you are showing or sending. In the case where you do need a form of security for your e-Portfolio, add a watermark to the presentation pages to ensure that they cannot be reused in any manner without your expressed permission. On each page, you should add your logo or name and easy contact information in an inconspicuous place such as the margins. You can also save a PDF file so that it cannot be printed or altered.

Preparing an e-Portfolio

If the e-Portfolio is to be viewed on a computer or projected, then use **landscape orientation**. Even though it is acceptable to use portrait orientation, you will not make good use of the screen size. Portfolios in **portrait orientation** use about half the screen size and make whatever is on the page even smaller than it would be in landscape orientation. The e-Portfolio is easy to assemble. Follow these steps to create one using your completed files from the tutorials in this book:

Step 1: Assemble the Contents of Your Portfolio

Your e-portfolio should contain one clear thought for a single group of apparel for one season. It should include:

- A cover page.
- A digital customer profile board. (See Tutorial 5.1.)
- A digital mood board. (See Tutorial 7.1.)
- A digital color board. (See Tutorial 7.2.)
- One or two pages of digital and/or freehand apparel illustration designs on croquis figures.
- A black-and-white technical flats line sheet. (See Tutorial 14.17.)
- Conceptual 3-D color flats as a showroom line sheet. (See Tutorial 14.17.)
- Several sample(s) of completed specification sheets with measurements. (See Tutorial 14.17.)
- A conclusion page with contact information.

Step 2: Import, Reduce, and Coordinate the File Size of the Pages

All the pages in an e-Portfolio should be the same size and orientation as discussed earlier. An ideal size is 17×13 inches because this is the current size of most standard portfolios. The format also matches the borderless prints of many desktop printers.

You need to reduce the file size of your pages so that the person receiving them can open the file with ease. To control this:

1. Flatten the file in Illustrator® via the hidden menu on the right side of the Layers panel. For Photoshop® files, see Tutorial 4.6, Step Five.
2. Save a copy of all the prepared files.
3. Open each file in Photoshop®.
4. Go to *Menu Bar > Image > Image Size*.
5. Change the Resolution to 72 dpi if you are sending the file by e-mail. A setting of 150 dpi is fine for files that are printed, so long as they have been originally saved at a higher resolution (see Chapter 1).
6. Change the Image Size to 17×13 inches.
7. Click OK.

Step 3: Add Your Identity to Pages

Use the Photoshop® Type Tool (T) to type your identity on each page. Use a universal font such as Arial or Helvetica at 10 pt. The type should be placed in the margins on the edge of the page.

Step 4: Save Each File into a Single Folder in the Adobe PDF File Format

Each software program that you will need for the e-Portfolio has the option to save files in the PDF format.

Step 5: Merge Files Into a Single PDF

1. Load Acrobat Pro®.
2. Go to *Menu Bar > Combine > Merge Files* into a single PDF. **Note:** *PC and Mac may have slight variations in the Menu Bar set up.*
3. In the **Combine Files** dialog box, click **Add Files**.
4. Select the files that will be combined, and then click OK. They will appear in your Acrobat® window.
5. To reorder the files, select them, and then click the *Move Up* or *Move Down* buttons at the bottom of the window.
6. Click the Combine Files button at the bottom of the dialog box.
7. In the Save As dialog box, give the e-Portfolio an appropriate name and save it in the folder that you created.

Step 6: Add Security

To add security features to your Acrobat Pro® e-Portfolio, follow these steps:

1. Go to *Menu Bar > Advanced > Security > Show Security Policies*.
2. Select the *Security* tab.
3. To the right of the *Security Method* section is a pull-down menu. Select *Password Security*.
4. In the Password Security Settings dialog box, check the box next to the statement *Require a password to open the document*.

Note: *Do this only if you require the receiver to use a password for the file.*

5. Enter your required password in the field below. Remember the password, so that you can give it to the recipient.

6. If you want to restrict editing and printing of the document, check that box under the *Permissions* section, and then enter a password. Remember to change the *Printing Allowed* and the *Changes Allowed* sections via the pull-down menus. You can also restrict copying of the text in this window.

Note: With this option, the receiver can open the document but not print it or make alterations. However, some devices may ignore your settings.

Step 7: Add Watermarks

To add watermarks to the pages of your Acrobat Pro® e-Portfolio, follow these steps:

1. Go to *Menu Bar > Document > Watermark > Add*.

2. Enter the text that you want to appear in the *Text* field. You can choose the font, adjust the Opacity, and change the appearance of the text in this window. Save the settings for multiple uses. Click OK when you are done.

Note: Exercise caution when creating watermarks because some companies may find them offensive. If the company is reputable, it is best not to include them.

Glossary

Abstractrealism: A contemporary painting style characterized by the fine art paintings of Stacy Stewart Smith using memories, visual and metaphysical experiences, and representations of the psyche in motion, which combines abstract, realist, and photorealist techniques.

Accessory: Any item such as handbags, sunglasses, or shoes that are usually worn to enhance, complete, and otherwise complement an apparel ensemble.

Accuracy: In digital design, the degree to which a task is performed with precision and meets a preset standard for excellence.

Action flats: Three-dimensional renderings of apparel as though it were worn by an invisible human form in motion. (See Floats.)

Adapters: A connector used to allow communication between two or more electronic devices, such as a video graphics array (VGA) or other devices.

Add Anchor Point Tool: A tool in both Illustrator® and Photoshop® that can be used to add anchor points along an existing path.

Add Files button: A button in the Combine Files dialog box of Acrobat Pro® that allows the user to add files to be merged into a single PDF file.

Add Noise filter: The Add Noise filter converts selected objects into tiny particles of color.

Adjustment Layer: Any layer created to provide the user with a temporary look at color changes in Photoshop® before they are accepted. Also described in this book as a temporary background layer between layers.

Acrobat Professional®: A software program created by Adobe Systems Incorporated used to view, create, manage, and edit its Portable Document Format (PDF) files that maintain the integrity of your work in a universal self-extracting format when shared.

Adobe Bridge®: An organizational program used to view and link files in the Adobe Creative Suite in an interface similar to a browser.

Adobe Creative Suite®: The current "A" series of products offered by Adobe System Incorporated encompassing a collection of bundled software packages for graphic design, web design, and video editing.

Adobe Flash: A software program distributed by Adobe Systems Incorporated and used to create animations on web pages.

Adobe Illustrator®: A widely used object-oriented, vector-based, digital graphics software drawing program created by Adobe Systems Incorporated used to generate digital animations and illustrations.

Adobe InDesign®: A software program created by Adobe Systems Incorporated. It is used for creating multiple-page layouts, import vector graphics and photos, etc., combined with text formatting to facilitate desktop publishing of books, pamphlets, etc.

Adobe Photoshop®: A widely used graphics pixel-based image-editing software program originally created by Thomas Knoll, now owned and distributed by Adobe Systems Incorporated. Photoshop® is used to manipu-

late photos, create digital animation, and create 3-D illusions.

Adobe Reader®: A free, downloadable software program, created by Adobe Systems Incorporated, that enables the user to open, view, and print PDF files without having Acrobat Pro® installed on the computer.

Adobe Systems Incorporated: An American computer software company, headquartered in San Jose, California.

Adobe TV: An Adobe online source of information and instruction in video format.

Aesthetic: Concerned with beauty or the appreciation thereof as a set of principles that guides an artist or particular group of artisans.

Age of information and technology: Open communication that would have been previously limited under industrialization, but is now free due to technology as a part of the digital age.

Algorithm: In mathematics, a finite sequence of instructions used to solve problems, such as calculations and data processing. Also, a step-by-step computer process or tutorial that if followed will yield an approximate outcome.

Align panel: A palette of organizational functions in Illustrator® and Photoshop®, that allows the user to position and distribute selected objects.

Align Dashes to Corners and Path Ends: A new feature of Illustrator® CS5 that allows the user to miter corners of selected Dashed Lines of a stroke by pressing a button in the Stroke panel.

Align Stroke: An option in the Illustrator® Stroke panel that allows the user to designate the position of a stroke in relationship to the edge of a shape or line segment.

Align the Stroke to Inside: This *Align Stroke* option, when selected, keeps a stroke from protruding out of the sides of a shape.

Alpha Channels: A time-saving production mask that can be created with the settings of the Channels panel. It allows Photoshop® users to save and edit selections within a file and to pick up where they left off in creating a selection.

Alt key: One of several modifier keys on a PC keyboard.

Anchor point: See *Vector*.

Animation: The technique of rendering two-dimensional or three-dimensional images in sequences that simulate movement.

Anti-aliased: A Photoshop® setting within the Illustrator® Export Options dialog box that if selected ensures a vector-smooth quality to exported images so they do not become bitmapped in Photoshop®.

Append: In digital art, a generic computer term denoting the process of adding on to an image, such as a filter or a finishing touch.

Apple icon: A branded logo of a silhouetted or outlined apple with a stem and a human bite taken from the right side. It was originally used on the two modifier command keys located at the sides of the spacebar of Macintosh computers, but currently represents keyboard shortcut operations in menus. To type this icon on most Macintosh computers, depending on the fonts you are using, press *Shift+Option+K*.

Apple Inc: A computer technology corporation presently headquartered in Cupertino, California, known for products that include Macintosh computers, iPod music players, the iPad, and the Mac OS operating system.

Application Bar: An interactive panel in Illustrator® and Photoshop® that houses those functions that assist the user and augment the programs including, software identification, a button that provides access to Bridge®, the Arrange Documents menu icon, and the Workspace Switcher. In addition, there is a search field for Adobe Community Help. The system and software menus are located in the Application Bar on PC versions, but are separate on Macintosh versions of the CS5 and higher software.

Application Frame: The window of Illustrator® and Photoshop® CS5 where various open files can be docked.

Arc Tool: An Illustrator® tool that creates arches with a marquee and twisting. The lines can be altered with the Stroke panel options.

Area Type Tool: An Illustrator® tool that is used to type only inside vector shapes.

Arrange Documents button: A button menu accessed from the Illustrator® and Photoshop® Application bars that allows the user to choose viewing options for multiple files open in the Application Frame.

Arrow pointer: An arrowhead shape that indicates the presence of a hidden menu. This icon can be tipped (turned with a click of the computer mouse) to reveal the menu.

Art: Any interpretation of life through visual representation, sound, literature, performance, etc. that also appeals to the senses or the emotions of the viewer. The generic term "art" encompasses all types of expressions.

Artboard: The printable area of the Illustrator® window interface, which is flanked by a solid black line and can be customized by the document size up to 227 x 227 inches.

Artboard panel: An Illustrator® panel that allows the user to work on multiple spaces within one file.

Artboard Tool: An Illustrator® tool used to realign the Artboard via a Bounding Box or Control Panel options.

Art History Brush Tool: This Photoshop® CS5 tool creates fine art painting techniques from images through various adjustment options available in the Brush panel.

Artistic filter: Any number of various filters located within the Menu options of both Illustrator® and Photoshop® that simulate the visual effects form major fine art techniques such as watercolor and paint daubs, etc.

Art movements: Distinct periods of artistic development and style characterized by the various disciplines of particular artists or groups, such as Cubism, Futurism, Dadaism, and others.

Auto Color: A filter in Photoshop® that automatically adjusts the color based on the calibration of the user's monitor.

Auto Contrast: A filter in Photoshop® that automatically adjusts the difference between tones.

Auto Tone: This setting allows Photoshop® to make adjustments to the tone of colors.

Avatar: An animated or digitized representation of a human in cyberspace. Often used as movable icons for players in 3-D games.

Avatar Model Agency folder: A folder in this book that contains finished digital croquis created by Stacy Stewart Smith that can be reused for various illustration purposes throughout the tutorials or otherwise. The term avatar is used to denote the fact that the images were mostly rendered using "Digital Duo" procedures from composite photos of human models.

Background Eraser Tool (E): This Photoshop® tool deletes pixels of any object below the one upon which the designer is working.

Baseline: In typography the baseline is where the type rests.

Basic CMYK Color Swatches panel: A color panel devoted to color swatch standards of the CMYK color mode.

Basic RGB Swatches panel: A color panel devoted to color standards of the RGB color mode.

Bevel and Emboss: The Bevel and Emboss Layer Style is commonly used to simulate 3-D realism and resembles relief sculpture. The size, spread, and opacity of this Layer Style all play an important role in its successful application.

Bézier Curve: A digital curved path between two vectors named after Pierre Bézier, a French designer of automobiles, who used them widely in his work for Renault. It is the principle feature of vector-based graphics software programs such as Illustrator®.

Bitmap: An invisible grid on a digital display, such as a television or a computer monitor.

Bit-mapped image: Any digital image with poor resolution in which pixel formations are visible.

Black & White: A Photoshop® filter used to desaturate objects within a color group. This setting allows the user to adjust the balance of the grayscale as to various presets or customized color balances.

Bleed: Bleeds indicate to a printer that the image is to be printed borderless (printed to the edge of the page).

Blend Mode: A Photoshop® Layer Style option that allows the user to adjust the intensity or type of blend.

Blending Options: A Photoshop® Layer Style option that allows the user an ability to merge aspects of images on layers by decreasing *Opacity* of certain color modes and/or settings.

Blend Tool: An Illustrator® tool that the designer can use to blend objects, set specified steps, distance selected objects, specify distances, and orientate objects on a path by selecting an anchor from the objects or selecting all and clicking on the tool.

Blob Brush Tool: An Illustrator® brush that creates organic freehand shapes.

Bluetooth: A trademarked protocol of short-range wireless wave radio transmissions for interconnectivity between computers, cell phones, printers, etc.

Blur Tool: This Photoshop® tool is used to defocus pixels.

Bounding Box: In Illustrator® a visual rectilinear nonprintable parameter of a selection that appears around a selected object path, and is primarily used to resize or reposition the shape manually in accordance with the Transform panel functions and the Zero Point.

Brand: A particular product or label, such as a designer known for a specific standard of quality and consumer base.

Branding: The process of creating particular identities for select products owned by a company.

Brightness/Contrast: A Photoshop® filter setting used to brighten the color and the variance between light and dark on selections or selected layers.

Bristle Brush Preview: A button at the bottom of the Photoshop® Brush panel that allows the user to see the virtual movement of a CS5 Bristle Brush in a small window within the canvas.

Brush Tip Shape: A Photoshop® Brush panel option that allows the user to adjust the tip of a brush and helps with digital painting fluidity similar to the manner by which artists choose different paintbrushes for various tasks.

Brush Change Alert: An Illustrator® dialog box that appears when adjustments are made in the Brushes panel. The alert allows the user the opportunity to choose whether or not to apply the changes to existing strokes in the document.

Brush Diameter: The size of a Photoshop® brush in pixels based on a radius.

Brushes Panel: The designer can use the options of the Illustrator® Brushes panel to access preset or create vector brush types including Calligraphic, Scatter, and Art, Bristle, and Pattern brushes.

Brush Hardness: The simulated stiffness of a Photoshop® Bristle Brush, which has an affect on the type of mark the brush will make.

Brush Libraries: Illustrator® preset brushes that can be access via menu options.

Brush Panel: The options in this Photoshop® panel are used to adjust the attributes of each brush preset.

Brush Presets panel: A new Photoshop® CS5 panel that offers preset options for each individual brush.

Brush Tool: This Photoshop® tool is used for digital painting and may be adjusted as to type, size, and function through the Options Bar and the Brush Presets panel.

Burn Tool: This Photoshop® tool darkens pixels with a brushstroke. It takes its name from actual burn tools used by photographers in darkrooms to underexpose areas in photos.

Byte: A unit of disk space.

CAD: An acronym for computer-aided design.

Canvas Size: In Photoshop® the canvas is a type of working space that defines the parameters of the page. It is literally the file size.

Cap height: In typography the cap height designates the vertical length of capital letters.

Cartoon: A rendering that portrays a caricature or a parody of an entity or thing. A cartoon may also be a preliminary drawing.

CD-R: A recordable CD-ROM.

CD-ROM: A compact disc used to store digitized information and readable by a computer.

CD-RW: A rewritable CD-ROM.

Central processing unit (CPU): A computer processor with a primary purpose to communicate to the computer how to function by means of a program.

Channel Mixer: This Photoshop® filter adjusts the intensity of the color modes by channels.

Character: A numeric or alpha-numeric digit. A character can also be the personification of an illustrated human personage. In this book characters can also be avatars.

Character panel: This panel provides access to word processing functions for type in Illustrator® and Photoshop®.

Chrome filter: The Chrome filter transforms the look of flat vector graphics to the look of 3-D metal in a Photoshop® Effects Gallery.

Chuck Close: (1940–) An important American contemporary photorealist painter and photographer.

Cleanup: Designers Cleanup in Illustrator® to rid the illustration of all unpainted paths and stray points.

Click: In computing, the act of pressing the mouse function once.

Click again: The second step to creating a Bézier Curve, it is the act of pressing the mouse function again after previously releasing it.

Click and drag: In computing, pressing the mouse function once, and then holding and intentionally dragging it in the desired direction before releasing it. This operation is used to create Bézier Curves.

Clicking sequence: Set protocols for using a mouse to access computer functions.

Clipping mask: Usually used on a vector shape to block out areas of images.

Clone Stamp Tool: A Photoshop® tool samples an area of pixels. The user holds down the Option key (Mac) or the Alt key (PC) and clicks an area, then places it elsewhere with another click.

Closed path: A finished digital shape composed of vectors and paths.

Clouds filter: Photoshop® mixes cloud formations on selected layers.

CMYK: An acronym for cyan (a turquoise hue), magenta (similar to fuchsia), yellow, and k, for key (or black). It is the default color model for Illustrator®. CMYK is a subtractive color mode, meaning that each color added masks or changes the one previously applied upon a white or light-colored surface. The masking continues from cyan to black.

Code key: A term given to a function key, such as F1, F2, etc.

Collage: An art form consisting of various two-dimensional flat shapes, such as paper, cloth, or printed matter, arranged and pasted onto a flat surface.

Colored Pencil filter: A filter available in both Illustrator® and Photoshop® that converts selections into a look resembling fine art color pencil strokes and color arrangements.

Color Guide Harmony Rules: A selector at the top of the Color Guide panel that allows the user to limit the color scheme to Photoshop®-generated color groups.

Color Guide panel: The Illustrator® Color Guide panel helps the user manage fashion color schemes, harmonies, and stories. It provides suggestions for these from the selected object's Fill and Stroke colors and patterns in the Tools panel. Illustrator® calculates color changes based on the selected artwork. This allows the designer to mix and preview various color combinations before accepting them and without having to redefine a pattern swatch.

Color Mode: A color mode (also color model) is a printing process, such as CMYK and RGB.

Color panel: The designer can use the Color panel to mix and save spot colors.

Color Picker field: The area of the Color Picker from which a user is able to choose all the variations of a single hue, including tints, tones, shades, pastels, chroma color, and grayscale by clicking.

Color Replacement Tool: This Photoshop® tool replaces the color of an object with applied strokes with a new color from the Set Foreground Color box. However, it does not work when the color is black or white. An attempt to replace a specific hue with these color absences will result in varied grays.

Color Sampler Tool: With this Photoshop® tool, the user can place up to four temporary color samplers in a file for referencing via the Info panel.

Color 6: A preset of Live Trace (now Image Trace) in Illustrator® that divides traced images into outlines of 6 colors based on those predominant in the selection.

Color 16: A preset of Live Trace (now Image Trace) in Illustrator® that divides traced images into outlines of 16 colors based on those predominant in the selection.

Combine: An option of the Pathfinder panel that makes two or more selected objects into a single object.

Combine Files: An Acrobat Pro® dialog box that allows the user to add and organize files to be merged into a single multiple-page PDF document.

Command key: The main modifier key on a Macintosh key-board and equivalent to the PC Control key.

Compatibility: In computing, the ability of two or more hardware devices and/or software programs to function together.

Composite image: A digital image composed of separate sources, such as those created with image-editing software.

Composition: In digital art, the arrangement, balance, proportion, and symmetry of a composite image.

Compound path: With compound paths, the user can make two or more objects into a single object.

Computer: A machine that manipulates data according to set functions, such as a Macintosh or a PC.

Computer-aided design (CAD): The act of using computer technology to generate visual art or concepts.

Conceptual flats: A generic term used by fashion professionals for color flats used for presentation purposes.

Content-Aware filter: A new filter in Photoshop® CS5 that can approximate the fill based on the adjacent area of a selection.

Content-Aware Scale: Photoshop® CS5 Content-Aware Scale setting can be used to increase the size of approximated fill in reference to the selected area.

Contour: A feature option of the Photoshop® Layer Styles dialog box. It allows the user to change the effects of a selected Layer Style via a preset menu.

Contrapposto: Italian for counterpose, this term describes when the weight of the body in a standing pose is all on one leg, and the action of the shoulders and waist are at angles opposite to those of the hips and legs. This makes a figurative composition more convincing and relaxed. Digital croquis posed in contrapposto prevent the development of a digital floating figure.

Construction Guides: A feature of Smart Guides in Photoshop® that creates highlighted lines to help users draw perfect paths based on preset angles of a radius.

Control key: The main modifier key on a PC keyboard and equivalent to the Macintosh Command key.

Control Panel: In Illustrator®, the Control Panel is a hub that provides quick access to other panel functions. Akin to the Options Bar in Photoshop®.

Convert Anchor Point Tool: One of five tools in the Illustrator® Pen Tool Suite that can be used to convert angles of vectors to curves and vice versa.

Convert Point Tool: A Photoshop® tool that converts curved paths into straight and vice versa. Similar to the function of the Illustrator® Convert Anchor Point Tool.

Creative focus: A term designating the concentration of the artistic mind.

Crop Tool: The user can use this Photoshop® tool to reduce the size of the canvas or change its orientation by performing a marquee, then clicking inside the highlighted area (except in the middle) to accept the changes.

Croquis: An idealized sketch of a fashion figure used to create additional illustrations and facilitate quick, proportioned design presentations.

Cross-platform: The ability to interface with both Mac and PC computers.

CS: An abbreviation of Creative Suite, this is the current "A" series of bundled software packages from Adobe Systems Incorporated.

CS5: A full version upgrade of the Creative Suite that was released in 2010.

CS5.5: A mid-cycle upgrade between CS5 and CS6 released by Adobe Systems Incorporated in 2011.

CS6: A full version upgrade of the Creative Suite released in 2012.

Cursor: The screen pointer of a computer mouse.

Current Colors Field: In Illustrator®, a selection that appears in a dialog box when the Recolor Artwork button is clicked. It reveals a breakdown of the colorways in a selected object and provides a way to change each color separately or as a group.

Current Tool: Any tool in Illustrator® or Photoshop® that has been selected in the Tools panel. The Current Tool field is a featured area of the Illustrator® Status Bar.

Curves filter: This Photoshop® filter lets the user make slight-to-dramatic adjustments of the overall luminosity and the tone of an image. Through Curves, light or shadow can be adjusted in a specific area of an image without completely affecting the whole.

Custom: A setting of any new document profile that is not standard.

Customize: A computer that is built to the preferences and lifestyles of the consumer in almost minute detail.

Custom Shape Tool: A Photoshop® tool that makes flat symbols from preset or saved vector masks, logos, and clip art libraries located in the Options Bar.

Cutout filter: An artistic filter that simplifies digital objects artwork.

Daub: A single mark of paint made with a paintbrush or an equivalent digital representation.

Define a pattern: The act of creating a digital pattern from a repeat.

Delete Anchor Point Tool: A tool in both Illustrator® and Photoshop® that can be used to delete anchors on a path.

Depth: A setting in the Photoshop® Layers Styles dialog box that adjusts how far the transition of a selected Layer Style goes into the image.

Desaturate: In Photoshop® to desaturate is to make a color image grayscale.

Deselect: To release a selected area.

Designer: One who creates the concept, form, and end use of something before it is released to the general public. In fashion any person who conceives and drafts original concepts, and then plans the production of samples to be previewed and sold to retailers.

Desktop: In computing, the visible area on a computer monitor with no open windows, revealing the system software interfaces, icons, etc.

Desktop publishing: The creation of layouts on a computer via graphics software for various types of literature and promotional materials, brochures, etc.

Dialog box: In computer software, any intermediary window that appears and requires a response before proceeding.

Digit: A symbol or character, such as A, B, 4, or $.

Digital: Any information that has been converted to binary numeric form.

Digital art: The use of computer software to create visual interpretations to appeal to the senses or emotions.

Digital artist: One who creates digital art.

Digital camera: A camera that takes photos and records video in a digital format.

Digital design: The process of creating functional designs, apparel, and accessories with computer technology.

Digital drawing: The act of using computers to render images.

"Digital Duo": The author's term for the process of using object-oriented vector-based digital software, combined with raster-based image-editing digital software to create fashion illustrations and presentations.

Digital Duo Fashion Week: A fictitious apparel market week associated with the tutorials of this book.

Digital fashion age: The period of digital acceptance and wide use in apparel design, manufacturing, and marketing as necessitated by changes in globalized trade and markets.

Digital floating figure: This occurs when freehand figurative drawings or photos are digitized and placed in front of a background photo, painting, illustration, etc. Because images scanned into computers are brought into a virtual environment—unlike flat paper—if the poses are not in contrapposto, they will appear as flat floating puppets.

Digital flats: Two-dimensional or three-dimensional black-and-white computer renderings of apparel used as technical drawings to facilitate production and marketing rendered as if laid flat on a surface.

Digital painting: The use of digital brushes, colors, tools, and filters in an image-editing software program to simulate the appearance of fine art painting.

Digital software: A software program that can be read by a computer.

Digital transparency: Colorless pixels.

Digitize: The act of converting a document or image to its binary numeric form.

Direct Selection Tool: A tool in both Illustrator® and Photoshop® that can be used to manipulate and reposition anchors and paths.

Direction line: In computer graphics Direction Lines are visible adjustment lines emanating from anchors clicked on with the Direct Selection Tool. They are used to determine the arc of a curved path. Also see *handle*.

Disk space: In computing, the amount of memory a computer or digital storage device has remaining as measured in bytes, kilobytes, megabytes, gigabytes, terabytes, etc.

Dock: A dashboard on a computer where application buttons can be positioned for easy access.

Document Setup button: A button that appears in the Illustrator® Control Panel that allows the user to return to the document setup and make changes to the page attributes.

Dodge Tool: This Photoshop® tool brightens pixels with a brushstroke. The term is borrowed from a photography darkroom technique that decreases the exposure of select areas in a photograph.

Domestic-based businesses: Any self-sufficient company that contracts manufacturing procedures and sells its goods in the country where it is headquartered.

Domestic manufacturing: The process of producing and assembling nonimported products in the country where the facility is headquartered.

Download: The process of transferring a digital file from one source to a computer.

dpi: An acronym for dots per inch. Used to measure disk space. Also see *ppi*

Drag-and-drop: The term drag-and-drop is used to describe the entire procedure of grabbing a selected image and moving it to another file or area.

Draw Behind: One of three drawing modes offered in the Illustrator® Tools panel that allows the user to render behind an object.

Draw Inside: One of three drawing modes offered in the Illustrator® Tools panel that allows the user to render inside an object.

Drawing modes: Illustrator® default settings for rendering accessible in the Tools panel, including Draw Normal, Draw Behind, and Draw Inside.

Draw Normal: The default Illustrator® drawing mode, which appears in the Tools panel.

Drop Shadow: A computer generated shadow beneath and/or offset to an object.

Drop Zone: In Illustrator®, the instance of meshing that occurs when panels are placed next to one another, allowing the user to arrange them in docked groups.

Dry Brush filter: An artistic filter that mimics the look of painting effects of actual fine artist

brushes when used with very little paint. Often the digital effect provides a twill-looking texture.

DVD: An optical disc storage media device used for storing video and data similar to a CD-ROM but with much more storage capacity. Depending the source, the acronym stands for digital video disc, digital versatile disc, or nothing at all.

DVD-ROM drive: An internal input and output device that runs the functions of DVDs and CD-ROMs on a computer.

DVI: An acronym for digital visual interface. A DVI adapter connects devices to computers.

E-portfolio: A digital multipage document containing a cover page, customer profile board, mood board, digital color board, one or two pages of digital and/or freehand apparel illustration designs on croquis figures, a black-and-white technical flats line sheet, a conceptual color flats line sheet(s), several sample(s) of completed specification sheets with measurements and a conclusion page with contact information. An e-portfolio augments the regular printed version and should be constructed to fit the particular needs of each recipient.

Edges: Any intersecting outline between Illustrator® Live Trace Faces.

Edit in Quick Mask Mode: A mode in the Photoshop® Tools panel that allows the user to create an immediate mask on a channel but manipulate the mask in the window.

Edit or Apply Colors button: A button (color wheel icon) at the bottom of the Illustrator® Color Guide panel that reveals the Recolor Artwork dialog box, and applies the color group of the Color Guide Harmony Rules selector.

Electronic drawing: The process of using electronic peripherals such as a stylus or a mouse to draw digitally on a computer.

Ellipse Tool: An Illustrator® tool used to make vector ellipses and circles.

Elliptical Marquee Tool: A Photoshop® tool that can be used to create ellipses and circles of selections.

Embed: The act of pressing the Illustrator® Embed button, which appears in the Control Panel when files are placed, so that they will become a part of the new document.

Equalize: To automatically adjust the color saturation and contrast of a selected object.

Eraser Tool: The Photoshop® and the Illustrator® Eraser tools both manually remove digital data.

Ethernet: A direct connecting port for computers with an Internet service provider through a modem and a cable.

Excel: A spreadsheet application that is part of the bundled Microsoft Office suite of applications.

Exclude: An option in the Illustrator® Pathfinder panel that can be used to create an immediate clipping mask from two overlapping objects.

Expand: The Expand button in the Control Panel allows the user to change the color sections into vector outlines in Illustrator® after using Live Trace on an object.

Export: The process of transferring data from one computer program to another. In Adobe software, the term also refers to a transfer that maintains the integrity of the layer compositing.

Export Options: A dialog box that appears when a file is being exported from Illustrator® to Photoshop® and offers custom features.

Exposure: A Photoshop® filter used to increase the amount of light in an image. Exposure is also an option of the Burn Tool (O), which can be used to adjust the intensity of the tool.

Eyedropper Tool: This Photoshop® tool samples a color with a click and places it in the Set Foreground box.

Faces: Shapes usually surrounded by Edges created when Live Trace areas are Expanded and made Live. When a Live Trace image is Live, it can be filled with color, gradients, and patterns.

Fades: A linear blend of transparency and one or more colors.

Fashion abstractrealism: The author's term for the combined techniques of virtual digital realism and realistic idealism as an all-inclusive means of creating digital fashion illustrations featuring fashion figures and other relevant objects simulating frozen movement in environments.

Fashion avatar: A moving or still avatar created for the purpose of representing a prototype for fashion and marketing presentations.

Fashion design: The applied art and science of creating apparel and accessories based on current trends, markets, lifestyle, etc.

Fashion icons: Any person, object, or symbol that represents the personification of style or a specific aspect of fashion.

Fashion illustration: Rendering of apparel for the purpose of communicating with consumers, usually seen in fashion magazines and other periodicals.

Fashion presentation: The process of preparing and exhibiting fashion design, illustration, merchandising, and marketing concepts during pre- or post-production to facilitate buying and selling.

Fashion prototypes: The wide use of the image of a specific fashion personality representing a fashion market, such as a celebrity model. Avatars can replace such a person to facilitate fashion presentations.

Fashion techie: A technical fashion enthusiast usually studying digital design for fashion, fashion graphics, and/or any nonprofessional or professional person interested in the field of fashion and computing.

File format: The file format is the character of the file and determines how it will communicate with the application, system software, and other applications. Each file format has its own extension beginning with a period or dot right after the file name.

Fill: The act of digitally placing color, gradients, or patterns into a path sequence, a closed path, or a selected area.

Fill Button: A button located in the Illustrator® Tools panel that allows the user to fill a selected object with a color gradient, fade, or a pattern.

Fill Path with Foreground Color button: A button located at the bottom of the Photoshop® Paths panel that allows the user to fill a path with the contents of the Set Foreground Color box of the Tools panel.

Filter: A preset computer program or process that performs a sequence and provides visual enhancement features.

Finder: The Macintosh user-operated management system for files, disks, downloads, ports, etc.

Finder icon: Currently, the trade-marked Apple happy face, likely inspired by the painting style of Pablo Picasso in tints and tones of RGB blue with black markings.

Fine arts: Art that is produced for its own sake—primarily for beauty—as opposed to that intended to fulfill a utilitarian purpose.

Fit-in-window: The act of fitting an image to the screen size of an open window in a software program. Also known as fit-to-screen.

Flash drive: In computing, a small portable input and output storage device that uses a USB port.

Flatbed scanner: A device that digitizes flat images, such as documents and textiles, when placed on a flat surface to be used in computer graphics.

Flat Blunt Brush: A type or preset Bristle Brush shape available in the Photoshop® CS5 Brush panel menu. This brush mimics the capabilities of an artist brush that is used to create flat strokes of paint.

Flats: Two-dimensional technical drawings presented as if they were laid flat on a surface.

Flare Tool: The Flare Tool creates the illusion of light flashes with a marquee formation. It is located in the Illustrator® Tools panel within the hidden menu of the shape tools.

Flare Tool Center: An option of the Illustrator® Flare Tool accessed by the Options menu and used to adjust the center of a selected flare.

Flare Tool Halo: An option of the Illustrator® Flare Tool accessed by the Options menu and used to adjust the ghosted translucent shapes that appear with the light illusion of a selected flare.

Flare Tool Rays: An option of the Illustrator® Flare Tool accessed by the Options menu and used to adjust the beams that extend from a selected flare.

Flare Tool Rings: An option of the Illustrator® Flare Tool accessed by the Options menu and used to adjust the amount of rings that compose a selected flare.

Flatten: To compress a file into a single layer, reduce its size, and maximize printing capacity.

Flatten Transparency: In Illustrator® the Flatten Transparency option allows the user to flatten a selected raster image in order to create from it editable outlines.

Floats: Technical or conceptual flats rendered as if frozen in action on an invisible person or as if on a coat hanger.

Forward Warp Tool: A Photoshop® Liquify filter tool, which twirls areas of pixels as if in water.

fn: Code for the function key.

Freeform Pen Tool: This Photoshop® tool creates anchors and paths, and performs like the Illustrator® Pencil Tool.

Freehand: The process of rendering by hand without a mechanical device.

Free Transform: A Photoshop® feature that allows the user to make adjustments to the scale, position, and rotation of selected objects on layers.

Free Transform Tool: An Illustrator® tool that helps to angle objects in perspective

Full Screen Mode: A setting that allows the user to view a window in an application at the largest dimensions relevant to the monitor, and usually without the application tools, panels, etc.

Function keys: F keys that perform preset macros when pressed.

fx icon: A symbol for Photoshop® Layer Styles.

Gamma Correction: An Illustrator® option of the Exposure filter that helps the user adjust the proportions of brightness and darkness of areas.

Gamut: The Photoshop® Gamut is the capacity of a computer to interpret colors. When a particular color or range of colors in a working file falls out of the color RGB color mode gamut, a warning signal appears in the Color Picker and in the Color panel. Colors that are out of the gamut will not print properly unless first converted to the CMYK color mode.

Gaussian Blur: A type of filter in Illustrator® and Photoshop® that gives selected pixels a hazy appearance based on a radius.

General Preferences: An area of the Preferences menu in Illustrator® and Photoshop® where the basic functions of the program can be adjusted and/or customized, especially those that relate directly to the computer keyboard, cursor, effects, etc.

Geometric: An aspect of fashion design that uses angular or curved lines based upon any number of forms relating to geometry, such as ellipses, triangles, circles, rectangles, and squares.

Gigabytes: A unit of disk space consisting of 1,000 megabytes.

Global Angle: When the Global Angle of a specific Layer Style is checked, it will automatically take on the light source of the other layers where the option is checked in the Photoshop® Layer Style dialog box.

Global communications: The ability, made possible by digital technology, to freely communicate with anyone worldwide.

Gloss: In the Photoshop® Lighting Effects filter, the *Gloss* settings saturate each color separately, giving the appearance that there is light in the color.

Gradient: A graduated radial or linear blend of two or more colors used to fill objects.

Gradient Overlay: A Photoshop® Layer Style that allows the user to cover objects on a layer with a gradient, fade, or vignette.

Gradient panel: A panel in Illustrator® that offers options for mixing blends of colors or color with transparency in either linear or radial formation.

Gradient Slider bar: A bar in the Gradient panel that allows the user to make adjustments to the sliders that represent color blends.

Gradient Tool: A tool in both Illustrator® and Photoshop® that provides the ability to blend two or more color fills or a fade with a color(s).

Graphic design: The applied art of combining text and visual art for the purpose of communication.

Graphics: In computing, of or relating to visual images.

Graphics tablet: An electronic drawing device that synchronizes freehand movements via a stylus on a surface to create digital objects on a computer screen in a software program as a method of electronic drawing.

Graphic Styles panel: An Illustrator® panel that allows the user to save combination filter and tool attributes.

Graph Tools: Any of the various Illustrator® tools used to create stacked column, bar, stacked bar, line, area scatter pie, and radar graphs.

Grid: A network of lines both perpendicular and parallel to one another, creating square spaces.

In software, the grid is used to assist drawing and spatial arrangement of objects.

Grid plane: A movable grid in the Illustrator® CS5 Perspective Grid Tool.

Grids in Back: An option available in the Illustrator® Guides and Grid preferences menu that the user can check to toggle the position of the grid.

Ground tile: A term in this book that identifies the rectilinear shape used to define the background of a pattern repeat in Illustrator® CS5 and earlier versions.

Group Selection Tool: An Illustrator® Tool that allows the user to select sets of grouped objects within other groups by double-clicking. It can also be used to select a single object in a group.

Guides: The customizable horizontal and vertical lines of basic Guides are used to assist alignment. Horizontal Guides can be pulled from the x-axis ruler and vertical Guides from the y-axis ruler. Guides can be locked, unlocked, repositioned, and deleted.

Guides & Grid preferences: A menu option of the Illustrator® preferences where the appearance and position of Guides and Grids can be adjusted.

Hairline fractures: Breaks in an Illustrator® defined repeat, which show as white lines or gaps due to the spaces created between ground tiles.

Handle: A line with a square on the end that protrudes from a Bézier Curve and is used to make direct adjustments to the curve. Sometimes the Illustrator® handle is referred to as a direction line.

Hand Tool: This tool is used to move around the page. It also works in conjunction with the Proxy Preview Area of the Navigator panel in both Illustrator® and Photoshop®.

Hard drive icon: On Macintosh computers, the hard drive icon comes installed on the desktop with the system software. It offers direct access to the computer's contents as made available by the operating system software and user-related files, ports, and drives.

Hard disk drive: In computing, an internal disk, usually in the main unit of a computer, that has the capacity to store information. It is the computer's memory device.

Hardware: Physical parts of digital devices, such as computers, monitors, and laptops.

HDR (High Dynamic Range) Toning: An all-in-one time-saving retouching filter hub introduced with Photoshop® CS5. HDR Toning offers a multiplicity of preset and manually adjusted editing options that can produce surreal effects by the user moving slider options rather than through a combination of filter dialog boxes and panels. The HDR Toning dialog box places the capability to see all of the adjustments in real time and takes the guesswork out of going back through the menu options. Simulations that are created can be saved for future use, but it will be a flattened file.

Healing Brush Tool: With this Photoshop® tool, the user can sample desirable pixels near a problem area by holding and clicking with the Option key (Mac) or the Alt key (PC).

Hierarchy: In computing the system of order in horizontal and vertical links of visual locations and interfaces via a computer's menu.

Highlight Mode: A setting in the Layer Styles dialog box that adjusts the intensity of highlights in selected Layer Styles, such as Bevel and Emboss, among others.

Histogram: The Illustrator® Levels Histogram panel is a graph that allows the user to adjust the lightness and darkness in an image based on the relationship of highlights, midtones, and shadows. The Photoshop® Histogram panel is a graph that can be used to correct the tonal value of an image based on its composite color channels.

History Brush Tool: This Photoshop® tool works as a brush to return areas gradually to their original state when the user first opened the file. The History Brush Tool (Y) is a great asset for the designer when retouching photos.

History panel: A Photoshop® panel that records stages of a file's development in layers that can be selected back to the opening of the file.

Horizon Line: In the Illustrator® CS5 Perspective Grid Tool, the Horizon Line is a level that can be set to represent the plane of the estimated horizon in reference to objects on the Artboard.

Horizontal Align Center: A feature of the Illustrator® Align panel that can be used to position two or more objects based on their centers in horizontal formation.

Horizontal Grid: In the Illustrator® CS5 Perspective Grid Tool, the Horizontal Grid helps to position the plane of perspective that governs the top or bottom of objects in relationship to the Vanishing Point.

Horizontal repeat: A pattern repeat that has a motif that only repeats itself on the top and the bottom of the Ground tile.

Horizontal Type Mask Tool: This Photoshop® tool is used to create horizontal type as selections that can be filled or stroked. Masked-out areas leave just the horizontal type, with whatever is beneath them showing through the characters.

Horizontal Type Tool: With this Photoshop® tool, the user can type across the file using a variety of fonts and sizes. In Photoshop®, type can be treated as an object and take on most of the features, with the various effects offered.

Hot key: A keyboard shortcut.

Hue Color Picker: A mode setting of the Color Picker that allows the user to select all the tints, tones, shades, and chroma color of one specific hue.

Hue/Saturation filter: A Photoshop® filter that allows the user to change the hue and adjust the saturation and the brightness of a selected object or layer.

Icon: A small pictogram on a computer used to represent programs, functions, etc.

Iconic: The quality of being a widely recognizable symbol.

Idealize: The act of rendering a person or object more perfect than reality according to accepted norms of the times. In fashion, the act of distorting rendered figure proportions simulating the tall, extra-slender stature of fashion models.

Illustrator® Community Help: An online resource and help menu for Illustrator® where users can interact, locate information about the program, and search for answers to frequently asked questions via links.

Image editing: The process of digitally altering images via the manipulation of pixels, through a program such as Photoshop®.

Image quality: The visual state of digitally created or altered images when printed.

Import: Converting a file into a format for a specific software application, such as video frames being separated into layers in Photoshop®. It is also used to denote the act of bringing apparel or other goods from abroad.

Impressionism: A nineteenth-century art movement that originated in France and is characterized by depicting the fleeting "impression" of an image.

Infinite loop: The symbol of a square with looped corners used as an icon for the Macintosh command key.

Inner Shadow: A Photoshop® Layer Style that darkens the outer edges of images on layers and can be used to simulate dimension.

Input: To import information into the computer (to digitize).

Intel: The world's largest semiconductor computer chip maker, whose primary business is supplying them for personal computers.

Intensity: A setting in the Photoshop® Lighting Effects filter that adjusts the illusion of bright light as if it were beaming onto an object or surface.

Interface: The process of interacting with computers or the use of any procedure, software, or equipment that allows communication with a computer.

Internet: A public international computer network accessed with a modem that facilitates global communications links via e-mail and the World Wide Web.

Inverse: A feature of Photoshop® that selects the outside space of a selected area.

Invert: A feature of Photoshop® that creates the opposite of any color image(s) much like photo negatives. Inverting generally shows the complement of colors.

JPEG: Short for Photoshop® Joint Photographic Experts Group, this file format dramatically reduces file sizes. The file is compressed but retains a high quality image. (The extension appears as .jpg.)

Kerning: A setting in the Character panel. In typography, kerning is the act of adjusting space between letters, numbers, or other characters.

Keyboard: An electronic input device consisting of a panel of keys with alphanumeric characters used to type and access a computer.

Keyboard & Mouse Preferences: An Apple Preferences menu option where the functions of both the keyboard and the mouse grid can be adjusted.

Keyboarding: The unofficial term given to proper use of a computer keyboard, which includes hand and finger positions for performing specific functions.

Killer software: Major software programs like Illustrator® and Photoshop® that are so widely used they popularize and increase sales on the computer platforms on which they run.

Knife Tool: An Illustrator® tool used to make freehand-like cuts through shaped and paths by clicking and dragging.

Kuler panel: An Illustrator® panel that is part of the online community and exhibits color schemes created by users. Colors stories can be uploaded to the panel for others to use.

Landscape orientation: A page layout that is wider than it is high.

Lasso Tool: With the Illustrator® Lasso Tool, the user can select objects by drawing freehand around it. It is especially useful for selecting abstract or organic shapes within complex groups and for selecting portions of paths that can be further transformed through Control Panel options.

Lasso Tool Suite: The three tools in this Photoshop® suite allows the user to freeform areas with the Lasso Tool, select freeform angular areas from point to point with the Polygonal Lasso Tool, and adhere digital pins to the outer parameter of objects close the shape with the Magnetic Lasso Tool.

Launch Bridge: A button in the Photoshop® Application bar that when pressed launches Bridge. Also, a similar button in Illustrator® labeled *Go to Bridge*, which launches the same application.

Launch Mini Bridge button: A new feature of Photoshop® CS5 that opens a Mini Bridge panel where the user can access saved files.

Layer Compositing: The process of creating separate layers for certain objects as a production technique to assist in the organization of multipart electronic drawings.

Layer Groups: Folders created by Photoshop® or the user to house files as groups on a single layer.

Layer Styles: Preset and editable Photoshop® filters that help give dimension to vector art on specific layers.

Leading: A setting option of the Character panel. In typography, leading is the amount of blank space between lines of text.

Left Grid: A movable vertical grid panel of the Illustrator® CS5 Perspective Grid Tool that helps create the illusion of perspective in relationship to a vanishing point.

Lens Flare: A Photoshop® filter that allows the user to place simulated camera flashes randomly.

Levels: An Illustrator® filter that contains a histogram and is used to adjust the lightness and darkness in an image based on the relationship of highlights, midtones, and shadows.

Lighting Effects filter: A special Photoshop® filter that adds moody, dimensional light effects to objects on layers. This filter only works in RGB mode.

Light Type: An option of the Photoshop® Lightning Effects filter that offers a pull-down menu where the user can choose to add *Omni*, *Spotlights*, or *Directional* light effects.

Linear gradient: A gradient composed of straight blends.

Line segment: In vector-based software, the line between two anchors.

Line Segment Tool: With this Illustrator® tool, the user can create a straight line by clicking and dragging and adjust the line through the Stroke panel options.

Line sheet: An organized display of associated items being marketed or manufactured that have been grouped by shipping cycle, fabrication, and/or trend. There are generally two types of line sheets: the line sheet used for showroom sales and the technical or production line sheet.

Link icon: A chain icon that denotes when two or more layers have been linked together.

Liquify filter: The Liquify filter allows the user to move selected portions of an image around as if they were being transformed by water.

Live: The state of Illustrator® Faces and Edges of a Live Trace and Embedded image that has been selected and can be affected by the Live Paint Bucket Tool (K).

Live Paint Bucket Tool: A color, gradient, and pattern distribution tool used to affect Live Trace areas.

Live Paint Group: Any grouping of selections made Live and therefore can be filled at the same time with the Live Paint Bucket Tool (K).

Live Paint Selection Tool (Shift + L): With this Illustrator® tool, the user can select Expanded areas of Live Trace (Image Trace CS6) images by holding the Cmd/Ctrl key, double-clicking, selecting, and moving.

Live Paint tip: A warning notification dialog box that appears when an attempt is made to use the Live Paint Bucket Tool (K). It informs the user that a live area has not been defined.

Live Trace: Live Trace allows the user to convert rasterized images into vector selections in Illustrator®.

Load Channel as Selection: A button at the bottom of the Photoshop® Channels panel that when pressed, restores the marching ants of a previously saved and selected Alpha Channel.

Load Path as Selection button: A button at the bottom of the Photoshop® Paths panel that when pressed, creates a selection from a path.

Lock icon: An icon in the form of a lock that indicates that a layer in Photoshop® is not writable.

Mac: A Macintosh computer.

Mac OS: The system software for Macintosh computers.

Mac OS X: A current level of the Macintosh system software.

Magic Eraser Tool: The Photoshop® Magic Eraser Tool (E) erases pixels of the same color. It is frequently used to erase a particular colored area within a pattern or photo.

Magic Wand Tool (Y): This Illustrator® tool selects multiple objects by color.

Magnetic Lasso Tool: With this Photoshop® tool, the user can select shapes by first placing magnetic sensors on their perimeters.

Manual: To perform a task totally by hand without the use of mechanical devices.

Manufacturers: Any company engaged in product development, production, and sale of goods.

Marching Ants: Flashing indicators in Photoshop® that a selection has been made.

Marquee: See *Perform a Marquee*.

Marquee formation: See *Perform a Marquee*.

Marquee Tool Suite: This Photoshop® suite of tools creates shaped selected areas and includes the Rectangular Marquee Tool (M), the Elliptical Marquee Tool (M), the Single Row Marquee Tool, and the Single Column Marquee Tool.

Masked Areas: In Photoshop® masked areas are those that are protected by a filter so that they cannot be affected by any changes that the user makes. The Photoshop® Tools panel has an Edit in Quick Mask Mode icon at the bottom that provides immediate access to this option.

Match Color: A Photoshop® filter setting that can be used to match the color in another open file on a specific layer.

Maximum Editability: An Illustrator® option in the Export dialog box that allows an exported file to be used efficiently by the version of the file format that it will become.

Measure Tool: An Illustrator® tool, used in conjunction with the Info panel, that allows the user to measure areas, objects, etc. as to their position on the Artboard by clicking from one point to another.

Megabytes: A unit of disk space composed of 1,000 kilobytes.

Menu: In computing, usually the manual interface via a mouse and cursor on a monitor that accesses pull-down and scroll window directories.

Menu bar: The main manual interface of options on a computer that provides access to system software and application menus.

Merchandiser: In fashion, any professional with the responsibility of moving goods (especially apparel and accessories) in niche markets that were purchased at wholesale and sold at retail in varieties, assortments, and categories, and arranged by their intrinsic and extrinsic cues for consumers.

Merge: The act of combining the contents of two or more layers.

Mesh Tool (M): With this Illustrator® tool, the user can create gradient blends based on an arbitrary mapping system to generate the illusion of dimension by clicking to add hues, and then manipulating paths and anchors.

Microsoft Corporation: A computer technology corporation that develops a wide variety of software products, including the Windows operating system and the Microsoft Office suite of software applications.

Mixer Brush Tool: This Photoshop® tool blends two or more colors, gradients, and/or patterns.

Modern art: A general term for twentieth-century art, which was a period of experimentation, when the former classical and traditional concepts of "fine art" were ignored in favor of succinct movements, characterized by specific processes and styles from individuals and/or groups of artists.

Modifier keys: Keys that are programmed to alter the normal function of other keys when pressed in conjunction.

Monitor: An electronic output device (screen) used to display high-quality text, graphics, and video on a computer.

Morph: The act of changing one 3-D object smoothly into another. In this book, morphing is the act of transforming one vector shape into another with the use of vector tools, especially those of the Illustrator® Pen Tool Suite and the Direct Selection Tool.

Mouse: In computing, a small input device used on a flat surface, connected to a keyboard. When dragged or clicked, the mouse moves the cursor on a monitor allowing an interface with software programs.

Mouses: The plural form of the computing term mouse.

Move Tool: The first Photoshop® tool in the Navigator panel, it is used to reposition objects, selections, etc.

Navigation controls for multiple Artboards: An area of the Illustrator® Status bar that allows the user to switch Artboards within the Application Frame.

Navigator panel: These tools help the user to move objects and navigate pages.

Neo-impressionism: A late nineteenth-century movement in French painting that sought to "improve" Impressionism through systematic approaches, especially pointillism.

New Brush Presets panel: This new Photoshop® panel offers preset options for each individual brush.

New Document Profile: A dialog box that opens a file with specified settings for document formatting.

New Layer: A layer created by pressing the New Layer icon as part of layer compositing.

New Layer icon: An icon at the bottom of the Layers panel next to the Trash icon that creates a new layer.

Noise scale: The amount of noise added to particular Layer Styles.

None icon: The Illustrator® None icon button specifies that a selected object should have no Fill or Stroke.

Normal Screen Mode: The default screen mode that is windowed with a menu bar.

Note Tool: The only administrative tool in Photoshop®; it allows users of a file to leave notes that can be posted as reminders or to give instructions.

Object-oriented: Any work created with vector graphics software.

Ocean Ripple filter: A Photoshop® and Illustrator® filter that can be used to simulate rippled texture on images.

Off Set: A slider option of the Photoshop® Exposure and CS5 HDR filters that darkens shadows and midtones.

Opacity: The amount of visibility of an object (translucency).

Operating system: A software program that runs a computer such as Mac OS or Windows.

Optical illusion: A trick of the eye, or *trompe-l'oeil*, is a visual deception whereby the mind processes what is seen but "thinks" it sees something else, such as perceiving an object as three-dimensional that in reality is two-dimensional.

Option key: A modifier key on the Mac keyboard between the Command and the Control key.

Options bar: In Photoshop®, the hub where the user can select options for the currently selected tool. Called the Control Panel in Illustrator®.

Organic: A term relating to or derived from living organisms and their inherent properties in nature.

Outer Glow: A Photoshop® layer style that simulates glowing edges around selected areas or objects on a layer.

Outline Mode: A mode of Illustrator® that allows the outline of objects to be viewed without regard to Fill or Stroke.

Output Devices: Devices that receive and display information from a computer's central processing unit or main memory. Examples include monitors, printers, etc.

Paintbrush Tool (B): An Illustrator® tool that can be used to create freehand strokes similar to a quill.

Paint Bucket Tool: This Photoshop® tool is used for the random fills of objects and/or color areas in conjunction with the Set Foreground box. It is located in a hidden suite with the Gradient Tool.

Paint Daubs filter: A raster filter offered in both Illustrator® and Photoshop® that converts selected objects to simulated fine artists' strokes of paint usually made by stippling with a round brush.

Panels: A range of options provided as a group in a computer graphics program, such as colors, navigation, and channels etc.

Pantone® Color Libraries: Illustrator® and Photoshop® libraries of universal color standard swatches used to decrease the margin for error when communicating with outside sources.

Paste Profile Mismatch: A warning that tells you that Photoshop® will convert the color profile of a pasted file to match the destination file.

Patch Tool: This Photoshop® tool is used to sample selected problem areas, such as tears or water damaged areas of photos. It can be used for retouching to create instant pattern fills, to reposition pattern repeats within a rendering, or even to remove tattoos.

Path: In computer graphics, a line between two vectors.

Path Eraser Tool: An Illustrator® tool that can be used to erase sections of a selected path.

Paths panel: The Photoshop® Paths panel works in conjunction with any shape. When a shape is rendered, a work path appears. Designers use the Paths panel when working with shapes (*work paths*) created on the same layer that he or she wants to keep separate. The panel can affect each path created as to its fill or its stroke. They can also be loaded as selections (*rasterized*).

Path Selection Tool: This Photoshop® tool functions like the Illustrator® Selection Tool. It selects and moves paths, but not the filled shapes they create.

Pattern: A term applied to any regimented motif or design.

Pattern Brush: A Photoshop® brush that paints selected defined patterns in freehand strokes.

Pattern Stamp Tool: The user can use this Photoshop® tool to sample an area of patterned pixels by holding and clicking with the Option key (Mac) or the Alt key (PC) and placing them with a click or a swipe in another area to continue a repeat.

PC: An abbreviated term designating a personal computer usually associated with the Microsoft Windows operating system.

PDF: The Illustrator® Portable Document Format is a transfer application that allows users to share work and retain its integrity. This includes an ability to write the layers so that when a file is opened in Illustrator® on another computer, it can be restored to its original state.

Pencil Tool: This Photoshop® tool acts like a brush. It is used to render fine to thick lines. The Illustrator® Pencil Tool acts as a freehand rendering tool that creates immediate anchor points and paths.

Pen Tool: A graphic software tool used in products to facilitate the rendering of straight and curved paths governed by anchor points created with movements of the cursor through clicking and dragging with either a mouse or a stylus.

Pen Tool Suite: A family of rendering tools in Illustrator® within the hidden menu of the Pen Tool in both Illustrator® and Photoshop® but chiefly used of the former.

Perfect repeat: In the procedure of creating a repeat, the copy of the ground tile that contains all of the essential motifs.

Perform a marquee: The act of selecting a tool and then clicking and dragging from an upper-left to a lower-right destination to create an invisible rectangular area that will be the base for the size and position of an object. A marquee may also be performed to select one or more objects or to activate an appropriate function of a tool, such as to increase the view of a particular area with the Zoom Tool (Z).

Perpendicular: A 90-degree angle from a plane, or surface.

Personal computer: A PC owned and operated by an individual consumer, as opposed to the concept of a supercomputer.

Perspective Grid Tool (Shift + P): An Illustrator® tool that can assist in the composition of page layout and images in one-point, two-point, and three-point perspective by the user repositioning a specialized grid with planes via a widget control.

Perspective Selection Tool (Shift +V): An Illustrator® tool that can be used to select objects and adjust them in perspective in relation to the composition of the Perspective Grid Tool (Shift+P).

Photo filter: A Photoshop® filter used to cast a color over another similar to the way photographers alter the mood of a composition by covering lights or lenses with color filters.

Photography: The art and practice of taking and processing photographs.

Photo High Fidelity: An Illustrator® Live Trace preset that provides fine details of raster images by creating many small Faces and Edges.

Photomontage: A technique utilizing a compilation of photographs arranged to create an entire image from cutout parts, often in conjunction with other graphics materials.

Photoshop® Effects Gallery: Photoshop® raster effects offered as a menu option in Illustrator® through the Effect section.

Photoshop® Import Options: A Photoshop® dialog box that offers the user the ability to place raster objects in Illustrator® without a white background.

Pixel: A minute square dot of color used to compose an image on a monitor or screen.

Place: The process of importing a file into an open file as artwork, media, etc.

Plane Switching Widget: A widget that appears with the Illustrator® CS5 Perspective Grid Tool in the upper-left hand corner that allows users to activate grids on different planes in reference to one-point, two-point, or three-point perspective.

Plastic Wrap filter: A raster filter that creates the illusion of clear plastic wrapped around an object.

Platform: In computing, the platform denotes a computer's system software.

Pointillism: A neo-impressionist movement created by French painter Georges Seurat whereby small dots of various groups of pure color are used to create compositions that are "mixed" or blended in the eye of the viewer from a distance.

Polygonal Lasso Tool: A Photoshop® tool that creates selections in the form of polygons.

Polygon Tool: An Illustrator® tool that creates polygons.

Pop art: Art based on popular culture, depicting objects and scenes from everyday life utilizing techniques borrowed from commercial art and popular illustration.

Pop Art colors: A color library containing bright color swatches significant of the art form made popular by the early and mid-career works of Andy Warhol, Roy Lichtenstein, and other fine artists of the 1960s through the 1980s.

Popular culture: Mainstream ideas, perspectives, and attitudes generally accepted by a society.

Portable external hard drive: A portable device used to store data outside of the computer.

Portrait orientation: A page layout that is higher than it is wide.

Posterize: A Photoshop® filter that creates dark outlines significant of early poster art.

Postmodern art: A term used to describe an art movement that challenged or contradicted certain aspects of modern art, or has emerged or developed in its aftermath.

Power adapter: A cable that connects a digital device via a port to an electrical outlet, usually used to recharge laptop batteries.

Power PC: A computer with an Intel processor.

ppi: Pixels per inch. Similar to dpi, however, ppi refers to the resolution of an inputted image, whereas dpi refers to an outputted image.

Preferences: In computing, preferences are preferred operating options available through adjustable menus.

Preferences menu: Menus that allow the user to adjust a computer's operating options.

Pre-rendered: A drawing that has been provided for instructional purposes.

Preview box: A small box on dialog boxes that allows the user to see changes by a filter or setting option in real time. The feature allows the user to choose a correct adjustment before accepting the changes and therefore saves time.

Printer: An output device used in conjunction with a computer to print images.

Printmaking: The process of creating duplicate images of an original, usually on paper and in limited numbered series.

Print Tiling Tool: An Illustrator® tool used to adjust the printable area of the Artboard.

Private label: An exclusive line of apparel, accessories, or products offered by a retailer to the consumer via a direct relationship with a contractor.

Production flats: Technical flats, usually created with a vector-based software program, that are used as diagrams for creating apparel production via a technical package.

Production technical flat: See *Production flats*.

Programming: The act of setting the parameters of instructions for a computer.

Projector: An output device that can be connected by a VGA adapter cable to a computer and used to project the desktop display onto a screen or a flat surface via a lens and a powerful light beam.

Proportionate: The visual correctness of scale between the concept of the human form and illustrations, especially in flat sketches.

Proxy Preview Area: A red outline (box) in the Illustrator® Pathfinder panel that mirrors the larger page view of the document window.

Pull-down menus: Menus that are accessed by clicking and scrolling downward to an option.

Puppet Warp: A new feature of CS5 that can be used it to change the position of images with controlled mapping and placed pins that act as joint stabilizers.

Quick Selection Tool: The Photoshop® tool selects freeform areas based on a brush. It has additional options in the Options Bar.

QuickTime® player: An Apple media player.

Radial gradient: A gradient that is in the form of a radius.

RAM: An acronym for random access memory.

Randomly change color order button: A setting of the Illustrator® Color Guide panel's Recolor Artwork dialog box that alters the colorways randomly based on the various hues in the Current Colors field.

Randomly change saturation and brightness button: A setting of the Illustrator® Color Guide panel's Recolor Artwork dialog box that alters the saturation, brightness, and colorways randomly based on the various hues in the Current Colors field.

Range: A setting option of the Photoshop® Dodge Tool (O) that allows the user to adjust from a menu which pixels will be affected by the tool as to *Highlights*, *Midtones*, and *Shadows*.

Raster: The use of a rectangular invisible grid on a monitor to assign numbered pixel spaces assisting the creation of composite images.

Raster art: Commercial or fine art created from image-editing computer software.

Raster-based: A figurative term referring to the foundation of an idea, process, tool, program, or anything that is reliant upon image-editing software.

Raster Effects: A setting control in the Illustrator® New Document dialog box that sets the resolution of raster artwork and filters in a file separately from the resolution-independent quality of the Illustrator® file itself. This feature also can increase the file size tremendously depending on the size and nature of files and filters used.

Realism: In art, the quality of representing things accurately just as they appear in life.

Realistic idealism: A term used by the author to denote an illustration process that begins with photo resources and/or idealized freehand renderings that are then digitized to create idealized illustrations in graphics software programs. Further applications of 3-D techniques, portions of photographic collage, filters, and digital painting are applied to generate creative effects.

Rectangular Grid Tool: An Illustrator® tool that creates instant grid areas with a marquee that can be filled and stroked.

Rectangle Tool: An Illustrator® tool that creates squares and rectangles by the user performing a marquee.

Rectangular Marquee Tool: A Photoshop® tool that creates square and rectilinear selections by the user performing a marquee.

Recycle Bin: The Windows operating system Trash used to delete items from a PC.

Red Eye Tool: A Photoshop® tool used to eliminate red eye or subjects. The tool can be adjusted in the Options Bar.

Reference point: Parameters used to govern digital drawings.

Reflect Tool: An Illustrator® tool that flips objects and patterns.

Reorder Layers: The act of rearranging the order of layers by pulling and placing them above and below one another in the Layers panel.

Repeat Bounding Boxes: A term used in this book to denote the box without a Fill or a Stroke that is a copy of the Ground tile, and used to tell Illustrator® CS5 to repeat what is inside the area as a defined pattern.

Reshape Tool: An Illustrator® tool that can be used to organically change the form of an object by clicking and dragging on a path similar to the process of using the combination of the Add Anchor Point Tool (+) with the Convert Anchor Point Tool (Shift + C).

Resolution: The amount of dots per inch (*dpi*) that determine the quality of a digital image for devices, such as computers, scanners, printers, etc.

Resolution independent: The status of Illustrator® having an ability to create images of high print quality and can be seen up close (zoom in) without a loss to visibility.

RGB: A three-color additive printing process whereby red, green, and blue light are mixed to produce various colors and illuminate darkness. The default color mode of Photoshop® is RGB.

RGB channel: The composite channel of the color RGB image in a Photoshop® file; also a layer of the Channels panel.

RGB Lights: A filter that creates the illusion of red, green and blue lights in the Photoshop® Lighting Effects filter.

Rotate: To change the position of a letter, an object, or an image based on a radius.

Rotate Tool: An Illustrator® tool that rotates selected objects and patterns.

Rotate View Tool: A Photoshop® tool that randomly changes the page orientation based on a radius.

Rough Pastels filter: A Photoshop® filter that gives objects the look of fine art created with colored chalk strokes.

Round Angle Brush: A type of new Photoshop® CS5 bristle brush that mimics art paintbrushes with a round angled tip.

Round Fan brush: A type of new Photoshop® CS5 bristle brush that mimics art paintbrushes with a fan spread.

Rounded Rectangle Tool: An Adobe Illustrator® tool that creates squares and rectangles with rounded corners.

Ruler Origin: The Zero Point between negative and positive integers identified as an area between the x-axis and y-axis rulers in Illustrator® and Photoshop®, which can be moved by clicking and dragging. The ruler origin governs the relationship of all objects created and certain functions of the programs such as Bounding Boxes and the Transform panel.

Ruler Tool: This Photoshop® tool measures distances with a click and drag. The recorded information as to position, width, and height appear in the Options Bar.

Satin: A Photoshop® layer style that overlays color to mimic the organic formations, highlights, midtones, and shadows of satin fabric.

Save: To save a file with an appropriate name, in a specific location, and with a proper file format.

Save Color Group to Swatch Panel button: A button at the bottom of any color swatches panel that allows the user to select a group folder of swatches

and save them to the default Swatches panel in Illustrator®.

Save Selection as Channel: A button at the bottom of the Photoshop® Channels panel that when pressed creates an alpha channel mask from a selection.

Scale Tool: An Illustrator® tool that resizes objects and patterns.

Scaling: The act of altering size and/or dimensions of an object.

Scan: A digitized file from a scanner.

Scanner: An input peripheral device used in conjunction with a computer to digitize two-dimensional documents and objects.

Scanning: The process of digitizing two-dimensional documents and objects.

Scissors Tool (C): An Illustrator® tool used to cut line segments by clicking on them.

Scratchboard: In Illustrator®, this is the nonprintable area outside the Artboard.

Screen mode: The view setting of an application window interface.

Screen resolution: The lowest amount of pixels per inch on an electronic display (72 dpi, for "dots per inch"), which the human eye can see without distortion.

Scroll: A tab, usually located on the right hand of a computer screen, that moves a display up or down rapidly.

Scroll menus: Menu options that can be accessed by selecting areas and then scrolling with the cursor to hidden menus beneath arrow pointers.

Selected areas: In Photoshop® selected areas are indicated by marching ants.

Selection & Anchor Display: A menu option in the Illustrator® Preferences that can be used to adjust the program's functions as to selecting, snapping to a point and the appearance of anchor points.

Selection Tools: These Photoshop® tools are used to generate selected or shaped areas.

Selection Tool: The Illustrator® Selection Tool is used to select, move, scale, and reshape paths and shapes via a Bounding Box.

Set Background Color box: In the Photoshop® Tools panel, the Color box at the bottom of the panel in the upper position used as a second color choice to fill or stroke objects. The Color Picker is accessed by double-clicking on the Set Foreground Color box.

Set Foreground Color box: In the Photoshop® Tools panel, the Color box at the bottom of the panel in the upper position used as the primary color choice to fill or stroke objects. The Color Picker is accessed by double-clicking on the Set Foreground Color box.

Sequences: In computing, a series of functions performed to generate a desired outcome.

Shadow Mode: A Photoshop® Layer Style option that controls shadow effects of a selected style.

Shadows: A selection in the pull-down menu of the Photoshop® Burn Tool's Range option located in the Options Bar.

Shadows/Highlights: These settings intensify and/or tone the balance of the exposure between areas within an image by the user adding or decreasing the amount of grayscale in shadows, highlights, and/or hues.

Sharpen Tool: Photoshop® tool used to focus pixels.

Shape Builder Tool: An Illustrator® tool that can be used to unite, delete, or exclude all or portions of several selected shapes by holding modifier keys and clicking and dragging within specific areas.

Shape Dynamics: A set of options in the Photoshop® Brush panel that can be used to adjust the function and performance of a selected brush.

Shape: Any closed path that covers an area.

Shape Tools: The shape tools in this suite create vector masks on the Photoshop® Paths panel and generate the forms associated with their titles.

Sharpen Tool: A Photoshop® tool used to focus pixels.

Shear Tool: An Illustrator® tool that turns and distorts selected objects on angles based on a radius to assimilate perspective.

Shift Key: A modifier key on a keyboard that alters the function of other keys, typically used for capitalization.

Shortcuts: A term for keyboard commands or *hot key* functions read by computers.

Shortcut commands: Computer macros used to perform computing tasks by the user pressing code keys on a keyboard instead of using a mouse.

Show Backdrop: A box that can be checked in the Photoshop® Liquify window allowing the user to see an object in front of a pixel grid.

Signage: In visual graphics, signage is text used to communicate to a target audience.

Single Column Marquee Tool: A Photoshop® tool used to make a single (1 point wide) vertical selection that can be filled.

Single Row Marquee Tool: A Photoshop® tool used to make a single, (1 point wide) horizontal selection, which can be filled.

Slice Select Tool: Photoshop® tool used to select and reposition slices.

Slice Tool: An Illustrator® and Photoshop® tool that is used to isolate areas of a layout or photo by clicking and dragging in order to save them or portions of them on web pages.

Smart Guides: An Illustrator® preferences setting that toggles tool tips and construction guides based on a radius, enabling the user to construct centrifugal structures, angles, and other geometric objects.

Smart Objects: See *Vector Smart Object*.

Smoothing: A Photoshop® Brush Tip Shape menu option of the Brush panel.

Smooth Tool: An Illustrator® tool that can be used to further append selected line segments and shapes by clicking on areas.

Smudge Stick filter: A Photoshop® filter that creates the illusion of marks made with artist's smudge sticks on selected objects.

Smudge Tool: This Photoshop® tool smears pixels.

Snap to Point: A Photoshop® setting that when checked will cause objects to automatically position themselves to the invisible grid.

Soft Spotlight: A light option of the Photoshop® Lighting Effects filter that simulates a spotlight.

Software: Programs that run on computers to make them able to perform tasks.

Software bundles: Prepackaging of several different software programs for one price, usually installed together.

Software program: Computer software composed of a set of specific instructions and functions to be read by a computer in order to generate specific functions based on programmed variables.

Spacebar: In computers, the long key located at the central bottom of a keyboard that adds space between characters.

Spacing field: A setting of the Illustrator® Pattern Options dialog box that adds spaces between the repeat of a defined brush.

Spectrum bar: A color bar that the user clicks on to select a particular color range. Spectrum bars are part of the Color panel and Color Pickers.

Spatter filter: A Photoshop® filter used to simulate paint spatters.

Specifications: A set of requirements to satisfy products or services, especially those needed to facilitate apparel production as a part of technical packages.

Specs: In fashion computing, a generic term for information or details concerning procedures or information related to garment measurements required to facilitate production.

spi: Samples per inch.

Spiral Tool: This Illustrator® tool creates pre-shaped spirals with a click and drag.

Sponge Tool: A Photoshop® tool that can be used to paint in the simulated texture of a sponge.

Spot colors: The term is borrowed from its original use in printing when inks are used for a single run. In the case of computers, it refers to hues mixed by the user for a single use.

Spot Healing Brush Tool: This Photoshop® tool eradicates blemishes, spots, and marks. Also used to reposition desirable pixels, color, patterns, etc., it is one of several used for photo retouching.

Spotlight: One of three Light Types in the Photoshop® Lighting Effects filter. The Spotlight creates the illusion of direct beams of light.

Standard Screen Mode: The default (windowed) screen mode.

Star Tool: An Illustrator® shape tool that creates stars by the user performing a marquee.

Status bar: A customizable screen indicator on the bottom of the Illustrator® window that is used to show and manage various functions of the program and those that will assist the work flow.

Storyboard: In fashion design and merchandising, a storyboard is a planning or marketing tool used to exhibit the direction of tends, color, inspiration, etc. Also, a printed or digital file used to do the same.

Straight path: Any path with a direct line from one anchor point to the next.

Stroke: The outline of an object.

Stroke Arrowheads: An option in the Illustrator® Stroke panel that controls the look, size, position, etc. of arrowheads on a selected stroke.

Stroke button: A button in the Illustrator® Tools panel that controls the look of the stroke on a selected object.

Stroke Cap: A button in the Illustrator® Stroke panel that controls the look of end points.

Stroke Corner: A button in the Illustrator® Stroke panel that controls the look of jointed bends.

Stroke Dashed Line: An option in the Illustrator® Stroke panel that controls the length of dashes and gaps.

Stroke Limit: An option in the Illustrator® Stroke panel that controls the point of mitered edges.

Stroke Profile: The Stroke Profile enables the user to transform the look of lines to various preset widths similar to what can be done with the Illustrator® CS5 Width Tool (Shift+W).

Stroke Weight: The thickness of a line.

Style sheets: Visual layouts containing flat sketches as well as merchandising and marketing information for the current line of a manufacturer.

Styles panel: A Photoshop® panel that allows the user to save combination filter and tool attributes.

Sublayers: Hidden layers of the Illustrator® layers panel that are access by tipping arrow pointers. Usually sublayers are used to house parts of objects on the same layer.

Supercomputers: A powerful mainframe computer.

Swatch: A single digital color standard.

Swatch libraries: A color collection of digital swatches.

Swatches panel: A panel that houses digital color standards to be used like an artist's palette. In Illustrator®. The Swatches panel holds gradients, fades, vignettes, defined patterns, and color group folders.

Symbols panel: An Illustrator® panel that houses available clip art and can be used with the Symbols tool suite.

Symbol Scruncher Tool: An Illustrator® tool used to control the spacing of symbols.

Symbol Shifter Tool: An Illustrator® tool used to move symbols.

Symbol Sizer Tool: An Illustrator® tool used to control the size of symbols.

Symbol Spinner Tool: An Illustrator® tool used to control the rotation of symbols.

Symbol Sprayer Tool: An Illustrator® tool used to apply symbols.

Symbol Stainer Tool: An Illustrator® tool used to tint symbols with the color of the Fill box.

System preferences: The adjustable controls of the various functions of a computer.

System software: Software that directs the basic functions of a computer.

3-D: A three-dimensional optical illusion of width, depth, and height created for the purpose of simulating reality, weight, and space on a flat surface.

3-D flats: Full-color technical sketches rendered to look as if they were moving on an invisible person or as sculptural objects.

Tear-off menus: Floatable menus such as the tool suites in Illustrator®.

Technical design: An area of fashion design that features the mechanics of production, such as digital technical flats, specification, grading, etc.

Technical package: A technical package contains all the information necessary to produce a particular garment, and the extended needs of production.

Tech-packs: Short for technical package.

Technology: The application of science to advance industry, especially computers.

Template: A precut shape used as a pattern to create designs.

Temporary folder: A storage folder on a computer used to save a file for an immediate purpose, such as with Vector Smart Graphics transfers between Illustrator® and Photoshop® .

Terabyte: A unit of disk space consisting of 61,024 gigabytes. Also 1 trillion bytes.

Texturizer filter: A Photoshop® filter that gives objects relief texture.

Tilde key: A character key above the tab key on a keyboard. In Illustrator® the user can use the tilde key to reposition pattern fills by holding it while clicking and dragging in an area.

Tipping: The act of clicking on an arrow to access a hidden menu.

Title Bar: The top area of a window or panel used to move it and often where the name of the file appears.

Tolerance: A Photoshop® option of the Magic Wand Tool (W) that allows the user to adjust the sensitivity of its selections.

Toggle: To click on and off functions.

Toggle off: To click off a function.

Toggle on: To click on a function.

Toolbox: In computer software, the palette that holds the visual interface for the main creative functions.

Tools panel: An important panel of both Illustrator® and Photoshop® whereby the user interfaces with the program.

Tool Presets panel: This Photoshop® panel shows which tools possess preset functions. It can also be used to set new presets for tools and will retain color information as well.

Tools: In computing, the interfaces that create or manipulate files and are generally the main features of a software programs, such as the Lasso Tool in Photoshop® or the Pen Tool in Illustrator®.

Tool tips: Information that appears as you scroll over tools, options, swatches, etc.

Tracing and Presets menu: A hidden Illustrator® Live Trace menu in the control panel that, when pressed, reveals preset or saved tracing options.

Tracking: In typography tracking is the adjustment of space between entire bodies of text. This is a setting in the Character panel.

Trackpad: A flat area of a laptop used to access the computer with touch-sensitive finger movements.

Transform: A feature of Photoshop® that allows the user to alter the shape, scale, position, illusion, distortion, etc. of selected objects or those on a selected layer.

Transform Distort: A Photoshop® feature of the Transform function that can be used to distort selected objects via an adjustable Bounding Box.

Transform panel: Designates positions on the Illustrator® Artboard and Workspace in reference to the Zero Point, the x-axis, and the y-axis. Use it to set up the dimensions of selected objects based on a reference point of the Bounding Box that contains them. In Illustrator®, every Bounding Box has nine reference points corresponding to the Transform panel, no matter what their shape.

Transform Perspective: A Photoshop® feature of the Transform function that can be used to simulate perspective of selected objects or those on a selected layer via a constrained Bounding Box.

Transform Rotate: A Photoshop® feature of the Transform function that can be used to rotate selected objects.

Transform Skew: A Photoshop® feature of the Transform function that can be used to rotate and skew objects.

Transform Warp: A Photoshop® feature of the Transform function that can be used to rotate and warp objects via an adjustable grid and Bounding Box.

Transparent button: An Illustrator® menu option that allows the user to rasterize an object and prevent it from being surrounded by a white box.

Transparent pixels: In Photoshop®, the checkered background is considered transparent or transparent pixels. Literally, unaffected pixel space on a screen display.

Trash icon: A symbol on a button that the user can press to permanently remove a selected object.

Tutorial: An interactive visual lesson that provides instruction on how to complete a specific task.

Two-point perspective: A view that has two vanishing points. A setting of the Illustrator® CS5 Perspective Grid Tool, it can be used to create renderings in two-point perspective via adjustable grids.

Type on a Path Tool: An Illustrator® tool used to type on any path (straight or curved).

Typeset: The act of setting type as to layout for the purpose of desktop publishing or printing.

Type Tool: A tool that creates type.

Typography: The term referring to the art of creating and modifying type and the process of setting type design for the purpose of desktop publishing or printing.

Typography Tools: Photoshop® typographic capabilities that can be adjusted through the Character panel, the Paragraph panel, the Options Bar, and additional features of the program.

Underpainting filter: A Photoshop® filter that creates the illusion of fine art underpainting on a textured surface.

Undo: In computer software, to undo is to reverse a modification.

Units: A type of measurement, such as inches, points, etc.

Upgrade: To update technology by adding the latest features of a program or by discarding old software and/or hardware and replacing them with newer versions.

USB: An abbreviation in computing for universal serial bus, a connecting port for peripheral devices.

USB flash drive: A self-contained portable storage device used to store date from a computer via a USB port.

Vanishing point: The imaginary point of infinite distance of a perspective view and where receding parallel lines converge. A plane on the Illustrator® CS5 Perspective Grid Tool that can be adjusted to represent the vanishing point, and then used to render objects in perspective.

Vector: A coordinate that consists of a magnitude and direction. In digital graphics software, an anchor point.

Vector animation: The process of creating images via an object oriented software program, and then setting them into animation frames to simulated movement.

Vector art: Computer art or illustration created with anchor points to make paths—paths to make shapes—and shapes that are filled with color. Illustrator® is an object-oriented software program that can be used to create vector art.

Vector-based: In computing, any software that utilizes vectors to create digital art.

Vector Smart graphics: Illustrator® objects pasted into Photoshop® that are set (via a dialog box option) to communicate with Photoshop® by means of a temporary folder. Vector Smart graphics can transfer vector objects to Photoshop® and maintain their features. The user can also edit an object repeatedly by transferring the object back and forth between the two programs by pressing a Photoshop® Layer option.

Vector software: A graphics software program that uses vectors as a means of creating digital drawings.

Vertical Align Bottom: An option of the Align panel that repositions two or more selected objects or layer contents vertically by their bottom planes.

Vertical Align Center: An option of the Align panel that repositions two or more selected objects or layer contents vertically by their centers.

Vertical Area Type Tool: An Illustrator® tool that is used to type from top to bottom only inside vector shapes.

Vertical dock: In Illustrator® the default stacking of panels that are meshed on the right side of the window area.

Vertical integration: The collaboration of one company with two or more stages of production and operated by different companies that have formed a relationship for profit and efficiency.

Vertical repeat: A pattern repeat with a motif that repeats itself from one side of the Ground tile to the other.

Vertical Type Mask Tool: Photoshop® tool used to create vertical type as selections that can be filled or stroked. Masked-out areas leave just the type, with whatever is beneath them showing through the characters.

Vertical Type on a Path Tool: An Illustrator® tool used to type characters from top to bottom on a path.

Vertical Type Tool: An Illustrator® Tool used to type characters in a stacked formation.

VGA: An acronym for Video Graphics Array, which is an adapter or port that communicated with video equipment such as a projector, television, etc.

Vibrance: A color setting filter that adjusts the luminosity of selected objects in Photoshop®. This filter setting intensifies color as to its tone at various levels of color saturation.

Vignette: A Fade in radial formation.

Virtual alias identity: The current practice of using an avatar as one's "virtual" personage in a cyber environment.

Virtual digital realism: The author's term describing the use of graphic software programs to create digital illustration from photos, giving the subject an ethereal, perfected, and/or unnatural doll-like appearance. Fashion models, interiors, landscapes, and textile scans are digitized, and then further appended to make them look three-dimensional. The technique is suitable for animated video, web animation, and 3-D games.

Visibility: The condition of an object being visible to the human eye via the toggling of an icon that looks like a human eye in the Layers panel.

Visibility icon: The icon in the layers pane that looks like a human eye and toggles visibility.

Warp: A Photoshop® setting that can transform the attributes of a selection via an adjustable grid and Bounding Box.

Water Paper filter: A Photoshop® filter that gives objects the look of water paper.

Web: The short name for the World Wide Web that links millions of pages via hyperlinks and URLs.

Wet Edges: A Photoshop® Brush panel Brush Preset option of the Brush Tip Shape menu, which creates the illusion of wet strokes by building digital coats of color similar to the effects of actual watercolor painting techniques.

Width Tool: An Illustrator® CS5 tool that adjusts the width of strokes at intervals with a click and pull of the mouse.

Widget: A small application program that usually appears in the menu of a computer.

Wind filter: A Photoshop® filter that distorts objects to give the effect that they are windblown.

Windows operating system: A brand name for a group of PC-based system software programs made and distributed by the Microsoft Corporation.

Windows start icon: A Windows operating system button that, when pressed, reveals a menu to access the basic functions of and applications on a PC.

Wireless router: A modem that converts hard-line ISP signals wirelessly to a computer.

Workspace: A preset or saved desktop interface and setup of Illustrator® or Photoshop® that includes particular panels and docks in various positions.

Workspace Switcher: A feature that allows the user to choose from preset or saved workspaces via a button in the Options Bar.

Write Layers: A setting of the Export dialog box that communicates to Illustrator® that layers should be transferred to Photoshop® .

X-axis: The horizontal ruler.

Y-axis: The vertical ruler.

Zero Point: See *Ruler Origin*.

Zoom in: The act of accessing a close-up page view via a tool or panel feature; usually a function of the Zoom Tool.

Zoom out: The act of accessing a distanced page view via a tool or panel feature; usually a function of the Zoom Tool.

Zoom Slider: An adjustment slider in the Navigator panel that can create zoomed views of the window via the Proxy Preview Area.

Zoom Tool: A tool in both Illustrator® and Photoshop® that allows the user to view areas of the Artboard at various distances. It also works with the options of the Navigator panel.

Index